WILEY PLUS +

for *Introduction to Business Information Systems*

W9-CDL-581

Check with your instructor to find out if you have access to *WileyPLUS*!

Study More Effectively with a Multimedia Text

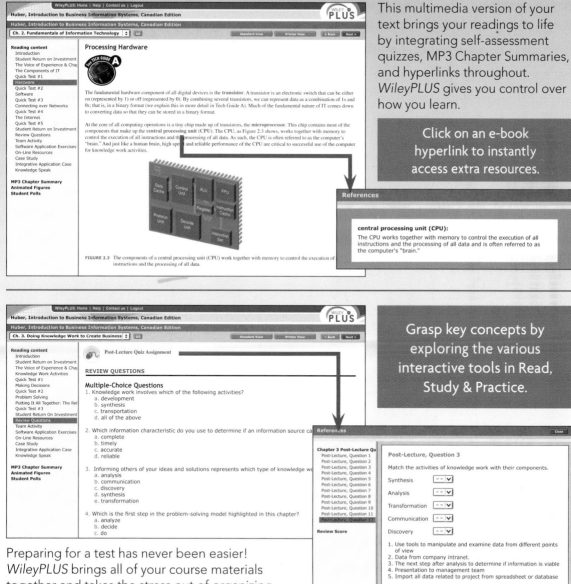

This multimedia version of your text brings your readings to life by integrating self-assessment quizzes, MP3 Chapter Summaries, and hyperlinks throughout. *WileyPLUS* gives you control over how you learn.

Click on an e-book hyperlink to instantly access extra resources.

Grasp key concepts by exploring the various interactive tools in Read, Study & Practice.

Preparing for a test has never been easier! *WileyPLUS* brings all of your course materials together and takes the stress out of organizing your study aids. A streamlined study routine saves you time and lets you focus on learning.

John Wiley & Sons Canada, Ltd.

WILEY PLUS
for *Introduction to Business Information Systems*

Complete and Submit Assignments On-line Efficiently

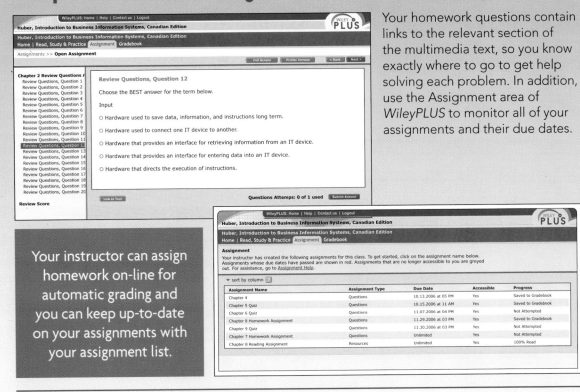

Your homework questions contain links to the relevant section of the multimedia text, so you know exactly where to go to get help solving each problem. In addition, use the Assignment area of *WileyPLUS* to monitor all of your assignments and their due dates.

Your instructor can assign homework on-line for automatic grading and you can keep up-to-date on your assignments with your assignment list.

Keep Track of Your Progress

Your personal Gradebook lets you review your answers and results from past assignments as well as any feedback your instructor may have for you.

Keep track of your progress and review your completed questions at any time.

Technical Support: http://higheredwiley.custhelp.com
Student Resource Centre: http://www.wileyplus.com

For further information regarding *WileyPLUS* and other Wiley products, please visit www.wiley.ca.

INTRODUCTION TO BUSINESS INFORMATION SYSTEMS

INTRODUCTION TO BUSINESS INFORMATION SYSTEMS

Mark W. Huber
University of Georgia

Craig A. Piercy
University of Georgia

Patrick G. McKeown
University of Georgia

James L. Norrie
Ryerson University

John Wiley & Sons Canada, Ltd.

Copyright © 2008 John Wiley & Sons Canada, Ltd.

Copyright © 2008 John Wiley & Sons, Inc. All rights reserved. No part of this work covered by the copyrights herein may be reproduced, transmitted, or used in any form or by any means—graphic, electronic, or mechanical—without the prior written permission of the publisher.

Any request for photocopying, recording, taping, or inclusion in information storage and retrieval systems of any part o this book shall be directed to The Canadian Copyright Licensing Agency (Access Copyright). For an Access Copyright Licence, visit www.accesscopyright.ca or call toll-free, 1-800-893-5777.

Library and Archives Canada Cataloguing in Publication
  Introduction to business information systems / Mark W. Huber ... [et al.].—Canadian ed.
  ISBN 978-0-470-84030-6
 1. Information technology—Management—Textbooks. 2. Management information systems—Textbooks.
I. Huber, Mark W.
  HD30.2.I58 2007
  658.4′038011   C2007-900432-6

Production Credits

ACQUISITIONS EDITOR	Darren Lalonde
PUBLISHING SERVICES DIRECTOR	Karen Bryan
EDITORIAL MANAGER	Karen Staudinger
DEVELOPMENTAL EDITOR	Leanne Rancourt
MARKETING MANAGER	Aida Krneta
MEDIA EDITOR	Elsa Passera Berardi
WILEY BICENTENNIAL LOGO	Richard J. Pacifico
COVER PHOTOGRAPHY	DynamicGraphics/maXximages.com
COVER AND INTERIOR DESIGN	Adrian So
PRINTING AND BINDING	Quebecor World/Taunton

Printed and bound in the United States
1 2 3 4 5 QW 11 10 09 08 07

John Wiley & Sons Canada, Ltd.
6045 Freemont Blvd.
Mississauga, Ontario L5R 4J3
Visit our website at: www.wiley.ca

DEDICATION

To my students, present and past, who have guided me both in the classroom and while writing this book; to my many colleagues and friends who encouraged me along the way; and most importantly to my family, whose indulgence and tolerance made this book possible. You are all awesome!

ABOUT THE AUTHORS

Mark W. Huber is Lecturer in Management Information Systems in the Terry College of Business, Director of the Terry College and Franklin College of Arts and Science Leadership Excellence and Development Program (L.E.A.D.), and a member of the UGA Teaching Academy. During the past six years he has won nine teaching awards including recognition as Outstanding Faculty at UGA Honors Day, a Terry College Regent's Professor Award Nominee, Outstanding MIS Faculty, a Student Government Outstanding Professor Award, Alpha Kappa Psi (professional business society) Outstanding Management Information Systems Teacher of the Year Award, and three UGA Career Center Student Development Awards. Dr. Huber recently completed a 21-year Air Force career that included the creation and command of a Combat Communications Squadron and the management and development of strategic information systems projects at the Pentagon. His research interests include group support systems and team and group development. He has written numerous papers for various professional and academic journals, and he has co-authored a lab manual published by John Wiley & Sons, Inc. in 2006.

Craig A. Piercy has been teaching large numbers of students in Introduction to Information Systems, Computer Programming, and Web Development classes at the University of Georgia since 2000. Previously, Dr. Piercy taught similar courses at Towson University. As an engineer and later as an academic, Dr. Piercy has long been interested in information technology and how it can be used to solve problems and improve our lives. He was the co-author of *Learning to Program with VB6,* 2nd edition, and he has co-authored a lab manual published by John Wiley & Sons, Inc. in 2006. His primary area of research is in developing algorithms to support decision making. In particular, Dr. Piercy explores decision models that include multiple conflicting objectives. Dr. Piercy has recently been named as the Director for the Masters of Internet Technology program at the University of Georgia.

Patrick G. McKeown is Professor Emeritus of Management Information Systems in the Terry College of Business at the University of Georgia. Until his retirement in 2003, he was the founding head of that department. He was on the faculty at the University of Georgia for 27 years. He has published close to 50 articles in the areas of management science and information systems and has also written more than 30 textbooks in these areas. He is a Fellow of the Text and Academic Authors Association, only one of 15 such honorees out of an organization of over 1,000 textbook authors. In addition, in 2003, he was given the Lifetime Service Award by the UGA MIS Alumni Association and had a student scholarship created in his name by the UGA MIS Department. Dr. McKeown was a Fulbright Scholar in Portugal in 1998 at the Catholic University of Portugal and has taught internationally at universities in France, Finland, South Africa, and New Zealand.

James L. Norrie, DPM, is an Associate Professor and currently Director of the School of Information Technology Management (ITM) at Ryerson University where he teaches in the areas of Introductory IT, Advanced Project Management, Systems Analysis & Design, Business Process, and Governance and Ethics. He also undertakes applied research, speaks regularly at industry events, and consults for numerous companies in these areas with a particular focus on aligning business and IT strategy to eliminate business risk and improve organization performance. Prior to joining the faculty, he was both an entrepreneur and F-1000 executive with a 15+ year track record of creating, growing, or managing high-tech and e-business ventures. In addition to his Ryerson appointment, he has served as either a  member or chairman of the board of directors or board of advisors of various corporate and charitable boards. He is the co-author of the best-selling title *The A to Z Guide to Soul-Inspiring Leadership* (Epic Press, 2003), now in its 2nd printing, as well as various articles in professional and academic journals.

PREFACE

WHY WE WROTE THIS BOOK

During our collective teaching careers, we have developed and taught introductory information systems courses to more than 15,000 business students. For most of our students, this was their first exposure to understanding both business and information systems. From them, we have learned that there is a significant need for an introductory information systems textbook that engages business students across all majors and creates a foundation for their understanding and strategic use of information systems and technology as future knowledge-enabled professionals. From our colleagues around the world, we have learned that providing a textbook that leads with the business context, rather than with a technology focus, helps them make introductory IT more interesting.

So why do a Canadian adaptation of this particular book? The answer is simple—innovation. The U.S. authoring team really believes in the value of teaching introductory IT well, especially to non-IT majors, something that is lacking in the current IT textbooks available today. When I was introduced to Mark Huber and Craig Piercy, it was clear that we shared a common perspective on the challenges of engaging those in business with IT. And this book is designed to reflect exactly that approach. So, beyond the simple fact that Canadian case examples, laws, and practices are different than those in the United States, we also added some elements that came from my own teaching experience (such as in-class discussion aids and a new integrative case study). Canadian students deserve the best experience we can give them so they will begin to share our passion about the value of IT, ensuring Canada remains as competitive, innovative, and successful a nation as any other place in the world. We hope that as a student or instructor of IT you will agree that this book represents an innovative and creative way of teaching an important subject.

HOW WE WROTE THIS BOOK

Our fundamental philosophy is that within organizations, knowledge-enabled professionals use information systems and technologies to enable and enhance the successful achievement of business goals. We believe that the effective integration of IS with knowledge can drive the creation of significant business value. As such, most students, regardless of their major, need to understand information systems and technologies and their importance to the success of business organizations.

To implement this philosophy, we incorporated our proven *spiral approach* to learning IT/IS fundamentals (for a visual of the spiral model, turn to page 7 of the text). You will learn more about this in the Logon, where we set the stage for learning by talking about how individuals, organizations, and business partnerships use IT systems to create competitive advantage. But there are some other unique features of this book that are designed to help students and teachers be successful.

INTEGRATION OF E-COMMERCE

As a part of our spiral approach to learning, we approach e-commerce as an important component of commerce and not as an aspect of business that stands alone from an organization's efforts to create business value. So, while we discuss e-commerce business models, strategies, and technologies in significant detail in Chapters 7 and 8, we integrate this topic into most other chapters where it applies and incorporate relevant examples throughout.

CORE BOXES

Four "CORE" (Connectivity, On-line Security, Relationships, and Ethics) boxes are included in each chapter as a way of highlighting the application of significant concepts from the chapter in real-world settings. For example, the Relationships CORE box in Chapter 6 focuses on why teams fail in organizations. Chapter 4 includes a Connectivity CORE box that discusses whether instant messaging is a toy or a tool. And in Chapter 1's Ethics CORE box, we discuss the issue of academic integrity and its connection to on-line fraud-detection systems. These boxes include references to relevant resources, on-line tools, or other supplementary information that you can use to learn more about how real organizations apply solutions to IT-related business problems.

TECH GUIDES

 We wanted to provide a way to extend students' learning experiences, as well as enable instructors to tailor the depth of the material to their course goals, without deviating from our goal of focusing on the business context first. To accomplish this goal, we've included five Tech Guides to provide more extensive coverage of hardware, software, networks, SQL and XML, and working in teams. Instructors can either cover these as links to appropriate introductory chapters or use them to motivate students to go beyond what is required for the class and enjoy a deeper look at base technology and systems architecture. Throughout the book, we include a Tech Guide icon in the margin to alert you to relevant information that can be found in the Tech Guides so both students and instructors will be able to make seamless connections between them.

FEATURES TO ENGAGE STUDENTS

In addition to the spiral approach and CORE boxes, we've added many other pedagogical features designed to engage students and enhance the learning process. These features include such things as our chapter opening student ROI, various within-chapter elements, relevant end-of-chapter material (including an integrative case study), and end-of-book material.

On the next few pages, we'll take you on a tour of some of the special features of our book. We strongly believe that our approach will enhance student engagement and help create a foundation for students' understanding and use of information systems and technology. We hope you'll agree! We'd love to hear from you regarding your experience using our book in the classroom. Please e-mail us with any comments.

Mark Huber	Craig Piercy	Patrick McKeown	James Norrie
mhuber@uga.ed	cpiercy@uga.edu	pmckeown@uga.edu	jlnorrie@ryerson.ca

FEATURES TO ENGAGE STUDENTS

PART
3

PART
3

PART
3

PART
3

PART
2

PART
2

PART
2

PART
1

PART
1

PART
1

GET STARTED ON THE RIGHT FOOT!

Student ROI

The *Student ROI* alerts students to the questions they will be able to answer after reading the chapter. In other words, this section helps students see the "return" on their "investment" of time to read and understand the chapter material.

STUDENT RETURN ON INVESTMENT

Through your investment of time in reading and thinking about this chapter, your return, or created value, is gaining knowledge. Use the following questions as a study guide.

1. How do different factors in a business environment, such as the Internet and globalization, impact the need for timely data, information, and knowledge?
2. What role does knowledge creation play in your success as a current student and future knowledge-enabled professional?
3. How do the different types of information systems (IS) help knowledge-enabled professionals manage data, information, and knowledge?

The Voice of Experience

The *Voice of Experience* is a Q&A session with a recent graduate who is employed as a knowledge-enabled professional using information systems. These interview boxes are designed to provide motivation for the reader to understand the content covered in the chapter by helping them to see how the chapter material might be useful in their future career.

THE VOICE OF EXPERIENCE
Michael Lee, Ryerson University

Michael Lee graduated in 2005 with a Bachelor of Commerce degree from the Information Technology Management program. Since then he has worked as an information technology consultant at IBM helping his clients achieve business results through technology.

application. It's like being able to talk to anybody on a moment's notice. If you need a quick answer, you simply message them and it pops up on their screen. IBM uses VPN extensively to connect remotely to these resources, so I can work on my project at any time re-

The Spiral Organization: Coloured Tabs

The spiral approach to learning information systems used in this text reinforces learning through expansion of topics from the individual level, to the organizational level, and then to the business-partner level. Within each set of three chapters in the spiral model, one chapter focuses on the organizational context (orange-tabbed chapters), one on technology fundamentals (yellow tabs), and one on the impact on business (green tabs). Coloured tabs appear on the edge of each page to remind you where you are in the spiral and how the chapter relates to others in the book.

MAKE THE CONNECTION!

Quick Tests

Quick Tests are short quizzes at the end of each major section within each chapter that provide the student with an opportunity to test their understanding of the material in that section.

Quick Test

1. Fill in the blank. Selling your CD collection on eBay.ca is a form of _____ e-commerce.

2. Fill in the blank. In general, companies already experienced in the physical order fulfillment and _____ process have been successful in e-commerce.

3. Fill in the blank. Consumers can easily download _____ products from an e-commerce site over a computer network.

Answers: 1. C2C; 2. returns; 3. digital

What Do You Think?

What Do You Think? boxes are scattered throughout the chapter and are designed to evoke critical thinking related to the topic just discussed. They pose questions to the students to help them think critically about an aspect of

WHAT DO YOU THINK?

Imagine that you have one or more items you want to sell. You can either put an ad in your local newspaper or sell it on-line. With this choice in mind, consider the following questions:

1: What factors would you consider in making the choice between selling the item on-line or off-line?
2: What steps would you take to put your item up for sale on-line? What site would you choose and why?
3: What makes you choose one site over another to list your item for sale?

the topic and to help them relate it to their own examples or experience. These boxes are further developed in the Instructor's Resources to provide a basis for leading in-class discussions or debates—techniques that we know are important to instructors who wish to engage students in the classroom.

CORE Boxes

CORE (Connectivity, On-line Security, Relationships, and Ethics) boxes are an important element of this book. We place four in every chapter, as opposed to covering these topics at the end of the book, in order to amplify the importance of these topics as well as to highlight significant issues relevant to the chapter.

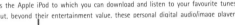

Connectivity

Podcasting for IT Knowledge

By now, most of you have heard of, and in many cases own, an MP3 player such as the Apple iPod to which you can download and listen to your favourite tunes. But, beyond their entertainment value, these personal digital audio/image players

On-line Security

Wireless Insecurity

Are you a knowledge-enabled professional who ha[s] your e-mail from your favourite sunny spot on cam[pus] to a classroom, coffee shop, or a hotel where a

Relationships

Virtual Teams

Today, Nick is about to have his first meeting with his new system project team. His company, Sodor Software, develops software that is used to schedule railroad traffic. The company has just formed a strategic partnership with the software

Ethics

Software Piracy

Have you ever shared software with someone else? Did you do something illegal, or were your actions simply unethical? Is there a difference?

The unauthorized sharing of software, or *software piracy*, is illegal. Software

ASSESS YOUR UNDERSTANDING

Student ROI Summary

The *Student ROI Summary* provides answers to the questions posed in the Student ROI at the beginning of the chapter. As such, it helps the student review what they have learned in the chapter.

Knowledge Speak

The *Knowledge Speak* section is a list of keywords found in the chapter, which the student should understand as a part of the terminology learned in the chapter.

Review Questions

The *Review Questions* contain a number of types of questions all aimed at having the student assess their understanding of the chapter material. Types of questions include true/false, multiple choice, fill-in-the-blanks, short answer, and essay questions.

Team Activity

The *Team Activity* provides an opportunity for the students to work as a team to carry out an activity pertinent to the chapter material.

Software Application Exercises

The *Software Application Exercises* ask the students to solve a series of related exercises using word processing, spreadsheet, presentation, database, and Internet software.

Case Studies

A *Case Study* at the end of each chapter is a short description of a well-known company's use of information systems to build business value. Case questions are included with the Case Study. There is also an *Integrative Application Case* at the end of each chapter that follows two students attempting to startup an Internet company. Each integrative application case builds on the material presented in that chapter, showing students how the content ties together. Case questions as well as a student task are included with each integrative application case.

CASE STUDY: DELL INC.

When it comes to purchasing new computers, for many individuals and corporations the top choice in this market has been Dell. What makes this somewhat surprising, considering the salesperson assistance generally required for these purchases, is that Dell sells only directly to its customers, without any retail stores. Dell initially did this by using telephone sales, but has aggressively moved into e-commerce as a way of connecting with its customers. Total 2003 on-line sales were over $50 million *per day*, resulting from more than 7,000

suppliers can see the same support information it uses internally.

Dell has always sought efficiency in its operations, as evidenced by the fact that its expenses dropped to an almost unheard of 9.9% of net revenue in 2003. With this level of efficiency, each Dell employee is generating over $1 million in revenue each year—three times the level of their competitors. This search for efficiency is also demonstrated by its move to the use of radio frequency identification (RFID) chips that it attaches

Integrative Application Case: Campuspad.ca

Sarah has been a great friend since you met in your student lounge during frosh week. Since you both live in residence, you hang out quite a bit. After IT class today, she approached you to talk about an idea she has for a new business and invited you to help her with it. You were curious—but cautious— as she told you about it.

Recently she had made the decision to live off-campus next year and was beginning to search for a place. Obviously, her first step was to hop on-line

ing for economical places to live, although she certainly wouldn't want to live in some of the places she saw on-line! The sites she had visited already left her pretty frustrated. Lots of them were focused on the United States, or mostly focused on general rental accommodation, and didn't seem to understand her specific search needs.

For instance, when she visited roommate-click.com she found that they did indeed serve Canada, but were only listed on google.com, not

Chapter Map

Navigating through a textbook, trying to remember where a certain concept was covered, or quickly looking up key information covered in a particular chapter can be difficult for both students and instructors. This is why we have created a Chapter Map, found at the back of book, which is your quick guide to locating common IT and business concepts within each chapter.

INSTRUCTOR AND STUDENT RESOURCES

ON-LINE INSTRUCTOR SUPPORT MATERIALS:
ALL CLASS-TESTED AND IN CURRENT USE BY THE AUTHORS!

www.wiley.com/canada/huber

As teachers, we understand the value of support materials for classroom activities. In fact, in creating this textbook package, we have tried to create a manageable "course-in-a-box" format. Our approach uses an integrated approach to teaching introductory IT/IS courses with a view to enhancing faculty effectiveness and decreasing workload while simultaneously increasing student interest in the discipline and level of engagement in the classroom. To create this course-in-a-box, the textbook is accompanied by a wealth of ancillary materials found on WileyPLUS. Materials are class-tested and in current use by the various authors (and other collaborators already using the text!) who are more than happy to help other colleagues implement them in their own classes. Using this book and its support package should provide a department with confidence that students will receive a rigorous and innovative introduction to IS and be better prepared to embark upon their future as knowledge-enabled professionals creating business value through IS. To achieve that goal, we provide extensive support materials for both the instructor and the student. Go to *www.wiley.com/canada/huber* to access the support materials for both students and instructors.

TEACHER'S MANUAL The *Teacher's Manual*, written by Mark Huber, Craig Piercy, James Norrie, and Michelle Nanjad, is based upon their experience teaching the course. Rather than calling it an instructor's manual, it is designed to be a useful teaching tool with a chapter overview, teaching outline and notes for each chapter, examples or links to examples that can be used in class, answers and solutions to the questions and exercises, and suggestions for team exercises. Also included are "pre-class entertainment" templates developed by Craig Piercy. These templates are PowerPoint presentations that highlight current IS topics, MIS facts, sports, brain teasers, and more. Designed to run prior to class, these presentations engage students and can serve as a springboard for class discussions. Lastly, our teaching manual will be a living document, as we will continue to share teaching resources as we develop them for our own classes.

TEST BANK The *Test Bank*, which has been carefully reviewed and class-tested by the authors, is a comprehensive resource for test questions. For each chapter, it offers a broad range of questions to choose from, including multiple choice, completion, true/false, matching, and short answer questions.

POWERPOINT PRESENTATIONS The *PowerPoint Presentations* consist of a series of slides for each chapter of the text that are designed around the text content, incorporating key points from the text and all text illustrations as appropriate.

IMAGE LIBRARY All textbook figures are available for download from the website. These figures can easily be added to PowerPoint presentations.

ANIMATIONS Selected figures from the text that involve dynamic activity have been animated using Flash technology. These animated figures can be shown as a part of instructor presentations to demonstrate multistep processes.

DEMONSTRATION OF LARGE CLASS TEAM EXERCISES Many instructors wonder whether it is possible to carry out team exercises in classes of more than 100 students. In these PowerPoint slides, master teachers Mark Huber and Craig Piercy demonstrate how to organize, carry out, and grade team exercises such as the "Egg Drop" or the "Tower Building" exercises in large classes.

LECTURE LAUNCHER VIDEO SERIES AND VIDEO CASES Prepared by James Clark, University of Lethbridge, the Lecture Launcher series will feature a series of short video clips (3–7 minutes in length) that will be tied to the major topics in each chapter. They are designed to provide an excellent starting point for lectures or discussion. A set of Video Cases will also be available. These videos will be 20–30 minutes in length and cover a range of topics. They will also include review questions and case notes.

WileyPLUS

WileyPLUS is a powerful on-line tool that provides instructors and students with an integrated suite of teaching and learning resources, including an on-line version of the text, in one easy-to-use website. To learn more about *WileyPLUS* and view a demo, please visit *www.wiley.com/canada/huber* and follow the link to *WileyPLUS*.

WileyPLUS TOOLS FOR INSTRUCTORS *WileyPLUS* enables you to:

- Assign automatically graded homework, practice, and quizzes from the end of chapter and test bank.
- Track your students' progress in an instructor's grade book.
- Access all teaching and learning resources including an on-line version of the text, and student and instructor supplements, in one easy-to-use website. These include teaching tips, full-colour PowerPoint slides, video, in-class activities, and animations.
- Create class presentations using Wiley-provided resources, with the ability to customize and add your own materials.

WileyPLUS RESOURCES FOR STUDENTS Within *WileyPLUS*, students will find various helpful tools such as learning links, interactive versions of the Quick Tests from the book, Knowledge Speak flashcards, downloadable MP3 chapter reviews, audio interviews, animations, and interactive versions of end-of-chapter materials and chapter quizzes.

- **Animated Figures** To aid students in understanding complex interactions, selected figures from the text that involve dynamic activity have been animated using Flash technology. Students can download these animated figures and run them to improve their understanding of dynamic processes.
- **Flash Cards** Key terms are available to students in a flash card format along with their definition.
- **MP3 Chapter Reviews** MP3 files that provide a review of the chapter are available for students to download and play back at their convenience using MP3 players.
- **Student polls** Surveys are integrated throughout the e-book, providing students with the opportunity to register their opinion on a variety of business information systems topics and issues. After they have voted, students can compare their vote with those of other students taking this course across Canada.

- **Pre- and post-lecture quizzes** Self-study practice questions located throughout the e-book to help students gage their level of understanding as they prepare for class time or a test. Immediate feedback is provided for this self-paced learning component.
- **CBC Video Cases** Relevant CBC programs have been integrated within the e-book. Accompanying video summaries and discussion questions are also provided.

ACKNOWLEDGMENTS

A large-scale textbook project such as this one is not the work of a single group of authors—rather, it is the combined effort of many people. In our case, we first wish to thank our students who have challenged us to develop new and innovative ways of teaching the concepts related to information systems and the value-creating role of IS in organizations. In many instances, you have been a willing audience as we learned what worked, and your pioneering efforts have allowed us to create a product that we feel will significantly benefit the next generation of students who study introductory IT.

Special thanks are due to many people who contributed and worked on this book. To begin with, the project would not exist had it not been for the vision and support of Darren Lalonde, our Acquisitions Editor. After turning him down for several other projects, he called me one day about this book and was honest, forthright, and easy to talk to. I am at Wiley because of his efforts. Similarly, it was Darren who suggested Leanne Rancourt, our Development Editor, and its been great to have her working by our side, day in and day out, bringing this project to completion. Our heartfelt thanks go out to the entire Wiley team who has made this book possible: Elsa Passera, Media Editor; Sara Dam, Editorial Assistant and Photo Researcher; Maureen Talty, General Manager and Publisher; Isabelle Moreau, Director of Marketing; Aida Krneta, Marketing Manager; and Adrian So, Designer.

And just as there is Leanne and a whole Wiley team behind Darren that makes it easy for him to do great work, I have a team behind me that makes me look good—only, it's a team of one! Michelle Nanjad and I have worked together for many years and still she comes back for more! I enjoy our collaborations immensely and could not do what I do without her research and editorial abilities, knowledge of the subject matter and, of course, her gentle prodding, pulling, pushing, and cajoling to create the best product we can. You're awesome. This book is what it is because of our efforts to be "better together!" I also wish to thank Carol-Ann Hamilton, who co-authored Tech Guide E: The Technology of Teams. Your help with this portion of the text is immensely appreciated.

Finally, all of the authors would like to thank our families for the gift of time they gave us to pursue a labour of love. Writing is not always an easy task and it is quite personal, requiring the indulgence of the many to make it possible for the few. To our spouses and children, you know who you are and your love means everything to us!

REVIEWERS

We also want to thank the many individuals who took the time to read and evaluate the draft manuscripts prior to production. Our reviewers generously provided their expertise to help us ensure the book's accuracy, clarity, and focus on the needs of today's information systems instruction. Without their many, many helpful comments, the book would not be what it is today. Thank you for your invaluable contributions.

Ron Babin
Ryerson University

Robert Goldstein
University of British Columbia

Bouchaib Bahli
Concordia University

Kamal Masri
Simon Fraser University

Bill Bonner
University of Regina

Al Pilcher
Carleton University

Danny Cho
Brock University

Harold Smith
Algonquin College

Jim Clark
University of Lethbridge

Ozgur Turetken
Ryerson University

Franca Giacomelli
Humber College

The reviewers of the U.S. text have also had a hand in shaping this Canadian adaptation, so thanks to all of you who helped create the base for our book to be built upon.

Chon Abraham
College of William and Mary

Nancy W. Davidson
Auburn University at Montgomery

Ihssan Alkadi
University of Louisiana, Lafayette

Charles DeSassure
Tarrant County College

Bay Arinze
Drexel University

Thomas Dillon
James Madison University

Janet Bailey
University of Arkansas at Little Rock

Charles E. Downing
Northern Illinois University

Kakoli Bandyopadhyay
Lamar University

Donna R. Everett
Morehead State University

Prasad Bingi
Indiana University-Purdue Fort Wayne

Stephane Gagnon
New Jersey Institute of Technology

Steven Burleson
Milwaukee Area Technical College

Frederick Gallegos
California State Polytechnic University

Megan Conklin
Elon University

Carl Gruel
The George Washington University

Gerald Cruez
Miami University

John W. Gudenas
Aurora University

Mohammad Dadashzadeh
Oakland University

Vipul Gupta
Saint Joseph's University

Shana Dardan
California State University, Sacramento

Mary Carole Hollingsworth
Georgia Perimeter College

Sergio Davalos
University of Washington, Tacoma

Wade Jackson
The University of Memphis

Brian Janz
The University of Memphis

Bhushan Kapoor
California State University, Fullerton

Anthony Kendall
Naval Postgraduate School

Sherry Kersey
Hillsborough Community College

Brian R. Kovar
Kansas State University

Kapil Ladha
Drexel University

Leonardo Legorreta
California State University, Sacramento

Ronald S. Lemos
California State University, Los Angeles

Keith Lindsey
Trinity University

Joan B. Lumpkin
Wright State University

Jane Mackay
Texas Christian University

Suzanne Markow
Des Moines Area Community College

Lee McKinley
Georgia Perimeter College

Donn Miller-Kermani
Florida Institute of Technology

Jarvis B. Moore II
The University of Memphis

Margaret O'Hara
East Carolina University

Timothy J. Peterson
University of Minnesota Duluth

Katie Pittman
Southern Oregon University

Mark L. Pranger
Rogers State University

Leonard Presby
William Paterson University

Robert S. Rokey
The University of Cincinnati

Arjan T. Sadhwani
San Jose State University

Subhashish Samaddar
Georgia State University

Stella Smith
Georgia Perimeter College

Raja Sooriamurthi
Kelly School of Business, Indiana University

Jeff Stewart
Macon State College

James Suleiman
University of Southern Maine

Eloisa G. Taméz
University of Texas, Brownsville

Giri K. Tayi
University at Albany, SUNY

Amrit Tiwana
Iowa State University

Ray J. Tsai
St. Cloud State University

Craig K. Tyran
Western Washington University

David Van Over
Sam Houston State University

William P. Wagner
Villanova University

John H. Walker
Brock University

Janice Warner
Florida Atlantic University

Dennis Williams
Orfalea College of Business, Cal Poly

Zachary Wong
Sonoma State University

David C. Yen
Miami University

BRIEF CONTENTS

CONTENTS

PART TWO

The Organizational Perspective 113

Chapter 4

Business Fundamentals and IT Strategy 114

Chapter 5

IT for the Organization 148

Chapter **9**

The Connected Enterprise: Business Partnering and Protecting 342

Logoff **390**

TECH GUIDES

Tech Guide **A**

The Details of IT Hardware 400

Tech Guide E

The Technology of Teams 516

CORE BOXES

Connectivity
Online Security
Relationships
Ethics

Connectivity

On-line Security

Relationships

Ethics

LOGON

Welcome to the start of our journey with you into the era of the knowledge-enabled professional. The new work world of today is quite different than that of the past. More and more, jobs require knowledge-enabled professionals who add value to business transactions by transforming data and information into knowledge and wisdom. In support of these activities, organizations acquire current technology and design information systems that help their workers create this value. We feel strongly that business strategy should drive these technology and system choices. This is often referred to as "alignment." This book will help you align your business choices, your career, and your understanding of technology required to make this happen.

WHAT ARE DATA, INFORMATION, AND KNOWLEDGE?

A timely and cost-effective flow of data, information, and knowledge is essential to your success as a university or college student and a current or future knowledge-enabled professional. Much of what you do, and will do, relates to data, information, and knowledge. You collect data about various subjects to transform it into information and knowledge. You learn where to look for quality information and how to store it for future use. Sometimes you share information with others. Information and knowledge are not just words on a page; they have tangible value, and knowledge becomes an important asset.

This is also the case in business. The flow of data and information to create knowledge is what creates value in organizations. You can likely think of occasions when the loss of information has had negative results; for instance, a misplaced order from an on-line supplier. Or a phone number that you didn't have a chance to put into your cell phone and now can't find. Or how about the registration mishaps where you are "sure" that you registered for that course that's now full? As a student of business information systems, learning to apply technology to enable this flow helps you and the organizations you will work for improve their results and avoid just these kinds of situations.

THE DATA–INFORMATION–KNOWLEDGE CONTINUUM

Now that you've begun to realize the importance of data, information, and knowledge, let's dig a little deeper into the meanings of each word and their relationship to each other. **Data** are raw unorganized facts, numbers, pictures, and so on. **Information** is data that have been organized and are useful to a person. In business, this person is often a manager or other knowledge-enabled professional. For example, a hair salon owner might include the names of clients, their phone numbers, and their e-mail addresses in an address-book program in a personal digital assistant. **Knowledge** is created when a person combines experience and judgement with information. Applying knowledge is how businesspeople create and add value to organizations.

For example, as an international sales manager, you may know the phone numbers and e-mail addresses of your best clients, but you also know your clients' time zones and normal business hours (information). Suppose you decided to e-mail rather than telephone one client. Why did you do this? Most likely, you based your decision on the information you have about the client and your personal judgement regarding past experience with this client. Maybe you've found the client doesn't like to be interrupted by the phone or doesn't have voicemail. Therefore, you made your decision based on the knowledge you had about that client.

As a student, you use data, information, and knowledge regularly. Remember your first day of classes during your first semester on campus? You had your schedule and the campus map. How did you find your first class? You probably looked on your schedule and found the building name and/or number (data). Once you knew this, you looked at your campus map (information). Were you on time for class? Maybe you were late because, based on the campus map, you decided to drive and park in a lot near your classroom. Unfortunately, the lot was full, and the only available parking was far away. You had good information (class time and class and parking lot location), so what went wrong?

Because you had never driven to this particular class and tried to park in a nearby lot, you had no experience with the process. Assume that the next time you decided to drive, you left earlier and found a space. Now when faced with the "when-to-leave-for-class decision," you use knowledge, which combines your class time, classroom location, and parking lot location with your "finding-a-space" experience.

Actually, we further believe that the data-to-knowledge continuum can be extended to include wisdom. **Wisdom** adds insight and ethics to the experience and professional judgement inherent in knowledge. Wisdom enables business leaders to perceive the underlying meaning and nuances of a business situation and ensures that knowledge from all relevant perspectives, disciplines, and sources is considered in the final decision.

Another important thing to note is that the cost and complexity of the tasks to be accomplished increase as we move up the pyramid from simply accessing data to applying wisdom (see the figure on the next page). We also propose that information technology and systems assist primarily with collecting, collating, and analyzing data and information. This is their strongest contribution. While technology is a key enabler, it is still up to humans to take this data and information and turn it into knowledge and wisdom.

Think of it this way: in its simplest form, we have data. These are the raw facts and figures related to the task at hand. By using information technology systems, we can transform this data into information by putting it into context, adding it up or sorting it out, and generally performing mechanical calculations and permutations that would be either boring or subject to error if performed by humans. The system can store and retrieve information quickly and disseminate it throughout the organization. At a higher level, we might also expect these systems to spot and identify basic patterns in the data or point out anomalies. They might generate warnings about potential problems or about process or values outside of expected or approved levels. However, after this point, the work of the information system is mostly done. It now falls to the knowledge-enabled professional to take this information and interpret it in context: turning it into

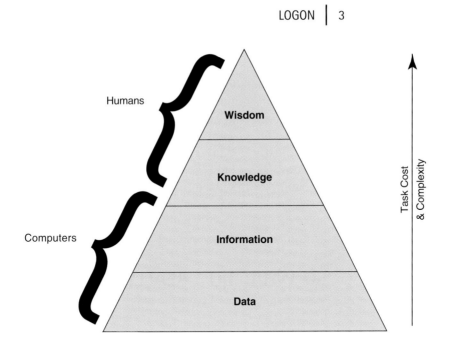

knowledge. An ethical or legal interpretation might also be added to the knowledge to ensure that all of the appropriate context has been considered before making a decision. Information that is not used to improve the outcome of a business decision is perhaps interesting, but certainly not useful. And we can clearly see the boundary of where information systems can and cannot be helpful.

DEFINING COMPETITIVE ADVANTAGE

In today's hypercompetitive business environment, all organizations must focus on improving results all the time. This is often referred to as continuous improvement and it is the hallmark of successful enterprises today—those that are never satisfied with good enough, but strive to set new standards and benchmarks.

To achieve this, every employee in an organization must be empowered to think and act at the top of their game. They must be encouraged to creatively seek ways to make things better. The notion of "better" is often thought of in terms of reducing the costs of a business process, decreasing the costs of goods sold or the price of raw materials, or improving revenue by increasing prices through branding or improved product quality. And while all of these are important and valid, we have a very distinct notion of what defines competitive advantage. We think of it as an equation that looks like this:

Competitive Advantage =
Quality of Insight + Speed of Execution + Cost Competitiveness[1]

1. Adapted from Carol-Ann Hamilton and James Norrie, *The A to Z Guide to Soul-Inspiring Leadership,* Epic Press, 2003, p. 129.

Simply put, unless your efforts at work improve the quality of insight of your organization (into markets, products, consumer needs, pricing, competitor behaviour, or anything else you can think of that matters in business) or improves the speed of execution or cost competitiveness of your organization's response to that insight, then your effort is futile and will not add value.

Similarly, good IT systems are deployed to improve the quality of insight of those making decisions, to improve the speed of execution, or to reduce costs. There is no other reason to spend money on a system. This text is primarily designed to help you make decisions about what kinds of technology can help an organization achieve competitive advantage.

SO WHAT DO I REALLY NEED TO KNOW?

Depending on the tasks at hand (which will be different if you are a marketing analyst, sales manager, accountant, operations analyst, human resources advisor, or plant manager), you may use different kinds of systems to provide information relevant to your role or function. Regardless of the work you perform, chances are good it will involve a system of some sort. But the degree to which you are interested in the underlying technology of the system, versus the opportunity to improve results you care about, is the essential question.

For example, think about a car that you might like to buy. Are you thinking about a red convertible with leather seats, a six-CD player, and speed to spare? Or maybe it's an SUV with a sunroof, DVD player, and 21-inch "spinners"? The way a car looks and how fast it will go are significant. But the real purpose of a car, or its value, is to get you from place to place safely and reliably.

Let's take this a step further. Think about what happens if you forget to fill the car's tank with gasoline. Like a car, a business will stall without its "gasoline," in this case, information. Drivers use gasoline to make cars go, and knowledge-enabled professionals use information to make businesses succeed. This is why we stress business value (transportation) and information (gasoline) first, and then the information technology (big engine) underneath the hood.

Those who are majoring in information technology or information systems (IT/IS) will obviously have a different level of commitment to and eventual understanding of the underlying technology being used in the systems—what is actually underneath the hood. However, they also need to make sure they understand the business context since this is where the systems will be used and where the car will be driven as a means of transportation.

We know that most of you reading this text will not be majoring in IT. And you probably care less about the engine of your car than you do about its features, comfort, and safety. In fact, this course may be your only required course in the subject matter and the level of interest that you have in it will vary, as it should. This is exactly why we wrote this book. We understand your dilemma: you want to understand the practical application of technology, but not necessarily the technology itself.

The authors of this text have all spent many years teaching introductory IT to university and college students around the world. We have come to learn that students vary in their level of interest in and involvement with the subject and their expectations of the course range from "just get me through it" to "I may want to change my major." Yet there are important opportunities available to you regardless of how much you initially want to study this subject. Information technology is everywhere. It is an essential component of most everything we do today. We find it in our homes, in our cars, and at the office. It is in our classrooms from preschool to university. We find it in our hospitals and in government offices. We use it to shop, socialize, and find out what's happening in the world. It may be hidden or visible; it may be a help or a hindrance, but it is omnipresent. And to succeed in business today, it cannot be ignored, but must be mastered.

Yet mastery is so often defined as understanding the definitions and origins of technology. In the Internet age, with its myriad search engines and information-laden sites, this is not the most optimal use of your time as a student. If it is definitions you want, those are easy to get. While we certainly include these in our text (especially in the Tech Guides at the end of the book), we try to provide them in the chapters on a just-in-time basis, to ensure you understand the application of technology in a business context. Only by first understanding the organizational use of the technology are we safe to assume you may be interested in the origins, operation, and acquisition of such technology. So this book's emphasis is on showing you how technology can be applied to create value and not on justifying the value of the technology itself! In short, our goal is to help you acquire knowledge about how to use IT to accomplish personal, organizational, and business partner goals—the really important stuff of business today.

OUR SPIRAL MODEL

Just as we see knowledge creation and application as a spiral, so too do we see understanding information systems as a spiral. To help prepare you for your future as a knowledge-enabled professional, throughout the book we highlight business and information applications first and then discuss the underlying technology. This is an important point. Technology itself is useless unless organizations can use it to create value.

The structure of this book follows closely our thinking about how organizations create valuable information systems. It follows a similar spiral path that deals with the organizational context, technology fundamentals, and business impact of systems.

In this book, we use a Spiral Model approach (see the figure on the next page) to help you learn about IT. After this Logon introduction, at the base of the spiral, we move toward a better understanding of IT hardware, software, and networks through an emphasis on an individual's perspective of these topics. Understanding the technological environment that an individual (you) works in, and how individuals might use information technology as knowledge-enabled professionals, will provide you with a sound foundation.

After covering the basics, we spiral upward toward a view of organizations as purposeful collections of individuals who use IT (hardware, software, and networks) to perform knowledge work activities. We try to answer the question, "How do organizations build and use technology to achieve their goals?"

The final spiral takes a business partner perspective. It moves beyond the organization to learning how technology can support new relationships among organizations and their customers, suppliers, and other stakeholders. It also considers the challenges and risks global organizations face, thereby highlighting the need for IT controls and enterprise risk management. The spiral is supported by additional, more detailed information on topics of interest in the corresponding Tech Guides at the end of the book. You will see an icon like the one in the margin to let you know when more information is available and which Tech Guide to go to.

Since in all cases humans actually operate information systems, we begin the first three chapters with the individual context. To be effective, we must never lose sight of the user, so we begin our journey with chapters that cover the fundamentals of business and its current context and describe why knowledge skills are so essential to any part of business today. We also cover the fundamentals of IT and begin to explore the concept of how individuals use technology to add value to an organization.

In later chapters, we learn about how systems operate within an overall organizational context, about connectivity and e-business and the dimensions of globalization that are affecting all organizations and their systems. What does the trade-off between security and usability mean, as an example? Or how do we make consistent information available to our workforce around the globe?

Finally, in the last chapters we discuss integrated operations and the interdependencies of business. No organization operates alone. It needs customers, suppliers, and partners. It must deal with regulatory issues and interact with government agencies. And it must often do so electronically and in real time. Employees in these organizations must use their skills and their employer's information systems to support complex business decisions that often have important

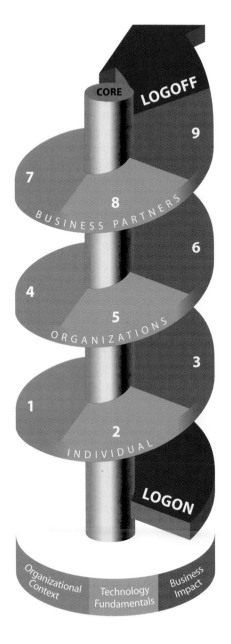

consequences. Problem solving is really the knowledge work of today, no matter your discipline or career choice.

Uniting these chapters and tying them together are the ever-
important concepts at the "CORE" of information technology systems:

- **C**onnectivity
- **O**n-line Security
- **R**elationships
- **E**thics

In each chapter, we will highlight important examples of connectivity, security, business relationships, or ethical considerations that will help you master information systems in the appropriate context of their risks and rewards.

At the beginning of each chapter, we also include a section called the "Voice of Experience." These highlight people just like you, perhaps with a little more experience, who are already putting knowledge about the strategic uses of technology to work in their careers and for the benefit of their organizations. They can help you see the value of learning to apply information technology in a variety of professions and different situations.

We intend for this book to be a journey through business and technology that begins and ends with you. With this Spiral Model approach, if you get lost at any point, simply retrace your steps in the spiral. Understand that a new topic simply expands on what you already learned in the first few chapters. By beginning with the familiar and moving toward the unfamiliar, we believe that this Spiral Model approach will provide you with the knowledge and tools you need to succeed as a future knowledge-enabled professional.

So, if you're ready, let's begin our journey into the world of information technology systems and the future world of knowledge work.

Integrative Application Case: Campuspad.ca

In all of the content chapters throughout the text (Chapters 1–9), you will find part of an Integrative Application Case that will help you apply what you have learned in each chapter to a real-world situation. The hypothetical creation of an on-line student business closely mirrors the real success story of four former students who began researching a new business concept in their first year of university after taking introductory IT—so it really does happen! As you move through the chapters, more and more information will be made available about the case. You will have to find out which opportunities and challenges facing this new business can be addressed using information systems and which cannot. You will analyze solutions and sort out problems using information presented in the relevant chapter, both from on-line sources and your own creativity and knowledge. The objective? To help this business get off the ground and succeed.

Your instructor may do this case in class or assign it as homework, perhaps asking you to work in a team during a lab or on your own. There are no completely right or wrong answers, but there are certainly essential things to think about and apply from each chapter. We hope that this case approach will help build your understanding of the material and the value of information systems.

PART I

The Individual Perspective

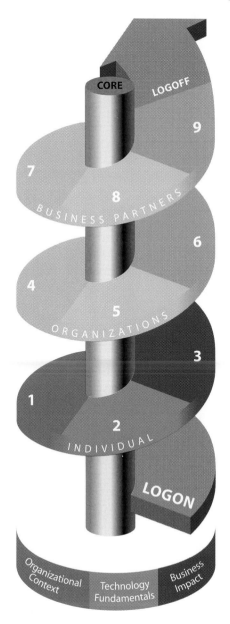

Chapter 1
Introduction to the Business Context
Chapter 2
Fundamentals of Information Technology
Chapter 3
Doing Knowledge Work to Create Business Value

In this book, we take you on a journey. You can visualize this journey as we do—a spiral path that will lead you to become a valued knowledge-enabled professional. We begin by focusing on you, the individual. In Chapter 1, we will introduce you to the concept of knowledge work and why knowledge work skills are important to business organizations. In Chapter 2, you will learn about the basic information technologies that knowledge-enabled professionals use. In Chapter 3, you will find out how knowledge-enabled professionals integrate their skills and use of information technology to support business decision making and problem solving. So if you're ready, get comfortable, and let's begin our journey!

1

WHAT WE WILL COVER

- Organizations and the Business Environment
- What Is Knowledge
- What Is an Information System?

C Connectivity   Podcasting for IT Knowledge
O On-line Security   How to Maintain a No-"Phishing" Zone
R Relationships   Thinking about Teams. . .
E Ethics   What Is Ethics?

Introduction to the Business Context

ROI ## STUDENT RETURN ON INVESTMENT

Through your investment of time in reading and thinking about this chapter, your return, or created value, is gaining knowledge. Use the following questions as a study guide.

1. How do different factors in a business environment, such as the Internet and globalization, impact the need for timely data, information, and knowledge?
2. What role does knowledge creation play in your success as a current student and future knowledge-enabled professional?
3. How do the different types of information systems (IS) help knowledge-enabled professionals manage data, information, and knowledge?

THE VOICE OF EXPERIENCE
Michael Lee, Ryerson University

Michael Lee graduated in 2005 with a Bachelor of Commerce degree from the Information Technology Management program. Since then he has worked as an information technology consultant at IBM helping his clients achieve business results through technology.

What do you do in your current position? I analyze the business requirements of projects from the client's perspective. Right now I'm part of a team that is implementing an enterprise resource planning (ERP) system using Oracle technology. The best ERP systems are customizable. It's not good enough to have a one-size-fits-all software; the software must be customized to the client's specific business functions because each company works differently. I do a "fit-gap" analysis and then tailor and implement the software to my client's specific requirements. To do this, I need to understand the features of the application, know its capabilities and limitations, and then apply it to my client's specific business needs.

What do you consider to be important career skills? Number one is a willingness to learn. Especially because I'm new, I need to take courses and learn the technology. Both IBM and Oracle have on-line courses. There's always a course you can take that will propel you further because you'll know a lot more and feel more confident.

Another important skill is communication. It is essential that I understand the technology and communicate it in a way my clients understand. They need to understand how technology can help create business value. I also work closely with technical people. In order to develop a customized ERP solution, the developers need to understand exactly what the client needs. This is more about understanding business requirements than it is about technology. The more skills you have—especially in the consulting industry—the more opportunities you'll have.

How do you use IT? I use applications on the Internet like MSN messenger, AOL messenger, and an IBM chat application. It's like being able to talk to anybody on a moment's notice. If you need a quick answer, you simply message them and it pops up on their screen. IBM uses VPN extensively to connect remotely to these resources, so I can work on my project at any time regardless of my geographical location. I always have important information and resources at my fingertips when I need it.

For all the projects I've worked on so far, the project team members have been working in different geographical areas. For my last project, there was an expert in the United States who would come into Toronto once a week. For the rest of the week he would work remotely from Chicago or New York. I've also worked with developers in India. I've had to dial in via VPN around 11 p.m. to catch them at the beginning of their work day and then I'd have to dial in around 6 a.m. and get caught up on what they did and answer any of their questions.

Can you describe an example of how you have used IT to improve business operations? IBM has a partnership with Oracle, which provides an on-line knowledge-based system called Metalink. You can search a database of key terms, documentation, FAQs, and previously resolved questions. It's an important tool when diagnosing and troubleshooting errors that are happening within any project. For example, I was implementing an Oracle business intelligence package, where there were a lot of set-up issues. When we ran into issues, we used Metalink to help diagnose the problem and find solutions faster.

Have you got any "on the job" advice for students seeking a career in IT or business? Choose a career, field, or industry that you think you'll enjoy. Your interest and enthusiasm will show, you'll want to learn the material, and you'll pick it up much quicker than you normally would. If you go with your interest, there's bound to be more opportunities and you'll enjoy yourself a lot more.

BUSINESS ORGANIZATIONS AND THE BUSINESS ENVIRONMENT

To learn about business organizations and the information systems and technology that support them, we need to start with a brief review of the world of business. Businesses are one type of organization. Other types include governmental, not-for-profit, and religious. For our purposes, when we refer to a **business,** we mean an organization with one or more people who:

1. decide on common goals to pursue
2. work together to locate and organize resources
3. create processes in order to achieve the desired goals

Typically a business's primary goal is to generate economic value (make a profit) over a sustained period of time. For example, when you order coffee at Tim Hortons this generates value for the company. Or when you sign up for a Rogers Wireless plan, this service creates business value for Rogers by giving you access to voice and data communication via a national wireless network of networks.

In reality, many different factors drive the selection of business goals. One of the most important factors influencing a business is its environment. As Figure 1.1 shows, a company's **business environment** is a complex collection of political, economic, social, and technological factors that organizational leaders must consider when making decisions regarding goals, organizational forms, and the creation of business value. And to respond to those factors, businesses are relying on information systems and information technology more than ever. Let's take a quick look at how.

THE CHANGING ORGANIZATION FORM

Increasingly, organizations are turning to technology and information systems to keep pace with dynamic business environments. Organizations rely on digital information to gain competitive advantage

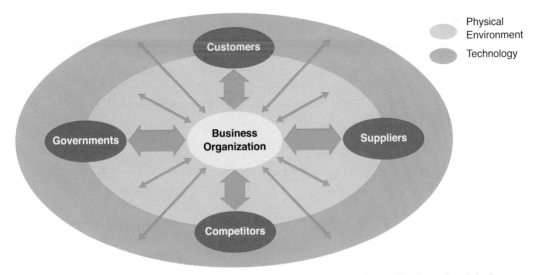

Figure 1.1 An organization's business environment is often a complex collection of political, economic, social, and technological factors.

and to respond quickly to opportunities. And as organizations strive to respond quickly, they are changing the way they organize or structure themselves.

Think about an organization from the point of view of a messenger carrying decisions between the top of the business and the bottom. The taller the organization, the more "stairs" the messenger must descend or climb to deliver the message. At each floor, people stop the messenger to read the message and to comment. This additional communication may or may not help the messenger efficiently and effectively deliver the message. Now imagine that the messenger can take an express elevator to deliver the message. The elevator "flattens" the business into two floors: (1) the floor where the messenger gets on and (2) the floor where the messenger gets off.

Organizations use advanced information systems (IS), such as *decision support systems (DSS)* and *enterprise resource planning (ERP) systems,* like the messenger uses the express elevator—to "flatten" the organization by eliminating unnecessary floors. Imagine the effect of such de-layering in a business. Now a chief executive officer (CEO) can use a DSS to view and understand corporate data. Such a system could very well eliminate the need for layers of middle managers to filter and interpret the data for the CEO. By eliminating the need for these management layers, the DSS helps "flatten" the organization and may make it more responsive to its business environment. As a student you do similar things using IS. You no longer need to visit several libraries and access specialized research resources individually to write term papers. You simply use a tool such as Google or your school's on-line library portal to find what you need.

GLOBALIZATION

While the organizational flattening is one of the effects of implementing information technology, advances in communications technologies have sparked an even greater change to the business environment: the globalization of business. **Globalization** means that modern businesses are using information technology to expand their market to customers around the globe, to find the lowest-cost suppliers regardless of location, and even to create 24-hour business days by shuttling work across time zones and nations. Much of the current globalization of business and business's worldwide reach is due to the use of the Internet and Internet-related technologies.

THE INTERNET

What is the Internet and why is it important to generating business value? To understand the Internet, you need to understand that much of today's economy is based on computer networks, in which a communications medium links together two or more computers, sort of how telephone networks link your phone to all others around the world. You almost certainly have a computer network in your college or university that links together the lab computers with other computers around the campus. You also probably have an ID and password that enable you to logon to this network. The **Internet** is then simply a large number of cooperating computer networks that use the same rules for sending messages.

The most widely used component of the Internet is the **World Wide Web,** or just "the Web." The Web is an Internet software application that allows us to transfer text, images, audio, and video. Its wide range of capabilities has led to new ways of doing business in the global marketplace.

So why has the Internet become such an integral part of our personal and business lives? There are three reasons for this: communication, information, and commerce. Communication generates business value by making it possible for knowledge-enabled professionals to share information both between themselves and with business partners. The Internet does this by providing newsgroups, chat rooms, bulletin boards, text messaging using cell phones, as well as e-mail and instant messaging. You may have only used a few of these Internet communication methods, but as you enter the business world, you will also find the others useful to you.

Another key to generating business value for any organization is the ability to both make information available to knowledge-enabled professionals and business partners, and for them to find information in a timely manner. Through the Web, the Internet has dramatically reduced the effort required to carry out both activities. For example, the Web makes it easy to publish information in a variety of ways. In fact, the Internet and Web have been called the greatest advance in publishing since the invention of the printing press over 500 years ago. After publishing information on the Web, efficient search engines make it possible to locate it quickly.

Finally, the Internet generates business value by being an avenue for the buying and selling of goods, also known as **commerce.** While still just a small proportion of the total commerce in the world, electronic commerce or e-commerce is growing dramatically. **E-commerce** is the use of information systems, technologies, and computer networks by individuals and organizations to create business value. This occurs especially in the information economy, such as travel, insurance, and banking, where often no physical product changes hands. We discuss e-commerce in more detail in Chapters 7 and 8.

WHAT DO YOU THINK?

Besides integrating communication, information, and commerce, there's another reason why the Internet has become such an important part of our daily lives—entertainment! This is one of the fastest-growing applications on the Web. To prove this point, just think about your own Web usage in this area and then consider the following questions:

1: What are some of the ways you use the Internet for entertainment?
2: Consider the site you prefer most for music or video downloading. What makes it so useful and interesting?
3: How could businesses use Web-based entertainment to create value for their customers? Can you think of any early examples of companies already doing this?

In whatever career you choose, in whatever business environment you find yourself, you need to understand your role in the organization (how what you do creates business value) and your organization's goals and information needs. Further, your success depends on understanding the technology solutions that help meet those goals and needs. Why? Ultimately, the need for and the use of information lies at the heart of every business decision and process.

Quick Test

1. The _____ is a worldwide network of networks.
   a. BusinesNet
   b. Internet
   c. TelcoNet
   d. World Wide Web

2. Which of the following factors has NOT contributed to globalization of business?
   a. Internet
   b. the search for low-cost suppliers
   c. managers' desire to travel overseas
   d. the ability to increase the amount of work done each day

3. The buying and selling of goods is also known as _____.
   a. revenue
   b. produce
   c. income
   d. commerce

Answers: 1. b; 2. c; 3. d

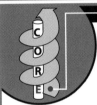

Ethics

What Is Ethics?

Ethics can be defined as "the discipline concerned with what is morally good and bad, right and wrong. The term is also applied to any system or theory of moral values or principles" (http://www.britannica.com).

At the personal level, ethics is the set of "rights" and "wrongs" we use to decide how to act in a given situation. Our ideas of right and wrong stem from our values, our culture, and other sources. One source, The Computer Ethics Institute (CEI), provides guidelines for the ethical use of computers: *The Ten Commandments of Computer Use* (http://www.cpsr.org/program/ethics/cei.html). Although these commandments are especially appropriate for professionals who use computers and information systems, they deserve consideration by all knowledge-enabled professionals.

Ethics and Academic Honesty

Your university or college most likely has an academic integrity policy for its students. As a student, you routinely transform data and information into knowledge in order to write papers, take tests, create programs, and so on. As you create this knowledge, it is generally accepted that you must not submit work that is not your own creation (work of another student or a published work) as your own. To take credit for another's work and then receive a grade for it is similar to stealing and then selling that "hot" item for a quick profit.

Web Resources

- Ethics Resource Center—http://www.ethics.org/
- Business Ethics Blog—http://www.businessethicsblog.com/
- BusinessEthics.ca—http://www.businessethics.ca/
- Canadian Centre for Ethics & Corporate Policy—http://www.ethicscentre.ca/

WHAT DO YOU THINK?

Academic dishonesty is a critical issue in higher education. To help you reflect on this issue, consider how your school defines academic integrity and why it considers it so important. And think about these questions:

1: As a society, should we protect intellectual property? Why?
2: Is there a link between intellectual property rights and business value? How does IP create value in business?
3: As a future IT professional, what responsibilities do you think you should have regarding the protection and upholding of intellectual property rights?

BECOMING A KNOWLEDGE-ENABLED PROFESSIONAL

Your ability to create knowledge is one of the key reasons a business will hire you. A business expects its employees to recognize opportunities, solve problems, and create business value. Regardless of your current major or chosen career, your success depends on your ability to find and process data, information, and knowledge, and to use it to make sound decisions. You are on your way to becoming what international consultant and management scholar Peter Drucker called a knowledge worker and what we call a **knowledge-enabled professional**.

According to Drucker, knowledge workers are at the heart of the new economy. And, in order to do their jobs successfully, they "require a good deal of formal education, the ability to acquire and to apply theoretical and analytical knowledge," and "they require a habit of continuous learning."[1] **Knowledge work** involves the discovery, analysis, transformation, synthesis, and communication of data, information, and knowledge. Examples include recommending an investment portfolio to clients or interpreting the monthly sales report in order to plan for the future.

LIFELONG KNOWLEDGE CREATION

To be a successful knowledge-enabled professional, you need to build on the two types of knowledge that you possess: explicit knowledge and tacit knowledge. **Explicit knowledge** is knowledge that is readily codified, such as the knowledge in this textbook. **Tacit knowledge** is knowledge that you gain through experience, insight, and discovery. These two types of knowledge are complementary halves of a lifelong knowledge-creation process. As highlighted in the CORE box "Podcasting for IT Knowledge," recent advances in portable electronic devices like the iPod™ offer additional ways to incorporate the explicit and the tacit knowledge of others into your own knowledge, thereby enhancing your personal knowledge-creation process.

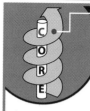

Connectivity

Podcasting for IT Knowledge

By now, most of you have heard of, and in many cases own, an MP3 player such as the Apple iPod to which you can download and listen to your favourite tunes. But, beyond their entertainment value, these personal digital audio/image players (shown in Figure 1.2) and personal computers with digital audio playback capabilities create new opportunities for discovering and learning from experts and others. The primary technology that has allowed for this arguably more productive use of audio devices is known as podcasting, a name derived by mingling the words iPod and broadcasting. Podcasting is a method of publishing audio programs via the Internet that allows users of just about any digital audio device to download broadcasts or to subscribe to a feed of new files (usually MP3s).[2]

1. Drucker, Peter F. The Age of Social Transformation. *Atlantic Monthly*, 1994:11, pp. 53–80.
2. http://en.wikipedia.org/wiki/Podcasting.

Podcasting makes all types of audio content portable and available on demand. So listeners can catch up on audio content—whether news, entertainment, or learning—while completing other tasks like working out at the gym. Like many Internet technologies, podcasting brings "power to the people" by allowing almost anyone to broadcast audio content. However, podcasting has more recently gained interest in the corporate world. Companies can use podcasts to spread the word about their products and services or to complement other media. For example, CBC Radio offers several podcasts that you can subscribe to at www.cbc.ca/podcasting.

One of the more well-known IT-related sites is PodcastAlley.com, which lists over 1,000 podcasts related to technology alone. So if you need to increase your knowledge of agile or extreme programming, or IT security, or even of what Microsoft is up to next, then the Internet and podcasting can provide you the knowledge you seek.

Figure 1.2 Today's portable digital audio and digital image devices, such as the one shown here, create new opportunities for increasing knowledge.

Finally, podcasting is one of the ways that professors are supplementing university and college classes. According to the University of Calgary, it was the first university in the country to introduce podcasting on a large scale when it launched four courses in 2006 featuring portable MP3 technology as a teaching tool.[3]

Podcasts will help you become more knowledgeable in the future. For now, you can become more knowledgeable in your classes by downloading audio files about topics in this book from WileyPLUS.

Web Resources

- http://canada.podcast.com
- http://www.itconversations.com/index.html
- http://www.rogic.com/canadapodcasts/
- http://www.podcastalley.com/podcast_genres.php?pod_genre_id=1

How does the knowledge-creation process work in the "real world?" Consider one of your first steps toward becoming a knowledge-enabled professional: the business internship or job interview. Interviewers often ask you about their company. They want to assess what explicit knowledge you may have gained about their company by visiting their website or reading the company's annual report. As the interview continues, the interviewer may ask you to describe a situation where you worked as a member of a project team. As you describe your experiences and the lessons you learned from them, you are highlighting your tacit knowledge of working in teams.

CHAPTER

1

3. http://www.ucalgary.ca/oncampus/online/march-06/ipod.html Retrieved July 19, 2006.

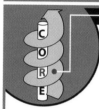

—Relationships

Thinking about Teams . . .

"A team is a small number of people with complementary skills who are committed to a common purpose, performance goals, and approach for which they hold them-selves mutually accountable."—Jon R. Katzenbach and Douglas K. Smith, *The Wisdom of Teams*, p. 45.

If there is one certainty in life, besides death and taxes, it is this: At some point in your life, you have been or will be a member of a team. Teams and teamwork are a significant part of many businesses. Your academic career will be filled with teams and teamwork. We designed this textbook and its companion website to provide you with tools and knowledge you need to become the best team member and team leader that you can.

Think for a minute about the teams that you've been a part of, and now answer the following questions: Did you work together well? Did some members work harder or seem to care more than others? Why do you think this was so? Does Katzenbach and Smith's definition of a team make sense to you, given your experiences with teams? Another researcher, Dr. Meredith Belbin, proposes that people fulfill different roles both within a single team and also across different teams. Do you always occupy the same role on all of your teams? Find out more about these roles by visiting the links listed below and reading about the "Technology of Teams" in Tech Guide E.

Web Resources

- Belbin's Nine Team Roles—http://www.belbin.com/belbin-team-roles.htm
- Microsoft's Net Meeting; hold a virtual meeting now—http://www.microsoft.com/windows/netmeeting/features/default.asp

You've learned that data are transformed into information, and information can be transformed into knowledge. Then what? If an organization is willing to hire you because you are capable of creating tacit knowledge that contributes to the organization's success, what does the organization do with the knowledge that you've created? How does it turn your tacit knowledge into explicit knowledge and/or information that others can use? In the next section, we show how organizations use information systems to manage the data, information, and knowledge that it creates.

Quick Test

1. If you add human experience and judgement to information, you can create _____.

    a. data   b. knowledge   c. resources   d. facts

2. To acquire tacit knowledge on how to use MS Excel's advanced functions to solve a business problem, which of the following sources would you consult?
   a. a lab manual for an introductory MS Excel course
   b. a textbook with an MS Excel–related appendix
   c. a DVD-based presentation by an expert user of MS Excel
   d. a textbook describing spreadsheet software capabilities

3. Following Drucker's definition, recommending an investment portfolio to a client is an example of _____.
   a. financial information interpretation
   b. knowledge work
   c. workflow portfolio data analysis
   d. data retrieval

Answers: 1. b; 2. c; 3. b

WHAT IS AN INFORMATION SYSTEM?

Like most students, you probably surf the Web, shop on-line instant-message with your friends on your personal computer, and send text messages on a cell phone. You may even go to the dentist and have digital X rays taken and then read on a computer. All of these things demonstrate information systems (IS) in action. So what is an IS?

> An *information system (IS)* is an organized collection of people, information, business processes, and information technology, designed to transform inputs into outputs, in order to achieve a goal.

As Figure 1.3 shows, businesses design their information systems to leverage the human ability to achieve business goals through the timely and appropriate application of technology, and

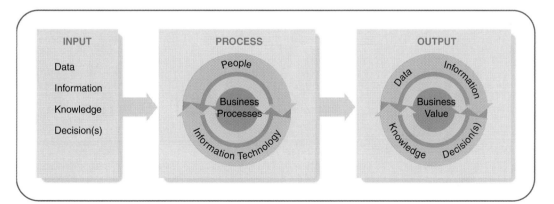

Figure 1.3 As this Input-Process-Output (IPO) model shows, a business should design its information system to leverage the human ability to use information technology to its best advantage. By doing this, the output is more than the sum of its parts (data 1 information 1 knowledge 1 decisions)—it is the creation of business value.

CHAPTER 1

the timely delivery of appropriate and useful data, information, and knowledge. That is, information systems enhance knowledge work, decision making, problem solving, communicating, and coordinating. Table 1.1 defines the components of our IS model (Figure 1.3) and gives examples for each component.

Table 1.1	Information System Components	
Concept	**Definition**	**Example**
Input Process Output	Items entered into a system in order to transform them into outputs. A series of one or more steps used by a business to transform inputs into outputs. The end result of a process. Information is the result of the transformation (processing) of data. From an organizational perspective, the output of a process is a product or a service.	(1) *Input:* Enter customer names, addresses, and income levels into a marketing IS in order to (2) *Process:* create (3) *Output:* an income-level-based customer mailing list.
Data **Information** **Knowledge**	Raw, unorganized facts. Processed/organized/transformed data that are useful to a person. Information plus human experience and judgement.	(1) *Data:* The Gucci sunglasses you purchased from the sidewalk vendor on Yonge Street, Toronto, cost $10.00; (2) *Information:* your total bill is $10.00; and (3) *Knowledge:* Since most genuine Gucci sunglasses sell for more than $100, you realize that you purchased a pair of fake Gucci sunglasses.
System	A recognizable whole that consists of a collection of interrelated parts that interact with each other to transform inputs into outputs in order to achieve a goal.	Humans, as a biological system, transform water, food, and air (inputs) into nutrients and oxygen (outputs), using their digestive and respiratory organs (interrelated parts) in order to survive (goal).
People	People or organizations that have both an interest in and an influence on the creation, implementation, or operation of an IS.	Marketing analysts push for the creation of a new IS to support their knowledge work.
Information Technology	The physical components, typically hardware, software, and connectivity, that make up an IS. Technology enables processes to perform the steps they were designed to accomplish.	The phone company's computers and networks rely on billing software to process monthly bills.
Decision	A choice made from one or more alternatives to follow or avoid some course of action.	I will study later, after I exercise and eat dinner.
Business Value	A positive return on the investment of resources that is created through the effective and efficient integration of an organization's people, information, information technology, and business processes.	A bank decides to reduce its number of tellers and increase the number of ATMs. The bank can assess the return on investment (ROI) and the amount of cost avoidance (fewer salaries and benefits to pay) based on this decision. If there is a positive ROI and overall cost savings result, then the bank's decision created business value.

Although we believe that ISs are a necessary and strategic part of all modern business organizations, and that it is important to understand modern information technology, we emphasize the need for organizational IS and IT to initiate, support, and sustain the creation of business value. In later chapters, we show you how these components come together to create business value and to support the organization.

WHAT DO YOU THINK?

Consider the components of a typical IS outlined in Table 1.1. In relation to the systems you use at your school to manage your enrolment, course selection, and payments, reflect on these questions:

1: What are the benefits to the user of an on-line information system versus a manual alternative? Does this make it worthwhile for you to use the system or would you prefer not to?
2: What are the benefits to the institution of an on-line system? Are these benefits critical for the institution to achieve in its current environment?
3: What would a smart organization do to encourage the acceptance and use of on-line systems among first-time users?

TYPES OF IS

Now that you have an idea of what a generic information system looks like and how it works, let's take a brief look at some types of IS that you'll find in a business. From transaction processing systems (TPS), management information systems (MIS), and decision support systems (DSS), to enterprise resource planning (ERP) systems and customer relationship management (CRM) systems, information systems perform a wide variety of tasks and services. These types of IS use all of the components of IS listed in Table 1.1, and each of these IS is vital to the efficient and effective operation of most modern businesses. As you read about the different types of IS in Table 1.2 on the next page, you'll see that, regardless of the type of IS, businesses connect people, information, hardware, and software to achieve goals and to create value.

IS COMPONENTS AND TYPES

The components of an IS are contained in each type of IS. Table 1.3 on page 26 illustrates each of the components for a transaction processing system (TPS).

IS SECURITY

As businesses increasingly rely on the use of IS to support and enable the creation of business value, the need for IS security also grows. In general, **IS security** (also known as *information assurance*) protects people, information, software, hardware, networks,

Table 1.2	The Business Value of IS Types	
IS Type	What Does It Do?	How Does It Help to Create Business Value?
TPS (transaction processing system)	Captures and processes transactions to make them available to the organization. A *transaction* is the exchange of something of value the business produces for something in return that the business values, e.g., revenue from product sales.	If a business cannot track its transactions, it will have no way of making decisions about the success or failure of its business processes.
MIS (management information system)	Through processing and reporting features, an MIS provides timely information to decision makers.	Timely reports enable managers to monitor critical processes and avoid costly mistakes.
DSS (decision support system)	Provides analytical and visualization tools to support and enhance decision making and planning.	Enables managers to make data-based decisions and to discover new business opportunities through the use of its tools.
ERP (enterprise resource planning) system	Integrates and standardizes processes, and centralizes and standardizes the storage and management of data.	Reduces costs associated with duplication of processes and effort. Also, can minimize decision-making mistakes due to multiple versions of the same data, information, and knowledge.
CRM (customer relationship management) system	Integrates data collection, transformation, storage, and analysis of customer transaction data, including purchases, service requests, and other forms of customer contact.	Greatly increases the understanding of customers' purchasing and service behaviours and needs. Facilitates the timely and proactive management of customers.

and organizations from the harmful actions of others. Harmful actions include unauthorized use of computing or system resources and unauthorized access to and use of private and/or proprietary data, information, and knowledge.

In fact, security is such an important aspect of IS that we include a security-related topic in every chapter. In this chapter, we start with a security topic known as *phishing*. The CORE box "How to Maintain a No-'Phishing' Zone" discusses phishing from an individual standpoint. However, due to the value of proprietary and other sensitive data used and stored by organizations, hackers and other cyber-criminals target businesses, too.

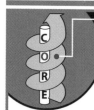

On-line Security

How to Maintain a No-'Phishing' Zone

Internet scammers casting about for people's financial information have a new way to lure unsuspecting victims: They go "phishing." Phishing, also called "carding," is a high-tech scam that uses spam to deceive consumers into disclosing their credit card numbers, bank account information, social insurance numbers (SIN), passwords, and other sensitive information.

According to Industry Canada, "Phishing is the impersonation of a trusted person or organization in order to steal a person's personal information, generally for the purpose of 'identity theft'. For example, an e-mail message may appear to be from a well-known bank asking recipients to visit a website to confirm their account details, but the website is actually controlled by a hostile party."[4]

Canada's Department of Public Safety and Emergency Preparedness and the United States Department of Justice recommend that Internet users keep the following three steps in mind when they see e-mails or websites that may be part of a phishing scheme:

Recognize it — If you receive an unexpected e-mail from a bank or credit card company saying that your account will be shut down if you do not confirm your billing information, do not reply or click on any links in the e-mail. Phishers typically have one purpose in mind: to entice people to react immediately by clicking on the link and inputting their password or credit card number before they take time to think through what they are doing. Internet users need to resist that impulse.

Report it — Contact your bank or credit card company if you have unwittingly supplied personal or financial information. You should also report the matter to your local police. They will often take police reports even if the crime may ultimately be investigated by another law enforcement agency. In addition, a creditor who mistakenly believes that you are the person responsible for a fraudulent transaction may want to see a copy of a police report before correcting your credit account or credit report. Finally, report your identity theft case immediately to the appropriate government and private-sector organizations. Canadian and American agencies are compiling information about identity theft to identify trends and assist law enforcement agencies in potential investigations.

Stop it — Become familiar with the practices of your financial institutions and credit card companies. They normally will not use e-mail to confirm an existing client's information. Keep informed of the latest advisories and steps on how to protect yourself from identity theft and fraud. A number of legitimate companies and financial institutions that have been targeted by phishing schemes have published contact information for reporting possible phishing e-mails as well as on-line notices about how their customers can recognize and protect themselves from phishing.[5]

Web Resources

- Public Saftety and Emergency Preparedness Canada—http://www.psepc.gc.ca/chan/cit/index-en.asp
- Privacy Rights Clearinghouse—http://www.privacyrights.org/identity.htm
- CERT® Coordination Center—http://www.cert.org/homeusers/HomeComputerSecurity/
- Computer Wellness at Western—http://wellness.uwo.ca/campaigns/phishing/
- The Globe and Mail—W3C: Phishing remains root of flourishing e-crime, http://www.theglobeandmail.com/servlet/story/RTGAM.20060526.gtcrimemay26/BNStory/Technology/einsider/ Retrieved July 19, 2006.

CHAPTER

1

4. Industry Canada http://e-com.ic.gc.ca/epic/internet/inecic-ceac.nsf/en/h_gv00170e.html#phishing Retrieved July 19, 2006.
5. Department of Public Safety and Emergency Preparedness http://www.psepc.gc.ca/prg/le/bs/phish-en.asp#how Retrieved July 19, 2006.

Table 1.3	IS Components of a Transaction Processing System (TPS)
Input Process Output	Sales records are gathered at point of sale (POS), when a product's bar code is scanned. The data are added to a sales database table and removed from an available inventory database table. The product is sold.
Data	 9 780470 840306
Information Knowledge	1 medium, white, Concordia University T-shirt, $19.95, Sept. 9, 2006, 4:06 p.m. Customers who purchased white Concordia University T-shirts were also likely to purchase Concordia University beer mugs.
System	As part of the TPS, the POS bar code reader allows for a sale to take place by managing the sale's inventory. The payment module enables the customer to purchase the T-shirt using their credit card.
People	The clerks in the university bookstore have been trained on the system and are able to serve customers efficiently.
IT	The POS hardware (the bar code reader) uses software to read data that are then input into inventory databases, the accounting system, and banks through network connectivity.
Decision	The beer mugs are to be moved closer to the T-shirts to encourage cross-selling of products during the first weeks of September.
Business Value	More beer mugs and T-shirts were sold in the month of September as students, and their parents, arrived for the start of the school year.

Quick Test

1. TRUE or FALSE. Fundamentally, all information systems transform inputs into outputs by carrying out one or more processes.

2. Of the following types of IS, which type primarily captures and processes data?
   a. DSS (decision support system)
   b. EIS (enterprise information system)
   c. MIS (management information system)
   d. TPS (transaction processing system)

3. IS security includes protection for _____.
   a. data
   b. people
   c. networks
   d. all of the above

Answers: 1. True; 2. d; 3. d

STUDENT RETURN ON INVESTMENT SUMMARY

1. How do different factors in a business environment, such as the Internet and globalization, impact the need for timely data, information, and knowledge?

A company's business environment is a complex collection of political, economic, social, and technological factors that organizational leaders must consider when making decisions regarding goals, organizational forms, and the creation of business value. Increasingly, organizations are turning to technology and information systems to keep pace with dynamic business environments.

The Internet is a global network of networks that supports communication, information, and commerce. All three generate business value for individuals and companies. Communication generates business value by making it possible for knowledge-enabled professionals to share information both between themselves and with trading partners. A second key to generating business value for any organization is the ability to make information available internally to employees and externally to trading partners, in a timely manner. Through the Web, the Internet has dramatically reduced the effort required to carry out both activities. Finally, the Internet generates business value by being an avenue for the electronic buying and selling of goods, also known as e-commerce.

2. What role does knowledge creation play in your success as a current student and future knowledge-enabled professional?

Data are raw unorganized facts, numbers, pictures, and so on. Information is data that have been organized and are useful to a person. Knowledge is created when a person combines experience and judgement with information. This relationship implies that once data are collected, transforming them into information and knowledge adds value to the knowledge-enabled professional and, consequently, the organization.

To be a successful knowledge-enabled professional, you need to build on the two types of knowledge that you possess: explicit knowledge and tacit knowledge. Explicit knowledge is knowledge that is readily codified, such as the knowledge in a magazine or book. Tacit knowledge is knowledge that is within you, gained through experience, insight, and discovery. These two types of knowledge are complementary halves of a lifelong knowledge-creation process. Creating new knowledge, transforming explicit knowledge into tacit knowledge, and applying knowledge are ways knowledge-enabled professionals can increase their likelihood for success for themselves and their organizations.

3. How do the different information systems (IS) help knowledge-enabled professionals manage data, information, and knowledge?

Information systems combine people, information, and technology to address business needs and to achieve business goals. An information system (IS) is an organized collection of people, information, business processes, and information technology, designed to transform inputs into outputs, in order to achieve a goal. Table 1.2 on page 24 summarizes the different types of IS and how they help to create business value.

KNOWLEDGE SPEAK

CHAPTER

1

REVIEW QUESTIONS

Multiple-choice questions

1. Enterprise resource planning (ERP) systems can reduce:

   I. costs associated with duplication of processes and effort.

   II. decision-making mistakes due to multiple versions of the same data, information, and knowledge.

   III. knowledge-enabled professionals' reliance on data and information as the basis for decision making.

   a.   I
   b.   II
   c.   I and II
   d.   I and III
   e.   I, II, and III

2. Data are _____.

   a.   letters
   b.   numbers
   c.   symbols
   d.   all of the above

3. To arrange the following terms in order from least complex to most complex, which of the following sequences is correct?

   a.   knowledge, information, data
   b.   knowledge, data, information
   c.   information, data, knowledge
   d.   data, knowledge, information
   e.   data, information, knowledge

4. Which of the following best reflects an ethical view of decision making?

   a.   getting the job done quickly
   b.   getting the job done cheaply
   c.   getting the job done correctly
   d.   getting the job done, whatever it takes

Fill-in-the-blank questions

5. _____ are raw unorganized facts, numbers, and pictures.

6. For a manager, examples of _____ might include the names of clients, their phone numbers, and their e-mail addresses in an address-book program in a personal digital assistant (e.g., a Palm Pilot™).

7. _____ is created when a person combines experience and judgement with information.

True-false questions

8. Wisdom enables business leaders to perceive the underlying meaning and nuances of a business situation and to respond in an ethical manner appropriate to the situation.

9. According to the definition given in your textbook, accountants are not knowledge-enabled professionals.

10. Tacit knowledge is knowledge that can be readily organized and displayed for anyone to access, view, and incorporate into their personal knowledge.

Matching questions

Choose the BEST answer from Column B for each item in Column A.

Column A
11. Data
12. Information
13. Knowledge

Column B
a. You listen to the weather report and discover that it predicts a blizzard.
b. Milk.
c. You need to buy milk at your grocery store before it starts snowing, or you may find that the stores have sold all their milk.
d. None of the Column B choices are appropriate matches.

Column A
14. Business process
15. Input
16. Output

Column B
a. Raw sales data.
b. Organize and format the sales data in order to create a monthly sales report.
c. A manager's monthly sales report produced by the IS department.
e. None of the Column B choices are appropriate matches.

Short-answer questions

17. Apply the model of an IS to an information system of your choosing. Based on the IS you choose, give an example for each of the following components:

    a. Input
    b. Business process
    c. Output

18. What are the two kinds of knowledge that make up the knowledge cycle? How do they differ from each other? Give an example of each kind of knowledge.

Discussion/Essay questions

19. Define the terms *knowledge work* and *knowledge-enabled professional,* and explain why you do or do not believe that you will become a knowledge-enabled professional when you graduate.

20. Using the Input-Process-Output model of an information system presented in the text, create an example that describes how an information system can create business value for an organization.

CHAPTER

1

TEAM ACTIVITY

As you probably have already discovered, teams can be both fun and frustrating. How can you maximize the fun and minimize the frustration? Here's one way that might help.

If your team is willing to use them, good agendas can facilitate productive meetings. How? By creating an agenda, it will require your team to think about why it is meeting and what it wants to accomplish. Agendas help teams to break down meetings and project discussions into manageable chunks. They also provide a way to structure discussions from start to finish. If you have access to Microsoft Word, open Help and use the Answer Wizard to find out how to create an agenda. You can find additional sample agendas by searching the Web.

SOFTWARE APPLICATION EXERCISES

We designed these exercises to complement the material covered in each chapter, as well as to help you as a student and as a future knowledge-enabled professional.

Internet

The Internet provides a number of resources for internship and job seekers, such as Workopolis.com. Although these sites are designed to help you obtain an internship or job, maybe you're not quite ready for that. If so, use your favourite search engine to locate government (federal, provincial, municipal) sites for information on careers and future job prospects.

Presentation

Assume that you have to give a presentation about your background and qualifications to a graduate school admissions committee or a prospective employer. You should therefore create a presentation that highlights your strengths and experiences, relates why you chose your major, describes your goals, and then ties it all together to describe why you should be accepted or hired. (This exercise will also help you focus your thinking about possible majors or careers.)

Word Processing

Regardless of where you are headed after graduation, you will very likely need two important documents: a cover letter and a résumé. However, many people postpone creating these documents because they don't know where to get started. Further, in the case of the résumé, it is often difficult to highlight and convey the importance of past accomplishments in the space of one page. You can find examples of effective cover letters and résumés by searching the Web. These resources will give you ideas for creating your own résumé. Your school's career centre can also help you create and fine-tune your cover letters and your résumé.

Spreadsheet

Are you applying for summer internships? Attending career fairs? Applying for scholarships? Who did you meet? When did you send the thank-you note for that interview? Throw in all your normal school activities, and things can get hectic. However, a well-planned spreadsheet can help you reduce the stress inherent in managing your activities. Visit the course website to view a PowerPoint presentation on creating effective spreadsheets. Then, use this knowledge to create a spreadsheet that will help you track important activities.

Database

Here's a chance to see how others create and send you those form letters you receive in the mail. Word processors typically have a MERGE function that will allow you to import or *merge* data from a database (or other source) directly into the document. For this exercise, use database software to create a database of potential employers or graduate schools. You'll have to decide what data you need to store, e.g., Company Name, Internship Title, School Name, Graduate Program Name, and so on. Once you've entered the data into your database, return to your word processor and use its merge function to merge the data into your cover letter (usually called the Merge document). If you've created your database properly, it's easy to add new companies or schools to your database and print out a cover letter that contains the new data. CAUTION: When using the MERGE function, in a matter of seconds, you may create 10 cover letters with the same error. So don't forget to carefully proofread your cover letter before merging your data into it!

Advanced Challenge

Why not create a database that will manage your activities and allow you to provide data for merged documents? If you track activities by date, you can see what has been done in your meetings as well as what you still need to do. For your internship or job-related activities, you can use a database to track contacts with companies, the type of contact (phone call, e-mail, thank-you letter, etc.), the employees you contacted, and much more.

ON-LINE RESOURCES

Companion Website

- Take interactive practice quizzes to assess your knowledge and help you study in a dynamic way.
- Review PowerPoint lecture slides.
- Get help and sample solutions to end-of-chapter software application exercises.

Additional Resources Available Only on WileyPLUS

- Take the interactive Quick Test to check your understanding of the chapter material and get immediate feedback on your responses.
- Review and study with downloadable Audio Lecture MP3 files.
- Check your understanding of the key vocabulary in the chapter with Knowledge Speak Interactive Flash Cards.
- Link directly to websites recommended in the CORE boxes.

CHAPTER

1

CASE STUDY: A DAY IN THE LIFE OF A UNIVERSITY STUDENT

Ashley Hyatt attends university, where she is majoring in business administration. The following is a typical day in the life of Ashley.

7:00 A.M. Ashley awakens to new music videos of her favourite artists, played by her computer. These files have been automatically downloaded overnight in compressed format and charged to her credit card. After five minutes, the flat-screen monitor switches from the music videos to a web page displaying news customized to Ashley's interests, including scores from the latest university sporting events.

8:00 A.M.–9:15 A.M. Ashley's first class is Globalization, Regionalism, and Information Technology Systems (commonly known as GRITS), an elective course examining how nations' leaders can use IT to solve global problems. Today the class features speakers from the School of Business Leadership at the University of South Africa as well as speakers from Botswana and Kenya. In addition to being seen by students in Canada, the live broadcast is also seen by students in Singapore, Norway, Brazil, and South Africa.

9:15 A.M.–10:30 A.M. After class, Ashley heads off to the combination computer lab–coffee shop where she purchases a bottle of fruit juice and a muffin. As she leaves the food area, she checks the wall-mounted LCD panel to verify that the correct amount was deducted from her account by the mobile device in her backpack, which communicates automatically with the checkout device. Since her university now uses contact-less smart cards that do not require swiping, all she needs to do is walk through the food area exit. Her mobile device handles all such transactions in addition to other chores. In fact, she can program her mobile device to display selected information on a regular basis; wireless access is continuous throughout the university. For example, for her Finance class, Ashley's team is managing a portfolio of mature Internet stocks, and she has programmed her mobile device to display the portfolio's latest value every 15 minutes. The bottom line of the LCD window shows that the portfolio is down 1.5 percent for the day based on a number of stock exchanges around the world.

Choosing a seat at a table with an available flat-screen display device, Ashley uses the school's wireless-access capabilities to logon to her network account. She checks her Web-based to-do list and is reminded she has to take a quiz for her Networked Economy class and finish a report on Toronto.com for the Strategic Management course. The quiz takes about 20 minutes, and she is relieved to immediately find out that she scored 92 on it. Next, to finish her Toronto.com assignment, Ashley consults an on-line collection of databases and checks a few websites. When she finishes the report, she e-mails it to the professor. Even though the professor is working with an MBA team on a consulting assignment in New Zealand, she knows that he will grade the report within a couple of days and return it with attached audio and text comments. She thinks this mix of classroom lectures and independent learning is good preparation for her business career because she is learning how to learn by herself. She could have done all of this on her mobile device using audio output, but she likes to see the graphics available on the flat-screen display.

10:30 A.M.–11:45 A.M. Ashley attends her Networked Economy class and, via the Web, participates in an interesting class discussion that includes the use of voice over the Internet. Whereas some of her fellow students are in her classroom, others are at home or in offices as many as five time zones away. However, all work from the same web page and wear a special headset–microphone combination that allows them to hear and respond to other class members' comments.

1:00 P.M.–2:30 P.M. After lunch, Ashley's team for her Data Management class (Ashley, Eduardo from Brazil, and Tore from Norway) meets to review their design for a data model. The team participates in an audio conference with a shared screen, so the team members all see the same model and can take turns changing it until they agree. It is a high-fidelity model of the timetable for the Sao Paulo subway. The Data Management class is simultaneously taught with the partner business schools in Brazil and Norway, and students learn how to design and query databases at the same time they hone their skills in working in cross-cultural teams. After completing the project, Ashley catches a bus to the recreation centre to play racquetball. During the trip to the recreation centre, Ashley listens to a podcast of her Strategic Management professor's latest lecture, to confirm her understanding of the class material.

5:00 P.M.–6:00 P.M. Ashley's team in her Strategic Management class meets at the video booth in a school lab. Jennifer, an alumna working in Vancouver, has agreed to review the team's presentation. As she watches the presentation on her computer in Vancouver, Jennifer's software tags her comments, so that Ashley's team knows the portions of the presentation that need more work.

6:30 P.M.–7:30 P.M. During dinner, Ashley's sound system stops playing the latest U2 music downloads stored on her computer and announces the receipt of a priority voice mail. Ashley uses the remote to instruct the system to play it for her; it is from the alumnus who viewed her team's presentation that afternoon. Impressed by Ashley's role in the presentation, the alumnus asks Ashley to cut and paste her section of the presentation and mail it to the company's recruiter. It takes Ashley about five minutes to locate the video on the university server, edit it, and e-mail it to the recruiter.

11:00 P.M. Before going to bed, Ashley takes time to add comments on her day to the blog she is keeping for the GRITS class.

Questions

1. How many of the innovations in Ashley's home or school life are available to you? How many are you actually using?
2. There are many acronyms and technical terms mentioned in this case. Research and write a short paragraph about each of the following terms:
   a. Blog
   b. Wireless access
   c. LCD display panel
   d. Podcast
3. Do you believe that any of the information systems involved in Ashley's daily life create only limited value for her?

Integrative Application Case: Campuspad.ca

Sarah has been a great friend since you met in your student lounge during frosh week. Since you both live in residence, you hang out quite a bit. After IT class today, she approached you to talk about an idea she has for a new business and invited you to help her with it. You were curious—but cautious—as she told you about it.

Recently she had made the decision to live off-campus next year and was beginning to search for a place. Obviously, her first step was to hop on-line and search for "off-campus housing" and "student accommodation." During her search, she found a huge number of sites offering help to students look-ing for economical places to live, although she certainly wouldn't want to live in some of the places she saw on-line! The sites she had visited already left her pretty frustrated. Lots of them were focused on the United States, or mostly focused on general rental accommodation, and didn't seem to understand her specific search needs.

For instance, when she visited roommate-click.com she found that they did indeed serve Canada, but were only listed on google.com, not google.ca. While homes4students.ca was clearly a Canadian site, it didn't allow her to search for places specifically near her downtown city campus, and she couldn't see the value in searching through the hundreds of listings posted. What to do? she thought.

A visit to the student housing office had been very helpful, but so many of the listings she saw had either expired or been rented by the time she got to them that she had given up already. This wasn't going to be as quick or easy as she had thought. And after all, finals were just around the corner, and this housing search had to take second priority to that for sure!

And that's when the idea for campuspad.ca had been born. In fact, she had already registered the domain name—the first step to launching an on-line business. As she continued excitedly, you became more and more excited yourself. She had some really good ideas and might be on to something...and she wanted your help!

Guiding Case Questions

1. Research organizations, businesses, and sites that exist to serve student renters.
2. List the inputs, outputs, and transactional processes that occur in this system today.
3. How could the power of the Web and other technologies improve this system?
4. What do you think some of Sarah's ideas for this market are?
5. What ideas do you or your team have to improve on existing sites?

Your Task

Write up your findings in a two-page summary. You will use this in the next phase of the case to continue your investigation of Sarah's business idea.

WHAT WE WILL COVER

- The Components of IT Systems
- Hardware
- Software
- Connecting over Networks
- The Internet and World Wide Web

C	**Connectivity**	What Does E-Commerce Mean to You?
O	**On-line Security**	Scanning and Disinfection: Keeping Your PC Safe
R	**Relationships**	The Flash Mob Phenomenon: Instant Teams?
E	**Ethics**	Software Piracy

Fundamentals of Information Technology

ROI STUDENT RETURN ON INVESTMENT

Through your investment of time in reading and thinking about this chapter, your return, or created value, is gaining knowledge. Use the following questions as a study guide.

1. What are the fundamentals of information technology that will help increase your productivity as a knowledge-enabled professional?
2. How do the six categories of IT hardware relate to an IT system?
3. What are the primary concepts associated with IT software?
4. How do software and hardware come together to create business capability?
5. What makes the Internet and World Wide Web so valuable?

THE VOICE OF EXPERIENCE
Derek Ball, University of Calgary

With a Bachelor of Commerce specializing in Finance, Derek Ball started out in banking. He recognized the ability that technology has to create business value and was soon involved in the start-up of several technology companies. His most recent business venture, Sonic Mobility, was sold to U.S. based, Avocent, in 2004 for over US$8M.

What do you do in your current position? I am currently the Entrepreneur in Residence with Calgary Technologies Inc, a non-profit group that assists early stage technology start-up companies. I help them with a variety of problems including financing and ensuring they're delivering a viable product to market.

What do you consider to be important career skills? Understanding the value technology can deliver and whether it can solve a real-world problem. Just after graduation, I was working in Zurich for a bank, doing financial control. The bank bought computers and dumped them on everybody's desk and didn't tell them how to use them. I was willing to learn and I figured out how to use Lotus 123 to automate financial control functions. Despite the fact that I didn't have any formal IT training, the bank ended up giving me the role of applying technology to streamline operations.

What I am doing currently is probably less about education or skill and more about experience. I have enough technical knowledge to know what is possible. I can be realistic about what problems technology can solve. I learned that technology is a tool. It's a means to an end, but not the end itself. It will always be changing, so it's important to be flexible and adaptable.

How do you use IT? Personally, I don't do voicemail. I try to focus all my communications through e-mail as a way of managing my time. I'm also big believer in mobile devices as productivity tools. I have one central point of contact for all my communication: email, con-

tacts, calendar—it's all there with me. I have used the Internet extensively for research and I'm a big fan of software as a service, something that is accessed on a remote server, not installed on an individual hard drive.

Can you describe an example of how you have used IT to improve business operations? In my most recent business venture, Sonic Mobility, we used IT to provide a secure connection from a handheld wireless device to a company's backend network. It was an encrypted TCP-IP connection with secure identification. The handheld would connect with the Sonic Admin server, which would act as a proxy and communicate with the servers that needed to be adjusted through a variety of different protocols, depending on the required action. As an example, the IT support staff at one of our client's were about to board a plane to go to a conference when they were contacted about a virus attack. They were able to connect remotely to the network from their BlackBerry devices and use Sonic Admin to stop the virus without returning to the office and missing their trip.

Have you got any "on the job" advice for students seeking a career in IT or business? Your most important resource is the people sitting on your left and right. There's no way that any one person is ever going to understand everything there is to know in any field. Information technology has grown exponentially and will continue to do so. The most important thing you can do is make as many contacts as possible.

Although Derek did not start out in the IT field, he recognized that IT plays a critical role in business success. Early in his career, he had a willingness to learn about new technology and continued to build that learning into successful businesses. This chapter will introduce you to the components and terminology of IT to equip you with a foundation for applying IT in business.

Think about how often you come in contact with information technology (IT) that is beyond your use of a desktop or laptop computer. For example, a grocery store uses IT to allow you to purchase items more quickly. A bank relies on IT to provide you with ATM access. You probably carry IT with you, such as a cell phone, PDA, or MP3 player. We could spend all day adding to this list!

Now think about what IT allows you to do. IT allows you to *communicate* with others, such as through cell phones and instant messaging. IT *enables transactions* between you and the organizations with which you deal, for example, through on-line purchases. IT helps you to *obtain, organize, analyze, and store data and information* that you need through on-line searches and specific software tools. Finally, IT can *provide entertainment* through MP3 players and Game Boys. Information technology can help us do all of these things and more, with greater efficiency and value.

However, most of us are uninterested in opening up IT devices and tinkering with the circuits or boards. We just want to be competent users of technology. But, your use of IT will improve if you know and understand some basic concepts. It's a lot like owning and operating a car. To be a competent driver, you must know when you need an oil change or that an unusual sound means a trip to the mechanic. And, just like paying for gas at the pump using your credit card, doing many things with your IT devices yourself can save you time.

In this chapter, our goal is to equip you with the IT knowledge that you will need to support your future career. That is, we help you become IT literate. Knowledge of fundamentals, and using available technical tools, will also help you understand new innovations. Further, you will find that the technology fundamentals we discuss in this chapter also form the basic components for the organizational information systems that we explore in later chapters. The CORE box "The Flash Mob Phenomenon: Instant Teams?" makes use of all the components of IT that will be discussed in this chapter.

Relationships

The Flash Mob Phenomenon: Instant Teams?

Imagine standing on the corner of Portage and Main in Winnipeg, Manitoba, when suddenly 100 people show up. Each person pulls out a Post-It™ notepad, writes down their favourite word, and posts their word within a pattern that eventually forms a fish. Or, you're standing in line at the aquarium in Vancouver, British Columbia, when a group spontaneously forms. The group members all wave their arms in the air and repeatedly ask "Are dolphins fish or mammals?" This goes on for three minutes. Then, as suddenly as they arrived, the group disperses.

Has the entire world gone crazy? Possibly, but there is an explanation for these activities: the flash mob phenomenon. Organizers of a *flash mob*, also referred to as "smart flock" or "smart mob," select a group of people to show up for a predetermined reason at a pre-established time through the use of such technologies as cell phones, text messaging, e-mail, instant messaging, and websites. Participants meet or "swarm" at an appointed time to engage in the specified activity and then disperse or move on to another activity. Many flash mobs are called together for fun or silly purposes, such as the above examples. On the other hand, flash mobs can swarm for political or social purposes as well.

CHAPTER 2

For example, former president Joseph Estrada of the Philippines was forced out of office in 2001 partly by a flash mob of over 1 million citizens called together by text messages.

With that in mind, what about having a "flash team"; that is, calling together a group of people through the Internet or mobile technologies? This is just the idea some defence experts at the Rand Corporation, a global policy think-tank, had when they generated a report titled "Swarming and the Future of Conflict" for the U.S. Defense Department. In this report, the authors suggested that swarming could lead to a revolution in military conflict. They forecast that a commander would draw up a list of objectives, assign importance to them, and then units in the field would pick one that had not been achieved to attack. Basically, the commander would review progress, reassign importance to unachieved objectives, and stay out of the way.[1]

While using flash mob technology to achieve military objectives could work, civilian organizations may also use flash technology to solve pressing problems. For example, the marketing vice-president (VP) might see an unexpected drop in demand for a key product. The VP might send out a text or e-mail message to all the organization's employees explaining the problem and asking them to join a chat group at a specified time to suggest solutions. In this case, the organization uses flash technology to create an ad hoc virtual team. Further, members of this virtual team may be located anywhere in the world.

Using technology, companies such as Cisco Systems and IBM have discovered that they can form teams less bound by space and time, and structure them specifically by task. They have found that Internet-based tools can foster collaboration and communication, and enable employees to access the information they need to do their jobs more effectively. When combined with flash technology, this can raise productivity across entire organizations.

Web Resources
- Center for Coordination Science—http://ccs.mit.edu/ccsmain.html
- Center for Collaborative Organizations—http://www.workteams.unt.edu/
- Information and Communications Technology Council—http://www.ictc-ctic.ca/
- FlockSmart—http://www.flocksmart.com

THE COMPONENTS OF IT

When you think about it, all IT, including computers, cell phones, and PDAs, are actually limited to the following capabilities:

- Accepting and storing information
- Performing mathematical calculations
- Applying logic to make decisions
- Retrieving, displaying, and sending information
- Consistently repeating the above actions many times

1. Joel Garreau, "Cell Biology." *The Washington Post*, July 31, 2002, p. C01.

WHAT DO YOU THINK?

Think about some of the IT systems you use daily and how they demonstrate basic IT capabilities by considering the following questions:

1: What capabilities can you identify in the IT system that allows you to select courses at your university or college?
2: What is the primary IT capability of your cell phone?
3: Chapters.indigo.ca and other e-businesses demonstrate all of the basic IT capabilities. How do the steps you go through to purchase a book on-line illustrate these basic IT capabilities?

The power of IT comes from the fact that it does these things amazingly well. IT devices combine these capabilities in a number of ways to help us more efficiently and effectively work with information. How is this possible?

Information technology consists of three basic categories: hardware, software, and networks. **Hardware** is the electronic and mechanical components that you can see and touch, such as your computer monitor. **Software** is the set of instructions that direct the hardware. While not necessary for all IT devices, **network** technology increases their power by allowing users to share resources, including hardware, software, and information. The three basic categories (hardware, software, and networks) together create a platform, as Figure 2.1 shows.

The complicated nature of IT, along with the vast number of options for each IT component, requires more knowledge for intelligent decision making than other items we might buy and use. With this in mind, we present basic IT terms and concepts so that you can become a competent user.

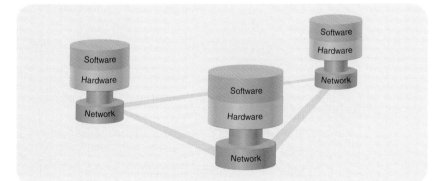

Figure 2.1 The IT platform consists of hardware, software, and network technology.

Quick Test

1. Which one of the following sentences best describes why IT is important to knowledge-enabled professionals?

   a. IT stocks provide higher returns on investment than stocks of other industries.

   b. Knowledge of IT is a great way to impress our co-workers.

   c. IT can help us do many things important to our work with greater efficiency and effectiveness.

   d. It's always useful and fun to obtain the latest IT devices.

2. Using an Internet search engine like Google or Yahoo! is an example of using IT for which of the following activities (choose the best answer)?

   a. communicating with others

   b. carrying out a transaction

   c. obtaining data and information

   d. analyzing data and information

3. Which of the following is one of the three primary categories of IT devices?

   a. hardware

   b. software

   c. networks

   d. all of the above

Answers: 1. c; 2. c; 3. d

HARDWARE

IT devices share a common set of system components. We can categorize these general components into six basic IT hardware categories (see Figure 2.2), as follows:

- **Processing**—Directs execution of instructions and the transformation of data.
- **Memory**—Temporarily locates data and instructions before processing.
- **Input**—Provides the interface used for data entry *into* a device.
- **Output**—Provides the interface used to retrieve information *from* a device.
- **Storage**—Stores data, information, and instructions for the long term.
- **Communications**—Connects one IT device to another.

The hardware components represent the physical (hard) parts of a system, as distinguished from the more adjustable (soft) parts, the

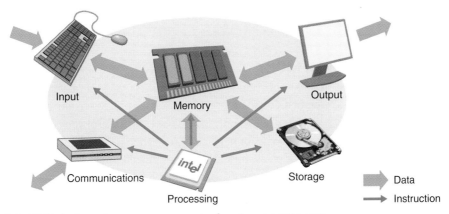

Figure 2.2 All IT devices share a common set of system components.

software. The working parts of IT hardware consist primarily of electronic devices (mostly digital) with some electromechanical parts used with input, output, and storage devices.

In our discussion of these six hardware categories, we focus on the personal computer (PC). However, the same architecture and components are common to most modern IT devices.

PROCESSING HARDWARE

The fundamental hardware component of all digital devices is the transistor. A **transistor** is an electronic switch that can be either on (represented by 1) or off (represented by 0). By combining several transistors, we can represent data as a combination of 1s and 0s; that is, in a binary format (we explain this in more detail in Tech Guide A). Much of the fundamental nature of IT comes down to converting data so that they can be stored in a binary format.

At the core of all computing operations is a tiny chip made up of transistors, the **microprocessor.** This chip contains most of the components that make up the **central processing unit (CPU).** The CPU, as **Figure 2.3** shows, works together with memory to control the execution of all instructions and the processing of all data. As such, the CPU is often referred to as the computer's "brain." And just like a human brain, high speed and reliable performance of the CPU are critical to successful use of the computer for knowledge work activities.

For example, the *clock speed* may be the most common measure of CPU performance. Clock speeds are measured in *megahertz (MHz)*, millions of cycles per second, and more recently *gigahertz (GHz)*, billions of cycles per second. Higher clock speeds usually translate into faster performance. A CPU that cycles at a clock speed of 2 GHz

Figure 2.3 The components of a central processing unit (CPU) work together with memory to control the execution of all instructions and the processing of all data.

CHAPTER 2

will generally perform processing tasks faster than a computer with a clock speed of 1 GHz.

MEMORY

Long-term memory helps us to keep track of facts, like the name of the first Canadian prime minister, or processes, like how to brew coffee when we're only half awake. Short-term memory, on the other hand, is only for items that we need to remember for a relatively short time, such as the start time of a movie. After leaving the theatre, you forget that time, or replace it with other things to remember.

Similarly, computers also have long-term memory (ROM) and short-term memory (RAM) stored on chips. Memory capacity is measured as the number of *bytes* that the ROM and RAM chips store. Capacities of memory devices range from thousands (kilobytes—KB), to millions (megabytes—MB), and on to billions (gigabytes—GB) of bytes.

ROM

Read only memory (ROM) contains instructions and data that only special devices can alter. ROM is present in most IT devices, from calculators to digital cameras. In a computer, the ROM holds the instructions used to control the start-up processes (booting up). After completing the booting-up process, most computer functions no longer need ROM. As a result, the largest number of memory chips in your computer is in the form of RAM.

RAM

Random access memory (RAM) stores data only until they are no longer needed, or until you shut down the computer. This type of memory is called random access because the CPU can access any item stored in RAM directly (randomly). The CPU takes operating system instructions and data from secondary storage and places them in RAM. The operating system instructions will remain in RAM as long as your computer is on. Further, whenever you load software, like Microsoft Word to work on that 10-page term paper that you've been putting off, the CPU retrieves the software instructions and loads them into main memory. As you begin typing the paper, the CPU stores the text that you see on the screen in RAM. As you have no doubt found, if your computer shuts down inadvertently, and you have not saved your paper, it will be lost, since the RAM is cleared at shutdown.

Eventually, your computer reaches its RAM capacity. What happens then? It becomes necessary to continuously exchange items stored in RAM with new items from slower storage devices. This can profoundly affect the overall performance of your computer. Consequently, increasing your RAM capacity can be one of the cheapest and most effective ways of extending the life of your computer.

INPUT HARDWARE

For an IT device to process information, you need to provide it with the data it needs. After processing the data into information, the IT device needs a way to present the information back to you. *Input devices*, such as the keyboards shown in Figure 2.4, provide the interface between the internal processes of the information system and its environment. In this role, input/output (I/O) devices represent our primary means of working with computers: entering data and commands. The usefulness of any one of these devices usually rests more on how well it performs in the role of human–machine interface than with its data conversion capability.

Figure 2.4 Input devices, such as the keyboards shown here, allow us to enter data and commands.

You should consider several criteria when selecting input devices, such as:

- Data format
- Accuracy and quality
- Compatibility
- Portability
- Speed
- Environmental limitations
- Ergonomic properties

Using these criteria, you should choose input devices according to the task, while considering individual differences and personal preferences when possible. We discuss next how these criteria are applied to use three different types of input hardware—the keyboard, pointing devices, and scanning devices—to their best advantage.

The Keyboard

Most people use a keyboard (shown in Figure 2.4) as the primary input device for computers. As input devices go, the keyboard is the most versatile, providing the capability to enter all types of data as well as instructions.

However, the keyboard does have disadvantages. For example, some people have suffered injuries due to the repetitive motions of typing in data. As a result, *ergonomic keyboards,* designed for a more natural hand and wrist position, are used to reduce the risk of injury. **Ergonomics** is the science of designing a job or tool to fit the worker. Ergonomically designed tools can help keep us safe as well as allow us to be more productive.

CHAPTER

2

As another example, consider knowledge-enabled professionals who travel frequently for their job. The need for portability can often preclude the use of a standard keyboard. Instead, several alternatives, such as a foldable keyboard that can be attached to a PDA (personal digital assistant), can be used. Even more common are mobile devices such as a BlackBerry (a Canadian invention) or text-enabled cell phone, which have a full keyboard on the device itself.

Pointing Devices

Many people use other input hardware, such as the pointing devices shown in Figure 2.5. Pointing devices, such as a mouse, allow users to provide instructions to the computer using physical movements, such as "point" and "click." As such, controlling a computer with a pointing

Figure 2.5 Controlling a computer with a pointing device, such as a touchpad, mouse, or power glove, allows more natural movements, thereby requiring less user training.

device allows more natural movements, thereby requiring less training. People most often use these devices to point to graphical items like buttons and icons on a display device. Thus, they are typically more useful for entering commands than for entering data.

Scanning Devices

Other input devices include scanning devices, such as the bar code scans used by most retail stores. In most cases, people use scanners to improve the speed and accuracy of entering data, or as new ways to perform a task more efficiently. For example, the ability to scan product and payment information has allowed some retailers, such as Loblaws, a grocery store, to set up self-service checkout lanes.

In addition to bar code readers, you can often find *magnetic ink character recognition* (*MICR*) devices for scanning cheques, devices to read the magnetic strip on a credit card or the data on a smart card, and even *drum scanners* to scan and determine the denomination and authenticity of your cash. Figure 2.6 shows a few important types of scanning devices. For a complete discussion of the latest input devices, see Tech Guide A.

Figure 2.6 People use scanners, such as those shown here, to improve the speed and accuracy of entering data, or as new ways to perform a task more efficiently.

Of course, another popular input device that you likely use often is a digital camera. This allows you to upload your images to on-line photo albums and content sharing websites.

? WHAT DO YOU THINK?

Have you used a Wii? The Wii gaming remote, invented by Nintendo, connects wirelessly to the gaming console and by sensing motion allows the gamer to move the remote to perform activities as if they were in the game itself (e.g., swinging a tennis racket or steering a car).

1: Did you realize that Wii is an input device? What type of input device is it?
2: What business applications can you think of for this technology?
3: Why might gamers prefer this method of input over others?

OUTPUT HARDWARE

Output devices convert IT-processed information into a usable form. When choosing output devices, knowledge-enabled professionals are concerned primarily with the quality and speed of the output. Secondary considerations may include ergonomics, portability, compatibility, and environmental considerations. Display devices make up the most common category of output device, such as computer monitors. However, most users also require printers. Further, many users now rely on other output devices, such as speakers or MP3 players. Let's look at a few output devices in more detail.

Display Devices

Many computer monitors have been built around the *cathode ray tube* (*CRT*), an electrical device for displaying images that has been available since 1901. However, with improvements in picture quality and decreases in cost of newer technologies, CRT displays are becoming antiques. In fact, **liquid crystal displays (LCDs)** (see Figure 2.7) are rapidly replacing CRTs as the display of choice. Having been used for many years[2] in portable devices such as digital watches, calculators, laptops, and PDA displays, knowledge-enabled professionals are now purchasing LCDs for the desktop. LCDs are slimmer, lighter, and consume less power than the CRTs.

Printers

Figure 2.7
LCDs are slimmer, lighter, and consume less power than the previously used CRTs.

Printers and plotters are used to obtain "hard copy" output from a computer. *Printers*, shown in Figure 2.8, produce both text and

2. Liquid crystals were first discovered in 1888 by Austrian botanist Friedrich Reinitzer. But 80 years passed before the first experimental LCD was made in 1968 by RCA. *Source:* Tyson, Jeff, "How LCDs Work," HowStuffWorks.com, http://electronics.howstuffworks.com/lcd.htm, 2006.

PART
1

Figure 2.8 The different printing devices shown here (inkjet, plotter, and multifunction printer) will produce both text and graphics at various levels of quality.

graphics at various levels of quality. *Plotters* provide high-quality printing of graphics, such as those used for blueprints. Knowledge-enabled professionals generally choose printing devices based on print quality, printing speed measured in pages per minute (PPM), and whether or not the device will print in colour. When considering cost, the price of the device itself is not the only consideration. The buyer should also factor in recurring costs such as paper, toner, and ink cartridges.

Other Output Devices

Other output devices include speakers and controllers. Speakers provide audio output that allows users to know the status of software, communicate with others using voice, and listen to their favourite MP3s. As its name implies, a **controller** is a device that controls the transfer of data between a computer and a peripheral device, such as a printer or disk drives. However, controllers can also be used to control specialized devices, such as a music keyboard or a robotic device.

STORAGE HARDWARE

Storage refers to various hardware media and devices used to contain large amounts of data and instructions for the long term. Storage devices retain data and instructions even after shutting

CHAPTER

2

Figure 2.9 USB flash memory will store large amounts of data and instructions for the long term.

Figure 2.10 Network interface cards provide the physical connection between a computer and a local network.

down the computer. Examples of storage include the computer *hard drive*, the *diskette*, *CDs* and *DVDs*, and *USB flash memory* (see Figure 2.9).

Storage is usually much slower to access than memory. Why? Imagine that you are in the office working at your desk. In the opposite corner sits a file cabinet, storing your important files. To retrieve information from the file cabinet, you must leave your desk, walk across to the cabinet, find the desired file, and bring it back to the desk. How much faster would it be to work with the information if you could, instead, simply recall it from your memory? Similarly, retrieving your file from the top of your desk (through RAM) is very fast compared with getting it from storage.

COMMUNICATIONS HARDWARE

Communications hardware, such as the **network interface card (NIC)** shown in Figure 2.10, provides the physical connection between a computer and a local network. This ability is vital to many knowledge work activities.

When you are not physically connected to a network, you can use a modem. **Modems,** both wired and wireless, allow you to connect to a remote network over a telecommunications line, such as the telephone or cable TV service. A modem converts (*mo*dulates) the digital signals going out from your computer into an analog signal appropriate for the connection medium used. When receiving a signal, it converts (*dem*odulates) the analog signal back into a digital signal that your computer can recognize.

Modem speeds, measured in bits per second (bps), significantly affect knowledge work activities. For example, if you frequently research information on the Internet, you will lose valuable time waiting for a telephone modem to download the data. At top transmission speeds of 56 Kbps, telephone modems cannot compete with cable or DSL modems, which offer higher transmission speeds—up to 3 Mbps and higher in many areas.

Finally, recent IT technology has increased knowledge work effectiveness by allowing mobile devices to connect to wireless networks by using wireless NICs. See Tech Guide A for a more detailed discussion of communication hardware.

We have now discussed the main categories of hardware that exist in any IT system. However, each and every IT device, from your MP3 player to your desktop PC, includes a component that you can't touch but that your device cannot work without. In the next section, we discuss this important component called software.

Quick Test

1. All other things being equal, which mix of components allows a computer to simultaneously run multiple programs faster?
   a. 1-GHz processor with 256 MB RAM
   b. 1-GHz processor with 512 MB RAM
   c. 1-MHz processor with 256 MB RAM
   d. 2-MHz processor with 512 MB RAM

2. Which of the following IT devices is used for long-term storage of data and software (which may be changed from time to time)?
   a. ROM
   b. RAM
   c. hard drive
   d. CPU

3. What IT device allows us to move around from place to place while remaining connected to a network?
   a. virtual keyboard
   b. USB flash memory
   c. wireless NIC
   d. MICR device

Answers: 1. b; 2. c; 3. c

SOFTWARE

As we just discussed, IT devices help us with knowledge work activities. As such, they always involve working with information in some way. You may be thinking: "Aren't instructions a form of information?" Certainly! So you can think about software as information that specifies how the device should work with other data, information, and knowledge.

However, you should also think about software as the result of creativity and hard work. That is, software is *legally protected*, just like other forms of information such as music and literature. Software is also considered to be technology, thereby included under the same protections that cover inventions. This dual nature of software allows developers to protect their work under both patent and copyright laws. These protections, along with the popularity and proliferation of IT devices, have provided an environment in which software is big business. In 2004 alone, revenue from the sale of packaged software has been estimated at over $179 billion.[3] The following CORE box, "Software Piracy," discusses the ethics of using unauthorized software.

3. "Packaged Software Industry Revenue and Growth," The Software & Information Industry Association, http://www.siia.net, 2005.

CHAPTER 2

Ethics

Software Piracy

Have you ever shared software with someone else? Did you do something illegal, or were your actions simply unethical? Is there a difference?

The unauthorized sharing of software, or *software piracy*, is illegal. Software piracy exists because when you purchase most software you do not really own it. Instead, you only have a licence to use it, usually on only one computer. Therefore, you *cannot share it* without violating Canadian copyright law. Penalities for violating Canadian copyright law can be as severe as 5 years imprisonment and up to $1 million in fines.[4] In addition to breaking Canadian copyright law, every time someone illegally shares software, the developer suffers a loss of one or more sales.

In fact, software piracy costs software developers like Microsoft a great deal of money each year—around $13 *billion* for Microsoft alone according to a 2003 study. Does that loss affect you? Absolutely. As a potential consumer of Microsoft and other software developers' products, it means higher costs for *you*. As a knowledge-enabled professional, it may mean that you or your organization cannot afford the tools you need to get the job done and to create business value.

If software piracy is illegal, is it also unethical? Doesn't Microsoft have more money than it needs? Isn't software piracy the modern equivalent of the fictional character Robin Hood stealing from the rich (Microsoft) and giving to the poor (students)? We often hear this argument as an ethical justification for software piracy. However, ethically this is considered "wrong" because the act and consequences of stealing knowledge work (e.g., software piracy) violates the "do no harm" and the "create the greatest good for the greatest number of people" principles found in many societies' and individuals' codes of ethics. Therefore, in our view, software piracy is not only illegal, it is also unethical.

Web Resources

• Canadian Alliance Against Software Theft (CAAST)—http://www.caast.org
• World Intellectual Property Organization—http://www.wipo.int/

To begin to understand the relationship between software and hardware, think about cooking from a recipe. Your mother makes an amazing chicken pot pie, and it has been a while since you had a home-cooked meal. She e-mails you the recipe and you buy the ingredients. You follow the recipe exactly: 2 cups of chicken, 2 carrots sliced, and so on. You also follow the baking instructions: 1 hour at 350 degrees Fahrenheit. Does the chicken pot pie turn out the same as your mom's?

By now you're probably wondering: "What in the world does this have to do with computer software?" Recall that a computer performs functions based on instructions; that is, software.

---

4. CAAST. http://www.caast.org/resources/default.asp?load=law, accessed January 20, 2007.

The process by which a computer follows instructions is similar to how we learn and follow instructions for the tasks that we do.

For example, even if your mother gives you the exact recipe, she may omit some of the steps that she takes to ensure the perfect chicken pot pie (such as adding a little more salt or pepper to taste). She is able to execute these instructions routinely and without thought. The instructions for this have become instinctual or built-in, like **firmware**. Similarly, when you turn on a computer, firmware built into ROM chips allows the computer to start and prepare for use (i.e., boot up). Once the computer is ready, the CPU loads more software into RAM, and the computer can get to work.

After your chicken pot pie is cooked, you begin to do more tasks, such as finding dishes and utensils to eat with. Your *personal application software* for setting the table may instruct your body which utensils (fork or spoon) to select. However, it's your *system software* that controls your hands as you place items on the table. Similarly, while you may select the Print command within an application software package, it is the operating system that takes over and carries out the actual print job.

As the previous example shows, we can divide computer software into two main categories: (1) system software and (2) application software. (We discuss software in more detail in Tech Guide B: The Details of Software.)

SYSTEM SOFTWARE

System software includes any software required to control the hardware components and to support the execution of application software. System software includes the operating system and utility software. The **operating system (OS) software** coordinates and handles the details of working with the computer hardware. **Utility software** provides additional tools that you can use to maintain and service your system.

Operating System Software

After the boot program in ROM successfully tests and starts up the hardware, the CPU loads the operating system (OS) software into the computer's memory. The OS software then directs the appropriate components to complete their tasks. Users may also interact directly with the operating system through the user interface, such as using your mouse to navigate and click on screen icons. Given its role of directing all computer operations, OS software has the most impact on our experience, efficiency, and productivity when using a computer.

CHAPTER 2

The OS software performs two main tasks:

1. Managing the hardware and software resources of the computer.
2. Providing a stable and consistent interface between application programs and the hardware.

To manage the hardware, the operating system works like a police officer who directs traffic at a busy intersection. As Figure 2.11 shows, the OS software directs each application to the appropriate resource, while attempting to use those resources in the most efficient manner. A stable and consistent interface allows applications to work on any computer system that uses the OS software.

Utility Software

Utility software provides additional IT capabilities. For example, users often add utilities such as file management software and security programs. There is a trend, however, toward integrating utilities into the core of the OS. For example, Windows XP comes packaged with a firewall utility. A **firewall** application helps guard your computer against unauthorized access when connected to a network. Previously, users had to obtain and install a separate firewall. Even newer OS software, such as Windows Vista, contains several new security features to prevent attacks from viruses and other malware. We discuss another important category of utility software next in the CORE box "Scanning and Disinfection: Keeping Your PC Safe."

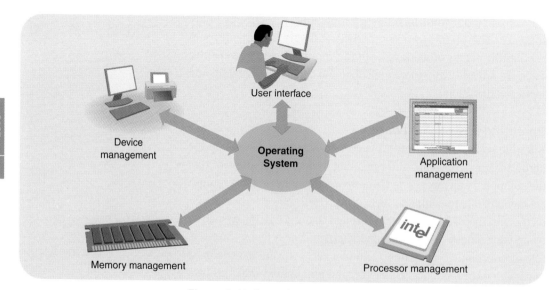

Figure 2.11 Operating system software functions much like a police officer at a busy intersection.

On-line Security

Scanning and Disinfection: Keeping Your PC Safe

A multitude of virus and worm programs, collectively known as *malware*, are making the rounds of the Internet with increasing frequency. A *virus* is a program that is designed to spread itself to as many computers as possible. It usually needs some human action, like opening an e-mail attachment, to occur in order to spread. A *worm* is destructive software that can spread by itself, such as MyDoom and its later version, DoomJuice.

The MyDoom worm was particularly nasty. Once started on a computer (by clicking an e-mail attachment), it automatically sends out infected e-mails to everybody in the user's address book, using one or more of the names on the address book as the sender. In addition to overwhelming e-mail servers around the world (at one point, the virus generated as many as one in three e-mails in circulation), MyDoom also marshalled an attack on the Microsoft Web server and that of another, smaller software company in an attempt to crash those sites.

Incidents of malicious programs like viruses and worms have increased along with the growth of the Internet. For example, the number of incidents reported to CERT (Computer Emergency Response Team) increased from 1,334 in 1993 to 137,529 in 2003.[5] Prior to MyDoom appearing in February 2004, many other worms and viruses had appeared with such names as Nimda, Slammer, and So Big—all with their own particular method of destructiveness.

How can you protect your computer from viruses like MyDoom? Follow these recommendations:

- First and foremost, don't open e-mail attachments *unless* you know the sender *and* are expecting an e-mail with an attachment from that person. While it's often impractical to ban attachments outright, you should *always* confirm with the source that the attachment is legitimate.
- Load the latest updates (patches) to your software. Many software updates include fixes for known security problems and are readily available from the software company's website.
- Load antivirus software on your computer and update it often. It's not enough to simply install an antivirus program; you need to keep its database of virus references up to date.
- If you don't have antivirus software running on your computer, visit McAfee.com and download a powerful program called Stinger.exe that you can use to scan and disinfect your computer. It is not a replacement for antivirus software, but you can use it in emergency situations.
- Obtain and run a firewall.

If all of these fail and your computer is infected, visit one of the following Web resources for information about removing the offending program.

Web Resources

- CERT (Computer Emergency Response Team)—http://www.cert.org
- CanCERT (Canadian Computer Emergency Response Team)—http://www.cancert.ca
- Symantec Security Response—http://securityresponse.symantec.com
- McAfee AVERT Stinger—http://vil.nai.com/vil/stinger/

5. "CERT/CC Statistics 1988–2003," CERT (Computer Emergency Response Team), http://www.cert.org, last updated: 1/22/2004.

APPLICATION SOFTWARE

Application software is a complete, self-contained program or set of programs for performing a specific job. For example, you would use a word processing application software, like Microsoft Word, to write your term paper.

An important group of application software for the knowledge-enabled professional is known as **productivity software.** Knowledge-enabled professionals frequently use productivity software to work with data, information, and knowledge more efficiently and effectively, as follows:

- **Document preparation software**, for creating documents composed of text, images, and supporting graphics.
- **Electronic spreadsheet software**, for performing general calculations and analyses, such as financial analysis, budgeting, and forecasting.
- **Presentation graphics software**, for preparing professional-quality slides and graphics for business presentations; often requires a knowledge-enabled professional to be able to access and manipulate large amounts of data.
- **Database management system (DBMS)**, for designing, creating, updating, and querying data.
- **Personal information management (PIM)**, for managing personal information, such as to-do lists, schedules, and electronic mail.

Finally, a new general type of application software has emerged alongside the popular use of the Internet: network application software. However, before discussing this type of software, we need to review networks in general.

Quick Test

1. Which one of the following types of software controls the primary functions of a computer system?
   a. application software
   b. communications software
   c. operating system software
   d. utility software

2. A firewall is an example of which type of software?
   a. application software
   b. communications software
   c. operating system software
   d. utility software

3. Imagine that you are in charge of tracking the dues paid by each member of a large student organization. To store these data in an organized form that allows you to easily look up data, which type of application software would you most likely use?

a. spreadsheet

b. database management

c. presentation

d. word processing

Answers: 1. c; 2. d; 3. b.

CONNECTING OVER NETWORKS

Look around. Networks are everywhere! We humans are networking maniacs, as the few networks shown in Figure 2.12 illustrate. We have social networks—linking people through family relationships, friendships, acquaintances, and business contacts. We have created global transportation networks—linking cities and towns via roads

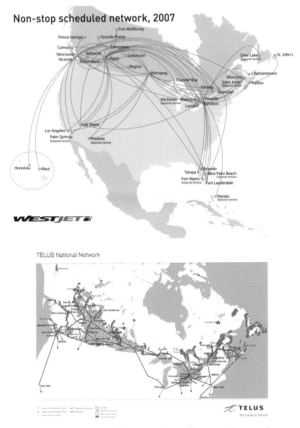

Figure 2.12 Networks are all around us. The top image is a network diagram of WestJet's travel routes, and the bottom image is a diagram of TELUS' national network.

and highways as well as by train, bus, and airline routes. We have a long history of communication networks, such as the Greek message runners, the Pony Express, telegraph systems, and the international telephone system. Today, the fastest-growing network is arguably our global computer network, known as the Internet.

A computer network consists of *nodes* that represent computer hardware and the network users, with various types of hardware, software, and *communications media* forming the links between nodes. As such, a computer network requires four primary components:

1. Data (the resource) that computers share on the network.
2. Special hardware.
3. Software that allows computers to communicate and share the data.
4. Communication media to link the computers together.

In the following sections, we briefly review network hardware and software. For a more in-depth discussion of networks, see Tech Guide C: The Details of Networking.

NETWORK CATEGORIES

To better understand why so many options exist for network technology, it helps to know the different types of computer networks that exist. The categories we discuss here (covered in more detail in Tech Guide C) are important because they represent why different networking components or techniques may be required.

One common method of describing computer networks relies on how much geography the physical size of the network covers. The two extreme sizes are local area network (LAN) and wide area network (WAN). Technology requirements are generally more complicated as the physical size of the network gets larger.

Local Area Networks

A **local area network (LAN)** is confined to a relatively small geographic area. Examples of LANs include school computing labs, private home wireless networks, and private networks over a few buildings of a corporate campus. While physical LAN sizes vary, LAN computers are rarely more than a mile apart. As Figure 2.13 shows, a good rule of thumb is: If you can walk from any one node in the network to any other node in the network in a reasonable amount of time, then your network is probably a LAN.

Wide Area Networks

Wide area networks (WANs), as Figure 2.14 shows, connect computers that cover entire regions, countries, and even overseas. While WANs are often collections of smaller networks, some differences are required in connection technology to cover the greater distances. For

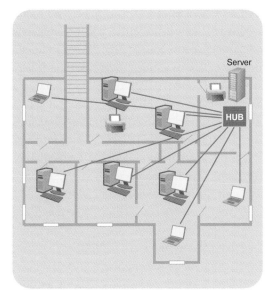

Figure 2.13 A local area network (LAN) is confined to a relatively small geographic area, such as a building.

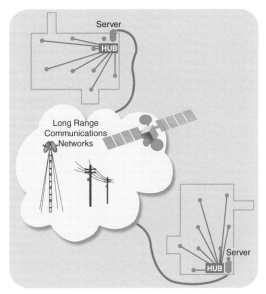

Figure 2.14 A wide area network (WAN) connects computers that cover entire regions, countries, and even overseas.

instance, many WANs rely on special transoceanic cabling or satellite connections, much like the international phone and television systems. Also, the usually higher network traffic requires more sophisticated routing and switching equipment in order for the multitude of messages that are sent over the WAN to find and reach their destination.

In addition to WANs and LANs, you may hear of other size networks. A *municipal area network (MAN)* is the name of a city-wide network. A *campus area network (CAN)* is a category that is sometimes used to describe a network that covers a university or corporate campus. Finally, a *global area network (GAN)* is a network that spans the globe. Each type of network will often require different network hardware.

NETWORK HARDWARE

Forming a network requires a number of devices for making network connections as well as for managing data transmission over the network. We can divide network hardware into three basic categories:

1. Hardware to connect a device to a network.
2. Specialized hardware for handling network traffic.
3. Specialized computers that control the network and the delivery of data on the network.

Network Connection Hardware

Hardware that connects computers or other devices to a network includes *modems*, *cable modems*, *network interface cards* (*NICs*), and *wireless cards.* Each of these devices serves to connect your computer or device to a network. The device that you use depends mainly on the media that connects to your computer. For example, you would use a standard *modem* to connect over a standard telephone line, offered by providers such as Bell or Telus. Similarly, a *cable modem* connects your device over the same coaxial cable that delivers your cable television service, offered by providers such as Rogers or Shaw. Finally, recall from above that a *network interface card* (*NIC*) provides the physical connection between the computer workstation and the network. As the name implies, you need a *wireless card* to connect your device to a wireless network.

A physical link that forms a network connection is referred to as a *carrier* or *communications medium.* There are several different options. Copper wire like that used for the *plain old telephone system* (*POTS*) network is the most common for transmitting electrical signals. Because it is currently installed in almost every home, it is the most inexpensive media to use. Coaxial and fibre optic cables that can transmit information at faster speeds are made of more durable, expensive materials. However, due to the materials and additional installation required, they cost more than copper wire. Networks with higher capacities, such as those used for cable television and broadband services, use coaxial and fibre optic cables. Finally, technologies such as infrared light, radio waves, and microwaves also allow networks to transmit signals through the air. This form of transmission is increasingly important as we seek more mobility with our IT devices.

Network Traffic Hardware

Devices that help coordinate the data traffic on a network include routers, bridges, repeaters, and hubs. A *bridge* is a device that lets you connect to networks or break a large network into two smaller, more efficient networks. A *router* can be thought of as an intelligent bridge. Rather than just provide connectivity, a router connects, translates, and then directs data that cross between two networks. A *hub*, also known as a *concentrator*, serves as a central connection point for cables from the devices on the network. A *repeater* is sometimes needed to strengthen or amplify signals that are sent along a long transmission route. Finally, a wireless *access point (AP)* is a special bridge that connects between wireless devices and a wired network.

Specialized Network Computers

On most networks, specialized computers, called *servers*, manage the various functions of the network. Servers are often assigned a specific task such as handling e-mail (*e-mail server*), Web traffic (*Web server*), or running programs (*application server*).

A **file server** is a fast computer that requires a large amount of RAM and storage space. Why? Because not only does it store and run the network operating system software, it may also store shared software applications and data files. Further, the file server manages all communication between the devices on the network. (Any computer that is connected to the file server on a network is called a *client* or a *workstation*.) Because many users may request services from the file server at the same time, you can also see why a computer that can store a lot of data and share it quickly is required. We discuss other types of network servers in Tech Guide C.

NETWORK SOFTWARE

Like PC software, we can divide network software into operating system software and application software. Network operating system software manages network functions and the flow of data traffic over a computer network. Network application software provides the instructions that allow for the creation of data and for this transformation to fit appropriate *protocols* for transmission over a network. A **protocol** is a standard set of rules that allows the communication of data between nodes on a network.

You have no doubt used network application software when you composed an e-mail to a friend and sent it over the Internet. These days, we can include just about every productivity software category as network application software. For example, modern word processing software usually includes features that allow you to e-mail or fax a document directly, or even transform and post the document as a web page.

HOW NETWORKS BENEFIT THE IT-LITERATE KNOWLEDGE-ENABLED PROFESSIONAL

Today, with the ability to do things like purchase the latest Harry Potter book over the Internet, we may take for granted the benefits derived from computer networks. Let's review some of the reasons why computer networks have not only become a necessity for most businesses and many homes, but also how they will enable you to be a knowledge-enabled professional.

- **Efficient communication:** E-mail and instant messaging have become everyday tools for most of us. Software tools, known as *groupware,* help individuals and teams keep up with their scheduled meetings, monitor projects, share work files, and even conference on-line.
- **Effective resource management:** A network allows easy sharing of software, hardware, and data resources. Examples include

CHAPTER 2

a single printer for an entire computer lab, software purchased at lower cost per user via a site licence, and a single database accessible to everyone in the organization.

- **Complete, accurate, reliable, recent, and timely information:** With a central database system, multiple users can access or update data quickly from multiple and remote locations. (However, access to the data can be limited while the data are being processed to maintain the accuracy.) Also, users can share files quickly as e-mail attachments, for example.
- **Expanded marketing and customer service capabilities:** On the Internet and World Wide Web, businesses and individuals can carry out remote business transactions anytime and anywhere. They can inform a larger number of customers about their products and services.

Let's take a closer look at how the last items, the Internet and the World Wide Web, benefit knowledge-enabled professionals.

Quick Test

1. Which one of the following is a primary component of a computer network?
   a. communications media
   b. data to share
   c. software
   d. all of the above

2. In relation to network size, the computer network that connects all of those within the boundaries of your university or college campus is best classified as a _____.

   a. CAN   b. GAN   c. LAN   d. WAN

3. Which one of the following is the name of a computer on a network that is assigned a specific task to manage the functions of the network?

   a. client   b. protocol   c. server   d. workstation

Answers: 1. d; 2. a; 3. c

THE INTERNET

Strictly speaking, any computer network that connects several networks together is an internet (short for internetworking). We simply refer to the single largest and most popular internet in the world as the "Internet." With the Internet, all of the IT components we have discussed so far—hardware, software, and networking technologies—come together to make what is arguably the most useful technological tool of the last few decades. An estimated 7.9 million (64%) of the 12.3 million Canadian households had at least one member who used the Internet regularly in 2003, either from home, work, school, a public library, or another location. This was a 5% increase from 2002, but well below the annual gains of 19% and 24% observed in 2000 and 2001.[6] In 2006 it was estimated that over 1 billion people worldwide had access to and were using the Internet, with this number predicted to rise to 1.8 billion users by 2010.[7]

WHAT MAKES THE INTERNET POSSIBLE?

The foundation technology that makes the Internet possible is the adoption of standard protocols. The Internet uses the *TCP/IP* suite of *packet switching* protocols. This is a very general, non-proprietary set of communication rules. By adopting these rules and making use of software compatible with the TCP/IP standards, any computer, regardless of the platform (processor and OS), can connect and communicate over the Internet.

Another aspect of the Internet, important to its near global adoption, is that no single organization or governmental entity owns it. Instead, several international organizations provide committees that discuss and propose Internet standards. These committees include the *Internet Engineering Task Force* (*IETF*), the *Internet Architecture Board* (*IAB*), and the *World Wide Web Consortium* (*W3C*). These groups, and others, have developed standard protocols, sometimes referred to as the Internet protocol suite. This suite offers many useful protocols, such as *HTTP*, *SMTP*, and *FTP*, which we discuss in Tech Guide C.

Obviously, most knowledge-enabled professionals use the Internet, often on a daily basis. But how do they actually access it?

ACCESSING THE INTERNET

At home, users access the Internet through dial-up (over traditional phone lines) or broadband (through cable or ISDN). At work, they often connect directly to the organization's LAN or WAN. The organization in turn will provide connection to the Internet if needed. All Internet-access methods require specialized hardware—a modem for dial-up access, a cable modem for cable access, and an NIC for direct connection to a network.

6. Statistics Canada, "The Daily: Household Internet Use Survey," July 8, 2004.
7. Enid Burns "U.S. Tops Broadband Usage, For Now," *Clickz* http://www.clickz.com/stats/sectors/geographics/article.php/3563966, November 14, 2005.

CHAPTER 2

Most users do not connect directly to the Internet. Instead, they contract with an **Internet service provider (ISP).** ISPs, like Sympatico, Primus, NetZero, and Rogers, purchase the expensive equipment needed to connect to the Internet. ISPs then provide connections for customers to use via dial-up or cable.

Internet access also requires software. Software used to make the connection includes OS utilities and special software that the ISP usually provides. To access and process content, Internet users also need application software, such as an e-mail client and a Web browser.

In recent years, Internet access has moved out of the home and office to such public locations as libraries, airports, and coffee shops. Access at these places is increasingly simple and universal with the increase in "Wi-Fi hotspots." **Wi-Fi** is the popular name for the 802.11 standards for wireless network access. A hotspot refers to any public space within which a wireless device can connect. With Wi-Fi and other forms of wireless access, knowledge-enabled professionals can now go mobile and stay connected to the Internet using laptop computers, PDAs, or a number of other wireless devices. You will find wireless access, free and paid, in all major cities in Canada. Toronto Hydro recently announced plans to provide a blanket of Wi-Fi coverage in the downtown Toronto core, giving Toronto the largest ubiquitous Wi-Fi coverage zone in Canada. Anyone who works, lives, studies, or plays in the downtown core will have access to this new network.[8] For a list of free Wi-Fi hotspots in Canada, the United States, and Europe, visit www.wififreespot.com.

WHAT DO YOU THINK?

There is no doubt that the ability to access the Internet anywhere at any time using wireless technology is changing the way we work and live. Just imagine, there was a time when you could only access the Internet or e-mail by using special terminals in the library! However, some argue that using wireless technology may make us too productive. Consider the following:

1: Have you ever heard the term 'Crackberry'? What does this mean to you?
2: Do you think being able to access your e-mail at all times using a wireless device keeps you more or less socially connected?
3: What do you think of the expectation some organizations have that if you are connected wirelessly, you are available 24/7?

For more on this topic, see the following article by two professors at Ryerson's School of Information Technology Management: Catherine A. Middleton and Wendy Cukier, "Is Mobile E-mail Functional or Dysfunctional? Two Perspectives on Mobile E-mail Usage," *European Journal of Information Systems,* June 2006, 15, p. 252.

THE WORLD WIDE WEB

For many, the Internet is synonymous with two of its most popular applications, the *World Wide Web* (*WWW*) and *electronic mail* (*e-mail*). However, the World Wide Web, often called simply the Web, is not the same as the Internet. Think of the Internet as the technology platform, and the Web as an application that works on that platform.

One of the most popular uses of the Web is e-commerce. Our next CORE box, "What Does E-Commerce Mean to You?" discusses how e-commerce has changed the way we shop.

Connectivity

What Does E-Commerce Mean to You?

Have you ever used credit/debit cards, ATMs, or the World Wide Web? Then you've used e-commerce! *Electronic commerce* (or e-commerce for short) is a transaction carried out using computer networks. Using credit or debit cards, withdrawing money from an ATM, and making purchases over the Web all fit this definition. To many people today, the term e-commerce often means making or researching purchases over the Web.

We can trace e-commerce over the Web to the introduction of the first "point-and-click" Web browser in 1994. Today, the Web ranks second only to e-mail in popularity among computer users with access to the Internet. E-commerce is a large reason for this popularity. Statistics Canada reports that in 2003, Canadian households spent just over $3 billion shopping on the Internet for everything from airplane tickets to books.[9] The largest on-line retailer, Amazon.com, said that it set a single-day sales record during the 2005 holiday period with more than 3.6 million units, or *41 items per second,* ordered across the globe.

The growth in e-commerce results from the ease with which computer users can search for information on a wide variety of products, jump to those products' web pages, and then purchase desired items with a few clicks of the mouse. While items like books, music CDs, DVDs, and computer games are the most popular items, it is now possible to purchase almost anything using e-commerce.

Even if you don't decide to buy an item over the Web, you can find comparative data on products that can help you with your purchase. For example, websites like www.pricegrabber.ca and www.shopbot.ca provide a wide range of price and quality information on electronics and computers, making you more knowledgeable when you visit an electronics store.

While not included in the on-line sales numbers mentioned above, travel continues to be a huge part of e-commerce, as more and more people take advantage of the tremendous amount of travel information and bookings that are now available on-line. Websites such as Travelocity.ca and Expedia.ca provide many of the same services traditionally offered by travel agents, but with no fees attached to the bookings. Other sites like itravel2000.com and Priceline.com specialize in providing low-cost tickets.

The future of e-commerce is virtually unlimited. You will encounter more information on this exciting application of information systems throughout this book.

9. Statistics Canada, "The Daily: E-commerce Household Shopping on the Internet," http://www. statcan.ca/Daily/English/040923/d040923a.htm, September 23, 2004.

CHAPTER

2

Web Resources

- Industry Canada—http://e-com.ic.gc.ca
- E-Commerce Times—http://ecommercetimes.com/
- E-Commerce Guide—http://www.bizweb.com/

The Web basically provides a hypertext system that operates over the Internet. **Hypertext** allows an easy way to publish information on a network. Hypertext documents can include references (hyperlinks) to other information on the network. Using **Web browser** software, you can view hypertext documents and use the hyperlinks to browse (or surf) other related documents.

To provide this hypertext system, the Web relies on three basic standards:

1. A **uniform resource locator (URL),** which specifies a unique address for each page that indicates the location of a document.
2. **Hypertext transfer protocol (HTTP),** which provides the rules used by browsers and servers as they communicate requests for data and responses between each other.
3. **Hypertext markup language (HTML),** which provides a language for encoding the information so a variety of IT devices can display it.

In addition to the three primary Web standards, the Web includes other standards that enhance its capabilities. These include programming languages, such as Java and Javascript, which can add interactive capabilities to Web documents. Newer standards were also introduced as the need arose. The *eXtensible markup language (XML)* organizes data based on its meaning rather than how it should appear. *Web services* provide a standardized way for one application to run another application over the Internet. We discuss these important protocols and technologies further in later chapters and in the Tech Guides in the back of the book.

Quick Test

1. Which one of the following represents the set of primary rules for transmitting and receiving data over the Internet using packet switching?

   a. FTP   b. HTTP   c. SMTP   d. TCP/IP

2. Which of the following is a true statement about the Internet?
   a. Dial-up access generally provides faster access to Internet resources than broadband.
   b. Most home users require an ISP to connect to the Internet.
   c. The Internet is owned by the U.S. government.
   d. It is impossible to use a wireless device to connect to the Internet.

3. The Web standard that provides a language that a browser interprets when displaying a web page is known as _____.
   a. eXtensible markup language (XML)
   b. hypertext markup language (HTML)
   c. hypertext transfer protocol (HTTP)
   d. uniform resource location (URL)

Answers: 1. d; 2. b; 3. b

 STUDENT RETURN ON INVESTMENT SUMMARY

1. **What are the fundamentals of information technology that will help increase your productivity as a knowledge-enabled professional?**

An information technology (IT) device can accept and store information; perform mathematical calculations; apply logic (e.g., compare values of numbers to make decisions); and retrieve, display, and send information. As such, IT allows you, a knowledge-enabled professional, to *communicate* your thoughts, ideas, and feelings with others. IT *enables transactions* between you and the organizations with which you deal. IT helps you *obtain data and information* that you can use. IT provides tools you can use to *analyze data and information* to aid in your decision making. IT can help you *organize and store data and information* that is important to you. IT can *provide entertainment*. Information technology can help you do all of these things more efficiently and with greater value.

2. **How do the six categories of IT hardware relate to an IT system?**

The main hardware categories are (1) Processing—directs the execution of instructions and the transfor-

mation of data; (2) Memory—location where data and instructions can wait temporarily for processing; (3) Input—the interface that we use for data entry into a device; (4) Output—the interface that we use to retrieve information from a device; (5) Storage—used for the long-term storage of data, information, and instructions; and (6) Communications—components used to connect one IT device to another.

3. **What are the primary concepts associated with IT software?**

We can define *software* as the collection of instructions that an IT device executes. Software is the component that allows you to use your IT hardware in the way that you want. The operating system (OS) software coordinates everything that goes on in your computer and handles the details of working with the computer hardware. Application software is a complete, self-contained program or set of programs that allows you to perform a specific job. Productivity software is commonly used by knowledge-enabled professionals to more efficiently and effectively create and work with data, information, and knowledge.

CHAPTER 2

4. How do software and hardware come together to create business capability?

A computer network is built with nodes that can represent computer hardware and the network users, with various types of hardware, software, and communications media forming the links. A computer network requires four primary components: (1) data represent the resources that are shared between computers on the network; (2) special hardware; (3) software to allow computers to communicate and share the data; and (4) communication media to link the computers together.

5. What makes the Internet and World Wide Web so valuable?

The Internet is arguably the most useful technological tool of the last few decades. The Internet uses the TCP/IP suite of packet switching protocols, a very general, non-proprietary set of communication rules. By adopting these rules and making use of software compatible with the TCP/IP standards, any computer, regardless of the platform (processor and OS), can connect and communicate over the Internet. Further, another aspect of the Internet important to its near global adoption is that no single organization or governmental entity owns it.

If the Internet is the technology platform, the World Wide Web is an application that works on that platform. The Web is the primary Internet application that supports many types of e-commerce. The Web basically provides a hypertext system that operates over the Internet. Hypertext allows an easy way to publish information on a network. Hypertext documents can include references (hyperlinks) to other information on the network. Using Web browser software, knowledge-enabled professionals can view hypertext documents and use the hyperlinks to browse (or surf) other related documents.

KNOWLEDGE SPEAK

PART

1

REVIEW QUESTIONS

Multiple-choice questions

1. What is the hardware location that temporarily stores data and instructions?

   a. hard drive
   b. RAM
   c. ROM
   d. USB flash drive

2. A _____ connects a computer to high-speed network access over the same connection that many use to obtain their television broadcasts.

   a. cable modem
   b. network interface card
   c. hub
   d. router

3. _____ software manages and controls the resources of a computer system.

   a. Application
   b. Operating system
   c. Productivity
   d. Utility

4. The main pair of protocols used by the Internet for all data transmission is known as _____.

   a. TCP/IP
   b. HTTP/HTML
   c. XML/Wi-Fi
   d. SMTP/HTTP

Fill-in-the-blank questions

5. The _____ speed of a processor can be measured in megahertz or gigahertz.

6. _____ displays usually take up less space and consume less power than CRT displays.

7. A major category of productivity software that knowledge-enabled professionals primarily use for quantitative analysis is known as a(n) _____.

8. Wi-Fi is the popular name of the _____ for wireless network access.

True-false questions

9. A pointing device is generally easier to use than a keyboard when entering text data.

10. The Internet is controlled by several independent, international organizations.

Matching questions

Choose the BEST answer from Column B for each item in Column A.

Column A
11. Communications
12. Input
13. Output
14. Processing
15. Storage

Column B
a. Hardware used to save data, information, and instructions long term.
b. Hardware used to connect one IT device to another.
c. Hardware that provides an interface for retrieving information from an IT device.
d. Hardware that provides an interface for entering data into an IT device.
e. Hardware that directs the execution of instructions.

CHAPTER

2

Short-answer questions

16. List the basic tasks that IT can accomplish.
17. What are the three basic categories of IT?
18. Briefly explain why more RAM can speed up your computer.

Discussion/Essay questions

19. The diskette has been one of the most popular media for secondary storage. Do you think that the USB flash drive will replace the diskette? Why or why not?
20. How do you think differences in network sizes and capabilities, such as for CANs, LANs, and WANs, affect security measures for data, information, and knowledge?

TEAM ACTIVITY

Effective teamwork relies on good communication among team members, as well as between the team and its organization. In this activity, you will explore how information technology can help you with each. First, organize yourself into a team of at least five people. At your first meeting, select a team coordinator and an assignment (e.g., a problem that you've noticed on campus or a team assignment for one of your classes). Then send everyone off with the task of thinking about possible solutions to the problem. Over a period of days, the team coordinator should use information technology to communicate with team members to come up with a set of possible solutions to discuss at the second meeting. The coordinator will also use information technology to schedule the second meeting and inform the team members. At the second meeting, in addition to discussing the problem, discuss how the team used IT to perform these tasks. What worked well and what didn't? How could your team use IT more effectively?

SOFTWARE APPLICATION EXERCISES

Internet

Information technology is constantly changing, and many new IT devices can seem exciting and "cutting-edge." Search the Web and select five new or future information technologies that interest you. Bookmark these sites for use in the Presentation activity that follows.

Presentation

Create a presentation to discuss the technologies that you found for the Internet assignment above. For each technology, use two or three slides to provide a brief description and possible uses of it. Give your presentation a professional look by incorporating an attractive layout, informative graphics, and appropriate slide transitions.

Word Processing

In this day and age, it is important for knowledge-enabled professionals to continuously update their IT skills. In order to keep up with your ever-increasing skill set, you should consider keeping a skills inventory that you can update as you acquire each new skill. The inventory will provide a record that you can use when you need to create or update a résumé, discuss your skills at an interview, or plan your next moves in your study of IT.

Use a word processing program to create a template for your skills inventory. You may begin your document with appropriate titles and introductory information. Be sure to include a last update date in the header of your document. For the bulk of the document, use a table to record your list of skills. You should divide the table by major categories such as General Skills, Application Software, and Programming Languages. Under each major category, include a row for the specific skill that you want to include. For each skill, record the name of the skill, an estimation of your skill level (beginner, intermediate, expert), and the date acquired. You may also want to record any courses that you have taken to gain the IT skill.

Spreadsheet

Acquiring information technology can be expensive! Personal computers and laptops can range from a few hundred to a few thousand dollars, depending on the capabilities and options selected. Assume that you are interested in purchasing a new computer. Create a spreadsheet to help you evaluate the relative costs of several options. For each system, include cells to record the possible options and their price. Be sure to include extras such as shipping or tax, which may apply to some options but not others. Use formulas to calculate the overall cost for each system. For a challenge, try to use special cells and IF statements to reflect various decisions such as CRT versus LCD flat-screen monitor, or 512M versus 1024M RAM.

Database

Create a relational database to keep up with your household belongings, including the IT devices that you own. Your database should include three tables: Room, Items, and Item Categories. The Room table should include fields for a room identification number and a room name. The Item Categories table should contain fields for category ID and a category name. You will record the bulk of the data in the Items table under the fields Item ID, Description, Manufacturer, Serial Number, Date Purchased, Place Purchased, Purchase Price, and Notes. You will also need to include the appropriate fields in your tables to represent a one-to-many relationship between the Room and Items table (e.g., a Room can contain many Items) and a one-to-many relationship between and Item Category and an Item (e.g., you can have many items from a particular category, but a single item can be from only one category). Can you think of other data or features that you might add to improve your database? Will your database allow you to answer a question such as "which items did I purchase during the past year?" If not, how can you add this capability to your database?

Advanced Challenge

Are you a "gadget-holic"? Do you need to have the latest technology? Create a multimedia dream system for your home. But wait, there's a catch. You also have to consider how you'll pay for it. So, based on your skills that you identified in the preceding Word Processing activity, choose a job that you think you will qualify for. Find the annual salary for this job and then

CHAPTER

2

deduct approximately 30 percent for taxes, employment insurance, and Canada Pension Plan contributions. Use a spreadsheet to calculate how long it will take you to pay for your dream system (based on a 40-hour workweek).

ON-LINE RESOURCES

Companion Website

- Take interactive practice quizzes to assess your knowledge and help you study in a dynamic way.
- Review PowerPoint lecture slides.
- Get help and sample solutions to end-of-chapter software application exercises.

Additional Resources Available Only on WileyPLUS

- Take the interactive Quick Test to check your understanding of the chapter material and get immediate feedback on your responses.
- Review and study with downloadable Audio Lecture MP3 files.
- Check your understanding of key vocabulary in the chapter with Knowledge Speak Interactive Flash Cards.
- Link directly to websites recommended in the CORE boxes.

CASE STUDY: SELECTING A COMPUTER

In the end-of-chapter case for Chapter 1, you met Ashley Hyatt, a student in business administration at university. In this case, we continue Ashley's story.

After a successful fourth year, during which she interviewed with a number of companies, Ashley has accepted a position with one of the large consulting firms. She'll start her new job within a few weeks. Because Ashley will telecommute one to two days per week, her company will fund the purchase of a Windows-based, desktop PC system for her home, up to $3,000. However, she is unsure of what system will work best for her job.

Ashley realizes that she should begin by considering her job requirements. Because she'll be carrying out extensive financial analyses, she needs a system with a significant amount of processing and hard disk storage. So, because she may be doing some serious "number crunching" in her new job, Ashley should probably go for the maximum processor speed she can afford. Because she will be storing large data files on her hard disk, she should try to purchase a hard drive with as much capacity as possible, but not less than 100 GB. Further, because Ashley will need to transport large files between work and home, she needs a system that reads and writes DVDs.

Finally, Ashley decides that a large (at least 19-inch) flat-panel monitor, which can also display high-definition television signals, will allow her to check breaking news stories while also working on her assigned projects.

Case Questions

1. Using a budget of $3,000 and the requirements mentioned by Ashley, make specific suggestions as to what computer system she should purchase, including a brand name, model, and options.
2. You realize Ashley has overlooked printed output. Considering her budget of $3,000, what options would you recommend?
3. Do you think that Ashley's choice of DVD as a portable secondary storage media is a good one? Why or why not?
4. What upgrades would you recommend that Ashley purchase in the future?

PART

1

Integrative Application Case: Campuspad.ca

After your chat with Sarah and agreeing to help, you decide that you probably need to know a little bit more about creating and running an on-line business. To begin with, although you hadn't wanted to admit it to Sarah, you didn't even really know how someone went about registering a domain name. So that was the first thing you researched, and you were surprised at just how easy it was. But of course, the first step is often the easiest and you knew there was much more to know about running an on-line business, especially if it was going to need full e-commerce capability.

At your last meeting you and Sarah had decided to divide the tasks based on your areas of expertise. Sarah is going to explore marketing, advertising, and regulatory or licensing issues, and you will be putting together a high-level technology plan and getting some estimates of costs. Between the two of you there should be some idea of how much money it would take to get this business started.

As always, you can only start with what you have and that was a simple laptop. Using that and your own ingenuity, you had some serious work ahead of you.

Guiding Case Questions:

1. Research what is required to register a domain name in Canada and how to do it.
2. List the various IT components required to support a transactional e-commerce site.
3. What additional information might you need before you can make cost estimates?
4. What assumptions would you make about this new business based on what you know?

Your Task:

Create two simple documents. The first is a brief description of what is required to register, launch, and host a simple e-commerce site in Canada serving the Canadian market. The second document (best done in Excel or other spreadsheet program) would highlight basic starting assumptions about the IT infrastructure and its associated costs (or cost options) to support the business. Assume that these documents have to be clear and concise enough so that Sarah, as someone with very limited IT knowledge and whose major interest is "the business," will be able to understand them.

3

WHAT WE WILL COVER

- Knowledge-Enabled Work Activities
- Making Decisions
- Problem Solving

CORE

Connectivity	Searching Beyond Google
On-line Security	Wireless Insecurity
Relationships	Meet Me!
Ethics	Intellectual Property Rights

Doing Knowledge Work to Create Business Value

ROI STUDENT RETURN ON INVESTMENT

Through your investment of time in reading and thinking about this chapter, your return, or created value, is gaining knowledge. Use the following questions as a study guide.

1. What are some activities that you, as a knowledge-enabled professional, will likely perform to add business value to your organization?
2. How do structure and quality information influence the nature of the decisions made by knowledge-enabled professionals?
3. How can knowledge-enabled professionals solve problems to create business value?

THE VOICE OF EXPERIENCE
Sherrill Burns, Carleton University

After earning degrees in psychology and sociology and graduating from teachers' college, Sherrill Burns built a career in leadership and organizational development in the high-tech industry. She is now a partner in the consultancy firm Culture Strategy-Fit Inc., which helps clients find ways to create business value and improve performance.

What do you do in your current position? As an organizational development consultancy, we provide diagnostics, particularly ones looking at organizational culture. We look at the way work gets done in organizations, the way people work together on a day-to-day basis, and the extent to which they collaborate, share information, trust each other, experiment, and innovate.

What do you consider to be important career skills? My first job was as a teacher. The most important skills were planning, organizing, relationship building, and conflict resolution. The skills I use now are surprisingly similar. It is also important that I retain strategic focus while being able to dive into tactical issues. Because I'm now a partner and have assumed the business development side of the business, I've added marketing and alliance building to my skill set. I'm not a "techie" (my partner is the "technical guru"), but I've learned that you need to leverage technology to gather the data required to analyze our clients' organizational cultures. We can then apply this knowledge to help our clients be more productive and have a competitive edge.

How do you use IT? In the past, we used face-to-face interviews and focus groups to do our organizational assessments. With clients all over the world, this became increasingly costly, difficult, and time-consuming. So we have developed Web-based diagnostics. We use our databases to analyze day-to-day behaviours and the practices that are in use in the organization to uncover culture patterns and to identify causal factors that inhibit the organization from getting to its strategy. These analyses also help us uncover the levers that could bring organizations a competitive advantage or help them accelerate their strategy.

Can you describe an example of how you have used IT to improve business operations? Once an assessment is complete, we use Web conferencing to communicate the results to clients. Because we do not often travel to clients, we have reduced the cost of our offering, which makes us more competitive. We also use IT to collaborate with nine other consulting firms in an alliance. We use Groove, a collaborative on-line space, to post course calendars, our marketing materials, research articles, sample reports, and proposals. Having this information available to other consultants, with whom we have a committed business relationship, improves efficiency and productivity for us. We are not constantly responding to requests for information.

Have you got any "on the job" advice for students seeking a career in IT or business? Whether you are working for an organization or client, you have to be willing to experiment to meet business needs. You need to think in three dimensions: first, focus on the work to be done and what you'll contribute; second, look at your workplace's technology enablers, processes, and the base of knowledge you can tap into; and third, examine the way the organization works, its culture, social networks, hubs of wisdom, and experience. You need to realize that you cannot do it all yourself and you will need to lean on capable people and use the resources at your disposal. Consider what you're going to be a master of and what you will outsource to others.

Sherrill has been in the high-tech industry, though not as a technologist, and now uses technology as an enabler in her own business. By using the Web and databases, her consultancy is able to analyze each client's situation, help them solve problems, and provide them with insight to make decisions about their business strategy. In this chapter we discuss knowledge work activities similar to those employed at Sherrill's consultancy, along with problem solving and decision making.

In this textbook, you are learning about knowledge-enabled professionals, information systems, and the creation of competitive advantage that enhances business value. At some point, you will likely apply that knowledge on an exam to earn a good grade. Your final grade (the outcome) will likely depend on how much time you have (an input to the decision), how much of that time you choose to devote to studying (the decision), and how well those study methods ultimately help you master the course content (problem solving) so you get a higher grade (the value added). Later, you will apply this same knowledge and decision-making process to create business value for the company you work for. So, what kind of knowledge will you need?

As a new hire, many of your early assignments will include responding to requests for data or information from managers, co-workers, or clients. They will ask you to locate data, analyze and organize it, transform it, and synthesize it (combine and shape the ideas from your analysis). Once this is done you need to communicate and share the results. You will likely use various kinds of information systems to help you with these tasks. In this chapter, we discuss how to strategically apply information technology to successfully perform these activities.

KNOWLEDGE WORK ACTIVITIES

Even as a preschooler, you were already performing knowledge-based activities. How? Say it was your fourth birthday, and you received a bucket of Lego™ blocks. Inside the bucket you made a *discovery*—plastic blocks in many colours. So, what did you do? You dumped the blocks on the floor and began to analyze the blocks and organize the big pile into smaller piles of colours and shapes. Maybe you first decided to build a car, but then realized, "who needs a car when I can build a really big tower and use all the pieces (*transform*)!" So, you started snapping together blocks, until what began as a collection of pieces came together as a magnificent tower (*synthesis*). You were so pleased with your successful creation that you showed everyone around you what you had built. You also probably told them how you built it. In other words, you *communicated* your Lego-building knowledge to others. If we apply this analogy to an organization, the steps you went through are referred to as "work flows" and the outcome of your building efforts as the "work product."

Figure 3.1 depicts these knowledge work activities and shows how they constantly interact around and through you. You did them when you were young (e.g., playing with Lego), you did them recently (e.g., selecting which university or college to attend), you do them now (e.g., preparing for your current classes), and you will continue to do them throughout your life: the discovery, analysis, transformation, synthesis, and communication of data, information, and knowledge. Because of their importance, we will discuss each activity in more detail in the following sections.

DISCOVERY: FINDING DATA, INFORMATION, OR KNOWLEDGE

Discovery is the finding of data, information, and knowledge relevant to a task, problem, issue, or opportunity (the context). You begin with

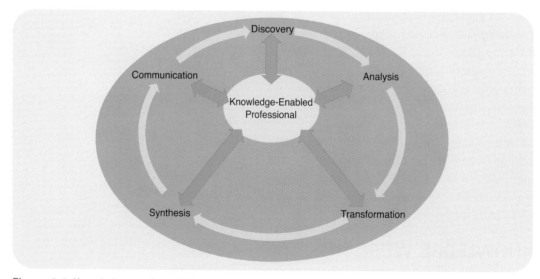

Figure 3.1 Knowledge work activities.

an idea of what to look for, and then reflect on where information related to the task may exist. You then retrieve relevant data from those various sources and assess its value to the decision at hand. For example, say you work as a marketing assistant for WildOutfitters.com, a hypothetical retail hiking store. Your manager asks you to find the weekly sales data for the store and its main competitors. This request frames your discovery activities. You now need to answer questions such as "Where is the sales data for our store located?" and "Who are our competitors?" This type of request is similar to the challenges you face in your search for information to create term papers and presentations.

Learning from your university or college experiences and course requirements will train you for many knowledge work tasks, especially discovering data and information. You already know how to search the Internet to locate specific data and information. As we see in the CORE box "Searching Beyond Google," strong Internet research skills balanced with an awareness of the limitations of this source of data can help you create business value for your organization.

However, discovering information often extends beyond the Internet. In fact, you may have even more powerful job-related

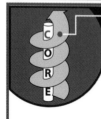

Connectivity

Searching Beyond Google

Do you use Google? So many people use the popular search engine Google (www.google.ca) that is has become part of our language. However, what does searching have to do with business value? Well, for an e-commerce transaction to occur on the

PART 1

Web, customers must locate the merchant's website. Prospective customers often find a website through a search engine. So, in some ways, search engines are the eyes and ears of the customers. And with the Web containing 7 billion pages at last count, without some type of search aids, customers might never find the exciting new stuff in the 38 pages that are being added to the Internet every second.

How do search engines work? Search engines collect, index (organize for retrieval), and store the addresses of web pages and varying amounts of content about those web pages. But what responsibility should they have to make sure that the information they are collecting and indexing is accurate and valid? Many search engines use information technology called *spiders* to increase the breadth of the search. These spiders *crawl* the Web by following links from one page to the next, and sending information back to a database or index of visited pages. And what if the information collected is deliberately vague, false, or misleading? It is this database that you search when you use a search engine to discover information. The largest search engines now claim to have over 4 billion pages in their databases, making the problem quite challenging.

Let's also consider the myriad business issues that arise with search engines. How can you structure your organization's on-line presence to ensure that the right information from the right source is displayed to those searching out your business? What are the ethical, legal, and related issues that arise if you try to manipulate or otherwise influence search engine "hits" to favour your business? And to what extent do the business models of search engines influence how, when, and what they display and how they disclose this to you once it is displayed?

Another tool that every knowledge-enabled professional should know about is the metasearch engine. A *metasearch engine* is a Web-based tool that allows you to review the search results generated by other search engines. A metasearch engine sends out a search query (formats the word or words that you enter for use by search engines) to other search engines, and then returns the list to you. The metasearch engine uses criteria to select which results it will display. So, if you use a metasearch engine like Mamma.ca (www.mamma.ca) or Copernic.com (www.copernic.com), your results will be the top listings from other search engines like Teoma (www.teoma.com), MSN (www.MSN.ca), LookSmart (www.looksmart.com), and Google.

So will using search engines help you find the information you are looking for? Not necessarily. This is where your experience and skills come into play. If you don't know which search criteria to enter, you may not be able to locate the information you need to succeed. Therefore, learning more about query languages, the construction of Internet search engines, and how that technology works is very useful. To improve your Internet-searching capabilities, you may wish to visit the following Web resources.

Web Resources

- Visit a how-to-search site like www.pandia.com, where, according to the website authors, "At Pandia you can learn how to search the web more efficiently; read about search engines, search engine optimization, and sites devoted to searching; and gain easy access to all the best tools and search engine resources on the Internet." You can also visit www.searchenginewatch.com and www.nielsen-netratings.com for similar information about search engines and how-to-search tutorials.
- Check out Canuckster.com, a search engine for Canadian websites only.
- A picture is worth a thousand words—http://images.google.com/ and http://www.alltheweb.com/?c=img
- Learn more about ethical and political issues in search engines from Lawrence M. Hinman, University of San Diego—http://ethics.sandiego.edu/LMH/Papers/Google/Google.html

information close at hand. The company you work for may have a private version of the Internet known as an intranet (which we will discuss in detail in Chapter 5). Basically, an **intranet** contains data about the company that only authorized employees can access. If your organization stores information on its intranet about where a similar problem has occurred before and how it was solved, or perhaps tracks the results of decisions made by competitors or partners, it may even help you to discover "best practices" for solving problems, thereby creating business value for your company.

ANALYSIS: INVESTIGATING AND EXAMINING THE AVAILABLE DATA, INFORMATION, AND KNOWLEDGE

Analysis may be thought of as breaking down the whole into its more discrete parts so as to better understand how it works. We often perform analysis under other names such as "process mapping" (if we are analyzing a business process), "quality assurance" (if we are analyzing product quality), or "performance testing" (if we are assessing fitness or standards). All of these types of business activities involve some form of root cause analysis to answer the contextual question: "What is happening and why?" Therefore, analysis is a critical knowledge work activity that will help you answer questions and gain understanding through a thoughtful investigation and examination of the available data and information. Once you complete the analysis, put it into the appropriate organizational context, and make a decision or recommendation, you have now created knowledge. If you can extend this to include consideration of any unintended consequences, ethical constraints, or risks so that this knowledge can be safely and quickly put to use to create a sustainable competitive advantage, then you have demonstrated wisdom.

To understand better what analysis entails, let's consider the presentation of the data in Figure 3.2. In analyzing the data, you might ask yourself, "What type of equipment sold the most units?" "What was our total profit?" "How did the sales of each type of equipment contribute to that profit?" Answering these questions helps you to turn this data into information. To better understand the weekly sales and to add business value, you need to continue to analyze the data until you can come to some conclusions. For example, you may come to realize that tents contribute more to profit due to their low cost. For this deeper analysis, you may need more data and advanced analysis techniques. In Chapter 5, we discuss data warehouses and data mining, two information technologies that can help answer questions about underlying patterns and correlations across large amounts of data.

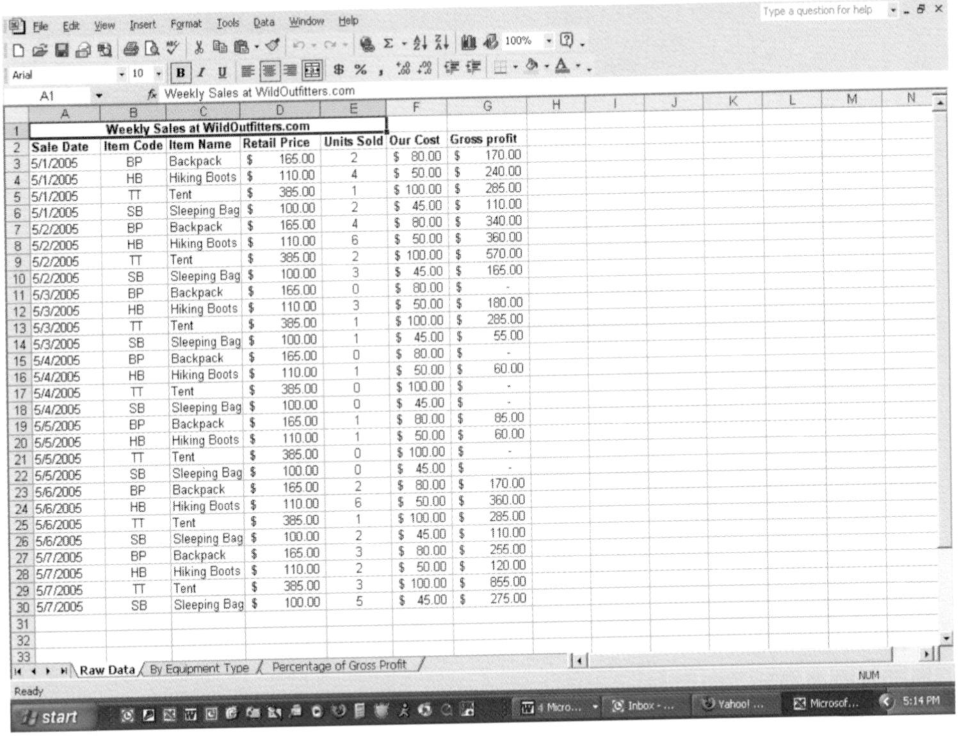

Weekly Sales at WildOutfitters.com						
Sale Date	Item Code	Item Name	Retail Price	Units Sold	Our Cost	Gross profit
5/1/2005	BP	Backpack	$ 165.00	2	$ 80.00	$ 170.00
5/1/2005	HB	Hiking Boots	$ 110.00	4	$ 50.00	$ 240.00
5/1/2005	TT	Tent	$ 385.00	1	$ 100.00	$ 285.00
5/1/2005	SB	Sleeping Bag	$ 100.00	2	$ 45.00	$ 110.00
5/2/2005	BP	Backpack	$ 165.00	4	$ 80.00	$ 340.00
5/2/2005	HB	Hiking Boots	$ 110.00	6	$ 50.00	$ 360.00
5/2/2005	TT	Tent	$ 385.00	2	$ 100.00	$ 570.00
5/2/2005	SB	Sleeping Bag	$ 100.00	3	$ 45.00	$ 165.00
5/3/2005	BP	Backpack	$ 165.00	0	$ 80.00	$ -
5/3/2005	HB	Hiking Boots	$ 110.00	3	$ 50.00	$ 180.00
5/3/2005	TT	Tent	$ 385.00	1	$ 100.00	$ 285.00
5/3/2005	SB	Sleeping Bag	$ 100.00	1	$ 45.00	$ 55.00
5/4/2005	BP	Backpack	$ 165.00	0	$ 80.00	$ -
5/4/2005	HB	Hiking Boots	$ 110.00	1	$ 50.00	$ 60.00
5/4/2005	TT	Tent	$ 385.00	0	$ 100.00	$ -
5/4/2005	SB	Sleeping Bag	$ 100.00	0	$ 45.00	$ -
5/5/2005	BP	Backpack	$ 165.00	1	$ 80.00	$ 85.00
5/5/2005	HB	Hiking Boots	$ 110.00	1	$ 50.00	$ 60.00
5/5/2005	TT	Tent	$ 385.00	0	$ 100.00	$ -
5/5/2005	SB	Sleeping Bag	$ 100.00	0	$ 45.00	$ -
5/6/2005	BP	Backpack	$ 165.00	2	$ 80.00	$ 170.00
5/6/2005	HB	Hiking Boots	$ 110.00	6	$ 50.00	$ 360.00
5/6/2005	TT	Tent	$ 385.00	1	$ 100.00	$ 285.00
5/6/2005	SB	Sleeping Bag	$ 100.00	2	$ 45.00	$ 110.00
5/7/2005	BP	Backpack	$ 165.00	3	$ 80.00	$ 255.00
5/7/2005	HB	Hiking Boots	$ 110.00	2	$ 50.00	$ 120.00
5/7/2005	TT	Tent	$ 385.00	3	$ 100.00	$ 855.00
5/7/2005	SB	Sleeping Bag	$ 100.00	5	$ 45.00	$ 275.00

Raw Data / By Equipment Type / Percentage of Gross Profit

Figure 3.2 Sales data for WildOutfitters.com.

TRANSFORMATION: ORGANIZING DISCOVERY RESULTS

Transformation is knowledge work that requires you to use the results of your analysis to deepen your understanding of the data and information. Why is transformation important? Imagine your university or college course calendar as simply an alphabetic list (e.g., Accounting 350, Acting 102, Art History 210). Each course may contain all the appropriate information, but it is not organized in a useful format. That is, organized this way, you would not know which course is applicable to which degree. When it is organized by course of study (e.g., Business, Fine Arts) or specialty (e.g., Business—Finance it is transformed into information that tells you what courses are required to achieve a particular degree.

Let's revisit your manager's request from the discovery phase, where you needed to obtain weekly sales data for WildOutfitters.com and its competitors. Through your intranet and Internet searches, you discovered a lot of information. In fact, you found more raw data than you can quickly process. This may be especially true if you work as part of a collaborative project team, where others may discover the data or information and pass it to you to analyze and transform. Fortunately,

CHAPTER

3

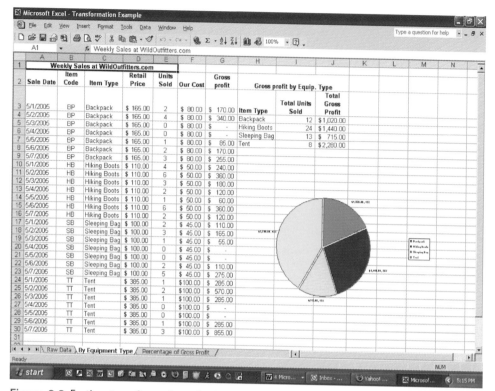

Figure 3.3 Further transformation of sales data for WildOutfitters.com.

information technology can help you transform data regardless of who did the discovery and analysis work. For example, spreadsheets and databases are effective tools for organizing and storing information, as Figure 3.2 shows. (We discuss these software tools in more detail in Tech Guide B.) Note that for this example, you could also use database software. Larger organizations, with many transactions, often use database software for storing and transforming data.

Figure 3.3 shows additional transformations of the data. Note that you (and your manager) can now easily see that hiking boots sold the most number of units, but tents contributed the greatest percentage to weekly gross profit. So by transforming the data into a useful form through the use of a spreadsheet, you begin to make sense of events and issues. You set the stage for the insight and understanding that often result from the next type of knowledge work: synthesis.

SYNTHESIS: THE SUM OF THE PARTS

Synthesis allows you to interpret trends or patterns that seem to explain the past and the present, and may suggest courses of action likely to favourably influence the future. Further, while some of these patterns will stand alone—for example, the WildOutfitters.com sales data for each week of the month—isolated information often paints an incomplete picture. As a result, you will probably need to bring together different pieces of data and information in order to form a complete picture of your current situation. The essential element of synthesis is in knowing which parts, when combined, will create higher total value than the value of the parts themselves. This is particularly true with the synthesis of information. For instance, national security issues often arise only when one piece of information (otherwise deemed irrelevant or uninteresting) is combined with a similarly unassuming piece of other information to begin to show a pattern of possible terrorist activity. While any one piece of information on its own may seem innocent, when correlated and synthesized into a discernible pattern, you have a potential terrorist threat to deal with.

Remember, you may need to integrate even more information before gaining a complete understanding or making recommendations. In the WildOutfitters.com example, the weekly sales data may be trending upward, but the last six weeks' data may be trending downward. A synthesis that excludes additional weekly sales data, competitors' sales data, and industry trends may result in an incomplete understanding. For example, if all additional data trend downward except the weekly sales data shown above, this week may be an anomaly (exceptional case). Or, if other weeks show a downward trend and the overall economy is slowing, you may want to investigate what occurred to generate the increased sales. While systems can provide the summary information, it is people who have the ability to put this information into the proper context and draw conclusions from it.

Once you have an accurate and complete analysis of your results ready you must then communicate them succinctly to others so you can help the organization make better decisions.

CHAPTER

3

? WHAT DO YOU THINK?

You have made your way to university or college by doing knowledge work activities. Of course, you may not have known the names of each of these activities or been aware that you were doing them! Consider the activities of discovery, analysis, transformation, and synthesis, and think about the following questions:

1: What activities did you undertake to come to this university or college? This course?
2: How you purchased a car? Are you thinking of purchasing a car? Which activities will you use to do this?
3: Are you thinking of getting a part-time job? Again, think about what knowledge work activities you will use to find suitable employment.

COMMUNICATION: SHARING ANALYSIS WITH OTHERS

As a knowledge-enabled professional, you will most likely work for and with others in a business or other type of organization. To help your employer create business value, you must have strong **communication** skills; that is, the ability to share your analyses, ideas, and solutions with others. Even if you work for yourself, you still need to communicate effectively with your customers.

Individuals and organizations can and do use information systems and technologies to help them communicate. Some of the technologies individuals use focus on physically sharing the message, such as e-mail and instant messaging. Others, such as those discussed in the CORE box "Meet Me!," help in scheduling meetings.

Information systems and technology can also allow you to share the meaning behind the message. For example, you can use Microsoft PowerPoint to create a presentation, or other software applications to communicate your knowledge, such as Inspiration (www.inspiration.com) and Visio (http://office.microsoft.com/en-us/

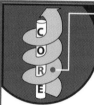

Relationships

Meet Me!

As a student, you've probably already discovered that you must often work in teams to complete tasks (e.g., a team presentation). However, scheduling meetings for all of these teams can be a nightmare. To ease some of this pain, consider using the free meeting scheduling software and other meeting-related tools and information at MeetingWizard.com (www.meetingwizard.com).

What can MeetingWizard.com do for you? After you enter each person's e-mail and select multiple suggested meeting times, the software will automatically send e-mails requesting a response to the meeting invitation. By clicking on the link in the e-mail, the invitees are taken to the meeting invitation on the MeetingWizard.com site. Once there, they indicate their availability by clicking in the RSVP section on the listed times that you initially entered (see Figure 3.4). Lastly, as Figure 3.5 shows, you can get a status update on the responses to the invitation. Although there may still be conflicting meetings, usually team members can find a time or times that are agreeable to all.

Web Resources
- MeetingWizard.com—http://www.meetingwizard.com
- Meeting Maker, Inc.—http://www.meetingmaker.com/home.cfm
- WebEx web conferencing, video conferencing, and online meeting services—http://www.webex.com/
- Microsoft Office Online Live Meeting (web conferencing system)—http://office.microsoft.com/home/office.aspx?assetid=FX010909711033

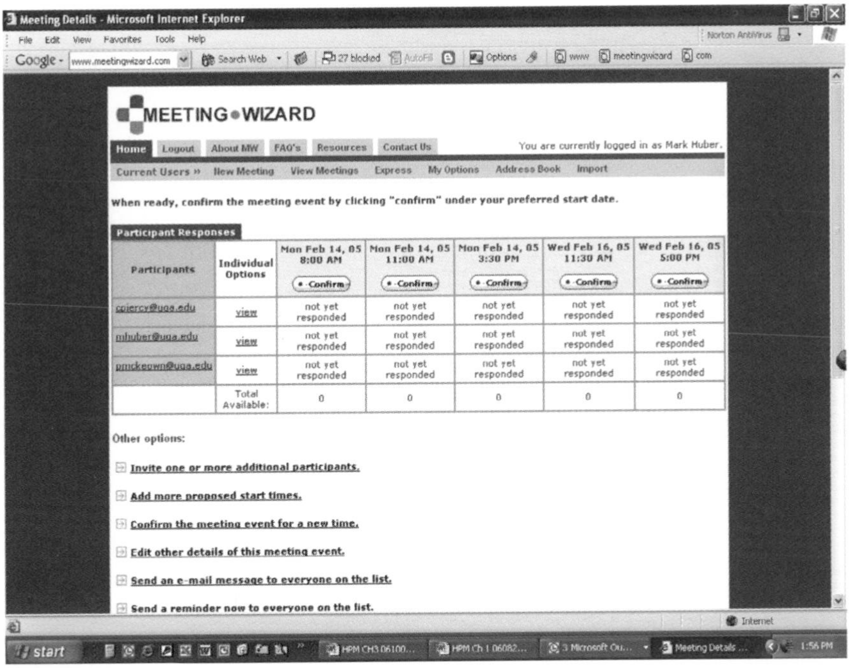

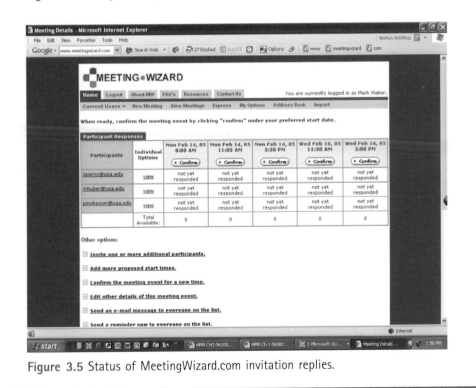

Figure 3.4 Using MeetingWizard.com.

Figure 3.5 Status of MeetingWizard.com invitation replies.

CHAPTER

3

visio/FX100487861033.aspx). These can be collaboratively enabled by using tools such as Groove (www.groove.net) or NetMeeting (www. microsoft.com/windows/ netmeeting/) to organize and disseminate information throughout a virtual team. In Chapter 6, we discuss additional tools used to communicate and collaborate that are the essence of today's complex, network-enabled business information systems.

SUMMARY OF KNOWLEDGE WORK ACTIVITIES

Table 3.1 summarizes and expands on the examples of knowledge work activities we just covered. However, knowledge work activities are only part of the larger picture of a rational decision-making and problem-solving process.

You'll find that any decision making and problem solving creates the need to engage in the knowledge work activities of discovery, analysis, transformation, synthesis, and communication. To help you understand this better, we'll begin by defining a basic decision-making process and then tackle that in the context of problem solving that creates business value.

Table 3.1	Expanded Example of Knowledge Work Activities	
Knowledge Work Activity	**Manager's Request**	**Helpful IT Tools and Activities**
Discovery	Find weekly sales data for our company and for our competitors.	Data from checkout/point-of-sales (POS) terminals, search tools (e.g., Google), and Web searching.
Analysis	Compare the sales data for the first week of May to similar data from our company for the previous two months.	Import the data into a database or spreadsheet application, and use its features and tools to organize the data. Find the previous months' data and import these as well.
Transformation	Identify any trends in the data by week, month, and day of the week. Indicate how our company's results compare with our competition and with the industry as a whole.	Use the data analysis tools in the spreadsheet application to examine the data from different aspects. Consider what your analysis of the data revealed and combine this with your knowledge of your company's goals to add focus to your analysis. Search the Web for other analyses of your company, industry, and competitors. Integrate this with your interpretation of the sales data.
Synthesis	Given your analysis of our company's relative success or failure, suggest ways to capitalize on our strengths and overcome our weaknesses.	With analysis in mind, obtain feedback about specific company products and services. Arrange a brief Web meeting (e.g., with NetMeeting) of the top sales associates in your company.
Communication	Present your findings and suggestions to management.	Import your spreadsheet data into presentation software. Add the insights gained from your Web meeting.

Given our constantly connected and wireless world, the knowledge work activities described above can occur 24/7 from almost anywhere. The CORE box "Wireless Insecurity" discusses Wi-Fi hotspots and wireless security concerns.

On-line Security

Wireless Insecurity

Are you a knowledge-enabled professional who has gone wireless? Are you checking your e-mail from your favourite sunny spot on campus? Have you taken your laptop to a classroom, coffee shop, or a hotel where a wireless local area network (LAN) makes access to the Internet possible? In all of these cases, as well as many more, wireless networks enable users to connect to computers without stringing cables between the computers.

The most popular method for setting up such wireless networks is the WiFi 802.11 (a, b, or g) protocols. The popularity of this form of networking has become so great that most new laptops come with a wireless chip built in, and free access points called *hotspots* are springing up in cities around the world. Jwire, a Wi-Fi hotspot directory (www.jwire.com), reports there are over 130,000 Wi-Fi hotspots worldwide, with 1,500 of those in Canada. Companies are also finding that wireless or mobile devices can bring increased business value for executives, sales representatives on the move, and field technicians. According to Gartner (a well-known research and consulting firm that releases industry and business trend information), 80 percent of workers will use wireless e-mail by 2008. Wireless e-mail adoption is growing very rapidly due to the growing use of BlackBerry devices, a Canadian invention by Waterloo, Ontario-based Research In Motion.[1]

However, if you are a wireless user, have you or your organization installed adequate security measures? After all, signals from within a building are accessible from a parking lot over 100 metres away and, if not encrypted, can be read by anyone with a mobile-equipped laptop. If you haven't installed security measures, you're not alone. One survey showed that 80 of 100 companies surveyed were at risk for security breaches, with 100 percent of educational institutions and 66 percent of banks transmitting sensitive information over their networks.[2]

Why should we worry about a few radio signals leaking out from a wireless network? In a word—hackers! Although we usually think of hackers breaking into computer systems through the Internet, the growing popularity of wireless networks for organizations and homes has created a new type: wireless hackers.

As an example of what could happen, a security expert noticed his physician using a notebook to set-up appointments and wondered about the level of security in this wireless network. Outside, he noticed a chalk mark on the side of the building put there by a hacker indicating an open network was available inside—so-called *warchalking*. Sure enough, when the security expert got to his car, he could access the physician's appointment notes, including the one just created for him! While data about appointments are relatively harmless, diagnoses and prescriptions could also have been on this network, leading to a

CHAPTER

3

---

1. "BlackBerry is driving market for mobile email, says Gartner", http://news.zdnet.co.uk/communications/0,1000000085,39167274,00.htm. Retrieved July 19, 2006.
2. "Wi-Fi Provides Convenient Access, but Security Remains a Challenge." *Electronic Commerce News*, June 7, 2004.

potential loss of privacy or other problems. So, if you're using an unprotected wireless network, be aware of the potential for the so-called *drive-by hackers* to be accessing your files. Think about adding security measures to protect your network and your data.

Web Resources
- Sierra Wireless, a Canadian company that is prominent in wireless networking technology— http://www.sierrawireless.com
- Wireless Toronto, a not-for-profit group dedicated to bringing no-fee wireless Internet access to Toronto— http://www.wirelesstoronto.ca
- Research In Motion, the Canadian company that produces BlackBerry products—http://www.rim.com

Quick Test
Fill in the blank for each question below.

1. Either database or spreadsheet software can be very useful as part of the knowledge work activity known as _____.

2. _____ is the knowledge work activity where you make suggestions and offer alternatives by combining and interpreting data and information from multiple sources.

3. In a business organization, the ultimate purpose of knowledge work activities is the creation of _____.

Answers: 1. transformation; 2. synthesis; 3. business value

MAKING DECISIONS

Before we can discuss effective decision making, we need to have a common understanding of what a decision is. A **rational decision** is a choice that you make about what actions you will take (or not take) in a given situation after analyzing the consequences of each option. It may involve trade-offs between options or trying to optimize an outcome given a set of current circumstances and preferences balanced with risk. There may be legal or environmental factors or ethical or moral concerns about certain aspects of the decision. However, rational decision making normally occurs, as a part of a larger problem-solving process within a specific context. This creates natural boundaries and limits around the available options. In other words, you usually make a decision, for example, choosing between University A or

College B, in the context of solving the problem of what you want to study and why (the problem-solving process). This involves considerations such as distance from home, climate and language preferences, tuition and living costs, your knowledge of the institution involved, recommendations or rankings by others, quality of program or faculty, accessibility, and perhaps likelihood of being admitted. Once all these factors are considered, the outcome will dictate the first step of choosing where you will go to school (the actual decision). Further, you may also need to consider the ethics of a decision, such as whether or not it is important for you to attend a public or private, institution whose selective admission criteria or policies you may not personally agree with but whose education might be superior. Should you attend such a school or not? Lastly we know that the more practice you have making decisions and learning to anticipate their consequences, the better you become at making them!

As the CORE box "Intellectual Property Rights" illustrates, not all decisions are the same, nor will everyone necessarily perceive them the same way. Some decisions may be routine, such as putting gas in a car in order to drive it, whereas some decisions are more difficult, involving ethical considerations. Think about some of the other decisions that you have made, for example, what to wear today, what route to take to school, and what career to pursue. These decisions are not equal in consequence or in the need for careful thought and planning.

CHAPTER 3

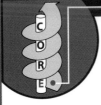

Ethics

Intellectual Property Rights (or Why Shouldn't I Download that MP3 Without Paying for It?)

Have you ever downloaded music, videos, or books over the Internet? Did you do something unethical? To understand why the *unauthorized* downloading of music files or other forms of copyrighted material may be unethical, it is important to be aware of a concept known as *intellectual property*. Intellectual property is any creation of the mind, including inventions, literary and artistic works, and symbols, names, images, and designs used in commerce. Canadian laws governing copyrights or patents, protect most intellectual properties, making unauthorized copies of such property illegal.

However, the problem is that there are not yet many good ways to enforce these laws. Illegal copying and distribution, brought about by digitization and high-speed networks, is easy. Further, the technological means of copyright enforcement that do exist, called *digital rights management (DRM)*, often seem to violate another important aspect of copyright law known as *fair dealing*. The fair dealing concept of Canadian copyright law allows the use of a copyrighted material for purpose of private study or research, or for criticism, review, or news reporting.[3] Material that uses DRM technology often does not allow any copies of the work to be made, including copies that would be allowed under fair dealing provisions.

Another challenge is to determine whether or not unauthorized use of copyrighted material has a negative impact on the owner of the material. For the case of music downloads, the jury is still out. Graham Henderson, who heads the Canadian Recording Industry Association, says downloading is damaging the industry, the economy, and the careers of artists: "Downloading, file-swapping, peer-to-peer networks—these are all euphemisms for piracy, pure and simple. It is devastating to the Canadian music industry." Henderson says the recording industry has seen music sales drop almost $500 million in just a few years. That's about a quarter of a million records a month.[4]

On the other hand, a research paper from Dr. Felix Oberholzer of Harvard and Dr. Koleman Strumpf of the University of North Carolina indicates that there has been little to no effect on the music industry from music file sharing. The paper, in fact, concludes that music file sharing has had a positive effect on the industry.[5] A Forrester Research report backs up this claim, which advocates that the music industry embrace music file sharing to improve sales.[6] Dr. Michael Geist of the University of Ottawa believes it is not peer-to-peer music file sharing that is negatively effecting the industry as a whole, but the Canadian Private Copying Collective, which collects tariffs on downloads, that threatens to kill the nascent on-line music industry.[7]

Despite the uncertainty surrounding music files, as a knowledge-enabled professional, how should you feel about the unauthorized use of intellectual property? Think about how you will earn your living as a knowledge-enabled professional—by creating business value through knowledge work activities, decision making, and problem solving. These activities are often highly creative and result in an information or knowledge product that has business value. If someone were to use the knowledge you create, they might be able to "steal" some or all of the business value that resulted from your knowledge work. Your organization might suffer financially. This in turn could adversely impact your salary, benefits for pensioners, and the value of the company to shareholders. So before you decide to download that MP3, you may want to think about how this practice might affect you some day.

Web Resources
- World Intellectual Property Organization—http//www.wipo.int
- Canadian Recording Industry Association—http://www.cria.ca
- Canadian Intellectual Property Office—http://strategis.ic.gc.ca/sc_mrksv/cipo
- Electonic Frontier Foundation—http://www.eff.org/

3. Canadian Intellectual Property Office (CIPO), http://strategis.ic.gc.ca/sc_mrksv/cipo/cp/copy_gd_protecte. Retrieved July 19, 2006.
4. "Musicians call for an update on copyright law," http://www.ctv.ca/servlet/Articlenews/story/CTVNews/110133117830_15?hub=Canada. Retrieved July 19, 2006.
5. Oberholzer, Felix and Koleman Strumpf (2004), "The Effect of File Sharing on Record Sales, An Empirical Analysis," Unpublished paper (Harvard Business School and Department of Economics, University of North Carolina, Chapel Hill), www.unc.edu/~cigar/papers/FileSharing_March2004.pdf.
6. Bernoff, J. "Downloads Save the Music Business," August 2002, www.forrester.com.
7. Geist, Michael, "Tariffs the real threat to music downloading," Toronto Star http://www.thestar.com/NASApp/cs/ContentServer?pagename=thestar/Layout/Article_Type1&c=Article&cid=1113774609428&call_pageid=968350072197&col=969048863851. Retreived August 25, 2006.

CLASSIFYING DECISIONS BY TYPE

Your college or university degree program likely requires you to take certain prerequisite courses. When you make your course selections, you know that you must register in these classes. Here, you carry out the required actions associated with a very structured decision. A **structured decision** is one that can be programmed; it is routine or repetitive.[8]

But, not all decisions are so clear cut. Sometimes even simple decisions may have increased uncertainty, or doubt about consequences and outcomes, associated with them. This is the case when you register for optional or elective courses. You may decide to take a course based on your interests or when the course is offered. Some of your classmates may have recommended an elective course that is "easy" or entertaining. Other classmates' opinions may have differed. The choice is not so easy. You are now faced with a **semistructured decision**.

Let's further complicate this example. You graduate from your course of study and are now faced with doing graduate studies or starting your career in the business world. You are now faced with a third kind of decision: the **unstructured decision**. This is a novel, complex situation, with no obvious and single correct decision or decision process. Further, your decision will significantly affect the next few years of your life. So what do you do?

To help you decide what to do, you may meet with some graduate students, survey some of the courses you would take, and talk to people working in the business area you are considering. You may also consult your family and friends. Money may also be a consideration. You do some research on the Internet and find that having a graduate degree does not significantly affect initial annual salaries. You've made your decision: you will enter the work world and not do graduate studies. But there is still a lot of uncertainty as to the correctness of this decision. If you don't do graduate studies now, when will you? Perhaps you will miss studying with an influential professor. However, given the available information, you've made the best decision you could.

USING INFORMATION IN DECISION MAKING

This is what rational decision making is all about: using information to reduce uncertainty in the outcomes of your decisions. The above example highlights aspects of the three different types of decisions and their relationship to uncertainty. In general, uncertainty complicates the decision-making process and underscores why information

8. Simon, H. A. 1960 and 1977 (re-release). *The New Science of Management Decision.* Harper&Row, New York; Keen, P. G. and Scott Morton, M. S. 1978. *Decision Support Systems: An Organizational Perspective.* Addison-Wesley, Mass.

CHAPTER

3

systems are so important to businesses: Information systems help businesses reduce uncertainty by providing information to decision makers. Less uncertainty due to more complete information can lead to better decisions, thereby enhancing the creation of business value.

However, as knowledge-enabled professionals, we also have a responsibility to recognize that there is no such thing as perfect information to eliminate uncertainty. Therefore, some of our responsibilty is also to know when we have enough valuable information to go ahead with a decision and then to push ourselves and our organizations to execute those decisions even when there is some lingering uncertainty.

Another important element of good decision making is what to do when we receive new information. Is it valuable and should it influence our decision? These are judgements you will be called upon to make throughout your career as you make important decisions about all kinds of things, both more and less certain, that can affect the organization you work for.

WHAT DO YOU THINK?

People can endlessly discover, analyze, transform, and synthesize—a neverending process known as *analysis paralysis*. Doing these knowledge work activities should lead to some conclusion—a decision or a solution to a problem. Often, organizations use knowledge work activities to investigate productivity. **Productivity** can be thought of as the ability to create business value with the least cost. Examining productivity forces organizations to look at efficiency and effectiveness, which we define as follows:

Efficiency: Getting the most output from a given input ("doing the thing right").
Effectiveness: Pursuing the goal or task that is appropriate for the given situation ("doing the right thing").
Therefore, productivity can be considered "doing the right thing, right."

Consider the following scenarios to better understand knowledge work and decision making concerning productivity:

1: Imagine that you are a sidewalk vendor of frozen drinks in Saskatoon, Saskatchewan. You get more drinks per amount of ingredients than your competitors; that is, you are highly efficient. But you sell only one frozen drink in January (when the average temperature is −17°C), so your efforts are ineffective.
2: Now imagine you are the owner of a T-shirt-selling business on campus. It is so successful that you always sell out of T-shirts by the end of frosh week. You know you could sell more if you were able to produce more T-shirts by the beginning of September.

For each of these scenarios, what decisions will you make to improve your productivity? What knowledge work activities will you undertake to assist in making these decisions? What role could IT play in improving productivity?

PART

1

Table 3.2	Information Evaluation Criteria
Information Characteristic	**Example**
Complete	Your new project team member's cell phone is 555-1212. Is this enough information? Maybe, but you may also need an area code.
Accurate	You check your printed course schedule and find out that your Intro to IS class meets at 11 P.M. You suspect the schedule is wrong.
Reliable	You receive an unsolicited e-mail offering you a share in millions of dollars if you will help this person transfer money out of his home country. You realize this is a frequent e-mail scam; and is, therefore, unreliable information.
Timely	When deciding what to wear, a forecast of yesterday's weather is recent information but could be worthless if today's weather is different than yesterday's. Timely information includes "recent" information but also requires that the information arrive close enough to the decision to be useful to the decision maker.

HOW TO MAKE MORE-INFORMED DECISIONS

As a knowledge-enabled professional, recall that your work often centres on finding and using quality data, information, and knowledge. As a decision maker, the quality of your decision often depends on the quality of the inputs you use to inform your decision.

In every decision that you make in life, you should always carefully consider the characteristics of the information you are basing your decision on. Obviously, you must have already considered the source when you either accessed or were provided with the information and you must assume that the source is a good one. However, beyond that are the nuances of the information itself. Is it complete? How accurate or reliable is it likely to be? If it is not, have any efforts been made to address the degree to which it is or is not accurate or reliable? And is the information up to date and provided in a timely way?

All of these information characteristics, which are summarized in Table 3.2, affect the usefulness of data and information for decision making. As someone living in the most intense knowledge era ever, you need to become a good judge of the quality of information.

THE DECISION-MAKING PROCESS

Figure 3.6 summarizes a typical rational decision-making process. Initially, decision making requires you to engage in knowledge work activities so that you can make an effective choice about some issue or challenge facing you. You have seen that not all decisions are the same with regard to the structure or uncertainty present in the decision-making environment, and normally, as you progress through the process, you will become more certain and the structure of the decision will become clearer. In order to make the best decision you can, you need to carefully consider the quality of the data, information, and

CHAPTER

3

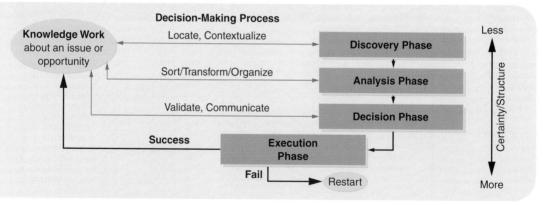

Figure 3.6 To make the best decision possible, you should carefully consider the amount of decision certainty and structure, as well as assess the quality of data, information, and knowledge available in the context of the decision to be made.

knowledge that you locate during the discovery phase and put it into proper context. During the analysis stage, you sort, transform, and organize the data to define options. Of course, in this sense, decisions are just like computer programs: Garbage in, garbage out! The quality of the final output of this process (the decision) will likely be based on the quality of the inputs (the information and analysis you create).

Once you have narrowed the options to a final decision, you communicate the conclusion so the organization can implement the decision. Obviously, the result will either be a success or a failure. Either of these contributes learning to the process for the next time. They lead to either tackling a new problem or refining your understanding of the current problem and repeating the process to make a new decision about a new course of action.

Quick Test

1. Fill in the blank. The level of uncertainty faced by a decision maker can be reduced through the discovery and use of _____.

2. True or False: The more you make decisions, the better you will be at anticipating the consequences of making them.

3. The need for data that are from a trusted source determines if the data are _____.

   a. accurate

   b. complete

   c. timely

   d. reliable

PROBLEM SOLVING

In general, a **problem** exists when we find ourselves in a current situation that fails to meet our goals, needs, or expectations. Further, that current situation often results from a past series of events, or lack of events, that did or didn't happen. For example, it's a problem if you studied and failed to make the desired grade on a test. But it's a different problem if you didn't study at all and failed to make the desired grade on the test. So the first step in problem solving is not only recognizing that a problem exists, but why it exists. We can then take effective and efficient steps to change the situation, to meet our needs and goals more productively.

For some problems, fixing them is relatively easy, for example, using an umbrella to stay dry if it's raining. For most business problems, however, resolving them poses a real challenge. So how do knowledge-enabled professionals reliably and consistently fix problems? They engage in problem solving. **Problem solving** refers to a series of steps or a process (logical sequence of activities) taken in response to some event or activity.

Let's use an example to help you understand the problem-solving process. It is January and it is time to pay the next installment of your tuition. Unfortunately, the first semester of the year cost a lot more than you expected and you do not have enough money to cover tuition (problem). You examine the alternatives and decide to ask your parents for a loan. This solves the problem; at least the original problem!

As a knowledge-enabled professional, you will often repeat the problem-solving process. And each stage of this process may require individual decisions that use the decision-making process we discussed above. Therefore, to make that process as effective as possible, you could use the IADD problem-solving model. If you follow the steps in this model, you'll have a tool that you can consistently apply to most problems, either as an individual or within an organization.

IADD[9] MODEL

The **IADD** model is a more formal expression of the problem-solving process that you probably already use intuitively. The model, as Figure 3.7 shows, consists of four major steps: **I**nvestigate, **A**nalyze, **D**ecide, and **D**o.

- *Investigate:* Determine if there is a problem or an opportunity, and if it is possible to solve the problem or take advantage of the opportunity.

9. This model is a synthesis of various problem-solving and decision-making models, especially Simon's Model of Intelligence, Design, Choice, and Implementation (Simon, 1977).

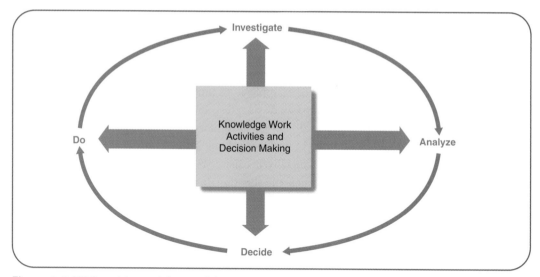

Figure 3.7 IADD problem-solving model.

- *Analyze:* Gather data that are relevant to the heart of the problem, or that pertain to the benefits, challenges, and risks associated with a given opportunity.
- *Decide:* Evaluate solutions, and make choices regarding how to implement the solution.
- *Do:* Implement the solution and monitor the results.

To demonstrate how to use the IADD model, let's take an example. Assume that you have not yet declared an academic major. To solve this problem, let's apply the IADD model in a question-and-answer format, integrating knowledge work activities as needed.

INVESTIGATE

In the *investigate* stage, knowledge-enabled professionals identify a challenge or problem and gather data to determine if meeting the challenge or resolving the problem is possible. Problems tend to be defined or identified in terms of what went wrong with a process or action. Or they may be defined by comparing a desired future state (profitability) to the current situation (expenses exceed revenues).

Problems can also be defined as opportunities or challenges. For example, Larry Page and Sergey Brin, frustrated with trying to find information on the Web, thought about how to overcome this problem and help others, too. Who are Page and Brin? They are the co-founders and chief executives of Google.

Let's use our example to illustrate how to work through the *investigate* stage. We begin by asking questions: "What's wrong?" "Is there a business or learning opportunity present?" You realize there is a learning *and* business opportunity here! You have the opportunity to decide what subject you wish to study and the courses you will most likely take for the next two years or so. You also realize this knowledge will help you in your future business career.

Now that you have identified the opportunity, you need to take action. As part of the investigate stage, you need to discover where to find more information about this opportunity.

Knowledge Work Highlight: Discovery

The *investigate* step is a major discovery effort. Recall that discovery is finding data, information, or knowledge on a given topic. In this case, you need to find data about academic majors.

Your academic advisor is a good place to start, as is your school's website. For example, on your school's website, you could search using the phrase "choosing a major" or "academic major." Where else can you find data, information, and knowledge about your major? You could talk to your friends who are majoring in the subject, or you could attend a meeting of the student organization related to your intended major. Also, you could contact a professor who teaches classes in the major.

ANALYZE

In the *analyze* stage, your brain needs to go into "detective" mode, looking for clues and evidence that will let you piece together what happened. Just as crime scene investigators do on television, you try to decipher what each piece of data means and how each piece relates to the other pieces. As you continue your analysis, you try to describe the problem or challenge, as well as all of the factors that influence the situation. Think of analysis as developing a list of suspects that you interview to try to develop a reasonable solution for the crime (problem).

Before we return to your "major" problem, let's think about how information systems can help with the *analyze* step of problem solving in general. If your problem or opportunity is complex, you will have an abundance of data that you will need to organize, classify, store, and so on. Fortunately, databases and database management systems (DBMS) software are excellent tools for organizing and storing data. Further, certain types of DBMS can even harness the power of the relationships that exist in the data (we discuss how in Tech Guide D). And once you've organized and stored the data and relationships, you can use other tools to manipulate the data. For example, you can ask questions of your database through Structured Query Language (SQL) queries, or use special software programs to "mine" the data to discover previously undiscovered relationships and patterns.

Let's return to the issue of choosing a major. Although you will want to effectively and efficiently analyze your data, the problem is not so large as to require huge amounts of data or complex information systems. As with other IADD stages, let's begin to analyze your situation by asking questions, such as: "If I am interested in learning about _____, or if I want to be a(n)_____ in the future, what subject should I major in?" Choosing good questions to focus your analysis is an important part of the problem-solving process. Your questions must fit the decision you need to make.

Knowledge Work Highlight: ALL

Obviously, you will engage in analysis during the *analyze* stage. However, you will also transform existing data to look at them in new ways. You may need to discover new data to aid your analysis. You will decide what data are relevant. Finally, you may communicate with others for ideas, assistance, and opinions. The *analyze* stage brings all your knowledge work skills to bear in grasping the problem and moving forward through the model.

Generate Alternative Solutions or Choices

Let's begin by thinking about the data that you gathered. Much of it will probably pertain to one or two majors in which you were already interested. However, there may be some surprises in there, too. Maybe you went by your university or college's career or student centre and took an aptitude test. You can use the results as data to generate alternative majors. Remember, as you generate alternative solutions or choices, you may need to gather more data. You should also take the time to think creatively to generate as many viable solutions as possible.

Determine Selection Criteria

Let's assume that you came up with three choices: (1) Accounting, (2) Finance, and (3) Management Information Systems (MIS). To analyze your choices, you need to determine selection criteria. **Criteria** are the factors that you think are important and relevant to solving the problem. For example, to solve your problem, think about your interests, or what you like or don't like to study. You might include your estimate of success in the course work required for the majors as criteria. Or perhaps you view your major as a stepping-stone to your future career. If so, your criteria may include future job opportunities, opportunities for travel and advancement, starting salaries, or lifelong earnings potential.

WHAT DO YOU THINK?

You have likely used brainstorming to solve problems or are familiar with it as a concept. The traditional method of brainstorming usually involves organizing a face-to-face meeting, introducing the topic or problem to be discussed, and having people voice their ideas or write them down on a piece of paper. A facilitator writes the ideas on a board or reads the papers out for the group to evaluate. If you have attended a brainstorming session, you know there can be issues: someone talks too much, some people are afraid to voice their ideas, and no one wants their ideas criticized.

Enter electronic brainstorming. Electronic brainstorming can draw on ideas of groups by using computers in the same room or around the globe. Each participant uses their computer and meeting software to enter their ideas anonymously on the topic being brainstormed. Research done by Brent Gallupe and William Cooper, professors at Queen's University, indicates that more and better ideas are produced using electronic brainstorming than through traditional methods.[10] Given this, consider the following questions:

1: Would you be more open with ideas if you were contributing them anonymously?
2: What types of problems could be solved using electronic brainstorming that could not be addressed through traditional brainstorming?
3: How could a business use electronic brainstorming as a way of creating business value?

Here's another approach that might help you develop useful and relevant criteria. Of the proposed solutions, think about the positive benefits or characteristics of each. As you list these characteristics, consider which ones you view as more important than the others. This method may help you develop criteria for choosing which solution to develop further.

What criteria you apply to your decision greatly concerns the data that you gathered. For example, if you select future job opportunities as a criterion, but you didn't gather the data, it will be difficult to use this as a meaningful criterion. You will then need to discover more data about your proposed solutions to complete your analysis.

DECIDE

At some point in the problem-solving process, you need to stop gathering and analyzing data, as well as stop generating alternative solutions. Your analysis may offer several good solutions to choose from, maybe even the "best" solution. However, if you don't choose a solution or fail to implement it, the problem remains unsolved. So, in the *decide* stage of the IADD model, knowledge-enabled professionals choose the best solution from those available and describe how that solution will solve the problem, meet the challenge, or capitalize on the opportunity.

CHAPTER

3

10. R. Brent Gallupe and William H. Cooper, "Brainstorming Electronically," *Sloan Management Review*, Fall 1993: Vol. 35, p. 27.

Table 3.3	Scoring Alternatives Based on Criteria				
Criteria Scale: 1 (low) to 5 (high)	Personal Interest	Estimated Starting Salaries	Forecasted Job Demand	Friends in Major	Total Score
Accounting	4	4 [$41,000.00]	5	3	16
Finance	5	3 [$40,000.00]	4	5	17
Management Information Systems	4	5 [$44,000.00]	5	4	18

Is it just that easy? No, not usually. As we discussed previously, decision making is often more complex and uncertain. One choice may not be clearly better than the others, or you may need to combine elements from one or more solutions to create a more comprehensive one. Or, if none of the proposed solutions seems workable, you may need to go back and generate more alternatives.

Knowledge Work Highlight: Synthesis

During the *decide* stage, you synthesize the best ideas from your alternative solutions into your "best" solution. How? By applying your criteria to and evaluating the merits of each proposed solution. You change ideas into reality, and begin the transition from thinking into doing. Through deciding, you determine how you will solve your problem and then translate these thoughts into planned actions.

Apply Criteria to Alternatives

How do knowledge-enabled professionals actually decide which solution to pick? It all depends on the criteria they established and the agreed-upon decision process. For your problem, you might enter the possible solutions in the rows of a spreadsheet, and the criteria for choosing in the columns (see Table 3.3). You can then score each possible solution by evaluating it against each criterion according to some scale [e.g., 1 (low) to 5 (high)]. Is this enough? Well, you may want to add some kind of emphasis or weighting on one or more of the criteria. For example, ask yourself if it is more important to study what you are interested in or to earn the highest possible starting salary upon graduation. In a sense, before you can rank your solutions, you may have to rank your criteria. Once you determine how to account for the scores you assign, then the solution with the highest point total could be the top candidate for implementation in the *do* stage.

After you select the "best" solution for you, you are ready to determine the what, when, where, and how of implementing your choice. Note, however, that although you select a solution in the

Table 3.4	Example of an Action Grid				
Person Responsible	Action Required	Resources Needed	Due Date	Date Accomplished	Comments
You	Make appointment with advisor	E-mail or maybe a Web-based form	MM/DD/YYYY	MM/DD/YYYY	Do this before midterm to ensure priority registration for major courses

decide stage, you can modify your solution in the future (e.g., you can switch majors if needed).

DO

Once you decide on a solution and a way to implement it, you must "conclude" the problem-solving process by carrying out the actions necessary to make the solution a success. This *do* step of the IADD model is where you implement tasks and other physical activities according to your solution. At the individual level, it is you who is responsible for doing these activities. It is you who completes the necessary paperwork, and enrolls in classes required by your intended major. You must carry out many of these tasks in sequence and by certain dates.

Knowledge Work Highlight: Communicate

Communication of your choice of major is important to your success in that field. For example, you may need to meet with faculty and/or advisors to enter into your chosen major, and to work with others to achieve your goal of graduating with a degree. You may also want to let others such as your parents and friends know of your choice. They can provide valuable insight and support as you work toward your goal.

Implement the Best Solution

Making a solution work is an especially important part of the problem-solving process. In fact, it can be as much or more of a challenge than the three previous steps. To help with this task, you can use an *action grid,* such as that shown in Table 3.4.

You can make the action grid even more effective by using information technology. For example, the action grid in Table 3.4 could represent a report that was the output from a database designed to track and manage activities. Or you might use project management software or CASE tools (we discuss these tools in Chapter 6). These

CHAPTER 3

sophisticated IS tools can help with your knowledge work activities, decision making, and problem solving.

Monitor and Modify the "Best" Solution

To monitor and modify (if needed) your solution, you need to establish metrics. Decision makers use metrics to determine what is measured and how to measure it. For example, you may select your major GPA as a metric. At the end of each semester, you can calculate your major GPA. You also need to determine what GPA you wish to attain that will indicate satisfactory progress. Or, if you think that a semester is too long to wait for feedback on your progress, you can calculate your major GPA after midterm. Depending on the outcome of your calculations, you may need to alter your studying habits. Basically, metrics should be those measurements that help you monitor the implementation and progress of your solution.

Review and Do

Ask yourself the following questions: (1) What was the solution designed to do? (2) What actually happened or is happening as a result of implementing (doing) the solution? (3) What might explain both the good and bad differences between planned solutions and results? (4) What can I learn from this effort so I can do a better job now and in the future? Based on your answers to these questions, you can modify or scrap your current solution. Simply return to the step(s) in the IADD model that will help you create and implement a more effective solution.

PUTTING IT ALL TOGETHER: THE RELATIONSHIPS BETWEEN KNOWLEDGE WORK, DECISION MAKING, AND PROBLEM SOLVING

You can see how much initial knowledge work is involved in decision making and problem solving. Figure 3.8 shows the relationship among knowledge work activities, decision making, and problem solving. It is this set of relationships that holds the key to the creation of business value.

Working outwards, we have the knowledge-enabled professional at the centre of the entire process (you). You are essential to its operation and critical in terms of your ability to perform knowledge work activities.

After sufficient knowledge work has occurred to define the problem or opportunity at hand, we use the decision-making process to

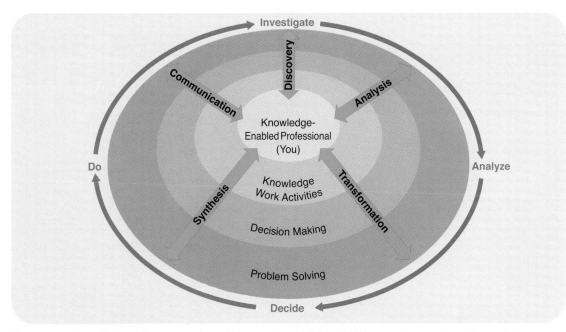

Figure 3.8 The relationships among knowledge work activities, decision making, and problem solving hold the key to the creation of business value.

establish what can be done about it. As we previously saw, all of these steps require the basic skills of discovery, analysis, transformation, synthesis, and the ability to communicate.

Of course, any specific decision occurs in the overall context of problem solving the big issues that face your organization. This is where our investigate, analyze, decide, and do (IADD) model can control the flow and order of activity within the organization to ensure it achieves its desired goals. Obviously, there is no point in doing knowledge work or making decisions about things that do not matter or that are less important than other issues in the organization. If we do, we risk making the overall efforts of the entire team suboptimal.

The best organizations use their most precious resource (people) to focus on their most strategic and urgent priorities (their goals). IT is used to automate the less useful and more routine tasks to free up resources to concentrate on these priorities. This is what makes them successful and also makes them great organizations to work for.

So, as a newly graduated knowledge-enabled professional, look for opportunities in organizations that are going to help you use your skills to make decisions and solve problems that make a difference for you and your employer.

CHAPTER

3

Quick Test

1. Fill in the blank. In order from first to last, the four steps in the IADD problem-solving model are _____.

2. An action grid is a tool that is especially useful in the _____ step of the problem-solving process.
   a. analyze
   b. decide
   c. do
   d. investigate

3. In the *decide* step, _____ are applied to evaluate each alternative's relative value and applicability.
   a. criteria
   b. action grids
   c. metrics
   d. queries

Answers: 1. Investigate, Analyze, Decide, Do; 2. c; 3. a

 STUDENT RETURN ON INVESTMENT SUMMARY

1. What are some activities that you, as a knowledge-enabled professional, will likely perform to add business value to your organization?

As a new hire, many of your early assignments will include responding to requests for data or information from managers, co-workers, or clients. They will ask you to *discover* data, *analyze* (organize) it, *transform* it, *synthesize* (combine and shape the ideas from your analysis) it, and then *communicate* (share) the results. Using IT as you perform these activities will help you increase your *productivity;* that is, create business value.

2. How do structure and quality information influence the nature of the decisions made by knowledge-enabled professionals?

A decision is a choice you make about what actions you will take (or not take) in a given situation. Decisions can vary in the amount of structure and

uncertainty, from structured and certain decisions (e.g., selecting prerequisite courses) to unstructured decisions that give little guidance about what to do, how to do it, and what the likely outcome will be. The amount of structure and the level of uncertainty can influence how much time knowledge-enabled professionals will spend in different knowledge work activities and how certain they might be about the outcomes of their decisions. Further, because the data and information that you gather (discover) form the foundation for your analysis and synthesis activities, the quality of your data and information directly affects the quality of your decision.

3. How can knowledge-enabled professionals solve problems to create business value?

The four steps in the IADD model are: (1) investigate, (2) analyze, (3) design, and (4) do. Knowledge-enabled professionals often focus on creating business value for their organization by solving problems and by

PART
1

recognizing and responding to new business opportunities. For example, they do this by gathering new information (*investigate*), considering which information is most important (*analyze*), outlining how to apply this information to the problem or opportunity at hand (*decide*), and then taking the necessary actions to implement and monitor the decided-upon solution or course of action (*do*).

KNOWLEDGE SPEAK

analysis   80

communication   84

criteria   98

discovery   77

effectiveness   92

efficiency   92

IADD   95

intranet   80

problem   95

problem solving   95

productivity   92

rational decision   88

semistructured decision   91

structured decision   91

synthesis   82

transformation   81

unstructured

  decision   91

REVIEW QUESTIONS

Multiple-choice questions

1. Knowledge work involves which of the following activities?

   a.   development
   b.   synthesis
   c.   transportation
   d.   all of the above

2. Which information characteristic do you use to determine if an information source can be trusted?

   a.   complete
   b.   timely
   c.   accurate
   d.   reliable

3. Informing others of your ideas and solutions represents which type of knowledge work?

   a.   analysis
   b.   communication
   c.   discovery
   d.   synthesis
   e.   transformation

4. Which is the first step in the problem-solving model highlighted in this chapter?

   a.   analyze
   b.   decide
   c.   do
   d.   investigate

Fill-in-the-blank questions

5. Data are a(n) _____ collection of text, numbers, or symbols.

6. During and after your search for and collection of data, you should apply the _____ model to ensure that your decisions are based on high-quality data, information, and knowledge.

7. Decision making may include making _____ to reach an outcome.

CHAPTER

3

True-false questions

8. Information is data that knowledge-enabled professionals have processed (organized) to make it useful to decision makers.

9. An unstructured decision includes little or no inherent uncertainty.

10. The investigate phase of the IADD problem-solving model generates criteria to evaluate options to help ensure the selection of the best solution.

Matching questions

Choose the BEST answer from Column B for each item in Column A.

Column A
11. Using the search engine Google
12. Creating a database to store the data from several sources
13. Applying the mathematical models present in a statistical software application

Column B
a. Analysis
b. Transformation
c. Discovery

Column A
14. Structured decision
15. Semistructured decision
16. Unstructured decision

Column B
a. How should I invest my money today to ensure a comfortable retirement 40 years from now?
b. What is the correct dosage of a prescription medicine that I should take in order to get well?
c. Given that I have decided to buy a hybrid car, which one should I buy?
d. None of the above

Short-answer questions

17. Apply the IADD problem-solving model to a problem or opportunity of your choosing. Based on the problem or opportunity that you choose, give an example for each of the following steps of the model:

    a. Investigate
    b. Analyze
    c. Decide
    d. Do

18. We can characterize decisions as structured, semistructured, and unstructured. Define each type of decision and give a personal example for each type.

Discussion/Essay questions

19. One of your friends is faced with a welcome opportunity: deciding between two internship offers. Apply the IADD problem-solving model to help him or her decide which offer to take.

20. Is decision making the heart of problem solving? Argue for or against this belief. Use examples from your own experiences to support your position.

TEAM ACTIVITY

Assume that your school will require laptop computers for all students and asks your class to provide detailed, written recommendations for the "best" laptop for incoming students. Form into groups of 4–5 and then apply the IADD model to complete this assignment. Be sure to list and discuss your criteria.

SOFTWARE APPLICATION EXERCISES

Internet

Many students pursue careers in the private (non-governmental) sector. For a listing of potential jobs, go to your school's homepage and search the website for "Career Centre" or "Job Placement." Use Google.ca or Mamma.ca to perform a similar search.

You may want to investigate careers with federal, provincial, or municipal governments. Although the starting salaries for government jobs are often lower than their private-sector equivalents, they have other benefits associated with them, such as job security and stability. We'll get you started at the federal level (www.jobs-emplois.gc.ca/), and you can use your favourite search engine to find your provincial and municipal governmental employment sites.

Presentation

Based on your research for the previous Internet assignment, prepare a presentation that highlights the essentials regarding three jobs that you would consider. For one job, discuss what companies you might work for, what you would be doing, and where you might live.

Word Processing

A critical business skill is the ability to communicate clearly and to the point. An executive summary (search the Web for an example) provides a brief background of the problem or issue; highlights the key factors, constraints, or opportunities; and may answer the question posed by the executive or decision maker for whom the summary is intended (e.g., recommends actions to take). Prepare an executive summary on the search process for jobs.

Spreadsheet

Prepare a budget for the salary that you anticipate that you'll receive upon graduation (for one of the three jobs that interested you in the previous Presentation assignment). Include items like savings, rent, car payment, food, auto insurance and maintenance, utilities, vacation, and entertainment. Assume that you have a choice of cities to call home. Visit www.homefair.com to use the salary calculator to compare salary relative to choice of city.

Database

As you continue through your academic and professional careers, start a hobby—collecting knowledge-enabled professional contacts. Although there are software packages that will manage your contacts, designing and creating your own database may prove more useful. Why? As you think about what data to store, you will recognize certain unique aspects of your relationships with certain knowledge-enabled professionals, for example, your professors. Maybe you'll need some fields to track if a professor wrote you a recommendation, what it was for, when he or she wrote that recommendation, and any follow-up actions (e.g., a thank-you e-mail). Also, you may need to complete and track different types of contacts or documents if you apply for government jobs in addition to private-sector jobs.

Advanced Challenge

Imagine that you and three friends are living off-campus, and you are all trying to discover which career is right for each of you. Much of your roommates' research is done through a dial-up Internet connection. You are the only roommate paying for high-speed Internet access through the cable company. Finally, you all have cell phones, and each of you has his or her own "traditional" phone connection through the local phone company. The others, tired of connecting via relatively slow dial-up connections, agree to help pay the bill if they can share your high-speed connection. You are willing to do this but are unsure how to go about it. You decide to use the IADD model to create a solution. Briefly outline your thoughts and actions for each step of the model, highlighting at least one knowledge work activity for each step. Then, fully describe your solution and how you will implement it.

ON-LINE RESOURCES

Companion Website

- Take interactive practice quizzes to assess your knowledge and help you study in a dynamic way.
- Review PowerPoint lecture slides.
- Get help and sample solutions to end-of-chapter software application exercises.

Additional Resources Available Only on WileyPLUS

- Take the interactive Quick Test to check your understanding of the chapter material and get immediate feedback on your responses.
- Review and study with downloadable Audio Lecture MP3 files.
- Check your understanding of the key vocabulary in the chapter with Knowledge Speak Interactive Flash Cards.
- Link directly to websites recommended in the CORE boxes.

CASE STUDY: USING IT TO BUY A CAR

After accepting a well-paying position with a consulting firm, Ashley Hyatt realizes that she can now replace the old car she has been driving since her first year of university. She has narrowed her choice down to two coupes—an import and a domestic brand with similar dealer prices. She has also looked at the interest rates that she could obtain for a car loan, but is unsure about which length of the loan—36, 48, or 60 months—to go with. She asks her father for advice.

Her dad begins by helping her understand the basic concept involved in the length of the loan: depreciation. Cars lose value very quickly, especially in the first year. In fact, after as little as 24 months, the residual value of a car can often be less than one-third of its original value. This means that if Ashley has a 60-month loan, even at *zero percent* interest,

she will still owe 60 percent of the original loan amount after the first 24 months but the car will only be worth 55 percent *or less* of the amount that she owes on the loan. This becomes a real problem if Ashley wants to trade or sell the car, or if the car becomes totalled in an accident.

Ashley realizes that she needs to compare the *residual values* (considering depreciation) to the amount owed on the loan at the same period of time. She knows that she can use a spreadsheet to calculate the amount she would owe on the loan after a given number of months. But she also needs to know the value of her trade-in to use in calculating the net amount of the loan she'll be taking out. She decides to investigate the wide variety of websites dedicated to automobiles—purchasing, selling, trading-in, financing, and so on.

	A	B	C	D	E	F	G	H
1		Import Coupe				Domestic Coupe		
2	List Price	$ 21,745			List Price	$ 21,995		
3	Trade-in	$ 3,450			Trade-in	$ 3,450		
4	Taxes	$ 1,098			Taxes	$ 1,113		
5	Net Loan	$ 19,393			Net Loan	$ 19,658		
6	Residuals				Residuals			
7	Year 2	$ 13,300			Year 2	$ 9,200		
8	Year 3	$ 11,325			Year 3	$ 7,375		
9	Year 4	$ 9,450			Year 4	$ 5,750		
10	Year 5	$ 7,850			Year 5	$ 4,450		
11								
12	**36 Month Loan**							
13	Interest Rate	5.25%						
14	Payment	$583.40			Payment	$591.37		
15		Loan Balance	Residuals	Difference		Loan Balance	Residuals	Difference
16	2 years	$ 6,805.67	$ 13,300	$ 6,494		$ 6,898.66	$ 9,200	$ 2,301
17	3 years	$ 0.00	$ 11,325	$ 11,325		$ 0.00	$ 7,375	$ 7,375
18								
19	**48 Month Loan**							
20	Interest Rate	5.50%						
21	Payment	$451.01			Payment	$454.93		
22		Loan Balance	Residuals	Difference		Loan Balance	Residuals	Difference
23	2 years	$ 10,227.90	$ 13,300	$ 3,072		$ 10,367.66	$ 9,200	$ (1,168)
24	3 years	$ 5,254.23	$ 11,325	$ 6,071		$ 5,326.02	$ 7,375	$ 2,049
25	4 years	$ 0.00	$ 9,450	$ 9,450		$ 0.00	$ 5,750	$ 5,750
26								
27	**60 Month Loan**							
28	Interest Rate	5.75%						
29	Payment	$372.67			Payment	$373.22		
30		Loan Balance	Residuals	Difference		Loan Balance	Residuals	Difference
31	2 years	$ 12,295.61	$ 13,300	$ 1,004		$ 12,463.63	$ 9,200	$ (3,264)
32	3 years	$ 8,429.80	$ 11,325	$ 2,895		$ 8,515.24	$ 6,899	$ (1,617)
33	4 years	$ 4,335.76	$ 9,450	$ 5,114		$ 4,374.41	$ 5,750	$ 1,376
34	5 years	$ 0.00	$ 7,850	$ 7,850		$ 0.00	$ 4,450	$ 4,450

Figure 3.9 Spreadsheet comparisons of car values.

CHAPTER 3

Table 3.5	MSRP and Residual at End of Yearly Periods	
Year	Domestic Coupe	Imported Coupe
MSRP	$21,995.00	$21,745.00
2	$9,200.00	$13,300.00
3	$7,375.00	$11,325.00
4	$5,750.00	$9,450.00
5	$4,450.00	$7,850.00

Using the information from these websites, such as Driving.ca and BankRate.ca, Ashley determines the trade-in value of her car is $3,450. Table 3.5 lists the residual values for the two cars that she is deciding between. She also found that the interest rates for a 36-, 48-, and 60-month loan are 5.25 percent, 5.50 percent, and 5.75 percent, respectively. Using this information, she calculates monthly payments for each length of loan for the net loan value (MSRP minus trade-in value plus 6 percent taxes) for both cars. She also determines the loan balance at the end of each year after the first from the amortization tables (in BankRate.ca) and enters this information along with that from Table 3.5 in a spreadsheet. Figure 3.9 shows the resulting spreadsheet.

Case Questions

1. Given the information shown in Figure 3.9, what would be Ashley's best decision if she can't afford more than $600 for a monthly car payment? What about $500? What about $400? Justify your recommendation using quantitative data.
2. If the car dealership offers Ashley a cash rebate of $1,500 or low-interest financing on the original price (assume the "low" interest rates are 2 percentage points lower than the standard rates), how will this affect her decision?
3. Should Ashley consider a lease instead? Research this lease-versus-buy decision and write a two-page report on your findings. List any on-line and IT devices that you use in your research.

Integrative Application Case: Campuspad.ca

You and Sarah have continued to reflect on your business ideas for campuspad.ca and remain quite excited. However, you still have lots of unanswered questions.

Having already reviewed the competitors in the student rental space e-world, you are pretty sure you are going to be the first to market a student-centric site design that really meets market needs. But you need to do even more than that to be successful; there are very few barriers to start an e-business, but you have to make sure that you continually innovate to stay ahead of future competitors.

You and Sarah had decided that you would each locate your five favourite websites and carefully consider *why* you liked them and *what value* they created for you when you used them. You had already discussed the need to pay careful attention to how technology was being used with the hope of inspiring ways of applying what you liked from other sites in your own site design for campuspad.ca. You had agreed to take a week to do this and then meet to sketch out how your homepage might look and define some high-level requirements of the site design. This had you really

excited and you wanted to dive right in. But analysis had to come before decision making, so you went off to do your on-line research.

Guiding Case Questions:

1. Identify your five favourite websites.
2. Analyze why you like them, how they create value for you, and their design features.
3. Do you pay for access to these sites? How do these sites profit from your presence?
4. What kinds of technology do these sites use to support their on-line business?

Your Task:

Use the knowledge you have acquired from this research to make some initial decisions about how your homepage will look when you launch campuspad.ca. Using whatever tools you prefer, sketch out how it will look, and add comments about how users will navigate and use the site to meet their needs. Briefly include descriptions of how your intended technology will meet specific user needs to justify your proposed design.

PART II

The Organizational Perspective

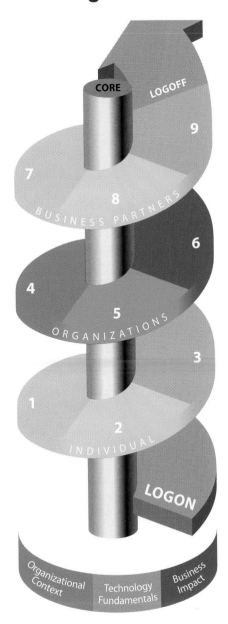

Chapter 4
Business Fundamentals and IT Strategy

Chapter 5
IT for the Organization

Chapter 6
Creating IS Solutions

Having mastered the context of individual productivity enabled by IT in Chapters 1-3 and the Tech Guides, we now turn our attention to IT in a business or organizational context. We will discover how analysis, problem solving, decision making are growing in scope and complexity and the critical role that information technology plays in these vital business processes. By the end of the next three chapters, you should be able to connect your understanding of the role of the individual knowledge-enabled professional with the larger organizational or business context and understand how IT can create long-term, sustainable competitive advantage and business value for any organization.

WHAT WE WILL COVER

- Businesses as Open Systems
- How Businesses Organize to Create Value
- The Value and Supply Chains
- Applying IT to Create Business Value
- Strategically Fitting IT to the Organization: A Business Example

C	**Connectivity**	Instant Messaging: Toy or Tool?
O	**On-line Security**	Protecting the On-line Organization
R	**Relationships**	Organizational Teamwork: Obey the Laws?
E	**Ethics**	Whose Data Is It Anyway?

Business Fundamentals and IT Strategy

STUDENT RETURN ON INVESTMENT

Through your investment of time in reading and thinking about this chapter, your return, or created value, is gaining knowledge. Use the following questions as a study guide.

1. Why can organizations be thought of and modelled as open systems?
2. How are organizations structured to optimize business value?
3. How do value and supply chains relate to business structure?
4. In what ways can organizations apply IT to build business value?
5. How can businesses strategically fit IT to the organization?

THE VOICE OF EXPERIENCE
Keith Powell, Concordia and McGill universities

After 20 years at Nortel Networks, including several across Nortel's value chain and four as chief information officer, Keith Powell established an information technology consulting practice, Keith Powell Consulting Inc., and is Partner of XPV Capital Corp., a venture capital company investing in early stage technology companies.

What do you do in your current position? I provide consulting services to large technology companies in the area of IT strategy development. I am also involved in executive coaching and development and I'm a partner in a venture capital company investing in small start-up technology companies. Much of my career has been in value-creating activities such as manufacturing, operations, and customer service so I have a lot to offer start-ups and executives who are trying to gain competitive advantage throughout their value chain.

I started out at Pratt and Whitney doing supply chain management and then I joined Nortel. Working directly in the supply chain helped me to understand the needs of customers first hand and showed me how applied IT can create competitive advantage. Because I worked so closely in Nortel's primary activities, I never thought IT was in my career plan. When John Roth, the CEO of Nortel, asked me to take over the IT portfolio for North America it was a shock to my system.

What do you consider to be important career skills? The ability to bring people, technology and business thinking together. A lot of my work focuses on using business thinking to translate how IT can add value to an organization. But I believe it has to go beyond just adding value. In today's environment, IT should be the strategic lever that organizations use to drive their business. If CEOs cannot understand what technology can do and incorporate it into their strategic thinking, they will fail. There needs to be a focused vision and strategy for information technology in an organization that is tied in with the strategic vision and plan.

Can you describe an example of how you have used IT to improve business operations? I was the chief information officer at Nortel for four years during which I saw Nortel through Y2K. I didn't have the technical background to be the CIO of a company like Nortel. I was lucky enough to have very strong technical people who were able to open their minds to the fact that there was a business that they were servicing. I counted on their expertise in technology, while I was someone who understood and operated in the business and could determine if we were getting a return on our investments in IT. Combining both of these perspectives helped us make the right decisions and have a positive impact on the company.

How do you use IT? I have a home office and I do all my business using high-speed Internet, voice communications, and VOIP. Without the IT capability available today, I would not have been able to perform the roles that I have, certainly not on a global scale. Information technology is a strategic competitive weapon for forward-thinking companies.

Have you got any on the job advice for students seeking a career in IT or business? The people side of business is very important: managing others, understanding people, their motivations, and how to work with people to get the best out of them. The relationships you have with people and your network are very important. When you need to find out something, when you need to get help, when you need to make a proposal, you really fall back on that network. Start building a network now and maintain that network throughout your career. It is the most powerful tool you have to help you move forward as an individual and as a businessperson.

Keith's early career experiences in supply chain management helped him to learn the primary activities of businesses. Later, in his career as a CIO, he used this experience to apply IT and create business value. In this chapter, we explore the value and supply chains and discuss how organizations use IT strategically to create business value.

Recall that a business or organization is made up of one or more people and creates products or provides services in order to earn a profit or satisfy a societal or client need. It does so through core processes it designs and manages that add value. Sounds easy enough, right? Not necessarily. To become successful, businesses must consider a number of items. Consider WestJet, a national airline.

WestJet provides a service by flying its customers to and from various destinations. To do this productively, WestJet must purchase or lease aircraft; hire pilots, mechanics, flight attendants, and other employees; safely procure, store, and dispense the fuel for its aircraft; and locate and secure capital for current and future operations. And these are just some of the many different resources and processes that WestJet must manage to create business value that customers ultimately pay for by flying WestJet.

Because of the sheer number of different tasks that need to be coordinated to deliver the end-result product or service, a company needs a strategy. Properly constructed, the strategy becomes the "road map" for what needs to be done to create business value and competitive advantage. In today's world, of course, IT is an essential element of any organization's strategy and IT professionals must ensure that their efforts are aligned to help the business deliver its intended end result. However, before we discuss how businesses use IT productively, you need a good understanding of business fundamentals. Let's begin by considering the analogy of business organizations as open systems.

BUSINESSES AS OPEN SYSTEMS

Looking at an organization as a system helps you see how organizations use various resources, processes, and structures to create business value. In Chapter 1 we used an Input-Process-Output model to define an information system. In this chapter, we expand the model into a general model of an organization, known as an open systems model.

As Figure 4.1 shows, the **open systems model** indicates that a business operates by transforming inputs into outputs and by constantly interacting with its environment. To understand this model better, let's look at it more closely. We begin by discussing two significant components of the business environment.

STAKEHOLDERS AND BOUNDARIES IN THE BUSINESS ENVIRONMENT

Different businesses have different business environments. How businesses adapt to their environment contributes greatly to how their structure develops and whether they succeed or fail as a business. What is it in this environment that can have such a profound effect on organizations? Stakeholders.

A **stakeholder** is a person or entity, for example a government agency or a shareholder, that has an interest in and an influence on how a business will function in order to succeed (or in order not to fail). A stakeholder may be external (in the environment) or internal

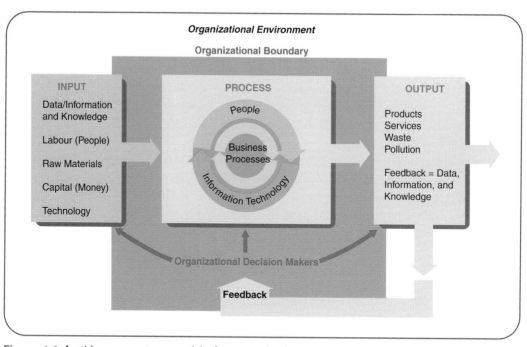

Figure 4.1 As this open systems model of an organization shows, a business operates by transforming inputs into outputs and by constantly interacting with its environment.

(within the organizational boundary) relative to the system. Note that influence is an important part of our definition of a stakeholder. That influence may be actual or potential, great or small. It all depends on how the organization's decision makers perceive it in relation to a stakeholder's interests.

For example, you or I may be interested in how a certain company handles on-line shopping transactions. But if we do not shop at the company's website, we probably have no influence over how the company conducts its e-commerce operations. However, if we are frequent customers and we then e-mail the company describing problems with its website, our suggestions may influence future e-commerce operations. Because we had both an interest and an influence, we are stakeholders in the organization's environment. Figure 4.2 shows other examples of external and internal stakeholders for a business. You should ask yourself why each of these stakeholders might have an interest in the operations of the business and how they might influence the business.

Another important aspect of an open system is the **organizational boundary** (the perimeter of the green rectangle in Figure 4.1). Businesses must remain open to their environment. Why? Primarily, an open boundary allows a business to receive inputs and to produce outputs. Further, a business must be aware of what is

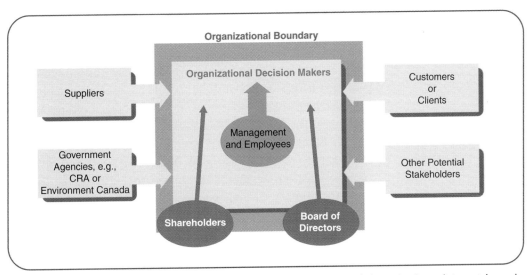

Figure 4.2 Organizational stakeholders, whether external or internal, have both an interest in and an influence on how a business will function in order to succeed.

going on in its environment so it can take steps to remain competitive by responding to opportunities or threats. In addition, a business needs external information to run its operations or processes on a daily basis. For example, soft drink manufacturers like Coke or Pepsi need information about purchases of their competitors' products in various regions of the country, the expected cost of high fructose corn syrup (sweetening ingredient), and even the government's recent changes to tax laws before making business decisions.

CHAPTER

4

WHAT DO YOU THINK?

In today's networked economy, organizational boundaries are not always clearly defined. Many organizations are blurring the boundary between their suppliers and their organization in order to gain greater efficiencies in their supply chain and create more business value. A recent evolution by some large retailers requires that suppliers manage the inventory bound for store shelves using sales data provided by the retailer. If supplies of a product are low, it is up to the supplier to recognize this and immediately ship whatever is needed to that store. With this in mind, consider the following questions:

1: How might the retail businesses gain or lose from having suppliers manage their in-store inventory levels directly?
2: Are suppliers who don't provide this level of service to retailers at a disadvantage? Do they ultimately have a choice about complying?
3: Are there any risks associated with expanding an organization's boundary in the way these retailers have?

However, interaction with that environment carries risk, especially when that environment changes constantly and new technologies (such as the Internet) can become a serious threat to an organization if they are not managed proactively. Organizations that use the Internet face threats that include the use of stolen or fraudulent credit cards and attacks against their on-line infrastructure by criminals. The CORE box "Protecting the On-line Organization" discusses these security threats in more detail, as well as how businesses can protect against them. Yet, for all of its security challenges, most businesses and organizations must use the Internet because so many customers and clients do business this way. So you can see it really is a double-edged sword: you have to be in the game to stay competitive but playing the game is risky!

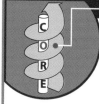

On-line Security

Protecting the On-line Organization

Is the fraudulent use of credit cards a problem? Well, consider that while consumers have a maximum liability of $50 for a lost or stolen credit card, the merchant is liable for the total amount of the illegal purchase. Further, because e-commerce credit card purchases lack a signature and the physical presence of the cardholder, which together verify the cardholder's identity, merchants must agree to pay the total amount plus any penalty imposed by credit card companies for accepting illegal cards.

Organizations are also susceptible to a number of other schemes, including investor fraud and on-line auction fraud. For example, in the first case, criminals use chat rooms to pump up the price of an almost worthless stock of a company, and then dump the stock at a high price. This causes the company to potentially lose money on its investments or on investments of employee pension funds. Finally, with more and more companies turning to on-line auctions like eBay to buy and sell goods, fraudulent auctions and payment systems can result in large losses.

A significant threat to the security of on-line organizations is through attacks, such as the denial of service (DoS) attacks. A DoS attack bombards a website with thousands of requests for web pages, putting the server out of action for several hours or up to a few days, depending on the overload. A DoS attack begins with a hacker installing software via the Internet on a large number of computers without the knowledge of their owners. Then, on a signal from the hacker, all of these computers send requests for information to a Web server at the same time. A DoS attack on an e-commerce site or credit card company can result in losses running into the millions of dollars. In some cases, the criminals try to blackmail the organization with the threat of a DoS attack.

To combat these security problems, organizations are taking a number of steps. In more and more cases, e-commerce companies are working with credit card companies to check the validity of a card before accepting it for on-line purchases. They are also educating their employees about the various types of fraud that the organization faces. Finally, while DoS and other attacks are still occurring, organizations are becoming more sophisticated in their efforts to repel them, including creating the position of chief information security officer (CISO) to supervise security.

Web Resources
- CERT Coordination Center at Carnegie-Mellon University—http://www.cert.org
- Information from the Canadian Government on Public Safety and the Internet—http://www.safecanada.ca/topic_e.asp?category=3
- For information on Internet fraud, check out the U.S. National Fraud Information Center—http://www.fraud.org/
- Competition Bureau of Canada, Fraud Prevention—http://www.competitionbureau.gc.ca/internet/index.cfm?itemID=17&lg=e

BUSINESS PROCESS

To transform inputs to their main outputs (products and services), organizations need to perform a series of steps known as a **business process.** Modern businesses are full of processes: Some, like manufacturing processes, directly create output—a product like a car or a DVD player—while others may create a service—, like a help desk for product support. For the help desk, a business needs at least three types of inputs—labour (employees), product information, and technology (e.g., phones and computers)—to create and implement the support process of providing the customer service output. Table 4.1 lists representative types of inputs that are essential to an organization.

Table 4.1	Inputs to Open Systems Organizations
Input Type	**Description**
Data, information, and knowledge	Raw facts, summarized data, information derived from research, and expert knowledge relevant to a business's goals, e.g., census data, consumer purchasing data, industry analysis, and a consultant's assessment of a business's IS security capabilities.
Labour	People hired to carry out all or part of the essential business processes or supporting functions, e.g., a production employee hired to make a product or a human resource analyst who manages an employee benefits program.
Raw materials	The "ingredients" from which the company makes its products. For an automobile manufacturer, a partial listing of its needed raw materials includes steel, plastics, glass, and rubber.
Capital	The money that businesses need to operate. Capital can assume different forms from cash, to debt instruments like bonds, to stock (shares of company ownership).
Technology	Available in many forms, and greatly extending beyond PCs and software applications. Examples of technology inputs include robotic welders, computer-controlled assembly lines, cell phones, and database and Web servers.

Now let's consider the special role that feedback plays in the business process. **Feedback** is a special kind of measurement created by a business process that is then returned to the system ("fed back") in order to control the system's future inputs, processes, and outputs. Normally, this feedback will include information such as error or failure rates, processing speeds, process costs, and information on approvals and controls required in the process and if they are being respected. Businesses often use this performance feedback to monitor the efficiency and effectiveness of a given process. For example, if a company assembles personal computer systems and has a lot of small parts left over, it should realize it needs to adjust its assembly and/or inventory management process to reduce unused or wasted parts and thus lower manufacturing costs. In fact, the perfect process would theoretically have no waste at all! However, the costs of creating a perfect business process outweigh the benefits in all but a few cases (such as medical services). In the case of extra computer parts, the physical presence of "too many leftovers" is feedback to the system that the process is not working as it should and the company must decide what to do about this.

As you can see, organizations must stay alert to their environment as well as to their business processes. If that sounds like a tall order, it is! So how do organizations manage to stay on top of all this *and* create superior business value? They do this through organizational structure, which we discuss next.

Quick Test

Select the appropriate response for the following questions.

1. Which one of the following is not an input to the organization as an open system?
   a. labour
   b. productivity
   c. information
   d. technology

2. True or False. Stakeholders are part of the environment of the open systems model of an organization.

3. Fill in the blank. A business needs a special kind of output known as _____ to help it control its operations or processes on a daily basis.

HOW BUSINESSES ORGANIZE TO CREATE VALUE[1]

If you want to get something done in an organization, you need to know where to go for the information and how to get to the authority required to accomplish your task. When you become a knowledge-enabled professional you will find that, to some degree, all business organizations possess structures that organize information, responsibility, and authority. When used appropriately, organizational structure helps get the job done. When misused, organizational structure can grow to an unmanageable size and density and can create a bureaucracy that seems to inhibit rather than facilitate productive work.

Figure 4.3[2] shows four types of organizational structures. Often companies will adapt these to their unique business situation.

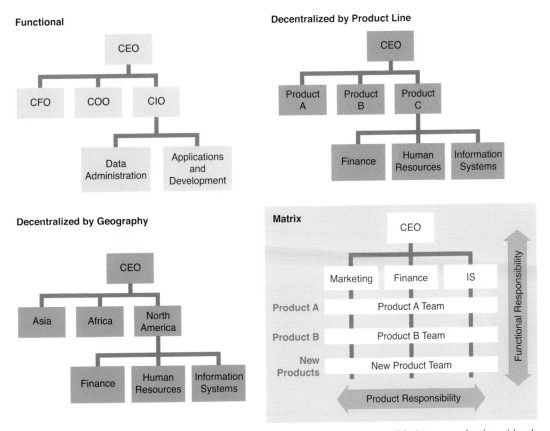

Figure 4.3 Functional, decentralized, and matrix organizational structures: Modern organizations blend and extend these forms to adapt to a complex and changing global business environment.

1. If you would like to learn more about these and other organizational topics, consult an introductory management book, such as *Management*, by John R. Schermerhorn, Jr., John Wiley & Sons Canada, Ltd.
2. Adapted from Weinshall, 1971, from *Understanding Organizations*, Charles Handy, Oxford University Press, 1993, p. 257. Matrix organization diagram added by authors.

For example, consider Federal Express, one of the world's largest logistics companies. The chief executive officer (CEO) of FedEx Corporation is Frederick W. Smith. Reporting to him are the presidents and CEOs of the various companies, like FedEx Ground and FedEx Kinko's, that make up FedEx Corporation, as well as FedEx Corp.'s chief financial officer (CFO), chief information officer (CIO), and other executives. FedEx is like the many other large organizations structured this way. More specific information about the company's structure and executive team can be found behind the "About FedEx" button at www.fedex.com. But this is not the only way a business can choose to structure itself, and Figure 4.3 depicts some other common organizational structures.

WHAT DO YOU THINK?

Is it your goal to be the CEO of a major corporation like FedEx? What about some of the other C-level roles: CFO, COO, or CIO? Perhaps you will be the president of your own company. Regardless of the company and its organizational structure, C-level executives are responsible for leading and managing businesses. Imagining that you are a CEO and consider the following questions:

1: Which organizational structure do you think you would like to work in? Why?
2: How would you ensure that the business continues to create business value?
3: How would you develop and communicate the business strategy throughout the organization?

Consider Figure 4.3 from the viewpoint of a CEO. What do you notice? In **functional** and **decentralized structures,** the lines of authority (who has the right to tell whom to do what) and communication are vertically oriented. However, the **matrix structure** blends the functional and decentralized organizational structures. From top to bottom, the matrix is organized as a functional structure. However, from left to right, the matrix follows a product-focused (or project- or customer-focused) structure. A matrix organization frequently uses teams of employees to accomplish work, as the CORE box "Organizational Teamwork—Obey the Laws?" discusses. Teams are an important part of any knowledge work. The technology of teams is discussed in greater detail in Tech Guide E.

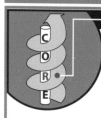

Relationships

Organizational Teamwork—Obey the Laws?

Organizations are complex entities that often use teams to accomplish work and help the organization achieve its goals. John C. Maxwell, a highly successful author of leadership-related books, wrote "The 17 Indisputable Laws of Teamwork." Regardless of whether you accept or reject some or all of his 17 laws, each law should spark your thinking about successful teamwork and your skills as a team member and a team leader.

1. The Law of Significance—One Is Too Small a Number to Achieve Greatness
2. The Law of the Big Picture—The Goal Is More Important Than the Role
3. The Law of the Niche—All Players Have a Place Where They Add the Most Value
4. The Law of Mount Everest—As The Challenge Escalates, the Need for Teamwork Elevates
5. The Law of the Chain—The Strength of the Team Is Impacted by Its Weakest Link
6. The Law of the Catalyst—Winning Teams Have Players Who Make Things Happen
7. The Law of the Compass—Vision Gives Team Members Direction and Confidence
8. The Law of the Bad Apple—Rotten Attitudes Ruin a Team
9. The Law of Countability—Teammates Must Be Able to Count on Each Other When It Counts
10. The Law of the Price Tag—The Team Fails to Reach Its Potential When It Fails to Pay the Price
11. The Law of the Scoreboard—The Team Can Make Adjustments When It Knows Where It Stands
12. The Law of the Bench—Great Teams Have Great Depth
13. The Law of Identity—Shared Values Define the Team
14. The Law of Communication—Interaction Fuels Action
15. The Law of the Edge—The Difference Between Two Equally Talented Teams Is Leadership
16. The Law of High Morale—When You're Winning, Nothing Hurts
17. The Law of Dividends—Investing in the Team Compounds over Time

Web Resources

- Free Management Library is a Web resource for many management topics, including team building—http://www.managementhelp.org/grp_skll/teams/teams.htm

In addition to the benefits of teams, a business might use a matrix structure in order to take advantage of the strengths, as well as make up for the weaknesses, of functional and decentralized forms. That is, the business would hope to combine the efficiency of a functional structure with the flexibility of a decentralized structure. Table 4.2 lists some advantages and disadvantages of matrix, functional, and decentralized organizational structures. Finally, although functional, decentralized, and matrix structures represent more typical forms, modern organizations blend and extend these forms to adapt to a complex and changing global business environment.

In the preceding sections, we provided a systems view of organizations to understand how they transform inputs into goods or services for their customers. We discussed how businesses organize to increase their efficiency and effectiveness in completing these processes. But how do they actually create value? How do they implement strategies that will increase their profit?

Table 4.2	Advantages and Disadvantages of Functional, Decentralized, and Matrix Organizational Forms[3]	
Organizational Form	Advantages	Disadvantages
Functional	• Economies of scale through efficient use of resources. • Significant technical expertise found in the functional areas. • Clear chain of authority and communications within a function.	• Poor communication and coordination between functional areas. • Relatively inflexible or slow to respond to change in the business environment. • Employees may focus on functional area goals rather than organizational goals.
Decentralized	• Faster response and greater flexibility. • Greater communication and coordination between organizational units. • Greater development of breadth of managerial skills.	• Duplication of resources and efforts across organizational units. • Technical knowledge not as in-depth relative to functional organizational form. • Less direct control by upper management.
Matrix	• Increased flexibility and responsiveness to business needs and environmental changes. • Enhanced problem solving, co-operation, communication, and resource sharing. • Decision making occurs lower in organization and closer to customer.	• Frustration due to dual lines of authority and responsibility. • Increased need for coordination between functional areas consumes time and resources. • Potential for goal conflict between functional and decentralized components of matrix (e.g., marketing manager vs. product A manager).

Quick Test

Select the appropriate response for the following questions.

1. Which one of the following is not an organizational form?

    a. matrix

    b. functional

    c. CEO-based

    d. decentralized by geography

2. Which one of the following is an advantage of the functional organizational structure?

    a. decision makers are closer to the customer

    b. economies of scale

    c. flexibility

    d. greater communication between organizational units

3. True or False. Teams are a key part of the matrix organizational structure.

Answers: 1. c; 2. b; 3. True

3. Based on R. L. Daft, *Management*, 3rd ed., pp. 300–312; and J. R. Schermerhorn, *Management*, 7th ed., pp. 259–264.

THE VALUE CHAIN

There are many ways to understand what businesses do to create value. Michael Porter provides one useful way, known as the value chain. In this section, we review all the components of the value chain, and then discuss how businesses use IT to optimize it, with particular emphasis on the five core processes of a typical supply chain.

BUILDING AN UNDERSTANDING OF THE VALUE CHAIN

The **value chain** is a connected series of activities, each of which adds value or supports the addition of value to the firm's goods or services.[4]

We begin our exploration of the value chain with the five core components of a typical supply chain as shown in Figure 4.4 *Inbound logistics* include the receiving, warehousing, and inventory control of raw materials required to create a product or service. *Operations* are the value-creating and often proprietary activities that transform the raw inputs into the final product. *Outbound logistics* are the activities required to get the finished product to the customer, including packaging, warehousing, and order fulfillment. *Marketing and sales* are all activites associated with getting buyers to purchase the product, including working with distributors, retailers, or on-line channels, marketing, advertising, and pricing. *Service activities* are those that maintain and enhance the product's value, including customer support, repair services, and warranty and recall.

Obviously, while these five steps are more often identified with traditional manufacturing businesses, they can also be associated

Figure 4.4 An organizational value chain is a connected series of activities, each of which adds value, or supports the addition of value, to the firm's goods or services.

4. M. E. Porter, "How competitive forces shape strategy." *Harvard Business Review*, 1979, pp. 137–145.

Figure 4.5 A customer using an ATM is a transaction between an individual (the customer) and an organization (the bank providing ATM service).

with IT-enabled businesses such as software companies. These firms use the same five-step process to hire programmers and other technical specialists, manage the project to create the software product, package and ship the software to the customer, create sales documentation, and provide after-sales technical support.

Now that you understand these five core processes in the supply chain, we move on to what happens when a transaction occurs. A **transaction** is an exchange of goods or services (value) between two or more parties (businesses, individuals, or a combination of the two) that creates a relationship between the parties. For example, a customer using a bank's ATM to withdraw money is a transaction between the customer and the bank (see Figure 4.5). When you download software you have purchased on-line, you have completed a transaction.

Normally, we think of *primary activities* as those directly related to the production and distribution of the organization's products and services. These are the activities that create business value for the organization and its customers when a transaction occurs.

? WHAT DO YOU THINK?

Every business has a supply chain. To manage the supply chain, businesses engage in **supply chain management (SCM)**. SCM manages the materials, information, and finances as they move from supplier to manufacturer to wholesaler to retailer to consumer. It is easy to see how a supply chain works in a manufacturing or retailing business, but what about a survices business such as an accounting firm, financial planning business, or an IT consultancy? Consider the following questions when thinking about the supply chain for a services business:

1: What would the supply chain look like for an accounting firm? Would it have the same primary and support activities as a manufacturing business? How might they differ?

2: What would the "materials" or other inputs be for an accounting firm?

3: How do you think services firms manage knowledge and knowledge-based products in order to create business value for their clients?

However, simply considering the supply chain is not enough. Most organizations also require additional *support activities.* Support activities are value chain activities that an organization conducts to support the creation of business value by the primary activities. In his original work, Porter identified four critical support activities: administration, technology development, human resource (HR) management, and procurement. For example, HR management and policy directly affect the people who perform the work that creates business value. HR manages the compensation and benefits that reward employees for their work (e.g., pay, bonuses and retirement plans). More motivated employees often create more business value. So even though employees

PART 2

might be engaged in operational activities (e.g., programming software or calling on possible customers to buy the software), the HR management efforts support them in their value-creating activities.

When you put this all together you can see that an organization's value chain is the sum of its primary and support activities, working together to create business value for the organization and its customers. As such, the value chain model is another way to view the organization as a system (inputs → processes → outputs).

The value chain is also a useful tool for defining an organization's core processes and the activities and competencies that it can pursue to gain a sustained competitive advantage[5] over its competitors. And through the intelligent use of IT, a business can increase its competitive advantage by incrementally changing the value-adding activities themselves or by making it possible to configure the value chain in a new way.

THE IT-ENABLED VALUE CHAIN

Figure 4.6 shows a number of ways in which an organization might apply IS to its value chain. The specific systems listed in this figure are discussed in detail in subsequent chapters, and by no means does the figure provide an exhaustive list of organizational IS. Further, note that some of the systems listed in the figure may support more than one activity. For example, Canada Post improved organizational efficiency and effectiveness by deploying an enterprise resource planning (ERP) system. This ERP system created value by providing visibility throughout its delivery network (inbound logistics, operations, outbound logistics), enabling new business (sales), and reducing costs through process standardization (organizational infrastructure). Canada Post's ERP demonstrates that the application of IS to its value chain's primary and support activities can support multiple important business processes and can create value for a business.[6]

Figure 4.6 also shows how IT, like Canada Post's ERP, supports and integrates both primary and secondary activities and supports the value chain horizontally (within a particular function of the value chain) and vertically (across the value chain). Some IT systems are specific to particular parts of the value chain or organizational departments. For example, logistics management systems may be specifically designed to support inbound logistics, and software development tools are generally used in technology development. On the other hand, some systems, such as ERP, are used in many or most parts of the value chain model. These systems are called

5. A company gains a competitive advantage over its competitors when it can maintain higher-than-average profits found in its industry.
6. Adapted from http://www.sap.com/services/customdev/pdf/CCS_Event_Management_Canada_Post.pdf. Retrieved August 25, 2006.

CHAPTER 4

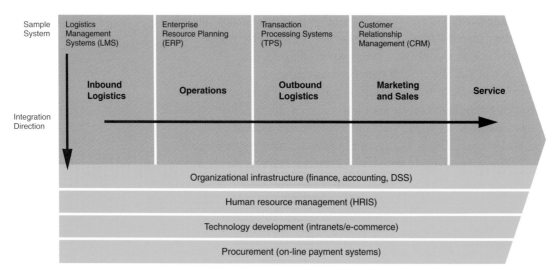

Figure 4.6 IT supports the value chain both horizontally and vertically, including some common applications in each component.

enterprise-wide systems and are used by the entire enterprise through a centralized database and coordinated software modules (applications or sets of applications) that are tightly integrated with one another. Integration between the parts of the value chain represents another very important application of IT: optimizing information flow between and across activities. This allows IT to have an impact throughout the entire value chain. For more information on the IT-enabled supply chain or enterprise resource systems, simply use a search engine and type in ERP or SCM and you'll find many interesting references.

In the next section, we discuss more specifically how firms strategically use IT as part of their value chain activities.

Quick Test

Select the appropriate response for the following questions.

1. Which one of the following is NOT a component of the value chain?
   a. primary activity
   b. secondary activity
   c. transaction
   d. support activity

2. An effective version of this type of IS could offer support to almost all activities in an organization's value chain.
   a. AIS
   b. CRM
   c. DSS
   d. ERP

3. True or False. IT can support business processes within a value
   chain activity as well as support the integration of activities across
   the value chain.

Answers: 1. b; 2. d; 3. True

APPLYING IT TO CREATE BUSINESS VALUE

In this section we focus on three aspects of strategically applying IT
in value chain activities to create business value: automating, informating, and transforming.

AUTOMATING TO DO THINGS FASTER

One of the first ways that a business seeks to apply IT is through **automating** (using automation to execute repetitive, routine tasks
without human intervention). This frees up knowledge-enabled
professionals to concentrate on tasks that have the potential to add
high value, or tasks that require judgement or insight to complete.
By automating, a business can also complete tasks with more
speed, economy, consistency, and possibly accuracy. Automation
may provide additional benefits by allowing a business to perform
work in different ways than before.

   When automating a process, a business first tends to apply technology in order to do the same things as before, but with greater efficiency and accuracy. Later, as the organization learns from the new
technology, it looks to use technology to do new things. Table 4.3

CHAPTER

4

Table 4.3	Using IT Automation to Create Business Value	
Industry	**Automation**	**Benefits Derived from Automation**
Banking	ATM machines, on-line banking	• Reduces costs associated with the processing of deposits, withdrawals, and money transfers. • Increases flexibility and improves access of services to customers.
Grocery/ Retail	Bar code inventory systems	• Increases speed and accuracy of product transactions. • Improves accuracy (assuming correct entry of products' prices into the system). • Reduces costs and transfers control to customers (e.g., self-service kiosks).
Travel	Reservation and scheduling systems	• Airline reps and travel agents can process reservations more efficiently and with less cost. • Allows transfer of processes to customers through on-line services.

presents several examples of how companies have used IT automation to increase business value.

When applying automation within an organization, management usually thinks in terms of improving a single process. It starts by considering answers to questions such as:

1. What is the main goal, and what are the steps of the process?
2. What data and information are required to carry out the steps? What data are generated in each step? How do data flow between the steps? (Keep in mind that IT works with data and information. The amount of data and information inherent in the process will determine the extent to which IT can automate the process.)
3. How is the process affected by other processes of the organization? When should it occur? What triggers the process to start? How does the output affect other processes?

These questions do not address specific IT hardware or software. Instead, the most critical issues when applying IT automation are related to how the process fits the business organization and its goals.

For example, consider automated teller machines (ATMs), which operate 24/7/365. Prior to ATMs, in order for a bank customer to withdraw cash, the bank had to be open and a teller had to be available. The bank customer had to fill out a withdrawl slip to present to the teller in order to receive cash. The teller would access the customer's account, determine if there were enough funds for the withdrawl and, if so, would update the account and give the cash and a receipt to the customer. The use of 24-hour ATMs, however, eliminated this requirement for serving customers. So, relative to the old way of serving customers who needed cash, ATMs met a bank's goals of increasing customer service (e.g., cash is "always" available) and saving money (e.g., no teller is involved in the transaction and bank need not be open).

INFORMATING TO DO THINGS BETTER

Another way companies view the application of IT is known as informating.[7] **Informating** is recognizing that executing processes (e.g., customers accessing their accounts to make deposits or withdraw funds) also creates new data and information. An organization may then process these new data to improve its decision making and to change or improve the process itself. However, as the CORE box "Whose Data Is It Anyway?" discusses, the organization should consider the source of the data before it uses them.

---

7. The concept of informating was first described by Dr. Shoshana Zuboff in 1988 in her book *In the Age of the Smart Machine*.

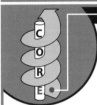

Ethics

Whose Data Is It Anyway?

When informating a process, an organization uses the created data with the goal of increasing business value. One huge source of created data comes from the continuing growth of e-commerce, as well as the general increased use of the Internet and World Wide Web. Whenever customers shop for items on the Web, purchase goods or services through e-commerce, or just visit a website or chat room, it creates data. This includes the so-called click-stream data that are generated when users move around a website—did they check the specials first or did they go to a specific area of the website right away—as well as the data generated whenever customers actually make a purchase.

Unbeknownst to us, some software that we install on our computers may contain additional software called spyware that tracks our actions related to the software installed. For example, a well-known company that markets popular media players was found to be gathering information on users' listening habits, preferred music types, and other information from those who installed its software. This use of the Internet to track data on users is termed *data surveillance.* There are anti-spyware products available, such as Windows Defender, which help users protect themselves from data surveillance.

If asked about the data being generated by website visits, purchases, and spyware, most companies will claim that these data are not specific to a person or user. Instead, these companies claim to combine the data with other similar data to help them better serve their customers by better understanding their shopping needs and habits. However, when companies get into financial difficulties, some of them, to generate cash, have sold their data to their competitors or companies that specialize in developing profiles of Internet users and shoppers.

The practice of capturing data and then selling it has generated a great deal of publicity, but no enforceable legislation to change it. In Canada, the law protecting personal data is the *Personal Information Protection and Electronic Documents Act* (PIPEDA). As of January 1, 2004, all private sector organizations located in Canada must act in accordance with PIPEDA. Private sector organizations that are not located in Canada, but are doing business in Canada, must also follow PIPEDA. That is:

- If a business wants to collect, use, or disclose personal information about people, they need the person's consent.
- Businesses can use or disclose people's personal information only for the purpose for which they gave consent.
- Even with consent, businesses have to limit collection, use, and disclosure to purposes that a reasonable person would consider appropriate under the circumstances.
- Individuals have a right to see the personal information that a business holds about them and to correct any inaccuracies.

There is oversight, through the Privacy Commissioner of Canada, to ensure that the law is respected, and redress if people's rights are violated.[8] Redress in this case involves an investigation conducted by the Privacy Commissioner and potential advice to the Federal Court to take action against non-compliant businesses. The Office of the Privacy Commissioner of Canada acts as an ombudsman that

CHAPTER

4

8. Retrieved from http://www.privcom.gc.ca/fs-fi/02_05_d_16_e.asp, September 25, 2006.

seeks to settle disagreements, not punish. Many wonder if the deterrent of action under PIPEDA is enough. There have been few cases elevated to the courts, giving the impression that PIPEDA enforcement is lacking. The European Union (EU) has come out much more strongly against invasion of privacy via the Internet. It even came close to outlawing the use of the small text files, called cookies, that are placed on users' hard drives by e-commerce sites. But this legislation would have effectively killed e-commerce in the EU. Cookies are essential to such e-commerce operations as remembering returning users and enabling them to make multiple purchases via an electronic shopping cart.

The Internet is also a vehicle for purchasing private information. In November 2005, *Maclean's* magazine illustrated how easy it is to obtain data by purchasing the mobile phone records of the federal privacy commissioner, Jennifer Stoddart, over the Internet from a U.S. information broker. The article asks several questions: How did the U.S. company obtain the data? Why was it released so readily despite PIPEDA? If the federal privacy commissioner cannot protect her own data, how can the Canadian public feel protected under PIPEDA?[9]

Privacy is an evolving issue with at least two sides to it. On the one hand, none of us wants to have our privacy intruded upon without our permission by software like spyware. On the other hand, a number of studies have shown that stringent privacy restrictions, like those almost instituted by the EU, may have negative effects, such as fewer free websites and less shopping convenience.

Information technology is the infrastructure of our modern economy, and information is the power that runs it. The impact of restricting the free flow of information is not fully known and may have a cascading detrimental effect on the economy. As a result, this is an area in which the ethics and legislation are still works in progress.

Web Resources

- For a discussion of issues concerning the future of the Internet, see the Internet Society website—http://www.isoc.org/internet/issues/privacy/
- Office of the Privacy Commissioner of Canada—http://www.privcom.gc.ca
- Electronic Privacy Information Center—http://www.epic.org/privacy/privacy_resources_faq.html

In most cases, companies derive informating and automating benefits from some of the same applications of IT. For example, Table 4.4 lists the same IT applications as those in Table 4.3, but note the additional benefits provided by informating the processes. As Table 4.4 suggests, with an informating view, IT can deliver more long-term benefits than from automation alone. In addition, an automation-only view may result in simply speeding up a "bad" process. Informating, however, allows a business to identify flaws in the process and then use its new-found knowledge to do things in entirely new ways. To gain the benefits of informating

---

9. Jonathan Gatehouse "You are Exposed," *Maclean's*, November 21, 2005. Retrieved from http://www.macleans.ca/topstories/canada/article.jsp?content = 20051121_115779_115779, September 26, 2006.

Table 4.4	Added Benefits of Automating and Informating	
Industry	Automation (IT Application)	Benefits Derived from Automating and Informating (the specific benefits of informating are shown in italics)
Banking	ATM machines, on-line banking	• Reduces costs associated with the processing of deposits, withdrawals, and money transfers. • Increases flexibility and improves access of services to customers. • *Tracks use of services to provide the most popular and profitable services to customers.*
Grocery/Retail	Bar code inventory systems	• Increases speed and accuracy of product transactions. • Improves accuracy (assuming correct entry of products' prices into the system). • Reduces costs and transfers control to customers (e.g., self-service kiosks). • *Improves the ability to track inventory and predict demand for various items.*
Travel	Reservation and scheduling systems	• Airline reps and travel agents can process reservations more efficiently and with less cost. • Allows transfer of processes to customers through on-line services. • *Enhances the ability to predict demand.* • *By better matching supply and demand, airlines can adjust pricing schemes for greater profitability.*

when applying IT to a process, a business needs to step back from the details of executing the process and ask three crucial questions:

1. Does the IT store data so that it can also be used for learning and decision making?
2. Is the business process that we are IT-enabling already optimized for high performance?
3. How could IT enable a better (more efficient or more effective) business process or capability that delivers higher value or additional competitive advantage?

TRANSFORMING TO GAIN COMPETITIVE ADVANTAGE[10]

The primary goal of most for-profit companies is to achieve a sustainable competitive advantage that results in high profits. In some cases, companies are concerned with competitive necessity: the need to stay in step with competitors and continue to stay in business.

10. The two types of competitive advantage were first identified by Michael Porter in his book *Competitive Advantage: Creating and Sustaining Superior Performance*, 1985, which is now considered a classic text on organizational strategy. "Transforming" is a term suggested by Professor Richard T. Watson to complement and extend the concepts of automating and informating.

CHAPTER

4

As a result, most businesses have a **transforming** view of IT; that is, using IT to help them acquire or continue a competitive advantage over or in line with their competitors. A company possesses a competitive advantage when it sustains higher-than-average profits for its industry. Organizations in the non-profit or government sector often have efficiency as their objective, but often see IT in a similar transformative light.

There are two basic ways of obtaining competitive advantage: cost and differentiation. A company gains a cost advantage when it delivers the same benefits to customers as its competitors but at a lower cost. A company gains a differentiation advantage over its competitors when it delivers superior benefits to customers. By trying to achieve a cost or differentiation advantage, a company can provide better value for its customers and increased profits for itself. It's often difficult to obtain both a cost and differentiation advantage, however, because attempts to achieve greater differentiation usually result in greater costs. This strategy will only work if the differentiation delivers higher market share that results in more revenue.

In a simple resource-based model of competitive advantage, a company gains competitive advantage through the development of distinctive competencies. A company forms its distinctive competencies from a combination of its capabilities and its resources. Distinctive competencies enable innovation, product quality, process efficiency, and customer responsiveness. Applying IT strategically can assist in all these areas.

Through automation with IT, a business can use its resources and capabilities more efficiently to achieve a lower cost structure. Through informating with IT, the business can learn new ways to increase or transform its capabilities and better ways to manage its resources in order to differentiate its products. For example, as the CORE box "Instant Messaging: Toy or Tool?" discusses, using IT has allowed one retailer to transform its on-line order capabilities.

Connectivity

Instant Messaging: Toy or Tool?

Is instant messaging (IM) a strategic use of IT? It certainly is a popular one. IDC estimated in 2006 that 1 *billion* IM messages were being sent every day by business users and consumers, with IM usage expected to surpass e-mail by the end of that year.

IM is an on-line communications service that allows users to communicate in real time over the Internet. As such, IM can play an important role in customer service. For example, the on-line clothing retailer Lands' End provides Lands' End Live service, which allows customers to get assistance, in real time, with a service representative while they shop on-line. The representative can even redirect the customer's browser to an appropriate page on the Lands' End site. Lands' End credits the technology as an integral part of the company's on-line success. The company notes that the average value of an order increases by 6 percent when a customer uses its IM service. A Lands' End customer who uses instant messaging is 70 percent more likely to buy something than a customer who does not use the service.[11]

There are two main categories of IM applications: public or enterprise (EIM). Examples of public IM include the well-known MSN Messenger and Yahoo! Messenger. EIM systems, on the other hand, provide features such as restricted access and security precautions such as encryption. Developed for corporate use, EIM services include Sun ONE Instant Messaging, IBM Lotus Instant Messaging & Web Conferencing, and Microsoft Office Live Communications Server.

Users of IM in the workplace cite improved teamwork, time savings derived from faster sharing of information, decrease in e-mail and voicemail, and moments of relief from the daily grind. Risks of using IM include a rise in needless interruptions and distractions, potential security problems, and increased workplace gossip. Many see that the benefits are starting to outweigh the risks, especially those already accustomed to IM. So when you walk into your new office on your first day of work, don't be surprised if you find that IM has gotten there first!

Web Resources

- For a description of how instant messaging works, see Howstuffworks.com—http://www.howstuffworks. com/instant-messaging.htm
- For a list of abbreviations used in text messaging, like LOL, see the following link on Webopedia— http://www.webopedia.com/quick_ref/textmessageabbreviations.asp

Some would go so far as to believe that companies can gain a unique advantage through an exclusive use or application of IT. This was a widely held view during the so-called dot-com years of the late 1990s and early 2000s. However, in recent years, some have challenged this view. In his provocative article, "IT Doesn't Matter,"[12] Dr. Nicholas Carr argues that since the core functions of IT—data processing, data storage, and data communications— are available and affordable for anybody, it isn't possible to develop sustained distinctive competencies on IT alone. In other words, if a company can put together an IT system that helps it automate a particular process, then so can its competitors. This

11. L. A. Lorek, "IM is a must in lots of offices," http://www.mysanantonio.com/business/stories/ MYSA010205.IR.IM.55538bcc.html, January 5, 2005
12. Nicholas, Carr, "IT doesn't matter," *Harvard Business Review*, 81(5), May 2003.

drives competitive necessity, the need to keep up with competitors to stay in business, rather than competitive advantage. A company can only gain a sustained edge over its competitors by doing things that they can't do.

The IS community continues to debate Dr. Carr's ideas. Dr. Carr maintains that IT is an essential part of the infrastructure of a competitive company, but inconsequential to strategy. Much of the business world agrees with Dr. Carr's view (those companies that create and sell IT naturally do not). They note that a sustained competitive advantage has never come from a particular technology itself, but from the intelligent application of IT to support business strategies and leverage distinctive competencies of an organization.[13] We will not attempt to settle that debate here. Rather, we encourage you to join the debate and continue thinking about the value and potential for competitive advantage offered by IT and that you continue to acquire knowledge about how IT can make you a more successful knowledge-enabled professional.

Quick Test

Select the appropriate response for the following questions.

1. The process of speeding up an existing task using technology is referred to as:
    a. informating
    b. transforming
    c. decimating
    d. automating

2. True or False. The process of learning to use technology to do things not just faster but also better is referred to as informating.

3. Fill in the blank. A company is said to possess a(n) _____ when it sustains higher-than-average profits for its industry.

Answers: 1. d; 2. True; 3. competitive advantage

13. E. K., Clemons, and M. Row (1991). "Sustaining IT advantage: The role of structural differences." *Management Information Systems Quarterly*, 15(3), pp. 275–292; L. M. Hitt and F. Brynjolfsson, (1996). "Productivity, business profitability, and consumer surplus: Three different measures of information technology value." *Management Information Systems Quarterly*, 20(2), pp. 121–112; J. B. Barney (1991). "Firm resources and sustained competitive advantage." *Journal of Management*, 17(1), pp. 99–120; and B. Wernerfelt (1984). "A resource-based view of the firm." *Strategic Management Journal*, (5), pp. 171–180.

STRATEGICALLY FITTING IT TO THE ORGANIZATION: A BUSINESS EXAMPLE

In the previous sections, we introduced four views of how a business can derive benefits by applying IT to support the organization and its processes: (1) support of the value chain, (2) automating, (3) informing, and (4) gaining a competitive advantage. These views, summarized in Table 4.5, demonstrate that a business can use IT not only to support current operations, but also to gain long-term or strategic benefits. In addition to listing the scope and benefit of each view, Table 4.5 provides a simple example of applying IT to handle a newspaper subscription transaction.

As you can see from the newspaper example in Table 4.5, the four different views are not mutually exclusive. By using IT to allow new customers to subscribe on-line, the newspaper company can gain benefits that coincide with all four viewpoints. By focusing on the subscription process itself, through automation it gains greater efficiencies. Through informing, it collects data that may help it improve the process further. The company may use the data it

Table 4.5	Comparing IT Application Views		
View	**Scope**	**Benefits**	**Newspaper Application**
Support of value chain	Organization-wide	Views organization as a system with need for integration of components and activities. Allows a focus on enabling value-adding activities. Helps to fit IT applications and infrastructure to organization.	Use subscription data to forecast demand and to better schedule inbound logistics, production, and outbound activities. Use demographic data for targeted marketing promotions and improved customer service.
Automating	Process/Transaction	Cost reduction, efficiency, quality, and consistency.	On-line subscription for newspaper reduces printing and handling costs of paper-based, mailed subscription forms.
Informing	Process/Transaction	Knowledge and learning of core competencies.	Use transaction data to understand subscription process. Collect demographic data during on-line subscription application and use it better understand customers.
Transforming/ Competitive advantage	Organization-wide	Connects automating and informing of processes to organizational strategy.	Can develop a unique competency for delivering targeted content to various customer segments as identified by demographic and subscription data.

CHAPTER

4

Figure 4.7 The overlap between people, technology and process creates an area called the productivity zone. It is in this zone that superior business outcomes are created.

collects when users subscribe to gain a competitive advantage by using it to support publications targeted at key customers or through some other means. While the process itself may fall within the marketing and sales activity of the value chain model, the company can use the collected data to make decisions about all of its primary activities.

Remember, information systems, like the organizations they support, consist of more than IT. When applying IT, a business must consider the interaction of the technology with the people who create and use it, the organizational structure and culture, the business processes, and the environment within which the organization resides. In fact, there is a substantial body of research in the field of information technology management (ITM) to suggest that organizations that "play at the top of their game" (however they may choose to define that) often incorporate definite thinking on how best to combine their people, processes, and technology resources to create superior business outcomes. This approach is shown in Figure 4.7. Keep in mind, too, that despite the almost constant excitement surrounding the potential value of IT, some IT systems do fail. As often as not, the failure of IT results from applying the technology in a way that fits poorly with the other components of the organization. To achieve a strategic IT fit, therefore, an organization must consider the IT within the context of its organizational system and its value-adding activities and ensure that its technology and business strategy are completely aligned.

Quick Test

Select the appropriate response for the following questions.

1. Fill-in-the-blank. _____ through application of IT would allow a newspaper company to create business value through on-line subscriptions.

2. Which of the following views of the application of IT would best explain a newspaper company's improved scheduling of inbound logistics?
   a. automating
   b. transforming/competitive advantage
   c. informating
   d. support of value chain

3. True or False. Support of value chain and competitive advantage are two organization-wide views of IT applications.

Answers: 1. Automating; 2. d; 3. True

STUDENT RETURN ON INVESTMENT SUMMARY

1. Why can organizations be thought of and modelled as open systems?

An open system is a useful way to view an organization because it reflects how a business is situated in and interacts with its environment. The environment that surrounds each organization creates a context or set of conditions in which that organization operates. How it adapts to its environment contributes greatly to how an organization is structured and whether it succeeds or fails as a business. This same approach works for other aspects of the model, i.e., the organization's transformation of inputs (e.g., capital, labour, and information) into outputs (e.g., products, services, waste, and pollution). Feedback is a special type of output produced by the system that an organization uses to control its processes, inputs, and outputs.

2. How are organizations structured to optimize business value?

A business must organize itself in order to strategically pursue its goals. Most businesses use either functional, decentralized, or matrix structures. A business might use a matrix structure in order to take advantage of the strengths, as well as make up for the weaknesses, of functional and decentralized forms. That is, the business would hope to combine the efficiency of a functional structure with the flexibility of a decentralized structure to optimize the creation of business value.

3. How do value and supply chains relate to business structure?

A value chain is a chain of activities whereby each activity adds value or supports the addition of value to the firm's goods or services. An understanding of value chains is important because it allows a business to focus its attention on activities (business processes) that create value for the business and its customers. It also allows a business to better understand the contribution of organizational activities in terms of primary activities, which directly create value, and supporting

activities, which support the creation of value. The value chain approach reinforces the systems view of an organization because a "value chain approach" involves obtaining and transforming inputs into outputs through the use of business processes.

4. In what ways can organizations apply IT to build business value?

Businesses can use IT to automate, informate, and transform organizational processes throughout the value chain to create a competitive advantage. Businesses use IT with a focus on automation to improve the execution of a process—simply doing it faster and more consistently. An IT-informating process recognizes the creation of new data and information about the business each time it executes a process. The business may then process the new data and use it to improve decision making in the organization and to change or improve the process itself. Lastly, transforming organizational processes to gain competitive advantage may involve automating and informating, as well as innovation through application of new technologies. Using IT may help a business differentiate itself or become the lowest-cost producer—two ways of gaining competitive advantage.

5. How can businesses strategically fit IT to the organization?

Information systems, like the organizations they support, consist of more than IT. When applying IT, a business must consider the interaction of the technology with the people who create and use it, the organizational structure and culture, the business processes, and the environment within which the organization resides. In other words, a business must consider the strategic fit of IT within the context of the organization as a system and what it is trying to accomplish. Table 4.5 and Figure 4.7 provide additional insights into IT and its strategic fit with organizations.

CHAPTER

4

KNOWLEDGE SPEAK

automating   131

business process   121

cookies   134

decentralized structure   124

enterprise-wide system   130

feedback   122

functional structure   124

informating   132

matrix structure   124

open systems model   117

organizational boundary   118

spyware   133

stakeholder   117

supply chain management
  (SCM)   128

transaction   128

transforming   136

value chain   127

REVIEW QUESTIONS

Multiple-choice questions

1. After months of declining sales and customer complaints, your manager asks you to analyze the company using an open systems model. Which one of the following elements should you consider first?

   a. feedback
   b. input
   c. process
   d. environment
   e. output

2. A business is a collection of people who must _____.

   a. agree on supply chain priorities
   b. create processes to achieve goals
   c. ensure outputs never exceed inputs
   d. verify process improvements before realigning organizational structures
   e. none of the above

3. If a company is inefficiently carrying out a business process that IT does not yet support, then it should consider using technology to _____ the process.

   a. automate
   b. informate
   c. renovate
   d. validate
   e. none of the above

Fill-in-the-blank questions

4. A(n) _____ is a person or entity that has an interest and influence on how a business must function in order to succeed.

5. A(n) _____ is an exchange of goods or services (value) between two or more parties (businesses, individuals, or a combination of the two) that creates a relationship between the parties.

6. A team is a relatively small number of people with _____ skills who are committed to a common purpose, performance goals, and approach for which they hold themselves mutually accountable.

7. The value chain model is a useful tool for defining an organization's goals and the activities that it can pursue to gain a sustained _____.

True–false questions

8. The application of IT to an organization can be seen from four different views: (1) automating, (2) informating, (3) competitive advantage, and (4) value chain support.

9. It is generally accepted that there is only one way that a business can achieve competitive advantage: by delivering the same results to its customers at a lower cost than its competitors.

10. In general, automating creates more business value than does informating.

Matching questions

Choose the BEST answer from Column B for each item in Column A.

Column A

11. Amazon.ca's use of patented "one-click" technology

12. Gathering data about search patterns of on-line purchasers

13. Having customers fill out their own on-line loan applications

14. Scanning of bar codes on incoming materials to determine if they meet purchase orders

Column B

a. Automating
b. Informating
c. Competitive advantage
d. Support of value chain

Short-answer questions

15. For each of the four basic organizational structures (see Figure 4.3), suggest a type of company or organization that might use that structure. (Hint: For a matrix organization, think of situations that require significant use of teams.)

16. Think of a business organization with which you are familiar, and list operations that would fall under each primary activity within Porter's value chain model.

17. Consider the Input-Process-Output (I-P-O) open systems model of an organization (see Figure 4.1). Apply this model to a business with which you are familiar. What are the inputs, processes, and outputs, environment, and feedback for the business?

Discussion/Essay questions

18. Some businesses are creating business value by extending their view of their organizational boundaries. From a value chain perspective, argue for or against outside contractors to manage support activities.

19. Considering your answer to the preceding question, how can information technology help transform organizational value chains?

20. How do you think managers in matrix organizations resolve the "love/hate" relationship that many people have with working in teams?

TEAM ACTIVITY

As a team, choose a business that you might like to own or work for. Create a diagram of the business that models it as a system. (Hint: I-P-O is at the heart of the model.)

SOFTWARE APPLICATION EXERCISES

1. Internet

Ever dream of owning your own business? If you own your own business, then you become CEO and custodian, CFO and customer service representative, and so on. Is such an idea more of a nightmare than a dream? Regardless of how you feel about it, thinking through the process of creating a small business can help you understand the business processes and challenges of much larger organizations. For this set of exercises, choose a small business that you would like to start. Visit the following websites to help you get started:

- Canada Business: Canadian government's small business portal at http://canadabusiness.gc.ca. This a great place to start for future and current small business owners.
- Canada One, an on-line resource for small businesses in Canada at www.canadaone.com
- British Columbia's (Canada) Business Services Portal at http://smallbusinessbc.ca/ offers a wealth of free information for starting a business and creating a successful business.

2. Presentation

To help obtain funding for your new business, create a business plan. To begin, open a new presentation in MS PowerPoint and use the AutoContent Wizard to find the Business Plan Template (choose Corporate/Business Plan/On-Screen Presentation). Be sure to include an organizational chart for your business.

3. Word Processing

Prepare a letter to potential customers that announces your business and includes your mission statement, business concept, and any additional information that your potential customers might find useful.

4. Spreadsheet

Develop a financial plan for your business. (Hint: Think I-P-O and visit the websites listed in Exercise 1.)

5. Database

Create a database of at least 10 potential customers for your business. Include the customers' names, addresses, e-mail addresses, and other relevant data. Using the Merge function in your word processor and the customer table that you just created, create a "form letter" version of your letter to mail to your customers.

6. Advanced Challenge

Finalize your business plan. Include links to the database and spreadsheets that you created in the preceding five assignments, and integrate them into a professional presentation about your business. Highlight how knowledge work activities and information systems can help make your business a success. Discuss the sources and types of information you will need to run your business, and the types of knowledge-enabled professionals that you might hire or whose services you might contract to help your business achieve its goals (e.g., an accountant).

ON-LINE RESOURCES

Companion website

- Take interactive practice quizzes to assess your knowledge and help you study in a dynamic way.
- Review PowerPoint lecture slides.
- Get help and sample solutions to end-of-chapter software application exercises.

Additional Resources Available Only on WileyPLUS

- Take the interactive Quick Test to check your understanding of the chapter material and get immediate feedback on your responses.
- Review and study with downloadable Audio Lecture MP3 files.
- Check your understanding of the key vocabulary in the chapter with Knowledge Speak Interactive Flash Cards.
- Link directly to websites recommended in the CORE boxes.

CASE STUDY: WAL-MART

From its humble beginnings in Bentonville, Arkansas, Wal-Mart has grown to be the world's largest corporation in terms of revenue. As measured by the Fortune 500 before the 2006 oil price rise, it surpassed such corporate giants as General Motors and Exxon Mobil, the only two other companies to hold this position. On top of that, *Fortune* named Wal-Mart as the "most admired" company in 2003, the first time the top Fortune 500 company has also had that honour. Reasons for this admiration? Wal-Mart's constant efforts to lower prices for consumers actually influences the U.S. economy by keeping inflation at low levels and forcing productivity up. Famed investor Warren Buffett calculated that Wal-Mart contributes $10 billion a year to the U.S. economy.

Founded in 1962 by Sam Walton, a large part of Wal-Mart's move to the top of the Fortune 500 ranking resulted from its aggressive use of information systems and technology. Unlike many of its competitors, Wal-Mart always considered information technology as a competitive advantage rather than an expense. Wal-Mart's technology-innovation history includes:

- 1969: The first company to use computer-supported operations.
- 1973: The first company to use electronic point-of-sale (POS) terminals.
- 1979: The first company to use a satellite network to link stores to headquarters.
- 1980: The first company to use bar codes to indicate prices at the checkout terminal.

Other retailers also eventually used this same technology, but Wal-Mart applied it innovatively. For example, rather than hoard or sell the data that bar codes and POS systems generated, Wal-Mart shared it freely with its suppliers, such as Procter & Gamble, as a way of improving its incoming logistics. The suppliers thus obtained the data necessary to replenish Wal-Mart's products without waiting for the retailer to order them. This process resulted in an average savings of 20 cents per shipping case for both Wal-Mart and the supplier.

In 1991, Wal-Mart took this sharing process one step further. It formalized sharing with an information system named Retail Link, which enabled suppliers to look up sales and prices of their products in any Wal-Mart store. This information helps the supplier plan its production and distribution to Wal-Mart, leading to better and cheaper products. Over 40,000 suppliers now use Retail Link. Wal-Mart is also pushing a Web-based version of EDI as a way to provide suppliers with even more information and data.

Another important part of Wal-Mart's philosophy of sharing information was the introduction in 1995 of collaborative forecasting and replenishment (CFAR). With CFAR, vendors can access Wal-Mart data from their home offices and adjust for causal factors themselves. Wal-Mart does not collaborate with vendors over public exchanges, but instead works with them through Internet connections to its Retail Link system.

This commitment to the use of IT is most obvious in Wal-Mart's supply chain; that is, the flow of products from its suppliers to its shelves. As one observer put it, "Grocers always invest in new stores. Wal-Mart invests in the supply chain, then

in new stores." By using the latest in technology to squeeze inefficiencies out of the supply chain, Wal-Mart keeps its costs down, which enables it to offer lower costs than its competitors. For example, recently Wal-Mart has been a leader in pushing the adoption of radio frequency identification tags (RFIDs) in products coming into its distribution centres. These RFIDs are tiny tags that are aimed at replacing bar codes as a way of identifying products. They have the advantage that they do not require direct contact or line-of-sight scanning to identify the product, and make it possible for retailers to know exactly what is in a pallet coming into the loading dock without having to be near it.

Wal-Mart also uses information technology for competitive advantage in product distribution. For example, Wal-Mart uses its POS data to minimize warehouse inventory. By using the warehouse as a "pass-through" point, where goods come in from the supplier at one side and go out to the store on the other side the same day over miles of conveyor belts, Wal-Mart saves time and money. To improve this process further, Wal-Mart was also an early member of UCCnet, the data synchronization and registry service of the Uniform Code Council that sets the codes used in bar code systems. This avoids problems with pallets with bar codes that fail to match the purchase order listing, which delays processing at the loading dock. If this pallet has a high-demand product on it, the result of the delay could mean lost revenue and unhappy customers.

Case Questions

1. In what ways does IT contribute to the growth of Wal-Mart?
2. How is Wal-Mart using IT to share data and information with suppliers? Why does this lead to lower prices for consumers?
3. What are Wal-Mart's recent IT innovations, and how will they lead to lower costs?

Integrative Application Case: Campuspad.ca

You and Sarah are now working as 50/50 partners in the business and are having planning meetings three times a week at the local coffee shop. In fact, if they ever write a *Canadian Business* article on you in the future, the journalist will surely be surprised to know just how much you can write on a napkin!

After compiling the information that Sarah has collected (available for you to review on WileyPLUS) and your work from last week, it's becoming clear that you still don't have sufficient knowledge to proceed—all you have is lots of input and supporting data, but no firm decisions on the path forward yet. You need some advice from someone more experienced who has done this before.

So you decide to approach your IT professor after class today. Turns out he had previously been involved in an Internet start-up and was quite pleased to spend a few minutes sharing what he could to help you launch your own idea. You were grateful and had distilled his rather long-winded comments into three simple points to share with Sarah at your next meeting:

1. **Follow the money!** If you can figure out who is paying who for what and how to do it quicker, better, or more cheaply than current business models, then you potentially have a sustainable e-business to pursue. If you can't follow the money then you won't make any... unless you're YouTube!

2. **Focus first!** In a start-up, don't try to be all things to all people, and don't try to do it all yourself. Figure out what's at your core, learn to do it better than anybody else, and outsource everything else. Make sure that if you rely on technology for your business it's the best technology you can buy or create because it's easily copied. You've got to stay one step ahead at all times.

3. **Segment your customer!** Where are they and how are you going to reach them? In every transaction there must be a buyer and a seller. Who do you serve and why? If you serve both buyers and sellers, how do you add value to both? What are the ethics of this and can it work? Are there regulatory or conflict issues? How will buyers find you? Can you find them? How much will it cost to reach them and let them know about you? Are you trying to create a new market or move an existing market on-line? Market makers are market winners!

It now seemed like you and Sarah are destined to become roommates. In fact, you had just recently located a place not far from campus and had *finally* gotten all the paperwork done—what a hassle! But it was an OK two-bedroom, one-bath place with a small balcony, and it was just a 15-minute walk or 5-minute bus ride from campus. Sweet! But the worst part was all the money you had to spend—first and last month's rent, damage waivers, key deposits. Oh, and did we mention you

needed proof of a tenant's insurance policy to lease here? Then there were the references, credit checks, and the notary fees to witness the approved standard lease form. Whoa... who knew living on your own could be so expensive?

And to top it all off, you are now gripped by your new idea and figure that the place is essentially going to become your office as well as your home. And that will probably mean a whole bunch of other problems, like the fact that your new lease prohibits you from running a business in your apartment. Oh well, all problems for another day. For now, it's off to meet Sarah for coffee.

Guiding Case Questions

1. Identify all the buyers and sellers in this market and make a diagram of the flow of money.
2. Figure out how you can use technology to add more value to buyers and sellers.
3. Based on this, decide if technology is core to your business or if it can be outsourced.
4. If you were to launch this business right now, how would you approach meeting its IS/IT requirements and why?

Your Task

Every new business ultimately needs money to get started. You and Sarah are struggling students—all one has to do is look at your bank accounts to figure that out! So if this business is going to go, it's going to need money... and it's not coming from you. To get money you have to have a simple business plan. Turns out your professor was also willing to share an example of what he thought was an outstanding business plan outline that he had given to a group of students last year (go to WileyPLUS to download a copy). He also said you could find lots of information on-line about writing good business plans. So, although the outline didn't have any specific information in it, the headings and tables seemed like a good place to start when you both looked at it. However, it also made you realize the many things you hadn't yet considered. As a result, you both agree that the next step is to fill this in with everything you know (or still have to find out through discovery) for campuspad.ca to become even more real and to eventually get it funded and launched.

WHAT WE WILL COVER

- The Technological Infrastructure of an Organization
- Databases: The Primary Data Storage for Organizations
- Storing and Accessing Data, Information, and Knowledge
- The IS Integration Challenge
- Information Systems that Support Business Activities
- Business Intelligence

C **Connectivity**
O **On-line Security**
R **Relationships**
E **Ethics**

XML: The Esperanto of the Web?

Disaster Recovery Planning

Habitat JAM: Solving Urban Issues Using Groupware

RFID and Privacy

IT for the Organization

Through your investment of time in reading and thinking about this chapter, your return, or created value, is gaining knowledge. Use the following questions as a study guide.

1. How do organizations use processors, networks, software, and storage?
2. What are the key concepts of data organization for an IS?
3. In what ways can organizations use IT to store and share data, information, and knowledge?
4. What is the software integration challenge, and how are organizations solving it?
5. How do organizations use IT to support transactions and business processes?
6. How does business intelligence enhance organizational decision making?

VOICE OF EXPERIENCE
Len Nanjad, University of Western Ontario

With an undergraduate degree in psychology and economics and an MBA, Len Nanjad journeyed from teaching business administration in Malaysia, to managing a knowledge base at a Toronto call centre, to his current position as organizational change consultant for IBM Global Business Services.

What do you do in your current position? I'm a senior managing consultant in organizational change strategy at IBM, providing management consulting services to our clients. When businesses are looking to change the way they work, often driven by new technology they want to implement, I look at that change from the perspective of the business and its people. I help my clients to understand what the impacts will be on how people are going to work and how they are going to accept and adopt the change.

What do you consider to be important career skills? My most important skill is communication. It's the ability to listen, understand, interpret, and then use information to take action. Communication also refers to the languages I understand—not only English, but technical and business jargon—and being able to translate among them. I need to understand what the technology is and translate it into business needs. I also need to understand business needs and what that means in terms of what information technology will or won't do. It is also important to be able to synthesize information from many sources. When I go to a client I have to learn about them, their business, their people, the technologies they're trying to implement, who it will affect, and how it will affect them.

How do you use IT? The technologies I use to do my job are the tools that make me a productive business person—primarily my laptop and software. The systems that enable me to connect with other people are the ones that make me the most valuable and generate the most value for me. The communications technology within IBM has enabled me to connect with experts across the planet. On any given day, I can have e-mail or chat conversations within minutes with people who are specialized in

any topic. I can also access the collective knowledge of IBM through our KnowledgeView information repository, where I can find information on client projects by industry, business type, and type of consulting engagement. I can also draw on best practices, methods, and approaches being used worldwide. This helps me learn and build on what's already been done.

Can you describe an example of how you have used IT to improve business operations? When I managed a knowledge base in a customer service contact centre, I used a knowledge management system to take knowledge from the physical "analog" world and "digitize" it into a software system. The system gave telephone representatives the ability to get to the answers they were looking for in a more intuitive and interactive way than having to do multiple searches or transfer the call. The technology increased the speed to an answer and the quality of the interaction, and offered a unique way to manage information by providing telephone representatives with a knowledge database they could rely on. We trained people on how to get to the answer rather than the answers themselves.

Have you got any "on the job" advice for students seeking a career in IT or business? Ask questions and learn to ask better and better questions. Ask early and ask often about everything and anything. From a business point of view, by asking lots of questions you can get to understand the root cause. From a technology point of view, you gather information to apply the right technology. You also need to understand that technology is critical to get things done; however, technology is there to help human beings achieve things, not the other way around.

Over Len's career he has helped a number of businesses create value by using IT, but has not been a part of an IT department. He has both created knowledge through building knowledge bases, and now uses similar tools in his work at IBM. In this chapter we learn more about the applied uses of IT and how it supports business knowledge and activities.

Data and information are as vital to an organization as the water we drink is to us. In addition, both individuals and businesses need these resources delivered in a usable form. Using this analogy, we can actually think of IT as the "plumbing" of a business information system (IS).

Let's take our water analogy further. First, we like to get our water when we want it—as soon as we turn on the tap, any time of the day. An organization also likes to get the data and information that it needs when it wants it as well. Constant access is therefore important. Second, in getting the water, we want a reliable system—the reservoirs, the processing facilities, the pipes that deliver it to our home, and the sewers that drain it away—to provide clean water. Similarly, a business counts on its IS technology to deliver accurate data and information.

However, it is perhaps more enlightening to think of how data and information differ from the water piped to our homes. With water, we basically need only one standard type—clear and clean. With data and information, an organization's needs are much more varied. It wants data in different forms (e.g., number, text, video, audio) and organized in different ways (e.g., tables, reports, graphs). Just think how complex a plumbing system would have to be to deliver water, coffee, or pop with just a twist of the tap!

In this chapter, we will discuss the equivalent of "organizational plumbing"—the IT systems designed to support different kinds of knowledge work: gathering and storing data, processing information, and making decisions. However, as businesses adapt to changes in consumer demands and needs, so will their IS. To keep current with these changes, knowledge-enabled professionals should realize that even new systems will continue to incorporate the *core components* of IT and information systems that we discuss in this chapter.

THE TECHNOLOGY INFRASTRUCTURE OF AN ORGANIZATION

All of the core components of IT that you learned about in Chapter 2—that is, hardware, software, and networks—also apply at the organizational level. The main differences in their use primarily relate to scale and complexity. At the organizational level, there is simply more of everything—more data to process, larger problems to solve, and more interconnected people and activities to support.

ORGANIZATIONAL HARDWARE—FROM SUPERCOMPUTERS TO PDAS

We discussed hardware at the individual level (your PC) in Chapter 1 and in more detail in Tech Guide A. Here we look at it from the organizational perspective. Just as processing hardware is at the heart of any individual IT device, processing hardware is at the heart of business IS. The main difference here is that rather than making decisions about a single processor, organizations typically need to select combinations of processors with varying processing power. A

Table 5.1   Computer Hierarchy

Computer Type	Relative Processing Power	Purpose	Example
Supercomputer	Largest and fastest	Performs processor intensive computations using parallel processing.	Environment Canada uses supercomputers to analyze data and forecast the weather.[1]
Mainframe	Large	Carries out many of the organizational processing needs using high-speed processing chips and large amounts of memory.	Health Canada uses mainframes to process health care benefit claims not covered under federal and provincial health care plans.[2]
Server farms	Medium/many	Allows multiple servers to handle network processing activities.	Google relies on its server farm—over 15,000 servers ranging from 533 MHz Intel Celeron to dual 1.4 GHz Intel Pentium III (as of 2003).[3]
Personal computer (PC)	Small to medium	Enables users to carry out processing tasks needed to perform their job; usually networked together.	All of the major Canadian banks provide Internet banking to their personal and business banking clients. Over their websites, the banks allow clients to manage their accounts, order cheques, apply for loans, and download their account activity in accounting software to manage household finances or create business financial statements.
Personal digital assistant (PDA)	Very small	Provides users with portable computing power; often used to communicate with PC or other users.	Real estate agents across Canada are able to access MLS home listings using their mobile devices (cell phone, BlackBerry, Internet-enabled PDA) while on the go with their clients.[4]
Embedded processors	Extremely small	Embedded in appliances and products to provide low-scale processing and/or identification.	Procter & Gamble incorporates embedded processors into packaging to monitor expiration dates.

common categorization scheme for processors used in IS is known as the computer hierarchy.

As shown in Table 5.1, the **computer hierarchy** categorizes processors according to their power. Note that processing power also often corresponds to the computer's physical size. However, comparing computer types on processing power alone can be deceptive.

1. Environment Canada, http://www.ec.gc.ca/press/2005/050110-3_b_e.htm. Retrieved August 23, 2006.
2. CGI Case studies, http://www.cgi.com/web/en/library/case_studies/technology_management/71037.html. Retrieved August 24, 2006.
3. Ding Choon Hoong and Rajkumar Buyya, "Guided Google: A meta search engine and its implementation using the Google Distributed Web Services," *International Journal of Computers and Applications*, 26 (1), ISSN: 1206-212X (202), ACTA Press, Calgary, Canada, 2004.
4. Wireless Realty, http://www.mosthomewireless.com/solutions.htm. Retrieved August 23, 2006.

For example, it is possible to combine the processing power of several smaller computers, like personal computers, to exceed that of a small supercomputer. An organization therefore has many options to meet its processing needs and will select the most efficient and cost-effective option possible.

In fact, the smallest type—embedded processors—may actually provide the greatest value to businesses. **Embedded processors** are programmable chips that are built into products to make them "smart." Like other processors, updating their operating system (OS) and application software is easy. Unlike other processors, however, businesses may design and make embedded processors to order. This allows organizations to use them, relatively inexpensively, for many applications that require only small amounts of processing power.

Figure 5.1 DSPs process signals in real time, perfect for applications that cannot tolerate any delays, such as cell phones.

For example, recent creative uses for embedded processors include **digital signal processors (DSPs).** DSPs are special microprocessors that include more math-related functions in their instruction set than the typical processor. DSPs can also process signals in real time. This makes this device perfect for applications that cannot tolerate any delays, such as cell phones (see Figure 5.1).

ORGANIZATIONAL NETWORKS—DATA COMMUNICATIONS IN ORGANIZATIONS

Networks of connected computers support the core function of data transfer in an organization (see Tech Guide C for more information on networks). But networks serve another critical function: Computer networks are the main technology supporting communication between managers and employees, between employee and employee, and between the organization and its suppliers and customers. They provide a platform for collaboration, allowing users to share data, information, and knowledge. As Table 5.2 indicates, organizations use all sizes of networks, including PANs, LANs, MANs, WANs, and the Internet, as well as networks based on the Internet protocols.

See TECH GUIDE C

WHAT DO YOU THINK?

Think about how business organizations you have experience with (as an employee, customer, or observer) use networks. Referring to Table 5.2, think of some examples and consider the following questions:

1: What type of network did the organization use?
2: Why do you think it used that kind of network? Was there a better option it could have used?
3: Did you notice any benefits associated with using that particular type of network?

Table 5.2	Organizational Networks		
Network	Size	Purpose	Examples
PAN (private area network) (private)	Covers a very small space that ranges from the size of a human body to a small office	Communication among computer devices in close proximity	A PAN allows your MP3 player to connect to a wireless headset, your PDA to "sync" with your PC, and your car to respond to commands from a Bluetooth-enabled cell phone.
LAN (local area network) (private)	Within the immediate location or building	Share files, resources, servers, and other hardware among the members of an organization	Common LANs include university computing labs, small office or household networks, and a wireless hotspot.
MAN (metropolitan area network) (private/public)	Ranges in size from a few blocks to an entire metropolitan area	Provides data and voice transmission typically at high speeds ($\approx$100 Mbps)	A university may use a MAN to connect LANs across campus; many city libraries use MANs to support centralized cataloguing and searching of resources.
WAN (wide area network) (private/public)	Over a large geographical area	Share data, information, and resources among units of an organization distant from one another	Connecting various university MANs/LANs to share research; a corporate network linking national and international locations.
Internet (public)	Worldwide	Share data and information with all stakeholders in the organization, as well as with the general public	The largest public WAN. Sometimes known as a global area network (GAN).

Intranets

For an organization, one of the most important types of networks is often the intranet. From a software perspective, an **intranet** is a set of services for distributing private information throughout the organization. From a hardware perspective, however, an intranet is a collection of private computer networks brought together to form an organization-wide, private network (ranging in size from LAN to WAN). Together these perspectives enable us to appreciate the value of intranets to organizations.

Unlike traditional network types, an intranet uses the technologies of the Internet and the World Wide Web. Intranets transmit data according to the TCP/IP and HTTP protocols of the Internet, and share the advantages of these protocols. For example, using the Internet as a bridge, an authorized user can access the intranet from any physical location—not necessarily within the organization's physical walls. Further, as with the Internet, employees can also access an intranet using a Macintosh, Windows, or any other PC platform. This is known as **platform independence,** which is usually not the case with traditional LANs and WANs. Finally, intranets can store data using Internet-compatible file formats, such as HTML and XML, thereby allowing users to access the data using a Web browser.

However, an intranet's use of Web technologies, which allows users to access outside resources over the Internet, also makes maintaining privacy of organizational information more crucial. An intranet, as Figure 5.2 shows, often incorporates security measures, such as a firewall, and requires users to authenticate themselves with usernames and passwords.

At first, most businesses used intranets to reduce publishing and distribution costs for such items as policy and procedure manuals, benefits information, and phone directories. Today, however, the use of intranets has moved beyond the goal of paper reduction to support automated internal transactions as well as to improve communication, teamwork, and knowledge management. For example, Ford Motor Company has been using an intranet since 1996 to connect its more than 350,000 employees worldwide. In addition

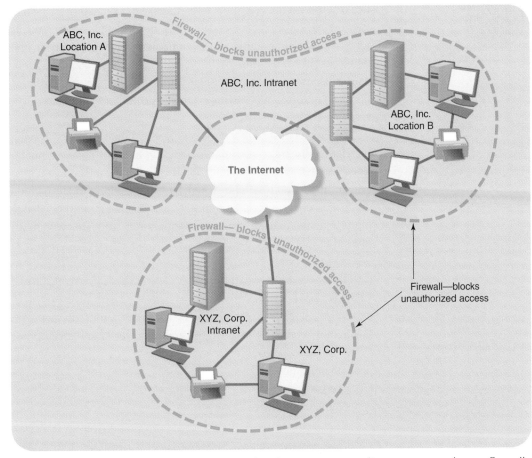

Figure 5.2 An intranet, as this figure shows, often incorporates security measures, such as a firewall.

Table 5.3	Individual vs. Organizational Software	
Type of Software	**Individual Use**	**Organizational Use**
Operating Systems	To manage a single computer	To manage a mainframe with many users or a server farm
Application Software	Personal productivity software, such as word processing or spreadsheets	Transaction processing, data storage, and organizational productivity software
Collaboration Software	To support communication between individuals, such as through e-mail or instant messaging	To enable members of the organization to share collaborative work electronically in a central repository

to providing access to documents and procedure manuals, the Ford intranet provides communication, collaboration, and other invaluable tools for its users.[5]

ORGANIZATIONAL SOFTWARE

Like other IT technologies, software at the organizational level is much like that used at the individual level. But like hardware processing and networking, organizations usually have more complex requirements for software. For example, large computers (like mainframes) and networks (like LANs and WANs) require operating system (OS) software (discussed in detail in Tech Guide B) that can handle large numbers of users and activities. Table 5.3 compares various types of software for individual and organizational use.

Our focus in this chapter is on organizational software. Having the right software is essential to ensuring efficient business operations and can give an organization a competitive advantage. Some critical application software used by organizations today include databases and their related applications, document and knowledge management applications, and collaboration software, which we discuss in more detail next.

Quick Test

1. Which category of the computer hierarchy represents the type of computer with the most processing power at any given time?
   a. embedded processors
   b. mainframe
   c. server farm
   d. supercomputer

5. Anne Stuart, "Under the hood at Ford," *WebMaster Magazine*, June 1997.

2. A network that connects computers and smaller networks together over a great geographic distance is known as a _____.
   a. LAN
   b. WAN
   c. MAN
   d. PAN

3. Which of the following is a benefit of using an intranet?
   a. Users can access information resources through a browser.
   b. Users can use the PC platform that they are comfortable with to connect to the intranet.
   c. An intranet can be secured so that only authorized users may access it.
   d. All of the above.

Answers: 1. d; 2. b; 3. d.

DATABASES: THE PRIMARY DATA STORAGE FOR ORGANIZATIONS

All business information systems rely on the use and storage of data. Data create useful information, which in turn helps organizations to make better decisions. The primary technology used to store, manage, and allow efficient access to data is the database.

Recall from Chapter 2 that a *database* consists of interrelated data that are stored in files and organized so that computer programs can quickly and easily access specific pieces of data. For example, a bank stores information about its customers in a database. The bank can then access and update the database as customers make deposits and withdrawals at an ATM. A **database management system (DBMS)** is a collection of software that allows users to create and work with a database. For example, that same bank uses a DBMS to obtain and print a customer's monthly bank statement. Together, a database and a DBMS make up a *database system.* As Figure 5.3 shows, the DBMS controls access to the data stored in the database.

Those people who create and manage the database, sometimes known as *database administrators,* use the tools in the DBMS to do their work. Other knowledge-enabled professionals who need to access the database typically do so through other application software that can connect to the DBMS and hence query the databases that it manages. In this section, we briefly introduce databases. As a knowledge-enabled professional, you will use business applications that depend on databases. Some of the more prevalent databases used today are provided by Oracle, Microsoft, and IBM. You

CHAPTER

5

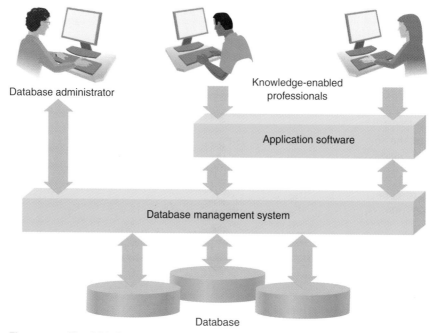

Database administrator

Knowledge-enabled
professionals

Application software

Database management system

Database

Figure 5.3 The DBMS controls access to the data stored in the database.

PART

2

may work closely with other knowledge-enabled professionals who are certified as database administrators for Oracle databases and/or Microsoft SQL servers. For more in-depth coverage, including a more thorough discussion of how to design and model a database, see Tech Guide D.

THE DATA HIERARCHY

To organize data in a database, most users rely on the **data hierarchy.** As Figure 5.4 shows, the data hierarchy organizes stored data in increasing levels of complexity. At the lowest level, the data hierarchy stores all data using electronic bits that can be 1 (on) or 0 (off). A specific combination of bits represents each data *character.* The exact number of bits needed for a character depends on the type of data and the encoding scheme. For example, the ASCII encoding scheme will use eight bits (one byte) to store a letter of the alphabet. Unicode will store the same letter using 16 bits (two bytes). A combination of characters representing a data item, such as a name or a price, is known as a *field.*

The next higher level of the data hierarchy stores collections of fields known as *records.* By using a record that includes fields holding values for FirstName, LastName, Gender, and Age, we find that Bob Smith is a customer who is a 21-year-old male (Figure 5.4). At the next level up, the data hierarchy assembles records into a collection called

Purchases   Products   Customers   **Database**

Customers

Bob, Smith, S7H 0W9, Male, 21
Sue, Jones, H3S 1Z7, Female, 23
Mike, Long, B3A 2K6, Male, 25

File (Table)

FirstName	Last Name	PostalCode	Gender	Age
Bob	Smith	S7H 0W9	Male	21

Record

FirstName

Bob

Field

B   **Character**

0101010   **Bit**

Figure 5.4 The data hierarchy organizes stored data in increasing levels of complexity.

CHAPTER 5

a *table* or *file.* For instance, at this level we would find a set of records listing the age and gender of all customers, not just Bob Smith. Finally, the top level compiles the organized collection of files into a database.

To implement the data hierarchy, most businesses at one time used a file processing approach to store and manage files.

USING FILE PROCESSING TO MANAGE DATA

Before the development of databases, most systems used a file processing approach for storing data. With **file processing,** each software application uses its own set of files. However, as Figure 5.5 shows, although the files for an application are related in that they work with the specific application, they are not necessarily stored or managed together. This type of data organization therefore has several drawbacks when dealing with large amounts of related data, such as:

- *Data redundancy:* Some files must be stored in more than one place, leading to inconsistent data if changes are made in some files but not in others.

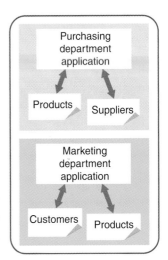

Figure 5.5 With a file management system, each software application uses its own set of files, which, as shown here, often results in data redundancy.

- **Data dependence:** Because files are designed for specific applications, their format may not be usable by other applications that need the data.
- **Data inaccessibility:** Data can be difficult to access in ways other than those allowed by the related application.
- **Poor file management:** It is difficult to manage the files for use by multiple users, secure use by only authorized users, and recover from file problems.

As a result, most organizations today turn to database systems to store and manage their data.

DATABASE SYSTEMS

Using a database system to organize data provides several advantages over the use of a file processing system:

- The organization of the data is independent of any one software application. This allows all applications to access the data in a standard manner.
- The organization of the data reduces data redundancy; a DBMS may need to store only one record of data for a particular product.
- The DBMS can include features for maintaining the quality of the data, handling security, and synchronizing access by simultaneous users.
- The database system allows for capabilities such as improved data access, allowing different views of the data for different users, and report generation.

These advantages improve the accuracy of the data stored (*data integrity*) as well as increase its use.

WHAT DO YOU THINK?

A database administrator designs the database; develops standards and processes to ensure data integrity; determines, acquires, and maintains physical storage hardware; administers users' privileges, authorization, and roles; and monitors the database system performance and responds to changing requirements. Further, the database administrator works with application developers to ensure compatibility between the applications and the database, and ensures that changes to the database system will not adversely affect the programs that rely on it. Considering all this, how would you respond to the following questions:

1: What business and technical skills do you think would be important for a database administrator to possess?

2: How do you think a database administrator determines what needs to be stored in a database, as well as maintain security of sensitive data?

3: What knowledge of other business disciplines might be helpful for a database administrator within a business context?

RELATIONAL DATA MODEL

In the early 1970s, Dr. E. F. Codd developed a method for logically organizing data in a database that was independent of the method used to physically store the data. In this method, known as the **relational data model,** databases store information about entities, such as suppliers and products for a retailer, and the relationships between those entities. Databases then use these defined relationships to store the connections between the entities, such as which suppliers provide which products.

The relational data model has since become the standard way of storing large amounts of data. Researchers at various universities and business organizations (notably University of California at Berkeley and IBM) developed systems based on Codd's relational model. These systems are now known as **relational database management systems (RDBMS).** While other database models exist, the relational data model has since become the most popular for organizing and storing large amounts of data. Figure 5.6 shows a typical relational database management system.

The relational data model stores data in one or more tables, corresponding to entities. Tables consist of records, represented by the rows of the table. The records generally hold data about a single instance of an entity. For example, a single record might store contact information for a single supplier. A record, in turn, consists of one or more fields that hold data about an *instance* of an entity. Because the data values in the fields often describe an instance of an entity, the fields are sometimes called **attributes.** The columns of the table represent the fields of all the records.

CHAPTER 5

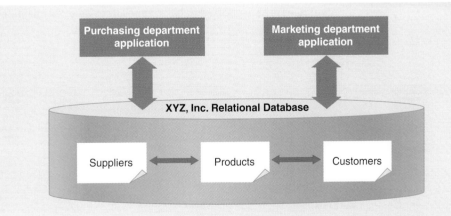

Figure 5.6 Because the relational data model overcomes many of the disadvantages of the file processing system, it has become the most popular method for organizing and storing large amounts of data.

For example, suppose that a company decides to create a relational database to store data about its products. It begins by identifying the generic category "Product" as an entity. The company then determines that an *instance* of the product category is a set of data about a specific product, such as "hiking boots." The attributes of the hiking boots product include ItemCode (HB), ItemName (hiking boots), RetailPrice ($110.00), and ItemCost ($50.00). Because the company wants to store data about the same attributes for all of the products that it sells, its product table will include fields for Item-Code, ItemName, RetailPrice, and ItemCost. (You can imagine that the field names are the column headings for a table.) When the company fills in a row in the table with values for the attributes—HB, hiking boots, etc.—then it has a data record for a product.

As an example of related tables, consider Figure 5.7, which shows a Product table and a Vendor table. Note that one row of the Product table contains our hiking boots example. The Product and the Vendor tables each store one field that has a unique value for each record, called the *primary key*. In the Product table the primary key is stored in the ItemCode field, while in the Vendor table the VendorID stores the primary key.

Note that the Product table also contains a VendorID field. To relate the data in one table to data in the other table, the company can simply use the VendorID as a reference. By matching a VendorID stored in the Product table with the unique record that it references in the Vendor table, the company can pull data about the product and vendor from both tables. When a second table uses the primary key of one table as a reference field in its table, the field is called a *foreign key*.

Of course, designing and storing data in a database is just the beginning. The power of a database comes from how organizations can use it. The relational database model provides powerful, standardized

ItemCode	ItemName	RetailPrice	ItemCost	VendorID
AM	Air Mattress	$100.00	$60.00	SFJ
BP	Backpack	$165.00	$80.00	BRU
CC	Child Carrier	$175.00	$85.00	SFJ
CK	Cookset	$50.00	$32.50	DOL
DP	Day Pack	$105.00	$60.00	WED
GC	Ground Cover	$20.00	$12.50	FEU
HB	Hiking Boots	$110.00	$50.00	DOL
HH	Heater	$75.00	$44.00	BRU
PL	Propane Lantern	$35.00	$20.00	FEU
SB	Sleeping Bag	$100.00	$45.00	DOL
TT	Tent	$385.00	$110.00	WED

Product Table

VendorID	VendorName	Contact	PhoneNumber	Discount
BRU	Backpacks R' U	Nick Estelle	415-555-8328	5.00%
DOL	Doleman Manuf	George Burdell	770-555-4505	6.00%
FEU	Feuters Campin	Chris Patrick	406-555-2103	4.00%
SFJ	SFJ Enterprises	Ashley Hyatt	239-555-0308	5.00%
WED	Waters End	Todd Keegan	715-555-1212	7.00%

Vendor Table

Figure 5.7 In this example of related tables, note that the VendorID field (stored as the primary key for the Product table and the foreign key for the Vendor table) provides the link between the two tables.

Backpack Profit SQL Statement:

```
SELECT Product.ItemName, Vendor.VendorName, Vendor.Discount, [RetailPrice]-[OurCost] AS Profit
FROM Product, Vendor
WHERE Product.VendorID = Vendor.VendorID
AND (((Vendor.VendorID)="BRU"));
```

Backpack Profit Query Result:

ItemName	VendorName	Discount	Profit
DayTripper	BackPacks R' Us	5.00%	$85.00
Mountaineer	BackPacks R' Us	5.00%	$31.00

Figure 5.8 Organizations often use SQL queries, similar to the one shown here, to obtain specific information from their databases, such as profit calculations. This example shows that of the two items BackPacks R' Us supply, the DayTripper provides more profit per item. Another query can be done to combine this profit information with sales information.

methods for maintaining and working with the data. The primary method for accessing and using data in an RDBMS is a query. A *query* is a method for asking a question of a database. For the relational database model, a standard and popular language called **Structured Query Language (SQL)** (often pronounced "sequel" for short) provides general rules for formulating the queries on relational databases.

For example, Figure 5.8, shows standard SQL queries, which use keywords in capital letters (e.g., "WHERE") and refer to the data by field names and the tables in which they reside (e.g., Product.VendorID). This example also shows that a query can produce values (Profit) that it calculates based on data stored in the database. With one or more SQL queries as a basis, organizations can create reports and forms to simplify data access and entry for their employees. A more detailed discussion of SQL is contained in Tech Guide D.

Most organizations rely on DBMS to operate efficiently and effectively. However, they sometimes need to use other methods to store data, information, and knowledge. We briefly review a couple of these methods in the next section.

Quick Test

1. A _____ is a collection of interrelated data that are stored in files and organized so that computer programs can quickly and easily access specific pieces of data.
   a. database
   b. DBMS
   c. program
   d. none of the above

2. Which of the following disadvantages of a file processing approach to data storage refers to problems that come up when the same data are stored multiple times?
   a. data dependence
   b. data integrity
   c. data locking
   d. data redundancy

3. A _____ key is a field that has unique values for each record in a relational table.
   a. primary
   b. foreign
   c. data
   d. relational

Answers: 1. a; 2. d; 3. a

STORING AND ACCESSING DATA, INFORMATION, AND KNOWLEDGE

As it turns out, databases are not the only, nor necessarily the best, form of storage for all business needs. For example, to analyze how a product change might affect sales, a marketing manager may need to access several databases. Or, the manager who needs to examine historical sales data may realize the database does not include it. In this section, we look at other ways that IT can support the organization, storage, and sharing of data.

DATA WAREHOUSES

A **data warehouse** is a means of storing and managing data for information access, typically composed of data from one or more transaction databases. It thus consists of *transaction* data, cleaned and restructured to fit the data warehouse model and to support queries, summary reports, and analysis. For example, the Royal Bank relies on its data warehouse to incorporate data from its many locations and business units, such as retail banking, investments, and mortgages. The Royal Bank uses the data warehouse to provide insight into customer behaviour, manage risks in its lending portfolios, and prevent fraud.[6] Table 5.4 lists several differences between a database and data warehouse technology.

Because data warehouses are very large (in terms of the amount of data stored) compared with the typical database, they work with

6. http://www.tdwi.org/education/display.aspx?id = 8011. Retrieved August 24, 2006.

Table 5.4	A Comparison of Database and Data Warehouse Technology	
	Database	Data Warehouse
Supported Activity	Operational (transactions)	Analytical (knowledge work)
Response Time	Fast response time (seconds)	Can be slower (minutes, sometimes hours)
Age of Data	Mostly data for current transactions	A lot of historical data
Scope	May support limited area within the organization	Should provide view of entire organization
Data Variability	Mostly dynamic, changes often	Mostly static, infrequent changes
Source	Transactions from operational domain; business rules	Combined from multiple sources (including operational databases)
Data Model	Based on business rules of operational application	Aligns with overall business structure

tools that allow users to more easily deal with these vast amounts of data. For example, a data warehouse may provide information to an area-specific data mart such as a marketing data mart. A **data mart** extracts and reorganizes subject-area-specific data to allow knowledge-enabled professionals to focus on a specific subject area.

Data warehouses often provide support for organizing multidimensional data, which are based on two or more characteristics (dimensions), such as time and place. Organizing data in this way allows businesses to more easily identify trends. For example, Figure 5.9 shows data with three dimensions for retail sales. The

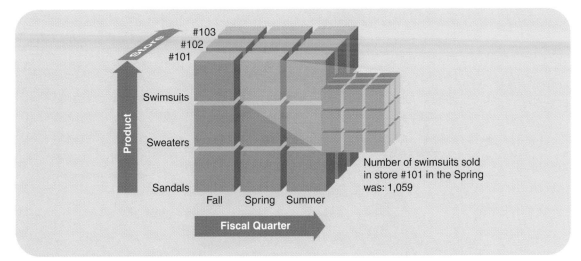

Figure 5.9 Data warehouses often provide support for organizing multidimensional data, such as the three dimensions for retail sales shown here, which allows businesses to more easily identify trends.

company can then organize each data item according to three dimensions: store, product, and fiscal quarter. Retrieving data from data organized in this way is sometimes referred to as **slicing-and-dicing;** that is, the process of cutting off portions of the data until obtaining the needed information.

As Figure 5.10 shows, businesses access and use a data warehouse for four main reasons:

1. *Automatic production of standard reports and queries:* When users need a particular report, they simply view the report that the data warehouse already generated rather than creating it themselves.
2. *Queries against summary or detailed data:* Data warehouse tools include simple query tools like those used with databases. Queries can involve summarized data or be drawn against stores of detailed data.
3. *Data mining in detailed data:* **Data mining** includes a set of techniques for finding trends and patterns in large sets of data. Data mining tools can incorporate advanced technologies such as *artificial intelligence.* Some provide aids for *data visualization*—organizing and presenting data in ways that allow humans to spot and analyze the patterns better.
4. *Interfacing with other applications and data stores:* A company will often connect a data warehouse to applications that use it as the source of data. A data warehouse may feed data to other data warehouses, data marts, or application programs.

Regardless of how a business uses it, maintaining a data warehouse (or DBMS) can be vital to a company's success. Just think what might happen to a business if it loses all of its data about products,

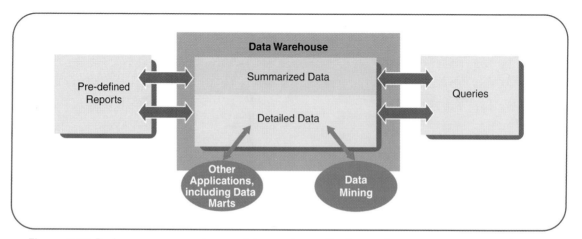

Figure 5.10 Businesses access and use a data warehouse for four main reasons: reports, queries, data mining, and applications.

vendors, or customers. As the CORE box "Disaster Recovery Planning" discusses, companies take a number of measures to reduce the risk of a catastrophic loss to their data.

On-line Security

Disaster Recovery Planning (DRP)

When we think of IS security, we usually think about prevention, such as preventing viruses or unauthorized access. However, an important aspect of security involves planning a response to a crisis. Many organizations have developed disaster recovery, or business continuity, plans. A disaster recovery plan allows an organization to resume operations after a major event that interrupts normal business processes. Such events may include data corruption, software bugs, network failures, network attacks, or natural and man-made physical disasters.

Even small amounts of downtime could result in lost transactions, diminished productivity, and reduced customer satisfaction. A business continuity plan addresses problem prevention, response to crises, resumption of business, recovery of losses, and restoration of systems and processes. When developing a plan, a company needs to determine its critical functions, the level of disaster, and appropriate procedures for recovery.

For IS, disaster recovery focuses on having and making available the important data needed to resume business. Reliable data storage and consistent backup procedures are essential in maintaining data integrity. An overall recovery plan will generally incorporate plans from each department in the organization, as the types of anticipated problems can vary. For example, the data centre may have a contingency plan for power outages or server downtime. Production facilities can have plans for network failures, employee strikes, or disruptions in supplies.

Disaster recovery plans are not necessarily easy or inexpensive to develop. However, they provide a type of insurance against business downtime caused by a catastrophe. Use the Web resources below to explore what is involved in disaster recovery planning.

Web Resources
- Disaster Recovery Journal—http://www.drj.com
- Disaster Recovery Information Exchange—http://www.drie.org
- Public Safety and Emergency Preparedness Canada—http://www.psepc-sppcc.gc.ca

Once captured and stored, businesses process data to create information, which they in turn use for decision making. Although a business can always develop information "on the fly" with queries to a database, this is not always practical. In addition, an organization may periodically need the same information. Therefore, rather than re-creating information from a database, storing that information "as is" using a management information system is often more efficient.

MANAGEMENT INFORMATION AND DOCUMENT MANAGEMENT SYSTEMS

In the early days of information systems, businesses typically developed systems, known as **management information systems (MIS),** specifically to meet the need of storing processed transaction data as reports for managers. These early systems were often rudimentary and produced large volumes of information because of their limited ability to sort and process data to specific user needs. MIS typically generate three types of reports:

1. *Periodic reports,* such as a company's annual financial statements or monthly sales reports, which are updated and generated after a specific time period has passed.
2. *Exception reports,* to monitor when, and perhaps why, exceptions occur of key values, defined as critical to the operation.
3. *Demand reports,* generated based on user requests. Many systems also include a library of such reports from which a user could choose.

As organizations and systems capability both progressed, many businesses began to create specific systems to serve specific needs. One example is **executive information systems (EIS)** designed to provide summary information about business performance to those making higher-level strategic decisions. This often involved creating "views" of data about business trends that gave rise to graphical displays of information.

Similarly, organizations began to recognize data management needs that revolved around business documents (as distinct from business information). These systems are known as **document management systems (DMS).** A DMS enters, tracks, routes, and processes the many documents used in an organization, including but not limited to the three types of reports that we just discussed. A DMS can create the documents electronically or convert them to electronic form using *imaging technology.* Imaging technology includes scanners like those discussed in Chapter 2, as well as special software that can recognize printed characters and convert them to specific data formats to work with application software.

Businesses can use DMS to support workflow systems by managing the storage and routing of documents. They can also use DMS to maintain large archives of forms and documents in a much more efficient and flexible manner than with traditional paper documents. The Canada Revenue Agency form shown in Figure 5.11 is an example of the type of document that a DMS might store.

PART

2

Canada Revenue Agency | Agence du revenu du Canada

GENERAL APPLICATION FOR REBATE OF GST/HST

Use this form to apply for a rebate of GST/HST for any of the reasons listed in Part B below. For detailed instructions on when to use this form and how to complete it, see our guide RC4033, *General Application for GST/HST Rebates.*

Mail to: Summerside Tax Centre
275 Pope Road
Summerside PE C1N 6A2

Please type or print

Part A ñ Identification

Are you registered for GST/HST? ☐ Yes ☐ No | Business Number (if applicable)

Claimant's last name or legal name of organization (include trading name if applicable)

Claimant's first name and initials (individuals only)

Mailing address (number, street, and apartment no.; P.O. Box no.; or R.R. no.)

City | Province/State | Country | Postal/Zip Code | Telephone no. ( )

Business address (if different from mailing address) (number, street, and apartment no, or R.R. no.)

City | Province/State | Country | Postal/Zip Code

Has your address changed since your last rebate application? ☐ Yes ☐ No | If *yes*, do you wish to have your file updated to reflect the address change(s)? ☐ Yes ☐ No

This claim is being filed by ☐ Head office ☐ Branch/Division | Does this application amend a previous application? ☐ Yes ☐ No

Language of correspondence ☐ English ☐ French | Period covered From Year Month Day To Year Month Day

Part B ñ Reason for rebate request

Put a check mark in the appropriate box to indicate the reason for this claim. Check only **one** box. Refer to our guide for specific details and documents that you have to file with this application.

Code	Reason	Code	Reason
☐ 1	Amounts paid in error	☐ 11	Non-resident recipient of a taxable supply of an installation service ñ rebate not paid or credited by supplier

Figure 5.11 A Canada Revenue Agency form stored in a document management system. (Source: http://www.cra-arc.gc.ca/E/pbg/gf/gst189/gst189-06e.pdf. Retrieved January 30, 2007.)

KNOWLEDGE MANAGEMENT

Of the three informational resources—data, information, and knowledge—knowledge is the most difficult to store and share. Why? First, consider that organizations rely on two types of knowledge—explicit knowledge and tacit knowledge. Recall from Chapter 1 that *explicit knowledge* includes anything that can be written down, stored, and codified. Examples include business plans, patents and trademarks, and market research. On the other hand, *tacit knowledge* includes the know-how that people have through learning and experience, which is difficult to write down and share. Tacit knowledge, while important to an organization, represents a major challenge in that organization's **knowledge management (KM)**; that is, how the company recognizes, generates, manages, and shares knowledge.

Organizations can use IT in several ways to support knowledge management. For example, businesses use expert systems, a type of knowledge management system. Expert systems originate from the field of **artificial intelligence (AI)**, which attempts to

PART

2

provide computer applications that mimic characteristics of human - intelligence. Many other applications use AI technology, from neural networks used for recognizing patterns in stock prices, to genetic algorithms that incorporate theories from genetics into programs that can find an optimal solution to a problem in a short time.

An **expert system** is used to capture and store the knowledge of a human expert so that the organization can permanently store and share it. To capture and codify tacit knowledge into an expert system, special techniques have been developed, such as observation and interview techniques, to capture how an expert performs work and makes decisions. Then, to store the knowledge, special formats capture how the facts relate to the decision rules used by the expert.

To support tacit knowledge, knowledge management systems often rely on **collaborative software,** which supports teamwork with technologies that enable communications and sharing of data and information. This software category, also known as **groupware,** can be a simple communication tool like e-mail. Or it can be more complex, providing shared workspaces to store common files and tools for conferencing and meeting support. Table 5.5 summarizes how we can divide groupware into three levels of support. The CORE box "Habitat JAM: Solving Urban Issues Using Groupware" illustrates how groupware's collaborative capabilities can even help to solve complex global issues.

Table 5.5	Collaborative Software Categories
Collaborative Software	**Comments**
Communication tools	• Facilitate the sharing of information and data with tools that enable people to send messages, documents, files, and data between each other. • Examples include e-mail, text messaging, voice mail, and Web publishing.
Conferencing tools	• Provide a more interactive facility for the sharing of information. At a minimum, a conferencing tool can provide real-time text discussions and a common "whiteboard" that each participant can edit. • Can also enable voice and/or video using special equipment or computer networks. • Some organizations build special facilities for conferencing that these tools support.
Collaborative management tools	• Can help to manage and facilitate the activities of a team. They can include electronic calendars for scheduling events and automatically notifying participants. • Shared workspaces can be provided in which to store and share work products that group members may modify. • May overlap with project management systems to keep the group aware of a project's status.

Relationships

Habitat JAM: Solving Urban Issues Using Groupware

In December 2005, IBM, the Government of Canada, and the UN hosted an on-line event called Habitat JAM, enabled by IBM's groupware technology. The purpose of Habitat JAM was to bring together people from all over the world to contribute to a discussion about urgent urban issues such as environmental sustainability, clean water, slums, safety, and security. IBM's collaborative groupware connected 39,000 participants from 158 countries via the Internet who, due to language, culture, and distance, would not have had the opportunity to interact and discuss the issues in person. In Kenya, people lined up for hours to have access to computers so that they could participate. "In just over 72 hours, the participants produced over 4,000 pages of dialogue and generated hundreds of actionable ideas on critical issues related to urban sustainability, including ideas for empowering women and the youth and suggestions for the opening of 'technology hubs' to give the urban poor access to meeting space, and the Internet."[7]

IBM's JAM technology created a chat-like environment for participants to communicate with one another. It also enabled forum moderators and subject matter experts to help guide discussions and provide input. Ideas were captured, circulated, and built upon by participants. Using data analysis tools, data were analyzed and provided to the in-person Habitat conference held in Vancouver a short time later. IBM has used JAM collaborative technology to join global project teams together for several years.[8]

A similar type of collaboration groupware used for group projects, Groove Workspace, allows teams to work together over a network as if they were in the same physical location. Groove differs from other groupware applications in that a Groove workspace does not reside on a central server. Instead, an individual team member's device stores synchronized copies of the workspace. After synchronizing the workspace when a user goes on-line, the user can then work off-line. When the user returns to the network, it synchronizes the workspace again. Other features of Groove include always-on encryption, bandwidth optimization, and the ability to traverse the user's firewalls. It is easy to see how teams operating in different locations can use Groove to store and work on documents they are collaborating on. In fact, team members can use Groove to communicate and work even if they do not have access to e-mail.

Web Resources

- Habitat JAM—http://www.habitatjam.com
- Groove Networks—http://www.groove.net
- Usability First Groupware Page—http://www.usabilityfirst.com/groupware/

CHAPTER

5

---

7. www.ibm.com/news/ca/en/2006/06/ 2006_06_20.html. Retrieved September 23, 2006.
8. www.answers.com/topic/habitat-jam. Retrieved September 23, 2006.

The benefits of knowledge management are often difficult to calculate. Some benefits directly increase revenue or reduce costs, while others do not. To derive the most benefits from knowledge management, clear business goals must drive the process for sharing relevant knowledge throughout the organization. For example, an effective KM program can allow knowledge-enabled professionals to streamline the supply chain. This in turn will improve customer service and boost revenues as the organization gets products and services out to the market faster. Further, an effective KM program can increase employee morale. Employees often feel greater appreciation when the organization recognizes the value and use of their knowledge. They are then often more eager to share their information and ideas, which can foster innovation throughout the organization.

As you might expect, as a company grows and applies IT to its operations, the number and types of hardware and software technologies that it uses will also grow. In this section alone we discussed many ways in which an organization can use IT to store and access data, information, and knowledge. While the IS that we have outlined is useful on its own, there is much to be gained by combining these systems. By enabling systems to integrate and connect with one another, organizations can achieve a higher level of efficiency and improved business processes and results. Integration, however, can be a significant challenge. This **integration challenge** is often faced by organizations seeking improvement and competitive advantage.

Quick Test

1. A _____ combines large amounts of data from many sources, including databases, to provide support for analysis.
   a. data mart
   b. data warehouse
   c. relational database
   d. file system

2. Which one of the following is the name of the modern IS with the focus on entering, tracking, routing, and processing documents used in a business?
   a. document management system (DMS)
   b. expert system (ES)
   c. management information system (MIS)
   d. domain name system (DNS)

3. _____ knowledge is based on intuition and experience and is more difficult to capture and store.
   a. Explicit   c. Precise
   b. Implicit   d. Tacit

Answers: 1. b; 2. a; 3. d

THE IS INTEGRATION CHALLENGE

To understand the advantages of integration, think about a simple personal productivity software example. In the 1980s, many knowledge-enabled professionals used a word processing application called WordPerfect. Later, they probably also added a spreadsheet software package called Lotus 1-2-3, which a different company developed and sold. However, the two programs could not share data or communicate directly with one another. Today, software companies (e.g., Borland, Microsoft, and Corel) bundle personal productivity software into **software suites.** These suites, which include word processor, spreadsheet, database management, and other applications, allow users to easily share data between applications through a simple cut-and-paste or linking of the files. By bundling the applications into a suite, these companies have integrated the software.

In this section, we review how businesses integrate IT tools and systems.

MIDDLEWARE

Middleware is software that links applications that use dissimilar software or hardware platforms. It acts like a specialized messenger/translator that manages the exchange of information.

Further, as more corporate networks rely on the same technologies and protocols as the Internet, middleware solutions are evolving to support applications on these networks. Figure 5.12 illustrates where a layer of middleware software would fit within an organization's IS to support efficient communication between various business applications and the system's environment.

An important class of middleware technology that is designed to work with Internet protocols is known as Web services. A **Web service** receives and processes data from a sending application and delivers the data over the network using a standard data format called **eXtensible Markup Language (XML)** to a receiving application. By using XML, the sending and receiving applications communicate in a language common to both. In the CORE box "XML: The Esperanto of the Web?" we discuss the universal application of XML. XML is discussed in detail in Tech Guide D.

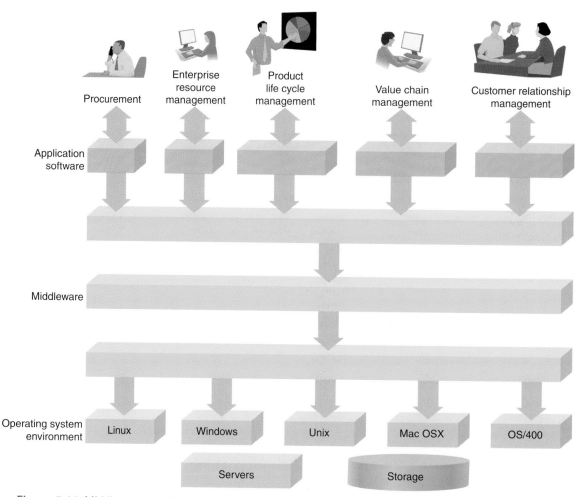

Figure 5.12 Middleware, as this figure shows, fits within an organization's IS to support efficient communication between various business applications and the operating system environment.

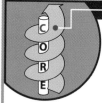

Connectivity

XML: The Esperanto of the Web?

In the 1965 feature film *Incubus,* starring William Shatner in his pre-Star Trek days, the dialogue was entirely in Esperanto. Esperanto is an "artificial" language that was designed to be a neutral, common second language useful for facilitating communication between speakers of different lands, languages, and cultures. First published in 1887, Esperanto is said to be easier to learn than national languages. Plus, Esperanto allows people to communicate on an equal footing by removing the advantage favouring a native speaker. The League of Nations, the precursor to the United Nations, even considered its use.

Much like Esperanto is meant to do for people, the objective of eXtensible Markup Language (XML) is to be a standard, neutral language to facilitate communication between computer systems.

XML is a standard from the World Wide Web Consortium (W3C) that facilitates the exchange of data between different computer applications. XML is similar to HTML, a language used for writing web pages, in that both use markup codes (*tags*). Computer programs can be written that automatically extract data from an XML document using its associated *data type definition (DTD)* as a guide.

Using XML would certainly make it much easier to integrate disparate information systems. However, for XML to succeed, everyone needs to agree on industry standards. Given some of the IT industry squabbles in the past, many wonder if this will occur.

Web Resources

- Multilingual Information Center about Esperanto—http://www.esperanto.net/
- World Wide Web Consortium XML Specifications—http://www.w3.org/XML

Web services continue to gain in use and popularity as they create value for companies. For example, Amazon.ca and Google both provide Web services that others can use to access their huge databases. One recent trend is to cobble together Web services from various sources to make an application known as a "mashup." A *mashup* is a Web application that seamlessly combines information from more than one source into an integrated experience. Mashups are not only creating new services for existing companies, but also entirely new companies. For example, Jobloft.com, a mashup site created by recent Ryerson University graduates, combines job postings and Google maps to help job seekers find jobs in their local area.

ENTERPRISE RESOURCE PLANNING (ERP)

Another way to integrate the departments and functions across an organization is to use **enterprise resource planning software (ERP)**. With ERP, a company runs all of its applications from a single database. Each functional unit of a company, such as finance, marketing, and sales, still uses its own supporting software applications, but ERP links these applications and ensures their compatibility via common data storage.

For example, imagine that a customer contacts a company's salesperson to place an order. Accessing the ERP sales module, the salesperson obtains all necessary information, such as the customer's contact and billing data, product data, and the product's forecasted availability. The salesperson enters the order data in the ERP sales module, which stores the data in a central database that everyone in the company and other ERP modules can access. This update creates an automatic trigger for all of the other required processes in the value chain related to filling this order. That is, the

CHAPTER 5

sales data are updated and the product is taken out of inventory, the financial data are updated to reflect an accounts receivable entry and a customer invoice is generated, the paperwork required for logistics is created (e.g., packing slip), and if the salesperson is working on commission, her commission is updated with the value of the sale she just processed. Further, any of the company's employees can quickly obtain the status of the order at any time by accessing the ERP system. All of these actions are undertaken by the ERP system without any additional human intervention.

As this example illustrates, a benefit of an ERP system is to streamline business processes. Companies want to get orders to customers faster and at less cost, and also receive sales revenue quicker. ERP can support all areas of the value chain, both primary and supporting processes, helping to achieve efficiencies not possible with independent systems.

WHAT DO YOU THINK?

We often hear the term "enterprise-wide computing" used by IT professionals. Reflecting back on this chapter's discussion of ERP systems and integration technologies, consider the following questions:

1: Can you come up with a definition of what this term means to you?
2: What would the benefits be to an organization if it could actually achieve standard enterprise-wide computing?
3: Can you find any information on the Internet about vendors who offer products or services to organizations to address the challenges of enterprise-wide computing? What do their products and services claim to do for a business that uses them?

However, the primary disadvantage of ERP is that, like the organizations that they support, the ERP system can become incredibly complex and difficult to manage as it grows. ERP systems need to be customized for the specific business processes and rules that it is supporting. Sometimes this customization is extensive and businesses come to rely on ERP vendors and service providers, such as SAP, Oracle, and IBM, to develop and maintain their ERP installation. These arrangements require close relationships between the client and the service provider. It is important that businesses do not become overdependent on service providers and end up paying expensive fees for support. In these situations businesses can find themselves losing the cost savings they have achieved through efficiency.

Regardless of which method companies use, overcoming the IS integration challenge allows them to combine IT components as needed to further their goals. In the next section, we look at other popular business information systems that create value for the organizations that use them.

Quick Test

1. Which of the following is true concerning the IS integration challenge?
   a. IS integration is a natural process that requires no additional thought.
   b. IS integration does not come naturally as new systems are added to the enterprise and can be difficult to obtain.
   c. There are no available solutions to the IS integration challenge.
   d. Businesses tend to operate just fine with no integration between their IS.

2. Software that is designed with the purpose of linking applications that use dissimilar software or hardware platforms is known as _____.
   a. firmware
   b. groupware
   c. middleware
   d. productivity software

3. Which of the following is a proposed solution to the IS integration challenge?
   a. XJL
   b. connectware
   c. jointware
   d. Web services

Answers: 1. b; 2. c; 3. d

INFORMATION SYSTEMS THAT SUPPORT BUSINESS ACTIVITIES

In this section, we show how organizations can combine the core technology concepts that we discussed earlier in various ways to support their specific objectives. We review three common business IS:

- transaction processing systems
- functional information systems
- workflow management systems

PART 2

Please keep in mind, however, that these do not begin to cover all of the various IS that organizations use to support knowledge work and business processes.

TRANSACTION PROCESSING SYSTEMS

In Chapter 4 we discussed the idea of a business transaction and its importance to the core activities of an organization. Now we take a more technical perspective. We discuss how businesses design their IS to include **transaction processing systems (TPS)**. The TPS enables transaction activities and captures the key data created by the transaction.

From a technical standpoint, a transaction is a unit of work that has the following characteristics:

- *Atomicity*—A transaction must be unequivocally completed. If an error causes the transaction to fail, then the entire transaction to that point should be undone and the data reset to its previous state.
- *Consistency*—All unchanging properties of data must be preserved. This means that the data captured by the transaction must fit within the rules of data storage.
- *Isolation*—Each transaction should execute independently of other transactions that may occur at the same time on the system.
- *Durability*—These characteristics of a completed transaction should be permanent.

These characteristics, together known as **ACID,** allow organizations to create systems that can handle large numbers of simultaneous transactions. Defining transactions that have the ACID properties also helps organizations ensure that the activities of any one transaction all succeed or fail as a group. Why is this important? Think about how a bank relies on its ATM transactions. Say a customer decides to transfer $100.00 from his savings to his chequing account. This account-transfer transaction has two simple activities: (1) subtract $100.00 from the savings account, and (2) add $100.00 to the chequing account. Imagine the problems that would occur if the first activity succeeds but the second one fails. Now think about this problem multiplied by the bank's daily ATM transactions. You can see why a TPS must handle both of these activities together as a single transaction.

Figure 5.13 shows how a TPS brings together the common components of IT—data storage, data processing, data capture, and software. Processing in a TPS must control the flow of both the activities and data involved in the transaction. Depending on the configuration of the system and the network connections, the processing power that

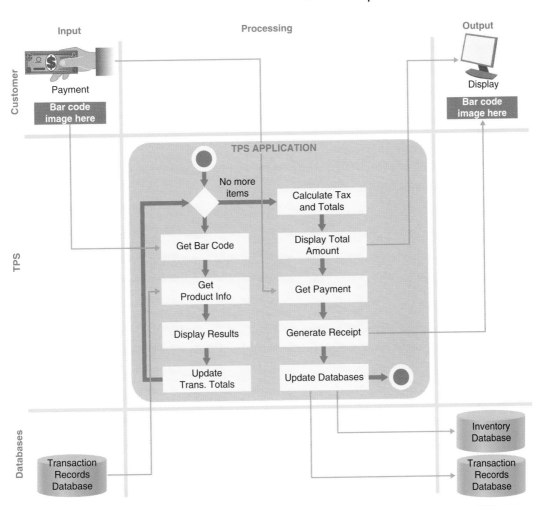

Figure 5.13 An Automated POS-TPS process brings together the common components of IT—data storage, data processing, data capture, and software—as it creates value for the organization.

handles the transaction can include PCs, servers, and/or mainframes. TPS software applications must incorporate the logic for controlling and enabling the transaction, the business rules of the organization that apply to the transaction, and necessary error handling logic.

Data storage, most often in the form of one or more databases, is very important as a source of input data and as storage for the captured data of a TPS. For example, most retail stores use a point-of-sale (POS) system to capture and store much of the data about their products. A bar code value, assigned as an ID for each product, serves as the primary key for accessing this data, such as the product name and price. However, as the CORE box "RFID and Privacy" discusses, some stores are now turning to a new technology, RFID, to identify their products.

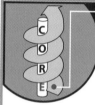

—Ethics

RFID and Privacy

Radio frequency identification (RFID) uses radio waves to automatically identify objects. The most common type of RFID stores a serial number on a microchip that is attached to an antenna. The antenna enables the chip to transmit the identification number to a reader. The reader converts the analog radio waves from the RFID tag into digital information. The ID number can then be matched against data stored in a database to obtain information, such as a product's name and price.

Because RFID tags are small and cheap, they may soon replace bar code technology for many applications. One advantage of RFID over bar codes is that it does not require "line-of-sight" scanning. For a bar code, the scanner uses a laser to read a printed label. To do this, the scanner must have an unobstructed "view" of the label. Since radio waves can pass through and around objects, a reader can read an RFID tag as long as it is in range. Another benefit is that an RFID tag can be read as soon as a tag is within range. This eliminates the need for a user to present the tag to the reader. Many expect RFID identification to be quicker and more accurate than other forms of product ID.

But, as with many new technologies, there is concern over the potential uses of RFID. Wal-Mart, a known leader in the use of IS for competitive advantage, is pushing the adoption of RFID by its suppliers. By requiring that products from suppliers have RFID tags, Wal-Mart is able to increase the efficiency of its warehouse and logistics processes. For suppliers, though, especially smaller ones, RFID can be costly to implement and will require them to transform many of their business processes. But since Wal-Mart has mandated the change, these suppliers have no choice but to follow or lose a lucrative customer.[9] Advocates of individual privacy worry that RFID could allow for the real-time tracking of customers. Privacy advocates caution that this could lead to abuses by RFID users who seek to collect data without the consumers' knowledge. For example, a clothing manufacturer might scan a theatre to measure the number of people in the audience wearing a particular brand. The data may then be used to make decisions about product promotions. While this may be innocent enough, the potential for abuse is there.

Web Resources

- The RFID Journal—http://www.rfidjournal.com/
- Privacy Rights Clearinghouse—http://www.privacyrights.org/
- Office of the Privacy Commissioner of Canada—http://www.privcom.gc.ca

Finally, a TPS uses network technologies to connect both its components as well as its system to the organization. The databases that the TPS accesses are usually stored on special database network servers. An important aspect of networks in a TPS is how the

9. David H. Williams, "The strategic implications of Wal-Mart's RFID mandate," *Directions Magazine*, July 29, 2004 http://www.directionsmag.com/article.php?article_id = 629&trv = 1. Retrieved January 6, 2007.

company uses the networks to update the central data stores of the organization with the new transaction data. Generally, firms do this either by batch or on-line transaction processing (OLTP).

With *batch transaction processing,* a local server first stores the transaction data captured at a location. Periodically, such as every night, the organization sends the collected data over a network to its central data stores as a group or *batch.* Batch processing is an older form of transaction processing. Less expensive than OLTP, batch processing is also useful when the actual processing time of a transaction is significant.

A downside of batch transaction processing is that organizational decision makers may not have the most recent data available. *On-line transaction processing* (*OLTP*) resolves this problem by processing and sending the data from each transaction as it captures the data. This type of processing generally requires a faster and more expensive network infrastructure than batch processing. Making the data available almost instantly to decision makers can result in significant benefits. However, systems capable of dynamic data processing also cost more money to build or buy and maintain.

FUNCTIONAL INFORMATION SYSTEMS

Traditionally, an organization divided its IS along lines that corresponded to its functional departments, such as operations, accounting, and marketing. Referred to as **functional information systems (FIS),** they focus on the activities of the functional department to improve its efficiency and effectiveness. For example, an accounting information system focuses on automating and informating accounting activities (see Table 5.6 for more detail).

FIS remain popular today. However, many companies now find that they need to integrate these systems with the rest of their organization by using middleware or turning to enterprise systems, such as ERP, that are integrated already. Functional information systems continue to be used in specialized areas like medicine (e.g., a patient information system) or for a specific purpose. You are familiar with an FIS at your university or college: the registration system.

WORKFLOW MANAGEMENT SYSTEMS

A **workflow** represents the steps, organizational resources, input and output data, and tools needed to complete a business process. By focusing on a business process from beginning to end, a **workflow management system (WMS)** (also referred to as **business process management** or **BPM**) supports activities that several departments of the organization may carry out.

CHAPTER

5

Table 5.6	Some Common Functional IS
System	**Description**
Accounting IS	• Typically dedicated to the reporting of a firm's financial health. • Relies on input from TPS since it must record all transaction data. • Provides both internal and external reports of a company's financial status.
Marketing IS	• Supports marketing research and decision making in developing and distributing products and services. • Input from TPS, strategic plans and corporate policies, and external sources. • Outputs include marketing research to support the four Ps of marketing: product development, pricing decisions, promotion, and product placement.
Human Resources IS	• Supports activities related to managing the employees of the organization. • Input from TPS, strategic plans and corporate policies, and external sources. • Supports human resources planning, recruiting, and hiring. Enables administration of salaries, benefits, and training.
Financial IS	• Provides financial information to the organization's financial managers. • Inputs include both internal items—TPS, financial objectives, and project needs—and external items—competitor and environmental data. • Generates both internal and external audits, supports management of funds.
Manufacturing IS	• Supports manufacturing processes and activities. • Input from TPS, strategic plans and corporate policies, and external sources. • Outputs used primarily for controlling processes: design and engineering, control of inventory, resource planning, and computer-aided manufacturing.

A WMS typically provides tools for modelling the steps of the process. The model shows the flow of work, along with the state of components. For example, Figure 5.14 shows an example workflow for a typical on-line product order. At each step in the workflow, information and documentation are needed and generated. However, workflow management is not just about how the documents and information flow through the process. A computer program manages the process itself, such as assigning the work and monitoring work progress.

A WMS often leads to several benefits. First, less misplaced or stalled work often occurs, which improves efficiency and quality. Second, managers can focus more time on business decisions rather than on tracking work. Third, because developing a WMS requires formal documentation of all procedures, more analysis and tighter control of the processes often result. This, in turn, leads to better work assignments—the best person for the job—and produces more efficient scheduling.

Workflow systems include tools and features that allow users to work with and manage the processes and the system itself. Administration and modelling tools provide a means for users to create and work with workflow models and definitions. Finally,

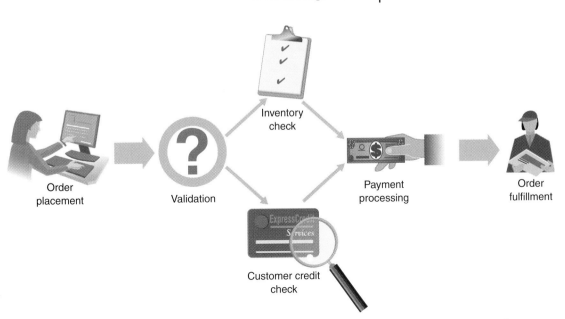

Figure 5.14 In a workflow management system (WMS), each step requires and generates information and documentation.

CHAPTER

5

particular workflow systems will generally not have all of the capabilities needed to support the business rules of the organization. However, the system can directly activate plug-in or custom-tailored tools to add capabilities to the system and the workflow client application manages the interactions between the system and added applications.

The IS that we have discussed in this section add value by enabling transactions and business processes and by capturing important data from these activities. They do this by gathering and storing data, and processing information. But IT systems can do more than that. Organizations can use IS to support decision making and problem solving. In the next section, we discuss an important class of IS for doing just that: business intelligence.

Quick Test

1. A _____ allows the data from a transaction to be processed and passed on immediately to organizational data storage.
   a. decision support system (DSS)
   b. functional information system (FIS)
   c. workflow management system (WMS)
   d. transaction processing system (TPS)

2. A _____ is an information system that an organization might use to support the activities of its marketing department.
   a. decision support system (DSS)
   b. functional information system (FIS)
   c. workflow management system (WMS)
   d. transaction processing system (TPS)

3. An IT system that automates and manages the steps in a business process is known as a _____.
   a. decision support system (DSS)
   b. functional information system (FIS)
   c. workflow management system (WMS)
   d. transaction processing system (TPS)

Answers: 1. d; 2. b; 3. c

BUSINESS INTELLIGENCE

Business intelligence (BI) is a process for gaining competitive advantage through the intelligent use of data and information in decision making. BI is, therefore, a key part of a corporate information strategy. It enables business leaders to make better decisions, which often translate into increased profitability.

USING IT TO SUPPORT BUSINESS INTELLIGENCE

To enable businesses to reach intelligent decisions, data and information must go through several stages. Table 5.7 lists the stages of business intelligence and how IT assists at every step. In the first stage, organizations get data, often from multiple sources. Then the data obtained generally need further analysis. Analysis may include

Table 5.7	The Stages of Business Intelligence
Stage	**Description**
1. Data sourcing	Mining data and information from text documents, databases, images, media files, and web pages.
2. Data analysis	Producing useful knowledge from the collected data and information, using tools such as data mining and text/image analysis techniques.
3. Situation awareness	Culling out and relating the useful facts and knowledge, while filtering out irrelevant data.
4. Risk assessment	Identifying decision options and evaluating them based on expectations of risk and reward.
5. Decision support	Using interactive software tools to identify and select intelligent decisions and strategies.

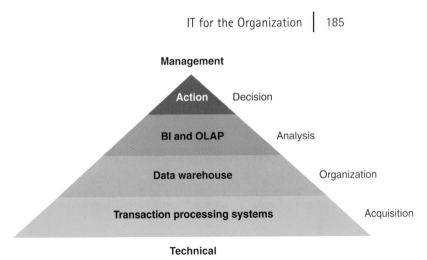

Figure 5.15 The Business Intelligence Pyramid.

looking for trends, combining and summarizing data from different sources, or filling in gaps by predicting missing information. Next, to ensure relevant analysis, knowledge-enabled professionals must match key items to information needs and filter out irrelevant items. With relevant data in hand, an organization can then evaluate plausible decision or action options. To do this, it may assess risks, compare costs and benefits, and weigh one option against another.

Figure 5.15 presents a model of how IT supports these business intelligence stages. The TPS at the base of the pyramid represent the primary source of data from business operations. Businesses store and organize the data in databases and, at times, data warehouses. Specialized BI and On-line Analytic Processing (OLAP) systems can help analyze, synthesize, and create knowledge. At the top of the figure, management uses the created knowledge to guide their actions and decision making. The BI systems in the third level of the pyramid, **decision support systems (DSS),** allow rapid and creative knowledge creation by decision makers.

WHAT DO YOU THINK?

Imagine that you were the CEO of a large global retailer. Recently, your CIO approached you to ask about the requirements for a new business intelligence system that is going to replace an aging MIS application. Answer these questions that you are asked during this meeting:

1: What kinds of information about our business would you like to see on a daily, weekly, or monthly basis?
2: How important is it to the kinds of decisions you normally make that this information is accurate and up to date? Does it have to be accurate by the minute, hour, or day, and why?
3: How would you like to have access to this information? Where and why?

DECISION SUPPORT SYSTEMS

DSS help businesses use communications technologies, data organization and access, knowledge, and models to perform decision-making activities. There are five types of DSS, shown in Table 5.8, each of which has a specific decision-making focus. Although businesses rely on all these types of DSS, model-driven DSS continue to make the most significant contribution to decision making.

Model-driven DSS provide tools that enable analysts to create and work with models, including the following:

- *Financial models,* which use financial mathematical models and financial data to support financial decision making.
- *Statistical models,* which use statistics and probability to describe or to forecast possible scenarios.
- *Optimization models,* which incorporate relatively certain data into a mathematical model of a situation. Solving the model helps to find the "best" solution.
- *Simulation modelling,* which is a technique for conducting experiments that test possible outcomes resulting from a quantitative model of a system.

Model-driven DSS use data and parameters to aid decision makers in analyzing a situation, but they are not usually data intensive. Instead, these systems often include smaller databases, with data that may be culled from the larger data stores of the organization. They often incorporate innovative user interfaces that provide analysts with graphical views of their models. Organizations often combine model-driven DSS with other types of DSS to form hybrid systems.

Table 5.8	Types of DSS	
Type of DSS	**Description**	**Examples**
Communications-driven DSS	Focuses on communications, collaboration, and shared decision making	Conferencing tools, on-line bulletin boards and chat facilities, e-mail, and meeting support applications
Data-driven DSS	Emphasizes access to and manipulation of internal company data and sometimes external data	Executive information systems (EIS), geographic information systems (GIS), and OLAP-enabled data warehouses
Document-driven DSS	Focuses on retrieval and management of unstructured documents	Document management systems (DMS); search services; tools for working with oral, written, and video documents
Knowledge-driven DSS	Provides special problem-solving tools that aid decision making by suggesting or recommending actions to users	Expert systems (ES), artificial intelligence applications, data mining tools
Model-driven DSS	Emphasizes access to and manipulation of a model	Financial, statistical, optimization, and simulation models

Quick Test

1. The process of gaining competitive advantage through the intelligent use of data and information in decision making is called _____.
   a. automating
   b. business intelligence
   c. value chaining
   d. modelling

2. _____ are interactive computer systems that support the decision and analysis stages of business intelligence.
   a. Decision support systems
   b. Groupware
   c. Transaction processing systems
   d. Workflow management systems

3. Which of the following is NOT a type of decision support system?
   a. document-driven DSS
   b. knowledge-driven DSS
   c. data-driven DSS
   d. information-driven DSS

Answers: 1. b; 2. a; 3. d

 STUDENT RETURN ON INVESTMENT SUMMARY

1. How do organizations use processors, networks, software, and storage?

These technologies enable the core IT competencies that are part of all organizational systems, namely data processing, data storage, data transfer, and the instructions that make these work. Computers with several levels of processing power are available for just about any processing need. Organizations use databases, data warehouses, and data mining tools to handle the vast data storage needs of the modern organization. Networks of connected computers support the core function of data transfer by supporting communication, providing a platform for collaboration, and allowing sharing of resources. Software at the organizational level focuses on handling the increased needs of multiple users.

2. What are the key concepts of data organization for an IS?

Organizations often store data in a database. The set of rules and concepts that describe entities and their relationships in a database is known as the data model. Relational databases store information about entities and relationships between those entities. Relational databases organize data in tables that consist of records (rows) and fields (columns). Each record provides data about a specific instance of an entity. A field value is a specific data item that is part of the record. Relationships are modelled using special fields known as primary and foreign keys. Each primary key value must be unique in the table, while a foreign key is a field in one table that is used to reference records in another table. Structured Query Language (SQL) provides a standard language that organizations can use to access and manipulate data in a relational database.

3. In what ways can organizations use IT to store and share data, information, and knowledge?

Databases and data warehouses are the primary systems in use to organize and store large amounts of organizational data. Management information systems (MIS) and document management systems (DMS) are two of several systems geared toward automating business reporting and the dissemination of information. Knowledge management (KM) systems provide tools for working with both tacit and explicit knowledge.

4. What is the software integration challenge, and how are organizations solving it?

The challenge of combining all of the disparate technologies into a single, overall system is known as the software integration challenge. This complex problem is one of the main concerns of the IS staff in modern companies. The software integration challenge increases as an organization grows and as it works with more and more business partners. Attempts to deal with this problem include middleware, ERP systems, and Web services.

5. How do organizations use IT to support transactions and business processes?

Transaction processing systems (TPS) enable transaction activities and capture the key data created by the transactions. A TPS can handle thousands of simultaneous users working independently on the same set of data safely and consistently. On-line transaction processing (OLTP) allows the data from each transaction to be processed and passed on to be used by the organization as they are captured. Functional information systems (FIS) are designed with a focus on the activities of the functional department, such as the accounting department, to improve its efficiency and effectiveness. A type of IS that corresponds more closely with the value chain model of an organization are workflow management systems (WMS), also referred to as business process management (BPM). A workflow represents the steps, organizational resources, input and output data, and tools needed to complete a business process.

6. How does business intelligence enhance organizational decision making?

Business intelligence (BI) is a process for gaining competitive advantage through the intelligent use of data and information in decision making. The goal of BI is to increase profitability by enabling business leaders to make better decisions. Decision support systems (DSS) provide computer-based tools designed to support business intelligence. There are five main categories of DSS: communications-driven, data-driven, document-driven, knowledge-driven, and model-driven.

KNOWLEDGE SPEAK

REVIEW QUESTIONS

Multiple-choice questions

1. Which category of the computer hierarchy includes computers that use high-speed processing chips and a large amount of memory to carry out organizational processing?

   a.   embedded processors
   b.   mainframes
   c.   personal computers
   d.   servers
   e.   supercomputers

2. The concept of _____ means that if an error causes the transaction to fail, then the entire transaction to that point should be undone and the data reset to its previous state.

   a.   acidity
   b.   atomicity
   c.   consistency
   d.   durability
   e.   isolation

3. Which of the following is a technique for conducting experiments that test possible outcomes resulting from a quantitative model of a system?

   a.   financial modelling
   b.   optimization modelling
   c.   simulation modelling
   d.   statistical modelling

4. An MIS system generates a(n) _____ report after a specific time period has passed.

   a.   demand
   b.   exception
   c.   knowledge
   d.   periodic

Fill-in-the-blank questions

5. Many appliances and products now include _____ that provide low-scale processing power.

6. A(n) _____ is a collection of interrelated data that are stored in files and organized in a way so that computer programs can quickly and easily access specific pieces of data.

7. A(n) _____ key is a field in a relational database table that is used to reference a record in another table and thus represents a relationship between the two tables.

8. A(n) _____ system is a specific type of TPS that enables traditional sales transactions.

CHAPTER
5

True–false questions

9. An intranet is a collection of public computer networks that uses http and www protocols.

10. There are virtually no differences between software at the individual level and software used by organizations.

11. A primary key is a field in a relational database table that must store a unique value for each and every record in the table.

12. A workflow represents the steps, organizational resources, input and output data, and tools needed to complete a business process.

Matching questions

Choose the BEST answer from Column B for each item in Column A.

Column A

13. Communications-driven DSS

14. Data-driven DSS

15. Document-driven DSS

16. Model-driven DSS

Column B

a. Emphasizes access to and manipulation of a model.

b. Emphasizes access to and manipulation of internal company data and sometimes external data.

c. Emphasizes communications, collaboration, and shared decision making.

d. Focuses on retrieval and management of unstructured documents.

e. Provides special problem-solving tools that aid decision making by suggesting or recommending actions to users.

Short-answer questions

17. Discuss why database systems are an improvement over file management systems.

18. Describe the different technologies that are being developed and used to deal with the software integration challenge.

Discussion/Essay questions

19. From an individual department's viewpoint, do you think functional information systems (FIS) provide more useful information than workflow management systems (WMS)? Why or why not?

20. Describe how your local government, whether at the city or county level, might use groupware to function more productively.

TEAM ACTIVITY

Search the Web or ask your instructor for a collaborative software (groupware) package to try out. Many vendors offer demonstration software for short-term use. Use the software to support one of your team projects for this or another course. After the project is over, write a short evaluation of the software. Discuss the features of the software that you found useful and those that you did not. What did you like about the software? What would you improve? Did the team benefit from using the software?

Possible sources:

Groove Virtual Office—http://www.groove.net/home/

phpGroupWare—http://www.phpgroupware.org/

Usability First—http://www.usabilityfirst.com/groupware/

SOFTWARE APPLICATION EXERCISES

1. Internet

Have a look at your university or college's website. Briefly answer the following questions: Is this an intranet? Explain why or why not. If it is not an intranet, how would you classify it? What would the developers of the site need to do to change it into an intranet? Ask a faculty or staff member if there are other Web-based resources at your institution that might qualify to be an intranet. If so, how do these resources compare with the main site?

2. Presentation

Assume that your boss asks you to present one of the technologies in this chapter to the CEO. Your presentation should provide an overview of the technology; that is, describing what it is and how the organization could use it. Include both the benefits and risks of using the technology, potential vendors, and one or two examples of how others have used the technology. Incorporate graphics as needed. Your presentation should be visually appealing as well as professional.

3. Word Processing

Business letters often follow a consistent format. While they can vary, most contain the following elements:

Date: Indicates when you wrote the letter. Write out the month, day, and year two inches from the top of the page and left-justify it.

Sender's address: Optional. If you include it, place the address one line below the date. Include only the street address, city, and postal code. Your name is in the closing and is not needed here.

Inside address: This is the recipient's address. It begins one line below the sender's address or one inch below the date. Left-justify it.

Salutation: It's best to use the person's title and full name, followed by a colon. If you don't know the recipient's name, use a salutation such as "To Whom It May Concern."

Body: Single-space and left-justify each paragraph within the body of the letter. Be concise. In the first paragraph, consider a friendly opening and then a statement of the main point. In the next few paragraphs, continue justification with background information and supporting details. The closing paragraph should restate the purpose of the letter and, in some cases, request some type of action.

Closing: Begin one line after the last paragraph of the body. Capitalize the first word only (e.g., Thank you) and leave four lines between the closing and your name for a signature. For this letter, write as an IS manager at your organization. You are experiencing problems with a software application that you recently purchased. Write a letter to the vendor to complain about the problem and to request some form of action.

4. Spreadsheet

Many companies have a lot of money tied up in physical assets such as machinery and IT hardware. To keep up with these physical assets and their value, companies typically maintain an equipment inventory. Create a spreadsheet to track the equipment inventory for a company. For each item, record or calculate values related to the physical condition and the financial status of the item as follows:

Physical condition: Provide columns to record an asset or serial number, an item description, a location, a physical condition, the name of the vendor, and the years of service left.

Financial status: Provide columns to record the initial value, a down payment, a date purchased or leased, a loan term in years, a loan rate, a monthly payment, monthly operating costs, total monthly cost, expected value at end of loan term, annual straight-line depreciation, monthly straight-line depreciation, and a current value. You should calculate some of these values as follows:

- *Monthly payment*—if an initial payment is entered and it is not equal to the down payment, use an appropriate function to calculate this value.
- *Total monthly cost*—monthly payment + monthly operating cost
- *Annual straight-line depreciation*—use an appropriate function and appropriate parameters to calculate this value. If you are unfamiliar with depreciation, search the Web for more information about it.
- *Monthly straight-line depreciation*—annual straight-line depreciation ÷ 12.
- *Current value*—use an appropriate formula to subtract the current depreciation amount from the initial value of the item. (*Hint:* use the now() function in your formula. This one is challenging.)

5. Database

Create a database to track your organization's assets. For each asset, you will need to include the following: the asset ID, description, category, and status; the employee to whom the asset is assigned; the department to which the asset is assigned; the vendor that provided the asset; the make and model of the asset; the date acquired; purchase price; and the date of the next scheduled maintenance. For each employee, store the following data: employee ID, first and last name, title, work phone number, and e-mail address. Store the following for each department: department ID and name. For each vendor, store the following data: name of company, first and last name of company contact, contact's title, and contact's phone number.

6. Advanced Challenge

Discuss how an intranet could allow you and your colleagues in a business to access inventory data and correspond with vendors. Include in your discussion how your team could use the intranet to share the inventory information found in spreadsheets and databases. Also include a discussion of how you could jointly work on and solve inventory problems using groupware. Capture your discussion in a business letter to your CEO, informing her or him of the value and challenges created by implementing a corporate intranet.

ON-LINE RESOURCES

Companion Website

- Take interactive practice quizzes to assess your knowledge and help you study in a dynamic way.
- Review PowerPoint lecture slides.
- Get help and sample solutions to end-of-chapter software application exercises.

Additional Resources Available Only on WileyPLUS

- Take the interactive Quick Test to check your understanding of the chapter material and get immediate feedback on your responses.
- Review and study with downloadable Audio Lecture MP3 files.
- Check your understanding of the key vocabulary in the chapter with Knowledge Speak Interactive Flash Cards.
- Link directly to websites recommended in the CORE boxes.

CHAPTER
5

CASE STUDY: DELL INC.

When it comes to purchasing new computers, for many individuals and corporations the top choice in this market has been Dell. What makes this somewhat surprising, considering the salesperson assistance generally required for these purchases, is that Dell sells only directly to its customers, without any retail stores. Dell initially did this by using telephone sales, but has aggressively moved into e-commerce as a way of connecting with its customers. Total 2003 on-line sales were over $50 million *per day*, resulting from more than 7,000 visits to its website each *minute* of the day.

The Dell website (www.dell.com) has made the direct sales model the heart of its approach to e-commerce. By providing greater convenience and efficiency to its customers, the site simplifies the process of selecting and purchasing a computer. Dell custom builds every computer so that customers get exactly what they want and the latest in technology. Dell also improved its support services by making its website work as a front end to its internal databases so that its customers and

suppliers can see the same support information it uses internally.

Dell has always sought efficiency in its operations, as evidenced by the fact that its expenses dropped to an almost unheard of 9.9% of net revenue in 2003. With this level of efficiency, each Dell employee is generating over $1 million in revenue each year—three times the level of their competitors. This search for efficiency is also demonstrated by its move to the use of radio frequency identification (RFID) chips that it attaches to parts. Using RFID allows Dell to convert on-line orders into radio signals that instruct automatic parts-picking machines to find the parts needed for each PC. These same radio signals transmit assembly blueprints to workers and track the shipping of the finished product, enabling Dell managers to watch the entire process on-line.

Recently, Dell has moved beyond personal computers by offering printers, personal digital assistants (PDAs), and plasma screen televisions. While it does not manufacture all of these products itself, Dell uses its e-commerce engine to sell these products in an innovative way. For example, if you have a Dell printer and it is close to running out of ink, a message will appear on your computer screen. If you agree to order a new ink cartridge, the e-commerce engine will automatically contact the Dell website and arrange to ship an ink cartridge overnight to your home or office. Compare this with the problems of determining which type of ink cartridge you need, finding a retail outlet that carries it, and then scheduling a trip to the store to purchase the cartridge.[10]

Case Questions

1. How does Dell use IT to differentiate itself from its primary competitor in terms of its sales and distribution of its products?
2. Discuss ways in which Dell is using its on-line capabilities to improve both sales and service.
3. Do you think that Dell will be successful in its move into the consumer electronics marketplace? Why or why not?

Integrative Application Case: Campuspad.ca

You and Sarah have now completed your initial business plan, and things are starting to come together. While you were doing this planning, it became evident that as your business grew, managing data flows was going to be critical to your success. Listings, members' information, transactional data, accounting data—there was so much to think about!

At the coffee shop today, the question of "device integration" came up. Last weekend during a party, when discussing your business idea with your potential customers, a student had said that what he really wanted was to get beeped or called every time a new listing came up that met his requirements. This made you both realize that you hadn't yet thought about how users might need to link to your system if they weren't at their computers. What other technologies do you need to support to make campuspad.ca work for users? What devices will they expect to be able to integrate with your system, and what information and in what forms needs to be available to them on those devices? This initiated a whole new set of analyses and questions, including the following critical ones.

Guiding Case Questions

1. Identify possible devices other than computers that your users might own or carry.
2. How could they be integrated into your site design?
3. What implications does this have for data flows, data integrity, and data security?
4. With your planning having progressed this far, have you thought enough about data types and flows to be able to figure out how the back end of your system might work?

Your Task

Pretend that campuspad.ca is going to be up and running within the next 30 days. The programmers are now at the point where they are getting ready to tackle issues around data flows, integrity, and security. The starting point for this was a "data dictionary" that would, at a high level, specify all the information that the system either needed to or intended to collect and store to support its business model. To help you along, the programmers had provided a template (provided

10. "e.biz 25," *Newsweek*, September 25, 2003, pp. 116–126. Todd Weiss, "Dell posts record revenue of $11.5B for Q4 2004," *Computerworld*, February 12, 2004.

on WileyPLUS for your use). They had asked you to map out all major transactional processes on the site (generic examples might include how new users sign up, how users change/edit/delete their information, how to search listings, how to post a new listing, how to update a listing, how to connect to sellers, etc.). These flow from your initial site design and business plan, of course. Once you have mapped out the process (with inputs, outputs, and associated data flows), you should be able to try filling in the data dictionary template so the programmers can stay on track for the launch of your new business! Do the best you can with the information that you have at your disposal.

WHAT WE WILL COVER

- The "Big Four" IS Development Questions
- The Stages and Activities of the System Development Life Cycle (SDLC)
- IS Development Teams
- Standard IS Methodology
- Managing an IS Project
- IS Development Tools

C	**Connectivity**	Software as an Outsourced Service
O	**On-line Security**	Developing Secure Applications from the Start
R	**Relationships**	Why Good People Can Make Bad Teams
E	**Ethics**	Ethical Project Management

Creating IS Solutions

Through your investment of time in reading and thinking about this chapter, your return, or created value, is gaining knowledge. Use the following questions as a study guide.

1. What major decisions do organizations make in obtaining an IS?
2. What important activities must an organization consider within each of the seven stages of the system development life cycle?
3. What considerations are important when creating an IS project team?
4. What methods do organizations use to ensure that they obtain the best IS to help meet their goals?
5. How do organizations provide effective and efficient management of IS projects?
6. What IT tools do many organizations rely on to obtain an IS that best meets their objectives?

PART

2

THE VOICE OF EXPERIENCE
Roshni Damani, Concordia University

Roshni Damani graduated with a degree in Management Information Systems in 2005 and now works in project management and systems analysis at Johnson & Johnson Inc. She is involved in their Information Management Leadership Development program, which rotates employees through different J&J operating companies, giving them the opportunity to learn about the impact of IS on the company as a whole.

What do you do in your current position? I am currently working in the consumer manufacturing group overseeing a project to implement an electronic records management solution. I'm working with our different business partners to figure out what their requirements are and make sure that everything is compliant with our internal records management regulations. I am also dealing with partners based in the U.S. who have already rolled out a solution in order to see what we can leverage. Once the system is completed, I will be involved with testing the software and training people on how to use it.

What do you consider to be important career skills? Number one is project management. That is, scheduling and dealing with time and resource constraints. Other skills I have found helpful are analytical skills, the ability to think logically, and having some basic knowledge of databases and programming languages. Basic knowledge of programming, the programming process, and the logic behind the system is sometimes crucial to understanding how the system will integrate with everything else. It also helps me to explain how the technology we're trying to put in place will help people in their day-to-day activities. Finally, collaborative skills are essential to succeeding in the workplace. You must be able to maintain strong relationships and partnerships within the business in order to understand the priorities of your business partners, and to help them achieve business goals.

How do you use IT? I create a lot of PowerPoint presentations in my role and e-mail communication is huge. At Johnson & Johnson, everything is on-line. Each oper-ating company has its own intranet portal that we have access to. When I was working in the medical products division, we wanted to implement a simple tool to track employee time. I was able to use the portals to see how other J&J companies were tracking time and decide whether we could leverage one of their systems, as opposed to developing something on our own.

Can you describe an example of how you have used IT to improve business operations? I recently worked on an on-line project management system. Johnson & Johnson has a number of consumer product websites and e-mail campaigns targeted to specific subscribers. There are a lot of different parties working on these campaigns—the developers creating it, the agencies that would actually deploy and send out the e-mails, brand management who came up with the concept, and the legal and regulatory groups that approve the campaign. Because there are so many players and so many steps, things were getting repeated and no one could clearly see what was going on. We used data flow diagrams and process mapping to identify who needed to be involved at what stage, and then applied this business logic to the on-line system. Prior to the project, more than half the campaigns were late; toward the end of the project, approximately 80 percent were on target.

Have you got any "on the job" advice for students seeking a career in IT or business? Teamwork and project-based work is everything when you get into the working environment. If you can communicate well and maintain a good rapport with your team members, you're on the right path. Also, every position is going to require some kind of understanding of IT, therefore the easier it comes to you, the more beneficial it will be for you in the long run.

Roshni is applying her knowledge of IS within business units to manage projects that create business value. She is using her knowledge of project management, the system development lifecycle, and modelling tools, which we discuss in this chapter, to help her succeed in this role.

Consider the following examples of successful information systems used in real companies:

• Barrett Steel Buildings of Great Britain is a leading structural steelwork contractor. A top 10 firm in its sector, Barrett was one of the first to develop a website to market its services. The website project resulted in the creation of an internal software development unit. The unit recently created a suite of programs called Fox, which includes FoxContact, a "tracker" program that maintains and updates information held in Barrett's accounting and MIS system, and FoxQuote, an estimating/quotation preparation application that uses data derived from 3D-model views.[1]

- A collection of three Toronto, Ontario, hospitals, the University Health Network (UHN), created an information system to streamline the delivery of medication to patients. Prior to the implementation of the Medication Order Entry and Administration Record System (MOE/MAR), patients did not receive their medication until forms were manually filled in, entered into a records system, and signed off by doctors, nurses, and pharmacists. With the improved ability to deliver medication to patients, UHN has enhanced patient care and increased the efficiency of caregivers. As an additional benefit, physicians, nurses, and pharmacists were brought together to discuss processes and policies, which resulted in needed organizational change.[2]

- The Ontario Ministry of Government Services had a collection of websites that were not meeting the needs of Ontarians. With the implementation of ServiceOntario, a new interactive website, the government reaches the public through the Internet, public kiosks, and access terminals and provides a variety of services including drivers' licence renewal and applying for a business licence. This implementation improved service substantially by allowing many transactions to occur on-line at any time, and helped to streamline operations.[3]

- 3L Filters of Cambridge, Ontario, manufactures custom pressure filtration vessels for global clients in the nuclear energy industry. 3L Filters faced the challenge of responding to clients' requests for quotations from its engineering department. As its products are custom made, an engineer would spend a significant amount of time analyzing the client needs and then preparing a quote. In 2005, 3L Filters developed and implemented a Web-based enterprise resource automation application that enables non-technical salespeople to design, price, and present engineering drawings for pressure vessels in just minutes—without engineering assistance. This increased the efficiency of the engineering department and boosted profits.[4]

1. In-house software development and integration at Barrett Steel Buildings Limited, http://www.cica.org.uk/integration-web/(2003).
2. University Health Network Medication Order Entry and Administration Record System, 2005 C.I.P.A Winner http://www.cipa.com/award_winners/winners_05/UHN.html, Retrieved August 24, 2006
3. ServiceOntario, ServiceOntario website, 2005 C.I.P.A winner. http://www.cipa.com/award_winners/winners_05/ServiceOntario.html; retrieved August 24, 2006.
4. 3L Filters Ltd. Automated Technical Quotation System 2005 C.I.P.A. winner, http://www.cipa.com/award_winners/winners_05/3L-Filters.html, retrieved August 24, 2006

PART

2

What do these examples all have in common? These information systems all created business value and helped to provide these organizations with a competitive advantage. So, what steps did they take to ensure that these systems matched their needs and were successfully implemented?

In this chapter, we provide the answers to these and other important questions that any knowledge-enabled professional in any business should be asking about their IT systems. So, let's turn our attention to the big four questions that many organizations face when considering the performance of their information systems.

THE "BIG FOUR" IS DEVELOPMENT QUESTIONS

In order to support a complex organization, employees often need complex information systems. And the more complex a system, the more difficult it can be to obtain and manage. Figure 6.1 shows some of the common activities that occur when a business seeks to install an IS. The small diamonds in this figure represent the major questions usually faced by decision makers. We will discuss each of these next in the context of four critical questions an organization needs to address before implementing a new IS for itself.

IS THERE A NEED FOR AN IS?

As we discussed in Chapters 4 and 5, organizations can improve their business processes by automating, informing, and transforming (to seek competitive advantage or out of competitive necessity). They also look for ways an IS can add value to their products and services. When they recognize that an IS can help them exploit an opportunity or solve a problem, the process of determining the best IS for their needs begins. At this point, an organization enters the first phase of the project, which is often known as *inception*, but can also be called the concept or idea phase, or proposal. During inception, an organization needs to determine whether or not the project has a reasonable chance of success. To answer this question, an organization often performs a feasibility study or produces a concept paper that outlines, at a high level, what the IS is going to accomplish and how.

IS THE PROJECT FEASIBLE?

The **feasibility study** is a detailed investigation and analysis of a proposed development project, to determine whether it is technically and economically possible. A project is technically feasible if

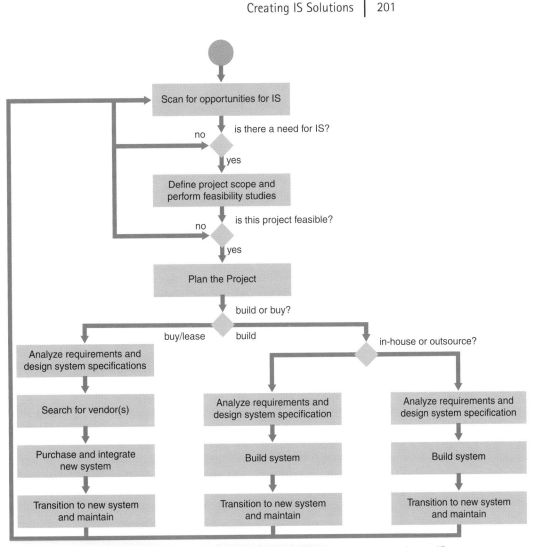

Figure 6.1 The common activities that occur when a business seeks to obtain an IS.

CHAPTER

6

the technology is available (or can be created—although this is a riskier proposition, as we will see below) to solve the IS problem. The study must conclude that the company is technically capable of acquiring and using the required technology. An organization can determine *technical feasibility* by examining potential solutions and evaluating these solutions based on its capabilities and the capabilities of any technology partners it may choose to work with.

A project is *financially feasible* if the company is able to pay for the project, and the project represents a good use of financial resources. To determine financial feasibility, an organization must show that it can afford to build or buy an information system and that the IS will financially benefit the organization. To do this, organizations often use several popular financial measures, such as return on investment (ROI), net present value (NPV), internal rate of return (IRR), and payback period. Other business texts discuss these in more detail and you may already be familiar with these measures from other courses. IS projects can be very costly to implement and these financial measures can be important in justifying their expense. For example, when a company is proposing to implement an ERP system (which can cost hundreds of thousands or millions of dollars), it will want to use these measures to estimate when it will see the benefits of implementing the system (payback period) and how much benefit it can expect (ROI, NPV, IRR).

The difficulty in calculating the financial measures is in obtaining the exhaustive list of all costs and benefits, and then placing a monetary value on each of them. Some costs and benefits are *tangible*, which means that a value can be easy to apply, such as the salary of software developers. Other costs and benefits are *intangible*, meaning they are difficult to measure in monetary terms. Sometimes a company will undertake an IS project for either offensive or defensive strategic purposes that are hard to justify on a purely economic basis.

For example, an intangible benefit of a cosmetics company's website might be the goodwill obtained after customers read about the no-animal testing of its products. How would the company measure this goodwill amount? As a result, due to the many intangibles that an organization must often consider in a major IS development project, the financial measures are, at best, good guesses of the project's final costs and benefits and some of the decision making around IS investments will still be based on the judgement and intuition of executives and managers.

Figure 6.2 shows example calculations for an IS project. You can see that the company is not expecting payback on the investment for either project for three years and that it is estimating that the returns on investment (ROI, IRR, and NPV) are greater for Project 2. In this spreadsheet analysis, the Project 1 software has a higher initial cost than Project 2 but a lower ongoing maintenance cost. If all other assumptions are the same, will an organization select Project 2? Not necessarily; financial feasibility and justification are just one piece of the IS development puzzle. Perhaps there is a technical, strategic, or other reason to prefer Project 1. Perhaps the organization is more confident in the maintenance cost estimates provided in Project 1 or is more comfortable working with the provider of the Project 1 software. Like any major decision, the financial context is only one element of the final business decision.

Assumptions		
Software Price		$1,800,000
Maintenance Costs (per year)		$75,000
Increase in Customer Revenues (per year)		10%
Decrease in Overall Marketing Costs (per year)		2%
Number of Customers (in Year 1)		80,000
Increase of Customer (per year)		5%
Average Revenue per Customer (no software)		
	Year 1	$75
	Year 2	$100
	Year 3	$125
Overall Marketing Costs (no software)		$2,000,000
Discount Rate		10%

Cash-Flows (in Dollars)	Software Project					Metrics
Year	0	1	2	3	Sum	
Costs						
Purchase of Software	($1,800,000)					
Software Maintenance		($75,000)	($75,000)	($75,000)		
Revenues						
Decrease in Marketing Expenditures		$40,000	$40,000	$40,000		
Additional Revenues by using Software		$600,000	$840,000	$1,050,000		
Number of Customers		$80,000	84,000	84,000		
Additional Revenue per Customer		$7.50	$10.00	$12.50		
Total Yearly Expenditures	($1,800,000)	($75,000)	($75,000)	($75,000)		IRR
Total Yearly Revenues	$0	$640,000	$880,000	$1,090,000		14.00%
Net Cash Flow	($1,800,000)	$565,000	$805,000	$1,015,000		
Discount Factor	1.00	0.91	0.83	0.75		
Discounted Costs	($1,800,000)	($68,182)	($61,983)	($56,349)	($1,986,514)	NPV
Discounted Benefits	$0	$581,818	$727,273	$818,933	$2,128,024	$141,510
Present Value for Period	($1,800,000)	$513,636	$665,289	$762,585	$141,510	
Cumulative Discounted Values	($1,800,000)	($1,286,364)	($621,074)	$141,510		ROI
				Payback Period		7.12%

Figure 6.2 Decision makers often use a spreadsheet, such as that shown here, to calculate financial feasibility metrics.

BUILD OR BUY/LEASE?

An organization usually chooses one of three primary options for obtaining an IS: (1) buying, (2) leasing, or (3) building. To select which option is best in any given set of circumstances, the organization needs to examine its requirements and the advantages and disadvantages of each option. Building a new system from scratch often ensures the best matching of an IS with an organization's requirements. It is also the best option for obtaining a sustainable competitive advantage because the system's capabilities are not easily copied by competitors if they are custom built. However, building a complete IS can be a long and costly process. When time and cost have greater importance than competitive advantage or customization, a firm often pursues buying or leasing.

Obviously, if there is a time-to-market factor in our decision; that is, unless we get to market fast, we are going to lose the opportunity. This may be the most important factor in any decision about buying or building a new system. CIOs today must deliver better systems faster than ever before to support their organization's competitive position, as shown in Figure 6.3.

CHAPTER 6

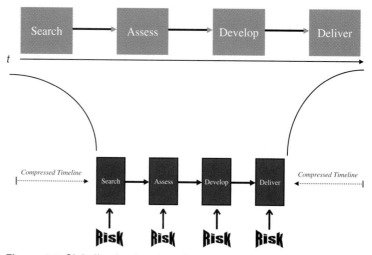

Figure 6.3 Globalization has forced organizations to speed up their processes, including systems development cycles, in order become or remain competitive. However, with increased speed comes increased risk.

When buying an existing system, an organization may still need to make adjustments, particularly by compromising its ultimate list of preferred requirements with the actual capabilities of the existing system. However, this option saves time and cost over building a new system. For some systems, like a customer service system, it may be possible to lease a system. This often involves a "pay as you go" approach based on transaction volumes or usage, or it can involve renting access to an application on a renewable monthly or yearly basis. In addition to lower development costs and time savings the major advantage with leasing a system is that the vendor is responsible for maintaining and updating it. Table 6.1 provides a more complete listing of the advantages and disadvantages of the three options.

Table 6.1	Buying, Leasing, or Building	
Development Choice	**Advantages**	**Disadvantages**
Buying	Generally faster and less costly than building entire system from scratch.	Little or no competitive advantage. May need to compromise on some features. Dependent on vendor for product updates.
Leasing	Lowest cost and fastest to put in place. Vendors are in charge of maintenance and updates. Does not require an in-house IS staff.	No competitive advantage. No control over system features. Dependence on vendor for entire system. Can get locked into an undesirable contract.
Building	Most likely to provide a competitive advantage. Retain complete control over system. Customization of system.	Longest time and highest cost to put in place. Requires IS staff with time and development knowledge.

IN-HOUSE OR OUTSOURCE?

If an organization chooses to build an entirely new system, the next big question is whether or not to use its own staff (**in-house development**) or hire another company (**outsource**), such as IBM, Accenture, or EDS, to build all or part of it. (When the outsourcing company is located primarily in a foreign country, the practice is known as *offshoring*.) An interesting offshoot of outsourcing is software as a service, as the CORE box "Software as an Outsourced Service" discusses. You should notice that providing software as a service is similar to leasing an IS. The primary difference is that with leasing an entire IS may be provided, while software as a service may be used to acquire components of a larger IS.

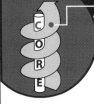

Connectivity

Software as an Outsourced Service

What if we stop thinking of software as a product and start thinking of the actions of software as a service? This is the realm of application service providers (ASP).

An ASP (pronounced ay-ess-pea) is an on-line technology company that develops and delivers software tools on the Internet. Payment for the service is often based on fees or subscriptions. And if you take a quick look on the Web, you will find many examples of ASPs. For instance, ASPNews.com has a directory of more than 1,800 companies that provide ASP services, such as BrightSuite's Web-based Groupware, Intranet, and Team Collaboration application. Further, services such as Hotmail or Google Maps are also considered to be ASPs. Many of these ASPs are now marketing their wares as software on demand.

ASPs provide several major advantages that are leading to their increasing popularity. When an organization uses an ASP, an external company builds and operates the system. This means that the organization does not need to acquire its own technical resources or hire knowledge-enabled professionals with technical expertise. Since the ASP is the primary service of the provider, it also bears the burden of keeping it up to date to provide it with a competitive advantage over other ASPs. Further, as ASPs deliver these services over the Internet, the software is available anytime and anywhere. In addition, any device can use it.

While the current ASP picture is rosy, it is not without risks. Just like building an IS using an outsourcer, going with an ASP means that an organization loses some control over its applications. In addition, if the Internet connection goes down or the ASP goes out of business, the organization loses its connection to its software applications.

So what do you think? Is software as a service here to stay? Before you answer, you might consider that in 2005 Microsoft, the undisputed champion in selling software as a product, announced two on-line services, Windows Live and Office Live. These services are designed to allow users of Windows and Office to expand what they do with these applications by connecting from anywhere on any device. Bill Gates, a founder and chairman of Microsoft, called the new services "a big change for every part of the [Microsoft] ecosystem." It seems that the "richest man in the world" sees a future for software on demand.

Web Resources

- The eNonprofit: A Guide to ASPs, Internet Services, and Online Software—http://www.compasspoint.org/enonprofit/
- News & Analysis for Application and Web Services—http://www.ASPnews.com
- IBM ASP services—http://www-03.ibm.com/services/ca/en/ams/asp/

An organization needs to carefully consider the advantages and disadvantages of outsourcing versus in-house development. So, as with the build-or-buy question, an organization must examine its present situation and capabilities, and choose the option that most closely matches its current needs. Table 6.2 compares these two options. Dimensions to be considered in this decision include any time-to-market imperative (which puts the priority on speed), current financial performance (businesses in crisis or that are underperforming must pay closer attention to costs), and an organization's risk tolerance (which must be greater to take on building a system from scratch).

Note that regardless of whether an organization decides to buy or build, to use in-house staff or outsource, it still needs to fully understand the IS project and define its requirements. This process of *system development* includes distinct stages and activities, known as the system development life cycle (SDLC), discussed in the next section.

Table 6.2	In-House Development vs. Outsourcing[5]	
IS Development Source	**Advantages**	**Disadvantages**
In-house development	Firm retains complete control of the project. Process builds internal knowledge through learning and experience.	Generally higher development time and costs. Distraction of in-house IS staff from other duties.
Outsourcing	High level of skill and expertise. Internal staff provides project oversight, which is less time intensive than full development. Generally lower time and costs.	Firm loses some control of project since it is necessary to give outsourcer some decision-making authority. Internal staff has less opportunity to build experience. Requires good contracts and oversight.

5. Adapted from McKeown, P. G. 2003. *Information Technology and the Networked Economy*, 2nd ed., (Boston: Course Technology, 2003) 328.

PART

2

Quick Test

1. A _____ study determines whether a project is technically and economically possible.
   a. hardware
   b. compatibility
   c. feasibility
   d. needs

2. True or False. In addition to lower development costs and time, a major advantage with leasing a system is that the vendor is responsible for maintaining and updating the system.

3. True or False. When the outsourcing company is located primarily in a foreign country, the practice is known as onshoring.

Answers: 1. c; 2. True; 3. False

THE STAGES AND ACTIVITIES OF THE SYSTEM DEVELOPMENT LIFE CYCLE (SDLC)

Like many projects and products, an information system goes through a life cycle. The **system development life cycle (SDLC)** is the common term used for the stages and activities of system development. The SDLC is composed of processes that occur from the start of a system to its end. The phases or steps of the traditional SDLC are typically shown in diagrams as flowing from one to the next from top to bottom, similar to a waterfall. This is shown in Figure 6.4. At a high level, the SDLC starts with an idea. We call this the concept. Early on, the person proposing the idea is unlikely to have details of what the final solution to the problem will be but realizes there is an opportunity that involves technology or information systems. The SDLC ends when the organization no longer needs the system or it is replaced with something newer. Between its start and end, and over time, the information system goes through the seven phases as illustrated in Figure 6.5 and described below.

1. *Concept* (also known as pre-inception or idea phase): The environment within the organization either promotes or inhibits the development of ideas for systems. Obviously, an organization prefers to foster an environment that promotes ideas that can improve its bottom line.

2. *Inception* (also known as the feasibility or planning phase): This phase begins when an organization has the idea to build an

PART

2

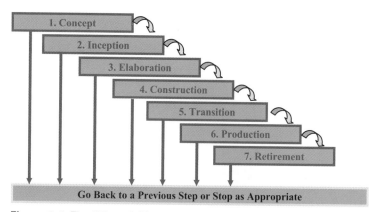

Figure 6.4 The "Waterfall" presentation of the SDLC steps.

information system. The focus is on understanding the problem to be solved or the opportunity to be addressed and planning the project. Early interactions with *stakeholders* of the system (discussed later in the chapter) take place at this time.

3. *Elaboration:* In this phase the project team finalizes the requirements for the system and the project plan, and designs the system architecture. The team also creates conceptual models of the systems and subsystems.

4. *Construction:* During this phase the team builds the initial running system. Usually, the team implements core functionalities first and then incorporates additional features.

5. *Transition:* At this time, the team finalizes the system and puts it in place. In addition, the team completes the final training of users and management of users during the transition.

6. *Production:* Once the system is up and running, the organization must continuously monitor, maintain, and evaluate it. The organization must also keep users of the system up to date with the latest modifications and procedures.

7. *Retirement:* At some point, the system may lose its value to the company. This phase often marks the concept of a new system to replace the obsolete one. The old system may retain some usefulness as it is phased out over time by the replacement system.

Let's illustrate the SDLC using an example. As the marketing assistant at WildOutfitters.com, a hypothetical retail hiking-goods store, you suspect that sales are not as high during December as they could be. You come up with an idea to increase website sales for the holiday season (Concept). You analyze sales data for the month of December for the past five years and prove that they are significantly less than sales during the summer. You call a meeting with your manager and your IT department to discuss this information and your idea. Your manager and IT agree that your idea is

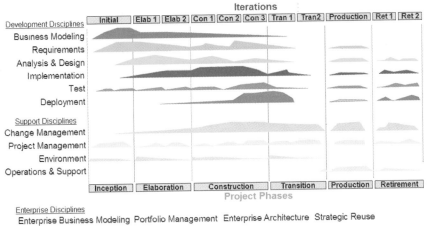

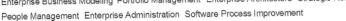

Figure 6.5 In its life cycle, an information system goes through seven phases (note that the concept stage is not shown here) and involves the activities of many disciplines.

feasible and should generate a favourable ROI (Inception). You now have the go ahead to determine the details of a website campaign.

With the help of IT and the advertising department, you design the content and the look and feel of a campaign that will be sent via e-mail to all WildOutfitters customers (using contact data contained in the customer database) with a link to a Christmas list generator that encourages them to add hiking equipment to their Christmas list (Elaboration). IT builds the mailing list and a new web page for the creation of a Christmas list with links to the on-line product catalogue and shopping cart. Marketing writes the content of the e-mail and website (Construction). You make sure that customer service and technical support are briefed on this campaign (Transition).

On November 30, the e-mail is sent to all WildOutfitters.com customers. Technical support monitors the website to ensure it is ready for customers to create their Christmas lists (Production). After a month of frantic activity and increased sales, the Christmas list generator web page is turned off (Retirement). The campaign was so successful you are promoted to website marketing manager and you are not sure how you are going to top this! You go back to your desk to look at more data and come up with more ideas (Concept again).

Figure 6.5[6] shows not only the stages of SDLC on the horizontal axis (note that the concept stage is not shown) but also lists the core activities related to the life of the information system on the vertical axis. These activities are grouped together primarily based on when they take place, with the coloured shapes illustrating when and how active each of these areas is during the life cycle.

6. Adapted with permission from Scott Ambler, "Adopting the Enterprise Unified Process (EUP)," http://www.enterpriseunifiedprocess.com/essays/adoption.html, 2005.

- *Development disciplines* represent the group of activities that focus on creating the new system. Activities in this group include business modelling, gathering requirements, analysis and design, implementation, testing, and deployment. Note that testing is a continuous process that occurs throughout the project. The testing task is sometimes referred to as quality assurance. *Quality assurance* of a project represents continuous monitoring and improving of the process, ensuring that any agreed-upon standards and procedures are followed, and identifying and resolving any problems.
- *Support disciplines*, as the name implies, serve to support the system over its lifetime. These include configuration and change management during the change/transition phase, project management during system development, environmental scanning to ensure compatibility of project plans, and operations and support at system deployment.
- *Enterprise discipline* activities are the most active prior to inception of an IS project. Effective use of these activities will create a promising environment for an IS project.

WHAT DO YOU THINK?

As you can imagine, answering the "big four" IS development questions and developing an IS involves a significant amout of decision making and problem solving. Review the sections on decision making and problem solving in Chapter 3 to consider the following questions:

1: What types of information will you gather to determine if the IS under consideration aligns with the strategic goals of the business?

2: How would you decide between building or buying a system? What types of information will you gather and how will you evaluate these data to come to a solution?

3: During the elaboration phase of the SDLC, many decisions are made about what the system must do. Many times there are a lot of requirements to consider. How would you determine which requirements are more essential than others?

Figure 6.6 The four pillars of a system analysis and design project; failures in any one of these areas can cause the whole project to come crashing down.

Over the years the process of completing an IS project has come to be known as **system analysis and design.** Any system analysis and design project involves four essential ingredients: (1) people, (2) methodology, (3) management, and (4) tools. As Figure 6.6 shows, like a pillar that holds up a roof, failures in any one of these areas can cause the whole project to come crashing down. In the next sections, we discuss each pillar in detail. Near the end of the chapter we discuss the trade-offs between this traditional approach and more modern approaches to system design and development.

Quick Test

1. True or False. The system development life cycle of an IS begins when the system is ready to be used by the organization and ends when the organization retires the system.

2. At which phase does an organization finalize an IS and put it in place?
   a. construction
   b. inception
   c. production
   d. transition

3. Which one of the following disciplines includes activities that are most active before an IS project begins?
   a. enterprise disciplines
   b. development disciplines
   c. support disciplines
   d. organizational disciplines

Answers: 1. False; 2. d; 3. a

IS DEVELOPMENT TEAMS

The people associated with an IS project usually fall within one or both of two groups: those on the project team and those who are stakeholders in the IS.

THE IS PROJECT TEAM

The size of an IS development team varies with the specific characteristics of the project. These factors can include the scope of the project, the budget, and the available resources. The project team's skill requirements also vary along these lines. However, most IS development projects require teams to possess the following:

- *Project strategy:* This ensures that the project goals correspond to the organization's business objectives. Any strategy needs to consider the strengths and weaknesses of both the business and the teams, identify opportunities and threats both internal and external to the organization, understand the financial aspects of the project such as budget and the project's return on investment, and manage risks and planning needs.
- *Project management:* This demands knowledge of methods and techniques to ensure delivery of the project on time and on budget, and the ability to communicate project goals and requirements to the project team.

- *Account management:* Typically, this group is part of the development team when the project team works as an outsourcer. This team is responsible for the sales and service of the project team. They provide the initial point of contact to the client (the people who need the IS) as well as daily communication with the client.
- *Architecture and design:* The members who work in this group must provide a well-designed user interface. Many user interfaces include multimedia components that require special skills in the areas of art and design.
- *Programming:* This group creates the technical infrastructure of the system, which can include the design and construction of the data architecture. It also includes the analysis and design of any software needed by the system.
- *Specialists:* This group handles unique aspects of the project. For instance, a system may need an artificial intelligence (AI) specialist on the project team. Likewise, a website for a news organization requires a resource with journalistic skills on the team.
- *Client interface:* A client may be an internal or external customer of the team's organization. In either case, the client has responsibilities toward the successful completion of the project. The client must define system requirements, negotiate contract terms, and maintain oversight of the teams as the project progresses. The client may also need to supply resources to the project team.

Figure 6.7 illustrates these roles, along with some common job titles that fit within each category. Recall, however, that the exact mix of jobs required will depend on the nature and scope of the project. It is the project manager's responsibility to assemble a team with talented people who can each fill one or more of these jobs.

In fact, the team composition is perhaps the most important aspect of project management. As the CORE box "Why Good People Can Make Bad Teams" illustrates, the lack of a good team composition can increase the risks to a project's successful completion. Most successful project teams consist of technical IT people as well as those with non-technical skills. Non-IT skills range from business skills, such as accounting or business strategy, to creative skills like artistic design and journalism. Thus, no matter what your major, you may have skills that an IS development team needs. Learn more about teams and team composition in Tech Guide E.

Client
Internal/External

Account Team	Project Management	Strategy Consultancy
Account Director Account Manager Account Executive	Project Director Project Manager Assistant Manager QA Tester	Strategy Consultant Technical Consultant Marketing Consultant

System Manager

Architecture and Design	Programming	Specialists
Information Architect Interface Design Manager Designer Art Director	Data Architect Programming Manager Advanced Programmer Programmer Database Administrator Specialist Programming	Animator Producer/Director Editor Journalist Researcher AI Specialist Marketing Manager

Figure 6.7 IS development team technical jobs; note that the exact roles will depend on the nature and scope of the project.

Relationships

Why Good People Can Make Bad Teams

Almost all IS development projects are accomplished using teams. These teams may be teams of developers, or they may be teams that include developers, subject matter experts (SMEs, pronounced "Smeez"), and users. However, not every team develops a successful IS. Why not? In his popular book *Rapid Development,* author Steve McConnell discusses why teams fail. He lists the following as reasons for team failure or "teamicide."

- **Lack of common vision**—A team's vision is its agreed-upon path to successful goal accomplishment. It is unlikely that a team will be productive without a common vision.
- **Lack of identity**—Teams need to have a sense of who they are—they need an identity. With an identity, they can embrace and assume ownership for the goals and objectives that flow from their vision. Without it, the team may be a collection of individuals, thereby losing the potential for the output of the whole (team) to exceed the sum of its parts (individuals).
- **Lack of recognition**—Although IS development requires teamwork, individuals need recognition, too. For outstanding job performance, appropriate recognition can generate a future willingness to perform at high levels and a greater commitment to the team.
- **Productivity roadblocks**—Organizations must provide the resources and processes to allow the team to meet its goals. Managers should try to remove productivity roadblocks such as conflicting goals and demands and insufficient resources.

PART

2

- **Ineffective communication**—Organizations must provide the means (e-mail, Web conferencing, etc.) and the motivation for teams to communicate. Effective communication enhances team cohesion and performance.
- **Lack of trust**—Management should not micromanage its teams by getting into every step of their work. Micromanaging sends a message of distrust, which destroys self-confidence and weakens the team's motivation toward high performance.
- **Problem personnel**—Not all team members work equally. In fact, McConnell cites a Larson and LaFasto study that found that "the most consistent and intense complaint from team members was that their team leaders were unwilling to confront poor performance by individual team members."

So, as a future team member and organizational leader, what should you do? One suggestion is to watch for the signs leading to teamicide and to be proactive in your steps to ensure a positive environment for teams. Another suggestion is to learn all that you can about being an effective and efficient team member. Tech Guide E can be an excellent resource for you in this regard since it helps you understand how to be a good collaborator and team member. Then, when you are placed in a leadership position, you will understand what it takes to succeed and how to accomplish organizational goals through the work of teams.

Web Resources

- Creating Highly Effective Teams—http://www.sideroad.com/Team_Building/
- Team Building Book Reviews—http://www.humanresources.about.com/cs/involvementteams/tp/teams.htm
- IS-focused teams—http://www.intelligententerprise.com/

IMPORTANCE OF STAKEHOLDERS

For most IS development projects, identifying the key stakeholders can be a very important task. Why? Because the attitude of a powerful stakeholder toward a project can dramatically affect the project's eventual success or failure. As a result, a **stakeholder analysis** should begin as part of the project feasibility study. The project manager should then continue to use it during the course of the project in order to reduce the risk of negative stakeholder attitudes.

A stakeholder analysis begins with a list of the stakeholders, including what each has at stake, as well as the degree of impact each stakeholder can have on the project. The analysis must also consider whether the team can expect resources from the stakeholders. Further, the analysis should also attempt to identify each stakeholder's attitude toward the project and any risks. Finally, a project manager should assign team members to different stakeholders, with an anticipated strategy for dealing with each one.

Figure 6.8[7] shows an example of a stakeholder analysis for a generic IS. Note that this analysis lists potential stakeholders, along with how they will affect and be affected by the project. The analysis

---

7. *Stakeholder Analysis Template*, JISC InfoNet, http://www.jiscinfonet.ac.uk/InfoKits/
project-management, 2004.

Stakeholder	Stake in the project	Potential impact on Project	What does the Project expect the Stakeholder to provide?	Perceived attitudes and/or risks	Stakeholder Management Strategy	Responsibility
CEO	Policy and process owner who determines organizational policy and procedures	High	Experienced staff to be involved in user group and user acceptance testing. Commitment to implementing change.	Lack of clarity about preferred approach. Views project team as too technically oriented.	Involvement in Project Steering Board, Regular updating meeting with project leader.	Project Manager
Department Head	Manages admin staff who will operate the new system at local level and secretarial staff who will indirectly input and directly extract data	Medium	Commitment to implementing change.	Lack of interest in project.	Involvement in briefing sessions at quarterly meetings.	Project Sponsor
Admin Staff	Will operate new system	High	Contribute to system and process design and testing.	Concern about increased workload. Worried about what training they will receive.	Involvement in user groups.	Project Team

Figure 6.8 A stakeholder analysis lists potential stakeholders, along with how they will affect and be affected by the project.

also estimates the potential impact on the project's success that each stakeholder can have, along with a strategy for dealing with the stakeholder. Finally, the analysis includes the assignment of a team member to oversee and carry out the strategy.

Quick Test

1. Which one of the following IS project team skills represents a knowledge of techniques for ensuring that a project is successfully completed on time?
   a. architecture and design
   b. client interface
   c. programming
   d. project management

2. True or False. A knowledge-enabled professional must possess technical skills such as the ability to design databases or write a computer program in order to be on an IS project team.

3. Which of the following is true about performing a stakeholder analysis?
   a. The group of stakeholders analyzed includes anyone who has a stake in the project and may affect the outcome of the project.
   b. An attempt is made to judge the attitude of a stakeholder toward the project.
   c. In order to mitigate the risk associated with each stakeholder, a project team member is assigned to implement stakeholder management strategies.
   d. All of the above.

Answers: 1. d; 2. False; 3. d

STANDARD IS METHODOLOGY

A **methodology** provides a framework for both the management and technical processes of an IS project. Selecting a methodology that matches a project's needs helps to ensure a successful IS.

WHY DO ORGANIZATIONS NEED AN IS METHODOLOGY?

Initially, system developers tended to work in a very ad hoc way, called the **build-and-fix model.** In this model, developers sat down briefly with the boss or a customer to find out the requirements. Then, they would write programs, create databases, and put together hardware. After building the system, developers would test and debug it. As you might imagine, this approach often led to problems. Because developers spent little time analyzing requirements or developing a design, systems developed using the build-and-fix model often did not satisfy customer needs or easily allow any changes and upgrades.

As a result, developers began to think about improving the process. A methodology, sometimes known as a **development life cycle,** provides a project team with structure to ensure that everyone works toward the same project goals. The methodology defines most of the development activities that are part of the plan developed by the project manager. Development tools are often designed to support a particular methodology. A formal methodology brings several benefits to an IS development project, as Table 6.3 shows. In the next sections, we discuss both traditional and modern development methodologies.

Table 6.3 Importance of Methodology to IS Development[8]	
Advantages	Disadvantages
• **Development fundamentals**—methodologies help team members use best practices.	• **Bureaucratic**—Some methodologies can be overly rigid and bureaucratic.
• **Avoiding rework**—the process can be oriented toward avoiding repeating tasks in the event of changing requirements.	
• **Risk management**—process helps identify and manage risks.	
• **Assures quality**—helps detect errors earlier, when they are easier to correct.	
• **Customer orientation**—focuses on customers' needs and desires.	
• **Improved planning**—makes it easy to identify and organize the activities required by the project.	
• **Targeting resources**—helps target resources toward the activities that need them.	

8. Steve McConnell, *Rapid Development*, Microsoft Press, 1996. p. 14.

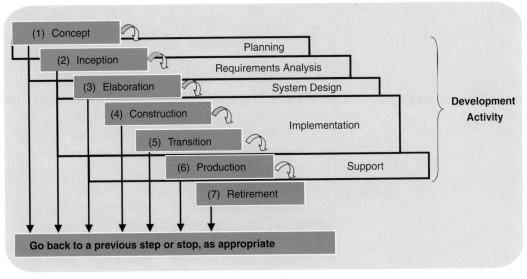

Figure 6.9 The Waterfall SDLC with Development Activities

THE TRADITIONAL IS METHODOLOGY:
THE WATERFALL MODEL

The first development model to gain wide acceptance among system developers was based on the **Waterfall model**, which was first illustrated in Figure 6.4. As discussed earlier, the Waterfall model defines a set of phases and a new phase begins only after acceptably completing the preceding phase. The same is true with the development activities that occur throughout the SDLC phases (see Figure 6.9). If developers discover mistakes or other problems, they then return if possible, to a prior phase. As a result, development activities tend to move downstream through the phases in a formal, detailed manner. The idea is that if things are done right in each phase, there will be little or no need to move back upstream to an already completed phase.

The Waterfall model is a document-driven and highly structured process. Work during each phase generally produces a document or another type of deliverable. For example, in the inception phase developers undertake planning activities that result in an initial project plan. During the inception phase, and often at the beginning of the elaboration phase, developers assist users with requirements definition and analysis. That is, they are developing the business requirements document for the system to be constructed. At the end of elaboration, a system design document, which often includes logical models (diagrams) that show how the system will satisfy business requirements, is produced. In the construction phase, developers are implementing the system. That is, they code its components and modules, integrate them, and create user interfaces. As these are

PART

2

completed, the system moves into the transition phase where the system is tested and implemented into the live production environement. The deliverables of the transition stage include program code, test documents, user documentation, and a completed system. Finally, during the production phases the developers support the system by keeping detailed records of changes and upgrades. As a result, one of the criticisms of this approach is that it is too focused on output (documents) and not sufficiently on outcomes (the results of the work itself).

While successfully used for many years, the Waterfall model does have other weaknesses. First, the Waterfall model is usually only effective when users can express their exact needs. Precisely defining the business requirements is crucial for this approach to work. Developers must understand the problem in detail so they can respond with an effective system design. Otherwise, developers may not detect errors or omissions until late in the transition phase when the system becomes available for testing. A closely related problem is that users often cannot adequately express their requirements until they have something to work with and see. This is called a prototype. With the Waterfall model, there is nothing to show the user until the entire process, through transition, is complete.

In addition, the sequential nature of the Waterfall process can delay progress. For example, construction must wait until approval of the system design. In truth, developers can often start some design work while still finalizing user requirements. However, a strict reading of the Waterfall model prevents earlier starts for tasks or for completing activities in parallel. As a result of all these constraints, developers today rarely use a rigid Waterfall model.

Regardless of its limitations, it is still important for you to know about and understand the Waterfall model and its associated development activities. It is the most common reference model for describing the development process, allowing developers to share a common language when discussing the development of an IS. The Waterfall approach also proved the need for consistent documentation and carefully defined system requirements. As such, the Waterfall model provided the basis for more modern methodologies.

MODERN IS METHODOLOGIES

With more modern methodologies, developers produce a partial running system that they evaluate and then revise and enhance. An **evolutionary model** fits this approach to development. With an evolutionary model, developers first investigate, specify, and implement an important core part of the system with minimal functionality. The team then tests and evaluates this version of the

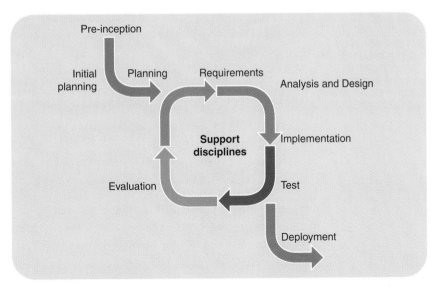

Figure 6.10 Using an evolutionary model of IS development, developers produce a partial running system that they evaluate and then revise and enhance.

system to plan for the next version. On each iteration of the cycle, the team then adds new functionality and features to the system. Figure 6.10[9] broadly depicts an evolutionary development method.

As we noted earlier, a common approach to the evolutionary model is to use **prototyping.** With prototyping, the project team works with customers to progressively build the system from an initial outline specification using visual mock-ups of screens, diagrams of data relationships, and similar tools that help users see what is going to be built. The final system essentially evolves from that initial *prototype.* This process can help the team members and the users better understand the requirements. However, one problem with an evolutionary model is that developers often neglect to create a well-defined set of documents. This makes it difficult to monitor and control the project, which in turn can cause other problems such as making it difficult to stay on schedule or estimate the true final costs of development.

A current trend is to develop systems using an **"agile" development** methodology. Because an agile process is designed to satisfy continuously changing requirements, the team develops software in short development cycles or increments. Each cycle may include all of the primary phases of the process, as Figure 6.11 shows.

Evolutionary and agile development methodologies are an attempt to reduce the somewhat constricting formality of the pure Waterfall approach. A well known agile development method is the

9. P. Krutchen, "What is the Rational Unified Process," *The Rational Edge,* Rational Software, January 2001.

Figure 6.11 Because an agile process is designed to satisfy continuously changing requirements, the team develops software in short development cycles or increments.

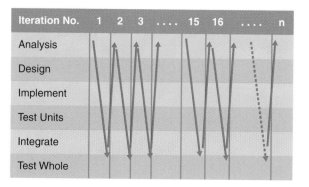

rational unified process (RUP). This is not only a development method and process, but also comes with software tools of its own to enable the method. RUP is built on the "six best practices" that occur in each development phase: (1) develop iteratively, (2) manage requirements, (3) use component architecture, (4) model visually, (5) verify quality, and (6) control changes.

The choice between any of these development methods can depend on the importance and complexity of the project itself. In general, the greater the complexity and importance of the project to the strategic mission of the company, the more formality needed in the development process.

WHAT DO YOU THINK?

There is much debate in the IT community about the use of Waterfall and evolutionary methodologies for system development. Given what you now know about these methodologies, consider the following:

1: Imagine if you were to do a term paper using "agile" writing. How would this work? What would be the benefits and drawbacks of completing your term paper this way?
2: Do you think that the type of system being developed (e.g. website vs. ERP) should determine the development methodology to be used, or should user preference determine the method?
3: Is it possible to use both methodologies in the development of the same system? How would this work?

IS MODELLING

Modelling system requirements is an important part of any IS development methodology. A **model** is a simplified representation of something real, such as a building, weather pattern, or information system that knowledge-enabled professionals can manipulate in order to study the real item in more detail. Models can be of many types, including mathematical equations, computer simulations, and graphs or charts. For IS development, the model usually includes one or more diagrams that developers can use to examine, evaluate, and adjust in order to understand the system and performance requirements that are derived from the design of the underlying business process that the system is trying to automate or support. Developers generally create models during the elaboration phase of the SDLC to help them align possible IS solutions to the requirements of each step in the business process.

Entity–Relationship Diagram and Logical Data Model

The **entity-relationship diagram** (**ERD**) and the **logical data model** are the two most commonly used models for designing the organization of a relational database. The ERD indicates the entities and relationships for the data that the IS will store (see Tech Guide D for a more detailed discussion of ERDs). The logical data model then translates the ERD into a diagram of the tables in the database. Figure 6.12 shows a partial ERD and logical data model for an electronic voting system.

Data Flow Diagram

As the name implies, a **data flow diagram** (**DFD**) is a traditional IS model that depicts how data move or flow through a system: (1) the external entities (boxes) that send input or receive output from the system; (2) processes (boxes with rounded corners) that show activities that move or transform data; (3) data stores (open-ended boxes) that usually correspond to tables in the data model; and (4) data flows (arrows) that connect the components.

Figure 6.13 shows a partial DFD for an electronic voting system. In this figure, one external entity, the voter, interacts with the system.

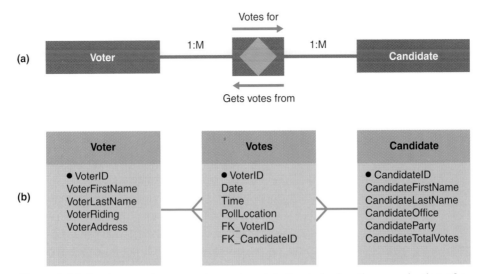

Figure 6.12 The two most commonly used models for designing the organization of a relational database are the (a) ERD and (b) logical data model, used here to represent an e-voting system.

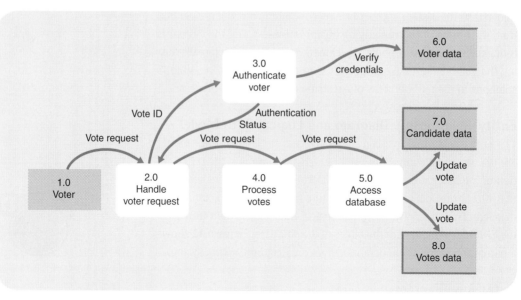

Figure 6.13 A DFD depicts how data move through a system; the partial DFD shown here provides more details building on the ERD and logical data model shown in Figure 6.12.

Three data stores (tables from the logical data model in Figure 6.12) indicate the need to store various data items. The boxes with rounded corners represent four processes, each of which transforms the inputs into outputs. At this point, the model focuses on identifying the need for these processes. Determining exactly what steps will be taken within each process occurs in a later stage of development.

The DFD uniquely identifies all of the components with a number. However, the model does not specify how to implement the components. For example, to authenticate a voter, the system may rely on either a computer program or a manual process (e.g., a polling volunteer).

UML Diagrams

Unified Modelling Language (UML) has become a very popular modelling tool as it works particularly well for developing object-oriented systems. The UML consists of several graphical elements that, when combined, form a set of diagrams.

The purpose of the UML diagrams is to show multiple views of a system. Together, the set of UML diagrams is known as the *system model*. Like the other models we discussed above, a UML model describes the purpose of the system but not how to implement it. The most commonly used UML diagrams include class, object, use case, state, sequence, activity (Figure 6.1 is an example), communication, component, and deployment diagrams. We focus on use cases and

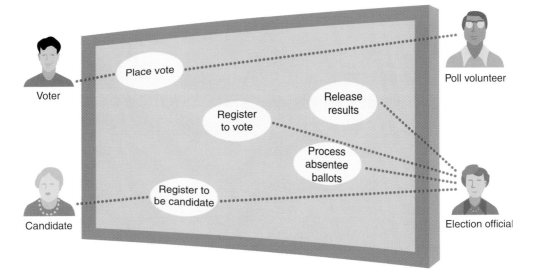

Figure 6.14 The UML use case diagram notation captures all the possible ways to use a system, in this case, an e-voting system.

sequence diagrams here, so that you can see how they help the IS development process.

The UML *use case* diagram notation captures all the possible ways to use a system. It shows which users employ which use cases, as well as the relationships both between the users and between the use cases. A use case describes a system's behaviour from a user's standpoint. Knowledge-enabled professionals often create use cases as a tool for determining user requirements. For example, Figure 6.14 shows a use case diagram for an electronic voting system. Here, the use case diagram identifies the possible users of the system and their primary interactions with the system (the ovals). The ovals represent activities that the system needs to support. Knowledge-enabled professionals can further investigate these activities by using other UML diagrams, such as activity or sequence diagrams. Use case diagrams are usually drawn while gathering user requirements during the inception and elaboration phases of the system development life cycle.

Organizations use a UML *sequence diagram* to view the interactions between system components as they occur. Figure 6.15 presents a sequence diagram of the voting process. The diagram in this figure, a software representation of a real-world entity, shows three main objects from the system: a voter, pollster, and election object. Over time, each of these objects performs tasks, represented by rectangles. Arrows represent messages that can be passed between objects. The solid arrows generally trigger another object to start a task, while the dashed arrows represent the results of that task.

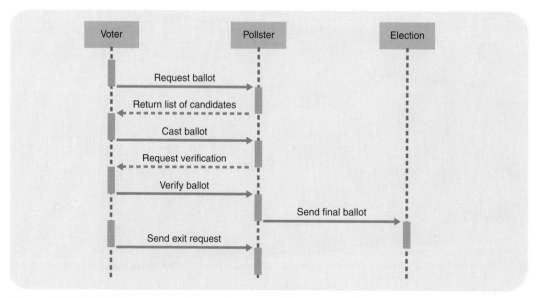

Figure 6.15 This UML sequence diagram for an e-voting system shows the interactions between system components as they occur.

Regardless of the method you use to identify information flows between entities, the important point is that they are understood, documented, and shared among the team. This enables the developers to ensure that when the system is programmed, it will actually function as it was intended to and that the data required are available to users.

Quick Test

1. Through _____, developers produce a partial running system, which they then evaluate, revise, and enhance.
   a. data flow diagrams
   b. prototyping
   c. use cases
   d. Waterfall development

2. A(n) _____ is a traditional IS model that depicts how data move through a system.
   a. entity-relationship diagram (ERD)
   b. data flow diagram (DFD)
   c. logical data model
   d. UML sequence diagram

3. True or False. Evolutionary development methodologies are considered to be less formal and more agile than the traditional Waterfall development method.

Answers: 1. b; 2. b; 3. True

MANAGING THE IS PROJECT

Project management is "the application of knowledge skills, tools, and techniques to project activities to meet project requirements."[10] For IS development, a project manager simultaneously oversees three main project elements: the scope of the project, the resources needed, and the time to complete it. The project scope defines what the project should accomplish. Resources can include people, equipment, material, and money. Time estimates consider project activity times and how they depend on each other.

Management of these elements is usually a balancing act. A manager often makes decisions to actively set the levels of two elements, and then calculates the third accordingly. For example, if the client requires specific software features, these features define the scope of the project. The client may also set a time deadline for receiving the final software. The project manager then calculates the resources, which then result in cost, needed to meet the scope and time constraints.

As Figure 6.16 illustrates, you can think of the three project management elements as the three sides of a triangle. And, as you might recall from geometry, once you know the length of two sides, you can calculate the length of the third. Note also that Figure 6.16 uses project scope/quality as the base of the triangle. That's because, among these three elements, project scope is often the most important to manage: increases in scope will drive increases in time and/or resources needed. Also, changes in time and cost can affect the quality delivered by the project.

Of course, for any particular project, choices are made not only about time, cost, scope, and quality, but even the choice of which projects to undertake in the first place must be aligned to an organization's overall strategy.

Figure 6.16 The project management triangle.

---

10. *A Guide to the Project Management Body of Knowledge (PMBOK® Guide) 2000 Edition*, p. 4, (2000).

PART

2

Previously, the project management triangle we referred to was often called the "triple constraint" or the "iron triangle" because it was perceived as nearly impossible to deliver on all three components successfully (on time, on budget, and on scope). However, competitive pressures often require the delivery of all three. In fact, we suggest that there is actually a quadruple constraint in most organizations today, where linking project outcomes to strategy is crucial to success. Therefore, the project management triangle, like any other part of the development methodology, must work inside the organization's strategy and mission, as shown in Figure 6.16. By selecting systems projects that enable faster and more certain execution of business strategy, and by executing those projects more successfully, an organization can "lock in" competitive advantages that make it a force in its industry.

OVERVIEW OF PROJECT MANAGEMENT TASKS

As shown in Figure 6.5, project management activities may occur as early as the inception phase. More often than not, these activities begin at the end of the inception phase and the beginning of the elaboration phase when the idea is approved and a project started. It is important to note that the system development life cycle (SDLC) is different from the project management activities to support a project. A project has a beginning and an end whereas the SDLC is a continuous stream of activities over time. As we discussed earlier, the SDLC can start at the beginning of an idea (concept), continue through to production and transition, where the IS is implemented, monitored, and maintained, and then finally retired and re-started with the idea for a new IS. The project for an IS starts with the approval to move ahead with the idea, bringing a project team together, planning the project, and elaborating the requirements. Many of the activities in project management occur before the system is constructed. The project ends when the system is in production and transitioned to day-to-day operational staff. These operational staff monitor and maintain the system until it is retired.

Figure 6.17 shows the nine key components of a project management methodology that support the life cycle of the project. Although the project manager should develop knowledge and skills in all of these areas, the following four core functions lead to specific project objectives:

1. *Time management:* estimating the duration of the project, developing an acceptable schedule, and managing the project to ensure timely completion.
2. *Cost management:* preparing a budget and managing the costs of the project to stay within budget.

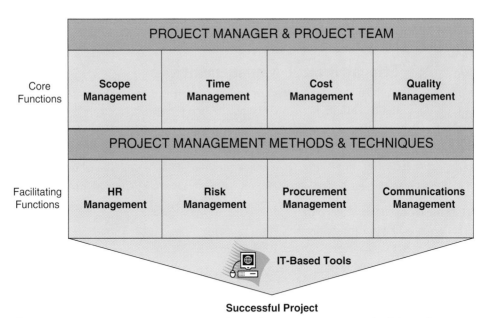

Figure 6.17 The nine key components of a project management methodology that create a successful project.

3. *Scope management:* identifying and managing all the tasks required to complete a project.

4. *Quality management:* ensuring that the finished project satisfies its defined goals.

The facilitating functions support the project activities. Human resources management focuses on making productive use of the team members. Communications management involves the supervision of shared project information. With risk management, the project manager seeks to identify and prioritize potential risks, and develop contingency plans in case a risk occurs. Procurement management involves acquiring the resources needed for the project. Of course, implicit in all of these concepts is that the organization has actually selected projects that are strategic. This is known as project portfolio management (PPM) and is emerging as a critical consideration for companies that are focused on competitive advantage. Therefore, project management should not only be about doing the projects right but also about doing the right projects!

Especially considering the large amount of resources that a project manager typically oversees, as well as the time pressure of completing a project quickly, ethics can play a large role. The CORE box "Ethical Project Management" explores this issue in more detail.

Project management requires strong organizational skills in addition to sound ethics. If you look at Figure 6.18[11], you can see the

11. With permission from *A Guide to A Project Management Body of Knowledge (PMBOK® Guide) 2000 Edition*, p. 8, (2000).

PART

2

Ethics

Ethical Project Management

At the organizational level, project management is an important part of an organization's efforts to transform problems into solutions that create business value. As such, project managers often operate with huge budgets, but limited time. However, despite the pressures that both factors can bring, project managers must use their resources in an ethical manner. In fact, the Project Management Institute (PMI), a professional organization that certifies project management professionals (PMPs®), has a member code of ethics. Members pledge to:

- Maintain high standards of integrity.
- Accept responsibility for their actions.
- Continually seek to enhance their professional capabilities.
- Practise with fairness and honesty.
- Encourage others in the profession to act in an ethical and professional manner.

Think of the many organizational systems that you interact with: your school's registration system or your bank's on-line banking system, to name a few. Each of these IS may identify you by your social insurance number (SIN). Think of the harm that could be done through the unethical or careless compromise of these data. It's very likely that the project manager (PM) of these systems was very concerned about protecting access to your accounts and sensitive personal information like your SIN. Regardless of what code of ethics knowledge-enabled professionals like PMs and programmers follow, the organizational and individual impacts of information systems demand that knowledge-enabled professionals involved in their development adhere to the highest professional standards of conduct.

Web Resources
- Canadian Association of Management Consultants Code of Conduct—
  http://www.camc.com/index.cfm?PID=12506&PIDLIST=12506
- Project Management Institute—http://www.pmi.org
- ACM Software Engineers Code of Ethics—http://www.acm.org/serving/se/code.htm

---

number of standard functions and tasks listed under each key component that a project manager must oversee. A project manager ties together all these functions through *project management integration.*

Project management integration includes the development of the project plan, execution of the plan, and the coordination of changes to the plan as they occur. The project manager uses a project plan to coordinate all project documentation and help guide the execution and control of the project. Figure 6.19[12] provides a sample outline of a software project management plan. Note that creating and managing the project plan is a job in itself!

12. "IEEE Standard for Software Project Management Plans," Software Engineering Standards Committee of the IEEE Computer Society, IEEE Std 1058–1998, p.4.

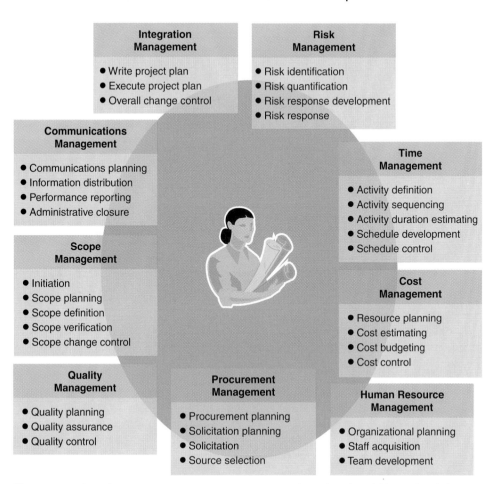

Integration Management

- Write project plan
- Execute project plan
- Overall change control

Risk Management

- Risk identification
- Risk quantification
- Risk response development
- Risk response

Communications Management

- Communications planning
- Information distribution
- Performance reporting
- Administrative closure

Time Management

- Activity definition
- Activity sequencing
- Activity duration estimating
- Schedule development
- Schedule control

Scope Management

- Initiation
- Scope planning
- Scope definition
- Scope verification
- Scope change control

Cost Management

- Resource planning
- Cost estimating
- Cost budgeting
- Cost control

Quality Management

- Quality planning
- Quality assurance
- Quality control

Procurement Management

- Procurement planning
- Solicitation planning
- Solicitation
- Source selection

Human Resource Management

- Organizational planning
- Staff acquisition
- Team development

Figure 6.18 A project manager must oversee any number of tasks within each of the nine key components of a project management methodology.

WHAT DO YOU THINK?

How do you know if what you are working on is a project or just part of your everyday job responsibilities? Believe it or not, this is a question individuals and organizations struggle with when determining what work to do and how to do it. Consider the following questions:

1: Make a list of projects that you have worked on in the past. Are you sure these are all projects? Does each have a distinct beginning and end and were started for a specific, unique purpose?

2: Think of some examples of projects in the business context. Could any of these be confused with everyday operations of the company?

3: Many times we manage projects without even realizing it. Were you the project manager on any of the projects on your list from question 1? If you were, what skills did you use to manage the project? Are these unique to project management?

Figure 6.19 Sample project management plan.

Title Page
Change History
Preface
Table of Contents
List of Figures
List of Tables
1. Overview
    1.1 Project summary
        1.1.1 Purpose, scope, and objectives
        1.1.2 Assumptions and constraints
        1.1.3 Project Deliverables
        1.1.4 Schedule and budget summary
    1.2 Evolution of the plan
2. References
3. Definitions
4. Project organization
    4.1 External interfaces
    4.2 Internal structure
    4.3 Roles and responsibilities
5. Managerial process plans
    5.1 Start-up plan
        5.1.1 Estimation plan
        5.1.2 Staffing plan
        5.1.3 Resource acquisition plan
        5.1.4 Project staff training plan
    5.2 Work plan
        5.2.1 Work activities
        5.2.2 Schedule allocation
        5.2.3 Resource allocation
        5.2.4 Budget allocation
    5.3 Control plan
        5.3.1 Requirements control plan
        5.3.2 Schedule control plan
        5.3.3 Budget control plan
        5.3.4 Quality control plan
        5.3.5 Reporting plan
        5.3.6 Metrics collection plan
    5.4 Risk management plan
    5.5 Closeout plan
6. Technical process plan
    6.1 Process model
    6.2 Methods, tools, and techniques
    6.3 Infrastructure plan
    6.4 Product acceptance plan
7. Supporting process plans
    7.1 Configuration management plan
    7.2 Verification and validation plan
    7.3 Documentation plan
    7.4 Quality assurance plan
    7.5 Reviews and audits
    7.6 Problem resolution plan
    7.7 Subcontractor management plan
    7.8 Process improvement plan
8. Additional plans
Annexes
Index

PROJECT TIME MANAGEMENT

After budgeting, the most important function for the project manager is developing and controlling the project schedule. In fact, delays in completing tasks usually go hand-in-hand with increases in costs. However, for many IS projects where gaining a competitive advantage is a goal, creating and maintaining a schedule that produces a quality project as quickly as possible can be more important than costs. For example, think about what might have happened if another company developed its website before eBay.com. Could a delay in eBay's development schedule have allowed a competitor to become the first big Internet auction site instead?

The main activities of project time management include:

- *Activity definition:* to identify the activities that the team members need to do to complete the project, including each activity's completion time, expected cost, and needed resources.
- *Activity sequencing:* to determine the order of activities, as well as the dependencies and relationships between them.
- *Activity duration estimating:* to determine a constant unit of time, called a work period, and then to estimate how long each activity will take in terms of work periods.
- *Schedule development:* to create a deliverable schedule document by analyzing the sequences of the identified activities, their durations, and their resource requirements.
- *Schedule control:* to keep the project on schedule, adjusting it as necessary.

To manage all these activities, project managers often use a **Gantt chart**.

Gantt charts (see Figure 6.20) provide a standard format for displaying the results of the first four time-management activities. This chart lists the project activities, along with the start and finish dates in a calendar format. On the calendar, horizontal bars that correspond to start and end dates represent activity durations.

ID		Task Name	Duration	January				February				Ma
	ⓘ			31/12	07/01	14/01	21/01	28/01	04/02	11/02	18/02	25/02
1		INCEPTION	14 days									
2	✓	Analyze market data	3 days	100%								
3	📝	Conduct market study	5 days	20%								
4		Examine feasibility	3 days	0%								
5		Create feasibility report	5 days	0%								
6		Present report for approval	1 day	0%								
7		Project approved	0 days	18/01								
8		ELABORATION	24 days									
9		**Create project plan**	4 days									
10		Do stakeholder analysis	2 days	0%								
11		Develop risk analyis and plan	2 days	0%								
12		Develop schedule	2 days	0%								
13		Develop budget	2 days	0%								
14		Project plan approved	0 days	24/01								
15		**Define requirements**	10 days									
16		Determine user requirements	10 days	0%								
17		Determine content requirements	10 days	0%								
18		Determine data requirements	10 days	0%								
19		**Design system**	10 days	0%								

Figure 6.20 A Gantt chart provides a standard format for displaying the results of activity definition, sequence and duration estimating, and schedule development; this chart lists the project activities, along with the start and finish dates, in a calendar format.

PART

2

Patterns or colours on the bars can represent various categories of activities. Arrows show when the start time of one or more activities depends on the completion of an earlier activity. While the project is ongoing, the project manager updates the chart to show actual project durations, to serve as a project evaluation and schedule control tool.

RISK MANAGEMENT

Every IS project contains an element of risk. Uncertainties or unexpected events can and do occur. For example, a key project team member might leave unexpectedly, or management might suddenly decide to reduce funding. But most project risks reflect the fact that much of an IS plan relies on estimates. Since these risks are inherent in the project plan, they can be manageable.

The job of **risk management** is, therefore, to recognize, address, and eliminate sources of risk before they threaten the successful completion of the project. This is the responsibility of all project team members. In general, risk management tasks fall into one of two main categories: (1) risk assessment and (2) risk control.

The first step in risk assessment is to identify potential project risks. A project manager often obtains an initial list of risks by asking several questions: What could possibly go wrong? How likely is this to happen? How will it affect the project? What can I do about it? Since the greatest risks often occur where there is an interface, such as between systems, departments, processes, or organizations, particular attention is paid to these areas. This is where the input of business team members becomes critical: what do you see as being a risky aspect of the project? What can be done to mitigate these risks? Table 6.4 lists some of the most common areas where risks can occur in an IS project.

After obtaining a list of potential risks, the next step is risk assessment; that is, to analyze each of them for likelihood and potential impact to the project. This assessment will come primarily from the experience and knowledge of project stakeholders and others consulted during the risk analysis process. As Figure 6.21 shows, the greatest effort to manage risk will focus on addressing the risks that are most likely to occur (high probability) and those that will have the biggest impact (high impact) if they do occur. In other words, project managers usually concentrate on those risks that fall in the upper right corner of the matrix.

To manage risk effectively, a project manager directs a team member to allocate each risk to an identified owner. This should be someone within the project team who is responsible for monitoring

Table 6.4	Common Areas of Project Risk[13]
Project Risk	**Description**
Feature creep	As the project progresses, user requirements may increase beyond the team's ability to handle them within the original project scope.
Requirements goldplating	A project has more requirements than is really needed from inception.
Shortchanged quality	If a project is rushed, corners are often cut in areas such as testing, documentation, and design tasks.
Overly optimistic schedule	Setting an overly optimistic schedule can cause abbreviations in critical planning and design tasks, as well as put undue pressure on team members.
Inadequate design	When not enough time is allocated to design, the quality of the design can suffer.
Silver bullet syndrome	Occurs when a project team latches on to a new practice or technology, and expects it to answer all of their problems.
Research-oriented development	This occurs when a design attempts to push the boundaries of what is technically feasible in too many areas.
Weak personnel	Occurs when the skills and knowledge of the team members is not up to the project tasks.
Friction with customers	Can be caused by perceived lack of co-operation on one side or the other or personality conflicts.

the situation and ensuring the initiation of any necessary mitigating actions. Table 6.5 lists responses to initial risk assessments.

Managing risk is an ongoing task throughout the project life cycle. The nature of the risks faced by the project team will change as the project progresses. For example, staff recruitment may be a big issue at the inception of a project, while staff retention becomes more of an issue as the project draws near to an end. Or, as the CORE box "Developing Secure Applications from the Start" illustrates, some risks, such as those involving security, may be avoided or reduced by using good development practices.

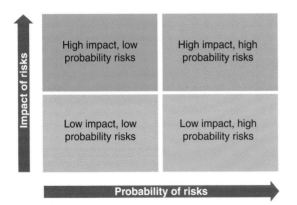

Figure 6.21 A project risk matrix helps managers focus on those risks that will have the biggest impact if they occur.

13. Steve McConnell, *Rapid Development*, Microsoft Press, 1996, p. 85.

Table 6.5	Responses to Risk[14]
Risk Response	**Action**
Risk transfer	Move the risk to someone who is more able to deal with it (e.g., a contractor).
Risk deferral	Adjust the plan schedule to move some activities to a later date when the risk might be lessened.
Risk reduction	Either reduce the probability of the risk occurring or lessen the impact; for example, increase staffing resources on the project.
Risk acceptance	Sometimes, we need to accept the risk and then ensure that contingency plans are in place.
Risk avoidance	Eliminate the possibility of the risk occurring; for instance, use alternative resources or technologies.

On-line Security

Developing Secure Applications from the Start

It smelled terrible. For over two months, hundreds of thousands of litres of sewage had been leaking into Australian parks, rivers, and the grounds of a hotel, and no one knew why. Marine plants and animals were dying, and the water in one creek had turned black. Police solved the mystery when they arrested a man who had been using a computer and radio to gain control over machines governing sewage and drinking water. His motive? He allegedly was trying to get a lucrative consulting contract to solve the problems he was causing.

The above example indicates the serious need for secure program development. But what can be done to create more secure programs and therefore more secure information systems? In her article "Tipping the Scales toward Secure Code," Rebecca Rohan collected 18 tips from software developers and listed them at the DevSource website (see below). Three of these ideas apply to secure programming and IS development in general: (1) Think security—have a security focus and get someone to specifically review the code for security; (2) separate "church" and "state;" that is, separate the "test and review" team from the development team; and (3) require frequent authentication to confirm identities and restrict user access to specifically needed areas.

Web Resources
- DevSource—http://www.devsource.com/article2/0,1759,1612685,00.asp
- Microsoft TechNet—http://www.microsoft.com/technet/security/topics/DevSecApps.mspx
- IBM's DeveloperWorks—http://www-128.ibm.com/developerworks
- Bitpipe—http://www.bitpipe.com/tlist/Secure-Application-Development.html

As the above discussion illustrates, the scope and complexity of an IS development project is often difficult to manage. To assist project managers and ensure that there are standards in the project management profession, the Project Management Institute (PMI) has developed a guide to the Project Management Body of Knowledge (PMBOK®). Much of the information in this section of the text can also be found in the PMBOK® guide. If project management interests you, we encourage you to visit www.pmi.org to learn more about the profession and project management standards.

Following standard practices helps project teams do the right things (be effective). Using technology helps project teams be more productive and efficient (do things right). In the next section, we discuss some of the IT tools that knowledge-enabled professionals, like project managers, use for IS development.

CHAPTER 6

Quick Test

1. True or False. After setting the project scope and time frame, an organization can then calculate the amount of resources needed to complete a project.

2. The job of _____ is to recognize, address, and eliminate sources of risk before they become a threat to the successful completion of the project.
   a. activity sequencing
   b. a Gantt chart
   c. risk management
   d. schedule development

3. The risk that the desired scope of a project will continue to increase as the project progresses is known as _____.
   a. feature (scope) creep
   b. requirements goldplating
   c. shortchanged quality
   d. silver bullet syndrome

Answers: 1. True; 2. c; 3. a

IT TOOLS FOR IS DEVELOPMENT

What types of IT tools can project teams use in IS development? Well, project teams routinely use personal productivity tools, such as spreadsheet software, to explore financial feasibility or create a budget. They also use word processing software to write reports and documentation such as the project plan. Collaboration software aids group decision making and communications between team members as discussed in Tech Guide E. As you are already familiar with these types of software, we focus next on software categories that are geared primarily toward the development of information systems.

PROJECT MANAGEMENT SOFTWARE

Project management (PM) software is designed to support and automate the tasks of project management and decision making. PM software is usually classified into three levels, as follows:

- *Low-level packages*, for entry-level users, include tools for basic scheduling, project control, reporting, filtering, and sorting.
- *Mid-level software* adds to these functions by providing resource-levelling, resource-allocation, cost-control, and flexible-charting capabilities. These functions allow effective management of large projects, with up to about 2,000 tasks.
- *High-level software* provides advanced functions including scheduling by user-defined rules, programming languages, resource management for multiple projects, and risk management. High-level software can identify conflicting demands for the same resources, as well as allow the manager to set priorities among projects that require the same resource.

Table 6.6 lists common capabilities of PM software.

Table 6.6	Project Management Software Features
Feature	Description
Task scheduling	Allows the project manager to assign start and end times to a set of tasks that is subject to certain constraints, such as time or resources.
Resource planning	Tools for determining and controlling what resources (people, equipment, materials) are needed, in what quantities, to perform the activities of the project.
Time tracking	Helps the project manager to ensure that the project is meeting the schedule, budget, and quality targets.
Estimating	Tools for estimating task-completion times and amount of resources needed for each task.
Risk assessment	Aids for identifying project risks and then developing strategies that either significantly reduce or avoid the risks altogether.
Reporting/charts	Include capabilities for reporting on the project status, for example, the use of charts.
Collaboration	May include a shared database as well as e-mail, chat, and virtual meeting capabilities.
Process/methodology	Many packages provide tools geared toward supporting a particular development method.
Hosted or local install	PM software may be locally installed or hosted on the Web by an application service provider (ASP).

Most PM software includes graphical tools for scheduling and tracking tasks, such as the Gantt chart shown in Figure 6.20. Another possible tool is the **program evaluation review technique (PERT) chart**. Like the Gantt chart, a project team uses a PERT chart to schedule and manage the tasks within a project. In Figure 6.22, the PERT shows the project as a network of tasks (represented by rectangles) that are linked by arrows. An advantage of the PERT chart is that it clearly shows the sequence and dependencies between tasks. (A dependent task cannot be started until another task is completed.) Each task in the diagram is labelled with a task number, the duration of the task, an estimated start date, and an estimated end date.

An important use of the PERT chart is to identify the critical path. The *critical path* is the sequence of tasks that determines the overall completion time of the project. If any of the tasks on the critical path are delayed, then the entire project will be delayed. Tasks not on the critical path may have the luxury of extra time, called *slack*, for completing the work. Note that as the project goes on, the critical path of tasks may change. This can occur if tasks on the critical path are completed early or tasks not on the critical path are delayed beyond their allowable slack time.

IS DEVELOPMENT TOOLS

Software also supports the IS development tasks themselves. The project team needs software to model the system, write the software, and develop the database. We describe several types of development tools next.

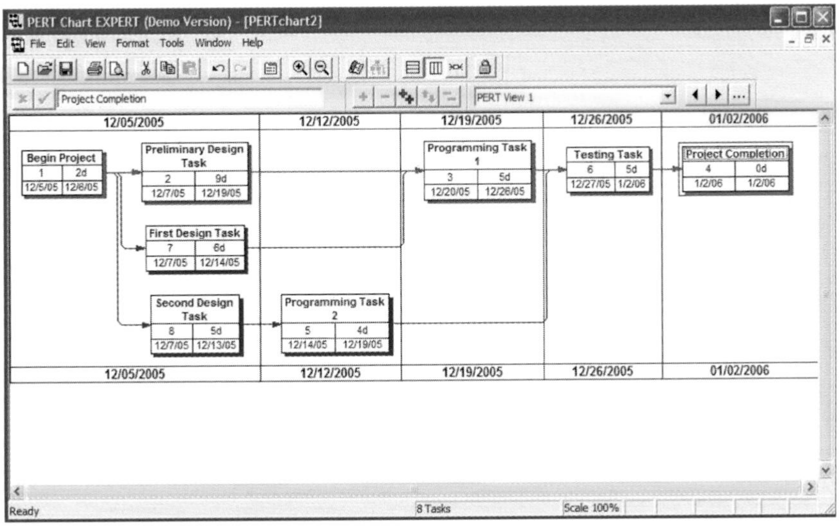

Figure 6.22 A PERT chart, such as the one shown here created from PERT Chart EXPERT software, clearly shows the sequence and dependencies between tasks.

Integrated Development Environments (IDEs)

Today most software programs rely on **integrated development environments (IDEs)**. Instead of using separate software packages, an IDE allows developers to complete several programming tasks within the same software application. The typical IDE includes a text editor to allow the user to write program code, a file system to store programs, a compiler to translate the program into machine language, and debugging tools to find and correct errors. Many IDEs feature visual editors that allow the programmer to develop graphical user interfaces by dragging and dropping components onto a palette. For example, Figure 6.23 shows the Microsoft Visual Studio IDE.

Modelling Tools and Code Generators

Using graphical diagrams in modelling systems is an important activity in information system development. A number of software packages offer a toolbox with common diagramming elements to make the building of diagrams easier. Perhaps the most significant trend in this category is the move toward code generation.

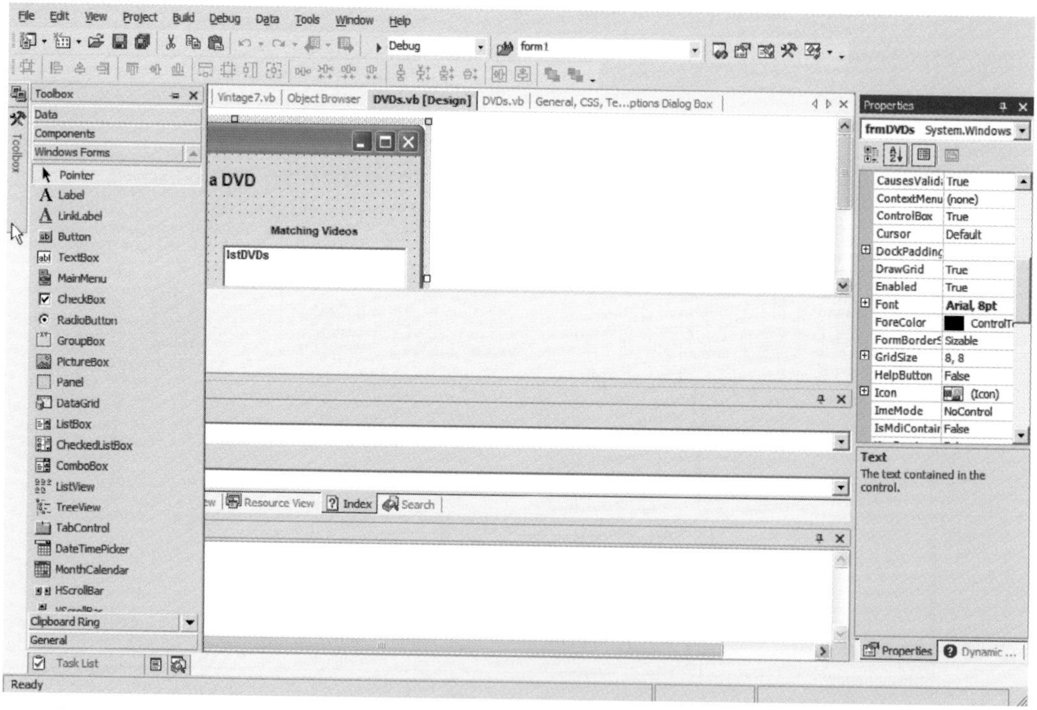

Figure 6.23 IDEs, such as the Microsoft Visual Studio IDE shown here, allow developers to complete several programming tasks within the same software application.

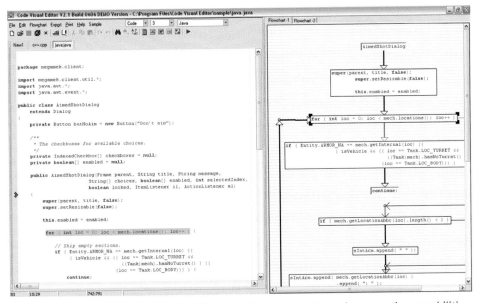

Figure 6.24 The Visual Browser for V/C++ Software provides code-generation capabilities.

With **code generation**, a developer can use graphical diagrams to define a system's components and how they are related. Then, with a simple click of a button or by selecting from a menu, a developer generates code that corresponds to the diagram in a language like C++ or Java. Figure 6.24 shows a screen shot of software that provides code-generation capability along with modelling features.

As Table 6.7 lists, a number of specialized tools are also available that focus on the development of specific IS components.

Table 6.7	Authoring Software Categories	
Category	**Description**	**Representative Software**
Database (DBMS)	Database management system software allows developers to build and manage the databases that are a key part of most IS.	Oracle Database, InterSystems Caché, MySql, MS Access
Web development	Provide tools for developing web pages and applications. Can range from simple HTML editors to full-blown IDEs.	Macromedia Dreamweaver, IBM Websphere
Animation/video	Provides tools for developing animation and video components.	Macromedia Flash and Shockwave
Graphics	Allows users to format and edit visual content.	Adobe Photoshop
Audio content	Allows users to format and edit audio content.	Adobe Audition

CASE Tools

Computer-aided software engineering (CASE) is the use of computer-based support in the software development process. CASE tools support the creation and maintenance of the many documents, diagrams, and data that the project team creates over the course of the IS development life cycle and integrates them in a CASE environment accessible to all users. A current trend in CASE environments is to support the analysis and design of business processes along with the technology to support business processes.

Although project management, development, and CASE tools have improved the IS development process dramatically, there are some risks in using these tools. One common error is to focus on managing the software tools rather than the project itself. Another common problem is known as the "silver bullet" syndrome. This occurs when there is an overreliance on the tools for the success of the project while neglecting the other pillars of a development project. For a successful project, it is important to keep the tools in perspective and view them as support for the primary activities of the project.

Quick Test

1. A _____ chart is used to show sequences of project activities and to identify the critical path.
   a. data-flow
   b. Gantt
   c. PERT
   d. sequence

2. A(n) _____ combines software development tools into one package.
   a. application software
   b. integrated development environment (IDE)
   c. project management software
   d. graphics package

3. _____ -level project management software is a good choice when managers have large projects but are usually focused on one at a time.
   a. Low
   b. Mid
   c. High
   d. Extreme

STUDENT RETURN ON INVESTMENT SUMMARY

1. What major decisions do organizations make in obtaining an IS?

There are four major questions that organizations need to ask when considering obtaining an IS: (1) Do we need an IS? Knowledge-enabled professionals in an organization are constantly looking for ways to improve their operations. (2) Is the project feasible? During project inception, an organization needs to determine whether or not the project has a reasonable chance of success. (3) Should we build, buy, or lease the IS? (4) Do we build the IS ourselves (in-house), or do we contract with an outside firm (outsource) to build it?

2. What important activities must an organization consider within each of the seven stages of the system development life cycle?

The system development life cycle is a series of events viewed over time from the initial concept through to the retirement of an information system. In other words, the system is born, develops, has a useful work life, and then retires. We can divide the life cycle into seven main phases: concept, inception, elaboration, construction, transition, production, and retirement. The retirement of one system often means that an organization is about to transition to another system. The vertical axis of Figure 6.5 lists the core activities related to the life of the information system, grouped together primarily based on when they take place.

3. What considerations are important when creating an IS project team?

As with any team, an organization should carefully consider the makeup of the IS project team. Many different kinds of knowledge-enabled professionals may be involved in the process of obtaining an information system, such as those with highly technical IS knowledge like programmers, those with time-management and budgeting-technique knowledge like project managers, or those with subject matter expertise essential to the future success of the information system, such as clients.

4. What methods do organizations use to ensure that they obtain the best IS to help meet their goals?

The ultimate goal of any IS methodology is to provide a thoughtful and thorough approach to the process of obtaining information systems. Without a methodology, developers and users usually attempt a make-and-fix or buy-and-fix approach. The Waterfall model is a well-known methodology that proceeds from concept through inception, elaboration, and construction to transition and production. More modern methods involve a more evolutionary approach and use prototyping and agile development to complete IS projects.

5. How do organizations provide effective and efficient management of IS projects?

For IS development, a project manager simultaneously oversees three main project elements: (1) the scope of the project, (2) the resources needed, and (3) the time to complete it. The project scope defines project goals. Resources can include people, equipment, material, and money. Time estimates consider project activity times and how they depend on each other. Several standard activities and practices have been developed to manage a project to its successful completion. The diagram in Figure 6.18 shows the nine key components of a project management methodology that support the life cycle of the project.

6. What IT tools do many organizations rely on to obtain an IS that best meets their objectives?

Various software tools are useful to a project team in enabling them to better develop an IS. These include personal productivity tools and collaborative software (discussed in earlier chapters). Three other categories of software tools are directly related to IS projects: (1) project management software, (2) development tools software, and (3) CASE tools. Project management software typically includes tools that help a project manager to plan, schedule, and manage a development project. Development tools include computer programming environments and

CHAPTER 6

special editors that allow developers to create specialized content, such as Web applications or multimedia. Computer-aided software engineering (CASE) tools provide automated support for the modern IS methodologies, as well as provide tools for creating and maintaining the many documents, diagrams, and data that the project team creates over the course of the project.

KNOWLEDGE SPEAK

agile development   219

application service provider (ASP)   205

build-and-fix model   216

code generation   239

computer-aided software engineering (CASE)   240

data flow diagram (DFD)   221

development life cycle   216

entity-relationship diagram (ERD)   221

evolutionary model   218

feasibility study   201

Gantt chart   231

in-house development   205

integrated development environment (IDE)   238

logical data model   221

methodology   216

model   220

outsource   205

program evaluation review technique (PERT) chart   237

project management   225

project management (PM) software   236

prototyping   219

risk management   232

stakeholder analysis   214

system development life cycle (SDLC)   207

system analysis and design   210

Unified Modelling Language (UML)   222

Waterfall model   217

REVIEW QUESTIONS

Multiple-choice questions

1. In the _____ phase of the IS life cycle, the project team finalizes the requirements for the system and designs the system architecture.

   a. inception
   b. elaboration
   c. construction
   d. transition

2. In the _____ phase of the IS life cycle, the organization recognizes a need for an IS and defines the project.

   a. inception
   b. elaboration
   c. construction
   d. transition

3. Which of the following is NOT a project management task?

   a. activity sequencing
   b. use case creation
   c. resource planning
   d. scope verification

4. Which of the following risk-mitigating tactics means that the project manager will act to eliminate the possibility of a risk occurring?

   a. risk reduction
   b. risk deferral
   c. risk acceptance
   d. risk avoidance

Fill-in-the-blank questions

5. _____ is perhaps the most important aspect of project management.

6. The _____ consists of graphical elements that are combined using rules to form logical diagrams of an information system.

7. A(n) _____ is a software package that combines several tools used to write software into one package.

True-False questions

8. The IS life cycle enterprise disciplines include configuration and change management, project management, environmental scanning, and operations and support.

9. Most IS development teams currently use the Waterfall model.

10. A stakeholder analysis is useful for understanding how well the team members will work together.

11. An important part of a CASE tool is the central repository of project items.

Matching questions

Choose the BEST answer from Column B for each item in Column A.

Column A

12. Buying
13. In-house development
14. Leasing
15. Outsourcing

Column B

a. Developing an IS by purchasing an already designed system, customizing it, and then installing and maintaining it in-house.

b. Hiring another company to design and build all or part of an IS.

c. Subscribing to IS services from another company, which also maintains and controls the IS.

d. Building an IS using internal staff members to analyze, design, implement, and maintain it.

e. Using computer-based tools to support IS development.

Short-answer questions

16. List and define the stages of an information system life cycle.

17. Modelling is an important part of many business applications in addition to IS development. List some examples of models that you have seen lately.

18. Discuss why an evolutionary development approach is an improvement over the Waterfall model.

Discussion/Essay questions

19. What is the ideal system development life cycle? Is this ideal possible to achieve? Why or why not?

20. Should managers rely on purely financial techniques when determining an information system's feasibility? Why or why not?

TEAM ACTIVITY

Form a discussion/study team to discuss the remaining weeks of your classes for the term. Think of the successful completion of the term as a project. Identify the goals and the tasks that you will need to complete in order to meet these goals. In your group, brainstorm the risks you might face that can keep you from meeting the goals, and then develop a risk checklist for the remainder of your class term.

SOFTWARE APPLICATION EXERCISES

1. Internet

As you've learned, there are many methodologies used to develop information systems. Use a search engine to locate and read about rapid application methodologies. Read the Database assignment below and decide which methodology you would use to develop the database if you were the project manager.

2. Presentation

Assume that you are an IS analyst working for the IS department in a large retail organization. The Database assignment below will be built for use by project managers (not just IS project managers) in your company. Create a stakeholder analysis that shows the interest and influence of organizational stakeholders for the Database project.

3. Word Processing

Based on your stakeholder analysis in the above Presentation assignment, your company should consider the benefits and costs of outsourcing the database development to a third party. Prepare a request for proposal (RFP) that lists the requirements for the projects and any other relevant items. An RFP is a document that an organization provides to vendors to ask them to propose hardware and system software that will meet the requirements of its new system. You can find many sample RFPs on the Web.

4. Spreadsheet

Create a spreadsheet that supports your financial analysis of the Database project. Use the financial feasibility metrics discussed in this chapter: return on investment (ROI), net present value (NPV), internal rate of return (IRR), and payback period. You will find built-in functions for some of these metrics in Excel. Use Excel Help and your own research to determine how to calculate these values. Create two sets of data for each metric: (1) in-house development cost and (2) outsourced cost.

5. Database

Create a database that a manager can use to track projects. The database will need to track information about projects, the employees who work on them, and the activities that they perform. We show a possible ERD for this database below. Add fields to your database that you think would be appropriate given what you have read about IS projects in this text.

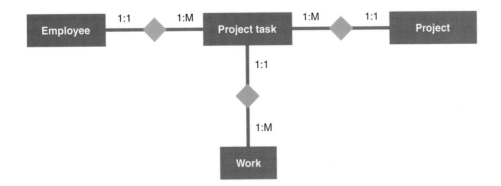

6. Advanced Challenge

Pull together all parts of your analysis and project management database project work. Create a seamless presentation for management that includes development options, stakeholder analysis, feasibility studies, responses to your RFP, and a prototype of the database. Make the presentation to your professor or to your class.

ON-LINE RESOURCES

Companion Website

- Take interactive practice quizzes to assess your knowledge and help you study in a dynamic way.
- Review PowerPoint lecture slides.
- Get help and sample solutions to end-of-chapter software application exercises.

Additional Resources Available Only on WileyPLUS

- Take the interactive Quick Test to check your understanding of the chapter material and get immediate feedback on your responses.
- Review and study with downloadable Audio Lecture MP3 files.
- Check your understanding of the key vocabulary in the chapter with Knowledge Speak Interactive Flash Cards.
- Link directly to websites recommended in the CORE boxes.

CHAPTER

6

CASE STUDY: GOOGLE INC.

"Do you google?" The search engine known simply as "Google" has become so well known that some people now use the word "google" as a verb. Google.com is currently the most popular search engine in use today, with over 4 billion web pages indexed and available in less than one-half second. At last count, 48% of all searches originated on Google. What spurred this popularity? Well, basically, Google found a better way to determine which pages match the user's term using an approach called PageRank, which ranks a page based on how many other web pages pointed to it. This approach usually avoids links to pages that have nothing to do with the user's query. This has made the work of knowledge-enabled professionals much easier.

Google Inc. is younger than many dot-coms, but this relative newcomer has managed to do almost everything right. Like Apple, Google actually started in a garage with two employees, Larry Page and Sergey Brin. Since 1996, these two entrepreneurs have built an organization that now has more than 2,000 employees working at its California headquarters, known as the "GooglePlex." Google-Plex's somewhat laid-back appearance masks a corporate drive for growth and superiority in the highly competitive search engine market.

What makes Google different than so many earlier failed dot-coms? First and foremost, Google added business value by making information much easier to find and much more relevant to the needs of the person doing the searching. Because of this, industry giant Yahoo! picked Google as its search engine, thus giving the company an early source of steady income. Second, Google made money from the very beginning by using innovative advertising on its website. Through a product called AdWords, Google allows anyone to create a simple advertisement for products or services that it displays on related Google search pages.

Third, Google remains open to accepting improvements to its system from its users. Google's open-system approach has resulted in innovative and profitable products being built on top of the Google search engine. Finally, Google constantly looks for new ways to leverage its search engine prowess into other areas, such as indexing images, groups, and products. The company has also added a Web log system called "Blogger," as well as a free e-mail system called G-mail, to compete with existing e-mail systems like Hotmail.

What does the future hold for Google? A number of recent events indicate that existing information industry companies are taking note of its success in the search engine field. Yahoo! has dropped Google as its search engine and has come up with its own engine. Also, Microsoft has announced plans to release its own search engine. These developments and others mean that Google will have more competition. However, by remaining most knowledge-enabled professionals' favourite search engine, Google Inc. expects that its IS-based business will continue to create business value well into the future.

Questions

1. How does the Google search engine create business value for the company? For others?
2. For which knowledge work activities might you use Google? Which knowledge work activity might benefit the most from the use of a search engine like Google?
3. As a dot-com business, what decisions did Google make that enabled it to succeed at a time when so many other dot-coms failed (went out of business)?

Integrative Application Case: Campuspad.ca

Unfortunately, development has not been going as smoothly as planned (see the issues log and project updates on WileyPLUS to see for yourself). Sarah is getting cranky and it appears as if you are on the verge of a second delay in the proposed launch date for campuspad.ca.

When your uncle (who is in the systems business himself) heard about this, he suggested you get in touch with some colleagues of his who run a software development company with a twist. In return for assuming the risk of development, they *lease* completed systems to you rather than selling you their services. After some initial contact, you met with them earlier in the week. Sarah wasn't available (she had a group project meeting) so you went on your own, but she was expecting a briefing. After your meeting, they had sent you a brief proposal (see WileyPLUS for your copy) and were hoping they could meet with you again next week.

You weren't quite sure what to do. After having invested some money upfront on development (funded by two of your angel investors attracted to your business plan), you didn't have much to show for it. This new proposal seemed pretty cheap, even if it might cost you more in the long run. And you had personally being toying with the idea of suggesting to Sarah that you invite Adam (a friend from way back…and a *total* technology-guru-geek kinda guy) to become an equal partner and take on the programming and technology stuff, which of course doesn't have any cost. "What to do, what to do?", you thought.

Guiding Case Questions:

1. How well do you think the current software development firm is doing and why?
2. Do you feel that a lease option is something worth considering? If so, what are the potential risks of that approach?
3. What risks does involving Adam bring?
4. What should your new company do to secure the development resources it needs?

Your Task:

You have scheduled a "coffee clutch chat" with Sarah tomorrow and you know all these topics are bound to come up. She is going to expect not only a briefing, but likely will accept your recommendation on how to proceed. What will you do and why? Write this in the form of a recommendation (no more than two pages), including the rationale that backs up the reasons for your proposed solution to the current system development issues.

CHAPTER

6

PART III

The Business Partner Perspective

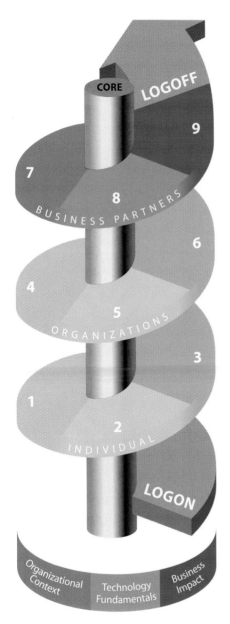

Chapter 7
E-Commerce for Consumers and Organizations

Chapter 8
E-Commerce Technologies

Chapter 9
The Connected Enterprise: Business Partnering and Protecting

As you learned in Chapters 4–6, at the heart of organizations are knowledge-enabled professionals working together to achieve business goals. Often, knowledge-enabled professionals use technology to help them achieve these goals, as well as to create solutions to business problems. While these activities are important to business success, knowledge-enabled professionals are also looking outside the organization for additional opportunities to create business value. They do this through e-commerce and global partnerships, which brings us to the next level of the Spiral Model. In the next few chapters, we discuss how a business connects with trading partners outside its boundaries, and how information systems affect and enhance these relationships.

WHAT WE WILL COVER

- E-Commerce Defined
- The E-Commerce Advantage
- E-Commerce for Consumers
- E-Commerce Between Organizations

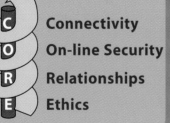

Connectivity	Advertising on the Internet with Google
On-line Security	Keeping Strong Passwords
Relationships	Virtual Teams
Ethics	Corporate Privacy Policies

E-Commerce for Consumers and Organizations

 STUDENT RETURN ON INVESTMENT

Through your investment of time in reading and thinking about this chapter, your return, or created value, is gaining knowledge. Use the following questions as a study guide.

1. What is e-commerce and how is it a part of today's economy?
2. How does e-commerce make a difference to businesses and consumers?
3. How does e-commerce allow organizations to create value for their clients?
4. How can organizations use e-commerce to enhance the delivery of products and services, manage trade with business partners, and improve their supply chain efficiency?

PART

3

THE VOICE OF EXPERIENCE
Colleen Fleming, Carleton University, Heriot-Watt University

With a B.A. in Psychology from Carleton University, a Certified Human Resource Professional designation from the University of Toronto, and a distance M.B.A. from Heriot-Watt University at the University of Edinburgh, Colleen started her career in retail management. She became the head of operations for Tabi International, followed by being senior vice-president at Nestlé and president of Laura Secord. Colleen left retail to start her own boutique management consulting and public speaking firm, and then in 2005, joined the Career Edge Organization.

What do you do in your current position? I am the president and CEO of Career Edge, a pay-for-service, not-for-profit organization where businesses post paid internships for recent graduates and where students apply for these positions. In 1999, Ability Edge was created for recent graduates with a self-declared disability, and in 2003, we launched Career Bridge, which integrates internationally qualified professional immigrants into the labour market via paid internships.

What do you consider to be important career skills? At the level that I'm working at, the business skill I'm using is identifying strategic advantage and then implementing it. You have to be at least IT literate to understand how to use it for competitive advantage. I can't imagine a job without some aspect of technology. In every job that I have had, I have been a change manager, leveraging technology. I have never worked in IT and have never studied IT, but it has been a key success factor in the things I have done.

How do you use IT? This morning I'm making a presentation in Vancouver, which I was asked to do yesterday. I have a laptop with me and can access our organization's intranet, where we have presentation material. I am working on this presentation on-line with my director of communications and project manager in Toronto. Mobility is also important. Much of my career has been on the road and if I wasn't able to access intranets and information, I could not be productive.

Can you describe an example of how you have used IT to improve business operations? Career Edge was the first Internet job-posting board that leveraged

business-to-consumer (B2C) e-commerce in Canada. As a not-for-profit, we have both small margins and operating budgets, and without technology, we never could have national reach, serve the number of organizations that we do, or work efficiently. We are also a business-to-business (B2B) organization in that we administer the payroll for interns with a customized technology platform. Our CRM system and our contact database are very important. By using these systems I can understand the sales outreach and marketing strategy—which are productive and which aren't, what clients we should focus on—and adapt the outreach and marketing to the productivity of clients.

E-commerce has made a huge impact on business operations, especially in the area of supply chain management. When I first started in retail, there were no bar codes and we had to manually track inventory. At Laura Secord, I would phone each store in order to compile national sales results. While at Nestlé we introduced SAP, which, of course, automatically accounts for inventory by store and compiles the information instantly.

Have you got any "on the job" advice for students seeking a career in IT or business? A key thing for me in university was creating formulas for attacking a problem. Even though a problem was daunting, through my education I learned how to approach any problem. My advice to students would be to love what you do. You're going to do better and learn more and give it more energy if you really care about what you're doing.

Colleen is at a not-for-profit organization that was a leader in its use of e-commerce technology. Now Colleen's challenge at Career Edge is to continue that use of technology to remain competitive, manage costs, and meet the needs of her clients, both students and businesses alike. In this chapter we discuss business strategy and e-commerce, B2C and B2B specifically, and how e-commerce is used, especially in the areas of business partnerships and supply chain management, to create competitive advantage.

Recall that in Chapter 4 we viewed organizations as open systems. In this view, organizations create competitive advantage through a chain of value-producing activities. We also noted that each organization operates in an environment of stakeholders, those individuals and other partners or suppliers with an interest in and an influence on that particular organization. A business uses these commercial relationships with its stakeholders, typically customers and suppliers, in order to achieve its financial goals. We have also learned how enterprise-wide systems such as ERP or CRM can help companies manage these internal processes and enhance the efficiency of their value chains.

Similarly, through the Internet, these relationships among customers, partners, and suppliers are evolving. Businesses now create relationships and carry out transactions either completely or partially through *electronic commerce,* or *e-commerce.* In this chapter, we discuss the many ways that e-commerce can create business value for organizations. To do this, we bring together the perspective of the individual and their information systems (Chapter 1) with the broader needs of an organization that processes transactions (Chapters 4 and 5) through networks (Chapter 2) and other information technologies to create the interconnected organization. We show the connections between transactions (Chapter 4 and 5) with information technologies and computer networks (Chapter 2 and Tech Guide C). By the end of this chapter, you will see that for an organization to efficiently and effectively engage in e-commerce, it must tie all of these things together and integrate them into its own unique value chain.

E-COMMERCE DEFINED

For as long as there have been merchants, there has been the desire to improve the efficiency of the retail channel. And advances in technology, product variety, and consumer demand have brought an accompanying change in retailing strategy (as seen in Figure 7.1). The arrival of the telegraph enabled orders to be placed rapidly and shipped by mail. Rail and airline transportation brought new and

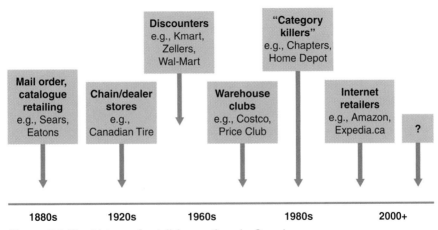

Figure 7.1 The history of retail innovations in Canada.

rapid possibilities for order fulfillment. And the telephone call centre has changed our definition of customer service. So it seemed inevitable that the invention of the Internet would create another revolution in commerce and specifically the arrival of "e-commerce" as a way of doing business around the world.

Some have tried to distinguish between e-commerce (transactions that involve buying and selling goods and services through the Internet) with e-business (the broader use of Internet technologies to reduce operating costs, such as extending the electronic supply chain to partners and suppliers). We have chosen not to make this distinction. Why? We believe that Internet technologies are still early in their development cycles and their evolution as a vital part of business operations continues even as you read this. There is still much unexplored potential in these technologies that relate to everything we do as a society. So for our purposes in this text we will group all of this together and call it e-commerce.

EXPANDING THE BASIC DEFINITION

When you hear of e-commerce, you may think of an on-line retail company like Amazon.ca. However, the wholesale or business-to-business level is far larger and more important to the global economy than the retail level. In fact, while on-line retailers measure sales in the billions of dollars, on-line wholesalers measure them in the *trillions* of dollars. But e-commerce is more than just sales. Consider this more formal definition of e-commerce:

> *E-commerce is the use of information systems, technologies, and computer networks by individuals and organizations to carry out transactions in order to create or support the creation of business value.*

This general definition of e-commerce therefore includes all types of computer networks, all types of transactions, and all types of business relationships.

To help us better understand the full potential of e-commerce in various settings, we describe the parties involved on each side of the transaction to identify the type of e-commerce that is occurring. For instance, we refer to a transaction where a consumer buys a product or service from a business as "B2C." The transaction types are summarized in Table 7.1

E-COMMERCE AND PRODUCTS: PHYSICAL AND DIGITAL

Think about the types of products that consumers typically buy. We can divide such products into two primary categories: *physical* and *digital.* Physical products include anything that requires an actual

Table 7.1 Types of E-Commerce Transactions and Example Websites

Transaction	Description	Example Websites
Business-to-consumer (B2C)	On-line equivalent of the retail store as well as other services	www.chapters.indigo.ca, www.telus.ca
Business-to-business (B2B)	Electronic exchanges between companies	www.worldwideretailexchange.org for the Worldwide Retail Exchange
Business-to-government (B2G)	On-line sales to government agencies, as well as electronic payment of taxes	www.ppitpb.gov.on.ca/mbs/psb/ psb.nsf/english/doingbus.html for businesses wishing to provide goods or services to the government of Ontario
Consumer-to-government (C2G)	Electronic payment of taxes as well as purchase of various types of licences	http://www.netfile.gc.ca/menu-e.html to electronically file and pay taxes to the federal government
Consumer-to-consumer (C2C)	Use of on-line auctions like eBay or Yahoo! Auctions	www.ebay.ca, www.auctions.yahoo.ca

CHAPTER 7

shipment of the item from a central distribution point to the buyer (whether an end-consumer, wholesaler, or another company). This also requires an off-line supply chain to handle the sales, order processing, and delivery of these goods. On the other hand, consumers can receive digital products directly over the Internet or other computer network (such as downloading an album on iTunes versus going to HMV to buy it). This usually requires the use of a completely IT-enabled supply chain. Table 7.2 provides examples of both types of products for all five types of e-commerce transactions.

The main difference between physical and digital products is in the delivery process, as shown in Figures 7.2 and 7.3. Even though a computer network can transmit information about the order, it cannot ship a physical good. For example, say you order a DVD of a recently released movie on-line. As Figure 7.2 shows, the company must still pick it from a shelf in a warehouse, pack it for shipment, and physically send it to you. So even though a web page and on-line

Table 7.2 Types of E-Commerce Transactions and Associated Goods

Transaction	Example Physical Goods	Example Electronic Goods
B2C	CD, DVD	iTunes song, ring tones
B2B	Office furniture like desks and chairs	Virus protection software, mailing lists, databases of product information
B2G	Technical manuals, regulations, and other printed documentation	Document conversion from hardcopy (printed) to XML/Web-based documents
C2G	Printed and mailed income tax return, paper-based fishing licence application	Electronically filed income tax return, fishing licence application and fee
C2C	Elvis Pez, comic books	Shareware program, self-published e-book

PART

3

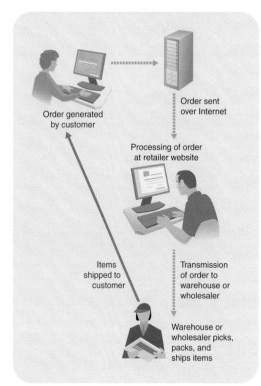

Figure 7.2 When buying a physical good over the Web, the company must still pick it from a shelf in a warehouse, pack it for shipment, and physically move it from the warehouse to the customer. The dotted lines indicate electronic communications, and the solid lines refer to physical shipments of products.

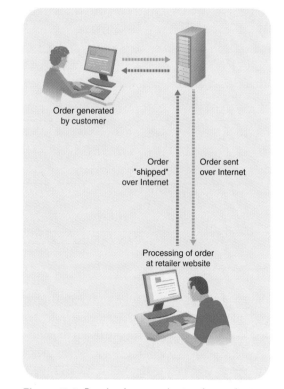

Figure 7.3 Purchasing an electronic product simplifies and speeds up the e-commerce process, as it avoids the need to physically pick, pack, and ship the product.

ordering system may be essential to many e-commerce systems, the business must still have these *back-office elements* in place to handle order fulfillment. Further, any company in the business of accepting orders and shipping goods to customers must also handle returns. This physical process is often as complicated as, if not more complicated than, the actual order fulfillment.

As a result, companies already experienced in physical order fulfillment and returns also tend to more successfully implement e-commerce. Dell and Lands' End are good examples of this type of company. Telephone and mail-order companies also have vast experience in handling returns, so returns from Web orders pose no special problems for them. In essence, e-commerce often simply extends an organization's existing business model. In some cases, it may be only adding another direct channel for interacting with customers.

Now consider digital products. Say that instead of receiving an actual DVD, the company electronically sends you the movie file that you can play back on your computer. In this case, as Figure 7.3 shows, the company can send you this electronic product directly over the Internet or a local network, thereby avoiding any picking, packing, and shipping issues. There are also no return problems. If a problem occurs with the electronic product, the company simply sends a new one for you to download as a replacement.

? WHAT DO YOU THINK?

Imagine that you have one or more items you want to sell. You can either put an ad in your local newspaper or sell it on-line. With this choice in mind, consider the following questions:

1: What factors would you consider in making the choice between selling the item on-line or off-line?
2: What steps would you take to put your item up for sale on-line? What site would you choose and why?
3: What makes you choose one site over another to list your item for sale?

Quick Test

1. Fill in the blank. Selling your CD collection on eBay.ca is a form of _____ e-commerce.

2. Fill in the blank. In general, companies already experienced in the physical order fulfillment and _____ process have been successful in e-commerce.

3. Fill in the blank. Consumers can easily download _____ products from an e-commerce site over a computer network.

Answers: 1. C2C; 2. returns; 3. digital

THE E-COMMERCE ADVANTAGE

The use of computer networks, especially the Internet, to carry out transactions between buyers and sellers is creating a significant "e-commerce advantage" in the worldwide economy. To understand this better, let's consider the technology, competitive issues, and strategy associated with e-commerce around the world.

THE GLOBAL REACH OF E-COMMERCE

When we consider the business use of computer network technologies, especially those associated with the Internet, we find that they offer a number of unique benefits, as Figure 7.4 shows.

People around the world now have Internet access to varying degrees. Some have it only in local Internet cafes; some have a connection directly to their homes or on cell phones, laptops, or personal

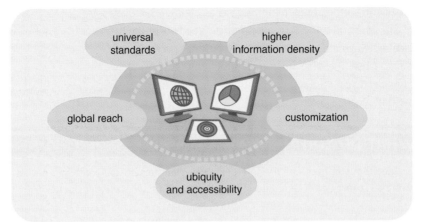

Figure 7.4 Impact of e-commerce technologies on business.

digital assistants (PDAs). This has resulted in the marketplace becoming a ubiquitous *marketspace,* with more than 1 billion potential customers (people with Internet access) as of the end of 2005.[1] In Canada, national Internet usage penetration rates are high, with over 80% of the population having some form of regular access to the Internet—one of the highest rates in the world. While still a minority of the world's total population, Internet users are a fast-growing group with significant buying power. Businesses cannot ignore this group when making marketing plans, especially not organizations in North America and Europe, where the Internet is a powerful and growing force for commerce.

The Internet relies on the use of universal standards to make it available in the same way no matter what corner of the world you access in. We will discuss these standardized Internet technologies more in Chapter 8. When combined with open source software applications and development tools, universal standards increase accessibility to the marketspace, while also lowering entry costs and encouraging innovation. This includes the innovative use of advertising on the Internet, as the CORE box "Advertising on the Internet with Google" discusses.

The innovative uses of the Internet in business have produced truly global competition. Sellers can reach virtually any potential buyer in the world, and sellers can create a global electronic presence easily. This moves us ever closer to the "perfect market" described for decades by economists as an ideal situation that theoretically produces the highest consumption at the lowest price for the most goods.

While this global marketplace is great for large retailers like Wal-Mart, it also allows the almost instant creation of niche businesses. Smaller businesses can compete successfully as well as

1. http://www.internetworldstats.com/stats.htm, as of November 2005.

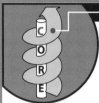

Connectivity

Advertising on the Internet with Google

A problem for many on-line merchants is attracting customers to their website. Simply having a great website is not enough; there has to be a way for customers to find it. A good way to make this happen, the same as in the physical world, is advertising! And search engine leader Google has created a number of economical ways that small on-line businesses can advertise.

One such advertising program is called AdWords. These are the advertisements that you see on the top of the page or on the right side of the screen when you do a Google search. These ads match the search and are therefore targeted to the needs of potential customers. For example, an advertisement for a beach-front property rental will appear on search pages that have something to do with vacations.

In addition to targeting advertisements, it is possible to control how much is spent on AdWords advertising by specifying a maximum cost-per-click (CPC) rate for prospective customers who "click through" to an ad. We say "maximum" CPC rate because the advertiser bids for a CPC rate, and Google only charges for the highest necessary bid rate. Google also uses this bid rate to determine the ad's position in the list of all AdWords advertisements.

The results from using AdWords can be dramatic, as prospective customers often visit websites that they see advertised on Google. This, in turn, can result in including a previously unlisted web page in the regular Google search page, as well as in the advertising section of the page. Finally, note that other search engines, such as Yahoo, have their own version of on-line search-related advertising.

Web Resources
- Google AdWords—https://adwords.google.com/select/
- Yahoo Search Marketing—http://www.content.overture.com/d/
- GoClick.com—http://www.goclick.com

CHAPTER 7

target customers for one-to-one marketing on the Internet in a way they cannot do by opening a small, local store.

E-commerce technology has also increased buyers' level of **information density**; that is, the quality and quantity of information about products and services of interest to them. For example, websites like PCMag.com or CNet.com offer product guides, reviews, and prices on many different kinds of technology, from PCs to printers to digital cameras. The ability of buyers to obtain dense information, however, creates business challenges. Some businesses have responded by choosing to create business value based on a customization-oriented approach to e-commerce, rather than solely on a low-cost producer strategy. Sellers use e-commerce to customize their products and services in at least two ways: *mass customization* and *personalization*.

Mass customization, or the ability to create custom products or services on-demand, is one way that Dell has succeeded in the consumer

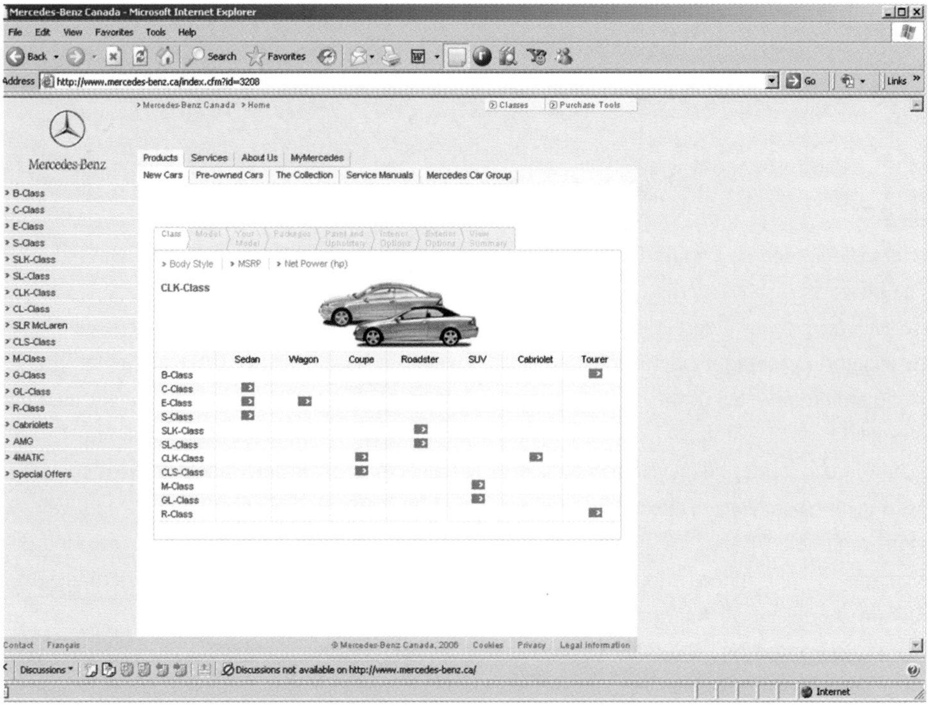

Figure 7.5 Some businesses use e-commerce to customize their products, such as this website that allows consumers to build their own Mercedes-Benz.

PC business. Through its website, customers can choose from a wide variety of ways to customize a "standard" Dell PC to match their needs and desires. Other manufacturers have tried this approach as well. For example, you can visit bmw.ca or mercedes benz.ca (shown in Figure 7.5) and customize a vehicle that the company will deliver to a dealer in your area.

Businesses also use personalization as another way in which e-commerce sites can better reach their customers. **Personalization** is a marketing message that a business customizes for each potential customer's interests, based on his or her searching, browsing, and buying habits. By using personalization, businesses can make marketing messages more effective and efficient. For example, as Figure 7.6 shows, if you register with Amazon.ca, you can view a list of book recommendations and why Amazon recommended the book to you. Personalization of this nature is often only possible because you previously shared information with a website through a registration or sign-up form, or through the data you provided to purchase items from the site.

E-COMMERCE DIFFERENCE IN COMPETITION

E-commerce dramatically affects competition between organizations in a number of ways, such as:

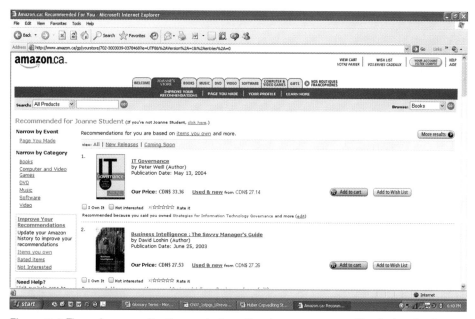

Figure 7.6 Through personalization, a strategy that Amazon.ca uses effectively, a business customizes its website for each potential customer's interests, based on his or her searching, browsing, and buying habits.

- Reducing barriers to market entry
- Preventing any company from "owning" the market
- Enhancing collaboration/alliances
- Multiplying market niches
- Changing marketplace drivers

To consider each of these impacts, let's use the example of a vacation home rental.

A vacation home is often a sound investment. As the owner, you can use it as well as rent it to others to help cover the costs of the property. Further, because you will probably purchase the vacation home in an area subject to significant increases in property value over time, you can later sell the investment for a large gain.

While investing in a vacation home can be a good idea, it does have problems, especially with traditional commerce. First, you might need to hire a rental agency located in the same area as your property, or advertise in newspapers in those areas where you believe your potential renters might live. However, a rental agency usually charges a significant commission (as much as 50% in some cases) and might neglect your property in favour of other rentals that it handles. Advertising in newspapers is expensive and is a "hit and miss" situation, depending on where potential renters live.

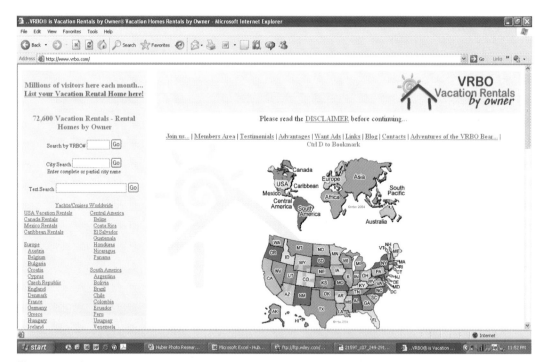

Figure 7.7 Co-operative websites, such as the one shown here, reflect one significant e-commerce difference in competition by reducing the barrier to entry.

An e-commerce solution to this problem is the use of a **co-operative website**, like VRBO.com, canadavacationrentals.ca, and A1Vacations.com, where owners of vacation properties co-operate by advertising on the same site. Such websites serve as a meeting place between property owners and renters. For example, the VRBO.com (Vacation Rentals By Owner) site shown in Figure 7.7 claims to list over 72,000 properties from around the world with "millions" of visits to the site each month.[2] Rental websites, such as those found through search engines like Google, Yahoo, and MSN, also provide an e-commerce solution. Potential renters will find these sites through search engines, advertisements on other websites, or even in traditional travel magazines.

Such websites have quickly become popular with both property owners and renters, for whom the website is basically a meeting place. The actual discussions of availability, price, and rental conditions are handled on a one-to-one basis between the potential renter and the owner.

2. http://www.vrbo.com, as of January 2006.

In looking at e-commerce co-operative websites, it should be easy to see how they have dramatically changed the face of the vacation rental market. They have reduced *barriers to entry* by not requiring that a rental agent have an expensive building in a well-travelled location near the vacation area, a list of rental properties to offer potential renters, or a well-known name among past and potential renters. Instead, owners can rely on a much less-expensive rental website that will act as a gateway to their individual vacation property website. Even another dominant website does not create any barriers to entry, given the wide open nature of the Internet.

In addition, e-commerce keeps any one rental agency or website from "owning" the market. The Internet, with the proliferation of search engines, is now the first way that many travellers look for a place to stay on their trips. This bypasses the traditional rental agencies, which often restrict themselves to travellers who happen by their building.

Further, many of the rental websites on the Internet today are co-operative sites that thrive on collaboration—even if the collaborators don't know each other! By co-operating on a popular rental website, property owners virtually ensure that search engines find the site so potential renters can visit it. Finally, a co-operative rental website also enables contacts between property owners in different parts of the world, which can result in alliances between them.

Traditional rental agencies also typically lack the resources to compete in a niche market, say, renting to travellers interested in visiting a specific beach known for its high-quality shells. Such agencies must rent to the broader market to cover the high fixed costs associated with having a physical location. On the other hand, vacation property owners can easily set up and advertise on a niche rental website. *Niche markets* are one area where e-commerce has shown itself to be superior to almost any existing form of marketing.

Finally, time, distance, and price all drive the traditional marketplaces, but e-commerce easily overcomes these limitations. For example, websites stay open for business on a 24/7/365 basis, and the owner and potential renter can communicate almost instantaneously from virtually anywhere in the world. This means that a property owner in Canmore, Alberta, can just as easily rent to somebody from Germany as they can to somebody from Edmonton. In terms of price, because the Internet generates so much data, a seller or renter can determine demand patterns based on prior experience or on data from other users. This means that negotiations on price between owner and potential renter can rely on availability and demand, rather than on a "one size fits all" pricing scheme.

CHAPTER

7

E-COMMERCE AND BUSINESS STRATEGY

Technology advances change business strategy. To understand this statement better, let's first consider **business strategy** in general. Henry Mintzberg, a professor at McGill University and a leading thinker on strategy and leadership, indicates that strategy is a plan, pattern, position, and perspective. He argues that strategy emerges over time. A strategy may start as a perspective (vision, direction) that calls for a certain position, such as being a low-cost provider, and then evolves into a plan that is implemented and emerges as a pattern that is evident in actions and decisions.[3]

Another view of strategy is by well-known business theorist Michael Porter, who states that *strategy* is "a broad-based formula for how a business is going to compete, what its goals should be, and what plans and policies will be needed to carry out those goals."[4] He suggested in numerous books and articles that the intensity of the competitive rivalry in any industry can be attributed to forces that define the industry. For instance, if the industry is attractive and there are few barriers to entry, then more competitors will enter the industry, increasing competition. If there are barriers to entry (such as requirements for large amounts of capital or it is a government-regulated industry), then it will be harder for new competitors to gain entry. Similarly we can look at the threat of consumers substituting a new product or service for existing ones and the bargaining power of both suppliers and buyers to determine strategies to create and sustain competitive advantage.

The potential competitive threat or opportunity in any industry that results from the introduction of e-commerce can be assessed using Porter's five forces model, shown in Figure 7.8. More detailed information on this model and how to apply it to an industry analysis can be found on the WileyPLUS site associated with this text.

We can visualize this interaction between strategy and technology in a business context by considering Figure 7.9. Any business strategy we are considering is likely going to be enabled and supported by technology. So, in developing our strategies, we must consider how technology will be used. Similarly, as technologies change (for instance as e-commerce has done in retailing), we must take advantage of new opportunities that they offer or we risk losing our competitive advantage.

We can modify Porter's general definition of strategy to specifically apply to e-commerce as follows: **E-commerce strategy** *is a general formula for how a business is going to use computer networks and*

3. Henry Mintzberg, *The Rise and Fall of Strategic Planning*, (1994). Basic Books.
4. Michael Porter, "What is strategy," *Harvard Business Review*, November 1996, pp. 69–84.

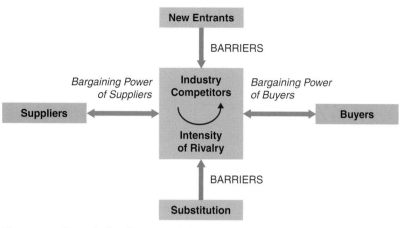

Figure 7.8 Porter's five forces model.

CHAPTER
7

information systems to compete in a global marketplace. For example, Manheim Auctions is the largest automobile auction company in the world. When the Internet became a reality, Manheim was also one of the first of such companies to explore ways to use it to protect its market share from potential encroachment by competitors. It strategically applied e-commerce to the wholesale used car market by creating an on-line purchase system, an on-line bidding system, and a co-operative system that enables individuals to sell their automobiles. Rather than ignore the Internet, Manheim changed its perspective and looked for ways to use the Internet to further its competitive goals of serving its customers better, demonstrating this co-dependence between strategy formulation and the impact of new technologies.

Building a meaningful e-commerce strategy requires two different views of an organization's strategy: what it wants to do (conceptual strategy), and how it will do it (technology strategy). Often there will be a gap between the two that must be addressed if we are to

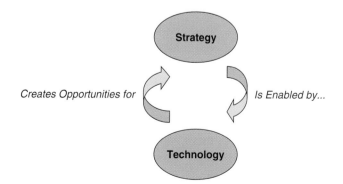

Figure 7.9 The intersection of strategy and technology.

successfully execute our strategy. Obviously, the two views are inter-linked. For example, having the technological capability to carry out an activity will result in business failure if no market exists. Similarly, relying on a new technology to create competitive advantage has both costs and risks associated with it that will have to be recovered in new sources of profit. Just ask all the people who lost money in one or more of the "dot-com" companies in the late 1990s about these two challenges! We consider some conceptual e-commerce strategies here, while deferring deeper discussions of technology strategies until Chapter 8.

An important strategy that many companies are using is *customer relationship management (CRM)* to create a one-to-one marketing experience for their customers. Recall that the Web generates a huge amount of data on customer buying habits and preferences. With these data, companies can use CRM to tailor the products on their website to the individual buyer. This creates a closer match to the customers' real needs, which, in turn, increases the probability they will return to the website for another purchase. However, as the

---

Ethics

Corporate Privacy Policies

Are you one of the many people who does their holiday shopping on-line to avoid the crowds at the mall? During the 2005 holiday season, B2C e-commerce sites generated approximately $30.1 billion in spending, up 30% from 2004.[5] Along with the large amounts of money and goods that are changing hands, consumers are providing on-line companies with vast amounts of private information that are necessary to complete the sales transactions.

This growth in e-commerce may reflect a growing sense of trust in e-commerce companies, despite an increased awareness of the dangers to private information that exists in cyberspace. Many companies have realized their moral and practical responsibility to protect private information. Guarding private information helps to maintain the trust and, hopefully, the loyalty of their customers.

As part of managing the relationships with their customers, most companies create and maintain privacy policies. In fact, in Canada, the Federal Personal Information Protection and Electronic Documents Act (PIPEDA) requires companies to adhere to specific rules regarding privacy and strongly encourages corporations have a privacy policy. A privacy policy is a set of procedures and philosophies that a company adopts to handle individually identifiable private information. A link to a privacy policy is available from the home page of most reputable e-commerce sites. For instance, look at rbc.com for the privacy policy of the Royal Bank of Canada as an excellent example.

The Online Privacy Alliance has developed a set of guidelines that represent the best practices for creating and maintaining an e-commerce privacy policy:

---

5. http://www.nielsen-netratings.com/pr/pr_051229.pdf

Adoption and Implementation of a Privacy Policy—Any organization, especially one engaged in e-commerce, has a responsibility for adopting policies for dealing with private information and making these policies public.

Notice and Disclosure—The policy should be easy to obtain and understand and be available before private data are collected. It should clearly explain what data will be collected and how they will be used.

Choice and Consent—Individuals should be given the right to choose how their identifiable information may be used when the use is unrelated to the purpose for which the data are being collected.

Data Security—Businesses that collect private information should take reasonable steps to make sure the data are reliable and protected from misuse.

Data Quality and Access—Businesses collecting private information should take reasonable steps to make sure that data are accurate, complete, and timely. They should also provide individuals access to their private data and the opportunity to correct inaccuracies if they are found.

As a consumer, you should read the privacy policies of the companies with which you do business. Check to see that the policies reflect the best practices of protecting private information.

Finally, as a knowledge-enabled professional, you should realize your responsibility for maintaining your customers' privacy. This is not only a moral obligation, but it also makes good sense as part of your overall management of customer relationships. Developing and following a good privacy policy can go a long way in fulfilling this obligation and retaining your customers' trust.

Web Resources

- Privacy.org—http://www.privacy.org/
- Electronic Privacy Information Center—http://www.epic.org/
- Computer Professionals for Social Responsibility—http://www.cpsr.net/
- Office of the Privacy Commissioner of Canada—PIPEDA Guide for Businesses and Organizations—http://www.privcom.gc.ca/information/guide_e.asp

CORE box "Corporate Privacy Policies" discusses, businesses also need to consider privacy issues when using these data.

In addition to privacy concerns, the use of CRM can also create *switching costs* for customers. Going to another seller means that they will have to retrain a new website to understand their preferences.

Other e-commerce strategies that companies are using to increase business value to consumers include virtual showrooms, increased channel choices, wider component choice, and use of mobile technology. For example, possibly the largest new channel is through mobile devices using wireless networks, or mobile commerce (m-commerce). **Mobile commerce** is the use of laptops, mobile telephones, and PDAs to connect to the Internet and Web to conduct many of the activities normally associated with e-commerce. Firms now have two-way interaction with customers through these mobile devices.

WHAT DO YOU THINK?

There has been an explosion in on-line sales in North America in the past few years and almost everybody has purchased something on-line at one time or another. In thinking about e-commerce sites you use, consider the following:

1: What features make you choose to do business with an on-line vendor?

2: How important is brand in your decision and what makes you trust one site or vendor over another?

3: What are some of the most interesting features you have seen that help make your on-line shopping experiences more enjoyable or useful?

Now that you have a better understanding of e-commerce and the difference it makes, let's look at the business-to-consumer (B2C) and business-to-business (B2B) sectors.

Quick Test

Match the term on the left with the application to e-commerce on the right.

1. CRM	a. Competing sellers partnering on a common website
2. m-commerce	b. Creating a one-to-one marketing system
3. Co-operative website	c. Transactions using hand-held devices

Answers: 1. b; 2. c; 3. a

E-COMMERCE FOR CONSUMERS

Let's start our discussion of consumer-oriented e-commerce by looking at the benefits that e-commerce brings to consumers and businesses, as well as its limitations for both parties.

BENEFITS AND LIMITATIONS OF E-COMMERCE FOR CONSUMERS AND BUSINESSES

In general, because having information about and access to larger markets increases the buyer's knowledge of a good deal, Porter's model suggests that e-commerce increases competition. This often results in lower prices and better services for all consumers, on-line or not. However, there may be disadvantages or limitations for consumers in the form of shipping time and costs, download speeds, security, and payment sizes that create some barriers to the use of this technology for some kinds of transactions or industries. On the flip side, the increased competition, lower prices, and better services

Table 7.3	Benefits and Limitations of B2C E-Commerce	
	Benefits	**Limitations**
Consumer	• Lower prices • Shopping 24/7 • Greater searchability of products worldwide • Shorter delivery times for digital products • Sharing of information with other consumers • Improved customer service	• Delay in receiving physical products, plus shipping charges • In areas without high-speed Internet, slow download speeds • Security and privacy concerns, especially with the rise of *phishing* • Inability to touch, feel, smell, try out, or try on products prior to purchasing • Unavailability of micropayments for purchases of small-cost products
Business	• Expansion of marketplace to global proportions • Cheaper electronic transactions • Greater customer loyalty through customized web pages and one-to-one marketing • Expansion of niche marketing opportunities • Direct communications with customers through website, often resulting in better customer service	• Increased competition due to global marketplace • Ease of comparison between competing products drives prices down • Customers want specific choices and will not accept substitutes • Customers control flow of information instead of companies

that consumers now expect can create problems for inefficient businesses as newer, more technology-savvy competitors enter the industry. Table 7.3 lists some advantages and disadvantages of B2C e-commerce for both consumers and businesses. You are probably familiar with most of these advantages and disadvantages for the consumer.

In looking at Table 7.3, note the number of advantages of B2C e-commerce for businesses. Expansion of the marketplace enables businesses to reach customers far beyond their local area with a minimal capital outlay. Businesses also reduce their cost of dealing with paper-based transactions by carrying out transactions digitally over a computer network.

Customizing individual web pages to the interests of customers also creates greater customer loyalty. Amazon.ca has turned this into a key advantage that keeps customers coming back since they don't have to train a new website to know their interests (see Figure 7.6). Use of niche marketing helps companies react to changing competition. For instance, many travel agencies have turned to specialized travel niches (for example, those specializing in a specific area such as www.findcroatia.com). Finally, more direct communication with

---

6. Some, but not all, of these are from E. Turban, et. al., *Electronic Commerce: A Managerial Perspective* (2002) Prentice-Hall: Upper Saddle River, NJ, pp. 26–28.

customers, even when an intermediary sells the product, results in better customer service. For example, a large company like Moen (moen.com), which markets kitchen and bath products, can provide customers detailed drawings of its products directly over the Internet as well as design information prior to the sale.

However, e-commerce carries definite disadvantages for inefficient companies that often mirror the potential advantages. A global marketplace means that companies from around the world can compete for a business's local customers, creating a very intense industry rivalry. More competition driving down prices is like having a Wal-Mart next to every business. If a business is not ready to compete on a price basis, then it must offer some service that its competitor cannot, like more customized products or more individual attention. Finally, with a wide variety of advertising media, companies must know how to attract customers to their websites.

WHAT DO YOU THINK?

Think about a product that you have purchased or would like to purchase from an e-commerce site. Think about a second product that you would *not* want to purchase from an on-line source and consider the following questions:

1: How do these two products differ? Specifically, why would you purchase one on-line but not the other?
2: For the second product, is there something the manufacturer might include on its website that would help to overcome your reservations?
3: What type of offers or features encourage you to purchase on-line?

One way to attract customers to websites is to ensure protection of sensitive data, such as credit card information. As a result of consumer concern, many on-line vendors resort to third-party endorsements of their security practices to help build consumer confidence. An example of this would be overlay brands (such as www.truste.org) that an organization qualifies for and then advertises on their site. It is important that on-line businesses are secure and that they safeguard consumer information. It is also critical that we take measures ourselves to safeguard our own privacy. One way of doing this is to by maintain strong password controls, as discussed in the CORE box "Keeping Strong Passwords."

All in all, however, the advantages of e-commerce continue to outweigh any limitations. As a result, businesses are turning to e-commerce business models to find more ways to compete in the global marketplace. Statistics Canada reported that in 2005, Canadian retailers had on-line sales of $5.4 billion, and the increase in on-line

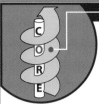

On-line Security

Keeping Strong Passwords

Come on, admit it! Is your password your account name or simply the word *password*, or a common name like that of a friend or relative? Do you use the same password for most or all of your accounts? According to research reported by the Computer Crime Research Center,[7] 21% of people use their own or their partner's nicknames for their passwords, 15% use their birthdays or anniversaries, and another 15% use names of their pets. About 14% had a family member's name as their password, 7% relied on a memorable date, and 2% even unimaginatively used the word *password*.

Why do so many people use weak passwords, especially considering that passwords are an important part of authentication for many computer systems? Authentication is the process of identifying an individual and ensuring that he or she is who they claim to be. Coupled with a username, a password is perhaps the most common authentication technique used today. Since most of us have important private information stored on various computer systems, using a weak password is like providing easy access to the key to our safety deposit box.

To ensure that your password is and remains as strong as possible, you should follow these guidelines:

1. Use at least eight characters.
2. Include digits, punctuation, and nonprinting characters.
3. Use both upper- and lowercase characters.
4. Use different passwords on different accounts.
5. Change your password regularly and don't reuse passwords or make minor variations such as incrementing a digit.

Of course, these are hard to do. The main reason we don't use strong passwords is that they can be hard to remember, and more difficult still to remember more than one. So what can you do? Try this: come up with one or more rules that you can use to derive a strong password from something easy to remember—your own password-making algorithm. For example, (1) start with something easy to remember such as a favourite song (the *key*) like "*Mary Had a Little Lamb*." (2) Take these initials: MHALL. (3) Make every other initial lowercase: MhAlL. (4) Insert a punctuation mark between each letter: M*h*A*l*L. (5) Append the initials of the account that you want to access; for the office desktop the password may become M*h*A*l*Lod. By memorizing just a few items—the song title, the punctuation, the account initials—a fairly strong password can be created and remembered that is different for each account. Warning: don't use these exact rules, but come up with rules that are all your own! Also, don't forget to change your password periodically by coming up with a new key or set of rules.

Web Resources
- GeodSoft: Good and Bad Passwords How-to—http://geodsoft.com/howto/password/
- Computer Crime Research Center—http://www.crime-research.org/

CHAPTER 7

sales was six times the rise in overall retail sales.[8] While these B2C numbers are impressive, they pale in comparison to the B2B sales results of $19.8 in 2004.[9]

E-COMMERCE BUSINESS MODELS

A **business model** defines how a company will meet the needs of its customers while making a profit. As such, a business model must also include a *revenue model*, which describes how the company will generate revenue from its business operations that exceeds the costs of conducting those operations. Simply put, the business model chosen should result in a profit (revenues > costs) for the firm. Businesses can do this by finding ways to increase revenue, decrease costs, or a combination of both.

In terms of e-commerce business models, there are a wide variety of ways to categorize them, including revenue generation, type of website, audience, or a combination of the three. Table 7.4 highlights the nine different B2C e-commerce business models that we believe represent the majority of e-commerce models. And while none of the business models in Table 7.4 is completely new, the ways in which some businesses have implemented them for e-commerce are quite innovative.

For example, people have been buying recorded music since the invention of the phonograph well over 100 years ago. However, the ability to use Internet-based e-commerce to purchase and instantaneously download songs directly to a personal music player or cell phone is a relatively new model for B2C transactions.

WEBSITE PURPOSE

Another way to understand e-commerce is to look at the purpose of the website used to implement the various business models. That is, having a great e-commerce business model like those listed in Table 7.4 will not generate a profit *if* it is not associated with a website that brings in customers or at least visitors. As with business models, there are a number of ways to classify websites by purpose. In our case, we use the eight classifications listed in Table 7.5 on page 274.

In looking at Table 7.5, note that the same website (Yahoo and Netscape) provides an example of two classifications. That's because most B2C websites are trying to serve as large an audience as possible, thereby making their sites more valuable to advertisers and as a source of information about their Web visitors to other companies.

8. Statistics Canada, http://www.statcan.ca/Daily/English/060420/d060420b.htm. Retrieved February 11, 2007.
9. Statistics Canada, http://www.statcan.ca/english/research/11-621-MIE2005033.htm. Retrieved February 11, 2007.
10. All but the last are taken from Michael Rappa, http://digitalenterprise.org/models/models.html

Table 7.4	E-Commerce Business Models[10]		
Business Model	**Description**	**Examples**	**Comments**
Brokerage	Brings together buyers and sellers for a fee.	eBay, Priceline, PayPal	There are many types of brokerage models in all types of e-commerce.
Advertising	An extension of the traditional broadcasting model in which ads appear on websites.	Yahoo Canada, Google	There are many different types of advertising, but all depend on a large volume of viewer traffic.
Merchant	Sells products, both physical and digital, to consumers.	Amazon.ca, Canadiantire.com, Walmart.ca, iTunes	Commonly referred to as *e-tailers*, merchants can use pure e-commerce or a combination (click-and-mortar).
Manufacturer Direct	Makes and sells products directly to customer.	Dell, Gateway, Microsoft, McAfee (antivirus products)	Products can be purchased (PCs), leased (servers), or licensed (software).
Affiliate	Receives a fee for their websites when purchases come through them.	Amazon.ca fees to affiliate websites.	Can also include banner ad exchange between affiliated sites as well as revenue sharing.
Community	Based on user loyalty because of high investment of time and emotion.	MySpace, Neopets, Evite, Linux.org	Generates revenue through sales of ancillary products or voluntary contributions.
Subscription	Charges a fee to users to subscribe to service or information source.	Classmates, globeandmail.com	Subscription may be for premium services; advertising model may be combined with this model.
Infomediary	Provides data on consumers and consumption habits.	DoubleClick, NetRatings, Edmunds	Usually aimed at helping businesses rather than consumers.
Co-operative	Enables competitors to co-operate on a website.	AutoTrader.ca, VRBO.com, Craigslist	Usually aimed at individuals or small businesses that cannot attract customers to their own website.

CHAPTER 7

For example, Yahoo started out as a type of search engine and then became a portal by using its popularity to charge for adding links to other websites. Similarly, Netscape started out as a portal for Netscape browser users and now contains links to a search engine as well as providing news and information.

Quick Test

1. Which of the following is NOT an e-commerce benefit for businesses?
   a. Expansion of marketplace to global proportions
   b. More expensive electronic transactions

Table 7.5	Websites Classified by Purpose		
Website Type	**Purpose**	**Example**	**Business Model**
Portal	Provides a gateway to many other websites.	Netscape, Yahoo, MSN	Advertising, Affiliate
Search Engine	Finds websites that contain a word or phrase.	Google, Netscape, Yahoo, MSN, DogPile	Advertising, Affiliate, Infomediary
Browse or Search and Buy	Sells goods and services.	Dell, Chapters.indigo.ca, iTunes, VRBO	Merchant, Infomediary, Manufacturer Direct, Co-operative
Sales Support	Provides information on a product before or after the sale.	Microsoft, Dell, McAfee, Telus	Community, Infomediary
Information Service	Provides news, information and commentary.	National Post, TSN, Economist	Subscription, Community, Affiliate
Auction	Facilitates sales between third parties.	eBay, Priceline, PayPal	Brokerage
Travel	Sells travel tickets and tours.	Expedia, Travelocity, Orbitz, itravel2000	Merchant, Brokerage, Co-operative
Special Interest or Services	Provides information, product sales and support, and contacts between visitors.	Microsoft support groups, Google Groups, Lavalife, Craigslist	Community, Merchant, Affiliate, Infomediary, Advertising

   c. Greater customer loyalty through customized web pages and one-to-one marketing

   d. Expansion of niche marketing opportunities

2. A business _____ defines how a company will meet the needs of its customers while making a profit.

   a. operation

   b. model

   c. division

   d. centre

3. An _____ website facilitates sales between third parties.

   a. advertising

   b. affiliate

   c. auction

   d. extreme

Answers: 1. b; 2. b; 3. c

E-COMMERCE BETWEEN ORGANIZATIONS

Even though most of the emphasis in the popular press has been on the B2C form of e-commerce, B2B is by far the larger market in terms of volume of transactions and dollar amounts. In this section, we discuss commerce between organizations using the various types of information that must pass between trading partners in order to complete a transaction. We review the concept of the *interorganizational system* as a form of IS to handle this information flow. We then consider the benefits that e-commerce provides the organizations in terms of improving their supply chains.

DOING BUSINESS WITH OTHER ORGANIZATIONS

One business or organization doing business with another markedly differs from the B2C process. For example, if you decide you need a new computer, you think about what you need in a new PC and then search for computer merchants that sell the product that meets your needs. You most likely make the purchase with a credit card and set it up yourself when it arrives. You then pay the bill from your personal bank account.

On the other hand, if an organization decides it needs new PCs, it's not just ordering one computer at a time, but potentially thousands of PCs. This larger-scale purchase results in a more complex decision-making process, like that discussed in Chapter 3, requiring a great deal of thought and preparation. One or more authorized individuals (knowledge-enabled professionals) must consider a number of factors, including the existing organizational technology infrastructure. That decision becomes even more complicated when the organization structure includes *virtual teams*, like those discussed in the "Virtual Teams" CORE box.

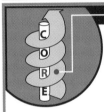

Relationships

Virtual Teams

Today, Nick is about to have his first meeting with his new system project team. His company, Sodor Software, develops software that is used to schedule railroad traffic. The company has just formed a strategic partnership with the software house Bagheera, Inc., located in Bangalore, India. As the project manager, Nick is looking forward to meeting with his lead programmer, Aditya, and the other team members from Bagheera. As he enters the conference room in Sodor's Ottawa headquarters, he notes that Breanna, his systems analyst, and

PART

3

Mark, his financial manager, are already seated around the table. There is no one else in the room. Nick smiles at his co-workers and says: "Looks like we're all here. Let's start the meeting."

Where's the rest of the team? They're waiting in a similar conference room in Bangalore. Nick and his group are part of what is known as a virtual team. A virtual team, sometimes called a *geographically dispersed team (GDT)*, is a group of people who work across geographic distance, time, and the boundaries between organizations. They stay connected through telecommunications technology. Like any team, however, the members should have complementary skills, focus on a common goal, and hold themselves mutually accountable.

The number of virtual teams has grown along with improvements in communications, especially with the file-sharing capabilities available over networks like the Internet. Reasons for virtual teams revolve around the differences in the locations and work times of team members. Like Nick's team, members may not be physically located at the same place, and it may be impractical or too costly for the team members to travel to meet face-to-face. In addition, the members may work at different times; for instance, Bangalore is about 14 time zones ahead of Ottawa.

Technology to support virtual teams includes hardware, software, and networking. Hardware may include computers, telephones, and videoconferencing apparatus, either connected over private WANs or more often using public networks like the Internet. The primary software category in use is groupware. Groupware features can include e-mail, meeting facilitation, group scheduling, and project management tools. In a nutshell, a team, plus groupware, plus a communication network, equals a virtual team.

An organization can derive several benefits by using virtual teams:

- People can work from any place and at any time.
- Organizations can recruit the best people regardless of their physical location.
- Expenses are reduced due to travel and sometimes facilities.
- There is greater flexibility for workers.

However, virtual teams may need to overcome time zone, culture, and organizational responsibility differences in order to function effectively as a group. Teams and teamwork and the technology used to support teams are discussed in more detail in Tech Guide E.

Web Resources

- Teamspace.com—http://www.teamspace.com
- Google has several free virtual team resources including spreadsheets and a calendar—http://www.spreadsheets.google.com and http://www.google.com/calendar
- Virtualteams.com: Collaboration in the Network Age—http://www.virtualteams.com

Whether it involves large-scale purchases or virtual teams, e-commerce between organizations is often more complicated than B2C. Let's consider some aspects of B2B e-commerce, in terms of types of transactions, marketplaces, and business models.

B2B TRANSACTIONS AND BUSINESS MODELS

We can broadly divide B2B transactions into two types: (1) spot buying and (2) strategic sourcing. **Spot buying** is much like what you do when you make a stock market transaction; you buy at market prices determined by supply and demand from someone you do not know. Companies often engage in spot buying to purchase goods and services that are commodities; that is, they are usually uniform in quality and differ only somewhat in price. Examples include gasoline, paper, and cleaning supplies. Whenever a company engages in spot buying, it needs to find a public marketplace or *exchange* that sells these desired products and services. Although it can be a physical marketplace, most B2B e-commerce exchange transactions occur through an on-line intermediary.

On the other hand, **strategic sourcing** involves forming a long-term relationship with another company. The companies set prices through negotiation. Both the buyer and seller are usually well known to each other and wish to continue a trading relationship into the future. A company's large-scale computer purchases probably result from strategic sourcing.

Strategic sourcing often relies on a one-to-one business model, although company-centric and exchange models are also used.[11] In the **one-to-one marketing model**, two companies collaborate to create a trading relationship that is good for both of them. In this form of B2B, both trading partners win from the relationship, as with strategic sourcing transactions. While they are not always of the same relative size, neither company dominates the trading relationship. From an e-commerce point of view, the two companies often seek to use computer networks to facilitate the supply chain from one to the other. (We discuss this model in more detail in a later section.)

With the **company-centric business model**, a company is either a seller to many other companies (one-to-many) or a buyer from many companies (many-to-one), as Figure 7.10 shows. In either case, the single company tends to dominate the market. It often completely controls the information systems that support the transactions, including the supply chains between it and its smaller trading partners. In this model, the large buyer or seller wants to use e-commerce to improve its profitability by increasing prices and/or reducing costs of doing business with the many smaller trading partners.

With the one-to-many model, the seller often provides a Web-based private sales channel through a private network, called **electronic data interchange (EDI)**, or through a protected form of the

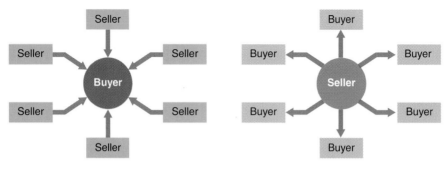

Many-to-one model   **One-to-many model**

Figure 7.10 With the company-centric business model, a company is either a buyer from many companies (many-to-one) or a seller to many other companies (one-to-many).

Internet, called an *extranet*, to link trading partners while keeping others out (we discuss both EDI and extranets in more detail later). Such sales can be at a set price or via an auction. For example, Carbid.ca uses an extranet to enable car dealers to purchase used cars on-line, thereby avoiding a costly trip to the physical auction. They have specified prices for cars as well as on-line auctions at which dealers can bid on automobiles.

Because the many-to-one model provides a single buyer with products that it needs to carry on business, this is a part of the *procurement process*. When using e-commerce, it is commonly referred to as **e-procurement**. A buyer can conduct this process in a number of ways, including reverse auctions, aggregating catalogues, or group purchasing.

With an e-procurement reverse auction, the buyer posts projects to a secure website to which sellers respond with bids for providing goods and services for that project. In this case, the bidder with the *lowest* bid wins, hence the name *reverse auction*. The aggregating catalogues model assembles together the catalogues from all suppliers on the buyer's server. The buyer then uses them to make all purchases. This tends to centralize the procurement process. Finally, with group purchasing, two or more buyers work together to achieve lower prices

Figure 7.11 From an e-commerce point of view, an exchange is typically a website where buyers and sellers post their needs and offerings.

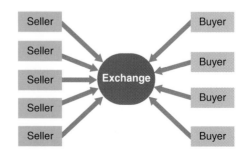

from their suppliers. Smaller buyers can do this through websites that aggregate demand and then negotiate prices with suppliers.

In the **exchange model**, many companies use an exchange to buy and sell from each other through spot-buying transactions. The exchange can be a co-operative venture among a number of the companies, owned by an independent organization like that run by the National Retail Federation for the benefit of its members. It can also be run by a larger company that has found a way to profit from the transactions. The airplane parts exchange created by Boeing (see the Case Study at the end of Chapter 8) is an example of the last type of exchange.

We can categorize exchanges into two groups: (1) verticals and (2) horizontals. *Vertical exchanges* meet the needs of a single industry, say, retailing. On the other hand, *horizontal exchanges* deal with products and services that all companies need, regardless of the industry (like office supplies). Figure 7.11 shows how buyers and sellers come together in an exchange. From an e-commerce point of view, an exchange is typically a website where buyers and sellers post their needs and offerings. For example, for a fee, the Workpolis.com website posts both résumés and job openings.

SERVICES IN B2B E-COMMERCE

Like consumers, companies need a variety of services and electronic goods, just in far greater quantities. Table 7.6 highlights some of

Table 7.6	B2B Services and Electronic Products
Service or Electronic Product	How Companies Use E-Commerce to Obtain
Software	The ability to buy a site licence on-line and then download one copy, which they then burn on CDs, reduces organizations' cost and time in procuring software.
Leasing	Companies can use e-commerce to negotiate the original lease price and to dispose of an item at the end of the lease.
Travel	Travel is a big item with companies that have more than one office or distant customers; using e-commerce to provide less expensive travel can save money.
Insurance	Companies must insure their buildings, people, vehicles, and so on; using e-commerce to find better insurance coverage can mean lower costs for the company.
Banking	As with consumers, businesses must pay their bills. They must also accept payments from customers. Moving banking on-line reduces the cost of writing and depositing cheques as well as making the transfer of funds much easier.
Stock trading	As a part of their overall financing process, businesses will often buy and sell other stock as well as their own. On-line trading makes this possible for much lower transaction fees.
Financing	Businesses often need to raise capital through debt; a number of services now make it possible to do this on-line for lower transaction fees.

these services and electronic products used by businesses, and how using e-commerce can help an organization effectively and efficiently obtain them.

USING B2B E-COMMERCE TO IMPROVE SUPPLY CHAIN EFFICIENCY

Recall from our discussion of the *value chain* in Chapter 4 that the inbound and outbound logistics (movement of goods or services from supplier to organization and from organization to customer, respectively) of a company are linked to the logistics of other companies via its supply chain. That is, a **supply chain** is a network of facilities and distribution options that performs the functions of procurement of materials, transformation of these materials into intermediate and finished products, and the distribution of these finished products to customers.[12] Procurement plays a large part in any supply chain, and the use of e-commerce for procurement has been an important way for organizations to save money. To understand why, we need to first review the traditional procurement process.

WHAT DO YOU THINK?

When we buy a product on-line, we might not stop to think about all the steps in the supply chain, or the number of partners or suppliers involved. For example, let's assume you are wearing a cotton shirt today that you purchased on-line from your favourite clothing retailer. Consider the following questions:

1: Where does the complete supply chain for this cotton shirt begin and end?
2: At the point at which you purchased it, how much of that supply chain has already happened versus how much was still left to happen to get your shirt delivered?
3: How do you think technology was used at every point in the supply chain to keep costs low enough that you were able to buy the shirt at such a reasonable price?

Traditional Procurement Process

For procurement to occur between businesses, there must be an information flow between the entities in addition to the flow of goods. Traditionally, this paper flow has involved three key elements: (1) the purchase order, (2) the invoice, and (3) the receipt of goods. Figure 7.12 shows the typical steps in the process, as follows:

1. The buyer sends a purchase order to a vendor. A *purchase order (PO)* is a document from an organization requesting another organization to supply something in return for payment. It

---

12. Ram Ganeshan and Terry P. Harrison, "An Introduction to Supply Chain Management," http://lcm.csa.iisc.ernet.in/scm/supply_chain_intro.html

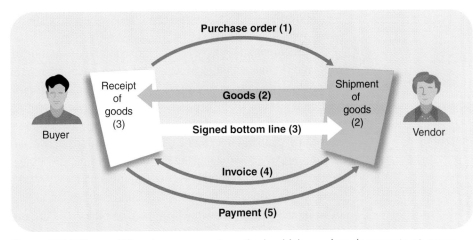

Figure 7.12 The traditional procurement method, which requires documents at every step, is often an inefficient process.

typically provides product specifications and quantities, with this information often coming from the supplier's catalogue.

2. The vendor responds to the PO by sending the goods to the buyer along with a *bill of lading (BOL)*, which describes the contents of the shipment.

3. After receiving the goods and BOL, the buyer sends back a signed copy of the BOL to the vendor and internally files a *Receipt of Goods*.

4. The vendor sends an invoice to the buyer. An *invoice* is a detailed list of goods shipped from the supplier, along with a list of all costs and discounts. In essence, it is a detailed bill and request for payment.

5. The buyer's accounting department compares the original PO with the Receipt of Goods and the invoice to ensure they match. After confirming a match, the buyer pays the vendor.

As you can see, the traditional procurement process relied on all paper-based documents. The employees in the accounting department had to pull all of them together and make an item-by-item comparison. Not only was this very tedious and time-consuming, it was also subject to errors and fraud.

Using E-Commerce to Improve the Procurement Process

E-commerce, with its digital information, replaces the paper documents in traditional procurement systems. Employees can quickly compare the digital files with far fewer errors and less opportunity for fraud. While companies still compare all three key documents— PO, Receipt of Goods, and invoice—prior to payment, automating the process is a giant step in the right direction. In fact, some companies have moved ahead by authorizing payment on receipt, thereby eliminating the need for invoicing (Steps 4 and 5).

E-procurement is also evolving into a tighter integration and co-ordination of the activities of a supplier–buyer relationship through the creation and use of interorganizational systems. An **interorganizational system (IOS)** is *a networked information system used by two or more separate organizations to perform a joint business function.*[13] IOS can help to create 24/7 communications between organizations and their suppliers and customers, as well as enable paper-less transactions throughout the supply chain. An IOS often involves electronically linking a production company to its suppliers or to its customers in such a way that raw materials are ordered, production takes place, and finished goods are sent to the customer with little or no paper changing hands. IOS can therefore enable supplier and customer organizations to carry out transactions almost as if they were parts of the same organization.

The two most common forms of IOS in use today are based on electronic data interchange (EDI), which uses value-added networks (VANs) or private networks instead of the regular telephone system, and **extranets**, which are collaborative networks that use Internet technology to link businesses with their suppliers, customers, or other businesses that share common goals.

EDI allows the exchange of structured information between two computer applications, using a minimum of human involvement. EDI works due to a set of agreed-upon message standards that allow both applications to understand and process the exchanged data. In EDI terminology, the organizations that send or receive documents from each other are called *trading partners*. These partners agree on which specific information to exchange and how to use it.

Although the initial purpose of EDI was to replace the exchange of paper-based documents with more efficient and flexible electronic documents, trading partners have since realized several additional benefits from its use. An EDI system can save unnecessary re-capture of data, which leads to faster data transfer, fewer errors, and a more streamlined business process. Firms can also use EDI as a platform for automating existing processes. This can help to reduce costs further, as well as improve the quality and speed of services. Finally, since EDI requires co-operation between trading partners, it can also serve as a catalyst for improving interorganizational processes and improving overall supply chain efficiency.

EDI is older technology that is often overshadowed by the newer cutting-edge technologies such as the World Wide Web and XML.

13. J. I. Cash, Jr., F. W. McFarlan, J. L. McKenney, and L. M. Applegate. 1994. *Corporate Information Systems Management: Text and Cases.* 4th ed. Homewood, IL: Irwin, p. 339.

Nevertheless, EDI remains an important part of business. It is still the engine behind a majority of all e-commerce transactions in the world.

An extranet uses Internet technologies to interconnect the intranet of an organization with the intranets of its business partners. Through the extranet, customers, suppliers, consultants, and other trading partners can access selected sites and data available on the internal intranet. Keep in mind that while an extranet extends access to the network outside the boundaries of the organization, usually over the Internet, it is still a private network. Security measures, such as usernames and passwords, usually control access to the extranet. Companies may also use the additional security measures of encryption and firewalls.

As companies realized the advantages of sharing data and information with trading partners, they began to develop extranets as a way to allow these trading partners to access limited areas available on the intranet. An extranet is somewhere in-between a private intranet and the public Internet. There is still a firewall between the intranet and public access, but it is now set to open for selected outsiders. We will consider the technology of extranets in more depth in Chapter 8.

Because EDI requires the use of expensive VANs or private networks, most businesses find it too expensive. However, through the use of an extranet, the Internet enables smaller companies to take advantage of IOS. Table 7.7 highlights some differences between EDI and extranet-enabled B2B e-commerce.

Does e-procurement work in the real world? Absolutely. For example, Scotland exploited technology to facilitate collaboration and change through use of a common platform, *eProcurement Scotl@nd*. The results, so far, have been very positive. Since its creation in 2002, governmental entities have placed more than 260,000 orders

Table 7.7	Comparing EDI and Extranet-Enabled B2B E-Commerce	
	EDI	**Extranet**
Security	More secure due to use of private network.	Less secure than EDI due to use of Internet, but can be made safer through use of security measures (e.g., strong passwords, encryption).
Cost	More costly due to proprietary software and use of VANS.	Less costly because with enhanced features, an organization's extranet can evolve as an extension of its intranet, allowing for the use of existing networks and possible reuse of Internet-enabled applications.
Flexibility	Less flexible, as proprietary software limits use primarily to standard business documents.	More flexible because it is based on the Internet, which permits greater customization and wider access to development tools.
Trend	Gradually being replaced by extranet-based applications.	Gaining wider acceptance due to lower costs and increased use of Internet.

for goods and services from thousands of suppliers, spending in excess of 271 million Scottish pounds. In fact, this effort has been so successful that *eProcurement Scotl@nd* was a finalist for Scotland's National e-Government Excellence Award.[14] The government of British Columbia has introduced procurement technology called BC Bid®. This software allows businesses that would like to sell to the provincial government the ability to access, create, browse, and compete on public sector opportunities anytime.[15] The federal government and other provincial governments have, at minimum, posted rules and procedures for selling to their governments on their websites in order to facilitate procurement.

Another example shows how small businesses can also benefit from e-procurement. One Canadian florist recognized the opportunity offered by RBC Financial Group's e-procurement initiative. This formerly regional florist implemented e-procurement into its supply chain and created alliances with other Canadian florists. By doing this, it became the central access point for all of the RBC Financial Group's floral purchases.[16]

Quick Test

1. True or False. Procurement paper flow involves three key elements: the purchase order, the invoice, and the payment of the bill.

2. True or False. An extranet is a semi-private network that enables organizations to electronically handle the trading process.

3. True or False. Extranets are typically more costly than EDI because users must lease network bandwidth.

Answers: 1. True; 2. True; 3. False

ROI STUDENT RETURN ON INVESTMENT SUMMARY

1. What is e-commerce and how is it a part of today's economy?

E-commerce is the use of information systems, technologies, and computer networks by individuals and organizations to carry out transactions in order to create or support the creation of business value. Almost all sectors of today's economy rely on it: business (B), consumer (C), and government (G).

The primary relationships between these sectors result in C2C, C2G, B2C, B2B, and B2G e-commerce.

2. How does e-commerce make a difference to businesses and consumers?

E-commerce makes a difference to businesses and consumers in a number of ways including technology, competition, and strategy. For example, the use of

14. The eProcurement Scotl@nd home page and other pages on the site. http://www.eprocurementscotland.com/default.asp?page=1
15. http://www.bcbid.gov.bc.ca/open.dll/welcome
16. http://www.rbc.com/sourcing/eproc_5.html

technology in e-commerce has resulted in information density, which businesses have responded to through mass customization and personalization. In terms of competition, e-commerce (1) reduces barriers to entry for consumers and new businesses; (2) helps keep any one company from owning the market; (3) provides more opportunities for collaboration and alliances among various stakeholders; (4) increases the number of market niches; and (5) affects the traditional marketplace drivers of time, distance, and price. Finally, e-commerce demands specific strategy, such as CRM, which allows businesses to create a one-to-one marketing experience.

3. How does e-commerce allow organizations to create value for their clients?

E-commerce provides both advantages and limitations to consumers and businesses; see Table 7. 3. To emphasize the advantages, most organizations rely on e-commerce models. Table 7.4 describes the primary e-commerce business models recognized. However, having a great e-commerce business model will not generate a profit if it is not associated with a website that brings in customers or at least visitors. As with business models, there are a number of ways to classify websites by purpose (see Table 7.5).

4. How can organizations use e-commerce to enhance the delivery of products and services, manage trade with business partners, and improve their supply chain efficiency?

B2B transactions are usually of two types: (1) spot buying and (2) strategic sourcing. Companies often engage in spot buying to purchase goods and services that are commodities; that is, they are usually uniform in quality and differ only somewhat in price. On the other hand, strategic sourcing involves forming a long-term relationship with another company. Strategic sourcing often relies on a one-to-one business model, although company-centric and exchange models are also used. Table 7.6 highlights some of these services and electronic products used by businesses, and shows how using e-commerce can help an organization effectively and efficiently obtain them.

In addition, e-commerce can benefit a company's supply chain. A supply chain is a network of facilities and distribution options that performs the functions of procurement of materials, transformation of these materials into intermediate and finished products, and the distribution of these finished products to customers. Traditional supply chains involve a number of paper-based transactions, but e-commerce-based supply chains involve an interorganizational system (IOS). An IOS can help create 24/7 communications between organizations and their suppliers and customers, as well as enable paperless transactions throughout the supply chain. The two most common forms of IOS in use today are based on electronic data interchange (EDI), which uses value-added networks (VANs) or private networks instead of the regular telephone system, and extranets, which are collaborative networks that use Internet technology to link businesses with their suppliers, customers, or other businesses that share common goals.

CHAPTER 7

KNOWLEDGE SPEAK

REVIEW QUESTIONS

Multiple-choice questions

1. Which of the following is considered a benefit of B2C e-commerce?

   a. Consumers are uncomfortable about the security of their personal data.
   b. Delivery of the product is delayed and may incur an extra cost.
   c. Distance to markets is shortened.
   d. Micropayment systems are not yet standardized.

2. Which of the following e-commerce impacts would best describe the ease at which new businesses may start an e-commerce site?

   a. reducing barriers to entry
   b. no one owns the market

   c. enhanced collaboration/alliances
   d. market niches multiply

3. Which of the following is an e-commerce site that facilitates how users find web pages of interest?

   a. information service
   b. auction
   c. sales support
   d. search engine

4. With _____, many companies use an on-line market to exchange products or services.

   a. an exchange
   b. a reverse auction
   c. spot buying
   d. strategic sourcing

Fill-in-the-blank questions

5. _____ is the use of information systems, technologies, and computer networks by individuals and organizations to carry out transactions in order to create or support the creation of business value.

6. A _____ is a broad-based formula for how a business is going to compete, what its goals should be, and what plans and policies will be needed to carry out those goals.

7. Companies can use the data collected using a _____ system to tailor their products and prices on their website to the individual buyer.

8. A _____ is a network of facilities and distribution options that performs the functions of procurement of materials, transformation of these materials into intermediate and finished products, and the distribution of these finished products to customers.

True–false questions

9. An intranet is a network for connecting an organization with external business partners using Internet protocols.

10. When you perform a banking transaction at your bank's ATM, you are performing an e-commerce transaction.

11. Due to the popularity of e-commerce, it is more difficult than ever to create business alliances.

12. E-commerce customers are frequently more demanding about the goods and services they purchase over the Web than customers using other channels.

Matching questions

Choose the BEST answer from Column B for each item in Column A.

Column A

13. Affiliate
14. Brokerage
15. Infomediary
16. Manufacturer

Column B

a. An e-commerce business model where products are shipped directly from the manufacturer to the consumer.

b. An e-commerce business model where websites are paid a fee when purchases come through them.

c. An e-commerce business model where data on consumers and consumption habits are provided.

d. An e-commerce business model that brings together buyers and sellers for a fee.

Short–answer questions

17. Why is it important for an e-commerce company to have a business model?
18. What are the three main categories of B2B business models?

Discussion/Essay questions

19. List and describe the benefits and limitations of B2C e-commerce.
20. Discuss how e-commerce is changing many aspects of business today.

TEAM ACTIVITY

Find two or three other students in your class who are in, or are interested in, the same major that you are. Think about creating an e-commerce/portal site for your major or your intended major. What information needs to go on the web pages that make up the site? What links are necessary? What about collecting membership dues? Could you also use the site to raise money for the student organization associated with your major? Plan the site on paper first, and then use the activities below to implement it.

SOFTWARE APPLICATION EXERCISES

1. Internet

Research how to build an e-commerce site for your major (see Team Activity assignment above). Look for open source tools that introductory IS students can use (for free) to create and maintain a website. Visit hosting sites to check on hosting plans, and ask your academic department to see if it is willing to host student sites.

2. Presentation

Create a presentation on how to build and host a major-related e-commerce site (see Internet assignment above). Present your ideas and solutions to your class and/or a professor in your major. Use presentation software to create prototypes of screens that give your audience insight into the look and functionality of your proposed website.

3. Word Processing

Create a promotional brochure to give to the students and faculty in your major. Use this as a basis for a press release to your student newspaper that announces the major-related site (see Internet assignment above) once it is up and working (simulate this if you are not actually implementing the site).

4. Spreadsheet

E-commerce sites cost money, whether or not you host them at school or offsite. Prepare a budget with projected costs, including an assessment of labour costs (e.g., your hourly rate—research these rates for a more realistic cost). Include charts from your financial estimates for the Presentation assignment above. If you decided to deploy this type of website across your entire school (organization), how would the costs increase? Would there be any economies of scale?

5. Database

Research open source databases, and design and create a database that will support the membership and e-commerce components of your website (see Internet assignment above). You may also use a commercial DBMS like MS Access if this fits better with your school's IT architecture.

6. Advanced Challenge

Think about some of the stakeholders mentioned in the preceding Internet assignment, e.g., fellow students and faculty in your major. Once you have their support, consider what other stakeholders might influence your ability to effectively implement your website. Assume that all stakeholders have approved your e-commerce site. Use an iterative development approach to create the site and test its functionality. Find a suitable hosting site (verify faculty approval to implement) and "go live."

ON-LINE RESOURCES

Companion Website

- Take interactive practice quizzes to assess your knowledge and help you study in a dynamic way.
- Review PowerPoint lecture slides.
- Get help and sample solutions to end-of-chapter software application exercises.

Additional Resources Available Only on WileyPLUS

- Take the interactive Quick Test to check your understanding of the chapter material and get immediate feedback on your responses.
- Review and study with downloadable Audio Lecture MP3 files.
- Check your understanding of the key vocabulary in the chapter with Knowledge Speak Interactive Flash Cards.
- Link directly to websites recommended in the CORE boxes.

CASE STUDY: NETFLIX

After returning a VHS movie and getting hit with a $40 late fee, Reed Hastings saw a business opportunity. He felt that he could successfully compete with the existing store-based rental services by sending DVDs to customers along with postage-paid return mailers. As it turns out, Hastings was correct, and consumers embraced the idea. His company, Netflix, has been able to ride the decrease in price for DVD players and the rapid expansion of availability to the Internet to have more than 4 million subscribers by April 2006, and revenue of over $600 million in 2005.

Initially, Netflix charged customers for each movie they rented, but when that idea failed to pan out, Hastings transformed the company into a subscription-based service in 1999. At that point, the company's revenues took off. Currently, subscribers can rent up to four DVDs at a time for a set fee, with no due date or late fees. Netflix pays the postage both ways. While four DVDs does not sound like much, dedicated movie buffs can watch many more movies each month (if they are conscientious about returning them immediately after watching them)!

The key to Netflix's success is its innovative use of the Internet for subscribers to order movies. Instead of requiring subscribers to order specific movies they want, the company encourages subscribers to create an on-line list ("Queue") of movies from a list of over 60,000. After viewing a movie, a customer returns the DVD to Netflix using a Netflix-provided envelope and, as soon as Netflix receives that DVD, the company sends the next available movie from the customer's on-line list, often resulting in a one-day turnaround. Customers can update their queue even before new movies are released by selecting soon-to-be released titles. Netflix also provides personalized film recommendations based on customer ratings of other movies.

While still small compared to industry giants like Blockbuster, Netflix has shown its business model to be a success. In fact, its market value is now greater than Blockbuster as investors have come to value its stock. In Canada, Rogers Video also provides a similar subscription-based service.

Competition

A successful innovation breeds competition. In the case of Netflix, Blockbuster and Wal-Mart initially moved into the on-line video rental business with business models that mimicked that of Netflix. In the case of Blockbuster, it also changed its in-store rental model to eliminate late fees and is looking at ways to rent and return DVDs both on-line and in its stores. It has been able to leverage its customer base of 40 million and 5,600 stores into 1 million on-line subscribers in its first year.

Wal-Mart started a subscription service in 2003 that had an estimated 250,000 subscribers by early 2005. However, by mid-2005, Wal-Mart decided that a partnership with Netflix was better than trying to compete with it.

While aware of the current and future competition, Netflix does not appear to be overly worried about these competitive threats. The company continues to concentrate on improving customer service to create satisfied customers.

VoD

A new technology that all competitors in the video rental marketplace, on-line or otherwise, will have to be aware of is *video on demand (VoD)*, a technology that enables movies to be downloaded over the Internet and then displayed on a computer monitor rather than a standard TV. While the current state of this technology is unsatisfactory to many movie fans due to often long download times and poor display quality of movies, this could rapidly change. So even though Reed Hastings believes that only one-tenth of 1% of Netflix's customers are interested in VoD, the company is actively investing in it.

Questions

1. In business, any company that finds a new way to market an existing product or to replace an existing product with a new one is often referred to as a "disrupter." Discuss whether Netflix fits this definition in the video rental market.
2. VoD is being considered a disruptive technology. Can you think of other examples of disruptive technologies that have recently occurred?
3. Of the existing or possible competitors in the on-line DVD rental market (Netflix, Blockbuster, and Rogers Video), in your opinion, which is better positioned to take advantage of VoD technology? Explain.

Integrative Application Case: Campuspad.ca

At your next meeting, Sarah is much less interested in discussing the development problems and much more excited about a call she'd received from the student union president. It turns out that the student housing office is a source of revenue for the union. If a successful tenant is referred to a landlord by the housing office, the student union receives a listing fee. Although not a huge amount of money, it mostly covers the operating costs, allowing the student union to offer a valuable service to students for free.

The student union president approached you because he had heard you might be launching an on-line business that would compete with the housing office. While not making the statement directly, he said the union had uncovered "unspecified privacy issues" that might force them to recommend students not use your site. On the other hand, he also hinted at wanting to meet to discuss the possibility of the union becoming a strategic partner. Although you and Sarah weren't sure what this meant exactly, you suspected they were interested in how your on-line business might help them actually improve the service they offer to students. Further, they felt that if they could pilot it successfully then it could be sold to student unions all over Canada.

The union has asked you to think about how you might work together and meet with them early next week. Sarah thinks this could evolve into something where they fund the launch of the business in return for some kind of stake in the enter-

prise, but you're not so sure; you don't feel like they "get it." Again, lots of decisions to make.

Guiding Case Questions:

1. What are the risks to an incumbent business with an Internet competitor?
2. How could e-commerce fit into the student union business model?
3. What business model will your new site use?
4. What privacy or other legislation in your jurisdiction might you have overlooked?
5. Could these laws have a negative effect on your future on-line business?

Your Task:

Make up eight to ten PowerPoint slides that help explain the potential value of the Internet in the student rental market that you will use in your meeting with the student union. Make sure the presentation "sells" the value of your strategic thinking to ensure that the student union, if it is truly looking for a technology partner, will choose campuspad.ca. Ensure that your presentation addresses the issues of privacy, on-line security, and secure commerce that you intend to use in the site to make sure it's compliant with local laws, and that it addresses any possible concerns the student union might have about your site's design.

8

WHAT WE WILL COVER

- The Evolution of E-Commerce Technologies
- First-Generation E-Commerce Technologies: Establishing a Web Presence
- Second-Generation E-Commerce Technologies: Providing Interaction
- Third-Generation E-Commerce Technologies: Supporting Transactions
- Fourth-Generation E-Commerce Technologies: Transforming Processes

Connectivity	Is it the Death of Software?
On-line Security	Securing E-Commerce with Encryption
Relationships	Finding Team Members by Using a Social Network
Ethics	Who is Responsible for Protecting Data?

E-Commerce Technologies

Through your investment of time in reading and thinking about this chapter, your return, or created value, is gaining knowledge. Use the following questions as a study guide.

1. How have e-commerce technologies evolved over the years?
2. Why do many businesses still rely on first-generation e-commerce technologies?
3. How do second-generation e-commerce technologies provide businesses with more effective customer relationship management?
4. How do third-generation e-commerce technologies support business transactions?
5. How do fourth-generation e-commerce technologies contribute to strategic alliances?

THE VOICE OF EXPERIENCE
Roger Ley, University of Windsor

Roger Ley graduated with a degree in computer science in 1997, just as the tech boom was starting. He has worked at IBM and DuPont and was director of product development for a VoIP (voice over Internet protocol) solutions startup. He now provides consulting services through his firm, RedShoe Technologies.

What do you do in your current position? I do website development, including credit card processing, e-commerce solutions, infrastructure database design, and development using Lotus Notes, Java Script, HTML—basically all the Web technologies. Most of the fun stuff has been more architectural, sitting down with customers to figure out exactly what they want and how to deliver it.

What do you consider to be important career skills? Communication. I am a geek in that I know how to write code, but I can also translate between what a tech team can build, what a sales guy wants, what marketing people want, and what customers need. Common sense is critical. I talk to customers who have grand ideas of what they want and technology guys who want to talk about the latest technology to persuade somebody to buy it so they can build it. I help my clients answer the questions: "What are you trying to do?", "Who are you trying to build it for?", and "Why are you trying to do it?"

How do you use IT? Although I am located in Nelson, B.C., most of my work is for clients in Toronto. I have a high-speed Internet connection so I can work anywhere. I still view personal face-to-face interaction as the best form of communicating, so I often use video conferencing over the Web. In order to do technical work with a client, I establish a secure remote connection to their systems. I use VoIP for my long distance phone calls. I use Google and on-line software documentation to help me solve problems. I go on the premise that if I run into a problem, it's likely that someone else in the world has, too. The trick is to know enough to separate the 'bull'

from actual solutions. I also spend time on forums posting my own solutions for others to use.

Can you describe an example of how you have used IT to improve business operations? My role with HelpCaster was to go on client calls with sales guys to find out how our product could help them and what enhancements they wanted. We created a product plan and requirements for developers and I did user-interface design, Java Script, and HTML. HelpCaster was one of the earliest companies to provide a voice and video over IP product, which is a Web-based application and allows two-way tech chats, two-way audio, and one-way video. We married this technology with experience in call centres and standard telephony allowing a call centre agent to pick up a call and demonstrate a product via the Web. We also introduced intranet-based hold music where our clients could stream custom advertising to their customers. This combined the utility of call centre live interaction and direct marketing and supported the way our clients worked.

Have you got any "on the job" advice for students seeking a career in IT or business? It is important to have diversity in your interests. I work in technology, but I'm also a musician. While I have been working steadily since 1997, I have also taken the opportunity between jobs to travel. It is important to get away from work as much as you get into work. Also, take advantage of the people at university—your professors and your colleagues. It is important to realize that when you graduate, regardless of your level of education, the most important thing you'll have is your network.

Roger has been working in e-commerce since its first generation and now helps his clients navigate the world of fourth-generation e-commerce technologies. This chapter introduces you to the generations of e-commerce and some its key underlying technologies. Having a working knowledge of these will help you make common sense decisions about e-commerce strategies, as Roger does.

As we saw in Chapter 7, computerized networks organized into the World Wide Web have profoundly changed both how organizations conduct business and how they manage their important relationships with consumers, partners, and suppliers. The *application* of using these networks to support business is often referred to as e-commerce or e-business. As mentioned previously in Chapter 7, for the purposes of this text we are not making the distinct between e-commerce and e-business. Instead, we consider the aspects of both under the term e-commerce. In this chapter, we discuss the enabling *technologies* that allow businesses to conduct e-commerce and the rapid rate of change this has caused in business around the world.

THE EVOLUTION OF E-COMMERCE TECHNOLOGIES

In its relatively brief history, e-commerce has been through several distinct generations of growth. These generations, shown in Figure 8.1, represent important shifts in the evolution of e-commerce and its enabling technologies. Note that the increasing heights of the bars in Figure 8.1 represent both the growing number of users and increased technology capability. Also, do you see how the time frames listed on the bottom of the figure overlap somewhat? That's because we can only approximate the dates when each stage began. Similarly, we can also only estimate the end of each stage; that is, the point at which most Web users adopted the technologies of that generation and began to move on to the next stage.

Knowing the exact dates of each stage, however, matters much less than understanding the business and technological advances made at each stage. For example, in the first generation of e-commerce, the available technologies delivered static content through a Web presence. **Static Content** refers to fixed information, such as

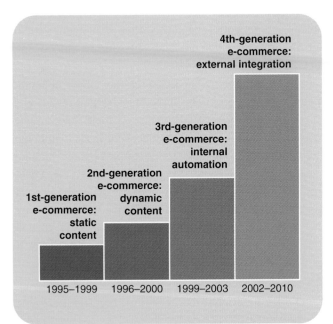

Figure 8.1 Generations of e-commerce.

CHAPTER 8

PART

3

company information, on-line marketing, and electronic versions of company brochures. A **Web presence** means the business has established its existence on the World Wide Web by creating a set of pages that users can access. In fact, a term often used to refer to sites with only static content is "brochureware"—a direct reflection of how consumers negatively view this low level of sophistication today.

At some point in the mid-1990s, newer technologies allowed for the delivery of dynamic content, moving us into the second generation of e-commerce. With **dynamic content,** information on a web page can change depending on a number of factors. For example, the time or date, user profile, or browser location might trigger web page changes. In addition, other capabilities became available, such as delivery tracking and personalization of content to match user preferences.

As the power of the World Wide Web became clear to businesses, demand for new technologies grew. Consumers liked using the Web and organizations moved to respond. The third generation of e-commerce saw demand for technologies that would extend to support real-time, on-line transactions. Companies began to automate both internal and external business processes. Automated transactions enabled advanced capabilities on the Web, such as data mining and the delivery of instant status information through portals (such as FedEx or Canada Post now do with full-cycle individual-item tracking systems). Companies sprung up around the globe with new business models that took advantage of enhanced technology and network capabilities, often challenging well-known incumbent firms to catch up and move more quickly into the e-commerce age.

Currently, we are in the midst of the fourth generation of e-commerce, characterized by increasing integration of all enterprise systems with external customers, partners, and suppliers all linked over the World Wide Web. The Web itself is undergoing a transformation, from enabling transactions between humans and Web applications to allowing transactions between two Web applications. Still more advanced capabilities are being adopted, such as the capability of making phone calls over the Web using voice over Internet protocol (VoIP) and advanced personalization. To grasp just how fast these enabling technologies are changing, VoIP (which allows us to make calls anywhere in the world and bypass traditional switched telephone networks) was only invented in the last few years. Now, pretty much anybody with a PC can use this technology to eliminate long distance charges! This remarkable rate of adoption of new technologies offered through the Web is nothing short of revolutionary in human history: no previous technology has spread as quickly to as many households as the Web. And only now are all of us beginning to grasp just how important this evolution is. While customers love technologies like VoIP, imagine how you might feel if you were a senior executive at Bell Canada? Or perhaps you know a family member who has lost a job in a restructuring related to the increasing cost pressures of competing in a world that no longer has boundaries and where businesses operate globally, 24/7. Every social revolution comes with both opportunities and threats, and the era of e-commerce is no different.

Of course, the evolution of e-commerce was only made possible by corresponding increases in IT capabilities. This, of course, is supported by the concept of **Moore's Law**. The most common interpretation of Moore's Law is that computing power (as measured by the maximum number of transistors in an integrated circuit) roughly doubles every 18 months (Figure 8.2). This formulation was printed in a volume of *"Electronics Magazine"* (v. 19, April 1965) and was based on the founding work not of Moore himself but of VSLI pioneer Carver Mead. However, it was Moore who connected the notion of underlying changes in the pace of technology

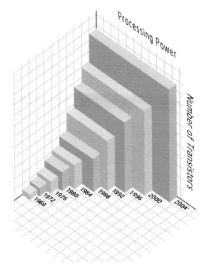

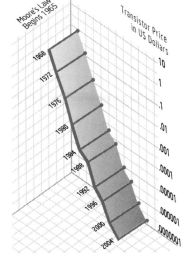

Moore's Law Means More Performance

Processing power, measured in millions of instructions per second (MIPS), has risen because of increased transistor counts.

Moore's Law Means Decreasing Costs

Packing more transistors into less space has dramatically reduced their cost and the cost of the products they populate.

1. Estimate only

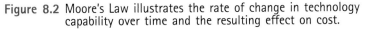

Figure 8.2 Moore's Law illustrates the rate of change in technology capability over time and the resulting effect on cost.

with consumer access to lower cost and higher performance computing over time.

Although Moore's Law was initially an observation on only one component of the technology industry (semiconductors), the more widely it became quoted and accepted, the more it served as the standard within this huge global industry. As technology engineering and marketing strove to keep up with Moore's Law, a technology revolution was born, eventually leading to the introduction of the personal computer, the forerunning technology to the rapid spread of the World Wide Web. Since every technology company always presumed that one or more of their competitors would soon introduce a newer, faster technology than theirs, the industry became hyper-competitive and one of the most productive and innovative industries in the world.

So what does this mean for business? Well, consider this. If you wanted to express Moore's Law on a different time scale, you could say this technology will improve at an average rate of 1% per week. Compounded, this means an increase of 11–15% per quarter, depending on the number of days and weeks in the quarter. If you're not in the technology business, but in a business where IT is a part of the business, what must you do to keep up with this ever-present rate of change? To see how IT has helped to create significant business value, let's take a closer look at the specific technologies that furthered each stage of this e-commerce revolution.

FIRST-GENERATION E-COMMERCE TECHNOLOGIES: ESTABLISHING A WEB PRESENCE

The basic technologies of the first generation of e-commerce are still used. These include:

- Client/server networks—the networks over which data travel
- Browser—application software that lets users request and view web pages
- HTTP protocol—the standardized rules for exchanging data over the Web
- HTML—the language that guides the display of a requested page

Businesses that use only these technologies for their websites are limited to providing static content. But these technologies also represent a low-cost and relatively easy way for new businesses to begin or expand e-commerce transactions.

Figure 8.3 shows how these technologies work together to form the basic first-generation e-commerce application. Since we have

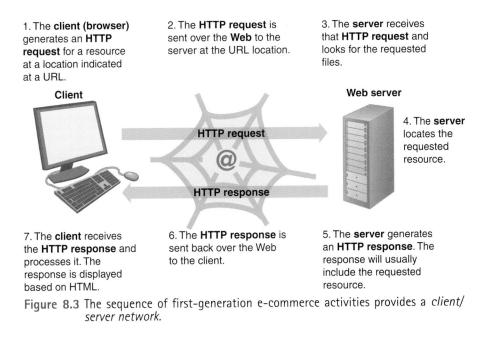

1. The **client (browser)** generates an **HTTP request** for a resource at a location indicated at a URL.

2. The **HTTP request** is sent over the **Web** to the server at the URL location.

3. The **server** receives that **HTTP request** and looks for the requested files.

Client

HTTP request

@

HTTP response

Web server

4. The **server** locates the requested resource.

7. The **client** receives the **HTTP response** and processes it. The response is displayed based on HTML.

6. The **HTTP response** is sent back over the Web to the client.

5. The **server** generates an **HTTP response**. The response will usually include the requested resource.

Figure 8.3 The sequence of first-generation e-commerce activities provides a *client/server network.*

discussed these technologies in other chapters and Tech Guide C, we'll simply provide a quick review here. However, as we learned earlier, given the huge impact that Web technologies have on organizations today, it is worthwhile for anyone interested in a career in business to have at least a general knowledge of these technologies.

CLIENT/SERVER NETWORKS

When you open a Web browser on your computer, you start a client application. If you type a URL into your browser or click a hyperlink, the browser sends a request out over the Web, to make its way to the corresponding server. The browser formulates the request under the rules of HTTP (discussed below) so that all computers on the Web, especially the destination server, will know how to handle it.

When the request reaches its destination, the server generates a response that includes the requested item and conforms to HTTP (note that a *Web server* is a software application that handles Web requests, not necessarily separate computer). The server then simply loads the text data from storage, adds the appropriate HTTP information, and sends the item back to the client. This sequence of activities provides a **client/server network.**

A static web page file will typically hold a combination of text content and *hypertext markup language* (*HTML*) commands. Other requests may include other static file formats such as images, sound, or video. While sound and video might seem interactive, they are nevertheless static because the file contents do not change.

CHAPTER

8

See TECH GUIDE C

WEB BROWSERS

A *Web browser* is a software application that allows you to easily navigate the Web and to view the content that you find there. At its most basic, a browser will let you request, either by typing a URL or clicking a hyperlink, and display a hypertext-based file. Hypertext organizes content into units that are connected using associations called **links.**

Figure 8.4 shows an example of a browser displaying a web page. In this figure, note the *GUI (graphical user interface)* elements that allow you to work with the browser and adjust your view of the web page. Several components of the browser in Figure 8.4 are common to most browsers. For example, most browsers provide a navigation bar for specifying the page that you want to load, and buttons for moving between the pages that you have viewed. A main window displays the body of the page, which often consists of a combination of text, hyperlinks, images, and other elements.

While a browser provides a simple client capability to a networked computer, it also offers two other major advantages for an organization. First, by allowing multimedia capabilities, a browser enhances information that a business wishes to convey to customers. Second, most browsers work similarly, presenting a common interface to all users. This can reduce the training required for those who previously used other software applications. However,

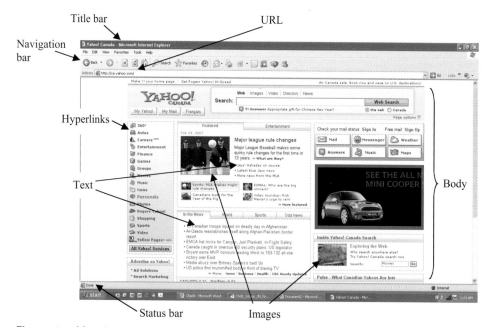

Figure 8.4 Most browsers, including Internet Explorer used here, provide similar components for displaying and viewing a web page.

sometimes websites must incorporate or leave out specific features if they want to be compatible with all browsers. This is why you sometimes have either browser compatibiltiy problems or may find a site recommending the use of a certain browser.

WHAT DO YOU THINK?

Users can get quite committed to one type of technology or another, such as a PC versus a Macintosh. This also happens with browsers, of which Internet Explorer, Netscape, and Mozilla Firefox are just three examples. If you are choosing a browser for yourself, consider these questions:

1: What features might be most important to you on a browser?
2: How important might it be to use the most popular browser? What are the risks of choosing a browser with less market share?
3: Which browser would you ultimately choose for yourself and why? Would you choose a different one for work than for home and if so, why?

An organization obviously benefits when it creates a common platform for delivering information and applications. Rather than having to develop several different versions of a report or a software application for each computer platform that an organization may use, it can instead develop only one report or application for delivery over the Web. That means a business no longer needs to convert a file created on a Windows machine for viewing on an Apple computer. With the Web, both platforms can view the same content without conversion, saving the business time and resources.

HTTP—HYPERTEXT TRANSFER PROTOCOL

A client and a server communicate with each other using messages. To do this, they need a standard set of rules for formatting and transmitting these messages. That is where HTTP comes in. The *hypertext transfer protocol (HTTP)* comprises the set of rules for exchanging messages on the World Wide Web. As Figure 8.3 shows, HTTP governs both the request for a file and the transmission of the requested file.

Tim Berners-Lee, the inventor of the World Wide Web, first implemented HTTP while at CERN, the European Centre for High-Energy Physics in Geneva, in 1990 and 1991. He developed HTTP to live at the application layer of networks. That is, once the application composes the HTTP message (request or response), lower-level protocols such as TCP/IP transmit the message. Berners-Lee originally designed HTTP as a lightweight, speedy method of sharing hypermedia information over a client/server network.

```
GET /index.html HTTP/1.1 ◄——— Requests file index.html using http1.1
Accept: image/gif, image/jpeg, */* ◄——— File Types Accepted
Accept-Language: en-us ◄——— Preferred language is English
Host: hostcom.mycompany.com ◄——— Host name for server that client is making request to
User-Agent: Mozilla/4.0 (compatible; MSIE 5.12; Windows NT)
                         ◄———————Type of browser and operating system
```

Figure 8.5 A typical HTTP message header.

An HTTP message consists of a header followed by data. The two main types of messages are known as *HTTP request* and *HTTP response*. Figure 8.5 shows a typical HTTP request message. In this figure, note that the browser has requested a file called *index.html* from a server with the name *hostcom.mycompany.com*. Recall that information about the browser passes to the server so that it can respond with the correct type of data. For example, this message indicates the browser type, file types that the browser will accept, and the acceptable language. The IP address of the client also passes along to the server, but is not included as part of the message file.

The greatest advantage of HTTP is that it provides a lean and fast method for exchanging hypertext information. However, to achieve this speed, HTTP must also be *connectionless* and *stateless*. This means that after the server responds to a client's request, the connection between the client and the server is dropped and forgotten. No memory or state is retained between different client connections. In effect, HTTP treats every request, even requests for more pages at the same site, as a new request.

This limitation of HTTP presents difficulties when supporting e-commerce. For example, how can a Web application keep up with the products that you put in your on-line shopping cart, if every time you browse to a new page it forgets about your connection? Later in this chapter, we discuss how more recent e-commerce generations used different technology innovations to help overcome this problem.

HTML—HYPERTEXT MARKUP LANGUAGE

Hypertext markup language (HTML) is the primary language for creating web pages. It is not a true programming language, as the computer does not generally process HTML instructions. Instead, browser software interpret HTML instructions through the use of *tags*, which are interspersed with content. The tags, surrounded by angle brackets (<and>), mark the placement and appearance of the various components of the page. A web page usually consists of several different types of components, such as page layout instructions, formatted text, hyperlinks, tables, graphics, and form objects. Figure 8.6 shows

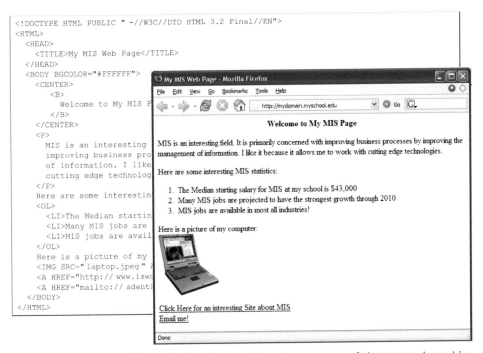

Figure 8.6 HTML tags determine the placement and appearance of the text and graphics of this web page.

an example of HTML marked content, along with how it is displayed in a browser.

While the first generation of e-commerce technology represented a significant advance in sharing information, it was the ability to exchange dynamic information that allowed e-commerce to really take off. Let's turn next to the second-generation e-commerce technologies that made this possible.

Quick Test

1. _____ is the primary language for defining how web pages are displayed in a browser.
   a. HTTP
   b. HTML
   c. Java
   d. VoIP

2. _____ defines the rules for sending messages with content and instructions over the Web.
   a. HTTP
   b. HTML
   c. Java
   d. VoIP

3. What makes it difficult for a server to remember a user who has previously visited a website?

a. Servers typically have low memory capacities.

b. The HTTP is stateless.

c. Browsers are not capable of storing data.

d. HTML tags can only describe content.

Answers: 1. b; 2. a; 3. b

SECOND-GENERATION E-COMMERCE TECHNOLOGIES: PROVIDING INTERACTION

On the Web, dynamic content changes according to a number of factors. For example, the same URL might display different results depending on the date or the name of the user. So how do second-generation e-commerce technologies overcome the stateless nature of HTTP? Dynamics and interaction occur based on input data and programming instructions. To create dynamic content, the following needs to occur: obtain input data, pass data to the server, hold data in memory, and execute programming instructions to process the data. Let's consider the enabling technologies that make each of these steps possible.

GETTING INPUT DATA

Web pages can change based on input data, which can come from several sources. For instance, the header in the HTTP request contains data about the client requesting the page. The server can also use its own resources, such as its system clock, to provide input data. In addition, the server can receive client data from a *cookie* along with the request. The server can store the data, which it can later retrieve based on a request. Finally, users can input data on a web page by using an HTML form.

You have probably come across a web page that asked you to enter data. The components of a page that allow you to enter input are called HTML **form controls.** Figure 8.7 shows some common form controls. For example, a textbox control obtains text input, such as a name. A text area control expands the textbox by allowing you to enter more than one line of text. Some form controls limit input to specific choices, such as radio buttons, listboxes, and checkboxes.

HTML forms are the primary means by which a business can get the data it needs for on-line transactions. For example, think about the type of information you may have input when ordering items on-line, such as your name, address, and credit card information. Because this information is critical to successful e-commerce transactions, a

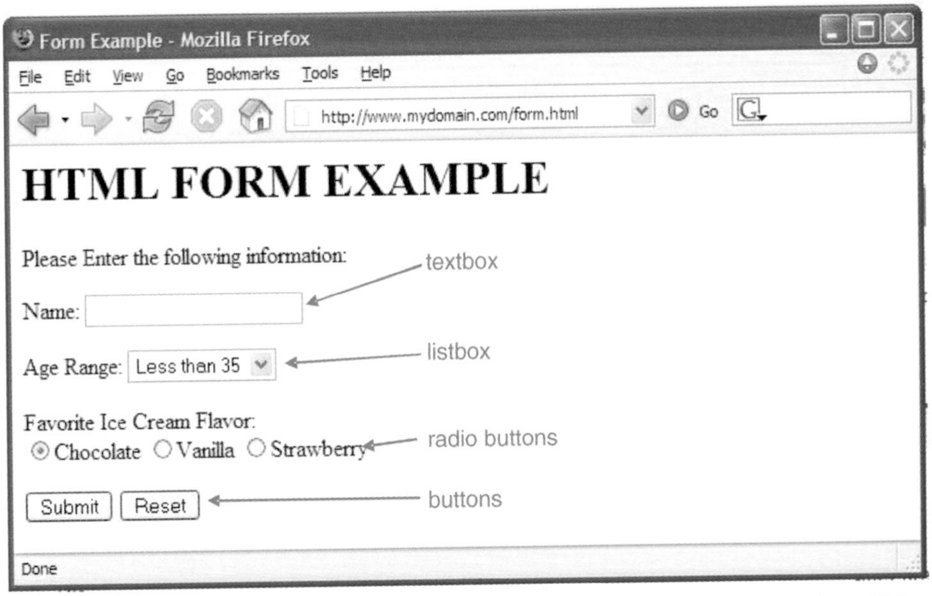

Figure 8.7 HTML forms, such as the one shown here, are the primary means by which a business can get the data it needs for on-line transactions.

business will carefully select the form controls with two major goals in mind. First, the form components must fit the data needs of the transaction. Second, a business selects the form components for ease of use and to minimize the chance of incorrect data entry.

STORING DATA ON THE CLIENT SIDE

Recall that the first-generation HTTP protocol is stateless and connectionless. As a result, every request is independent of any other. So how, then, can a server recognize that a new request is from a previous client? One solution is to store some type of identifying data on the client's computer, in the form of a "cookie."

A **cookie** is a small bit of data, usually created by programs running on the server, stored on the client machine, and passed back and forth in the HTTP request and response. The cookie sent by the server will be passed back to the server when the client makes a request for a new page. With a cookie, the server can store one or more data items on the client that it may need for subsequent requests, making it appear as if there is a persistent connection even though there is not.

In most browsers you can view the data that a cookie stores. For instance, the Netscape browser stores all cookies combined in a file called cookies.txt. (For other browsers, the cookies are usually available but may be more difficult to find or read.) Figure 8.8 shows an example of a file of cookies stored by the Netscape browser. Note that each cookie stores a variable name and value that the browser and server can reference in their programs. The cookie also stores data

```
cookies.txt - Notepad
File  Edit  Format  View  Help
# Netscape HTTP Cookie File
# http://www.netscape.com/newsref/std/cookie_spec.html
# This is a generated file!  Do not edit.

kcookie.netscape.com      FALSE   /       FALSE   4294967295      kcookie <script>location="."</script><scri
www.nytimes.com FALSE     /2005/04/11/international/africa         FALSE   1144335996          5501_uu 1
statse.webtrendslive.com          FALSE   /dcss910ug21e5h6ugmb32ovpd_2s8i FALSE   1424436302          WEBTRENDS_
www.itconversations.com FALSE     /L10Apps        FALSE   1134825826      L10HC   27281%7C2004%2F2%2F27%7C%7
imageads.googleadservices.com     FALSE   /pagead FALSE   2147483647      GoogleCookieTest            1
.zdnet.com      TRUE    /       FALSE   1262321998      cqversion       5
.doubleclick.net          TRUE    /       FALSE   1145875741      id      8000023aa65707
.techtv.com     TRUE    /       FALSE   1146141052      visitor 80c5989d.79e72633.67.30.248.202.1051533110
.verisign.com   TRUE    /       FALSE   1582122480      v1st    3EBFE8692C27D1AC
.priceline.com  TRUE    /       FALSE   2051222400      SITESERVER      ID=a8ed4843c5bcae16d5fec902d38f766
www.course.com  FALSE   /       FALSE   2137622401      CFTOKEN 30056215
.yahoo.com      TRUE    /       FALSE   1271361601      B       97q542kvcanpv&b=2
www.meetingwizard.com     FALSE   /       FALSE   2137622399      CFGLOBALS       HITCOUNT%3D6%23LASTVISIT%3
www.meetingwizard.com     FALSE   /       FALSE   2137622480      CFID    361752
www.meetingwizard.com     FALSE   /       FALSE   2137622480      CFTOKEN 75098540
www.active.com  FALSE   /       FALSE   2000893265      CFID    342769
www.active.com  FALSE   /       FALSE   2000893265      CFTOKEN 39141014
www.cnn.com     FALSE   /       FALSE   1157838035      nnselect        1063230035374
.cnn.com        TRUE    /       FALSE   1281665508      CNNid   d87fc7f6-21367-1063230043-147
www.mathtools.net         FALSE   /       FALSE   1127045930      webtrans        67.30.249.30.9541106397392
www.mathtools.net         FALSE   /       FALSE   1293840003      MathtoolsRedirect          http://www.nist.go
www.mathtools.net         FALSE   /       FALSE   1293840003      MathtoolsLocation          http://www.mathtoo
.searchenginewatch.com    TRUE    /       FALSE   1293840051      RMID    4433e52e4038a9f0
.cirquedusoleil.com       TRUE    /       FALSE   2147144398      MSCSProfile     95385A1F52DEA1A229D5B37542
.microsoft.com  TRUE    /       FALSE   1159858803      MC1     GUID=d4bd9fa05fe84f4e8da24209543329f5&HASH
.ucomics.com    TRUE    /       FALSE   1293840213      RMID    44be2890407a85b0
counter.hitslink.com      FALSE   /       FALSE   2147403596      VISID   2CD5EC36
counter.hitslink.com      FALSE   /       FALSE   2147403596      VNO     SaferSite-1
counter.hitslink.com      FALSE   /       FALSE   2147403595      PriorPage       SaferSite=/PestInfo/t/theu
counter.hitslink.com      FALSE   /       FALSE   2147403595      PriorPageTime   SaferSite=4%2f12%2f2004+8%
```

Figure 8.8 The cookies.txt file for the Netscape browser.

such as the domain name of the Web server that created the cookie, the date and time the cookie was created, a date and time when the cookie will expire, the path on the server for which the cookie will be active, and a security flag that determines if the cookie will be encrypted when it is sent over the Internet.

By allowing a cookie to store data on the client side, the cookie data can remain until the user returns to the website. When data remain available for a period of time, it is known as **persistent data**. Persistent data allow Web applications to benefit both users and the businesses that run the sites. Because the main use of the cookie is to identify the user, this allows websites to provide *personalization* (recall this advantage of e-commerce from Chapter 7). Businesses also often use cookies to keep up with data, such as a shopping cart of products that customers want to buy.

However, cookies also pose concerns. Some users may worry that others can use cookies to steal data off of their hard drive, or that they can get a virus from a cookie. This cannot occur. However, cookies do allow others to track the sites that you browse on the Web. Most services that use cookies to track your browsing habits do this in order to collect data about what sites and pages are popular. But some users view tracking on-line behaviour as an invasion of privacy. With this in mind, e-commerce businesses need to be careful in how they use cookies and make responsible use of the data collected with them. The issue of data protection is discussed in the CORE box "Who is Responsible for Protecting Data?"

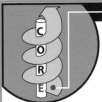

—Ethics

Who Is Responsible for Protecting Data?

Frequently, we read about a case of some company exposing data about its customers or having data stolen. In many cases, the data contain personal information about the customers including their name, address, social insurance number (SIN), and even credit card numbers. Some examples include:

- A customer brought her laptop to the store where she purchased it for repair. When it was not fixed within the time limit prescribed by store policy, the company gave her a new computer. A few months later, she received a phone call from an individual who had purchased her original laptop from the store including the personal information that was saved on it.[1]

- For more than three years, a large Canadian bank had been faxing client fund transfer requests containing confidential client information including phone numbers, names, addresses, and SINs to a scrapyard in West Virginia.[2]

- In 2003, a hard disk containing the details of 176,000 insurance policies was stolen from an IBM data centre in Regina, Saskatchewan. The policy information included client names, addresses, SINs, and bank and credit card information.[3]

Unfortunately, unscrupulous individuals can use the lost or stolen data to carry out identity theft, in which criminals steal a person's identification to impersonate someone else and perhaps buy goods and services using their credit. Identity theft has become one of the fastest-growing crimes in Canada and the United States. In the United States, identity theft complaints to the Federal Trade Commission have increased five-fold in just three years. In Canada, the PhoneBusters National Call Centre received 7,629 identity theft complaints in 2002 that reported total losses of more than $8.5 million, and an additional 2,250 complaints in the first quarter of 2003 that reported total losses of more than $5.3 million. In addition, two major Canadian credit bureaus, Equifax and Trans Union, indicate that they receive approximately 1,400 to 1,800 Canadian identity theft complaints per month, mostly from Ontario.[4]

Who is responsible for protecting private customer data? The truth is that individuals, companies, and governments all have some responsibility for protecting it. Individuals should hesitate to give out personal data, especially their social insurance number, as this is a key identifier that criminals can use to carry out identify theft. Individuals should also carefully consider the data they provide on the websites they visit. While many companies are harvesting clickstream data to help them improve their website and services, some unethical groups are also looking to collect data from site visitors that they can use to carry out crimes.

1. Office of the Privacy Commissioner of Canada, http://www.privcom.gc.ca/ser/2004/s_040623_e.asp. Retrieved October 9, 2006.
2. David Akin, "CIBC faxes go to scrapyard, "Globe and Mail, http://www.theglobeandmail.com/servlet/story/RTGAM.20041126." wxcibc1126/BNStory/ Business. Retrieved October 9, 2006.
3. Patrick Thibodeau, "Canadian Insurer Rejects 'Don't Tell' Approach on Data Theft" Computer World, http://www.computerworld.com/securitytopics/security/story/0,10801,78746,00.html. Retrieved October 9, 2006.
4. Public Safety and Emergency Preparedness Canada, Public Advisory: Special Report for Consumers on IDENTITY THEFT. http://ww2.psepc-sppcc.gc.ca/publications/policing/Identity_Theft_Consumers_e.asp. Retrieved October 9, 2006.

In Canada, the Personal Information Privacy and Electronic Data Act (PIPEDA) ensures that companies are responsible for the data they collect, yet many have not moved aggressively to ensure that personal information does not get into the wrong hands in the first place. Data loss primarily occurs through criminal activities, accidents, or employee error. Recent statistics show that the number one cause of data loss is non-malicious employee error, with 39% of data losses for the surveyed companies resulting from this source.[5] Clearly, companies can do more.

So while companies that collect data should be responsible, they may need a "push" from government before they actually take action. The Office of the Privacy Commissioner of Canada acts as an ombudsman. It has the ability to bring parties together to mediate a dispute involving the Privacy Act, but this office does not dictate punishment. The Commissioner can, however, make a recommendation to the Federal Court if mediation fails. In Canada, more often than not, organizations are depended upon to regulate themselves. Often the real threat against organizations that do not protect their customers' data is negative publicity.

Web Resources

- Privacyinfo.ca (a website maintained by Professor Michael Geist of the University of Ottawa, Faculty of Law, which highlights privacy issues in Canada and summarizes cases settled by and before the Privacy Commissioner)—http://www.privacyinfo.ca
- Identity Theft: Office of the Privacy Commissioner of Canada—http://www.privcom.gc.ca/fs-fi/02_05_d_10_e.asp
- RCMP: Phonebusters (a way to report identity theft)—http://www.rcmp-grc.gc.ca/scams/identity_e.htm
- Identity Theft: Public Safety and Emergency Preparedness Canada—http://www.psepc-sppcc.gc.ca/prg/le/bs/identhft-en.asp

STORING DATA ON THE SERVER SIDE

A database is an essential component for any interactive e-commerce site. In fact, the ability to store and retrieve data quickly is a crucial capability if you want a site to be more interactive. So understanding database technologies helps us understand how an organization can use the Web more effectively. Recall that businesses use databases to track customers and registered users; store content, such as news articles or catalogue product descriptions; and support on-line searches. More than that, though, databases provide another means of maintaining the state of client interaction with the server and storing persistent data on the server side. We discuss below how databases fit into the infrastructure of an e-commerce application. For more information on database technologies, see Tech Guide D.

5. Tom Zeller, Jr., "The Scramble to Protect Personal Information." *The New York Times*, http://www.nytimes.com/2005/06/09/business/09data.htm.

WHAT DO YOU THINK?

Web hosting is the business of housing, serving, and maintaining files for one or more websites. Sometimes a local internet service provider (ISP) will provide this service. Or there are specialized firms (such as Q9 in Canada) and global IT firms (such as IBM or EDS) that can host commercial sites for you. This makes it very easy to get into a Web-based business. Imagine you are choosing a Web hosting company and consider the following questions:

1: Do the service offerings differ among companies? How?
2: On what basis might you make this decision, besides cost? How would you compare costs for a decision like this?

EXECUTING PROGRAMMING INSTRUCTIONS

For interaction, a computer needs to execute programming instructions. The server, the client, or both may execute instructions. Let's take a look at the primary technologies used for executing program instructions with Web applications.

Making the Client-Side Dynamic and Interactive

On the client side of a Web application, the browser generally executes instructions by using a scripting language, downloadable code components, or a plug-in. A **scripting language** is a high-level computer language that another program—in this case the browser—interprets when executed. The HTML can include scripting languages in a page, thereby adding dynamic interaction. For example, companies may use script code to display interactive visual components, such as dynamic advertisements.

Businesses often use client-side scripting for **data validation,** to ensure that user information is in the correct form before sending it to the server. The most common client-side scripting language is **JavaScript** (related to but not the same as the popular language known as Java). Figure 8.9 shows a simple JavaScript program that ensures that users enter their names and e-mail addresses on an HTML form. You can tell where script has been added in a web page source by locating the < script > tags.

Scripts are primarily used for simple processing tasks. For more complex tasks, a browser relies on specialized components designed to interact with the user and perform advanced instructions, such as *ActiveX*, *Java applets*, and *plug-ins*.

ActiveX is a set of technologies that Microsoft designed to support the sharing of information among different applications. The ActiveX technology allows you to link data from one document to

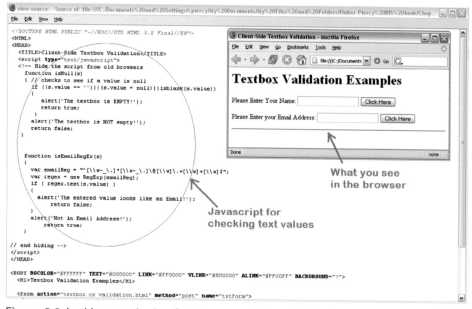

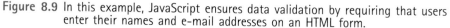

Figure 8.9 In this example, JavaScript ensures data validation by requiring that users enter their names and e-mail addresses on an HTML form.

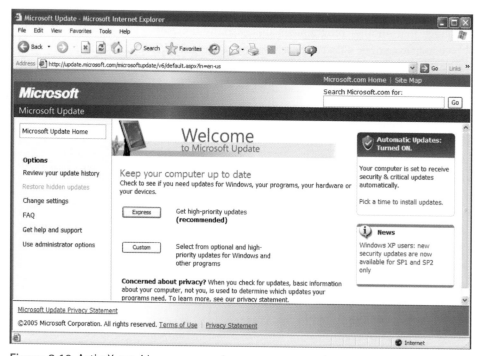

Figure 8.10 ActiveX provides more complex e-commerce actions, such as allowing users to update their Microsoft software.

another. For example, a marketing report created using a word processor might link to a chart in a spreadsheet. Businesses generally use *ActiveX controls* in their e-commerce applications for more complex actions, such as in the Microsoft Update page, shown in Figure 8.10, which allows customers to update various Microsoft programs. Without ActiveX, you would not be able to update your Microsoft software through this page.

A Java **applet** is a small Java program that a browser can download and execute. Java applets are small and fast, so a network can easily transfer them. Applets use browser features to decrease the size of the applet file, which in turn increases download speeds. This design has made applets a popular means of delivering interactive features like on-line games (see Figure 8.11). Applets have limited file and network access, which restricts their applicability, but does lessen the chance of someone using an applet for malicious purposes.

Finally, a browser **plug-in** is a small software module that is compatible and can work along with your browser. As such, it adds features to the browser software. The idea is that the browser developer, such as Microsoft or Mozilla, will develop the main browser software with the ability to extend it. Then, outside programmers

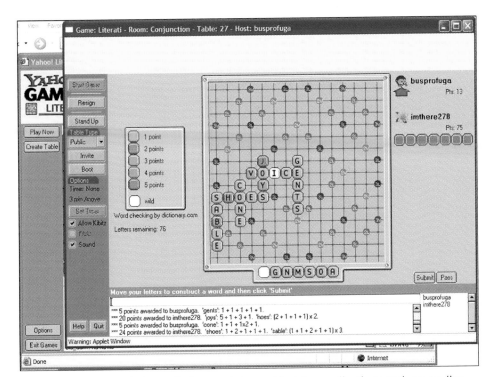

Figure 8.11 Due to their small size, applets are ideal for applications such as on-line interactive games.

Figure 8.12 Plug-ins add features to the browser software, such as the Macromedia Shockwave Player used here to display interactive media.

can write small extension programs that you can download and simply plug in to the browser framework.

You have probably already used plug-ins. For example, most browsers rely on plug-ins, such as RealPlayer by RealNetworks or the Windows Media Player by Microsoft, to allow the browser to play video and audio. You have also probably used Adobe Acrobat, a very popular plug-in that allows you to view and work with documents that are specially formatted for the print medium. Over time, the more popular plug-ins tend to get built into new releases of the browser software.

Figure 8.12 shows the Microsoft Internet Explorer browser with a couple of plug-ins. In the main window, you can see an interactive animation that uses the Macromedia Shockwave Player. Shockwave works with the browser to display interactive media for demonstrations or entertainment, using a proprietary format known as Flash. Along the top of the browser window is the Google Toolbar, to allow quick Google searches without browsing to the Google website. This is a good example of how businesses can strategically use browser plug-ins to extend a company brand name.

Delivering Dynamic Responses from the Server

Most businesses use server-side programming to deliver truly dynamic content. **Server-side programming** is just what it sounds like—programs that run on the server in response to browser requests. Server-side programming is more powerful and can therefore do much more than client-side scripting. It also allows the owners to retain control over their programs so that they can better manage their websites.

Almost every major e-commerce site that you have visited uses server-side programming. When a site requires you to log in, a program on the server checks that you are a registered user. When you type keywords into a search engine, a server-side program queries a database and returns the results to you. When you shop at an e-tailer, server-side programs display the products and handle your transactions.

A server-side program runs after receiving a request to the Web server. The request can occur when a user enters a URL into the browser. However, it more frequently results from a user clicking a button or selecting an item from a list box on an HTML form. When the Web server receives the request, it triggers the execution of a server-side program. It then passes the request on to another server, known as an *application server*. Along with the request that tells it which program to run, the application server also receives any other data that the user entered on the HTML form. In addition, the application server will usually get data from a *data server,* which provides server-side storage.

A short listing of some things that server-side programming can do should convince you why it is important for e-commerce applications. With server-side programming, a business can:

- Deliver content that it customizes for the individual user
- Dynamically modify content for any page
- Access data stored in a server-side database and send it to the client's browser
- Take action on queries and data sent from HTML forms
- Provide access control and security for a website
- Optimally manage the traffic to the site

Several server-side technologies are available to create interactive e-commerce Web applications. Table 8.1 lists the most prominent of these. Note, however, that developing websites using these technologies is much more involved than simply creating a static HTML web page. Working with these technologies requires knowledge of computer programming and project management skills (discussed in Chapter 6).

THE N-TIER INFRASTRUCTURE

If you were to create an on-line business using the technology that we've identified in the first and second generation of e-commerce, you would have the enabling infrastructure used by most e-commerce applications today. Conceptually, if you were describing the system to others, you might consider it as being composed of several main

Table 8.1   Server-side E-commerce Technologies

Server–Side Technology	Programming Languages	Description
CGI (common gateway interface)	Perl	• Provided the first standards for sharing HTML form data received by the Web server with the application server. • Programs can be written using just about any computer language. Perl, a scripting language, has become the most popular. • As the first server-side programming technology, there is a vast library of CGI programs available.
PHP (PHP hypertext processor)	PHP	• A script language and interpreter that is available for free under an open-source licence used primarily on Linux Web servers. • Script is embedded within a web page along with its HTML. • Before the page is sent to a user who has requested it, the Web server calls PHP to interpret and perform the PHP script instructions.
Microsoft.Net	Visual Basic.Net, C-Sharp, and others	• Microsoft's family of software development technologies; ASP.Net (Active Server Page) is the main component used for Web development. • ASP.Net supports code written in compiled languages such as Visual Basic, C^{++}, C#, and Perl. • Features server controls that can separate the code from the content, allowing WYSIWYG editing of pages. • Only servers that use Microsoft Web server software can deliver ASP.Net pages.
Java Servlets and JavaServer Pages	Java	• A servlet is a small Java program that runs on a server. • Java servlets can execute more quickly than CGI applications on servers with lots of traffic. • Java servlets can run on several types of Web servers, including Netscape Enterprise, Microsoft Internet Information Server (IIS), and Apache servers. • Java Server Page (JSP) uses HTML and Java to control the content of web pages and works in conjunction with servlets.

parts. Each part is called a tier. The number of tiers can vary depending on what components are actually used. For example, in Figure 8.13, we depict a four-tier system. When you connect to the Internet using your browser, you are part of the client tier. Depending on its capabilities, the e-commerce application that you connect to may consist of one or more of the Web, application, and data tiers. Just as there may be many users accessing a website as part of the client tier, a large e-commerce site may have multiple computers set up as servers for each of the server-side tiers.

The typical transaction using a four-tier system works like this:

1. By entering a URL, clicking a button, or any of several other ways, you send an HTTP request to a Web server.

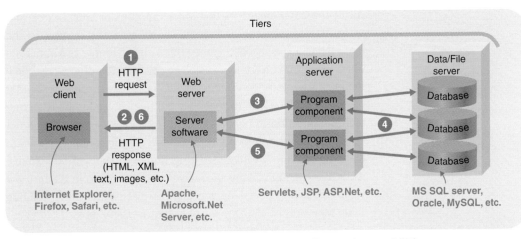

Figure 8.13 A four-tier e-commerce infrastructure; depending on its capabilities, any e-commerce application that you build or use might consist of one or more of the Web, application, and data tiers.

2. The Web server receives the requests and determines how to generate a response. If the request is for a static HTML file, the server simply retrieves the file and sends it back as part of the response to the client's browser.

3. If the request requires a dynamic response, the Web server acts as a controller that routes messages and data between the client and the application server.

4. When needed, applications contact the data server to perform queries on the databases that it controls. The application uses the data to perform its tasks.

5. The results of an executed application will be formulated into a browser-compatible web page that combines the output of the application with the appropriate HTML tags.

6. The Web server includes the dynamically generated page in an HTTP response and then sends the result to the browser.

The three tiers that compose the server side in Figure 8.13 are sometimes referred to as a *solution stack of technologies* for supporting e-commerce applications. The technologies listed in Table 8.1 are also often key parts of the solution stack.

Another increasingly popular set of technologies used in the solution stack is known as **LAMP**, which stands for:

- Linux—used as the operating system for the servers (and possibly the clients)
- Apache—a Web server software application
- MySql—a database management system
- Perl, PHP, or Python—a selection of script programming languages

All of the components of this stack are popular *open-source software;* that is, users can look at the source code of the software and make changes as needed. In addition, open-source programs are often free or have very low cost. The combination of low cost, flexibility of use, and decreasing reliance on a single software vendor has made this stack an increasingly popular choice for many e-commerce applications.

The use of e-commerce technologies described above has led to many new and innovative uses of technology to support knowledge work. For example, many sites have been developed in the last few years to support social networking, as discussed in the "Finding Team Members by Using a Social Network" CORE box.

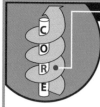

—Relationships

Finding Team Members by Using a Social Network

Your boss, a venture capitalist, invests in companies that are attempting to exploit cutting-edge technologies. He has heard about a new technology that combines the physics of nanotechnology with techniques from evolutionary biology and computer science. He wants you to put together a team to assess the viability of this new technology. In a panic, you wonder how you are going to do this. You don't know any physicists or biologists! Your little sister, who likes to program her Lego robots, is the closest person you know to a computer scientist.

Relax. With today's social networking tools, you only need to know someone who knows a physicist, someone who knows someone who is related to an evolutionary biologist. Social networking tools are a hot Internet application that seek to exploit the network of people with whom we are socially acquainted for both business and entertainment. For example, many of you may have had fun using the social networking site called *The FaceBook* to keep up with friends and make new acquaintances.

Other social network applications, however, have a more serious goal. For example, sites like *LinkedIn* include tools that allow you to search the network for people with various professional backgrounds or skills. If you find a likely candidate, you might be able to contact them directly. More likely, you will need to trace the network of acquaintances back to yourself. To contact this person, you will start with your closest acquaintance on the path and ask for an introduction to the next closest person. After a few such introductions, you may then find yourself directly linked to the target of your search. This may seem time-consuming, but the requirement of an introduction goes a long way toward establishing your credibility as someone who should be safe to work with.

So far, on-line social networking tools have been in a trial phase, as users try them out with mixed success. Even large organizations are starting to pursue these technologies to map the knowledge and expertise of their members. So, in the near future, when you need to build a team, it may be more important to be connected to a large web of contacts.

Web Resources

- LinkedIn Business Social Network—http://www.linkedin.com
- The FaceBook Social Network—http://www.facebook.com

Quick Test

1. Computer programs that run on the server are created using _____.

   a. client-side programming
   b. two-tier infrastructure
   c. server-side programming
   d. plug-ins

2. Which of the following is a small data file that can be used to store data on the client's computer?

   a. ActiveX
   b. cookie
   c. crumpet
   d. plug-in

3. Which of the following components of a four-tier client/server e-commerce system will handle requests from the Web and then generate responses to the requests?

   a. application server
   b. data/file server
   c. Web client
   d. Web server

Answers: 1. c; 2. b; 3. d

THIRD-GENERATION E-COMMERCE TECHNOLOGIES: SUPPORTING TRANSACTIONS

Early in the evolution of e-commerce, businesses recognized that they must contend with several important aspects of commercial transactions in order for e-commerce to work. In this section, we discuss three of these aspects: the ability to (1) find information, (2) order and pay on-line, and (3) provide secure and private transactions.

SEARCH TECHNOLOGIES

Have you searched the Web for information lately? If you have, you realize the vast amount of data available. In fact, many claim we are at the point of information overload, where huge volumes of useless, old, or unsubstantiated information lives just because it was once posted on the Web. So, without search technology, how would you locate the best source of specific information on any product, service, or topic?

Internet **search engines** generally follow the process shown in Figure 8.14. For most sites, users access an HTML form-based web page that allows them to enter their specific search criteria to a greater or lesser extent. Search criteria generally consist of one or more keywords and possibly other data to limit the search and keep the list of results to a manageable level. The search criteria data are sent to the search engine Web server, which in turn passes it to the application server to search through the sites' databases. In reality, when you search the Web, you are actually searching a database that was compiled from previous Web searches.

The main difference between most Internet search engines is how the database of Web locations is created and organized. To search the Web and compile location data in their databases, most Internet search engines use either special software called **Web crawlers,** human submissions, or a combination of the two. Many

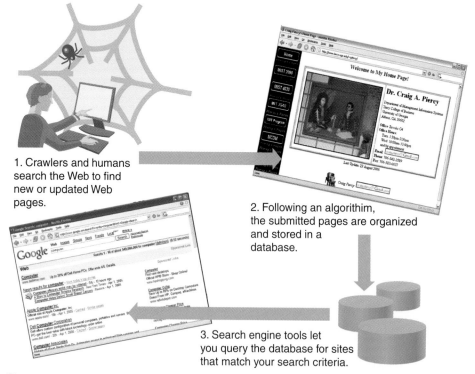

1. Crawlers and humans search the Web to find new or updated Web pages.

2. Following an algorithim, the submitted pages are organized and stored in a database.

3. Search engine tools let you query the database for sites that match your search criteria.

Figure 8.14 How search engines work.

web pages incorporate special tags, known as *meta tags,* which contain information that describe what a site is about. Crawlers, or spiders, move around from site to site, read these meta tags, and report the data back to their database for storage.

People can also submit sites, which the database also stores. Since people often discriminate between sites better than crawlers, human submissions are often of higher quality or fit a specific profile better than sites found by crawlers. In either case, the actual sites stored in each site's database can vary, depending on what the crawlers and humans find and submit.

Perhaps more important than how the sites are found is the manner in which the database organizes, or *indexes,* the Web data. Each search engine will typically use a different algorithm for indexing the data and applying the search criteria to query the indexed data. For example, a search engine may rank web pages based on the frequency and location of keywords in the page content. Those pages with a higher frequency of relevant keywords may receive a higher ranking. Another method, such as the one made popular by the Google search engine, ranks each page based on the number of other pages that link to the page. A page with a larger number of relevant linked pages is considered to be more important to the Web community, and thus would receive a higher ranking.

After honing their technologies with Web search engines, several of the major players, such as Google, Microsoft, and Yahoo, now offer desktop search tools. Once installed, a desktop search tool will automatically browse through your hard drive and index the files stored there based on the file names and extensions. After creating the initial inventory of files, the desktop search tool will then automatically catalogue and index any new items. You can then use tools similar to those on Web search sites to search through the growing number of files that you store locally. Many companies are using this "local search" technology to improve their use of the vast amount of unstructured data that they have stored.

ORDER AND PAYMENT SYSTEMS

An e-commerce site needs to include components for processing orders and accepting payments. The four primary components of a typical e-commerce site are: (1) the shopping and ordering system, (2) the merchant account, (3) the payment gateway, and (4) the security system. As you will see below, the merchant's site handles some of these tasks, while other tasks require connections to third parties.

Many e-commerce firms manage the shopping and ordering processes on their own servers or privately leased servers. The main tasks are to track the products that the user selects to purchase during browsing of the site, and then to record the order for those products so that the firm can gather and ship them to the user. A site may use several methods to do this, such as:

- A nonsecure HTML order form, with the results sent to the firm's e-mail address
- A secure HTML order form, with the results sent to the firm's e-mail address
- A "shopping cart" system that tracks customer orders using a database
- A shopping cart service provided by a third party

Possibly the best and most popular choices are to use a secure HTML order form or an in-house shopping cart system. The secure HTML order form is simpler to use and a viable choice if users typically order a small number of items. Firms use shopping carts for more complex sites with lots of shopping options. This makes the users' shopping experience easier, by allowing them to continue their browsing after selecting each product and then checking out only once. Figure 8.15 shows an Amazon.ca shopping cart page.

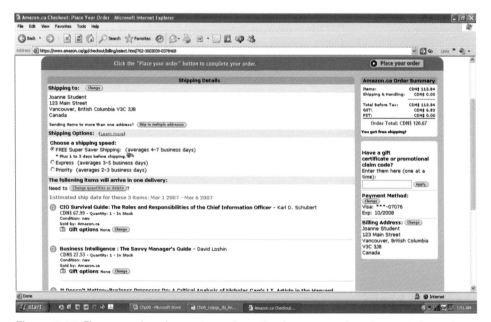

Figure 8.15 Firms use shopping carts, such as the Amazon.ca shopping cart shown here, to allow their customers to continue their browsing after selecting each product and then checkout only once.

Concerning the payment process, firms again have several options. In fact, many sites offer more than one of these options. Businesses can allow payment in more traditional ways, such as billing for payment by cheque or by manually processing the credit card information. This is known as *deferred payment*. Smaller sites with limited infrastructure can also use third-party merchant accounts like those provided by PayPal, CCBill, or ClickBank. These sites process payments between the customer and merchant for a transaction fee. While this can be a good solution for those with limited site capabilities, the fee can eat into profits. However, consumers love services like PayPal. Originally born by a group of entrepreneurs who worked together at eBay, and later purchased by them, PayPal essentially created a form of on-line currency that made a series of smaller consumer transactions possible and convenient by aggregating them through one account that is settled automatically. Especially popular with eBay and other trading site addicts, PayPal has now become an essential part of on-line commerce.

For large sites, the preferred method for processing payments is to use real-time credit or debit card authorization that they process themselves. This eliminates a "middle man" and improves margins on sales. However, it also makes the sites responsible for all of the issues (security, privacy, etc.) that come with accepting payment information directly into their own systems. This method is compatible with the most popular form of payment by customer, namely a credit card. With real-time processing of credit cards, the merchant handles the payment almost immediately. The merchant then simply needs to ship the goods. This type of payment system, however, requires the merchant to set up a merchant account and to establish a connection to a payment gateway. The same or a similar system is used for debit card payments.

A *merchant account* is basically a bank account that allows merchants to receive the proceeds of credit card purchases. After establishing a merchant account, the acquiring bank agrees to pay the merchant for all valid credit card purchases in exchange for the right to collect the debt owed by the consumer. A **secure gateway provider** is a company that provides a network to process encrypted transactions from a merchant's website. It then passes the transactions on to the issuing banks of the customers' credit cards for approval. Some of the most popular gateway providers include Verisign, Symantec, and AuthorizeNet.

A secure gateway provider will generally offer a payment gateway and a processor. A *payment gateway* links an e-commerce site

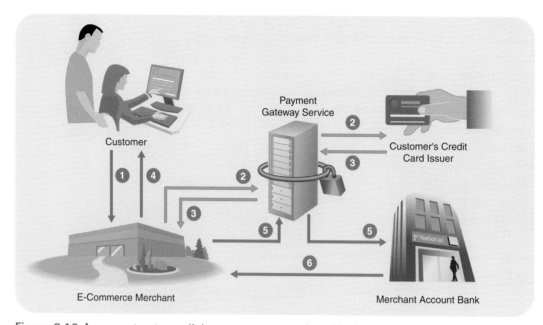

Figure 8.16 A payment gateway links an e-commerce site with the banking network.

with the banking network. The processor handles the financial data submitted by the shopping cart application. The processor will accept the data from the shopping cart, properly format it, and enter it into the banking network. It is then handled just like any other credit card transaction. Figure 8.16 shows the steps involved in this payment system, as follows:

1. The customer places an order with the merchant through the e-commerce site.
2. The payment gateway provider detects the placement of an order. The provider securely encrypts the transaction data (discussed in the next section) and passes an authorization request to the bank to verify the customer's credit card account and available funds.
3. The gateway provider returns a response, indicating whether or not the transaction is authorized, to the e-commerce merchant. This process typically takes less than 3 seconds.
4. Upon approval, the e-commerce merchant notifies the user and fulfills the customer's order.
5. The gateway provider sends a settlement request to the merchant account's bank.
6. The merchant account's bank deposits the transaction funds into the e-commerce merchant's account.

WHAT DO YOU THINK?

What stalled e-commerce in its early days was consumer distrust of on-line payment systems, especially if that involved giving out their credit card information. Over time, this has become less of an issue as secure computing has gained consumer trust and as various new types of "digital cash" systems have emerged on the Web, such as PayPal. Consider these questions as an Internet user:

1: Have you ever used an on-line payment system like PayPal? If so, for what? Did you trust it would work the first time and why?

2: What are the signs of legitimacy that you look for in a website before providing your credit card information for payment?

3: Have you ever had a payment problem on the Internet? What were the consequences or solutions to the problem?

SECURITY

The order and payment systems must be secure to protect both the customer and the merchant. Several technologies have been developed to keep these e-commerce transactions safe from prying eyes.

Most e-commerce security technologies relate to the **secure socket layer (SSL)** protocol. SSL, developed by Netscape and RSA Data Security Inc., allows a client and a server to communicate in a way that prevents eavesdropping, message forgery, or tampering. A server that encrypts data using the SSL protocol is known as a *secure server*. How do you know if you are connected to a secure server? You just need to look at the URL. The URL of a secure server starts with HTTPS in place of the usual HTTP. You may also see a closed lock icon in the lower corner of your browser. In addition, organizations may build this level of security into their own private extranets and intranets, especially for secure remote access to sensitive company networks (see Figure 8.17).

A website can signal that it uses SSL to encrypt data by purchasing an *SSL site certificate*. The site can own the SSL certificate itself, or a hosting service can provide it. When you connect to a secure server, the server will first identify itself to your browser using the SSL certificate. The SSL certificate works to verify the identity of the secure server, much like your driver's licence can be used to identify you (except the SSL certificate is much more difficult to fake).

When a customer connects to a secure server, the server and the browser use SSL to provide each other with the information needed to encrypt the data. This encryption is done using a public-and-private key encryption system. When the SSL session begins, the server passes its public key to the browser. The browser uses it to send a randomly generated secret key back to the server. SSL fits

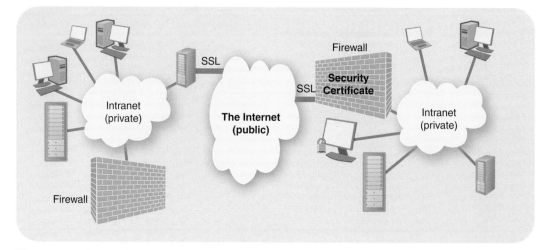

Figure 8.17 Companies can build security technologies into their own intranets and extranets when transmitting through the Internet.

between the TCP/IP connection protocols and the application protocols like HTTP, SMTP, and FTP. SSL is currently being replaced by a newer protocol called the **transport layer security (TLS).** TLS and SSL cannot work together, but a message sent with TLS can be handled by a client that uses SSL.

Microsoft, Netscape, Visa, MasterCard, and others also endorse another security standard called the **secure electronic transaction (SET)** protocol. SET combines several security standards to provide a system that can ensure private and secure transactions. SET makes use of SSL, Microsoft's secure transaction technology (STT), the **secure hypertext transfer protocol (S-HTTP),** and some aspects of *the public key infrastructure*. S-HTTP extends HTTP to allow the secure exchange of data on the Web. Each S-HTTP message is either encrypted, contains a digital certificate, or both. We discuss another use of encryption in the CORE box "Securing E-Commerce with Encryption."

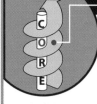

On-line Security

Securing E-Commerce with Encryption

The most common method of providing security to e-commerce transactions, as well as most other Internet activity, is encryption. Encryption is the process of scrambling a message so that it is meaningful only to the person holding the key to deciphering it. To everyone else, the message is gobbledygook. The reverse process, *decryption,*

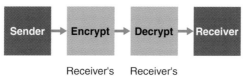

Receiver's   Receiver's
Public Key   Private Key

Figure 8.18 The process of public key encryption.

converts a seemingly senseless character string into the original message. There are two primary forms of encryption systems: (1) private key and (2) public key encryption.

Private key encryption uses the same private key to encrypt and decrypt a message. A key is an algorithm used to encode and decode messages. While private key encryption may sound like the simplest method, there are significant problems with it. For example, how do you securely distribute the key? You can't send the private key with the message, because if the message is intercepted, the key can be used to decipher it. You must find another secure medium for transmitting the key. Do you fax or telephone the key instead? Neither method is completely secure, and each is time-consuming to use whenever the key is changed. In addition, how do you know that the key's receiver will protect its secrecy? Another problem with private key encryption is that you have to create a separate private key for each person or organization with which you will exchange encrypted messages.

In contrast, a *public key encryption* system has two keys: one private and the other public. The public key is freely distributed and used to encrypt messages coming to you. In contrast, the private key remains secret and is only used to decrypt the messages encrypted with your public key. For example, you would distribute your public key to anybody who might need to send you encrypted messages. They would encrypt a message with your public key. Upon receiving the message, you would apply the private key, as shown in Figure 8.18. Your private key, the only key that can decrypt the message, must be kept secret to permit secure message exchange. Public key encryption is widely used in e-commerce to ensure the safety and privacy of transactions.

A free form of public encryption is Pretty Good Privacy (PGP), developed by Phil Zimmerman, a software engineer, in 1991. After inventing PGP, rather than trying to sell it, Zimmermann gave it away to anyone requesting it. That got him into trouble with U.S. authorities, because it was illegal at that time to export encryption technology. In spite of government efforts to stop his work, PGP quickly became the most widely used encryption software in the world. After a three-year effort to prosecute him, the U.S. Justice Department dropped its case. Although he has received a number of awards for his work, he is most proud of the fact that many human rights activists are documenting the atrocities of their governments by encrypting documents with PGP.

Web Resources

- E-commerce and Encryption—http://cyber.law.harvard.edu/ecommerce/encrypt.html (contains many other links to the same subject)
- More Information on PGP—http://www.pgp.com
- Download site for PGP—http://www.pgpi.org/
- Information on Phil Zimmermann—http://www.philzimmermann.com

PART

3

Finally, we should also mention the importance of cookies to payment and security technologies. Previously, we mentioned how businesses use cookies to track activities on the Web. However, the payment and security systems that we have discussed in this section may not work without cookies. For instance, these systems often use cookies to authenticate users or to hold data to match the user with their shopping cart. In this case, businesses and consumers must consider the trade-off between convenience and security.

Quick Test

1. Special software tools that scour the Web for pages and sites and then store the results in a database of a search engine are known as _____.
   a. search gateways
   b. payment systems
   c. shopping carts
   d. Web crawlers

2. Which of the following is a company that provides a network to process encrypted transactions from a merchant's website?
   a. merchant account gateway
   b. payment processor server
   c. secure gateway provider
   d. shopping cart system

3. A server that encrypts data using the _____ protocol is known as a secure server.
   a. HTML
   b. HTTP
   c. FTP
   d. SSL

Answers: 1. d; 2. c; 3. d

FOURTH-GENERATION E-COMMERCE TECHNOLOGIES: TRANSFORMING PROCESSES

Recall that in Chapter 5 we briefly mentioned Web services and how XML technologies present possible tools for dealing with the software integration challenge that afflicts many organizations. Together, these technologies are fast becoming important factors in linking organizations, or rather the systems of organizations. Well, they are also critical for fourth-generation e-commerce capability.

In fact, fourth-generation e-commerce technologies are moving to the realm where computers at one business automatically interact with computers at another business. These newer technologies are improving the ability to exchange small amounts of data via the Web and to standardize the support of transactions. We will look at the primary fourth-generation e-commerce technologies of XML and Web services in this section.

EXTENSIBLE MARKUP LANGUAGE (XML)

Recall that XML (eXtensible Markup Language), like HTML, uses tags to mark up content and/or data so that software applications can recognize it. However, the goal of XML is to describe data and focus on what they mean, while the goal of HTML is to describe how to display data. As such, XML complements HTML, and the two are often used together.

Using XML, companies can define their own tags that their trading partners can understand. For example, the tag < PARTID > would indicate that the field that followed was a part number. And, depending on how the application in the receiving computer wanted to handle the part number field, the data could be stored or displayed, or some other operation could be performed on them. Figure 8.19 shows an example of the use of XML to describe data about a fictitious company named ABC Metals that is located in Victoria, B.C. Note that the data item is surrounded by a beginning and ending tag to clearly identify it.

Note that by itself, XML does not do anything. As a result, to send, receive, display, and process XML files, the software industry needed to develop modern programming languages to work with it. For example, Microsoft's Visual Basic.Net and C# (C-sharp) include XML "baked in." Sun's Java language, perhaps the dominant language for Web and network application development, includes many tools for working with XML. Table 8.2 lists the many potential uses for XML, including e-commerce. You can find more details about XML in Tech Guide D.

```
< CompanyName > ABC Metals < /CompanyName >
< Address > 550 Montgomery Street < /Address >
< City > Victoria < /City >
< Province > BC < /Province >
< Postal > V8W 6T9 < /Postal >
```

Figure 8.19 Using XML, companies can define their own tags that their trading partners can understand, such as this figure, which provides the location of ABC Metals.

Table 8.2	Uses for XML
XML Use	Description
B2B e-commerce	XML provides a tool for exchanging transaction data between applications with a minimum of human interaction.
Basis for new languages	XML has been used to create new languages, such as wireless markup language (WML), which is used to mark up Internet applications for handheld devices like wireless PDAs and mobile phones.
Data exchange	Real-world systems often work with data in incompatible formats; however, because XML is self-descriptive and usually transmitted as plain text, it can be read by many applications.
Data storage	XML stores data in plain text files, which allows the development of generic applications to store, retrieve, and display the data.
Increased usefulness of data	Because XML is platform independent, data can be made available to more applications than just the standard browser. Diverse applications can access XML files as data sources.
Separate data from HTML	Developers can create "separate concerns" by storing data in separate XML files. HTML can be focused on display that will not require any changes as data changes.

Lately, XML is a major component in a set of technologies that are helping to make the Web even more interactive. By combining XML with JavaScript and dynamic HTML and HTTP protocols, a technology called AJAX is being used to allow web pages to respond more quickly to user actions. With AJAX, much of the processing related to user actions happens on the client side rather than sending a request to the server and having the user wait for the server's response. Instead, requests for only a small amount of XML formatted data are made when needed and then used to adjust the web page interface. This speeds up overall interaction for the user because any action that doesn't require a request from the server, like simple data validation, can be handled by an AJAX engine on the client side. These cutting-edge uses of JavaScript and XML provide a much richer user experience.

WEB SERVICES

Recall from Chapter 2 that **Web services** are a standardized way for one computer program to request and run another computer program over the Internet. The two applications may reside on different computers that are connected in some way, for instance by a LAN or more commonly by the Internet. The most popular and most discussed Web services are self-contained business functions that operate over the Internet.

A Web service is a platform-independent software component that can be:

- Described using a standard description language
- Published to a public registry of services
- Discovered using a standard method
- Requested through an application program interface (API)
- Combined with other services and procedures to compose an application

Web services are important because they enable different systems to interact more easily than before. Partners can more efficiently and quickly link and share data. Web services give companies the ability to do more e-commerce business, with more potential business partners, and in more different ways than before at a reasonable cost.

Along with the usual programming methods that we discussed in Chapter 6, Web services rely on specially created programming standards, listed in Table 8.3. Since Web services are written according to standards, all parties work from the same basic design. A company can then add value and business advantage to the basic design to meet the needs of its customers. Web services provide the basic messaging and service-description functions for this kind of relationship. Suppliers can build on the basic features to provide better services to the customer.

The standards in Table 8.3 are perhaps best understood if we think of them in terms of the actual message that is exchanged using a Web service. The message is composed using XML and SOAP. The main part of the message contains XML marked-up data. A SOAP header and footer "wrap" the body. Together, XML and

Table 8.3	Primary Web Service Standards	
Standard	**Description**
eXtensible markup language (XML)	The language used by Web services for marking the exchanged data according to their meaning.
Simple object access protocol (SOAP)	A simple XML-based protocol to let applications exchange information over HTTP.
Web service description language (WSDL)	A standard based on XML for formally defining a Web service.
Universal description, discovery, and integration (UDDI)	A standard for setting up directories of Web services. UDDI will allow you to discover what Web services are available on the network.

SOAP thus allow recognition of the message as it travels over the network. WSDL is used to create a document that is provided by the owner of the Web service to describe what the service will do and what it will return. UDDI is used to set up libraries of Web services through which we can search for a service that meets our needs.

The above explanation may seem fairly technical, so let's consider an example to see how a Web service might work. Suppose that Nick's Coffee Shops, a national coffee chain, wants to add a feature to its website. The company would like to allow a customer to visit its website, enter his or her postal code, and then view a list of the nearest Nick's Coffee Shops, including the approximate distance to each.

After searching a UDDI registry of Web services, the company found the URL for a Web service that will send back a number representing a distance in kilometres between two postal codes that it receives as input. Using the information from the WSDL for the Web

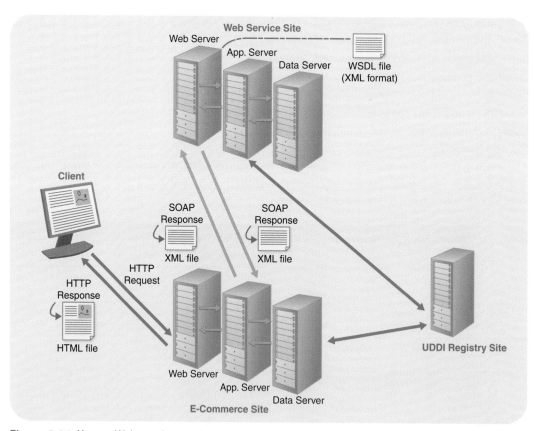

Figure 8.20 How a Web service works.

service, the webmaster for Nick's adds the appropriate code to the application, which will call the Web service when needed. As you can see, the request for the Web service is just one part of the Web application that serves web pages to Nick's customers.

After completing the website, Nick's potential customers may now use it to search for locations of nearby shops. The customers will enter their postal code into a textbox and then click a button to generate a request to Nick's Web server. Nick's Web server will start an application on Nick's application server to generate the dynamic page.

This will probably require queries to Nick's data server to create a listing of Nick's Coffee Shop locations. Then, for each shop in the listing, the postal code and the customer's postal code will be incorporated into a SOAP request to the Web service. The Web service will then calculate the distance between the two postal codes and return the value in a SOAP response. XML will format the data sent within both the SOAP request and SOAP response.

Finally, the application server at Nick's website will use the data generated from the data queries and the Web service to compose the response to the customer. After checking the listing displayed in the browser using HTML, the thirsty customer can head to the nearest coffee shop for a jolt of java. Figure 8.20 summarizes the general process of how a Web service operates. You can read about a real-world example of a company that is successfully using Web services in the "Is it the Death of Software?" CORE box.

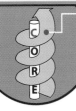

Connectivity

Is it the Death of Software?

"I've said it before, I think it's the end of software." This is a quote from Marc Benioff,[6] the flamboyant CEO of Salesforce.com. Mr. Benioff's company delivers on-demand *customer relationship management* (*CRM*) over the Web. Services at Salesforce.com include sales force automation, customer service and support, and document management, to name just a few.

SalesForce.com is to date the most successful example of a company that provides *on-demand* or *utility computing services*. Instead of the traditional approach of a firm developing its own IS to support its business applications, utility computing provides services hosted on servers, which can be accessed from anywhere. So software is not really dead, but the concept that a company has to create

6. Alorie Gilbert, "The End of Software," http://news.zdnet.com/2100-3513_22-5281034.html.

systems and install the software just may be close to extinction. The goal of utility computing is to provide computing resources when and where an organization needs them. Like electricity, clients pay for services only to the extent that they use them.

What makes services like Salesforce.com possible are the e-commerce technologies that we have discussed in this chapter. Using a combination of server-side programming to create the software, payment, and security systems to process and authenticate clients, and Web services for quick delivery of CRM data, Salesforce.com has built a viable utility with which clients can replace the need for local CRM applications.

Advantages for clients include:

- The clients no longer have to develop or maintain the applications.
- Applications are available anywhere a client can gain access to the Web.
- Reduced cost, as clients pay for only what they use and for only as long as they use the service.

These advantages provide powerful motivation for companies to move to an on-demand service provider, but there is a cost. Clients must be willing to relinquish some control over the applications. Further, they must realize that they will probably not be able to gain a competitive advantage by using the applications. This implies that these types of services would be best suited for business processes that are common to most organizations.

Could Mr. Benioff be right? Does utility computing represent the end of the way we currently think of software? Probably not for all cases, but the 267,000 subscribers from about 15,500 companies worldwide[7] that use Salesforce.com seem to provide strong backup for Mr. Benioff's argument.

Web Resources

- SalesForce.com—http://www.salesforce.com/
- The Executive's Guide to Utility Computing—http://www.cio.com/archive/080104/utility.html

There's no doubt that Web services are valuable for e-commerce. First, a Web service is like a spare part, which can be incorporated into any program that has access. Once written and made available, developers can simply request a Web service as needed. This saves time. Second, Web services provide a way for two computers to automatically pass data between each other. This saves more time. These two advantages are so important that many organizations are setting up an infrastructure to support full-scale use of Web services. This infrastructure is known as **service-oriented architecture (SOA).**

7. Reported on the SalesForce.com website on June 9, 2005.

WHAT DO YOU THINK?

As a means of allowing computer programs to communicate with other computer programs over the Web, the use of Web services has seen tremendous growth in recent years. Check to see if any of the websites that you use are using Web services and consider the following questions:

1: In what ways are they using them?
2: Some popular sites that use Web services include Amazon.ca and Google. How are these sites using Web services?
3: What benefits do you think these companies derive from the use of Web services?
4: What benefits are provided to the customers of these sites?

CHAPTER 8

BEYOND FOURTH-GENERATION E-COMMERCE TECHNOLOGIES

As you have seen in this chapter, the short history of e-commerce has been one of constant change. And this pace of technological advance is continuing. Many initiatives are underway to continue to improve the networks that provide the infrastructure for e-commerce. Some of the ongoing initiatives are primarily focused on improving the technology of e-commerce, while others are more application driven. For example, consider the following three projects:

- **The Next-Generation Internet:** This project is working on replacing the basic protocols that make the Internet possible, namely IP (currently version 4), with a next generation protocol called "Internet Protocol Version 6" (IPv6). IPv4 is already more than 20 years old and is sorely in need of an update in order for the Internet to continue to grow. IPv6 seeks to repair a number of problems with IPv4.[8] These include increasing the number of available IP addresses, and improvements to routing and network configurations. You can think of the Next-Generation Internet project as giving the Internet an overhaul.

- **Internet2:** A consortium of professionals, from more than 200 universities, industry, and government agencies, is developing advanced network applications and technologies to enable the development of revolutionary Internet applications and ensure the rapid deployment of new technologies and services to the global community.[9] Internet2 applications are already in use. Check at your school to see if some of the Internet sites that you visit are already part of Internet2.

8. "What is IPv6?," www.ipv6.org, 2003.
9. "About Intenet2," www.internet2.edu, 2006.

- **Web 2.0:** Not to be confused with Internet2 described above, Web 2.0 is an industry-led group that is seeking to define what will make the next generation of Web applications and companies successful. According to this group, an application is part of Web 2.0 if it strategically uses the Web as a platform. While this concept does not present much of a change from the previous generation of Web applications, Web 2.0 also defines more specific ways in which this is done. For example, Web 2.0 applications allow users to control their own data. In addition, a Web 2.0 application will demonstrate a number of core competencies: provide services, not packaged software; utilize an architecture of participation derived from existing social computing sites; provide cost-effective scalability; make data sources and transformation remixable; keep software independent of a single device; and harness collective intelligence.[10]

These are just a few examples of how e-commerce technologies continue to change the landscape of business. And they provide a valuable reminder that knowledge-enabled professionals must continue to possess a good grounding in both technology and business fundamentals.

Quick Test

1. Which of the following is true regarding XML?
   a. XML tags define the "look and feel" of a web page as it is displayed in a browser.
   b. XML is platform independent and can be used by many different applications.
   c. All devices using XML must use primary XML with no new tags defined.
   d. XML is only used for database query data.

2. Which of the following is the Web services standard that may allow programs to discover other Web services that are available on the network?
   a. XML
   b. SOAP
   c. UDDI
   d. WSDL

---

10. Tim O'Reilly, "What Is Web 2.0: Design Patterns and Business Models for the Next Generation of Software." www.oreilly.com, 2005.

3. An important new IS infrastructure that is built with the goal of supporting Web services is known as _____.
   a. active service provider network
   b. public–private key encryption
   c. service-oriented architecture
   d. voice over IP

Answers: 1. b; 2. c; 3. c

ROI STUDENT RETURN ON INVESTMENT SUMMARY

1. How have e-commerce technologies evolved over the years?

Currently, we can divide the evolution of e-commerce into four major stages or generations. The first-generation e-commerce technologies were capable of delivering static content, while the second-generation technologies allowed for the delivery of dynamic content. The third-generation e-commerce technologies provided increased support of Web-based transactions. We are currently in the fourth generation and can use e-commerce to become increasingly integrated with our external partners over the Web.

2. Why do many businesses still rely on first-generation e-commerce technologies?

First-generation technology allowed for the delivery of static content over the World Wide Web through client/server networks, browsers, HTTP protocol, and HTML. These components allow low-cost entry to e-commerce and are still major components of more recent Web applications.

3. How do second-generation e-commerce technologies provide businesses with more effective customer relationship management?

In the second generation of e-commerce, capabilities for interaction and dynamic content were added. Key technologies included server-side and client-side programming; plug-ins, applets, and ActiveX controls; three-tier server-side infrastructure; client-side storage using cookies; and server-side programming infrastructure. Interaction lets businesses deliver more interesting content, which in turns attracts more visitors to their website.

4. How do third-generation e-commerce technologies support business transactions?

Third-generation technologies have been developed to improve support for e-commerce transactions. Some of these include search, payment and order processing, and security technologies. Search technologies are available for the Internet, specific websites, and local storage. Order processing supports the capture of customer orders and ensures that the appropriate data are captured and routed where they need to go. E-commerce payment technologies allow customers to use several different payment methods such as credit cards or direct billing. Security technologies ensure that the transaction data are encrypted and protected.

5. How do fourth-generation e-commerce technologies contribute to strategic alliances?

Fourth-generation e-commerce technologies are allowing computer programs to communicate directly with computer programs of the Web. XML, which can be used to mark content according to what it means, allows transmitted data to be more easily processed. Web services are programs that can be called by other programs over the Web to deliver XML-formatted data. Service-oriented architectures are being developed to support the increasing use of Web services.

KNOWLEDGE SPEAK

ActiveX   309

applet   311

client/server network   299

cookie   305

data validation   309

dynamic content   296

encryption   324

form controls   304

hypertext markup language (HTML)   302

JavaScript   309

LAMP   315

links   300

Moore's Law   297

persistent data   306

plug-in   311

scripting language   309

search engine   318

secure electronic transaction (SET)   324

secure gateway provider   321

secure hypertext transfer
 protocol (S-HTTP)   324

secure socket layer (SSL)   323

server-side programming   312

service-oriented architecture (SOA)   332

static content   295

transport layer security (TLS)   324

Web crawler   318

Web hosting   309

Web presence   296

Web service   328

REVIEW QUESTIONS

Multiple-choice questions

1. Which of the following technologies can be used to make a website dynamic?

   a.   a Java applet
   b.   an ActiveX control
   c.   server-side programming
   d.   all of the above
   e.   none of the above

2. A small data file that is stored on the client side so that data can be persistent between visits to a website is known as a(n) _____.

   a.   cookie
   b.   tag
   c.   applet
   d.   schema

3. Which of the following is the standard format for a file that describes how a program can access and use a Web service?

   a.   XML
   b.   SOAP
   c.   UDDI
   d.   WSDL

4. Which of the following components of a four-tier client/server e-commerce system will display results of a request in a browser?

   a.   application server
   b.   data/file server
   c.   Web client
   d.   Web server

Fill-in-the-blank questions

5. A _____ is software that sits at the interface between an internal network and the outside to monitor the traffic that enters or exits the internal network.

6. A _____ is a high-level computer language that is interpreted by another program like a browser when executed.

7. The message that contains the web page sent to a client from a server is part of an HTTP _____.

8. A _____ is a small Java program that can be downloaded and executed within a browser window.

True-False questions

9. A static web page can change every time it is viewed.

10. Server-side programming occurs when the browser interprets and executes a script of instructions.

11. ActiveX controls are supported by all Web browsers.

12. Web services use XML for marking the exchanged data according to their meaning.

Matching Questions

Choose the BEST answer from Column B for each item in Column A.

Column A

13. SET
14. HTML
15. CGI
16. SSL

Column B

a. An early e-commerce technology that allowed server-side programs in scripting languages such as Perl.

b. A security protocol that allows a client and a server to communicate in a way that is designed to prevent eavesdropping, message forgery, or tampering.

c. A security protocol that combines several security standards to provide a system that can ensure private and secure transactions.

d. The language that is used to guide the display of a requested web page.

Short-answer questions

17. List the tiers and their purpose that make up the typical four-tier e-commerce infrastructure.

18. Describe XML and how businesses can effectively use it to create value.

Discussion/Essay questions

19. What features do you look for in an e-commerce website that will attract you as a potential customer? What characteristics make you nervous about using an e-commerce site?

20. In this chapter, we discussed a number of technologies that businesses can use to build e-commerce Web applications. See if you can discover other technologies that businesses can use, and then compare what you find with the technologies that we have discussed here.

TEAM ACTIVITY

With a group of classmates, get together and brainstorm to generate ideas for a new e-commerce-based company. Together, discuss the following questions. What will you sell as a primary product or service? Who will your customers be, and what value can they expect to get from your website? How will your company make revenue? Be sure to keep in mind the business models that we discussed in Chapter 7.

SOFTWARE APPLICATION EXERCISES

1. Internet

Search the Internet for e-commerce sites that are similar to one you or your team might want to create (see the Team Activity above). Compare the sites that you find with the site that you want to create. Do these sites sell similar products and/or services? If not, how do they differ? What customers are the sites aiming for? What value do the customers of these sites derive from the sites? How do you think these sites gain revenue? Finally, what would you do on your site to differentiate it from those of your competitors?

2. Presentation

In order to raise money for a new business (such as a Web start-up), potential businesspersons often must present their ideas to potential investors. Based on the ideas discussed in the Team Activity and Internet assignments above, prepare a presentation designed to convince potential investors to finance your new company.

3. Word Processing

A very important aspect of an e-commerce site is the user interface. The designers must make sure that they design the site to convey the right message (e.g., that supports the business strategy). Several design factors are important to consider for any website. For example, the content must be appropriate to communicate your message to the user and to hold their attention. In addition, the overall site must be organized so that the user can easily understand how to use it (as well as navigate it). Most of today's word processors can be used to create quick web pages. Use a word processor to create "mock-ups" of how your pages (see assignments above) will look on your website.

4. Spreadsheet

Assume that you will be hosting your website (see assignments above) on your own equipment and that you will be developing the site in-house. Use a spreadsheet to develop a budget for the Web development project. You will need to list the technologies needed and estimate the quantity and prices of each. You will also need to list the required elements and estimate how much it will cost to complete them. You may need to do some additional research to come up with realistic figures. Assume that you have two years to complete the first version of your site. Use logical functions in Excel to assess budgetary impacts (e.g., what if the scope is increased?) and create plausible alternative development scenarios.

5. Database

Creating an e-commerce site can be a big project. As the project progresses, there will be many issues (problems) that your team will need to resolve. A database to keep up with the issues in a big project can therefore help to ensure that no issues are overlooked.

Create an issues database to track the issues that will inevitably come up in your Web development project (see above assignments). Your database should include at least two tables. One table should hold the names and all contact information for each person on the development team. The other table should hold the data related to each issue. At a minimum, you should record an issue ID, an issue description, the date when work on the issue began, the date when work on the issue ended, and the issue status. Assume that each issue will be assigned to only one development team member for resolution.

6. Advanced Challenge

To organize your team's efforts on your e-commerce project (see above assignments), research and develop a "digital dashboard" or project management portal for your project. If you think through the functionality of a dashboard and complete the activities above, you'll discover that you can use MS Excel, Word, or Access to create a single entry point for the management of your project. Remember that although the worksheets in an Excel workbook appear two-dimensional, a collection of worksheets can make Excel "3-D." Also, you may want to investigate a specialized form in Access known as a *switchboard*.

ON-LINE RESOURCES

Companion Website

- Take interactive practice quizzes to assess your knowledge and help you study in a dynamic way.
- Review PowerPoint lecture slides.
- Get help and sample solutions to end-of-chapter software application exercises.

Additional Resources Available Only on WileyPLUS

- Take the interactive Quick Test to check your understanding of the chapter material and get immediate feedback on your responses.
- Review and study with downloadable Audio Lecture MP3 files.
- Check your understanding of the key vocabulary in the chapter with Knowledge Speak Interactive Flash Cards.
- Link directly to websites recommended in the CORE boxes.

CASE STUDY: USING B2B E-COMMERCE AT BOEING

Assume that you are the spare parts manager for an airline operating a fleet of Boeing 737s in Asia, and you need to order spare parts in a hurry. At one time, this process would have involved your digging through the Boeing parts manual, finding the correct part numbers, and then calling, faxing, or telexing your order to the company parts warehouse in Seattle. Upon receipt of your order, Boeing would then send you a number of automatic faxes or telexes to acknowledge the order and to let you know its status. And this assumes that you have updated your maintenance manual with the continual revisions sent by Boeing—a process that usually took 60 to 90 days.

Sound like a big job? It was! However, today, with Boeing's MyBoeingFleet.com, customers and suppliers have a portal to Boeing's Web-enabled, B2B extranet. This site, and the functions it offers, makes the parts-ordering process much less painful for companies operating Boeing aircraft. The password-protected website is open to airplane owners and operators, as well as maintenance, repair, and overhaul shops—basically anybody who needs products or information for their Boeing airplanes. While it is not open to the general public, you can take a guest tour by going to www.boeing.com/commercial/aviationservices/myboeingfleet/.

In mid-2005, there were 30,000 industry professionals from 550 companies who had access to the extranet site, with more than 4,000 logins per day and 4 million hits per month. In addition to ordering parts from MyBoeingFleet.com, customers can access engineering diagrams, up-to-date maintenance and flight manuals, service bulletins, and other pertinent information.

The PART Page

A key part of Boeing's global B2B e-commerce effort is the sale of spare parts for the more than 7,000 Boeing aircraft in operation. These parts are handled out of spare-parts centres in eight cities with the largest such centre being located near the Seattle-Tacoma airport. This centre contains over $1 billion (U.S.) in spare parts stored in a building covering over 6 hectares! In 2004, the centre shipped an average of 3,000 orders each day. These orders contained almost 300,000 different parts and weighed 3 million kg. The centre handled all of these orders using an automated conveyor delivery system more than 3 kilometres long.

To handle this huge spare-parts e-commerce operation, Boeing created a special element of the overall MyBoeingFleet.com website. Termed the PART page, this site allows customers to order spare parts on a 24/7 basis and provides tracking information on the orders. Customers can work with the latest information without having to deal with reams of paper updates. Currently, this site lists more than 6.5 million types of spare parts and handles an average 130,000 transactions per week. This on-line supply chain management process is a win–win process for both Boeing and its customers: Boeing dramatically reduces its staff required to handle telephone calls, faxes, and telexes, while customers save hundreds of thousands of dollars each year in paper and distribution costs. For example, a customer can now access information equivalent to 80,000 pages of text—a stack of paper 7.5 m high weighing 360 kg!

Spare Parts Economics

Why does Boeing concentrate on the spare-parts business as the keystone of its e-commerce system? There are actually several answers to this question. First, it simply is not possible to sell multimillion dollar airliners over the Web. Second, Boeing makes a great deal of money from its maintenance program. In fact, aircraft maintenance is a much higher-margin business than selling the original aircraft. While Boeing has a 9% margin building planes, it has a 20% margin servicing them. Finally, even if Boeing stopped building aircraft tomorrow, it would still have a very profitable aircraft maintenance business for many years into the future. So finding ways to more efficiently handle this business, through e-commerce, is just smart.[11]

11. Sources for this case include: James Wallace, "Aerospace Notebook: Boeing's Got Parts—15 Whole Acres of Them," *Seattle Post-Intelligencer*, March 2, 2005. Elizabeth Davis, "Portal Power: E-business at Boeing Gaining Velocity." http://www.boeing.com/commercial/news/feature/ebiz.html. Fred Vogelstein, "Flying on the Web in a Turbulent Economy." *Fortune*, April 30, 2001.

Case Questions

1. What aspects of the website MyBoeingFleet.com qualify it as an extranet?
2. How does this website help enable the Boeing supply chain to operators of aircraft built by Boeing?
3. Why is the PART page referred to as the key e-commerce element of the MyBoeingFleet.com website? Do you agree with the economic analysis for concentrating on spare parts? Why or why not?

Integrative Application Case: Campuspad.ca

During your meeting with the student union last week the issue of your search engine strategy came up—and you didn't even have one! Well, you know they exist and use them all the time, but you hadn't really thought proactively about how campuspad.ca was going to appear on them, except that you knew it would.

You and Sarah had decided that you would now turn your attention to site marketing and refining your business plan since the site now seemed to be on track for launch based on your decisions about development two weeks ago. Adam, who agreed to become a partner in the business, is doing a great job and has found some co-op students to help him. More progress has been made on programming the site in the past two weeks than in the past two months! Launch seems closer than ever.

However, once launched, how are you going to get recognized? You know search engines are critical to e-commerce site success, but how do they work and what can you do to influence your results?

Guiding Case Questions:

1. Identify the search engines you or your group use most frequently. Why?

2. How do these search engines rank various sites?
3. Can you buy your way to the top of any of them by paying fees? If so, how much does it cost?
4. What Web marketing, besides search engines, might work for your new site?
5. What kind of partnering, associate or other, could build traffic for campuspad.ca when it launches?

Your Task:

In no more than one to two pages (because your angel investors who are funding the company won't read past that anyway!), identify the three most important search engines that you would want campuspad.ca to be listed on. Establish how they rate and weigh content for their listings and what this implies for your site design and marketing efforts. Look through their sites and determine if they have any programs, offerings, or methods that you could sign up for that would help market your new business post-launch.

WHAT WE WILL COVER

- Corporate and IT Governance
- Global Perspective on IS/IT
- Enterprise Risk Management
- Enterprise Information Security

Connectivity	Using RFID Around the Globe
On-line Security	Internet Security: A Global Problem
Relationships	Hail to the Information Chief
Ethics	Transborder Data Flows

The Connected Enterprise:
Business Partnering and Protecting

 STUDENT RETURN ON INVESTMENT

Through your investment of time in reading and thinking about this chapter, your return, or created value, is gaining knowledge. Use the following questions as a study guide.

1. Why are corporate and IT governance important?
2. What does it mean to have a global perspective?
3. How does global IT create business value?
4. What is enterprise risk management, and what can be done to prevent business loss?
5. What is enterprise information security?

The Voice of Experience
Jennifer Jewer, Memorial University, University of Waterloo

After completing a bachelor of commerce (co-operative) degree in 1998, Jennifer Jewer has worked as an IT consultant in Canada, the United States, and France, received a master's degree in management sciences, and is now pursuing her Ph.D.

What do you do in your current position? I'm doing my Ph.D. in Management Sciences at the University of Waterloo. My job at KPMG inspired me to research IT governance and the impact of how IT contributes to organizational success. I am also working as a sessional lecturer and an independent consultant.

What do you consider to be important career skills? You need to be able to learn different skills for different situations and to embrace any training opportunities. I started out in technical roles working in software development. One of those roles was to take business requirements, translate them into a CRM module design, and customize the software accordingly. I was able to go to France for a similar role in customizing CRM software on a database platform. In addition, especially because of my international experience, I have had to be able to work with a diverse group of people with different backgrounds, educations, and experiences. Overall, it's important to take your technical and non-technical skills from one job and adapt them to the particular situation you're in.

How do you use IT? In my current doctoral studies, one example of an important use of IT has been as a tool to collaborate with other researchers. I'm a member of a health informatics research group with participants from universities across Canada who meet almost exclusively on-line to discuss our ongoing research. We use real-time discussions, on-line presentations, and text messaging to share our research and the research of guest speakers. I also do a lot of research on-line.

Can you describe an example of how you have used IT to improve business operations? When I was an independent consultant working in France, I was helping to implement CRM software. The system managed the customer relationship from initial contact to billing and receiving of orders. This system improved customer satisfaction and helped maintain current customers by improving customer service. The system was implemented in many locations across Europe and allowed for consistent marketing, sales, and support for the company. It included the inventory system as well, which was revolutionary for our client. Before this new system, the company didn't know what products the offices in other countries offered or what parts they had on hand. I was also there during the transition to the euro currency. Without this system, I don't know how they would have done it.

In addition, as a member of KPMG's information risk management group, I worked in the areas of audit and risk management in response to the regulations under the U.S. Sarbanes-Oxley Act (SOX). I looked at how clients' financial systems operated and what controls they had in place to ensure they were adhering to standards and meeting regulations like SOX. With the introduction of SOX, one of the things public companies needed to do was to evaluate and disclose the effectiveness of their internal controls of financial reporting and to ensure that an independent auditor attested to their disclosure.

Have you got any "on the job" advice for students seeking a career in IT or business? You can't consider technology and business as two separate entities. You need to understand how systems work and how businesses work. You also need to be open to change. As an undergrad, I sometimes didn't see the value of non-technical courses, but if I hadn't taken those courses, I would never have been able to do my job at KPMG and I certainly would not have been able to pursue my Ph.D. in management sciences. Be prepared for change, and be able to adapt to your situation.

Jennifer has had a diverse career in academics and global business. She has been involved in multinational technology implementations and projects to ensure compliance to government regulations and to manage risk. In this chapter you will learn about some of the challenges in global business, the regulatory environment (including Sarbanes-Oxley), and enterprise risk management.

In the previous two chapters, we discussed how e-commerce can extend an organization's ability to create business partnerships with important stakeholders, such as customers, suppliers, and partners. You've seen that e-commerce and other information technologies make it easier than ever to conduct business without regard for time, distance, or location. Now we are ready to tackle some of the challenges and issues created when organizations use IT to extend their business reach, efficiency, and effectiveness.

Many of these challenges relate to the creation, processing, storage, and use of data, especially sensitive financial, customer, and employee data. Numerous stories detail the misuse of data. For example, one of the largest known breaches of information security occurred in May 2005 when hackers penetrated an Atlanta-based credit card payment processor, CardSystems Solutions, Inc. Banks that issue Visa- and MasterCard-branded credit cards reported that the breach affected their customers. Officials in Japan claimed that just one month after the loss of customer data, "at least $1 million in fraudulent charges were made on Visa, MasterCard and JCB cards issued by Japanese banks."[1] This same scenario was reported in news media around the world when TJX, owner of Winners, HomeSense, and other retail stores, publicly announced that a hacker had breached its IT security, compromising the credit card information of millions of customers in Canada and the United States.[2] Another such example involved the credit files of Canadians held by Equifax, a credit reporting agency, being compromised on several occasions by criminals posing to be legitimate creditors. These reports detail customer credit histories as well as private personal information.[3]

Given the reliance of most businesses on information systems and communication networks and the growing requirement to provide personalized service to customers, how can businesses expand and at the same time protect their customers and themselves? In this chapter, we answer this question by discussing the following topics:

- The important laws, regulations, and frameworks that affect IT governance and the creation of business value.
- The need for knowledge-enabled professionals and businesses to have a global perspective and to understand the globalization of IT.
- The opportunities and risks when organizations seek to create business value through partnerships and global sourcing.
- The requirement for all parts of the organization to manage risks to the enterprise, to establish and maintain enterprise information security, and to ensure the proper control of financial and other sensitive data and information.

1. P. C. Paul "Fraud in Japan tied to data breach," *Atlanta Journal Constitution*, Thursday, June 23, 2005, p. E-1.
2. CBC Newsworld report, January 27, 2007.
3. "Canadian Credit Agency Reports Data Breach," Joris Evers, Cnet news.com, June 16, 2005. http://news.com.com/Canadian+credit+agency+reports+data+breach/ 2110-1029_3-5750434.html, retrieved October 24, 2006.

Let's start our discussion with an overview of corporate and IT governance.

CORPORATE AND IT GOVERNANCE

To succeed in today's interconnected, global economy, businesses need effective corporate governance, including of IT. Effective governance is a critical enabler for success in the global economy, for securing the enterprise's information resources, and for creating competitive advantage. Noted MIT business scholar Peter Weill estimates that businesses with strong governance create 20 percent more business value than like firms with less-robust governance.[4] In Canada there is an ongoing debate about the financial value of corporate governance. Some contend that good governance is linked to good performance. Others say that there are examples of companies that are following all the rules of good governance but still face challenges and suffer from poor performance. We agree that there are more factors contributing to performance than simply governance. However, one thing is certain: all companies are re-evaluating their governance in light of high-profile corporate scandals such as Enron and Worldcom, to bring it into line with emerging global standards and legislated requirements.[5]

Corporate governance means that the leadership and management of a business are directly accountable to its owners (e.g., shareholders) for proper operation and financial control of the organization. Given the global expansion of businesses, and public demand to control what many see as massive corporate excess and global fraud, it is no surprise that stakeholders such as national governments have increased their involvement in ensuring effective governance. Government and business leaders around the world are enacting laws, writing regulations, and establishing policies and guidelines for the control of financial systems and data as well as the security and confidentiality of sensitive personal information.

However, most businesses today still need to take corporate governance one step further than they have in the past. Since managers and employees are the knowledge-enabled professionals who implement and follow governance policies and processes, they need to understand technology and its impacts on both corporate *and* IT governance. Why? Because most modern businesses are heavily invested in and dependent on information systems, technologies, and data. It certainly would not be prudent to simply assume that because

4. Peter Weill and J. W. Ross, *IT Governance: How Top Performers Manage IT Decision Rights for Superior Performance*, Harvard Business School Publishing, Boston, 2004, p. 2.
5. J. McFarland, and E. Church, "Do better boards make better companies?, *The Globe and Mail*, October 24, 2006, B1.

something is "in the system" then it must be right! Therefore, in order for an organization to understand and manage its operations, it must provide governance for all its information-related assets. In this chapter, we focus on the aspects of corporate governance directly associated with information systems.

IT governance is the "distribution of IT decision-making rights and responsibilities among enterprise stakeholders, and the procedures and mechanisms for making and monitoring strategic decisions regarding IT."[6] This means that IT governance begins as a very high level process that specifies (1) how the organization will set goals, objectives, priorities, and policies for IT; (2) how it will integrate IT with business strategies and goals; and (3) which organizational members will make decisions regarding, and be responsible for, the successful completion of these tasks (the "who" of IT governance).[7]

THE CIO: MANAGING IT GOVERNANCE

So who within a business addresses the IT governance challenges mentioned above? In many businesses, this is the responsibility of the **chief information officer (CIO)** (other titles could include VP of IS, director of IS or IT). This person normally reports to the CEO/Chair, COO/President, or sometimes the CFO, depending on the scope of the position. He or she leads the organization's information and technology efforts, especially as it relates to the creation of business value, and should sit as part of the organization's top executive team. Additionally, the CIO must ensure proper and secure use of all the organization's information resources. We discuss the role of a CIO in greater detail in the CORE box "Hail to the Information Chief." However, since not all organizations have a formally designated CIO, we use the term *IS leadership* to refer to the person or persons responsible for IT governance within an organization.

-Relationships

Hail to the Information Chief

It has been said that the right leader makes the team right. In many businesses, the leader of the information systems and technology team is the *Chief Information Officer (CIO)*. In most companies, the CIO is a high-level position only one or two ranks removed from the chief executive.

---

6. R. Peterson, "Crafting information technology governance," *Information Systems Management*, www.ism-journal.com. Fall 2004.
7. Adapted from IT Governance Institute ® website, http://www.itgi.org, retrieved June 15, 2005.

What does it take to become a CIO? A survey conducted by *CIO* magazine suggests that businesses around the world expect similar skills and experience. The skills most often cited by survey respondents include strong communication skills, the ability to think strategically, and a thorough understanding of the business processes and operations of the company. CIOs in Sweden added "being a good leader" near the top of their list.

These skills closely match those cited in the IS research literature. Dawson and Watson state that the attributes of an effective CIO are important for maintaining both a strategic and a structural orientation. A *strategic orientation* means that the CIO aligns the strategic direction of the IS team with the long-term goals of the business. For the *structural orientation,* the CIO must also understand and effectively manage the people, processes, and technologies of IS. Many scholars assume that the strategic view is more important for the success of the organization. The CIO survey seems to back this up, as the respondents, particularly those from the United States, ranked "strategic thinking and planning" second only to "good communications skills."

What about technical skills? Do you need to be a computer expert to be a CIO? No, not an expert, but definitely someone who has significant technical competence and experience. Although according to the CIO survey, technical skills were not as high on the list as the business skills previously mentioned, they are still very important. For example, in Sweden and in the United States, technical skills ranked fifth and eighth in importance, respectively. The survey indicated that CIOs in Canada spend the bulk of their time meeting with their company's executives and working with both IT vendors and non-IT business partners.

So, as you near the end of this text, keep in mind that you have gained the basic foundation for becoming a CIO. Through experience and increased business and technical knowledge, you may one day aspire to fill the CIO position.

Web Resources

- itWorldCanada.com—features CIO Canada—http://www.itworldcanada.com/publication/CIO.htm
- *CIO* Magazine—http://www.cio.com
- "The State of the CIO around the World," *CIO Research Reports*—http://www2.cio.com/research/, May 1, 2005, and G. Dawson and R. Watson, "All Effective CIOs Are Strategic, Right? Disagreement among Experts In Defining Public Sector CIO Effectiveness," working paper, July 2005.
- CIO Executive Council—an international organization of CIOs including contacts in Canada.—http://cioexecutivecouncil.com/

ROLES OF IT GOVERNANCE AND LEADERSHIP IN CREATING BUSINESS VALUE

Recall our discussion of Porter's value chain model, which shows the activities that create business value. Effective IT governance and leadership combine Porter's competitive strategies with the value chain model to help create business value. To see how IT governance and leadership can do this, consider Figure 9.1. The figure includes numbered boxes that correspond to our discussion here.

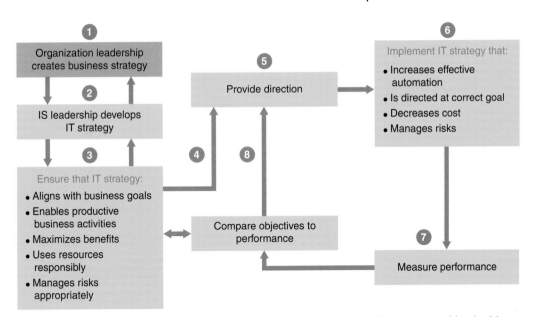

Figure 9.1 As this figure shows, effective IT governance and leadership, when combined with Porter's value chain model, can help create business value. (*Source:* IT Governance Institute ® website, http://www.itgi.org, retrieved June 15, 2005.)

For example, IS leadership can suggest how a business can integrate technology to reduce or eliminate costs throughout its value chain, until it becomes the lowest-cost producer or retailer (1). From this overall business strategy, IS leadership can develop a specific IT strategy, which enables the business to implement its lowest-cost strategy (2–5). Two possible ways for IT to help reduce costs are to automate a process or to support the *outsourcing* of a process to another location or vendor that can perform the process more efficiently and effectively. This is often referred to as business process outsourcing (BPO). This could include processes in IT, such as desktop support, help desks, hosting (often called IT outsourcing), or non-core processes in other parts of the business, such as accounting, human resources, or sales. The reduced process cost helps the business offer a lower price for its products or services, thus improving global competitiveness (6). If outsourcing a business process to another country, IS leadership will need to develop a strategy that includes how to support global operations (back to 1). Another way to support the low-cost strategy is to find efficiencies within the supply chain. Some businesses do this now by closely integrating business processes and systems with their suppliers to reduce time spent executing supply chain activities.

Regardless of whether implementing automation, outsourcing, or optimizing the supply chain, the business must measure the performance and total costs of the effort against the unit cost savings for the product or service. This determines if the IT strategy aligns with and meets the needs of the "lowest-cost" business strategy (7–8). If not, the IS leadership must act to bring performance in line with expectations (5). Especially while pursuing a low-cost strategy, a business may not only be trying to create enhanced business value, but simply be trying to stay in business. As Dr. Nicolas Carr has suggested, if a company can put together an IT system that helps it automate a particular process, then so can its competitors.[8] This suggests some companies may have to engage in constant improvements to their use of IT out of sheer competitive necessity.

Quick Test

1. True or False. All knowledge-enabled professionals who use organizational technologies should understand how technology can affect corporate and IT governance.

2. True or False. IT governance includes the distribution of IT decision-making rights and responsibilities among enterprise stakeholders.

3. The _____ usually leads the organization's information and technology efforts, especially as it relates to the creation of business value.
   a. CEO
   b. CFO
   c. CIO
   d. COO

Answers: 1. False; 2. True; 3. c

A GLOBAL PERSPECTIVE

In our preceding discussion, we mentioned that IS leadership might outsource a process to lower a company's costs. Through outsourcing, a business can also leverage its IT capability, extend and connect the business beyond its boundaries, and create workable partnerships with other firms that have relevant global expertise. However, as we mentioned in the Boeing case study in Chapter 8, some people might mistakenly equate outsourcing with only the *loss* of jobs. In fact, the reverse is often true. By adopting a global perspective regarding businesses, economies, and

8. Nicholas Carr, "IT doesn't matter," *Harvard Business Review*, 81(5), May 2003.

employment, outsourcing can also mean creating employment opportunities for successful companies.

Do you drive a Honda Civic? If so, you might be surprised to know that it was assembled in Alliston, Ontario. According to the World Trade Organization (WTO), if you drive a traditional "American" made car like a GM, Ford, or Chrysler, it is possible that 30 percent of the value of your car could be attributed to its Korean assembly, 17.5 percent to its Japanese components and advanced technology, 7.5 percent to its German design, 4 percent to its Taiwanese and Singaporean parts, 2.5 percent to the United Kingdom for advertising and marketing services, and 1.5 percent to the Ireland and Barbados for data processing support. If you add up all of these percentages, it leaves only 37 percent of the value of this "American" car created from U.S. work.[9] And, of course, many "American" cars are actually manufactured right here in Canada! What does all this mean for business organizations and for knowledge-enabled professionals? We think that it means that to be successful, twenty-first-century businesses and knowledge-enabled professionals will need to adopt a broad global perspective.

WHAT IS A GLOBAL PERSPECTIVE?

In his book, *The World Is Flat,* award-winning author Thomas L. Friedman describes a new view of the global competitive playing field: *flat.*[10] According to Friedman, in a flattened world:

> It is now possible for more people than ever to collaborate and compete in real time with more other people on a more equal footing than at any previous time in the history of the world—using computers, e-mail, networks, teleconferencing, and dynamic new software.[11]

Strategy guru Kenichi Ohmae defines the global economy similarly. He sees it as borderless, invisible (money moves around the globe in electronic format), cyber-connected (nobody is far away who has an IP address and access to the World Wide Web), and measured in multiples (the premium over current sales or profits that investors are willing to pay for the sustainability of these streams into the future versus the present).[12]

Finally, another internationally known strategist, C. K. Prahalad, suggests that global success can only come from discarding old ways of viewing the global marketplace as simply a geographic expansion of current business processes and existing product sales.

9. World Trade Organization, *Annual Report 1998,* cited in G. M. Gorssman and E. Helpman, "Outsourcing in a global economy," *Review of Economic Studies,* 72, 2005, p. 135–159.
10. Thomas L. Friedman, *The World Is Flat.* Farrar, Straus, and Giroux, New York, 2005, p. 8.
11. Ibid, p. 8.
12. Kenichi Ohmae, *The Next Global Stage: Challenges and Opportunities in Our Borderless World.* Pearson Education Inc., publishing as Wharton School Publishing. Upper Saddle River, N.J, 2005.

He further suggests that businesses should seek to serve the global market with new products and new processes, based on the needs and constraints of the specific market being served.[13] In other words, not only do you have to think globally, but you must act locally in multiple locations. In fact, some have coined the term "glocal" to represent firms that benefit from global scale with the ability to act with local sensitivity.

Based on the thoughts of these leading thinkers, we define a **global perspective** as:

> *A worldwide approach to business that seeks to create business value in an economic world that is largely flat, borderless, and cyber-connected.*

Note that "global" does not always assume that U.S. businesses are the "globalizers" or initiators of a global effort to create business value. In fact, many Canadian firms already operate extensively in the U.S. and around the world. A global perspective realizes that a non-U.S. firm may acquire or partner with a U.S. firm. For example, the Chinese government has encouraged its companies to "go global" to expand their business opportunities. The Chinese computer manufacturer Lenovo followed this suggestion by purchasing IBM's PC division for $1.75 billion. As a part of this acquisition, Lenovo also partnered with IBM and vice versa: Lenovo will become the preferred PC supplier to IBM's customers, and IBM will be Lenovo's preferred customer services and financing partner.[14] Although acquisitions of this size are unusual, some estimate that the worldwide impact of China's "go global" acquisition initiative could hit $15 billion.[15]

A GLOBAL PERSPECTIVE ON PARTNERSHIPS

As the above example illustrates, part of the "go global" movement includes business partnerships. Fundamentally, businesses partner with each other for many of the same reasons that you work in teams—complementary talents or more efficient work processes, for example. Although partnerships between large firms garner the most press, small businesses also create competitive partnerships. For example, GFI Solutions and IDR Business Solutions, two leading Canadian providers of business process consulting services, signed a strategic partnership agreement aimed at expanding their ERP solution offerings. The alliance gives IDR access to the Quebec marketplace, and enables Montreal-based GFI Solutions to reach new Canadian

---

13. C. K. Prahalad and Kenneth Lieberthal, "The end of corporate imperialism," *Harvard Business Review;* 7/1/1998.
14. Thanks to Dr. James Suleiman for additional insight into the Lenovo/IBM PC unit acquisition.
15. Paul Kaihla, "Why China wants to scoop up your company," *Business* 2.0 (May 25, 2005), p. 29–30.

markets. IDR is based in Kitchener, Ontario, and also has offices in Calgary and Vancouver. The two firms will pool their resources in order to better serve their Canadian customers in the ERP market. In addition, GFI will now have access to the SAP Business One product, which is one of IDR's core service offerings.[16]

Partnerships can span the globe, too. An example of an organization reaching out to partners around the globe is Finland's Nokia (cell phones, wireless solutions), which initiated "a series of collaborative efforts with other vendors in order to broaden its wireless mobile product portfolios, including those with voice over Internet Protocol (VoIP) capabilities." The partner companies include Avaya, Cisco Systems, OnRelay, and IBM.[17] In Canada, examples of this might be the Rogers partnership with Yahoo or the efforts of the large Canadian chartered banks to buy regional American banks to gain entry to the U.S. market.

One way that partnerships and IT have enabled companies to go global is through the almost worldwide usability of credit cards and their associated payment systems. As Figure 9.2 shows, these systems are part of a network of global information systems that link businesses and financial institutions. Although retailers partner with a single entity known as "Visa," Visa is actually a giant partnership-like association of more than 20,000 financial institutions worldwide.

Similarly, there are emerging global IT standards (such as ITIL and CMMI) that help organizations doing business around the globe to source and apply common definitions to various IT capabilities regardless of geography. This helps them ensure a higher level of consistent quality in their global operations. More detailed information can be found about these global standards in Table 9.4.

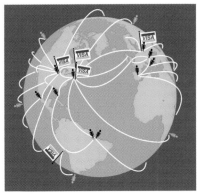

Figure 9.2 Visa ® and its merchant banks and their customers are part of a network of global information systems that link businesses and financial institutions.

? WHAT DO YOU THINK?

One of the powerful aspects of e-business is that an organization can offer its products and services worldwide. Consider the following questions about global Internet business:

1: Have you ever purchased something on the Internet that is not available in Canada? Were you aware of what location you were ordering from? Did it matter?

2: When you order something on-line, do you pay with PayPal or a credit card? Are you nervous about providing your credit card on-line? Why?

3: What do you think are some of the issues businesses need to think through in making their products available worldwide on the Internet?

---

16. "GFI Solutions and IDR Business Solutions sign a partnership agreement to offer ERP solutions for small and medium sized Canadian businesses" Canada Newswire, July 4, 2006, p 1.
17. http://www.telecomweb.com/news/1118691510.htm, retrieved June 18, 2005.

GLOBAL SOURCING

We use **global sourcing** to describe how businesses use partners to perform all kinds of activities, including IT functions and services, in order to reduce costs, gain access to new skills and diverse expertise, and focus on value-adding activities. As Figure 9.3 shows, we can classify sourcing choices as any of four major types: (1) in-sourcing, (2) onshoring, (3) nearshoring, and (4) offshoring. Note that the last three types all represent outsourcing; that is, partnering with an outside firm.

In-sourcing refers to the strategic decision made by a business to bring various services or functions back in-house, or keep them in-house, rather than globally source them. In-house IS development, discussed in Chapter 6, is an example of in-sourcing. Firms concerned with security, quality, and even cost reduction may decide to bring a formerly outsourced IS development, call centre, or other business application back in-house. For example, in 2003, Farmers Insurance Group, an American insurance group with revenues of $11.5 billion and 19,000 employees, in-sourced its IT processes, reassuming operation and control of mainframe IT support, application, and development. According to former Farmers' CIO Cecilia Claudio, Farmers realized an annual savings of $6 million within one year.[18]

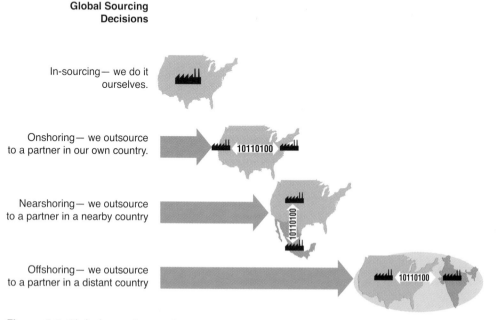

Global Sourcing Decisions

In-sourcing— we do it ourselves.

Onshoring— we outsource to a partner in our own country.

Nearshoring— we outsource to a partner in a nearby country

Offshoring— we outsource to a partner in a distant country

Figure 9.3 Global sourcing options.

18. S. Overby, "Bringing I.T. back home," *CIO Magazine*, March 1, 2003.

Onshoring occurs in the same country as a business. On-shoring is a very common practice within Canada. Companies of all sizes turn to large outsourcing providers such as EDS or IBM to provide application development in-house and operate their technical infrastructure. An example of onshoring between two Canadian companies is the $1.8 million agreement between Chapters-Indigo and Q9 Networks. Q9 Networks is a Canadian provider of out-sourced data centre infrastructure. In 2002 Chapters-Indigo awarded Q9 a contract to host its entire on-line infrastructure, including their website, in-store kiosks, and back-end applications, such as order entry and inventory management, for all 280 stores. In addition, Q9 hosts the bookstore chain's on-line test and staging environment.[19]

Nearshoring is outsourcing to a business partner located outside your country but in the same general geographic area as your business. Canada has been the leading nearshore centre for the U.S. for years. Many successful Canadian companies market their services south of the border, or are actually an in-sourcing centre for a U.S. parent.[20] Canada is the perfect nearshoring partner for the U.S. given its promixity, time zones, and cultural and linguistic similarities.

Xwave, based in St. John's, Newfoundland, offers nearshore application development and maintenance, as well as enterprise applications and systems integration services to U.S.-based customers. In October 2004, the firm won a contract to deliver its Corrections Information Systems (CORIS) to the Virginia Department of Corrections.[21]

Offshoring results from a partnership with a business in a distant country. Although we previously discussed offshoring in the context of IS development, this is only one part of the global off-shoring market. According to *A Fine Balance: The Buying and Selling of Canada,* which was compiled by PricewaterhouseCoopers in association with independent analyst David Ticoll, more than 70 percent of companies in Canada are taking action to lower costs and improve productivity in response to the offshoring trend. But they lag behind the United States and other global competitors in the use of offshoring.[22] One example of offshoring by a Canadian company is the acquisition of India's CuTe Solutions by the Canadian graphics chip company ATI Technologies Inc. in 2004. CuTe Solutions created software to compress and decompress audio and video data for hand-held game and cell phone developers. With this acquisition,

19. Q9 Networks, http://www.q9.com/news/pr32.html
20. Patricia Pickett, "Firms split on outsourcing development: National survey also finds that overall IT spending will drop over next two years," *Network World Canada,* Vol. 14, Iss. 12, July 9, 2004.
21. Patricia Pickett, "Recruiter eyes Maritime talent: Nearshore outsourcing contracts are creating a skills demand in the region," *Computerworld Canada,* Vol. 21, Iss. 3, February 4, 2005.
22. "A new kind of brain drain?," *CA Magazine,* Vol. 139, Iss. 2, March 2006, p. 16.

ATI, based in Markham, Ontario, created ATI Technologies India and immediately transferred control of the audio components of its product to this new division. ATI was no stranger to India, having previously outsourced various projects there.[23] Proving the global nature of business today, ATI was subsequently purchased by AMD of California in October 2006![24]

As companies gain confidence in their ability to manage partnerships around the globe, and as offshore vendors' abilities to provide transparent services improve, high-quality services also increase. It is no wonder that more companies are turning to offshoring as a means to increase business value.

Although businesses can gain benefits from global sourcing, failures also result. Some problems include increased costs due to additional or hidden costs, vendor complacency, inflexible contracts that reduce operational flexibility, loss of the firm's knowledge due to vendor employee turnover, and the vendor's failure to provide expected levels of quality and cost savings.[25] In addition, ethical concerns have been raised as business partners from different countries share data and sensitive information, as the CORE box "Transborder Data Flows" discusses.

Ethics

Transborder Data Flows

You're a busy person. You have neither the time nor the expertise to do your taxes, so you, like millions of others, employ the services of a tax accountant. As it turns out, the accountant is also busy with lots of clients, so she outsources some of the work to tax-preparation firms in India and China. This means the data associated with your taxes are being passed around the world over computer networks. Where is your private information going? Who makes sure that others responsibly use your private data as they zoom around global computer networks?

Not only are tax data sent overseas for processing, but other data as well. In fact, many companies globally outsource their data-processing activities. The movement of data from country to country over global information networks is known as transborder data flow. The difficulty with transborder data flows for consumers and countries alike is that it is often unclear which countries' laws have jurisdiction over the data. For instance, if your private data are created in Canada and then sent to India for processing, which country's data security laws apply? Since 2004, Canada has had the Personal Information and Electronic Documents Act (PIPEDA), which is strictly enforced within our boundaries.

23. Andy Holloway, "Hand-helds across the water," *Canadian Business*, Vol. 78, Iss. 13, June 20–July 17, 2005, p. 63.
24. "AMD completes takeover of ATI," http://money.canoe.ca/News/Sectors/Technology/2006/10/25/2125347-cp.html, Retrieved October 27, 2006.
25. "Calling a change in the outsourcing market: The realities for the world's largest organizations," *Deloitte Consulting*. April 2005, http://www.deloitte.com/dtt/cda/doc/content/us_outsourcing_callingachange.pdf

But what about information collected by Canadian companies in other countries? Or sending information from Canada to other countries?

The Organization for Economic Co-operation and Development (OECD) addresses data flows across borders of its member countries with its "Guidelines on the Protection of Privacy and Transborder Flows of Personal Data."

These guidelines, adopted in 1980, list a set of fair information practices including the following:

Collection Limitation Principle: There should be limits to the collection of personal data and data should be obtained by lawful and fair means and, where appropriate, with the knowledge or consent of the data subject.

- **Use Limitation Principle:** Personal data should not be disclosed, made available, or otherwise used for purposes other than those specified except with the consent of the data subject, or by the authority of law.
- **Security Safeguards Principle:** Personal data should be protected by reasonable security safeguards against loss or unauthorized access, destruction, use, modification, or disclosure of data.
- **Openness Principle:** There should be a general policy of openness about developments, practices, and policies with respect to personal data. Means should be readily available for establishing the existence and nature of personal data and the main purposes of their use, as well as information regarding the identity and usual residence of the data controller (the organization transmitting the data).
- **Individual Participation Principle:** An individual should have the right:
  a. to obtain, from a data controller or otherwise, confirmation of whether or not the data controller has data relating to him;
  b. to have any data relating to himself communicated to him in a reasonable manner and in a form that is readily intelligible to him, within a reasonable time, and at a charge (if any) that is not excessive;
  c. to be given reasons if a request for information is denied and be able to challenge either such denials or any data relating to himself, and, if the challenge is successful, to have incorrect data removed or amended.

With such guidelines, it might seem that our data would be safe. Unfortunately some countries not only ignore these guidelines but see an opportunity in becoming data havens. A data haven, much like a tax haven, is a country that offers a place for the unregulated use of data. This means that once a company transfers data to a data haven, the company is free to use it without restrictions. Countries that have allegedly been providing data havens include Bermuda and Anguilla.

Much concern of late has been raised regarding the U.S. Patriot Act the ability under this act to access the information of Canadians in the interest of U.S. national security. Because of data outsourcing agreements, a substantial amount of data about Canadians may be crossing the U.S. border. Under the Patriot Act, the U.S. government can access this information and use it to investigate individuals suspected of terrorist or other activities undermining U.S. national security without the data subject's knowledge.[26]

In some cases, organizations such as the OECD and legislation such as PIPEDA put guidelines and safeguards in place to help us protect our private data. In other cases, it is up to us to protect our own data by disclosing it only in secured transactions and taking actions against organizations that violate our data privacy. Safe transborder data flow is an important subject, but one that is difficult to solve.

26. P. Hillier, "Transborder Data Flow—Intruding on Privacy?", http://www.globalsecurityweek.com/
Transborder_paper_Peter_Hillier.pdf, retrieved October 27, 2006.

Web Resources

- The Treasury Board of Canada Secretariat: Privacy Matters: The Federal Strategy to Address Concerns About the USA PATRIOT Act and Transborder Data Flows—http://www.tbs-sct.gc.ca/pubs_pol/gospubs/tbm_128/pm-prp/pm-prp07_e.asp
- Office of the Privacy Commissioner of Canada—http://www.privcom.gc.ca
- OECD Guidelines on the Protection of Privacy and Transborder Flows of Personal Data—http://www.oecd.org/document/18/0,2340,en_2649_34255_1815186_1_1_1_1,00.html
- Laws Affecting Data Processing and Transborder Data Flows—http://www.lectlaw.com/files/elw01.htm

---

Global sourcing remains both an opportunity and a challenge to businesses competing in today's global marketplace. And as with most business challenges, management must stay actively involved and diligent when selecting outsourcing strategies and partners.

MULTINATIONAL AND TRANSNATIONAL COMPANIES[27]

Global partnerships are not the only type of global business model. Two other types of global business organizations are the multinational company and the transnational corporation. **Multinational companies (MNCs)** engage in global business but are identified most strongly with a "home country." MNCs like Microsoft, Nike, GM, and Ford all have operations and facilities in many countries, but strategic decisions and direction flow predominately from their U.S. corporate headquarters. Alcan and Nortel are examples of Canadian multinationals.

Transnational corporations (TNCs) go beyond this model to a more "borderless" view of global operations. A TNC is an MNC that is not strongly identified with a "home" country or national identity. Often a TNC decentralizes its decision making to give greater flexibility to the geographically dispersed parts of its organization, which allows them to function relatively independently. For example, the Logitech organization, maker of many popular peripheral devices for PCs (Figure 9.4), has sales offices in major cities in Asia-Pacific, Europe, and North America, and distribution in over 100 countries. Did you guess that Logitech was a Swiss company? Logitech's global competitiveness relies less on its Swiss identity than on its globally dispersed design, distribution, logistics, and manufacturing operations' abilities to respond to rapidly changing market conditions.[28] Harlequin Enterprises, the publisher of the popular romance book series, is a Canadian transnational, owned by Torstar Corporation. Surprised?

---

27. Following practice, we use global IT to mean worldwide information technology and information systems taken together and not just the technology portion of global information systems.
28. http://www.logitech.com.

Figure 9.4 Logitech, a TNC that makes many popular peripheral IT devices such as those shown here, has sales offices in major cities in Asia-Pacific, Europe, and North America, and distribution in more than 100 countries.

Quick Test

1. Which of the following is defined as outsourcing to a business partner located outside your country but in the same general geographic area as your business?

   a. geo-shoring
   b. nearshoring
   c. onshoring
   d. seashoring

2. True or False. A global perspective believes that the economic world is largely flat, borderless, and cyber-connected.

3. True or False. Multinational companies engage in global business but are not identified with a "home country."

Answers: 1. b; 2. True; 3. False

GLOBAL IS/IT

Today's global economy will only function as well as the underlying networked information technology and information systems. In this section, we focus on how individual businesses respond to the challenges and opportunities associated with the globalization of IT.

Recall from Chapter 1 that we defined an information system as an organized collection of people, information, business processes, and information technology designed to transform inputs into outputs in order to achieve a goal. Now, we expand that to define a **global information system (GIS)** as:

> *An organized collection of people, information, business processes, and information technology that creates business value by capturing, creating, storing, sharing, and transforming data across cultural environments.*[29]

Businesses that expand their operations worldwide, supported by global IS, benefit in a number of ways. They obtain low-cost, effective, and efficient communications and collaboration technologies such as e-mail, text messaging, VoIP, and video conferencing. They can share data over these same networks, giving employees, suppliers, and customers immediate access to product information and services regardless of location.

For example, consider TransAlta Utilities, an Alberta-based utilities company with operations across Canada, the United States, and Mexico. The company embarked on a differentiation strategy that was prompted by energy deregulation. They determined that they could differentiate themselves by creating a brand focused on low cost power generation and social and environmental responsibility. They recognized that a key enabler of this strategy is their human capital. With this in mind they partnered with SAP, a global provider of integrated business solutions, to implement SAP's human capital management (HCM) module of the enterprise resource program (ERP).

The HCM ERP first allowed TransAlta to eliminate the costly manual administration of more than 2,500 employees across three countries. Second, it allowed TransAlta to focus on value-adding activities such as automating HR business workflows, creating an employee portal, enabling e-recruiting, and providing an information repository to faciliate HR planning. TransAlta estimates that this initiative saves them $1.65 million per year in operating costs and helps them achieve their position as a low cost provider in the utilities industry.[30]

Although there are many successful cases like TransAlta's, operating globally remains complex and challenging. Many of these challenges include bridging or accommodating differences in technology as well as in cultural, political, and legal systems.

From a global IT perspective, Ives and Jarvenpaa list four key issues that businesses must address if they are to successfully deploy and manage global IT:

29. Although Ives and Jarvenpaa were referring to global IT applications, their attributes are easily extended to our definition of a system. *Source:* B. Ives and S. L. Jarvenpaa, "Applications of global information technology: Key issues for management," *MIS Quarterly*, March 1991, p. 34.
30. "A business value assessment: mySAP ERP human capital management at TransAlta," http://www.sap.com/solutions/business-suite/erp/hcm/pdf/CCS_Transalta.pdf, retrieved October 27, 2006.

- Linkage of global IT to global business strategy
- Information technology platforms
- International data sharing
- Cultural environment[31]

LINKING GLOBAL IT TO GLOBAL BUSINESS STRATEGY

This is an issue that affects even the smallest of businesses, but it is magnified when the business in question is global. This was the case for Manpower Inc., a global employment service with a world-wide network of 4,300 offices in 67 countries and territories, serving 400,000 customers per year and employing almost 2 million people. Two of its five corporate strategies were "to improve efficiency 'by con-tinuously improving profit margins and returns through disciplined in-ternal processes and increased productivity' and 'to aggressively ex-plore and implement the transformational opportunities of information technology and e-commerce to continuously develop defensible com-petitive advantages in all aspects of the company's activities.'"[32]

According to Rick Davidson, senior vice-president and global CIO of Manpower Inc., "We were looking for a partner that could support our long-term IT strategy, . . . continue leading the staffing industry in effective and efficient use of technology to improve our business processes and accelerate the implementation of customer-facing applications." Manpower Inc. chose BT (a UK-based global business communications services provider) to develop "a fully managed, global Wide Area Network (WAN) for 3,200 of the com-pany's offices in 63 countries. When completed, this WAN will increase speed of access to critical applications and data as well as provide cost savings through standardizations of Manpower's global communications platform."[33] By choosing BT and using its capabil-ities, Manpower Inc. supports its business strategy.

INFORMATION TECHNOLOGY PLATFORMS

According to a *Datamonitor* research paper on global reach, global companies have three key issues to consider: (1) linking globally dis-persed offices, (2) centralizing and standardizing processes, and (3) connecting to customers and partners.[34] In an effort to meet chal-lenges similar to these, the Intercontinental Hotels Group (IHG) part-nered with MediaSurface to build a 30,000-user, worldwide intranet

31. B. Ives, and S. L. Jarvenpaa, "Applications of global information technology: Key issues for management," *MIS Quarterly*, March 1991, p. 34.
32. http://www.manpower.com/mpcom/content.jsp?articleid = 60.
33. http://www.btglobalservices.com/business/global/en/business/business_zone/issue_02/manpower.html.
34. "Global reach: Extend networks, share information, and improve communications," *DataMinitor white paper*, December 2003, http://www.datamonitor.com. © DataMonitor, 2003.

and extranet to enhance collaboration between IHG employees and its franchisees. MediaSurface is a leading provider of enterprise content management software and related services. IHG views the development of the intranet and extranet as a strategic decision that will save at least £1.6 million (approximately $3.7 million) and allow it to sell more franchise agreements.[35] By having a single platform, IHG ensures all its locations are connected and collaborating.

Global companies are also relying on specific IT devices to increase their competitive advantage, such as RFID. We discuss why in the CORE box "Using RFID around the Globe."

Connectivity

Using RFID around the Globe

Radio frequency identification (RFID) technology, as we discussed in Chapter 5, has the promise to improve the accuracy of inventory counts and provide real-time information on the status of orders and shipments in transit, as well as what items customers are purchasing. It is currently being deployed across the supply chains of industries around the world and provides real-time, automatic tracking of goods in the global supply chain. Recall that an RFID system consists of tags, printers, readers, and middleware that allow products to be identified using wireless technology.

RFID technology has two major advantages over the use of bar codes. First, while the amount of data stored on an RFID tag is small, it can still include a lot more than the simple product ID that a bar code can store. With bar codes, the product ID only allows a product to be identified generically, i.e., that the item is one of a batch of similar products of a particular type from a particular vendor. With RFID, the code identifies each item individually so the exact history of an individual item can be traced.

Second, RFID is wireless, which allows an RFID tag to be read over greater distances and without a direct view of the tag. As a result, an individual product tagged using RFID moves through the supply chain, and tag readers along the way can easily track its every movement until it reaches the customer. This increased knowledge of the whereabouts of goods can help global companies to identify and improve their supply chains, resulting in benefits to their customers and reduced costs by streamlining operations. It's no wonder Wal-Mart has mandated its suppliers to use RFID to support its efficiency goals and low-cost provider strategy!

Web Resources

- RFID Journal—http://www.rfidjournal.com
- Canadian RFID Centre—http://www.canadianrfidcentre.ca/
- Supply Chain Brain—http://www.supplychainbrain.com/.
- Sarma, Sanya "Integrating RFID," *Queue Magazine,* October 2004. (From the *ACM Digital Library* www.acm.org.)

---

35. "InterContinental Hotels Group plans major worldwide intranet development; solution expected to save at least GBP1.6m a year in employee productivity," M2 Presswire; February 2, 2005.

INTERNATIONAL DATA SHARING

As we discussed above, global businesses need to share data to be efficient and to facilitate global out-sourcing. However, in some cases sharing data can be problematic technically, culturally, and legally. From a technical perspective, global businesses need to align their systems to share data in a uniform way. Imagine if the CRM system in the Canadian division of a company stored customer names as Lastname, Firstname, and the Indian division stored this data as Firstname, Lastname. Combining customer lists would result in mismatched data. From a cultural and legal perspective, some countries allow the collection and storage of different types of data. In Malaysia, for example, the government requires companies to register the religion of their employees; this is unheard of in Canada and would be considered a privacy violation. If employee data was transferred from Malaysia to Canada, religion would need to be removed. The issues of transborder data flow, security, and privacy, as discussed above, are also considerations in international data sharing.

CULTURAL ENVIRONMENT

As a business goes global, it spans time zones, nations, and cultures. Culture is the "learned behaviour of people, which includes their belief systems and languages, their social relationships, their institutions and organizations, and their material goods—food, clothing, buildings, tools, and machines."[36] In our daily life, cultural norms often guide our decisions and relationships. For instance, in Canada we see ourselves as a bilingual country with a need to offer services in both French and English. For a business, cultural norms may influence its success or failure in any given location. A U.S. firm doing business in Canada must adapt to the demands of a bilingual country.

Yet, one can imagine how easy it is to forget this even living in Canada. Although many people regard English as the first language of business, one analyst calculates that of the estimated 1.082 billion Internet users worldwide in 2005, only 27.2 percent of them speak English as a first language. Some global sites address this by allowing users to customize the corporate website either by country or language, or both. So what does this mean for Canada, for those doing business in Canada, and for Canadians doing business abroad?

36. www.mdk12.org/mspp/vsc/social_studies/bygrade/glossary.shtml

WHAT DO YOU THINK?

Imagine you are the global product manager for the Toyota Corolla and consider the following questions:

1: It is important for brand image that Toyota be known as a Japanese company?
2: What business issues would you need to address on Toyota's website for it to be useful around the world? How would you address these?
3: What other global companies would you refer to in making decisions about the marketing of your product? Are there other global companies facing similar challenges from which you can learn?

But there are bigger challenges than translating and adapting websites. In fact, global IT industry research firm Gartner Inc. cites cultural differences as one of the top five reasons why offshore deals fail.[37] Managers must not assume that workers in foreign countries will appreciate or react "appropriately" to leadership and managerial behaviours acceptable in the manager's country of origin. This holds true even if those behaviours are considered best practices, such as those listed in Table 9.1.

There are also important legal risks in operating globally. Many organizations rely on the value of their intellectual property (copyrights, trademarks, patents, and trade secrets) to sustain their business. In some parts of the world, the lack of a consistent legal code or enforcement of commercial intellectual property protections can lead to piracy, theft, or reverse engineering of products. So, while culturally or legally a behaviour may be seen as prohibited in one

Table 9.1 A "Best Practices" Approach to Handling Cultural Differences[38]	
Cultural Differences	**Language Barriers**
Take time to understand the history and culture of the country of your business partners, and accommodate the differences in work habits and forms of communication.	Do not confuse language fluency with an understanding of culturally specific idioms.
Use a mix of *asynchronous* (e.g., e-mail) and *synchronous* (e.g., face-to-face) communication to accommodate cultural preferences for different means and styles of communicating.	Speak clearly and repeat yourself often, until you are sure that everyone is on the same page. Regional dialects, accents, and pronunciations vary from standard forms of a language (e.g., think of a Newfoundland vs. a French-Canadian accent).
Ensure that the managers and employees that you assign to work with your business partners are experienced working with that country's people and culture.	

37. http://www.computerworld.com/careertopics/careers/story/0,10801,102677,00.html
38. M. T. Rao, "Key issues for global IT sourcing: Country and individual factors," *Information Systems Management*, Summer 2004, pp. 20–21.

country, it might be considered acceptable in another, creating a need to monitor this risk when operating globally.

Nonetheless, many organizations are able to successfully address cultural differences, as well as the other three global IT issues identified by Ives and Jarvenpaa. However, there is another issue that all businesses, whether local or global, must contend with: risk.

Quick Test

1. True or False. A global information system (GIS) is an organized collection of people, information, business processes, and information technology that creates business value by capturing, creating, storing, sharing, and transforming data across local environments.

2. Which of the following is NOT a key global IT issue identified by Ives and Jarvenpaa?
   a. the linkage of global IT to global business strategy
   b. information technology platforms
   c. international data sharing
   d. ethical environment

3. According to Gartner Inc., what is one of the top reasons that offshoring deals fail?
   a. incompatible technology
   b. failed geopolitical states
   c. cultural differences
   d. time zone differences

Answers: 1. False; 2. d; 3. c

ENTERPRISE RISK MANAGEMENT

All businesses face threats and risks to current and future operations, regardless of whether they are global or local. Obviously, businesses cannot anticipate or plan for all risks and threats. However, when creating and implementing a business strategy, a business must attempt to identify, address, and eliminate elements of risk before they threaten its success. To do this, businesses apply **enterprise risk management (ERM)**, defined by the Committee of Sponsoring Organizations of the Treadway Commission (COSO) as:

> *A process effected by an entity's board of directors, management, and other personnel, applied in strategy setting and across the enterprise,*

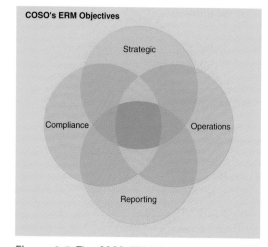

COSO's ERM Objectives

Figure 9.5 The COSO ERM framework identifies four overlapping categories of business objectives for focusing on risk assessment and management. (*Source:* Adapted from the Committee of Sponsoring Organizations of the Treadway Commission (COSO) ERM Integrated Framework Executive Summary, September 2004, p. 3.)

designed to identify potential events that may affect the entity, and manage risk to be within its risk appetite, to provide reasonable assurance regarding the achievement of entity objectives.[39]

What this means is that everyone involved with planning for and enabling the success of the organization, including any external directors, is responsible for figuring out what can go wrong and how to manage it. This includes deciding how much risk they can stand (*risk appetite*) and still achieve their business goals.

To help businesses identify risks and threats, the COSO developed an ERM integrated framework. This framework, shown in Figure 9.5, identifies four overlapping categories of business objectives for focusing on risk assessment and management.

How do businesses apply this framework? They first identify and categorize potential risks. For example, if you are the CEO of a specialty e-tailer (strategy), your customers will buy your goods using the Internet (operations). Accordingly, you need to have secure Web servers (compliance and control) to provide shopping and account management services to your customers (operations), as well as to collect, analyze, and communicate financial, transactional, and other data (reporting and compliance).

The next step is to assess risks and threats using two primary criteria: impact and likelihood. Continuing on with our example, you realize you risk loss of business due to a denial of service (DoS) attack launched against your servers. How would you assess this risk? You might begin by estimating the dollar-value impact (cost) of your servers' inability to respond to customers' requests. Say your business averages daily sales of $1 million. What if the server problem persists for several days? What if they are outsourced to an offshore vendor in a different time zone? You can see that an extended denial of service would severely affect your current operations and the execution of your business strategy.

You next need to determine the likelihood of a DoS attack. How do you estimate this? You can collect data from a reliable source, such

39. Committee of Sponsoring Organizations of the Treadway Commission (COSO) ERM Integrated Framework Executive Summary, September 2004, p. 2. COSO (http://www.coso.org) is a "voluntary private sector organization dedicated to improving the quality of financial reporting through business ethics, effective inter-control, and corporate governance." *Source:* ITGI, "IT Control Objectives for Sarbanes-Oxley," April 2004, p. 27.

as the widely cited 2004 E-Crime Watch Survey™.[40] Using the data from the survey, you realize that there is an 83 percent chance that you will experience some type of e-crime-related loss and a 44 percent chance that this will be a DoS attack. Therefore, you estimate the likelihood of a DoS attack as a 36.5 percent chance (0.83 × 0.44).

Now you have to decide whether or not this risk is acceptable. If your business suffers a DoS attack, recall that you previously estimated $1 million in lost sales per day. As a result, you decide to implement improved security procedures and invest in IT security infrastructure improvements as necessary.

In general, the greatest effort to manage risk should focus on addressing high-probability risks that will have the greatest impact (upper-right corner of the ERM matrix shown in Figure 9.6). However, businesses should also manage applicable risk (red area in Figure 9.6) *before* it evolves into high-impact/high-probability risk. Finally, businesses should note the *immediacy* of a risk. Due to the diminished amount of time available to discover and implement mitigation policies or processes for immediate risks, businesses need to proactively manage these risks rather than react to them.

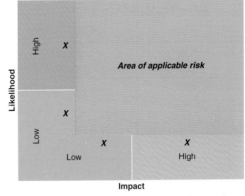

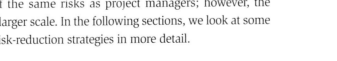

Figure 9.6 Organizations use the Enterprise Risk Matrix (ERM), where X indicates a potential risk, to ensure that they focus their efforts on addressing high-probability risks that will have the greatest impact (upper-right corner of the ERM matrix) (*Source:* Applicable risk as defined by the Institute of Chartered Accountants of England and Wales, cited in "How 7799 works," *Gamma,* http://www.gammassl.co.uk/bs7799/works.html)

RISK-REDUCTION METHODS

Table 9.2 lists some examples of organizational responses to enterprise risk. You may recognize the risk responses from Chapter 6, where we discussed project risk and responses. Corporate leaders confront many of the same risks as project managers; however, the risk is on a much larger scale. In the following sections, we look at some of these specific risk-reduction strategies in more detail.

Compliance

Recall that COSO identifies compliance as one of the four objectives critical to sound ERM. **Compliance** reduces risk through policies and processes that ensure proper financial and accounting procedures, as well as protect employee and customer data that corporate IS stores, processes, and transmits. Compliance also increases organizational stakeholders' abilities to trust the integrity and accuracy

40. "2004 eCrime watch survey," CSO Magazine/U.S. Secret Service/CERT ® Coordination Center, http://www.cert.org/archive/pdf/2004eCrimeWatchSummary.pdf, retrieved July 8, 2005.

Table 9.2 Types and Examples of Organizational Responses to Risk	
Risk Response	Action
Risk transfer	Move the risk to someone who is more able to deal with it, possibly using an insurer or outsourcing it to another type of business partner.
Risk deferral	Postpone exposure to the risk until circumstances are more favourable or resources are available to address the risk.
Risk reduction	Either reduce the probability of the risk occurring or lessen the impact, such as through a strong commitment to security and frequent and secure offsite backup of data and applications.
Risk acceptance	Realizing that some risks are unavoidable, make sure that contingency plans are in place.
Risk avoidance	Eliminate the possibility of the risk occurring; however, that may close the doors on some business opportunities as well.

of information reported by corporations. Compliance with laws and regulations (Table 9.3) ensures that stakeholders and the general public can trust that organizations are performing as stated and are prudently managing risks as they try to achieve their business goals.

Trust is an important cornerstone of global economic and financial systems. Trust is supported through effective continuous compliance practices while noncompliance destroys trust and opens the door to fraud, waste, and mismanagement. For example, after the publication of the financial scandals of Enron and WorldCom, people lost trust in the entire financial market, not just the banks. This mistrust caused markets to decline sharply, resulting in global repercussions for governments, corporations, and individuals. In response, the U.S. Congress intervened in the form of legislation, most notably the **Sarbanes-Oxley Act** of 2002. The impact of these scandals was not only felt in the United States but all over the world. Canada's response to this has been to implement strict governance practices and adopt practices in line with Sarbanes-Oxley. Organizations such as the Canadian Public Accountability Board (CPAB) and the Auditing and Assurance Standards Oversight Council (AASOC) have been formed to encourage complaint practices. And because Canadian and U.S. capital markets are co-dependent, the Canadian Securities Administrators (CSA) have adopted **multilateral instrument (MI) 52-109,** which essentially demands the same level of certification of financial statements for Canadian public firms that the U.S. does.

Sarbanes–Oxley Act of 2002

To restore public and investor confidence in the financial accountability and reporting of publicly traded companies, the U.S. Congress passed the Sarbanes-Oxley Act of 2002. Now often known simply as Sarbox or SOX, the act has generated significant costs for

Table 9.3	Selected Governance and Compliance Related Laws and Regulations
Laws and Regulations	**Description**
EU Data Protection Directive	Each EU member nation is required to pass legislation requiring confidentiality and integrity controls for networks, systems, and data containing personal information for both employees and customers.[41]
Basel II Accord: International Convergence on Capital Measurement and Capital Standards	The regulations from the Bank for International Settlements designed to encourage banks to adopt and follow rigorous risk assessment, management, and controls practices.[42]
Sarbanes-Oxley Act	The U.S. act that holds a company's officers personally responsible for providing accurate public financial information to investors. Emphasis is on internal controls.[43]
Multilateral Instrument 52-109	Since March 2005, CEOs and CFOs (or persons performing similar functions) of reporting issuers are required to personally certify in each interim and annual filing that: 1. He or she has reviewed the filing; 2. Based on his or her knowledge, the filings do not contain any untrue statement of a material fact or omit to state a material fact required to be stated or that is necessary to make a statement not misleading in light of the circumstances under which it was made; 3. Based on his or her knowledge, the financial statements together with the other financial information included in the filings fairly present in all material respects the financial condition, results of operations and cash flows of the issuer; 4. He or she and the other certifying officers are responsible for establishing and maintaining disclosure controls and procedures and internal control over financial reporting, and they have designed disclosure controls and procedures and internal control over financial reporting (or caused them to be designed under their supervision); and 5. He or she has caused the issuer to disclose changes in internal control over financial reporting with material affect or reasonably likely material affect on internal control. In each annual certification, the certifying officers must also disclose under item 4 that they have evaluated the effectiveness of disclosure controls and procedures and caused their issuers to disclose their conclusions regarding their evaluation.[44]
Privacy Act	This federal government act that imposes obligations on some 150 federal government departments and agencies to respect privacy rights by limiting the collection, use, and disclosure of personal information. The Privacy Act gives individuals the right to access and request correction of personal information about themselves held by these federal government organizations.[45]
Personal Information Protection and Electronic Documents Act (PIPEDA)	The federal government act that sets out ground rules for how private sector organizations may collect, use, or disclose personal information in the course of commercial activities. The law gives individuals the right to access and request correction of the personal information these organizations may have collected about them.[46]

41. http://www.cdt.org/privacy/eudirective/EU_Directive_.html
42. http://www.bis.org/publ/bcbsca.htm
43. http://www.aicpa.org/info/sarbanes_ oxley_summary.htm SOX Act—
   http://www.law.uc.edu/CCL/SOact/soact.pdf
44. http://www.kpmg.ca/unitymail/accountability/en/issues/elert2006-007.html
45. Office of the Privacy Commissioner of Canada, Privacy Legislation in Canada Fact Sheet,
   http://www.privcom.gc.ca/fs-fi/02_05_d_15_e.asp, Retrieved October 27, 2006.
46. ibid.

Table 9.3	Selected Governance and Compliance Related Laws and Regulations *(Continued)*
Bill 198	This Ontario legislature bill amends to the Securities Act and Commodity Futures Act. Among the amendments are those giving the Ontario Securities Commission (OSC) rule-making authority to require reporting issuers to appoint audit committees and to prescribe requirements relating to the functions and responsibilities of audit committees, including independence requirements. The OSC would also have rule-making authority to require reporting issuers to establish and maintain internal controls, disclosure controls, and procedures and require CEO, and CFO, to provide certifications related to internal controls and disclosure controls and procedures.[47]
Provincial Privacy Legislation	Every province and territory in Canada has privacy legislation governing the collection, use, and disclosure of personal information held by government agencies. British Columbia, Alberta, and Quebec are the only provinces with laws recognized as substantially similar to PIPEDA. These laws regulate the collection, use, and disclosure of personal information by businesses and other organizations and provide individuals with a general right of access to, and correction of, their personal information. Alberta, Saskatchewan, Manitoba, and Ontario have passed legislation to deal specifically with the collection, use, and disclosure of personal health information by health care providers and other health care organizations.[48]

businesses, as well as significant revenues for firms that specialize in helping other firms become SOX compliant. At the heart of SOX's growing impact on firms are the requirements set forth in its many sections, such as the following:

- *Section 302*—CEOs and CFOs must personally certify financial statements and disclosures in periodic reports as well as the effectiveness of the company's internal controls. In Canada, Ontario's Bill 198 was enacted to allow the Ontario Securities Commission (OSC) to issue rules related to information certification.

- *Section 404*—Requires a separate annual internal controls management report and mandates internal controls that are well defined, documented, and periodically evaluated by internal (management) and external audits. In Canada, this area is also covered by Ontario's Bill 198.

- *Section 409*—Decreases the time between reporting deadlines into a potentially "real-time" reporting environment and increases reporting requirements for material changes to business operation that affect financial reporting; e.g., if a main factory burns down, current financial projections are no longer valid.

- *Section 906*—Requires additional CEO/CFO personal certifications of financial reporting and imposes criminal penalties of up

47. Ontario Securities Commission Notice of Proposed Amendments to the Securities Act and Commodities Futures Act, http://www.osc.gov.on.ca/Regulation/Confidence/pic_20021115_amend-act-futures.jsp, Retrieved Oct 27, 2006.
48. Office of the Privacy Commissioner of Canada, Privacy Legislation in Canada Fact Sheet, http://www.privcom.gc.ca/fs-fi/02_05_d_15_e.asp, Retrieved October 27, 2006.

to $5 million in fines and up to 20 years in jail for knowingly falsifying certifications.[49]

- *Section 201*—Prohibits a public accounting firm from performing both audit and nonaudit services for the same client. Compliance with this section caused several of the major accounting and IS consultancies like PricewaterhouseCoopers (PwC) to restructure their organization. In 2002, PwC sold its existing global management consulting and technology services practice to IBM, in part, to comply with this section of SOX. The Canadian Institute of Chartered Accountants (CICA) has made several amendments to its *Handbook* in line with the rules contained in Section 201.

Why should a piece of legislation that focuses on corporate financial reporting and accounting practices become so important? And why is it relevant to understanding and using information systems in a global business environment? Consider technology author Ben Worthen's suggestion: "Imagine, if you will, that Sarbanes-Oxley is a water purity test. What ultimately matters is the quality of the water coming out of the faucet. But no responsible organization would let its water be tested before thoroughly examining and repairing its plumbing, especially when failure means multimillion-dollar fines, a ruined reputation, and possibly jail time for top executives."[50]

Worthen's suggestion continues our plumbing analogy from Chapter 5, where we described IT as the plumbing, and data and information as the water. If the plumbing is clean and intact from source to spigot, then as long as the source is clean (IT governance and auditing), so will be the water. Because information systems store the majority of a modern business's financial data, these systems must have proper controls in place if the data and the financial reports are to be accurate, reliable, and trustworthy.

CONTROL AND CONTROLS

The impact of Sarbanes-Oxley is creating significant requirements for IT organizations within public corporations and financial institutions in both the United States and Canada and elsewhere around the world. Given that organizations increasingly depend on IT to compete and even gain competitive advantage, it is also likely that organizations will seek to gain an internal "control advantage" through IT. We define **control advantage** as the strengthening of internal controls and compliance through the application of IT-based controls to business processes, policies, and procedures. Table 9.4 lists some frameworks that organizations rely on to attain this control advantage.

49. http://www.law.uc.edu/CCL/SOact/sec906.html
50. B. Worthen, "Playing by New Rules: Part 2," http://www.cio.com/archive/051503/rules.html

Table 9.4	Selected Compliance and Control Frameworks and Standards[51]
Frameworks and Standards	**Description and URL**
COSO (Committee of Sponsoring Organizations of the Treadway Commission)	Framework—A framework for internal controls. Also, an Integrated Enterprise Risk Management framework. (See www.coso.org/)
CoBiT (Control Objectives for Information and Related Technology)	A framework for effective governance and control of enterprise IT and information. (See http://www.isaca.org and http://www.ITgovernance.org.)
ISO 17799 and BS7799	ISO 17799 framework from the International Organization for Standardization focuses on information security controls. BS7799 is "a specification for an Information Security Management Systems (ISMS). An ISMS is the means by which Senior Management monitors and controls their security, minimizing the residual business risk and ensuring that security continues to fulfill corporate, customer, and legal requirements. It forms part of an organization's internal control system." (See http://www.computersecuritynow. com/ and http://www.gammassl.co.uk/bs7799/works.html)
Information Technology Infrastructure Library (ITIL)	Provides a set of best-practices standards for IT and service management. The U.K. Central Computer and Telecommunications Agency (CCTA) created the ITIL in response to the growing dependence on information technology to meet business needs and goals.[52] (See http://www.itil.co.uk/)
Capability Maturity Model Integration (CMMI)	Guides process improvements across those organizations especially associated with software development. (See http://www.sei.cmu.edu/cmmi/adoption/cmmi-start.html)
UCCnet	A standards organization that provides an Internet-based supply chain management (SCM) data registry service for e-commerce companies and companies that have an e-commerce component. (See http://www.uccnet.org)[53]
RosettaNet	An organization set up by leading information technology companies to define and implement a common set of standards for e-business. (See http://www.rosettanet.org)[54]
Institute on Governance (IOG)	A non-profit organization that promotes effective governance, including technology governance.[55]
Communication Security Establishment (CSE)	Canada's national cryptologic agency. It provides the Government of Canada with two key services: foreign signals intelligence in support of defence and foreign policy and the protection of electronic information and communication. It also provides an IT security program.[56]
Standards Council of Canada (SCC)	Facilitates the development and use of national and international standards and accreditation services. The SCC offers IT security evaluations and accreditation.[57]

51. Adapted: from D. Cougias, "Moving into compliance mode: Realizing the benefits, cutting the costs," Hospitality Today Special Report, March 2005, http://www.hotel-online.com/News/PR2005_1st/ Mar05_MovingIntoCompliance.html
52. http://searchsmb.techtarget.com/sDefinition/0,290660,sid80_gci535709,00.html
53. http://search400.techtarget.com/sDefinition/0,sid3_gci930408,00.html
54. http://search400.techtarget.com/sDefinition/0,290660,sid26_gci214634,00.html.
55. http://www.iog.ca/knowledge_areas.asp?pageID = 19
56. http://www.cse.dnd.ca/it-sec/it-sec-e.html
57. http://www.scc.ca/en/programs/lab/it_secureval.shtml

To help you understand how IT can enhance corporate control efforts, we first discuss control and controls in general (specific actions). We then review the overall process of internal controls, using an example to highlight how IT can enhance the effectiveness and efficiency of controls.

Defining Control and Controls

Businesses generally base control around three key concepts:

1. Control is a process that runs throughout the organization.
2. Control influences how people behave at work.
3. Control can only provide reasonable, not absolute, assurance of achieving objectives.[58]

Controls are specific actions, including policies and procedures, designed to ensure the achievement of business objectives. *Effective controls* prevent, detect, and correct actions that increase the enterprise's risk of failing to meet business objectives, such as inappropriate financial and accounting practices, fraud, misuse of resources, and ineffective physical and electronic security practices.

COSO defines **internal control** as

a process effected by an entity's board of directors, management and other personnel, designed to provide reasonable assurance regarding the achievement of objectives in the following categories:

- *Effectiveness and efficiency of operations.*
- *Reliability of financial reporting.*
- *Compliance with applicable laws and regulations.*[59]

All these categories should incorporate three broad types of controls: preventive, detective, and corrective. *Preventive controls* are designed to prevent increased exposure to risk by stopping some action or process before it occurs. An example of preventive control is requiring employees to change their corporate network password every 30 days. *Detective controls* reduce risk by discovering when preventive controls have failed and providing notification that action must be taken. For example, if an employee has not changed his or her password in 25 days, then he or she may get a warning e-mail message asking them to do so immediately. Lastly, *corrective controls* aim to remedy the situation and try to keep it from recurring. If the employee did not change his or her password by the 30th day, then he or she could be locked out of the system.

---

58. K. H. S. Pickett, *Internal control: A manager's journey,* New York: John Wiley & Sons, 2001
59. Committee of Sponsoring Organizations of the Treadway Commission (COSO) Internal Control—Integrated Framework Executive Summary, http://www.coso.org/publications/executive_summary_integrated_framework.htm

Specific Internal Control Processes

Now that you have an understanding of controls, we next discuss seven generic categories of controls, highlighted by K. H. Spencer Pickett in his book *Internal Controls: A Manager's Journey*.[60] The seven categories are:

1. Segregation of duties
2. Authorization
3. Security
4. ID codes
5. Verification
6. Control totals
7. Supervisory review

Segregation of duties (Figure 9.7) means that jobs do not span lines of control that would allow mistakes or fraud to go undetected. For example, say you only have one programmer who creates your critical e-commerce applications. A problem can arise if she is also the only person responsible for testing, debugging, and certifying the system. Further, if she leaves the company, who would know if she had created a back door in the e-commerce software, allowing her to later hack the system and steal sensitive data? Another person should review the code and the changes, even if this means sourcing the testing, debugging, and certification to another programmer.

Figure 9.7 Segregation of duties helps to prevent any mistakes or fraud from going undetected.

60. K. H. S. Pickett, *Internal control: A manager's journey*, New York: John Wiley & Sons, 2001

Authorization controls prevent scope creep and cost overruns (see project management in Chapter 6). Allowing an individual programmer to make minor system changes is efficient. But some changes to the system can be very costly and may commit resources that are already assigned. As a result, another person, such as the project team leader, should sign off (authorize) any significant changes.

If the team leader and programmers are working on an e-commerce application, they will need access to a development database to develop their application. However, for the majority of their application development process, they do not need to access the organization's actual transaction database (production database). Executing untested new code against a production database is a recipe for disaster. To provide *security* for the production database, application developers should therefore log in separately to the development and production databases.

It is also a good idea to track the login IDs and activities of all users, as login IDs are a useful type of *ID code* (and so is your student ID number). Tracking login IDs and other ID codes creates an audit trail that organizations can follow to ensure proper controls are in place and working. Organizations can also use them to detect and document attempts at unauthorized use.

Depending on how the application is implemented ("goes live"), *verification* controls can confirm that the application is accomplishing e-commerce functions (e.g., order placement, payment) without error. For example, verification controls can monitor return of merchandise counts, to ensure that the new system is sending customers what they ordered.

Control totals can help detect fraudulent actions. Imagine that you return a product. Now say a dishonest employee credits not your account but a fictitious account that he created. If the organization lacks control totals, which compare a customer's paid orders with credits received, it cannot detect this fraud. The item would have been returned and a "proper credit" in the correct amount given to a customer, just not the right customer.

Finally, supervisors should periodically audit and review processes and transactions. In the case of our e-commerce system, *supervisory review* could consist of ordering an item, calling customer service, returning the item, receiving credit for the item, and documenting the process. The supervisor would share any discrepancies with the responsible person(s), and then make improvements or take corrective actions.

Quick Test

1. Which one of the following is NOT an organizational response to risk?
   a. risk acceptance
   b. risk avoidance
   c. risk behaviour
   d. risk reduction

2. Fill in the blank. _____ reduces risk through policies and processes that ensure proper financial and accounting procedures, as well as protects employee and customer data that corporate IS stores, processes, and transmits.

3. True or False. Corrective controls reduce risk by discovering when preventive controls have failed and providing notification that action must be taken.

Answers: 1. c; 2. Compliance; 3. False

ENTERPRISE INFORMATION SECURITY

In this section, we look at how the convergence of people, policy, and technology can result in robust enterprise information security and enhance the enterprise's ability to manage risk and meet objectives despite the growing global risk. PricewaterhouseCoopers defines *security* as "a strategic business process that includes the organization, the processes, and the technologies that enable access to, and protection of, an enterprise's information assets." This perspective elevates security from something that a business's IS department does for the company, to a strategic process that engages the entire organization. With this in mind, we therefore define **enterprise information security** as an ongoing, strategic business process of risk and threat assessment and management, which helps to ensure safe and continuous business operations and the availability, confidentiality, and integrity of an enterprise's information resources wherever they may be located.

Our definition requires consideration of security issues and policies for people, technology, and processes, not just the information itself. As a result, we use a people-policy-technology (PPT) framework[61] to anchor your understanding of enterprise information

---

61. The authors of the textbook have direct practical experience with people-policy-technology information security frameworks. However, the following reference provides a concise guide and a very useful example. Our presentation of the PPT framework is adapted from this guide. and we wish to thank the authors for their succinct and informative paper. R. Pal and D. Thakker, "Defining an enterprise-wide security framework," *Network Magazine*, November 2002, http://www.networkmagazineindia.com/200211/guest.shtml

security. This understanding is critical to your success because, as the CORE box "Internet Security: A Global Problem" below discusses, this is a global problem, something that we all must deal with, wherever we live and work.

On-line Security

Internet Security: A Global Problem

In the last few chapters, we have explored how the creation and phenomenal growth of the Internet has spawned the emergence of a global information society and an increasingly global IT infrastructure. Internet security is seen as a serious issue in Canada. In 2003, the RCMP and Symantec, an IT security firm, released the results of a study called "Pulse of Internet Security in Canada." The study revealed that 61 per cent of Canadian "C-Suite" executives polled identified Internet security among the top five priorities in their organizations. There is good reason for this. Over recent years there have been numerous news reports of hackers originating in Canada attacking not only Canadian organizations, but prominent organizations around the world. This has lead some to call Canada a "hacker haven". Hackers undertake many activities from splashing graffiti on a website, to spreading a destructive virus, to theft of valuable data using a Trojan horse.

A *Trojan horse* is a small, malicious program that Internet users may pick up through e-mail attachments or websites. And once picked up, the malicious program can perform a number of functions. For instance, a *keylogging program* can gather passwords and other sensitive data. The security firm Sophos reported that it had seen a threefold increase in the number of keylogging Trojans alone in 2004.

Other security experts are reporting similar trends. Marcus Sachs, director of the Internet Storm Center sees the use of malicious code *(malware)* as part of a subversive, organized scheme. Such schemes are resulting in massive intrusions into sensitive financial and intellectual property areas.

How can you do your part to protect the Internet from these global threats? The first step is to secure your own computing resources. Be sure that you do the following on a regular basis:

- Install, and keep up to date, both antivirus software and a personal firewall.
- Update your software, such as Windows, to patch security holes.
- Do not open e-mail messages or attachments from unknown sources.
- Follow safe computing practices, such as effective password policies.

Web Resources

- "Canada called 'hacker haven' for criminals," *The Globe and Mail*, May 19, 1999, Jen Ross—http://www.efc.ca/pages/media/globe.17may99b.html, retrieved October 27, 2006
- "Internet Security Top Priority for Canada's Fortune 800 Executives," Symantec. http://www.symantec.com/region/can/eng/press/2003/n030610b.html, retrieved October 27, 2006
- "Today's hackers code for cash, not chaos," Naraine Ryan, *E-week,* July 3, 2005—www.eweek.com
- CERT Coordination Center—http://www.cert.org/

PEOPLE–POLICY–TECHNOLOGY ENTERPRISE INFORMATION SECURITY FRAMEWORK

Pal's and Thakker's version of a PPT framework stemmed from their work as technical consultants for PricewaterhouseCoopers. Figure 9.8 shows the three pillars that support enterprise information security—people, policy, and technology—which in turn rest on a foundation of business and IT governance, and security training and awareness.

However, while security awareness and training and governance compose the foundation of the framework, people are at its core. In order to better understand how the elements of people, policy, and technology interact, we need to take the roof off our model and use a top-down view of the pillars. This view, as Figure 9.9 shows, gives us three equal and overlapping circles (the tops of the pillars). When we refer to the framework element *People*, we mean organizational members and their roles and responsibilities within the organization. Examples include senior management, other employees, and also specialized employees working in areas like security, IT, and systems administration. *Policy* is all written documentation related to the vision, standards, and rules for governance and operation of organizational IT. *Technology* includes tools, methods, and mechanisms to support organizational processes, such as

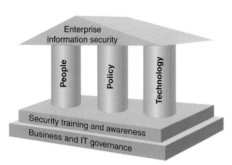

Figure 9.8 The three pillars that support enterprise information security—people, policy, and technology (PPT)—in turn rest on the foundation of business and IT governance, and security training and awareness. (*Source:* Adapted from R. Pal, and D. Thakker, 2002.)

Figure 9.9 As this top-down view of the PPT framework shows, the overlapping areas among the three circles indicate where two or three of the elements combine to enhance enterprise information security. (*Source:* Adapted from R. Pal, and D. Thakker, 2002.)

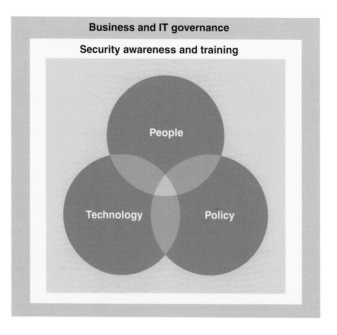

OS, databases, applications, Web services, and security tools (e.g., firewalls).[62]

Further, note the overlapping areas among the three circles. These areas, which indicate where two or three of the elements combine to enhance enterprise information security, follow the same principle as writing a paper with a classmate. You (people in the model) have built-in spelling and grammar controls. However, if you word process your term paper, you can use the word-processing software's spelling and grammar checker (technology) to further reduce the risk of error.

Let's continue with the example. To get the best grade possible on the paper, you and your teammate agree that each of you will submit your part of the paper to the other for proofreading (policy). So, as Figure 9.10 shows, you can use both elements (technology and policy) to achieve your objective (a high grade) and to provide control.

Businesses, too, can apply this PPT framework to increase information security. One industry whose members must establish effective enterprise information security is the health-care industry. For example, Kaiser Foundation Health Plan (a division of Kaiser Permanente) was fined $200,000 for exposing confidential health records for 150 of its members by mistakenly posting the data on a publicly accessible website.[63] Similar incidents convinced the U.S. Congress to pass the Health Insurance Portability and Accountability Act of 1996 (HIPAA).

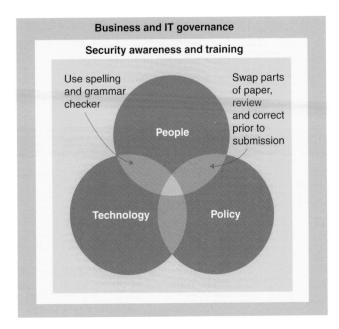

Figure 9.10 Combining the PPT framework elements enhances enterprise security, following the same principles as writing a paper with a classmate. (Source: Adapted from R. Pal, and D. Thakker, 2002.)

62. R. Pal, and D. Thakker, "Defining an enterprise-wide security framework," *Network Magazine*, November 2002, http://www.networkmagazineindia.com/200211/guest.shtml
63. L. Rosencrance, "Kaiser Permanente division fined $200K for patient data breach," *Computerworld*, June 21, 2005, http://www.computerworld.com.

The HIPAA established four key requirements for covered entities (e.g., hospitals, medical insurance providers, and physicians):

- Ensure the confidentiality, integrity, and availability of all electronic health information that the covered entity creates, receives, maintains, or transmits.
- Protect against any reasonably anticipated threats or hazards to the security or integrity of such information.
- Protect against any reasonably anticipated uses or disclosures of such information that are not permitted or required under the privacy rule.
- Ensure compliance by its workforce.[64]

Given the risks and possible civil or criminal penalties for compromising sensitive medical data, it is easy to see why HIPAA and other statutory and regulatory requirements are causing the health-care industry to seriously examine how it treats data and other sensitive information. For U.S. health-care firms, HIPAA has meant a significant investment of resources in information systems, technology, and information security measures.

There have not been any similar, documented breaches of health information confidentiality in Canada. There have, however, been isolated incidents reported to both the Ontario and British Columbia Privacy Commissioners. These situations, along with the U.S. HIPAA and health-care technology projects initiated to unify patient health records, has prompted some provinces to enact or propose privacy legislation specific to health information. Under these conditions, Canadian health organizations will be forced to evaluate their information security.

WHAT DO YOU THINK?

In the United States, following the terrorist attacks on September 11, 2001, businesses learned many lessons regarding continuity of their operations. For example, some businesses based in New York City had backup facilities in the southeastern United States. Therefore, if an IS crashed and lost data, a business could fly a back-up tape to New York to get its system back up and running. This seemed a prudent plan until all U.S. flights were grounded. The tapes were then driven the 1,500 km to New York, only to be turned back at the New York–New Jersey border, due to border closures.

This situation illustrates that in order to achieve organizational goals and objectives, businesses need to ensure the protection of critical people, data, and systems, regardless of circumstances or events. Enterprise risk management and enterprise information security work toward that end. Consider the following questions as you think about business continuity and information security:

64. 42 U.S.C., Section 1320-2(d)(2); 45C.F.R Section 164.306(a) as cited on page 20 of P. Litwak, "Practical issues your organization may face when developing a security management program: Several ideas to consider to better ensure compliance," *Journal of Health Care Compliance* (July–August 2004), pp. 19–27.

1: What do you personally do to ensure you can continue your operations as a student? Do you have safeguards in place if your computer were stolen, for example?

2: Have you been in organizations that were exemplary at ensuring business continuity and security? What did they do?

THE PPT ENTERPRISE INFORMATION SECURITY FRAMEWORK: AN EXAMPLE

Earlier in the chapter, as a part of our overview of preventive, detective, and corrective controls, we discussed an organizational use of passwords. Using the PPT framework, let's re-examine the use of passwords in a hypothetical hospital to see how each element of the framework contributes to effective enterprise information security.

Passwords are an essential control for medical information networks and databases. Passwords are preventive controls, as they limit access to authorized users, thereby reducing the risk of compromised data. If the hospital also tracks incorrect authentications (bad logins), then it is adding a detective control using technology. Also, if someone fails to follow policy and periodically changes his password or abuses access rights, then the hospital can revoke access, which is a corrective control.

What about the policy requiring people to have mixed characters in their passwords? Is this a form of control? Yes, it is preventive control. It adds to the security of the passwords and to the security of the information that the passwords protect. The "password-change-warning" acts as all three types of controls by detecting that time is running out and then correcting users' forgetful behaviour by reminding them of the policy. In a sense, this also prevents users from forgetting about the policy. You can see as Figure 9.11 shows, that the controls that combine people, policy, and technology are ultimately the most effective. If one fails, e.g., the employee forgets, then the technology can provide additional control as a reminder. By implementing critical parts of the password policy through the technology, people must comply or lose access to the on-line database, which could affect their job performance.

In addition to providing controls, effective information security efforts can also serve another important function: litigation risk mitigation. Just think about the many times you hear about major software companies' issuing critical software patches.[65] In the example, in addition to strong password management, the hospital may have the proper technology (proxy servers, firewalls); policies (patch management, mandatory user security education requirements,

---

65. For example, see http://news.zdnet.com/2100-1009_22-5778406.html. What if your company were attacked before Microsoft released its patch?

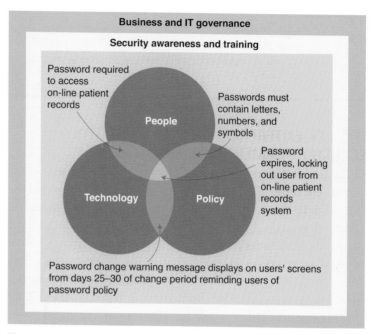

Figure 9.11 Organizations, such as hospitals, can use the PPT framework to implement information security procedures, such as password management.

need-to-know-type limited access); and people (technically expert managers, highly trained end users) yet still be vulnerable to an undocumented threat. However, if the hospital can establish that it had an ongoing and robust information security program and took all reasonable precautions, it will reduce its exposure to the risk of litigation succeeding against it.

Given this simple example, you can see the importance of implementing effective controls via a PPT framework. Further, we suggest that regardless of the location of the risk to an organization, effective enterprise risk management and strong IT and corporate governance are the critical links between a successful business strategy created by an organization's leaders and the high-quality data that support the development and execution of business processes. A sound enterprise information security program will help ensure the availability, confidentiality, and integrity of data that are critical to sound business decisions and proactive corporate and IT governance practices.

Quick Test

1. True or False. The three pillars that support enterprise information security are people, policy, and structure.

2. True or False. Governance provides a foundation of the framework for ensuring enterprise information security.

3. Which of the following is Canadian legislation designed to protect the availability, confidentiality, and integrity of sensitive health care-related data and information?
   a. HIPAA
   b. PIPEDA
   c. Sarbanes-Oxley Act
   d. none of the above

Answers: 1. False; 2. True; 3. d

 STUDENT RETURN ON INVESTMENT SUMMARY

1. Why are corporate and IT governance important?

Corporate and IT governance are processes for allocating the decision-making rights and responsibilities for corporate and IT decision making, respectively. They are the link between the business strategy and the IT strategy. As such, they lay the foundation for the implementation of strategy. Governance also includes risk assessment and control.

2. What does it mean to have a global perspective?

A global perspective to business seeks to create value in an economic world that is largely flat, borderless, and cyber-connected.

3. How does global IT create business value?

Simply put, global information systems are IS that link employees, companies, and business partners in more than one country or global region. Global information systems create business value by allowing organizations to (1) share value data and knowledge; (2) gain from worldwide economies of scale (the idea behind "buy in bulk"); and (3) gain a greater awareness and understanding of the global business environment in order to take advantage of opportunities and to manage current and future risks.

4. What is enterprise risk management, and what can be done to prevent business loss?

According to COSO, enterprise risk management is "a process effected by an entity's board of directors, management, and other personnel, applied in strategy setting and across the enterprise, designed to identify potential events that may affect the entity, and manage risk to be within its risk appetite, to provide reasonable assurance regarding the achievement of entity objectives."[66] Organizations should identify the impact and likelihood of risks to their organization. Risks range from traditional forms of risk, such as competition from other businesses, to more modern physical risks such as terrorist acts. After identifying risks, organizations should implement one or more of the risk-reduction responses found in Table 9.2.

5. What is enterprise information security?

Enterprise information security is an ongoing, strategic business process of risk and threat assessment and management, which helps to ensure safe and continuous business operations and the availability, confidentiality, and integrity of an enterprise's information resources wherever they may be located.

---

66. Committee of Sponsoring Organizations of the Treadway Commission (COSO) ERM Integrated Framework Executive Summary, September 2004, p. 2. COSO (http://coso.org) is a "voluntary private sector organization dedicated to improving the quality of financial reporting through businessethics, effective inter-control, and corporate governance." *Source:* ITGI, "IT Control objectives for Sarbanes-Oxley," April 2004, p. 27.

KNOWLEDGE SPEAK

Bill 198   370

chief information officer (CIO)   347

compliance   367

control advantage   371

controls   373

corporate governance   346

data haven   357

enterprise information security   376

enterprise risk management (ERM)   365

global information system (GIS)   360

global perspective   352

global sourcing   354

in-sourcing   354

internal control   373

IT governance   347

multinational companies (MNCs)   358

multilateral instrument (MI) 52-109   368

nearshoring   355

offshoring   355

onshoring   355

Personal Information Protection and Electronic
  Documents Act (PIPEDA)   369

Sarbanes-Oxley Act   368

transborder data flow   356

transnational corporations (TNCs)   358

REVIEW QUESTIONS

Multiple-choice questions

1. The primary focus of IT governance is on _____.

   a. decision rights associated with IT
   b. information processing
   c. network vulnerabilities
   d. technology acquisition and modernization

2. If you respond to risk by moving the risk to someone who is more able to deal with it, that strategy is called risk _____.

   a. acceptance
   b. avoidance
   c. deferral
   d. reduction

3. The Canadian legislation governing personal information disclosure by federal government organizations is _____.

   a. Sarbanes-Oxley
   b. PIPEDA
   c. HIPAA
   d. Privacy Act

4. Organizations generally consider control as _____.

   a. a process that runs through the organization
   b. based around people and how they behave at work
   c. providing reasonable, not absolute, assurance that objectives will be achieved
   d. all of the above

Fill-in-the-blank questions

5. _____ is outsourcing to a business partner outside your country but in the same general geographic area as your business.

6. _____ _____ can create sourcing issues because employees in one firm are awake while members of the sourcing firm are most likely to be asleep.

7. A(n) _____ is an organization that is not readily identified by its country of origin.

8. The area of _____ _____ contains a set of risks that are predominately high likelihood and high impact.

True-false questions

9. Integrity of data or information refers to the ability to see and use the data whenever and wherever you need them.

10. Manpower Inc. failed to find ways to link its IT systems with its global business strategy.

11. As evidenced by its home page, IKEA considers accommodating customers from different cultures as part of its e-commerce strategy.

12. The most cited and reported benefit of offshoring is attributed to labour cost arbitrage.

Matching questions

Choose the BEST answer from Column B for each item in Column A.

Column A

13. Preventive

14. Detective

15. Corrective

Column B

a. Electronic petty cash reimbursement tracking system.

b. Two signatures required to authorize payment using a corporate cheque.

c. ATM card seized by ATM machine due to an overdraft condition in the customer's account.

Short-answer questions

16. What is Sarbanes-Oxley and, briefly, what is its intended purpose relative to publicly traded U.S. businesses? How has Canada responded to Sarbanes-Oxley?

17. What is a global perspective?

Discussion/Essay questions

18. IT globalization presents serious challenges for organizations. Discuss the challenge that you feel is the most significant, and suggest at least two ways to meet and overcome it.

19. Define enterprise information security and discuss threats and risks to the availability, confidentiality, and integrity of an enterprise's information resources. Use examples of recent failures in each area to highlight the magnitude of the threat or risk.

20. Draw and correctly label the PPT framework. Give an example for each of the areas, and discuss why each adds to risk reductions and why each enhances enterprise information security.

TEAM ACTIVITY

Ask one of your instructors for the name of a colleague who teaches in a different country (or part of the country as an alternative). This colleague must also be willing to help you contact several of his or her students, so you can set up a virtual team with them. As a team, set up one or more chat sessions and discuss the issues presented in this chapter, such as IT globalization, global perspective, and cultural and business customs and norms. Prepare a written summary and presentation about the issues, as well as the process of working in your virtual team.

SOFTWARE APPLICATION EXERCISES

1. Internet

Choose a country that you have visited or that you are interested in learning more about. Use the Web to learn about that country's business environment, business culture, and culture in general. To discover what kinds of information are important, you may want to review what the Australian government has done to support its organizations that wish to do business in other countries (www.austrade.gov.au).

2. Presentation

(1) Prepare an informational presentation that a business traveller might review prior to travelling to and conducting business in the country that you researched (in the Internet assignment above). (2) As an alternative focus for your presentation, research the most recent and most common threats and risks present in the business environment of your chosen country. Create an "Enterprise Information Security" profile for that country and suggest actions that businesses and knowledge-enabled professionals can take to lessen the risks and threats.

3. Word Processing

One challenge of globalization is how to present your corporate information to a different culture. While English is one of the primary languages for business, it is often useful to create a local version of your website. Find a corporate website that is written in a language different than your native language. Using the translators available on the Internet, translate the business's website into your native language. By cutting and pasting pictures and other graphical images, you can create a mock-up of this site using your word processor. If possible, show your translated website to a native speaker from that country. How did you do? Did the essence and cultural subtleties translate as well as the text?

4. Spreadsheet

Select an industry that interests you, e.g., the pharmaceutical industry. (1) Research to identify the 10 largest publicly traded firms in your chosen industry and then create a spreadsheet to track financial data about these firms. As a minimum, you'll need the name of the firm, country of origin, stock symbol, and stock price. Use the link_data feature of your spreadsheet to help you keep the data current. (2) Create three charts from your data. The first chart should track the relative prices for all 10 stocks for a 12-month period. The second chart should show the relative percentage of the market captured by each firm (you'll need more than the minimum data for this to work). The third chart should highlight the firm's country of origin and give other knowledge-enabled professionals an idea of the level of globalization for your chosen industry.

5. Database

Create a B2B database of potential buyers/distributors of the products for the industry you chose for the Spreadsheet assignment above (or choose an industry that interests you). Remember that the consumers you identify should be businesses, not individuals. You should focus on the global market, and can include potential buyers/distributors from your country of origin. Be sure to capture relevant information on each business that you plan to contact. You'll need to understand the business, identify the leaders and other key people, and obtain contact information for these people. Add data to your database to support your strategy for expanding your business into your chosen market(s).

6. Advanced Challenge

(1) Using hyperlinks and OLE, prepare an interactive report (word-processed document) that discusses the current business situation in a country of your choice for one particular industry. Assume that the company you work for is in the industry you chose and that it wants to expand its business sales and/or business operations to the country that you pick. Address the challenges of going global as they relate to your company. Recommend how you might efficiently, effectively, and securely expand globally. You can use links to spreadsheets, databases, and/or websites to support your suggestions.

(2) As an alternative assignment, create a report that discusses only the technology needed to expand globally. Include estimates of costs and provide links to product or service-provider websites for detailed product information. Estimate the costs of your recommendations, and then use a spreadsheet to develop three alternatives for globalizing your IT. Be sure to address enterprise information security issues in your report.

ON-LINE RESOURCES

Companion Website

- Take interactive practice quizzes to assess your knowledge and help you study in a dynamic way.
- Review PowerPoint lecture slides.
- Get help and sample solutions to end-of-chapter software application exercises.

Additional Resources Available Only on WileyPLUS

- Take the interactive Quick Test to check your understanding of the chapter material and get immediate feedback on your responses.
- Review and study with downloadable Audio Lecture MP3 files.
- Check your understanding of the key vocabulary in the chapter with Knowledge Speak Interactive Flash Cards.
- Link directly to websites recommended in the CORE boxes.

CASE STUDY: INFOSYS TECHNOLOGIES INC.

When you hear of outsourcing jobs, you probably think of jobs in Canada being outsourced to other countries worldwide. That view no longer presents a complete picture. The current and future global market for knowledge-enabled professionals is now definitely a two-way proposition, with foreign firms offshoring some of their jobs to Canada in order to compete and to better create business value. In fact, employment statistics show that the global market for knowledge-enabled professionals and services is hot and getting hotter.

One of the international companies at the forefront of this trend is the Indian company Infosys Technologies Inc. Headquartered in Bangalore, India, Infosys is a global IT-services provider with more than 46,000 employees and offices in more than 40 cities worldwide. Infosys is rapidly growing, increasing revenues from $100 million (U.S.) to more than $2 billion (U.S.) in just five years. In 2005, *Business 2.0* magazine ranked Infosys as the eighth fastest-growing technology company in the world. *Wired* magazine ranked Infosys as the ninth on its "Wired 40" list.

How is Infosys a part of the outsourcing trend? Consider that it opened Infosys Consulting in Fremont, California and hired 500 employees in a $20-million (U.S.) move into high-end IT consulting. This move is unusual for Infosys, given its strategy of dividing projects into parts and executing them simultaneously in several different locations, including development centres in India, the client's site, and other areas around the world. Infosys recently opened a 300 person development centre in Canada to serve its U.S. clients in the same time zone. This global network enables Infosys to use its lower cost structure while maximizing efficiencies spanning many time zones to reduce product delivery times.

An important component of Infosys's success is that its business strategy emphasizes high quality. With their location in India, they have direct access to Indian universities, which produce large numbers of highly educated, English-speaking graduates. Add to this Infosys's willingness to hire and train the best candidates from around the globe, and the result is that in 2003–2004 Infosys had over 1 million applications for positions from which it selected only 10,000 knowledge-enabled professionals. After selective hiring, the company continues to invest in its knowledge capital through continual training and development and a strong emphasis on its people.

What does the future hold for Infosys? Given its emphasis on hiring the best and brightest, Infosys will experience more competition for knowledge-enabled professionals from companies such as IBM and Accenture. While this is great for the knowledge-enabled professionals, it will drive up Infosys's cost of acquiring and retaining talented individuals. This may create business risk for Infosys. On the other hand, Infosys has expanded into its competitors' backyards, and Infosys's strategy includes an increased emphasis on its own version of offshoring. One thing is certain: Infosys and its competitors will continue to help fuel a global economy that is knowledge intensive, borderless, and interconnected through IT.

Case Questions

1. How does Infosys Technologies's global perspective create business value for (a) others and (b) itself?

2. If knowledge-enabled professionals' salaries and other costs of doing business are potentially higher outside of India, what competitive advantages does Infosys hope to gain by globalizing its services through offshoring?

3. What are the business risks to Infosys created by its competitors? How has Infosys already responded to these risks? How might it respond in the future?

Sources: http://www.infosys.com/about/quick_facts.asp; http://www.findtechinsights.com/1697/insightDetail.htm; "The Fastest-Growing Technology Companies," *Business* 2.0 6 (5), June 2005, p. 120–128; Sachitanand, R., "India's Best Managed Company," *Business Today*, March 25, 2005, http://www.infosys.com/media/BT_infosys.pdf; "Infosys to set up development centre in Canada," *Top-Consultant*, February 4, 2004, http://www.top_consultant.com/US/news/Article_Display.asp?ID=1284

Integrative Application Case: Campuspad.ca

It's live! Campuspad.ca has been launched and is now operating successfully in North America although your transaction volume in Canada (with the help of your student union partnership) has been higher than in the United States so far.

The journey has been interesting. You, Sarah, and Adam (who is now called your CIO) have all learned a lot. The prospects for the future are significant enough that you have all stopped your post-graduate job search and plan to work on the business full time. Soon campuspad.ca will be the largest on-line student accommodation referral system in the world! Your search engine strategy has paid off, and funds spent on marketing have clearly started to drive new sign-ups on the site from both landlords and prospective tenants.

But you know that *true* e-business success will only come if you can take your business into the global arena. For a start, you feel that Europe and Australia are good prospects, since they seem quite similar to your North American market. You know a little less about Asia, but feel there must be selective opportunities there, too. Of course, expansion brings new issues with it, but you no longer shrink from them.

As the company has grown, so have its resources. Campuspad.ca now has eight employees, including the three of you. However, that is still not enough to tackle all the opportunities that you have before you, so the board of directors has secured sufficient funding to support future growth, including the approval of two additional full-time hires in the next three months. However, you're not sure where to focus these resources. As a growing e-commerce business you attract tons of interest from prospective employees and have had lots of good résumés submitted to your site through your Apply to join us button on the home page. Off you go back to the coffee shop. There is still so much to do and its not even lunchtime!

Guiding Case Questions:

1. What issues arise in the expansion of a site from North America to the rest of the world?

2. Can you easily design a site to work in languages other than English?

3. Are there new security or legal issues that you need to consider?

4. What kinds of skills and experience do you need to add to your team?

Your Task:

On WileyPLUS you will see a résumé bank of recent applicants to campuspad.ca. There are more than 30 waiting for screening in terms of fit and contribution. You intend to hire only two new employees in this quarter and you have to select carefully. Getting ready for the task, you have decided to:

1. Determine as a group the skills and experience you are aiming for.

2. Define two positions you intend to hire for.

3. Rank up to six of the résumés for in-person interviews (three for each position).

To accomplish this, your group must first write the two job descriptions/postings you will work from. These should each be approximately 1–2 pages in length and should summarize what the job entails, how its contribution will be measured, the qualifications you seek, and may even include possible compensation ranges for the role.

Once you have done this, search through the résumé bank and identify up to three candidates for each job that you would select to come in for an interview. Discuss as a group why you selected those candidates in relation to the job descriptions you wrote for each of the two roles.

LOGOFF

We hope that you have enjoyed this journey, learning to combine your business skills with IT/IS knowledge in ways that create value for the organizations that you will be a part of in the future. We also hope that the practical approach we took helped make the subject matter accessible to you.

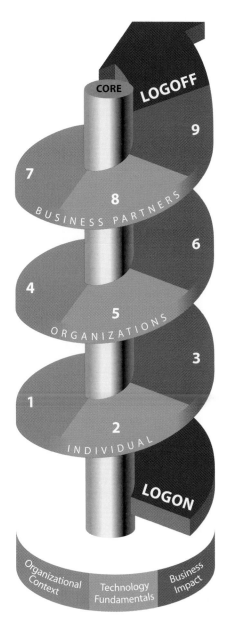

THE SPIRAL MODEL CONTEXT

This book was a journey through business and technology that begins and ends with you. We started by showing you that effective systems begin with the individual user, extend to the organization level, and then expand across to business partners, vendors, and those connected to the organization. This creates the connected enterprise—an organization that uses information technology to create global competitive advantage.

Effective system design ties these levels together into seamless, connected systems that enable the processes your organization uses to do its work and be successful. Those systems are best designed with the input of those closest to that work: knowledge-enabled professionals like you. You will ultimately use those systems to increase your own productivity and create business impact. The examples found in the CORE of our spiral model show you the practical application of technology in the business context. These are real business issues and real businesses operating in our technology-enabled world.

We are now at the end of our journey. You should be equipped with an understanding of the role technology plays in organizations, from your own productivity to enabling global e-commerce. But are you still wondering why technology matters so much?

WHAT'S IN IT FOR ME?

We could interpret this question in two ways: either what's in it for you personally, or what's in IT for you. Either one is important. It is impossible to be a fully functioning professional today and not use personal productivity tools or have a basic understanding of the Internet, for instance. But more fundamentally, no matter your ultimate career choice, IT knowledge can be a key contributor to your success. We saw this in a number of the Voice of Experience features, where even non-IT professionals find themselves engaged with IT systems. Let's consider just a few common examples of careers you may be thinking of.

I Want to Be an Accountant . . .

All basic accounting functions today are done in automated systems, and while they respect the ledger system, they have replaced the ledgers! This also means that all of the audit trail you need access to, either as an external auditor or as an internal accountant performing business analysis, is contained in systems. The ability to understand systems, validate the integrity of the systems operation, and assure management that what is being reported is accurate all require IT knowledge.

Marketing Is What I Want to Do . . .

As any good marketer will tell you, information is power. In this field it is essential to understand how consumers behave, what influences them, and how to reach them to deliver your message. Increasingly, this is done on-line. An understanding of the power of new media and its impact on society is fundamental for a marketer to figure out how to reach new and younger audiences. Furthermore, the information on current customers and their purchasing behaviour is likely all collected by the company's CRM or ERP systems and reported through a data warehouse or data mart. Part of your job will be structuring these systems to capture critical information you will need to analyze customer behaviour.

I'm All about Human Resources . . .

Have you signed up on-line lately with an employer for benefits? Or reported your time into an automated time-tracking system connected to payroll? Today's modern HR systems are all IT-enabled, and companies increasingly expect professionals in this area to be able to assess the cost-benefit trade-offs of making investments in automation to serve employee and employer needs. IT knowledge is essential to investigating these potential opportunities and making the final business decision about how to proceed.

Finance Is My Game . . .

Financial analysis, complicated or simple, is always conducted using systems, and like your colleagues in accounting, the trail of information you need to access is only going to be available in company databases. You will need to interact with the IT professionals in the company to structure these systems to provide not only the knowledge you need, but also to automatically flag important exceptions so management can deal with them before they become a problem.

The Law Is Where It's at . . .

Lawyers today could not cope with the information overload they face without systems. Looking up precedents and codes of law in any jurisdiction around the world in an instant, dealing with colleagues and clients in the firm's offices across the country, or checking on possible conflicts of interest before taking on a new client are all essential IT applications in the legal profession.

No one today can work effectively in any knowledge-intense profession without superior systems. This means you need to be knowledgable in the applications of technology in your chosen field and ensure that you have well-trained and systems-savvy professionals on board as well.

WHY TECHNOLOGY MATTERS SO MUCH

These few examples could be extended to just about any profession in any part of the world today. Technology has become and will remain ubiquitous. It is virtually impossible to identify a career path in business today that does not require a command of related IT knowledge.

Ignoring the impact of technology on businesses would mean risking the business itself. Since the presence of the Internet is irrevocable, organizations must learn to thrive on change. The speed of technology change is greater today than ever before. Consumers have completely adopted the Internet in less than a decade, when previous technology shifts, such as from radio to television, took many decades. Organizations must learn to keep up with these rapid technology changes or risk becoming obsolete.

The same could be said of each of us. As we progress through our careers, it will be more important than ever that we keep up with changes in technology that affect the world of work. As knowledge-enabled professionals, we must continually examine everything that we do to ensure that it is optimally efficient, effective, and makes use of the latest technologies required to do our jobs well, both now and in the future.

FUTURE TRENDS

The future often belongs to those whose creativity and innovation we rely on to advance our society and change the world. Of course, one could apply this to a technology executive like Bill Gates, or to

> One can never consent to creep when one feels an impulse to soar.
> —Helen Keller

> Success is a lousy teacher. It seduces smart people into thinking they can't lose.
> —Bill Gates

someone like Helen Keller, whose role in changing the world was less reliant on technology but more on her personal character. And a few of you who are reading this textbook right now will likely change the world of business, of technology, or both. One day we may be reading your quotes.

So this brings up another point: how do we predict the future of technology? Well, we can't. However, we can be sure that the only constant is likely to be change itself. What we can anticipate about the future is that technologies will evolve and change and increasing amounts of base computing power (as predicted by Moore's Law in Chapter 8) will bring more and more possibilities to the world of work and to our society.

One current example of that might be media convergence. A topical press release that we have reproduced below proves the point. Consider this interesting example of how a media company needed technology business partners to help it address a significant gap in capability required to produce and air a hit TV show in Canada. With the knowledge you now possess as a result of your studies, this case study should make you realize how technologically literate you have become. And perhaps your interest in the content of this press release is just a little bit higher because you can understand the business issues raised and conquered and some of the required underlying technology. You will also truly understand the point that is being made,—that technology is pervasive and persuasive and its use in business can create an undeniable competitive advantage.

Let's look at the actual press release from Bell Canada now.

UNPRECEDENTED TEAMWORK AND TECHNOLOGICAL INNOVATION CONTRIBUTE TO *CANADIAN IDOL* SUCCESS[1]

Canadian Idol mania took the country by storm during the summer of 2003 and accounted for establishing an astonishing telecom industry record. The popular television show became Canada's most-watched English-language Canadian series since the advent of electronic measurement in 1989. Almost 6.5 million viewers watched the two-hour finale to see Kingston's Ryan Malcolm become the first *Canadian Idol*. But there would have been no *Canadian Idol* without exciting new technology and unprecedented teamwork among cellular and wireline carriers coast-to-coast, led by Bell Canada.

The incredibly popular *Canadian Idol* TV series generated the highest call volume in Canadian history in the two hours following its finale on September 15th. An impressive 3.3 million phone and

---

1. Reprinted with permission of CTVglobemedia. Please note that Bell Globemedia changed its name on January 1, 2007, to CTVglobemedia.

text message votes from viewers were logged during the two-hour window.

This record was made possible through technological innovations, proactive communication and cooperation from regional and national telecommunication organizations, led by Bell Canada. The solution Bell designed for *Canadian Idol* merged three essential elements—a robust toll-free network, Interactive Voice Response (IVR) technology and text messaging. All of this, in addition to the near-live call detail reporting, helped to make *Canadian Idol* such a huge success.

PIONEERING A CANADIAN INDUSTRY FIRST

In October 2002, CTV announced that it had partnered with FremantleMedia, one of the largest international producers of entertainment programmes in the world, to produce and air a Canadian version of the "Idols" series. The television series had become a huge international hit following the success of *American Idol* in the United States and *Pop Idol* in the U.K.

Similar to those programs, *Canadian Idol* would feature undiscovered Canadian singing talent vying for the title of *Canadian Idol*. The show's interactive format allowed viewers to vote for their favourite performers each week via toll-free phone numbers or text messaging to determine who advanced to the next round.

Based on the popularity of the *Idol* shows around the world, CTV anticipated that it would need to partner with a communications service provider that could manage this voting process nationwide. CTV's requirements for *Canadian Idol* were simple: ensure all Canadians had equitable access to vote for their favourite performer and make sure that all votes were counted.

A number of factors contributed to the complexity of this challenge:

- It was not possible to replicate the communications processes used by other *Idol* shows and no similar projects had ever been undertaken in Canada. CTV needed to partner with a company that could design and manage a voting platform for *Canadian Idol*, charting unknown territory. The communications provider would be pioneering a process that could potentially be replicated for commercial applications, such as telephone voting or polling.
- Different telecommunications providers operate in different Canadian regions. These service providers would have to work closely together to ensure seamless communication and network integration.
- Based on the success of other *Idol* shows, CTV anticipated that the show could generate the highest volume of calls over a two-hour time span in Canadian history. This heightened call volume

had caused problems in other countries, where *Idol* shows had placed a significant strain on local phone networks. Call and messaging volumes were expected to reach peak levels in the communities where the *Idol* contestants resided. This necessitated the close monitoring of network performance and back-up plans in these regions.

- A flexible and intuitive IVR system needed to be rolled out nationwide to automate and process viewer calls and votes.
- Eleven sequential toll-free numbers—one allocated to each finalist—were required by *Canadian Idol* to simplify and streamline viewer voting.

CTV LOOKS TO BELL FOR SUPPORT

After reviewing all requirements, CTV—Canada's largest private broadcaster and a Bell Globemedia company—decided to turn to Bell Canada, the country's leader in communications. Over the next few months, CTV worked closely with Bell to develop and implement a plan to deliver a seamless and reliable platform for *Canadian Idol* voting.

Bell's expertise in wired and wireless voice and data communications for residential and business markets was a strong selling feature for CTV. In addition, Bell Canada was uniquely positioned to manage and integrate the complex communications components of the *Idol* voting strategy. CTV knew that Bell had the scalability and technological expertise it needed to maintain network integrity and meet the demanding requirements of high volume voice and text-based voting.

The timeline was tight and the specifications were daunting. Bell began working on the project in January 2003. The company was faced with a hard deadline of June 11th, the air date of *Canadian Idol's* premiere.

A NATIONAL NETWORK BUILT ON COOPERATION AND INNOVATION

"We recognized that *Canadian Idol* could only succeed if our communications requirements were managed on a national basis," said Sam Dynes, Director of Production at CTV. "With its extensive footprint and partnerships with 80% of Canadian telecommunication service providers, we were confident that Bell could manage our project on the scale we required."

Bell's team of network professionals worked closely with specialists at the wireline and cellular divisions of companies such as Aliant, Microcell (Fido), MTS, NorthernTel, Rogers AT&T, SaskTel, Télébec, and TELUS to help ensure the risk to telephone networks would be minimized. This close relationship between CTV, Bell and the major Canadian telecommunication service providers resulted in an integrated platform that enabled an easy, reliable and consistent voting process for viewers coast-to-coast.

Communications conference bridges were established throughout the country. Led by Bell, these calls brought together network management personnel from each of the major telecommunication service providers to ensure that calls were being processed quickly and accurately. This task was a challenge because of the variety of IVR systems and networks across providers. Cooperation between regional providers was essential to the success of *Canadian Idol* due to the strong regional nature of voting.

Live communications bridges used during the show enabled telecommunication providers to contact each other as they monitored voice and data traffic and take the proper action should a network issue arise. Essential public-facing service organizations, such as 911, Operator Services and 611, were also included in discussions so that contingency plans could be implemented instantly if networks suddenly became overtaxed with calls.

ADAPTING THE SOLUTION TO FIT EVOLVING NEEDS
Delivering a reliable and integrated network nationwide through industry partnerships was the essential first step in the *Canadian Idol* project.

Bell Canada also applied its networking expertise to ensure the integrity of the network week-to-week, as call volumes increased. A near-live streaming of call detail reporting was introduced to provide instant information regarding voting activity across the country. Using this system built specifically for *Canadian Idol*, Bell could identify and monitor potential high volume calling areas and respond quickly to peaks by applying the appropriate routing measures. This system also provided CTV with an additional audit to ensure voting accuracy.

As *Canadian Idol* entered the final few weeks and the number of contestants diminished, high call volumes were expected to be concentrated in the regions where the remaining *Canadian Idol* contestants lived. Innovative actions, such as segregating the toll-free lines, routing 911 on dedicated lines to lower volume areas, and using the cell network to divert calls from high volume areas, were some contingency plans that were applied with great success.

As *Canadian Idol* finalists were selected, each was assigned a dedicated toll-free number to ensure voting accuracy and simplicity. Locating eleven sequential toll-free numbers was a difficult task since toll-free numbers are not typically assigned sequentially. After searching national toll-free databases, Bell was able to identify an available block of toll-free numbers and reserve these numbers for *Canadian Idol* voting.

PLANNING AND PREPARATION DELIVERS RESULTS

"The strong partnership between Bell and CTV, along with hundreds of hours devoted to anticipating and planning the right strategies to cover off every aspect of project and network management, were key to the success of the show," commented Ms. Dynes.

For instance, to manage network volume, Bell created key messages for CTV to publicize prior to the broadcast through regional media, as well as live during the show, advising viewers on how to maximize the likelihood of their votes going through. This included instructions such as wait for dial tone; use a cell phone for toll-free or text messaging; and avoid calling during peak periods. CTV also used other vehicles such as its Web site, discussion board, and Bell operators, to communicate its key messages about voting. These actions not only supported the high performance of Bell's network, but also benefited regional service providers by redistributing cell phone calls and text message votes processed to available networks.

Bell's commitment to the project extended from its team of network professionals to the president of operations for Bell Canada. Each week, this group worked with CTV to monitor the performance of the national network, acting quickly and decisively when contingency plans needed to be put in place to maintain essential telecommunications links.

CHALLENGING THE IDEA OF WHAT'S POSSIBLE

From a network perspective, the success of *Canadian Idol* was largely due to three important factors: technological innovations that enabled Bell to manage the largest call volume in Canadian history; cooperation between the major Canadian telecommunication providers that resulted in a seamless, high performance national network; and proactive communication to encourage viewers to use a variety of voting methods and tactics to log votes.

As the *Idol* format evolves to include new shows, such as *World Idol,* CTV will continue to depend on Bell to deliver innovative and responsive network solutions that push the boundaries of telecommunications in Canada.

"We are excited to have collaborated with CTV to deliver a scalable, national network capable of handling over three million calls in two hours," said David Southwell, President, Network Operations at Bell Canada. "The success of *Canadian Idol* is a powerful example of how we work with customers to apply technological innovation and creative thinking to their business problems, challenging the idea of what's possible."

You may have watched *Canadian Idol* or even voted for your favourite singer using text messaging. You now have the insight of what it takes to make this type of business product, in this case a TV show, a reality. Did you recognize some of the technology factors: bandwidth, voting database, audit capabilities? Did you see that this endeavour was managed as a project involving a highly diverse team of knowledge-enabled professionals, including wireless telecommunications competitors and vice-presidents? Do you understand how this program created revenue and business value for all of the partners involved? CTV gained ratings and was able to sell premium advertising, and all of the wireless providers gained revenue from increased network usage. This is just one example of applying your new knowledge!

Now consider the many phenomena that are a part of our culture that didn't exist only a few short years ago: blogging, Googling, MySpace, FaceBook, or YouTube. The entire concept of social computing (such as on-line connections, profiling, and chatting) is only a decade old and yet it has changed the way an entire generation interacts with others. And who can even imagine what the next "big thing" is? Any of these innovations in isolation would be an interesting enough study about how technology affects society; but all of them together and over such a short period of time is a form of revolution rather than evolution!

FINAL THOUGHTS

One of the most powerful concepts that we keep returning to in our professional and academic lives is the power of properly combining and balancing people, processes, and technology to achieve productivity. It might help you to think of it like we showed you in Chapter 4, as seen in the margin.

We hope this book has helped you realize the power of this simple concept. So many of those profiled in our Voice of Experience sections spoke about the need to remain on top of technology in order to master its use in business, and we hope they have convinced you of its importance as you progress in your career. If your interest in technology stops at how to make yourself and others more productive and how to ensure business processes run more smoothly in your organizations, then we have accomplished what we set out to do. Good luck!

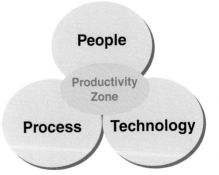

TECH GUIDE A

The Details of IT Hardware

⟲ROI STUDENT RETURN ON INVESTMENT

Through your investment of time in reading and thinking about this guide, your return, or created value, is gaining knowledge. Use the following questions as a study guide.

1. What factors should knowledge-enabled professionals consider to optimize their use of an IT device?

2. How do the electronic components of IT hardware allow the transmission and storage of data?

3. What elements affect the processing capability of hardware?

4. How does internal memory work to enable processing of data into information?

5. How can the type of input hardware help to make knowledge work more productive?

6. Why should knowledge-enabled professionals keep current about new developments in output hardware?

7. What types of secondary storage should be used to safely store data?

Recall that hardware is the physical component of information technology (IT). The working parts of IT hardware consist primarily of electronic devices (mostly digital) with some electro-mechanical parts used with input, output, and storage devices.

In this Tech Guide, we provide a more detailed look into commonly available hardware. Much of our discussion will focus on the personal computer (PC), as its architecture includes components common to all information devices. Our objective here is to provide you with enough knowledge of the technology to allow you to make savvy decisions.

EVALUATING HARDWARE DEVICES

If you've ever been to an office supply store, such as Staples or Office Depot, or an electronics store like Future Shop or Best Buy, you'll know that selecting the right IT devices can be an overwhelming decision. How do you know which ones will serve you best now and in the future? These decisions often include evaluating the following factors:

- *Cost*—We want the device to be within our budget and to provide the most value for each dollar we spend.
- *Compatibility*—Hardware devices work together to form a system. Each device needs to work correctly with the other devices.
- *Data and Information Needs*—We choose devices based on a desired task. We need our IT devices to work with data and/or information in a specific way.
- *Accuracy*—We rely on our devices to handle data and instructions without errors.
- *Speed*—We would like to work with our data and instructions as quickly and efficiently as possible.
- *Portability*—Because we often want to work with information as we travel, we need to easily move the devices as well.
- *Form Factor*—The size, shape, and physical arrangement of IT hardware can affect how and where we use a device.

Some, or all, of these factors influence your selection and use of hardware devices, whether the device concerns processing, memory, input, output, communication, or storage. Throughout this Tech Guide, we will be looking at various types of hardware devices. For each type, we evaluate the options based on the above factors, to help you determine which IT devices will be most suitable for your use. However, before considering many of the types of hardware devices on the market, we first examine the electronics behind them.

THE ELECTRONICS OF HARDWARE

The primary electronic component of IT hardware is the transistor. A *transistor*, as we defined in Chapter 2, is a very small device made out of semiconductor material that acts as a switch to control electronic signals. Millions of transistors, each too small to be seen by the unaided eye, are combined to make the microprocessor and memory chips of the computer. Both types of chips are quite small themselves.

Microprocessor chips carry out many different processing operations within a computer, including handling input and output as well as the actual conversion of data into information. Over time, the number of transistors on a microprocessor chip has expanded, resulting in the increasingly powerful computers we see today. For example, a recent version of Intel's Pentium microprocessor chip has 140 million transistors in it. Intel chips power the vast majority of all PCs in the world today, including those built by Apple Computer. Microprocessor chips are also built into virtually all electronic devices.

Memory chips also use transistors to store data within the computer. As with microprocessor chips, the amount of internal memory stored on chips has also risen dramatically as more transistors are built into the memory chips.

HOW TRANSISTORS WORK

Think of a transistor as an electronic switch, which can be in one of two states, off or on. We can represent the two states of a transistor using **binary** mathematics, which uses ones (on) and zeros (off). Thus, transistors store and transmit all data in a computer as combinations of 1s and 0s. Data that transistors store as a sequence of discrete symbols from a finite set, like the set {0,1}, are referred to as **digital data.** So when you speak of technologies like digital cameras or MP3 players, you can bet that the data processed in these devices are represented as binary numbers. Let's take a closer look at binary data.

BINARY DATA

In binary, the basic unit, a **bit,** corresponds to a power of two, or as they say in mathematics, binary is *base 2*. For example, we can use binary to describe the *base 10* decimal number 234, as follows:

$$11101010_2 = 1_{10}*2^7 + 1_{10}*2^6 + 1_{10}*2^5 + 0_{10}*2^4 + 1_{10}*2^3$$
$$+ 0_{10}*2^2 + 1_{10}*2^1 + 0_{10}*2^0$$
$$= 128_{10} + 64_{10} + 32_{10} + 8_{10} + 2_{10} = 234_{10}$$

Similarly, we can convert other binary values to decimal values; and vice versa, we can convert decimal numbers to equivalent binary values simply by taking the decimal number and repeatedly dividing it by two. In each case, the remainder of the division will be 0 or 1. The composite of all such remainders is then the binary equivalent of the decimal number. Let's use the number 234_{10} again. If we take all of the remainders and put them in reverse order from the divisions, we have the corresponding binary number 11101010_2.[1] See Table A.1.

You may be questioning the usefulness of binary data if they only concern data such as decimal numbers. But many other types of data can be stored as binary, like the letters and punctuation characters on

---

1. For an explanation of why this works, see http://en.wikipedia.org/wiki/Binary_numeral_system.

Table A.1	Finding the Binary Equivalent to Decimal Number	
Beginning Number	After Division	Remainder
234	117	0
117	58	1
58	29	0
29	14	1
14	7	0
7	3	1
3	1	1
1	0	1

your keyboard, as well as graphics, music, and videos. How do hardware devices use binary codes to store different types of information?

CHARACTER ENCODING

Binary codes represent letters and numbers through character encoding. **Character encoding** permits a specific combination of bits to represent each character. Figure A.1 shows an example of how this works. Can anyone design his or her own character-encoding scheme? Yes, but that would make it virtually impossible for all types of hardware and software to work together. When software works with a hardware device or when two hardware devices work together they are said to be compatible. Therefore, independent national or international committees write most schemes, including ASCII, Unicode, and EBCDIC, to ensure IT compatibility.

Standard ASCII

The oldest encoding system used on mainframe computers is the **Extended Binary Coded Decimal Interchange Code (EBCDIC)**, which is an eight-bit coding system. For personal computers, the first encoding system was the **Standard ASCII (American Standard Code for Information Interchange)**. Standard ASCII uses seven bits to represent the unaccented letters of the English language, a-z and A-Z; basic punctuation; numbers; space; and some control codes, such as the Enter key. Using binary-to-decimal conversion, we see that the maximum number of characters that standard ASCII can code is $01111111_{binary} + 1_{decimal}$ (for 00000000_{binary}) = $127_{decimal} + 1_{decimal} = 128_{decimal}$ characters. This limits standard ASCII mostly to English characters and punctuation. However, virtually all computers recognize an extended form of ASCII that uses eight bits to provide 256 characters, thereby adding accented characters from common

Roommate Message Coding System– Imagine that you and your roommate want to give signals to each other before entering the room. You could do this using a hook and tag system. Each combination of different coloured tags can be assigned a different meaning. How many different meanings you have depends on how many hooks you have and how many different coloured tags you have. For example, assume you have green and red tags.

One Hook

I'm Not Here

0

I'm Here

1

With one hook you can have two different meanings, $(2^1 = 2)$

Two Hooks

I'm Not Here

00

Shh! Studying

01

I'm Sleeping

10

I'm Here

11

With two you can encode four different meanings. $(2^2 = 4)$. Do you see a pattern?

Three Hooks

000

001

010

011

100

102

110

111

3 hooks, 8 meanings, $(2^3 = 8)$. The pattern is; $\#colours^{\#hooks} = \#meanings$

4 hooks = ??
How about 2 hooks and 3 colours?

Figure A.1 A character encoding system, such as the roommate message coding system shown here, permits a specific combination of bits (0s and 1s) to represent data (each character).

Table A.2	Comparison of Coding Schemes—Binary Representations		
Character	EBCDIC	ASCII	Unicode
A	1000 0001	0110 0001	0000 0000 0110 0001
A	1100 0001	0100 0001	0000 0000 0100 0001
Esc	0010 0111	0001 1011	0000 0000 0001 1011
%	0110 1100	0010 0101	0000 0000 0010 0101
2	1111 0010	0011 0010	0000 0000 0011 0010
π	Not available	Not available	0000 0011 1100 0000
$\frac{2}{3}$	Not available	Not available	0010 0001 0101 0011

foreign languages. However, even with 256 characters, with the increasing global use of computers, this limit has become a problem.

Unicode

To deal with the increased globalization of business and use of PCs, most IT devices now rely on a more recent standard called **Unicode,** which extends ASCII by providing a 16-bit character set. Unicode adds eight characters to the extended ASCII eight-bit character assignments to include the characters of the major modern written languages. As with standard and extended ASCII, Unicode is available on virtually all recently manufactured PCs.

Today, virtually all computers can work with all three types of encoding systems. Table A.2 lists some examples of character codes under each of these standards.

MACHINE INSTRUCTIONS

We've seen how a computer can represent numeric and character data, but what about instructions? Hardware devices, such as a computer or PDA, execute instructions as a sequence of binary strings known as **machine instructions.** The sequence used to represent a specific instruction is assigned in a similar manner as that used to assign binary sequences to character data (e.g., the ASCII code). For example, Figure A.2 shows the machine language instructions for a Pentium chip, seen as a series of instructions to sum the digits 1 to 100.

Instruction	Explanation
10111000 00000000 00000000	Set Total Value to 0
10111001 00000000 01100100	Set Current Value to 100
00000001 11001000	Add Current Value to Total Value
01001001	Subtract 1 from Current Value
01110101 11111011	If Current value is not 0, repeat

Figure A.2 The machine language instructions for a Pentium chip.

Table A.3	Important Powers of 2	
Power of 2	Decimal Value	Description
2^3	8	Number of bits in a byte
2^8	256	The number of characters that a byte can code
2^{10}	1024	1 kilobyte (KB)
2^{20}	1,048,576	1 megabyte (MB)
2^{30}	1,073,741,824	1 gigabyte (GB)

However, there is one significant difference for machine instructions: no default standard exists for how to encode instructions. Instead, this is left up to the manufacturers of microprocessors, which can therefore result in incompatibility between software and hardware. For example, a machine language instruction for an Intel chip will differ from the same instruction on the chips used in larger computers.

The importance of binary mathematics goes beyond the coding of data. We can express most important measures of performance and capacity in computers based on powers of 2. Table A.3 lists some important binary values that you will often encounter when determining hardware capabilities. For example, we typically use a **byte** to represent a character in ASCII, *megabytes* to measure the amount of memory in a computer, and *gigabytes* to measure the storage on a hard disk.

Now that you have a basic understanding of the electronics involved in hardware devices, we look next at how they affect processing hardware capabilities.

Quick Test

Match the type of computer input with the way that it is usually encoded.

1. A letter typed on the keyboard.

    a. Machine language instructions.

2. An instruction to print a document.

    b. Conversion to binary number.

3. A number entered for processing.

    c. Character encoding.

Answers: 1. c; 2. a 3. b

PROCESSING HARDWARE

At the core of all computing operations is the microprocessor. It contains the majority of the components that make up the *CPU or central processing unit.* The CPU works together with memory to control the execution of all instructions, and the processing of all data. The CPU is located on the system's **motherboard,** the main circuit board in an electronic device. As Figure A.3 shows, the motherboard contains the microprocessor as well as other chips and circuits. The motherboard and CPU chip are found in the **system unit,** the box that we often think of as the computer when we look at it.

Figure A.3 A computer motherboard, the main circuit board in an electronic device.

Often, the speed and performance of the CPU are the key considerations in determining the processing capability of IT devices. Because it's so vital to IT hardware, let's look at the CPU in more detail.

THE CPU

The CPU consists of several components shown in Figure A.4, as follows:

- *Control Unit (CU):* Performs the following four basic functions: fetch, decode, execute, and store. One time through each of these tasks in a sequence is called a *cycle.*
- *Arithmetic Logic Unit (ALU):* Executes mathematical and logic calculations. Logic calculations make comparisons between values.
- *Floating Point Unit (FPU):* Executes mathematical and logic calculations on non-integer values (values that may have a fractional portion after the decimal point).
- *Decode Unit:* Fetches machine language instructions from the instruction cache and translates them into binary code that the ALU processes.
- *Cache Memory:* Provides a staging area for instructions and the data. Because cache memory is faster than RAM, the processor can keep working without waiting on data.
- *Prefetch Unit:* Provides a small amount of memory that stores incoming instructions in a queue while awaiting execution, thereby reducing CPU waiting time.
- *Registers:* Small sections of memory that store data while the microprocessor needs it. A register address is expressed with a small number of bits, making it much faster to access than normal memory.
- *Clock:* A crystal that sits on the motherboard and vibrates regularly, many times per second. The clock speed refers to the

Figure A.4 The CPU components, connected by the data bus.

number of cycles a CPU performs in the span of a tick of the computer's internal clock.

- *Bus:* A bus is a set of wires that transports data from one location to another. A CPU can have internal buses and address buses. Figure A.4 shows the bus as yellow lines.
- *Instruction Set:* A collection of machine language instructions that governs how the processor interprets and executes various tasks that it performs.

Figure A.5 shows how these components work together to execute instructions. Data and/or instructions are input into memory (initially RAM and then into data or instruction cache, or the prefetch unit). After fetching instructions, the control unit then directs the other components based on the instructions. For example, the control unit may direct data either to the ALU or FPU for processing. Memory stores the processed data, which are then available for further processing or output. These four functions—fetch, decode, execute, and store—provide the basic framework for this process.

The Instruction Set

Each microprocessor has a permanently stored set of machine language instructions called the *instruction set.* The instruction set governs how the CPU interprets and executes the tasks that it performs to run computer software. Two main types of instruction sets exist: **complex instruction set computer (CISC)** instructions and **reduced instruction set computer (RISC)** instructions. Usually, processors that use an RISC instruction set are faster than those using CISC, because an RISC processor needs to understand and execute fewer commands. RISC processors tend to be used in small

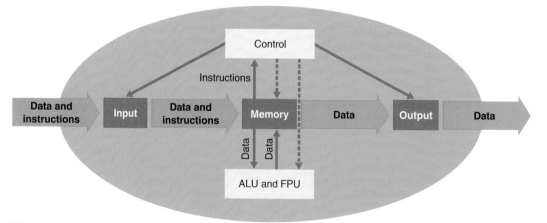

Figure A.5 How the CPU components work together to execute instructions.

electronic devices such as cell phones or MP3 players. Modern chips like the Intel Pentium combine the speed of the RISC approach with the power of CISC to provide increased speed.

Bandwidth

The size of a CPU's buses determines its **bandwidth,** which is the number of bits the CPU can process in a single instruction. Recall that a **bus** is a set of wires over which data travels from one location to another. In a computer the main bus is the *data or system bus,* which sends and receives data to and from the CPU to other components. However, the *internal buses* control the bandwidth. Internal buses carry data between the components that reside within the chip and *address buses,* which then connect them to main memory.

Bus capacity is expressed as the number of bits of data that can travel over the bus simultaneously. Usually, higher bus capacities mean faster processing of instructions and data. For example, assume that a PC has a CPU with a 64-bit internal bus and uses a 32-bit system bus. The CPU internal bus would be about twice as fast as the system bus.

Clock Speed

The clock speed is probably the most common measure of CPU performance. Clock speeds are measured in *megahertz (MHz),* millions of cycles per second, or *gigahertz (GHz),* billions of cycles per second. In general, higher clock speeds translate to faster system performance. However, other considerations, such as internal memory and video speed, can also affect overall speed. As a result, clock speeds can be a little misleading. Different internal structure and instruction sets can cause two different models of processors with similar clock speeds to perform at different levels.

CPU PERFORMANCE CHARACTERISTICS

Microprocessors are typically differentiated by their instruction set, their clock speed, and their bandwidth. As we noted above, the clock speed is the most commonly used performance characteristic. All other things being equal, the faster the clock speed, the faster the capability of the CPU chip to process instructions. Many of our devices not only contain one CPU, but at least two. Dual core processor systems contain two complete processors, often on the same circuit board. The advantage of this configuration is the increased ability to multi-task, which allows your computer to do more than one thing at a time.

In addition to the CPU or microprocessor chip, all computers need internal memory to operate.

Quick Test

Fill in the blanks for the following statements.

1. The component of the CPU that executes mathematical and logical calculation is the _____ .

2. The bandwidth of the CPU is determined by the size of its _____ .

3. The four functions of the CPU that provide the basic processing framework are the fetch, decode, _____ , and store functions.

Answers: 1. arithmetic logic unit; 2. buses; 3. execute

INTERNAL MEMORY

Like humans, computers have both long-term memory (ROM) and short-term memory (RAM). However, the analogy falls short when we look at the physical implementation and the relative capacity of computer memory. That is, memory stores data and instructions on computer chips. Further, unlike humans, computers require a greater capacity of short-term, temporary memory than long-term memory (keep in mind, we're talking about memory, not storage). In IT devices, from MP3 players to digital cameras to computers, the main purpose of ROM is simply to hold instructions that control the device's start-up processes (booting up). This small set of instructions, known as the *BIOS (basic input/output system),* activates the hardware components and loads the operating system.

Because ROM's instructions and data cannot be altered and ROM is usually not part of the decision when selecting IT, we focus our attention on RAM.

RAM

The largest number of chips in your computer used for memory is in the form of *random access memory (RAM),* so named because the CPU can access any item stored in RAM directly (randomly). In personal computers there are usually two types of RAM: dynamic RAM (DRAM) and static RAM (SRAM). RAM can also be found on other components of your computer system such as the printer and video and sound cards. This type of RAM is often referred to as peripheral RAM.

When people talk about *main memory,* they are usually referring to the DRAM in your computer. Like the CPU, **dynamic RAM**

(DRAM) has improved over the years to provide faster access and greater capacity. It turns out that one of the easiest and least expensive ways to upgrade an older system is to increase the amount of main memory (DRAM).

Static RAM (SRAM) is so called because it does not need to be constantly refreshed in order to maintain the data that it stores. This makes it faster and less volatile than DRAM, but it also makes it much more expensive. Due to its high cost, SRAM is typically used for smaller sections of memory known as **cache.** Typically, cache memory contains the most recently accessed pieces of main memory.

RAM can also be found on other components of your computer system such as the printer and video and sound cards. This type of RAM is often referred to as **peripheral RAM.** Peripheral RAM serves as a buffer area between the main system and a peripheral device. For example, the DRAM that exists in most printers is known as the *printer buffer.* This buffer temporarily holds the data until the item is printed. Without a printer buffer, the data processed by the CPU can begin to back up, since the CPU can send the data to the printer faster than the printer can print.

Video cards use another type of RAM, known as **video RAM (VRAM).** The main difference between VRAM and DRAM is that two devices can access VRAM at the same time. This allows the card to receive data from the CPU and transmit data to the monitor simultaneously.

RAM PERFORMANCE

Two factors affect RAM performance: (1) capacity and (2) address bus bandwidth. Let's consider each factor, starting with memory capacity.

When you open other applications, such as a program to chat with your friends on-line while you write a report with a word processor and listen to some tunes, the main memory stores the software and data for these applications. Eventually, you reach your main memory's capacity. Now when you open your favourite game program—and who hasn't done this when they should be working—there is no room in main memory for its instructions. In this case, the CPU either leaves some of the game's instructions on secondary storage until needed or it bumps instructions and data from other software out to secondary storage until needed again. Remember that access to secondary storage is much slower than accessing main memory. As a result, your system may also noticeably slow down.

Thus, the memory capacity in a computer can profoundly affect the overall performance of the computer. Memory capacity is measured in terms of the number of bytes that it may store. Capacities of most types of memory are in the range of thousands (kilobytes, KB), millions (megabytes, MB), and in some cases billions (gigabytes, GB) of bytes. The memory in your computer is primarily a hands-off component. In most cases, once you make your initial purchase, you will not need to configure or troubleshoot the memory. Mostly what you need to know is that the more main memory available to your system, the better. For example, Microsoft recommends that you have a *minimum* of 128 MB of RAM memory in order to install and use Windows XP. The new Windows Vista OS requires at least 512 MB. For two systems, with all other things equal, the one with the most RAM will be able to process more work.

While capacity is the most important consideration when measuring the performance of memory, another limiting factor on the memory capacity exists. Here we refer to the bandwidth of the *address buses* that connect the CPU and other devices to main memory. An **address** is a number that a computer uses to specify the location of a particular piece of data within memory.

The size of the address bus determines the maximum number of memory locations. Early address buses had an eight-bit bandwidth, which limited the amount of addressable memory to 2^8—256 locations. As it turns out, the address bus size is not much of a problem in today's computers. For example, in 2006, Pentium microprocessors used an address bus with a bandwidth of 64 bits. This means that the CPU could access up to 264—18,446,744,073,709,551,615 (18.45 extrabytes!) eight-bit locations of internal memory. Currently, space and cost limitations with the average personal computer make a comparable amount of RAM impractical. But a 64-bit address bus can handle that much if needed.

Quick Test

Determine if the following statements are True or False.

1. ROM instructions and data cannot be altered.

2. Most RAM in our personal computer is in the form of SRAM.

3. Because RAM is permanent memory, it is unnecessary to frequently save your work.

Answers: 1. True; 2. False; 3. False

INPUT HARDWARE DEVICES

Any hardware device must have methods for inputting data. The primary input methods include the keyboard, pointing devices such as the mouse, scanning devices such as bar code readers, and the Internet or other network connection. We consider all of these *except* the Internet/network connection, which we discuss separately in Tech Guide C.

THE KEYBOARD

The keyboard is generally recognized as the primary and most common input device for computers. As its name implies, it uses keys that you press to transmit letters, digits, or other characters to the CPU for processing. When you press a key, a microprocessor in the keyboard determines the location of the button. It then sends the appropriate character in binary encoded digits to the computer. Most keyboards allow you to type ahead; that is, to keep typing while the computer processes earlier entries. In order to do this, the keyboard stores characters in a memory buffer (a temporary storage area) before sending it on to the system processor. Since it includes its own processor and memory, a keyboard is itself a small, dedicated computer.

Keyboard Performance

Some people take a long time to learn to use a keyboard. Indeed, classes exist with the sole objective of teaching "keyboarding." Further, even after becoming a competent user of a keyboard, there are few who can type rapidly with few mistakes. (This fact has helped to make the spellchecker one of the most appreciated inventions in software history.) So why use a keyboard? The primary value of a keyboard as an input device relies on its ability and versatility to input text data. As a result, most people continue to rely on keyboards for certain tasks.

When considering a keyboard, an important aspect is the *tactile response*. This relates to how it feels to us when our fingers press a button. This is the reason most computer buyers like to try out the keyboard, especially on a laptop computer, before making the final purchase. The size of the keyboard can also be a factor. It can be difficult to type on a keyboard on which the keys are too small or too far apart.

Ergonomics are a consideration when choosing a computer keyboard or a laptop. As discussed in Chapter 2, ergonomics is the science of designing a job or tool to fit the worker. Most keyboards today are more ergonomic than in the past and are less likely to cause a variety of hand and wrist problems than was previously the case.

POINTING DEVICES

Second only to the keyboard are pointing devices including the mouse, trackball, touchpad, lightpen, touch screens, and even wearable devices that interpret a user's movements. Pointing devices, which work along with *graphical user interfaces (GUI)*, allow the user to provide data and instructions to the computer using physical movements such as "point" and "click." As the user moves the pointing device, the graphical interface echoes the movement.

Most pointing devices, such as a mouse, also include one or more buttons with which to further control the on-screen activities. You are undoubtedly familiar with the standard mouse, which comes in many shapes and sizes. A *mechanical mouse* uses moving parts, such as a ball and rollers. An *optical mouse* does not require moving parts. Optical mice, having no moving parts to detect motion, use the light from an LED (light-emitting diode) reflected off a surface to measure the mouse movement. Figure A.6 shows the bottom of the two types of mice—mechanical with a rollerball on the bottom and an optical mouse with no moving parts.

A laser mouse is one that incorporates wireless technology. A laser mouse uses an infrared laser instead of LED and can be more sensitive than other types of mice.

Many other pointing devices exist. Table A.4 lists and describes the most popular ones in the approximate order of their level of use, along with a photo of the device. Considering this extensive list, how do you select which pointing device to use? Ergonomically speaking, the setup of the workspace can be an important consideration in selecting a pointing device. For example, if space is tight or a flat surface is unavailable, trackballs or touchpads present better choices than a mouse. Pointing devices should also provide a proper fit with the user. Users should consider whether or not the device places undue stress on their arm, hand, or fingers, and if the buttons' location makes them easy to reach and use.

Figure A.6 A mechanical mouse (top) uses moving parts, such as a ball and rollers, whereas an optical mouse (bottom) does not.

Environmental conditions can be another important factor when choosing a pointing device. Dust or moisture can make standard mice and trackballs function erratically or require frequent cleaning or repair. Touchpads or optical mice are sealed and contain few moving parts, which help make them more suitable for harsh conditions.

Pointing Device Performance

Compared with the keyboard, pointing devices are simple to use. Pointing is a natural human movement. Coupled with a good GUI, controlling a computer with a pointing device can be intuitive and

Table A.4	Pointing Devices	
Device	Description	
Mouse	The most common pointing device.	
Touchpad	Commonly used on laptop computers, touchpads provide a small, flat surface that you slide your finger over using the same movements as you would a mouse. "Clicking" is accomplished by finger tapping, either directly on the pad or on nearby buttons.	
Joystick	A device often used to control games. A joystick consists of a handheld stick that pivots on one end and transmits its angle to a computer. A joystick usually has one or more buttons for entering instructions.	
Touch screen	A device that allows the user to interact with a computer by touching the display screen. Using a combination of sensing technology and software, the location where the display is touched is interpreted to perform the required operation. Often used in public kiosks where a mouse would be a problem.	
Trackball	Basically an upside-down mouse, a trackball consists of a ball that rests in a socket containing sensors to detect the ball's rotation. Users roll the ball with their hand to move a cursor. Used to replace a mouse in situations where physical movement is a problem, in the case of users with a physical disability, for example.	

Table A.4	Pointing Devices *(continued)*	
Device	**Description**	
Pen input	A pen looks like a ballpoint pen but uses an electronic head instead of ink. Also called a *stylus*, you can use a pen with a digitizing tablet or touch screen. A stylus is often used with PDAs, which also incorporate a form of handwriting recognition that allows you to write directly on the screen.	
Light pen	A device that uses a light-sensitive detector on a display screen. A light pen allows you to move the pointer and select objects on the display screen by directly pointing it at the objects. Similar in use to a mouse except that you point directly at the objects on the screen.	
Wearable device	There are any number of pointing devices that a user can wear. For example, a data glove can be worn on the user's hand. The computer interprets hand movements to move the cursor. Buttons may be added on the sides of the fingers to provide command input. Often used with virtual reality games. The newly introduced Wii from Nintendo is a recent example of a wearable device.	
Digitizing tablet	A digitizing tablet consists of an electronic tablet and a cursor that lets you draw and sketch into a computer. A *cursor* is like a mouse, but it has a window with crosshairs and as many as 16 buttons. The *tablet* contains electronics that enable it to detect movement of the cursor and translate the movements into signals to the computer. Used by graphic artists, engineers, and cartographers to convert drawings to digital form.	

require little training. Pointing devices are most often used to point to items on the GUI, so they are typically more useful for entering commands than for entering data content. For example, you may click on a scroll bar and move it to page through a document on your screen, while you would most likely use a keyboard to enter text.

Accuracy of a pointing device can be gauged by its resolution and tracking. **Resolution** in this case refers to how precise the device can pinpoint its location on the screen. **Tracking** refers to how close the screen cursor follows the movement of the device. For example, an optical mouse usually tracks better than mechanical, but can provide less resolution.

SCANNING DEVICES

Scanning devices read data and information stored on some form of non-connected media. Most scanning devices work closely with special software and databases. Software encodes the image in binary, or recognizes characteristics of the scanned image. Databases store and retrieve the remaining information needed. For example, most grocery stores use a bar code to encode a product code. Upon reading the bar code, the software then matches the resulting product code with the database records, to retrieve such details as the product price, description, and inventory level. A representative list of scanning technologies includes the following:

- *Bar Code Reader* A device that reads a printed horizontal strip of vertical bars. The bar widths and spaces between the bars vary in a standard way to represent a group of decimal digits.
- *Biometric Scanner* Any device that can scan and digitize human body parts. Most commonly used for identification and access purposes, based, for example, on a scanned thumbprint.
- *Document Scanner* A peripheral device on which you scan a printed document. The scanner will then use reflected light to obtain the image, digitize it, and transmit it to the computer. Flatbed scanners are often built in to other devices such as facsimile and copy machines.
- *Magnetic Strip Reader* A device that reads the data stored on a small magnetic strip as the strip is swiped through the device. They are commonly found on the back of credit and library cards. This device could also be considered a form of secondary storage.
- *MICR (magnetic ink character recognition)* A system that uses a special magnetized ink that can be read by a special scanner. MICR is primarily used in the banking industry to print information on cheques for efficient processing.

- *OCR (optical character recognition)* Usually implemented as software, it converts scanned print documents directly to electronic text.
- *OMR (optical mark reader)* It uses a special scanning device to read carefully placed pencil marks on specially designed forms, such as those used in standardized school tests.
- *Smart Card Reader* A plastic card that has an integrated circuit embedded inside on which to store information, used for such purposes as credit and debit cards, phone cards, and ID cards. Current (as of 2007) smart cards can hold about 8 KB of data.

The most widely used scanners are document scanners, bar code readers, and biometric scanners. We look at these next in more detail.

Document Scanners

Document scanners can be an important part of reducing an organization's paper documents in favour of more efficient and useful electronic documents. All document scanners convert areas of light and dark into digital data by reflecting light off of the page.

Although several types of document scanners are available, *flatbed scanners* are the most popular. To use a flatbed scanner, you place a document face down on a piece of glass and close the cover. The scan head moves underneath the document along the bed of the scanner. A light bar moves over the image, and the reflected light falls on a bed of photosensitive cells. The cells read the image, interpreting it as a series of dots, called *pixels* (picture elements). After scanning the document, its image appears on the monitor.

Other document scanners use similar technology but present the document to the scanner differently. With a *handheld scanner,* you physically drag the scanning devices across the page. *Sheetfed scanners* have a slot where you insert the page, and a motor draws the page, across the scanner. On the high-end pricewise, a *drum scanner* uses very sensitive sensors to read the document as it whirls around inside a cylinder.

Bar Code Readers

A bar code is basically just a horizontal strip of vertical, variable-width black bars. But these bars, introduced in 1973, revolutionized how companies identify products. The layout of black bars separated by white space is actually a binary code that represents a set of numbers used to uniquely identify products. Companies number and code all consumer products to a worldwide standard called the **Universal Product Code (UPC).**

Bar code readers interpret the codes through software that matches them to a database record. Basically, the bar code scanner sees and measures the absence or presence of light in the pattern of bars and spaces. It then converts that information into an electrical signal that can be translated into computer-compatible data. Common bar code scanning technologies include lasers, wands, and charged coupled devices (CCD).

Laser scanners project an oscillating beam that appears as a red scan. Laser scanning is automatic in the sense that it generates multiple scans activated either by sensing an object that is placed in front of it or by simply pulling a trigger. In comparison, a *wand*, a pen-type scanner, requires physical contact with a bar code. It must be moved manually across a bar code by hand. CCD technology photographs and digitizes bar codes by built-in photodetectors. A CCD reader is often considered the easiest to use. The user simply covers the bar code with the head of the scanner and pulls the trigger to activate the scanner. The next time you're at your favourite department store, see if you can identify the type of bar code scanner in use. Figure A.7 shows the process of using a bar code scanner in a consumer purchase.

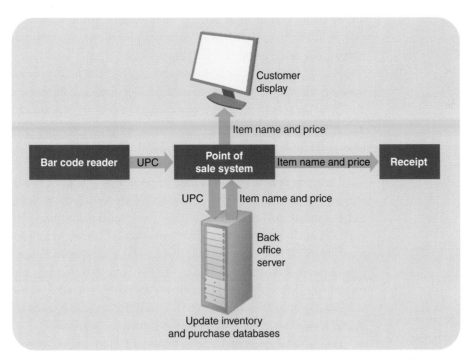

Figure A.7 Bar code readers convert UPC information into an electrical signal that can then be translated into computer-compatible data.

Biometric Scanners

Biometric scanners scan human physical characteristics. These devices may be used for identification, medical applications, and computer control. Devices that scan fingerprints or the patterns that exist in the retina of the eye can be used to uniquely identify a person and allow access to a facility, computer, or ATM bank account (see Figure A.8). Sonogram devices can use sound to provide images of the interior of the human body in order to view the growth progress of an unborn child or to check for tumours. Other devices may scan for body movements. With one device a user can control the movement of the screen pointer by simply moving the eye to look at an icon. You can expect biometric scanners to become more prevalent in coming years as their use for surveillance, security, and user authorization increases.

Figure A.8 Biometric input devices scan human physical characteristics such as a thumbprint, for identification, medical applications, and computer control.

Scanning Device Performance

The primary performance measures for scanning devices are the accuracy and speed of the scan. Accuracy is measured in terms of resolution. *Resolution* refers to the clarity and level of detail of an image that a scanning device can capture. It is measured using the number of individual dots scanned in a unit distance, often given in *dots per inch (dpi)*. A higher dpi indicates higher resolution, which allows you to capture more detail from the source medium. While it may seem different, this type of resolution is related to the resolution we discussed earlier for pointing devices.

If scanning for colour is important, consider the *bit depth* and the *dynamic range*. These values measure the range of colours, and quality of the colour, that the device captures. Accuracy of scans can also depend on the quality of the scanned media. For example, bar codes need to be clearly printed on a flat surface to achieve acceptable scanning performance.

There are two aspects to scanning speed. First, the device category can be selected to improve the physical processing of the items to be scanned. For example, you'll see more fixed-mount bar code scanners at the grocery checkout line due to their ability to process more items quickly than handheld scanners can. A second speed consideration is the time required by the device to scan an image and transmit all of the data to the computer. This varies depending on the size, bit depth, and resolution to be scanned. However, the speed required for similar scans can be compared between scanners.

Finally, environmental and ergonomic factors affect scanner performance. Because most scanners depend on the reflection of light off of a medium, surrounding light levels can affect them. Or, the presence of particles in the air can impair their performance. Ergonomic properties can also be a factor in the productive use and safety of a scanning device. Biometric scanners must be comfortable and safe. Handheld devices should fit neatly into your hand. Laser scanners should not be unsafe to your eye.

OTHER INPUT DEVICES

With the increasingly popular use of multimedia information, audio/video input has become a major category. *Audio input* is primarily obtained through the use of a microphone. Applications range from simply storing audio comments within presentations or analysis files, to dictation of text input using specialized voice recognition software. For music, **musical instrument digital interface (MIDI)** devices allow note and effect information like pitch and loudness to be captured from a device and stored in a special format in a computer. MIDI devices include music keyboards, controllers, and other electronic music devices.

Video input is captured using a digital video camera, a Web-Cam, video and DVD players, or from broadcast and cable emissions. A **WebCam** is a video camera that delivers its output for viewing over the Internet. Typically, a WebCam is a slow-scan video camera that captures images about every half-second. This slow rate of capture accounts for the choppiness of the picture relative to full-motion video cameras. Input from cable and broadcast television antennas can allow the computer and its monitor to serve as a television.

Often, both audio and video input require equipping the computer with special cards. A microphone is connected to a port in the audio card, while a video card processes video input. These cards process the input into a form that the computer can use and store. These cards will usually include their own processor and memory. Figure A.10 shows some of these other input devices.

Finally, sensory input is another important category of input device. A **sensor** is an electronic device that measures a physical quantity like temperature or pressure, and then converts it into an electronic signal. Sensors are of two types—analog and digital. *Analog sensors* generally produce a voltage proportional to the measurement. The CPU then converts the signal to a digital form. A *digital sensor* captures the measurement digitally, which therefore can be sent directly to the computer for processing. A multitude of applications rely on sensors, such as proximity sensors used in smoke alarms, temperature sensors that control office heating and air conditioning, and pressure sensors used in automatic garage doors.

Quick Test

Match the input hardware device with its use:

1. Keyboard

2. Pointing device

3. Scanning device

a. Reads data and information stored on some form of non-connected media.

b. Creates text by transmitting letters, digits, and other characters to the CPU for processing.

c. Works with GUI to provide data and instructions to the computer using physical movements.

Answers: 1. b; 2. c; 3. a

OUTPUT HARDWARE DEVICES

Output devices deliver the result of processing operations to the user. Output devices include display and printed output devices, storage devices, the Internet or other network connection, and a wide variety of other electronic devices. We will consider all but the Internet or other network connection here, as we consider those in Tech Guide C.

DISPLAY DEVICES

Because most of us prefer images, display devices continue to be, by far, the most common category of output device. When coupled with speakers, display devices deliver to the user just about every data format, ranging from plain text documents to movies with sound (of course, the sound itself is output by a speaker). Display devices are also a significant component for input. Using a display, mouse, and GUI-based operating system allows the user to interact with the computer by manipulating a pointer on the screen over graphic objects.

The display system is made up of two primary parts: the graphics card and the monitor, as shown in Figure A.9.

The Technology Behind LCD Monitors

Display devices vary in shape, size, and underlying technology. Most monitors in use today are LCD monitors. At the heart of an LCD monitor is a piece of liquid crystal material, placed between a pair of transparent electrodes. This combination of materials takes advantage of four facts from physics:

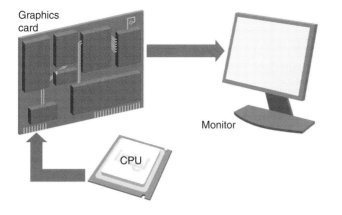

Graphics card

CPU

Monitor

Figure A.9 This simple display system is capable of delivering to the user just about every data format, ranging from plain text documents to movies with sound.

1. Light can be polarized.
2. Liquid crystals can transmit and change polarized light.
3. Electric current can change the structure of liquid crystals.
4. Transparent materials can conduct electricity.

A liquid crystal can change the phase of the light that passes through it. Moreover, applying a proper voltage controls the phase change. An LCD display consists of an array of cells (pixels) that can be controlled individually to create the image.

An LCD may be colour or monochrome. For colour LCDs, each pixel consists of three subpixels, one for each of the colours red, blue, and green. By carefully controlling the applied voltage, the intensity of each subpixel can range over 256 shades. Combining the subpixels produces a possible palette of 16.8 million colours. LCDs may also be either backlit or reflective. Liquid crystals do not emit light; they can only change the phase of light as it passes through. Small, inexpensive LCDs are often reflective, which means to display anything they need to reflect light from external light sources. However, most LCDs are backlit. Backlit displays have built-in fluorescent tubes above, beside, and sometimes behind the LCD. Combined with a white diffusion panel behind the LCD, this redirects and scatters light evenly through the display.

Display Device Performance

Display device performance depends on the resolution; that is, the maximum number of pixels that the screen can show, typically measured by dot pitch. The *dot pitch* of a display is the distance between a pixel and the closest pixel of the same colour. For computer monitors, dot pitch is usually less than 0.30 mm. For a display screen of given physical width and height, a higher dot pitch results in a lower resolution.

For LCDs, the voltage to each pixel is refreshed many times a second. How often this occurs is called the *refresh rate,* measured in hertz (Hz). The monitor's horizontal scan rate and the vertical resolution limit the refresh rate, since a higher resolution means more vertical lines to scan. Higher refresh rates mean less flickering, thereby reducing eyestrain. Anything above 60–72 Hz is fine for most users.

The physical dimensions of the screen can also be an important consideration. For LCD displays, screen size is measured on the diagonal in inches. For example, a 20-in. monitor will measure approximately 20 in. from a lower corner to the opposite upper corner of the display. In addition, LCD monitors are generally rated in degrees for their visible *viewing angle* for both horizontal and vertical. A problem with the LCD screens is that the colour in the image can only be accurately represented when viewed straight on. The farther away from a perpendicular viewing angle, the more the colour will tend to wash out. A higher viewing angle is usually preferred over a lower angle, unless you want to reduce attempts of others looking over your shoulder.

Touch Screens: The Future of Display Devices

An interesting and increasingly useful twist on display technology is the touch screen monitor. A **touch screen monitor** is a computer display screen that is sensitive to human touch or a special pen. Kiosks (such as ATMs and self-service checkout lanes), PDAs, and newer tablet PCs frequently use touch screens. Using a touch screen, the user can interact with the computer by touching images or words on the screen. Because of this interactivity, touch screens are both input and output devices. PDAs and tablet PCs can also include special software that allows the user to write using a special pen directly on the screen in "digital ink."

There are currently four types of touch screen technology in use. A *resistive* touch screen panel uses a specially coated resistive layer. Touching this layer sends an electrical charge to the controller for processing. *Surface wave* technology uses ultrasonic waves that pass over the touch screen panel. Changes in the ultrasonic waves that result from touching the panel are registered and sent for processing. A *capacitive* touch screen panel is coated with a material that stores electrical charges. Touching this panel draws a small amount of charge to the point of contact. Circuits located at each corner of the panel measure the charge and send the information to the controller for processing. Finally, newer tablet PCs use an *electromagnetic digitizer* that accepts input only from a special pen containing an electromagnetic coil. Using the pen can prevent inadvertent movements of the cursor that can sometimes occur with other touch technologies. Figure A.10 shows two types of touch-sensitive displays used for tablet PCs.

PRINTED OUTPUT DEVICES

The increasing use of PDAs and tablet PCs should reduce our dependency on paper. Think about the ease and lower cost of storing, editing, transmitting, and copying electronic information as opposed to paper documents. Yet we often need printed information. As Table A.5 indicates, a variety of printing devices allow a range of quality and options in outputting both text and graphics. We discuss the most widely used personal computer printers in more detail.

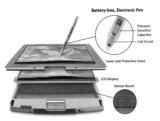

Figure A.10 LCD touch-sensitive displays respond to human touch or a special pen.

An *inkjet printer* sprays small ink droplets from a nozzle onto the paper. As paper is fed through the printer, a print head sweeps back and forth to spray coloured dots in the appropriate locations. When completed, the array of dots forms the image. Inkjet printers typically use cartridges that contain black ink, and ink in the colours red, yellow, and blue. Like the pixels on a display, the proper combination of the ink colours can result in a multitude of colours. Inkjet printers print fairly high quality text and graphics at moderate speeds.

A *laser printer* uses a non-impact technology similar to that used in copy machines. After receiving a print job, a laser beam "draws" the document on a specially coated drum using electrical charges. After applying the charge to the drum, the drum is rolled in a dry powder called *toner*. The toner sticks to the charged image on the drum. As the paper passes through, the toner is transferred onto it and then fused to the paper using heat and pressure. Laser printers can be either monochrome (black and white) or colour, with colour laser printers being several times more expensive than monochrome laser printers.

A *plotter* uses one or more pens that are raised, lowered, and moved over a page to draw high-end graphics or text. Unlike a regular printer, the plotter draws continuous lines. There are several different types of plotters. A *drum plotter* draws on paper wrapped around a drum. The drum turns to produce one direction of the plot, while the pens move to provide other directions. A *flatbed plotter* draws on paper that is stationary on a flat surface. An *electrostatic plotter* draws on negatively charged paper with positively charged toner. Because plotters are typically more expensive than printers, they are used mostly for architect blueprints or full-size engineering drawings.

Table A.5	Printed Output Devices	
Type	**Description**	
Dot matrix	Older style printer that uses a type of hammer and a ribbon to print characters using arrays of dots. Typically used for printing multipart business forms.	
Inkjet	A popular type of printer for home use that prints by spraying dots from an ink cartridge. Capable of high-quality graphics and text printing at speeds over 80 characters per second.	
Laser	A popular type of printer for business and home use that prints by applying dots from a toner cartridge. Capable of very high quality graphics and text printing at speeds as high as eight pages per minute.	
Multifunction device	A device that combines several types of input and output. Typically, a multi-function device will include a printer, fax, flatbed scanner, and copy machine—all in one device.	
Plotter	Prints very high quality graphics, although at slow speed, by manipulating a pen over a page.	
Thermal	Uses heat to transfer an impression onto paper either by adhering a wax-based ink from a ribbon or by burning dots onto coated paper. Used in early fax machines and still used for printing receipts like those at pay-at-the-pump gas stations.	

Printed Output Device Performance

Printer performance centres on colour, resolution, speed, and memory. Colour is important for most users these days. In addition to needing colour pages for presentations or maps, colour printers can print near-photo quality, reducing the need to pay for digital photo developing. However, colour printers are more expensive to operate, because they require two or more different colour ink or toner cartridges.

Printer resolution is measured similarly to the resolution of display devices. The sharpness of text and images on paper is usually measured in dots per inch (dpi). Higher dpi means higher quality printing. Many inexpensive printers provide sufficient resolution at 600 dpi.

The more print jobs, the more important the speed of the printer. Printer speed is measured as the page rate in pages per minute (ppm). More expensive printers can print faster at about 8–10 ppm, while typical inexpensive printers print only about 3–6 ppm. Note that colour and extensive graphics can reduce these rates.

Most printers come with a small amount of memory called a *buffer*. With a large enough print buffer, the computer can download an entire job for printing and then process other items, without having to wait for the print job completion. As you might expect, higher capacity print buffers perform more efficiently.

Quick Test

Fill in the blanks for the following statements.

1. At the heart of the _____ is a piece of liquid crystal material placed between two transparent electrodes.

2. For a display device, the _____ is the distance between a pixel and the closest pixel of the same colour.

3. A(n) _____ uses non-impact technology similar to that used in copy machines.

Answers: 1. LCD monitor; 2. dot pitch; 3. laser printer

STORAGE HARDWARE

Because of the limited amount of internal storage and the volatility of RAM, some form of storage external to RAM is necessary to permanently store data and programs. This **secondary storage** usually comes as magnetic storage media, optical disks, or chip-based flash memory. With all of these, stored information is accessed by internal memory when the control unit decides that this information is needed. Because the secondary storage unit must locate the information, read it, and then transfer it to internal memory, secondary storage is a much slower form of memory than internal memory. However, this slow transfer of information is balanced by the virtually unlimited storage capacity. Table A.6 lists the main types of storage used with personal computers.

MAGNETIC DISKS

Some secondary disk storage uses a *magnetic disk* to store information as a form of **direct-access storage** in which information may be accessed in any order, regardless of the order in which the information was stored. A magnetic disk is composed of metal or plastic that is covered with an iron oxide whose magnetic direction can be arranged to represent symbols. This magnetic arrangement is carried out on a *disk drive,* which spins the disk while reading and writing information onto it using a *read/write head.* Depending on the type of disk, the read/write head rides either directly on or immediately above the disk. Types of disk storage include diskettes, high-capacity disks, and hard drives.

At one time, the most popular form of portable secondary storage was the diskette. They are housed in a sturdy plastic case, and their small size ($3\frac{1}{2}$-in. square) offers easy portability. Diskettes are slower to access than hard disks and have far less storage capacity (1.44 MB), but they are inexpensive. They have been, to a large degree, replaced by CD-ROMs and flash memory storage, but you may still see one around and many desktop systems still have a diskette drive in them. Laptops may also come with a removable diskette drive. Higher capacity diskettes are now available that hold 750 MB, but require a special drive.

Almost all computer systems include a hard disk. *Hard disks* serve as the main storage device for programs and data. They have greater capacities and allow for faster access than most other storage technologies. Hard disks can store anywhere from 10 MB to 200 GB or more on the latest drives. A single hard disk usually consists of a stack of several platters. Each platter contains two read/write heads, one for each side. Each read/write head is attached to a single access arm, so that they cannot move independently. Each platter has the same number of tracks, and a track location that cuts across all platters is called a cylinder. Each track is divided into sectors, which are the smallest unit accessible on the disk. Each sector has the same capacity, 512 bytes. When storing data to a disk, the data are divided into portions

Table A.6	Storage Devices		
Storage Technology	**Type**	**Description**	**Capacity Range (as of 2007)**
CD-ROM, R, RW	Optical	Optical disk capable of storing large amounts of data; some types can be recorded upon (R) or rewritten (RW).	Up to 1 GB, most common is 650 MB
Diskette	Magnetic	Uses a soft, magnetic disk housed in a $3\frac{1}{2}$-in. rigid, plastic shell.	1.44 MB
DVD, DVD-R, DVD-RW, DVD-HD DVD-Blu-ray	Optical	A faster, higher capacity type of optical disk than CD-ROM; some types can be recorded upon (R) or rewritten (RW).	4.7 GB–17 GB
Hard disk drive	Magnetic	Very fast and with very high capacity. Generally used for permanent but stationary storage of programs and data.	10 MB–500 GB
High capacity diskettes	Magnetic	Higher capacity diskettes such as Zip and Superdisk that provide higher capacity while retaining the portability of a diskette.	120 MB–750 MB
Tape	Magnetic	A magnetically coated strip of plastic used to store data.	100 KB–100 GB
USB flash drives	Chip-based	Devices that use a special type of ROM chip and plug into a USB port.	1 GB and rising

that can fit within a sector. The operating system and the drive list where data are stored by noting their track and sector numbers.

Hard disk drives are known for their access speed. High-speed disks have an access time of 9 milliseconds or less. Hard disks are generally considered to be stationary, but there are also removable hard disks.

OPTICAL DISKS

Unlike diskettes and hard disks, which use electromagnetism to encode data, optical disk systems use a laser to read and write data. The two main categories of optical disk are *compact disk (CD)* and *digital versatile disk (DVD)*. Optical disks have very large storage capacity, but they are not as fast as hard disks. A compact disk is a small, portable plastic medium that includes in its makeup a reflective surface. To record bits of data, the surface of the disk is altered to affect how light is reflected when applying a laser. CDs are commonly used to store large files that need to be portable such as software, music, and video files. The original CDs were read-only memory (CD-ROM) that only the distributor wrote on, and that the user could only read. More recently, *CD-recordable (CD-R)* and *CD-read/write (CD-R/W)* have become widely available, with most computers now coming with a CD drive that writes to CDs as well as reading them.

DVD is an optical technology, expected to rapidly replace CD technology. One side of a DVD has a capacity of 4.7 GB, enough to hold an entire feature-length movie. With two layers on each of its sides, a DVD can hold up to 17 GB of data on a disk that is basically the same size as a CD. Because standards for recordable or rewritable DVDs (DVD-R or DVD-RW) have yet to be agreed on, several possible formats exist. More and more computers now come with a DVD drive that will write as well as read disks. Emerging types of DVD storage are high definition (HD) and Blu-ray, both driven by media producers and the need to store more high quality images such as movies.

CHIP-BASED STORAGE

Flash memory is a special type of chip-based memory that can be written to as well as read into internal memory. This form of storage has quickly become a very popular way of transporting data between computers. These devices are known as *USB flash drives* and plug into the **universal serial bus (USB),** an external bus standard that supports transfer rates of 12 Mbps (megabits per second). All personal computer systems sold today contain USB ports so flash drives are becoming widespread as a portable form of memory.

USB flash drives have advantages over many other storage media, especially over 1.44-MB diskettes. Strong points include higher capacity, smaller dimensions, high reliability, and noiselessness. As a result, this technology has, for the most part, driven the 1.44-MB diskette out of the portable storage market.

STORAGE PERFORMANCE

Most personal computer systems include several types of storage devices, such as a hard disk, CD-RW drive, and DVD drive as well as multiple USB ports that allow attachment of additional units including the flash memory modules. With all of these available, you should choose the format that is appropriate for the data you wish to store and the method you choose to use. Keep in mind that capacity, portability, and the ability to write to the media are important factors. Also, think about using networks for storage. Storage services exist on the Internet, which allow you to store your data at very little cost. Network storage could provide the ultimate in portability, as most computers have access to the Internet.

Quick Test

Determine if the following statements are True or False.

1. Until recently, the most popular form of portable storage has been flash memory, but it is rapidly losing favour among computer users.

2. Most forms of optical storage remain as read-only devices.

3. The unique static bus (USB) is an external bus standard that supports transfer rates of 12 Mbps.

Answers: 1. False; 2. False; 3. False

 STUDENT RETURN ON INVESTMENT SUMMARY

1. What factors should knowledge-enabled professionals consider to optimize their use of an IT device?

The factors that a knowledge-enabled professional should consider when purchasing an IT device include the cost of the device, its compatibility with other devices in the current system, data and information needs, the device's accuracy and speed, its portability, and, finally, its form factor—that is, its size, shape, and physical arrangement. Of these, the most important criteria are meeting one's information needs, since this is the reason for its purchase in the first place.

2. How do the electronic components of IT hardware allow the transmission and storage of data?

The primary electronic component of IT hardware is the transistor, which is a very small device made out of semiconductor material that amplifies electronic signals. These transistors are combined by the millions into microprocessor chips and memory chips used by hardware devices. Transistors act as an electronic switch that can be in one of two states—off or on—and these states are represented by binary mathematics. Transistors store and transmit all data in a digital form as combinations of 1s and 0s. Binary codes are used to represent letters and numbers through character encoding, using the ASCII, EBCDIC, and Unicode encoding systems. Instructions to the computer use binary machine instructions.

3. What elements affect the processing capability of hardware?

The microprocessor contains the majority of the components that make up the central processing unit (CPU). The CPU works together with memory to control the execution of all instructions, and the processing of all data. The CPU is located on the system's motherboard, the main circuit board in an electronic device. In a PC, the motherboard contains the bus, the microprocessor, and other chips and circuits. The CPU contains a number of components including the ALU, FPU, decode unit, cache memory, prefetch unit, registers, clock, one or more buses, and the instruction set, which enable it to carry out the required processing. Microprocessors are typically differentiated by their instruction set, their clock speed, and their bandwidth, which is the number of bits that the CPU can process in a single instruction. The CPU clock speed is the most commonly used performance characteristic.

4. How does internal memory work to enable processing of data into information?

Computers have both long-term memory (read-only memory, ROM) and short-term memory (random access memory, RAM). Both types of memory store data and instructions on computer chips. The main purpose of ROM is simply to hold unalterable instructions known as the BIOS (basic input/output system), which control the device's start-up processes (booting up). Most memory is in the form of RAM. Most personal computers include two types of RAM: dynamic RAM (DRAM) and static RAM (SRAM). DRAM is used in main memory, and SRAM is used in cache memory. All data and instructions in DRAM are lost when the computer is turned off. RAM can also be found in other computer system components such as the printer and video and sound cards. This type of RAM is often referred to as peripheral RAM. Memory capacity is measured in terms of the number of bytes that it may store. Capacities of most types of memory are in the range of thousands (kilobytes, KB) and millions (megabytes, MB) of bytes.

5. How can the type of input hardware help to make knowledge work more productive?

The primary types of input hardware are the keyboard, pointing devices such as the mouse, scanning devices such as bar code readers, and the Internet or other network connection. The keyboard is generally recognized as the primary and most common input device for computers. It uses keys to transmit letters, digits, or other characters to the CPU for processing. Pointing devices, which work along with a GUI, allow the user to provide data and instructions to the computer using physical movements such as "point" and "click." As the user moves the pointing device, the graphical interface echoes the movement. Scanning devices read data and information stored on some form of non-connected media. Most scanning devices work closely with special software and databases. Software encodes the image in binary, or recognizes characteristics of the scanned image.

6. Why should knowledge-enabled professionals keep current about new developments in output hardware?

Output devices deliver the result of processing operations to the user. Output devices include display and printed output devices, storage devices, the Internet or other network connection, and a wide variety of other electronic devices. Display devices continue to be the most common category of output device. When coupled with speakers, display devices deliver almost every data format, ranging from plain text documents to movies with sound. Display devices are also a significant component for input. Most display devices today use the liquid crystal display (LCD) technology, which uses a piece of liquid crystal material placed between a pair of transparent electrodes. An LCD display consists of an array of cells (pixels) that can be controlled individually to create the image, and they can be active-matrix or passive-matrix displays. Display performance is a function of its dot pitch, refresh rate, and physical size.

A variety of printing devices allow a range of quality and options in outputting both text and graphics. The most popular technologies for printers are ink-jet, laser, and thermal. Ink-jet shoots ink on paper to create text and images, while laser printers use the same technology as copiers. Thermal printers use heat to create text and images on a specially coated paper.

7. What types of secondary storage should be used to safely store data?

Because of the limited amount of internal storage and the volatility of RAM, some form of external storage is necessary to permanently store data and programs. This secondary storage comes as magnetic storage media, optical disks, and chip-based flash memory. Stored information is accessed by internal memory when the control unit decides that this information is needed. Because the secondary storage unit must locate the information, read it, and then transfer it to internal memory, secondary storage is a slower form of memory than internal memory. However, this disadvantage is balanced by virtually unlimited storage capacity.

Magnetic disks store information in a form of direct-access storage that allows information to be obtained in any order. Types of disk storage include diskettes, high-capacity disks, and hard drives. Optical disk systems use a laser to read and write data. The two main categories of optical disk are compact disk (CD) and digital versatile disk (DVD). Optical disks have very large storage capacity, but they are not as fast as hard disks. Flash memory is a special type of chip-based memory, located at a universal serial bus (USB) port.

KNOWLEDGE SPEAK

TECH GUIDE

The Details of Software

WHAT WE WILL COVER

- Overview of the Operating System

- What Does the Operating System Do?

- Overview of Application Software

- Developing Customized Software

ROI STUDENT RETURN ON INVESTMENT

Through your investment of time in reading and thinking about this guide, your return, or created value, is gaining knowledge. Use the following questions as a study guide.

1. Why is the operating system so important to the use of all types of computers?

2. What are the functions of the operating system?

3. How do knowledge-enabled professionals obtain and use application software?

4. What are the purpose and tools used in the software development process?

Software provides the instructions that IT hardware needs. The two major categories of software are operating system software and application software. Except in special situations, both software types run at the same time, each serving a different purpose. In this Tech Guide, we discuss operating systems and application software and the process of programming that IT professionals use to create software. We begin our discussion with an overview and comparison of operating systems.

OVERVIEW OF THE OPERATING SYSTEM

The operating system (OS) serves as the computer's "traffic cop," "office manager," and "chauffeur." As traffic cop, the OS manages all of the message traffic that flows from the user, to the application software, to the computer, and back again to the user. It is an "office manager" because it handles the allocation of resources and the assignment of tasks to various software programs. Finally, it is a "chauffeur" because the operating system enables users to get to their destination—that is, carry out needed tasks with application software—without worrying about the hardware interfaces.

For example, the OS monitors the keyboard and mouse to determine when users provide input to the computer. It also manages the video screen and printer to provide output from the computer. The operating system controls the operation of secondary storage, to transfer data back and forth between secondary storage and main memory. Finally, the operating system controls the execution of application programs.

For desktop PCs and laptops, the most common operating systems include Microsoft's Windows family, the UNIX family (including Linux), and Macintosh operating systems (Mac OS X). In the next sections, we look at operating systems in more detail, how they work, and what tasks they perform. We also compare these operating systems with those for mainframes, networks, and hand-held devices such as mobile phones and PDAs.

COMPARISON OF OPERATING SYSTEMS

The functions of the operating system apply to all computers, regardless of size. However, there are important differences between the operating systems for mainframes, networks, personal computers, and hand-held devices. The primary differences among the four operating systems are the numbers of users and the complexity of the peripheral devices that they manage. Mainframes and network operating systems manage multi-user systems, while most personal computer and hand-held device operating systems deal with only a single user.

Further, dealing with multiple users requires mainframe and network operating systems to have sophisticated security systems. For personal computers and hand-held devices, most users maintain a minimal security system, depending on their location and use. However, security is becoming more of an issue with hand-held devices due to additional wireless capabilities and storage of important data.

Mainframes must manage a large number of storage, input, and output devices. A network operating system must manage numerous hard drives, backup devices, and printers. On the other hand, a personal computer system usually has at most three or four storage devices, keyboard and mouse, printer, monitor, and set of speakers. Hand-held devices usually do not have peripheral devices. Because of these differences, mainframe operating systems are extremely large programs that require a staff of systems programmers to maintain them. Network operating systems may also be quite large, requiring support from individuals with special training and certification on the particular network operating system. On the other hand, operating systems for personal computers and hand-held devices are usually simple and need only periodic maintenance.

All four types of operating systems are multitasking systems, enabling the computer to work on more than one job or program concurrently. Table B.1 compares the mainframe, network, personal computer, and hand-held device operating systems in terms of number of users, security, number of peripherals, number of tasks performed, and support that each requires.

HOW THE OPERATING SYSTEM WORKS

The operating system is the foundation upon which all other software works. As such, the operating system is crucial to the operation of the computer. Yet, it is the least visible form of software in a computer. The only direct outputs from an operating system, to either the screen or the printer, are login requests (when the system asks for your user ID and password), error messages, and configuration choices (the settings that you can choose for your system).

All operating systems consist of two parts: the kernel and the command interpreter. The **kernel** is the essential part of the operating system, which internal memory must always include. It handles requests from either application programs or hardware (often printers

Table B.1	Comparison of Operating Systems			
Feature	Mainframe	Network	Personal Computer	Hand-held Device
Number of simultaneous users	Multiple	Multiple	One	One
Security	Sophisticated	Sophisticated	Minimal/ user-enabled	Minimal/ user-enabled
Peripherals	Complex	Numerous	Few	Few
Number of tasks	Many	Many	Many	Few
Support	Systems programmers	Networked-certified personnel	User	Provider
Example	OS390	Novell NOS	Windows XP	Windows Mobile

or input devices) and then determines the processing order of the requests. Regardless of how fast something seems to happen from a user's perspective, most computers can accomplish only one task at a time (in actuality, this depends on the number of processors—one task per processor at a time). The kernel also handles demands for internal memory from competing applications, by parcelling out the limited amount of internal memory as needed.

The **command interpreter** (often referred to as the *shell* in UNIX operating systems) accepts commands from users and translates them into language that the kernel can understand. Users typically communicate with the command interpreter through a *graphical user interface (GUI)*, like that used in Windows or Macintosh operating systems. The GUI acts as a shell to interact with the command interpreter. For UNIX systems, the GUI converts the user's mouse clicks into the appropriate text commands, which the operating system understands. The primary exception to this is the OS390 operating system used on most IBM mainframes and application servers. That OS command interpreter requires entering text commands that use a special syntax.

In addition to accepting commands from users through text commands or a GUI, the operating system also accepts commands from application programs through its **application program interface (API)**. The API is a specific process that allows the application program to make requests to the operating system or another application. For example, when you click the File|Print command or the Print icon on a Windows program, an API accepts this command and sends it to the operating system. The OS then communicates with the printer hardware to generate the desired output. Figure B.1

Figure B.1 Layers of an operating system.

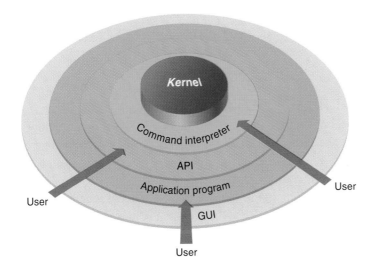

shows how the kernel, command interpreter, and API work together. Note that the user either communicates with the operating system kernel through an application program and API or through the command interpreter.

Quick Test

Match the operating system characteristic with the type of computer system.

1. Multiple simultaneous users	a. Mainframe and networks
2. Multiple tasks	b. Personal computers and hand-held devices
3. Minimal or no security	c. All types of computers

Answers: 1. a; 2. c; 3. b

WHAT DOES THE OPERATING SYSTEM DO?

For any computer, regardless of whether it is a mainframe or other large server, a stand-alone or networked PC, or a stationary or hand-held device, the operating system is a collection of software programs that manages the following tasks:

1. Starting the computer
2. Managing hardware
3. Controlling access to the computer
4. Providing an interface for the user
5. Ensuring efficient use of the CPU
6. Providing services to application software

STARTING THE COMPUTER

Users must start, or **boot**, all computers. This start-up procedure relies on the use of the *read-only memory (ROM)* chip, which permanently stores the booting instructions. Because of its size and the number of hardware elements attached to it, booting a mainframe, termed the *initial program load (IPL)*, often takes many steps and some amount of time. On the other hand, to start a personal computer with a hard disk, users simply turn on the computer. The time it takes to start a personal computer depends more on how many

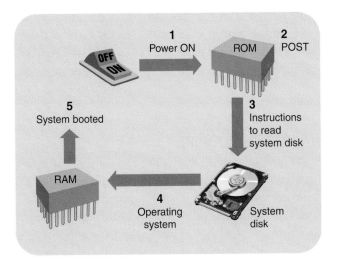

Figure B.2 The boot (start-up) process of a computer.

application programs will be initially started than how long it takes the OS to boot up. The ROM chip and hard drive then take care of the following booting steps, as Figure B.2 shows:

1. Turning on the computer's main power sends a flow of electricity to ROM.
2. The flow of electricity to ROM causes the BIOS (basic input/output system) to provide instructions to the CPU to perform a **power-on self-test (POST)**, which checks the various components of the computer, including memory, to ensure that they are working correctly.
3. After the POST, ROM/BIOS tells the CPU to find the system disk (usually the hard disk) and read operating system programs from secondary storage.
4. The CPU loads operating system files into internal memory (RAM).
5. The CPU implements instructions in the operating system files and then displays the OS interface.

At one time, a floppy disk (1.44-MByte capacity or smaller) contained the system programs, which the user had to insert in the computer before booting. Now the hard disk stores the operating system (Microsoft says that your system needs 1.5 GByte of available hard disk space to run Windows XP Professional and 15 GByte for Windows Vista[1]) and your PC is instructed, via the BIOS, how to start up the operating system. The BIOS is specific to your PC and

---

1. "Windows XP Professional System Requirements," www.microsoft.com/windowsxp/pro/evaluation/sysreqs.mspx, retrieved August 24, 2001; "Windows Vista System Requirements," http://www.microsoft.com/windows/products/windowsvista/buyorupgrade/capable.mspx, retrieved February 16, 2007.

prepares it so that other software can load and execute. In the case of booting your computer, you can access the BIOS to change the boot instructions if you want to start your computer from a floppy disk, or more likely, from a CD. Why would you want to do this? This is a common cure for a system failure or when your PC has a virus.

MANAGING HARDWARE

One of the most important tasks of the operating system is to act as a go-between for the user, software, and the hardware system. To do this, the operating system must control a large number of hardware elements. It must also manage the flow of data into the computer as well as information out of it. Finally, the OS monitors the use of internal memory by tracking application and user memory space, and protecting one from encroaching on the other.

Hardware management includes **input/output (I/O) tasks**. For example, the OS accepts input data, such as commands from a keyboard, and coordinates its output, such as the printing of a document. Other I/O tasks include the transfer of data, instructions, and information between the CPU, internal memory, and secondary storage elements (e.g., CD-ROM drive, flash memory). I/O also includes the transfer of data and information over the telephone modem, cable modem, DSL connection, or LAN connection.

Since mainframes serve multiple users, their operating systems must manage numerous hardware elements, including disk drives, tape drives, printers, communications equipment, and user workstations. Further, a mainframe OS must accomplish all this while minimizing delays for users and ensuring their access to the needed hardware elements. On the other hand, with only one user, the hardware control problem for a personal computer is much less complicated. However, it does involve many of the same elements as the mainframe system, plus such items as the mouse for GUI, speakers for audio output, and DVD players. Finally, in addition to the devices a stand-alone PC operating system must control, a network operating system controls the communications between the local PCs on the network and other network resources such as various printers and a tape backup for the file server. (We discuss networks in greater detail in Tech Guide C.)

CONTROLLING ACCESS

Once the computer is up and running, unless it is a stand-alone PC, the OS must control access to it. For mainframe computers or networked PCs, the operating system must provide security to users' data, information, and programs against unwarranted intrusion. The most recent operating systems require users to enter a password to access the computer, limiting their access to specific "areas."

PROVIDING AN INTERFACE

No matter the size or type of computer, it must have an interface with which the user interacts. Currently, most mainframe operating systems and some server computer operating systems, like *UNIX*, are still command-driven and use text commands. The commands necessary for a mainframe operating system tend to be very complex. In fact, they constitute a computer language of their own, called a **job control language (JCL)**. To work with a mainframe, you must learn this language of operating system commands just like you learn a programming language to create computer software. Figure B.3 shows an example of the JCL to run an application program on an IBM 390.

On the other hand, virtually all personal computer operating systems like Windows, Mac OS, and UNIX use a GUI. However, prior to the widespread use of these operating systems, users had to learn to use a text-based command line system called **DOS (disk operating system)**. In fact, it is still possible to use DOS commands with Windows by requesting the DOS window from the Start| Programs menu. For example, Figure B.4 shows the use of the DOS DIR/W (wide) command to list files and folders in multiple columns. Note that since DOS does not support long file names, the program uses the tilde (~) and a number as abbreviation. For example, the second file in the first column, named misresources.xls, becomes misres ~ 1.xls. To distinguish them from files, folders are enclosed in brackets []. Microsoft includes DOS with Windows to ensure *upward compatibility* for application software; that is, Windows will run software written for DOS.

```
000100 //@DPCTAPE JOB USER=@DPC,PASSWORD=&PW,NOTIFY=@DPC,
000200 //           GROUP=I143,MSGCLASS=X,TIME=99,REGION=999K
000300 //*MAIN     CLASS=PD,LINES=99
000400 //*****************************************************************
000500 //***==>THIS JOB WILL PRINT &REC RECORDS FROM SYSUT1.
000600 //***==>IT ASSUMES A CATALOGUED TAPE.
000620 //*****************************************************************
000700 //UFAU02    EXEC PGM=DSDUMP,PARM='/LRECLSYSIN=72'
000800 //SYSUT1    DD DSN=BA.PMMP06.YTD99,DISP=SHR,
000900 //           UNIT=TAPE62,DCB=DEN=4
001200 //SYSPRINT DD SYSOUT=F
001300 //SYSIN    DD *
001400 HARDCOPY='PRINT',STOPAFT=&REC;
001500 /*
001600 //
```

Figure B.3 Sample job control language (JCL) code for a mainframe computer.

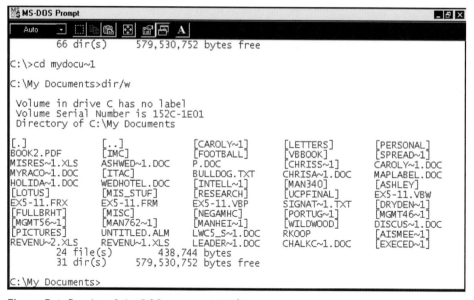

Figure B.4 Results of the DOS command DIR/W.

EFFICIENT USE OF CPU

In any computer system, the CPU always works much faster than the I/O operations. As a result, a key task of the operating system is to ensure that the slow I/O does not hold up the CPU. This is especially important for a mainframe, so that the processing for one user does not delay other users' I/O. Even on a personal computer, it would be inefficient for the CPU to wait on one task—for example, printing a job—before continuing its work.

To keep the I/O from interfering with processing, the OS directs the CPU to run programs concurrently. That is, the CPU processes part of one program, then part of another, then part of a third, and so on until the CPU has worked on all of them. The OS places the jobs in a queue (waiting line) to be executed according to their level of priority. It gives each job an extremely small amount of CPU time, called a time-slice, during which the CPU executes a portion of the job. Thus, the OS allows CPU **multitasking**, which mainframes have done for many years. Personal computers now also widely use multitasking, due to the increase in CPU speed and amount of internal memory. Because a mainframe has multiple users as well as multiple tasks, it usually also has a secondary processor to handle I/O, while the CPU handles the multiple tasks and users. Network operating systems usually handle the problem of efficiently using the server's CPU by shifting a significant portion of the processing burden from the central file server CPU to CPUs of the local PCs.

Multitasking is often confused with **parallel processing**, but they are quite different. With multitasking, the CPU only handles a part of one task at a time. With parallel processing, the multiple CPUs in the same computer handle either multiple different jobs or multiple parts of the same job at the same time. Think of the difference between multitasking and parallel processing as playing catch with yourself with five different balls.

If you multitask, you pick up one ball, toss it, catch it, put it down, pick up the next ball, and repeat the "toss-and-catch" process. If you parallel process, you are juggling: tossing and catching all five balls at once. We all know that juggling is harder than catching one ball at a time. Similarly, this is why multitasking is much more widespread than true parallel processing. Incidentally, newer microprocessors are being made as *dual-core* or *multi-core processors*. This is like having two or more processors on one chip. Having more than one processor enables PCs to parallel process, to some extent, and begins to address our need to multitask. Intel has introduced its Core™2 Quad microprocessor that contains four processing cores to power demanding PC functions for games and entertainment.

PROVIDING SERVICES TO APPLICATION SOFTWARE

While the operating system tasks just discussed are important to the operation of all computers, the main objective of an operating system is to provide services to application software. After all, the primary reason that most knowledge-enabled professionals use a computer is to run application software to create business value. Operating systems provide a number of services to application software, including the following:

- Running the application software and ensuring the availability of needed resources
- Determining the processing order of concurrently running programs
- Coordinating file/disk management
- Providing memory management

Running Application Software

The operating system must make it possible for the user to run application software. It does this by interpreting the instructions from the other software to the CPU and providing resources in the form of hardware devices when needed by the other software program. For example, when the user instructs a word processing program to print a document, the application software issues a command to the operating system, which handles the printing job. Network operating systems are not usually involved in running application software. Instead, the operating system on each individual PC handles this role. It is important to note that only certain applications run on certain operating systems. For example, you cannot run MS Office applications on the Linux operating system without special APIs. Even with the APIs, the full functionality of the application may not be available. Therefore, your choice of operating system may determine the application software you can use.

Determining the Processing Order

Modern computers are multitasking machines running multiple programs concurrently. For example, you may create a document, work with a spreadsheet, query a database, and print a series of presentation slides, all *seemingly* at the same time. In most cases, one job runs in the foreground, with other jobs processed in the background. The Windows operating systems show programs running concurrently as buttons on the task bar, usually displayed at the bottom of the screen. Figure B.5 shows an example of this process for Windows XP, where the foreground application is Microsoft Word. Background programs include Excel, Microsoft Project, Internet Explorer, Adobe Acrobat, and iTunes.

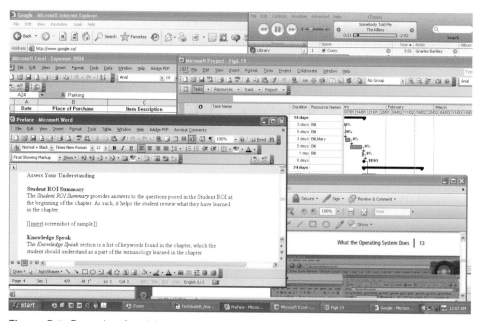

Figure B.5 Example of multiple programs running concurrently in Windows.

The operating system must decide which task takes priority, not just between foreground and background jobs, but also between the various background jobs. Setting priorities depends on various criteria, some of which the user may set, others which the operating system defines.

Coordinating File/Disk Management

The operating system must manage files on secondary storage (usually some form of hard disk) in such a way to make them available when needed, while also protecting them from unwarranted use or loss. A variety of file types are necessary to use application software, including data files, program files, and utility files. For example, program files execute application software, data files include specific information already entered by the user, and utility files provide assistance, such as spell-check ability.

For example, say you want to create a letter. To run a word processor in the Windows operating system, you click the appropriate icon. The operating system must know the location of the word processor program files, as well as the location of a variety of utility files known as *dynamic link library (dll)* files. After you specify the location, the OS must also know where to save the result of your work (or where to find a previously saved document). On the other hand, if you click on a data file, the OS must detect the corresponding application software to launch. The file management element of the Windows operating system handles all of these operations. The same is true of the Mac OS X and Linux operating systems. It is important to note that often files, such as dll's, are not stored in the application folder on a PC, but in the case of Windows, they are saved in the Windows folder. When you want to delete an application, you should always uninstall it, not delete the application folder directly. Uninstalling ensures all of the application is removed from memory.

Mainframe and PC network systems have multiple users storing their files on centrally located disk and tape drives, so their operating system must track where files are stored and who may receive access to them. For this reason, security is an important element of a mainframe operating system. For networks, the operating system must also monitor software on the file server, to restrict access to only those who have rights to use it.

On personal computers, the operating systems must accomplish the same file management tasks as for mainframes and network servers but usually for only one user. While security is slightly less important, file management continues to be crucial. Also, files on a personal computer hard disk are usually not stored as one contiguous unit. As a result, the operating system must be able to reassemble the parts of a file from many separate locations on the disk. The OS handles this via a table of the various files parts and their locations on the disk, called the **file allocation table (FAT)**. Because files are not contiguous, file fragmentation can occur. When this occurs, fragments of files are not stored efficiently, making it hard for your PC to recombine them, which reduces system performance. To solve this problem, you can run a defragmentation utility on your PC. After you have "defragged," you will usually notice an improvement in the speed of your PC.

The OS also provides file management tools to help users organize files for easy access and retrieval. Virtually all operating systems now use a *hierarchical* (tree) structure that divides a long list of files into several shorter lists, called folders. For example, assume that a company stores personnel files on disk for the employees in its 12 branches around the world. Each branch has between three and six departments. If the company has at least 10 employees in each department, the computer would store at least 360 ($12 \times 3 \times 10$) files. With a single folder on the hard disk, finding a particular employee's file might take time. However, as Figure B.6 illustrates,

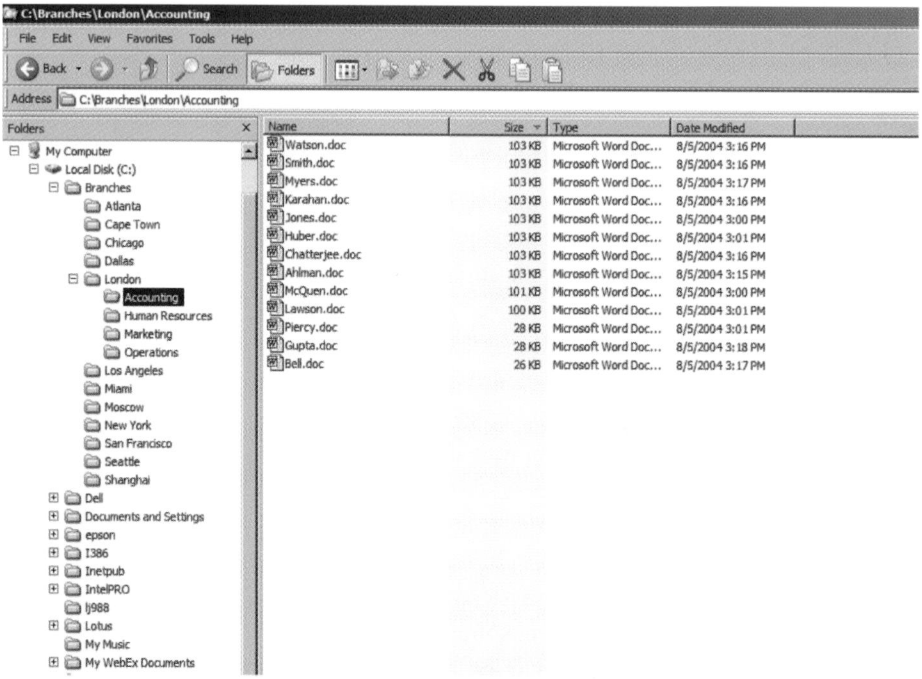

Figure B.6 The Windows hierarchical-based file structure.

using the Windows Explorer utility to create a hierarchical structure to organize files resolves this issue.

Providing Memory Management

Unlike the nearly unlimited secondary storage, internal memory continues to be a scarce resource and must be managed in several ways. First, because multiple programs often run concurrently, the operating system must ensure that these programs don't conflict when using memory or that there is even enough memory to run them. The operating system also tries to partition the various applications in such a way that an error in one does not cause the entire system to fail or lock up (commonly referred to as "crashing").

Second, even with the large amounts of memory in modern computers, they still need more. One technique, which began with mainframe computers in the mid-1970s, provides the appearance of additional memory: virtual memory. **Virtual memory** divides the internal memory into pages, or sections, that match equal-size sections of memory on disk. The process then exchanges, or swaps, internal memory with the disk or virtual memory when needed. As long as the processing needs only data or instructions that are currently in internal memory, it proceeds as usual. However, when the needed information is on disk, virtual memory swaps a page into main memory. The CPU tries to "think" ahead, to determine which pages from virtual memory will be needed next. As a result, the apparent memory exceeds the actual internal memory without great loss of processing speed. Virtual memory greatly enhances the ability of mainframes to run multiple jobs at high speeds. Personal computers also use virtual memory to expand their apparent memory capacity.

Has your PC ever been so slow that you could have grabbed a coffee before it was finished saving your Word document? This could be an indication that your PC is not managing memory well. Sometimes this occurs simply because you have too many applications open and your RAM is overloaded. Other times it could be because you have a memory leak or your hard drive needs to be defragged. In the case of a memory leak, you can use the task manager in Windows to identify applications and processes that are using a lot of memory and end them. Because RAM is constantly accessed to randomly write, read, and store to memory, it can get fragmented. You can use your PC's defragmentation utility to correct this. Of course, a reboot, which ends all processes, can also be effective in the short term.

Quick Test

Fill in the blanks for the following statements.

1. The ROM chip is most important in the _____ operating system function.

2. Subdirectories are important in the _____ operating system function.

3. _____ uses disk storage to give the appearance of additional internal memory.

Answers: 1. boot; 2. file management; 3. virtual memory

OVERVIEW OF APPLICATION SOFTWARE

You should now have a better understanding of how operating system software allows us to use hardware devices effectively. However, by far, the largest amount of software available to the computer user is in the area of application software. Knowledge-enabled professionals typically use either commercially developed (also known as *commercial off-the-shelf [COTS] software*) or custom-developed application software.

COMMERCIALLY DEVELOPED APPLICATION SOFTWARE

Commercially developed application software is used for a wide variety of tasks and is often mass-marketed. The most widely used commercially developed software categories used by knowledge-enabled professionals include the following:

- Word processing programs to create documents
- Spreadsheets and accounting software to carry out financial and other quantitative analyses
- Database programs to manage lists and tables of data
- Presentation programs to create electronic slide shows
- Web browsers and other Internet-related software
- Specialized software for specific industry needs

Many of these applications are often sold together in a bundle known as a **software application suite** such as Microsoft Office. The major benefit of a software suite is that each application in the suite has similar functions (e.g., Copy/Paste) and these functions can be executed across applications (e.g., copy a table in MS Excel and paste in MS Word). In the next sections, we will briefly discuss six types of common software.

Word Processing Software

Word processing software, part of a larger category known as *document preparation software,* allows us to easily compose, edit, save, and print various types of documents. Because word processing software almost directly replaces handwritten documents, most knowledge-enabled professionals often learn it first (other than games). Among other advantages, word processing software allows efficient creation and editing of text documents. **Desktop publishing software** takes word processing one step further. It combines word processing, graphics, and special page definition software to create documents that rival those available from professional typesetting companies.

Spreadsheets

If we consider word processing as a replacement for handwritten documents, the spreadsheet is an even more powerful replacement for the calculator. Knowledge-enabled professionals use it as the tool for almost any type of financial or quantitative analysis. To understand why, let's consider it in some depth. To start, a **spreadsheet** is an electronic table of rows and columns, with the intersection of a row and a column being termed a **cell**. The column letter and row number identifies each cell. For example, in Figure B.7, the highlighted cell, cell B5, is located in column B and row 5.

Knowledge-enabled professionals enter column values, labels, and formulas into cells to create business models. The formulas typically use the addresses of other cells to create relationships between them. For example, Column G in Figure B.7 automatically calculates the margin for a given item, equal to the selling price (column D), times the number sold (column E), minus store cost (column F) times the number sold (column E). For backpacks (G4), the margin formula in G4 is thus $=D4*E4-(F4*E4)$. Note the use of the asterisk (*) for the multiplication operation in this formula. Note also that the spreadsheet performs mathematical operations in the same order that we do, e.g., multiplication first, then subtraction. The spreadsheet software uses the "mathematical horsepower" of your computer to efficiently determine the correct solution.

Spreadsheet software accomplishes other tasks to help knowledge-enabled professionals. In the preceding example, the sales manager used the *Sort* tool in this spreadsheet software to automatically list the items according to item type. He or she also added a section to allow the spreadsheet to automatically calculate the total margin for

Microsoft Excel - WildOutfitters.xls

Weekly Sales at WildOutfitters.com

Sales Date	Item Code	Item Type	Retail Price	Units Sold	Our Cost	Margin
05/01/06	BP	Backpack	$165.00	2	$80.00	$170.00
05/01/06	BP	Backpack	$165.00	2	$80.00	$170.00
05/02/06	BP	Backpack	$165.00	1	$80.00	$85.00
05/03/06	BP	Backpack	$165.00	1	$80.00	$85.00
05/04/06	BP	Backpack	$165.00	1	$80.00	$85.00
05/05/06	BP	Backpack	$165.00	2	$80.00	$170.00
05/06/06	BP	Backpack	$165.00	2	$80.00	$170.00
05/07/06	BP	Backpack	$165.00	1	$80.00	$85.00
05/01/06	HB	Hiking Boot	$110.00	4	$50.00	$240.00
05/02/06	HB	Hiking Boot	$110.00	6	$50.00	$360.00
05/03/06	HB	Hiking Boot	$110.00	3	$50.00	$180.00
05/04/06	HB	Hiking Boot	$110.00	2	$50.00	$120.00
05/05/06	HB	Hiking Boot	$110.00	1	$50.00	$60.00
05/06/06	HB	Hiking Boot	$110.00	6	$50.00	$360.00
05/07/06	HB	Hiking Boot	$110.00	2	$50.00	$120.00
05/01/06	SB	Sleeping B	$100.00	2	$45.00	$110.00
05/02/06	SB	Sleeping B	$100.00	3	$45.00	$165.00
05/03/06	SB	Sleeping B	$100.00	1	$45.00	$55.00
05/04/06	SB	Sleeping B	$100.00	2	$45.00	$110.00
05/05/06	SB	Sleeping B	$100.00	1	$45.00	$55.00
05/06/06	SB	Sleeping B	$100.00	2	$45.00	$110.00
05/07/06	SB	Sleeping B	$100.00	2	$45.00	$110.00
05/01/06	TT	Tent	$385.00	1	$100.00	$285.00
05/02/06	TT	Tent	$385.00	2	$100.00	$570.00
05/03/06	TT	Tent	$385.00	1	$100.00	$285.00
05/04/06	TT	Tent	$385.00	1	$100.00	$285.00
05/05/06	TT	Tent	$385.00	1	$100.00	$285.00
05/06/06	TT	Tent	$385.00	1	$100.00	$285.00
05/07/06	TT	Tent	$385.00	1	$100.00	$285.00

Margin by Item Type

Item Type	Total Units Sold	Total Margin
Backpack	12	$1,020.00
Hiking Boots	24	$1,440.00
Sleeping Bag	13	$715.00
Tent	8	$2,280.00
Total		$5,455.00

Percentage Sales by Item

- $1,020.00, 19%
- $2,280.00, 42%
- $1,440.00, 26%
- $715.00, 13%

Legend: Backpack, Hiking Boots, Sleeping Bag, Tent

Figure B.7 Spreadsheets are an effective tool for tracking and analyzing product sales.

each product type. Finally, they used the software to automatically generate a chart showing percentage sales by product type.

Another useful aspect of a spreadsheet is that, when a value changes in a cell that is involved in a formula cell, the value in the formula cell may change also, depending on the relationship. For example, say WildOutfitters (from Figure B.7) sells three backpacks instead of two and updates the value in the spreadsheet. The spreadsheet then automatically changes both the margin for backpacks and the margin for the seven-day period to reflect the increased number of backpacks sold. This capability enables knowledge-enabled professionals to perform *what-if analyses* by changing the values in cells and quickly seeing the results.

For example, assume the WildOutfitters marketing department suggests running an advertising campaign for the four products shown in Figure B.7; that is, hiking boots, backpacks, sleeping bags, and tents. The marketing department believes this campaign will generate a 15 percent increase in unit sales for the four products. However, the cost of this campaign will result in a 10 percent increase in the cost to the company for each of the four items, which, due to competitive pressures, *cannot* be passed along to customers in the form of higher prices. The question is: Given these assumptions, should

Microsoft Excel - WildOutfitters.xls

File Edit View Insert Format Tools Data Window Help Acrobat

Weekly Sales at WildOutfitters.com

Sales Date	Item Code	Item Type	Retail Price	Units Sold	Our Cost	Margin
05/01/06	BP	Backpack	$165.00	2	$80.00	$170.00
05/01/06	BP	Backpack	$165.00	2	$80.00	$170.00
05/02/06	BP	Backpack	$165.00	1	$80.00	$85.00
05/03/06	BP	Backpack	$165.00	1	$80.00	$85.00
05/04/06	BP	Backpack	$165.00	1	$80.00	$85.00
05/05/06	BP	Backpack	$165.00	2	$80.00	$170.00
05/06/06	BP	Backpack	$165.00	2	$80.00	$170.00
05/07/06	BP	Backpack	$165.00	1	$80.00	$85.00
05/01/06	HB	Hiking Boo	$110.00	4	$50.00	$240.00
05/02/06	HB	Hiking Boo	$110.00	6	$50.00	$360.00
05/03/06	HB	Hiking Boo	$110.00	3	$50.00	$180.00
05/04/06	HB	Hiking Boo	$110.00	2	$50.00	$120.00
05/05/06	HB	Hiking Boo	$110.00	1	$50.00	$60.00
05/06/06	HB	Hiking Boo	$110.00	6	$50.00	$360.00
05/07/06	HB	Hiking Boo	$110.00	2	$50.00	$120.00
05/01/06	SB	Sleeping E	$100.00	2	$45.00	$110.00
05/02/06	SB	Sleeping E	$100.00	3	$45.00	$165.00
05/03/06	SB	Sleeping E	$100.00	1	$45.00	$55.00
05/04/06	SB	Sleeping E	$100.00	2	$45.00	$110.00
05/05/06	SB	Sleeping E	$100.00	1	$45.00	$55.00
05/06/06	SB	Sleeping E	$100.00	2	$45.00	$110.00
05/07/06	SB	Sleeping E	$100.00	2	$45.00	$110.00
05/01/06	TT	Tent	$385.00	1	$100.00	$285.00
05/02/06	TT	Tent	$385.00	2	$100.00	$670.00
05/03/06	TT	Tent	$385.00	1	$100.00	$285.00
05/04/06	TT	Tent	$385.00	1	$100.00	$285.00
05/05/06	TT	Tent	$385.00	1	$100.00	$285.00
05/06/06	TT	Tent	$385.00	1	$100.00	$285.00
05/07/06	TT	Tent	$385.00	1	$100.00	$285.00

Margin by Item Type

Item Type	Total Units Sold	Total Margin
Backpack	12	$1,020.00
Hiking Boots	24	$1,440.00
Sleeping Bag	13	$715.00
Tent	8	$2,280.00
Total		$5,455.00

Analysis of Advertising Campaign

Item Type	New Cost	Total Units Sold	Total Margin
Backpack	$88.00	14	$1,078.00
Hiking Boo	$55.00	28	$1,540.00
Sleeping E	$49.50	15	$757.50
Tent	$110.00	9	$2,475.00
Total			$5,850.50

Percentage Sales by Item

- $1,020.00, 19%
- $2,280.00, 42%
- $1,440.00, 26%
- $715.00, 13%

Legend: Backpack, Hiking Boots, Sleeping Bag, Tent

Figure B.8 Using existing spreadsheet information, such as that shown in Figure B.7, knowledge-enabled professionals can perform a series of "what-if" analyses.

the campaign be run? On the face of it, it seems like a "no-brainer." A 15 percent increase in unit sales should more than outweigh effects of a 10 percent increase in costs. Modifying the spreadsheet by inputting this revised information should back up this assumption.

Figure B.8, the revised spreadsheet, shows the new costs, the new units sold, and the margin figures (columns M through P). Note that the new total margin is $5,850.50, as compared with the existing total margin of $5,455.00. So, while there is a higher total margin using the assumptions for the advertising campaign given by the marketing department, the increase is far less than expected, with less than a 1 percent increase in total margin. Based on this what-if analysis, the company should study this issue further before initiating the advertising campaign.

Performing analyses requires the knowledge-enabled professional to explore many different possibilities to determine the meaning of the raw data after the data have been transformed. As a knowledge-enabled professional, you can expect that your early positions will require that you analyze a question or proposal, like the advertising proposal discussed in the preceding example.

Database Software

Another popular way to transform data into a usable form is to organize them by entering the data into *database management software.*

(We cover database management systems in greater detail in Tech Guide D.) Although the data are often input in a tabular form similar to that of a spreadsheet, the purpose differs. Spreadsheets assist in quantitative analysis, whereas a database locates information that matches some criteria. That is, it can be difficult to alter a database table to calculate margin as easily as you can change a spreadsheet, but you can use it to easily search for all sales of a particular item, say, the backpack.

A database often results in less redundancy than if using a spreadsheet. Why? The data in a database can be spread over a series of *related* tables. So while Figure B.7 shows the name, item code, price, and store cost for every transaction, using related tables in a database, as Figure B.9 shows, reduces this redundant information. Note how Figure B.9 shows the data on hiking item sales as they would appear in two related tables—a Transaction table and an ItemData table—for a popular database management system, Microsoft Access.

Further, databases allow users to locate information quickly, through queries. A **query** is a specially structured request to a database to locate a desired set of records. In our example, say you want to locate information on backpacks. You would therefore

TranNum	DateSold	Code	Number
5	5/1/2006	BP	2
6	5/2/2006	BP	1
10	5/3/2006	BP	1
15	5/4/2006	BP	1
18	5/5/2006	BP	2
22	5/6/2006	BP	2
26	5/7/2006	BP	1
4	5/1/2006	BP	2
1	5/1/2006	HB	4
7	5/2/2006	HB	6
11	5/3/2006	HB	3
17	5/4/2006	HB	2
19	5/5/2006	HB	1
23	5/6/2006	HB	6
27	5/7/2006	HB	2
3	5/1/2006	SB	2
9	5/2/2006	SB	3
13	5/3/2006	SB	1
14	5/4/2006	SB	2
21	5/5/2006	SB	1
25	5/6/2006	SB	2
29	5/7/2006	SB	2
2	5/1/2006	TT	1
8	5/2/2006	TT	2
12	5/3/2006	TT	1
16	5/4/2006	TT	1
20	5/5/2006	TT	1
24	5/6/2006	TT	1
28	5/7/2006	TT	1
0			

Record: 1 of 29

ItemData : Table

ItemCode	ItemName	ItemPrice	ItemCost
BP	Backpack	$165.00	$80.00
HB	Hiking Books	$110.00	$50.00
SB	Sleeping Bag	$100.00	$45.00
TT	Tent	$385.00	$100.00
		$0.00	$0.00

Record: 1 of 4

Figure B.9 Databases often result in less redundancy than spreadsheets.

BackpacksSold : Select Query					_	□	×
ItemName	ItemPrice	ItemCost	DateSold	Number	Gross Profit
▶ Backpack	$165.00	$80.00	5/1/2006	2	$170.00
Backpack	$165.00	$80.00	5/2/2006	1	$85.00
Backpack	$165.00	$80.00	5/3/2006	1	$85.00
Backpack	$165.00	$80.00	5/4/2006	1	$85.00
Backpack	$165.00	$80.00	5/5/2006	2	$170.00
Backpack	$165.00	$80.00	5/6/2006	2	$170.00
Backpack	$165.00	$80.00	5/7/2006	1	$85.00
Backpack	$165.00	$80.00	5/1/2006	2	$170.00
*					

Record: ◄◄ ◄   1   ► ►► ►* of 8

Figure B.10 A query can provide specific information as well as perform calculations.

enter a query to find and display, or in database terminology, *return*, all records with the BP item code. You can indicate specific information as part of the query, such as the item name, price, and cost, the date of the transaction, the number sold, and even the calculated gross profit. Figure B.10 shows the result of just such a query.

Presentation Software

Presentation software allows knowledge-enabled professionals to use text in many sizes and fonts, graphics, photos, and even audio and video files to inform an audience. Because of its ease of use, presentation software has become extremely popular for making business, academic, and instructional presentations. For example, Figure B.11 shows a slide from a presentation on teamwork. Presentation software can be used both in situations that support a person giving a speech and in presenting information on its own. For example,

Figure B.11 Presentation software allows knowledge-enabled professionals to create slides to inform an audience.

a product marketing manager may use presentation software to create a slide show that can display automatically on an information kiosk or at a conference booth.

Web Browser and Internet-Related Software

Since its widespread introduction in 1994, the Web browser has rapidly become one of the most popular (if not *the most* popular) types of software in use today. The main reason for the popularity of the Web browser is its access to billions of pages of information available on the World Wide Web.

Browsers rely on "point-and-click" methodology to carry out desired operations. If you know the address of a web page, you simply enter it in the address box and press the Enter key to retrieve it. Once you have a web page on the screen, you can jump to other related pages by clicking on underlined content called a **hyperlink**. Of all the types of software that we discuss here, the Web browser is almost certainly the one that you have already used. As an example of a web page in a browser, consider the one for the publisher of this book, shown in Figure B.12.

Beyond simply accessing web pages, browsers have become the "jack of all trades" for Internet operations. Web browsers enable searches for web pages based on a word or term; communications with others through e-mail, instant messaging, groups, and chat rooms; and downloading of files of all types, including audio and

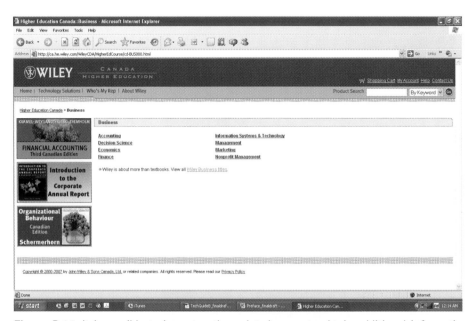

Figure B.12 It is possible to jump to other related pages to obtain additional information by clicking on hyperlinks.

video files. The power and versatility of the Web result in its almost universal use by knowledge-enabled professionals.

Using search engines from a Web browser enables you to search the Web and all of its billions of pages, as well as to search discussion groups and even chat sessions. Many public and governmental agencies now put their data on the Web in a form that can be searched and downloaded for use in problem solving. For example, in the Wild-Outfitters example shown earlier, a marketing analyst in the company could use a search engine to compare their prices and features with those of all possible competitors.

In addition, many organizations now enable their employees to search for internal data and information using search engines on their intranet using a browser. In many cases, employees can send out questions to other employees using e-mail to determine if a problem has already been solved within the organization. This makes it possible for an employee to access the accumulated organizational memory to answer questions and solve problems.

Specialized Software

In many cases, knowledge-enabled professionals rely on other developed software to handle specific situations. For example, while spreadsheets are the most general form of financial software, most organizations use other financial packages. These include accounting packages, real estate calculators, on-line stock and bond trading software, and retirement-planning software.

You can see how most knowledge work activities rely on commercially available application software. However, specific tasks require specially created software. Let's look next at developing customized software.

Quick Test

Determine if the following statements are True or False.

1. Spreadsheet software is not as good as database software for storing data records because it often includes redundant information.

2. Word processing is an improvement on desktop publishing software because it can be used to create professional-looking documents like books, pamphlets, and so on.

3. Boldfaced words in web pages provide connections to other parts of that web page or to other web pages.

Answers: 1. True; 2. False; 3. False

DEVELOPING CUSTOMIZED SOFTWARE

Companies usually buy commercially developed software, like word processing programs or spreadsheets, for routine business tasks. However, to achieve a competitive advantage, a company must often custom develop software to meet its particular needs. As one analyst notes, "software needed to be competitively different is generally not available from off-the-shelf packages" and "building . . . systems for unique [competitive] capability is often the single most important activity for an . . . organization."[2] As a result, there will always be a demand for programmers.

Computer programs are based on algorithms. An **algorithm** is a detailed sequence of actions that, when followed, will accomplish some task. For example, when making the bed, you may follow the steps in this algorithm:

1. Strip the covers and sheets from the bed.
2. Smooth out the fitted sheet.
3. Fluff the pillows and place them in their proper locations.
4. Tuck the sheet under the mattress at the foot of the bed and spread to cover the mattress.
5. Tuck in the comforter and spread it over the top of the sheet.
6. Crease comforter under the pillows and fold it over the top to cover the pillows.
7. Drop a quarter onto the bed to see if it bounces!

Defining an algorithm is just the first step in developing software. The next step is making a computer follow the algorithm; this is known as **programming**. A *computer programmer* takes the algorithm and translates it into instructions written in a programming language that the computer can understand. The set of instructions that follow the algorithm, written using the **programming language**, is known as a **program**.

Programming languages, like the machine language of the CPU, is a set of binary codes. With the first computers, programmers actually had to input binary instructions to their machines. As you can imagine, this was a difficult and error-prone process. Since the 1950s, there has been a trend toward abstracting the machine language instructions into a language that is more natural to human programmers. Unfortunately, the strict rules required for communicating instructions to the CPU confine programming languages to a formality that is still today far from natural and often difficult to master.

Table B.2	Commonly Used Computer Languages
Language	**Common Use**
C (including C++ and C#)	Writing a wide variety of applications for PCs or network servers.
Java	Writing software for all types of computers; also, for writing browser and server-side Web software.
PHP	Writing Web-based applications.
SQL (Structured Query Language)	Writing queries to relational database management systems.
VB.NET (Visual Basic .NET)	Writing software for PCs; also, for writing browser and server-side Web software.

Programs are written in a number of computer languages. Table B.2 lists some of the more commonly used languages and their uses.[3] Each computer language, like a human language, has its own vocabulary and grammatical rules. However, most share a similar logical approach to communication with the computer.

Of special interest is the **Java** language, originally developed to run on networks. Programmers now use it in many different ways, particularly in e-commerce applications. It actually runs differently than many other programming languages, in that it is platform independent. This means it can work on many different kinds of computers.

Microsoft's main competitor to Java is the .Net platform of languages including VB.NET, C++ .NET, and C# (pronounced "C-sharp") .NET. As an example of a .NET language, consider

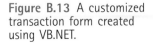

Figure B.13 A customized transaction form created using VB.NET.

---

3. Popularity is based on job openings for each computer language on the Craig's List website as quoted in http://www.dedasys.com/articles/language_popularity.html.

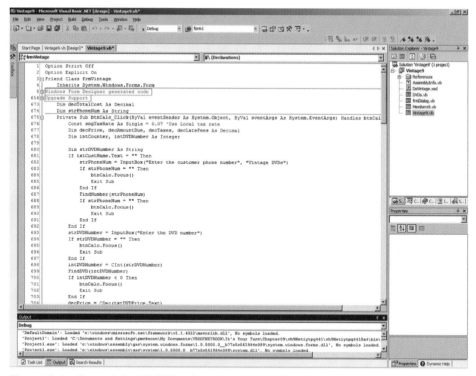

Figure B.14 Part of the VB.NET code written to produce the customized transaction form shown in Figure B.13.

Figures B.13 and B.14, which show an application in VB.NET for a video store. The figures show both the interface for this application and some of the corresponding programming instructions (code) necessary to implement the logic behind it.

OPEN-SOURCE SOFTWARE

One ongoing argument in the world of software is the use and development of open-source vs. proprietary software. **Open-source software** refers to programs for which the authors allow anyone to view the *source code*—the programming instructions—and make changes. Many open-source software applications are freely available for downloading over the Internet. The only requirement is that any programmer who makes changes to the open-source code must also make those changes freely available to others. Examples of open-source software and languages are the Apache Web server software, the Linux operating system, MySQL database software, the Mozilla Web browser, and the PHP Web development language. Open-source software is supported by a community of users who actively participate in newsgroups and websites like www.linuxforum. com and MySQLFreaks.com.

On the other hand, **proprietary software** requires a purchased licence and typically restricts access to the source code to the company employees. Examples of proprietary software are the Microsoft Windows operating system and IBM's DB2 database software. Proprietary software is supported by the company that sells it through technical support centres and websites.

The trade-offs between open-source and proprietary software include cost and support. Open-source software is typically free but often provides no centralized support centres. Proprietary software has a cost associated with it but does have a centralized support system.

There can be cases of software or a language being free but requiring the use of proprietary software to run. For example, it is possible to develop a website using a Microsoft language like ASP.NET using any text editor free of charge, but the website must run on the proprietary Microsoft Internet Information System Web server. An exception is Java, a proprietary language licensed by Sun Microsystems. Java is typically associated with the open-source movement because it will run on the Apache Web server software or under the Linux operating system, both of which are also open-source software.

As with hardware, software is changing rapidly to meet the needs of users. This is true for both application and operating system software. Further, the continuing contest between proprietary and open-source software will be one to watch. It may greatly influence both the software you use in the future and how much it will cost. If you use a PDA and mobile telephone, this is an especially fluid area for software, as companies vie to provide you with more ways to use your mobile device.

Quick Test

Fill in the blank for the following statements.

1. A(n) _____ is a detailed sequence of actions that, when followed, will accomplish some task.

2. _____ software allows anyone to view the programming instructions and make changes.

3. _____ software requires a purchased licence and typically restricts access to the programming instructions to company employees.

Answers: 1. algorithm; 2. open-source; 3. proprietary

STUDENT RETURN ON INVESTMENT SUMMARY

1. Why is the operating system so important to the use of all types of computers?

The operating system manages all of the message traffic that flows from the user to the application software to the computer and back again. It also handles the allocation of resources and the assignment of tasks to various software programs, and it carries out needed tasks with application software, without worrying about the hardware interfaces. However, there are important differences between the operating systems for mainframes, networks, personal computers, and hand-held devices, depending on the numbers of users and the complexity of the peripheral devices that they manage.

All operating systems consist of two parts: the kernel and the command interpreter. The kernel is the essential part of the operating system that handles requests from application programs or from hardware and determines the processing order of the requests. The kernel may also handle demands for internal memory from competing applications by parcelling out the limited amount of internal memory as needed. The command interpreter accepts commands from users and translates them into language that the kernel can understand.

2. What are the functions of the operating system?

The operating system is a collection of software programs that manages the following tasks:

- Starting the computer: The operating systems finds instructions on the ROM chip to start or "boot" the computer.
- Managing hardware: The operating system acts as a go-between for the user, software, and hardware system by controlling the many hardware elements that can be connected to a computer and by managing the flow of data into and information out of the computer.
- Controlling access to computer: The operating system must provide security to users' data, information, and programs against intrusion. The most recent operating systems require users to enter a password to access the computer, which limits their access to specific "areas."
- Providing an interface for the user: In order for the user to accomplish any task with the computer, he or she must be able to communicate with it through the interface provided by the operating system, whether it uses text commands or mouse clicks.
- Ensuring efficient use of the CPU: Since the CPU works faster than other hardware elements, including the I/O system, the operating system must ensure that the speed and power of the CPU are efficiently used—usually through running programs concurrently.
- Providing services to application software: This is the primary reason that most knowledge-enabled professionals use a computer.

3. How do knowledge–enabled professionals obtain and use application software?

Knowledge-enabled professionals rely on both commercially developed and custom-developed application software. The most commonly used commercially developed application software categories include word processing, spreadsheet, database, presentation, Web browsers and other Internet-related software, and specialized software.

4. What are the purpose and tools used in the software development process?

Knowledge-enabled professionals rely on custom-developed software, composed of multiple computer programs, to meet specific organizational needs. Developing each of these programs first requires an algorithm to be defined. The next step is writing the program in a computer language that can be understood by the computer. Computer languages that have been used for programming include SQL, C and C++, Java, PHP, and VB.NET. Of these, VB.NET is an example of a proprietary language from Microsoft, and PHP is an example of an open-source language that is not "owned" by any one company or organization. Java is a computer language that is proprietary but is often associated with open-source development.

KNOWLEDGE SPEAK

TECH GUIDE C

The Details of Networking

WHAT WE WILL COVER

- Network Architecture
- Network Layer Model
- Local Area Networks
- The Internet: A Network of Networks
- The World Wide Web

ROI · STUDENT RETURN ON INVESTMENT

Through your investment of time in reading and thinking about this guide, your return, or created value, is gaining knowledge. Use the following questions as a study guide.

1. What is the client/server architecture, and how does it work?
2. How does the network layer model describe a wide area network?
3. How are local area networks configured?
4. How does the Internet work?
5. What makes the World Wide Web valuable to knowledge-enabled professionals?

In Chapter 2, we briefly introduced you to the concept of computer networks and how they can benefit you as a knowledge-enabled professional. We described the basic types of networks, network connections, and protocols, as well as network hardware and software. Finally, we discussed the Internet and World Wide Web. In this Tech Guide, we provide you with more details about these important topics.

We start with the topic of network architecture and its most common type, client/server networks. After that, we review the network software, protocols, and data component using a network layering model. Next we discuss local area networks in more detail, because they are the network that you will work with in your university or college environment. Finally, we take a closer look at the Internet and World Wide Web.

NETWORK ARCHITECTURE

Much like a building, **computer architecture** refers to the design of a computer system or network. The term usually covers the overall combination of the hardware and software that makes up the network infrastructure. An *open architecture* is one where anyone can know the design, thus allowing anyone to develop software and hardware to work with it. A *closed architecture* network has a proprietary design, making it difficult for outsiders. Most of today's computer networks are open to allow easy growth.

In this section, we discuss the most common architecture for computer networks: client/server.

CLIENT/SERVER ARCHITECTURE

In the *client/server architecture,* each computer on the network is running either server software or client software, or both types of software simultaneously. *Server software* provides data or resources to other computers in the network. Computers running server software are typically referred to as **servers**, with each server typically focusing on a specific task. For example, a *file server* stores and delivers shared files. A *print server* manages one or more shared network printers. A *network server* manages the traffic on the network. Other servers manage databases (*database server*), e-mail (*e-mail server*), and access to the World Wide Web (*Web server*).

Clients are network computers running client software that request services from the servers. The clients depend on servers for shared network resources like software, files, devices, processing power, and access to the Internet. Figure C.1 shows a client that is requesting database records from a server.

Client computers can have various levels of processing power and capabilities. A network computer with little or no processing power or storage is a **dumb terminal** or **thin client**. On the other hand, a network computer with lots of processing power and storage of its own is a **fat client**. Determining whether or not to use thin or

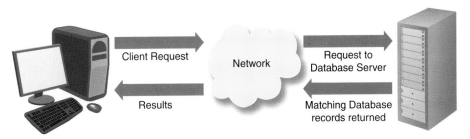

Figure C.1 Client/server architecture.

fat clients depends on many factors. For example, if an organization has a customized application that many people need to access, it may be implemented as a thin client, with the majority of the application residing on the server for everyone to access. This method would also be used if the application required frequent updates. Technical support would not want to release updates to individual fat clients when most of them could be applied to the server and used by thin clients instead. The use of fat clients makes more sense, however, when a user does not want to be dependent on servers for their applications. When a user has a thin client and the server is unavailable, that user cannot access their applications. Imagine if you were dependent on your university or college servers for MS Excel or Word!

Clients on the network typically consist of standard PCs and workstations. A **workstation** is a type of high-powered small computer, often used for tasks that require processing capabilities beyond those available on a standard PC, such as simulating complex business situations.

Note that while we use *client* and *server* to refer to hardware devices, it is actually the client software and server software running on the hardware that enable client/server processing to occur. In fact, it is possible to run several different types of client or server software on the same machine. For example, you probably have both Web browser and e-mail client software simultaneously running on your computer.

How is the client/server architecture valuable to knowledge-enabled professionals? Recall that mainframes store and process data on a central machine that is remote from the user, while PCs store and process data locally to the user. However, knowledge-enabled professionals frequently need both the power of a mainframe and the ease of use of a PC. Thus, the client/server architecture combines the best of mainframes and PCs. This combination of local and remote data storage and processing leads to four basic computing architectures, shown in Figure C.2. Note that the client/server system overlaps both local and remote storage and processing.

The simplest form of client/server computing involves a file server, which controls access to the network, manages communications between PCs, and makes data and program files available to the individual PCs. The computing load, however, is still distributed among the individual PCs. This can actually pose a significant problem for many businesses. If a large number of clients attempt to access the server, the client/server performance declines. Therefore, to increase processing efficiency, many client/server networks involve a three-tiered architecture.

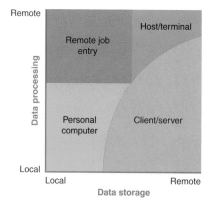

Figure C.2 Four basic computing architectures. *Source:* R. T. Watson, *Organizational Memory,* 4th ed. (New York: John Wiley, 2004), p. 354.

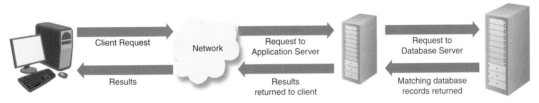

Figure C.3 Three-tiered client/server architecture.

THREE-TIERED ARCHITECTURE

In many cases, there is actually a series of clients and servers working to provide the data or application software that an end-user client requests. The most common form of series is the **three-tiered client/server architecture**, which uses a client, an application server, and a database server. In this client/server environment, a user working at a GUI-based client PC or workstation requests data or processing from an application server, which decides what data to supply. The application server then sends a query to the database server to retrieve those data. The database server processes the query and returns the matching data to the application server, which processes the data into the form required by the user. Figure C.3 illustrates this process.

One of the strengths of three-tiered client/server computing, therefore, is the capability to string together a series of servers to respond to a client's request while maintaining a single, central database. This allows an organization to maintain data in only one place, which avoids the difficulties of partitioning stored data. In the next section we discuss more advantages of client/servers.

USING CLIENT/SERVERS TO INCREASE KNOWLEDGE WORK EFFICIENCY

Today, the client/server environment serves a variety of purposes. Table C.1 shows the most commonly used servers along with their purpose in a client/server network. For example, Web server software

Table C.1	Types of Servers
Server Type	Purpose
Application	Handles high-speed processing.
Database	Handles queries to a large database and returns matching records.
Fax	Sends and receives faxes for entire organization.
File	Provides both software and data files to users.
Mail	Sends and receives e-mail for entire organization.
Web	Handles requests for web pages.

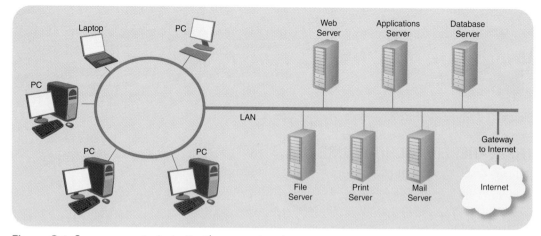

Figure C.4 Servers on a typical client/server network.

handles requests for web pages, whereas e-mail server software sends and receives e-mail. In fact, many organizations now use the application server to replace mainframes for handling large-scale processing tasks. For example, IBM refers to its large computers as *enterprise servers* to emphasize their use in client/server computing as application servers. Figure C.4 shows a typical client/server network that includes file, fax, mail, database, application, and Web servers and a variety of clients.

Similar to the other types of computing, client/server computing has advantages and disadvantages, listed in Table C.2. The primary advantage of client/server computing lies in its ability to share processing and data storage responsibilities among multiple machines and to use specialized servers to meet specific needs. The primary disadvantage is the complexity inherent in sharing responsibilities among multiple machines. Overall, however, the trend is toward wider use of client/server computing because of its increased flexibility.

Table C.2 Advantages and Disadvantages of Client/Server Systems	
Advantages	**Disadvantages**
Share computing burden among servers and clients.	More complex programming relationship between clients and servers.
Specialized servers to handle one particular type of task.	System upgrades require upgrading of all clients and servers, regardless of location.
Can upgrade system in small steps.	More complex computer and network security issues due to increased numbers of users and client machines with access to networked resources, including data.
Loss of one client does not stop other clients from accessing server.	

PEER-TO-PEER NETWORKS

As mentioned earlier, it is possible for computers on a network to run both server and client software at the same time. This enables organizations to set up a **peer-to-peer network**, where each computer in the network is on the same level as other computers and each computer is equally responsible for overseeing the functions of the network. Depending on the network connection, two computers in a peer-to-peer network may communicate directly with one another, or they may communicate through intermediate peer computers. In a pure peer-to-peer network, the two computers that are communicating with each other share the responsibility for carrying out the communication. There are no central computers or servers to manage the correct functioning of the network. Figure C.5 shows how peer-to-peer networks differ from client/server ones.

Prior to 1999, most knowledge-enabled professionals primarily used peer-to-peer networks on small LANs. In June 1999, however, Napster, a famous service for sharing files, began operation. Napster demonstrated how to share files using a virtual peer-to-peer network over the Internet. Peer-to-peer networks are generally easier to set up and manage than client/server networks, but they are not as efficient at handling heavy traffic on the network. Today, many companies use peer-to-peer networks for the legitimate purposes of sharing data, information, and services.

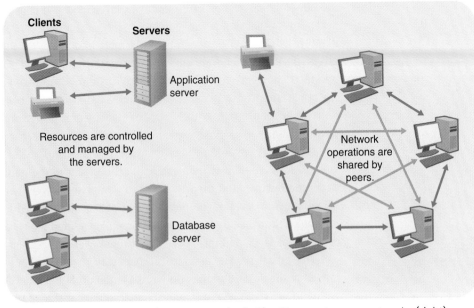

Figure C.5 Comparing client/server networks (left) with peer-to-peer networks (right).

Quick Test

Fill in the blanks for the following statements.

1. The most common form of networking architecture is the _____ architecture.

2. A(n) _____ architecture network has a proprietary design, making it difficult for outsiders.

3. In a(n) _____network, the computers are running both client and server software with no centralized server.

Answers: 1. client/server; 2. closed; 3. peer-to-peer

NETWORK LAYER MODEL

Now that you understand network architecture and how its design benefits knowledge-enabled professionals, how does the network actually operate? Recall that networks include a data component, as well as network connections, which deliver messages between computers in a network. In addition, networks rely on a wide variety of application software to actually generate the message. To understand how these three elements work together, we use a **network layer model** in which each layer handles part of the communications between computers.

The International Organization for Standardization (ISO) created the original version of the network layer model. It consists of seven layers that define the standards with which networks must comply. Our simplified version of this model contains only three layers: the *application software layer*, the *network connections layer*, and the *data component layer,* as Figure C.6 shows. In this model, the application software generates the message, which the connections layer then relays to the data component of the network for transmission.

Looking at Figure C.6, note that at the sender end of the network, a message moves from the application layer to the network connections layer, and then to the data component layer. The reverse process occurs at the receiver end of the network, with the message first traversing the data component layer, then the network connections layer, and finally the application layer.

The postal system provides a good way to think about this model. In the postal system, you write a letter, put it in an envelope with a friend's address on it, and then place the envelope in a mail box. Think of this as the application layer. A postal worker picks up

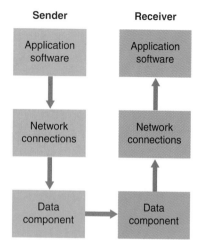

Figure C.6 The network layer model.

the envelope and takes it to the post office (the network connections layer), which decides how to send it to your friend (the data component layer). At the other end, your friend reverses this process to reply to your letter.

APPLICATION SOFTWARE LAYER

The application layer includes well-known software applications such as Web browsers and e-mail. This software formats user data by adding information to make it conform to a specific standard or *protocol*, the specific set of rules for communicating. Protocols for the application layer of the Internet include **simple mail transfer protocol (SMTP)** for e-mail, *hypertext transfer protocol (HTTP)* for web pages, and *electronic data interchange (EDI)* for large-scale exchange of data between organizations. The resulting message to the receiver thus combines the message generated by the application software and the protocol.

Application software may also encrypt the data (place the data in a secure, unreadable form) to protect it from unauthorized readers. For example, suppose a customer goes to an e-commerce website and fills out and submits a form to order a product. In this case, the application is a Web browser, the message is the contents of the form, and the protocol is HTTP. In addition, the message is encrypted. Figure C.7 shows the components of the application software layer for any message. For a product order, the message would include the message protocol (HTTP) and encrypted message and encrypted order data.

Figure C.7 The components of the application software layer for a message.

NETWORK CONNECTION LAYER

In the network connection layer, the application software layer formats the message according to the network protocol. For example, the protocol for the Internet is the **transmission control protocol/ Internet protocol (TCP/IP)**, as Figure C.8 shows.

With the TCP/IP Internet protocol, the network connection layer conducts a series of operations to prepare the message for sending across the Internet to a destination computer. It must first convert the address of the server at the destination from a text form (e.g., somecomputer.somewhere.org) to an *IP address*, which consists of four groups of numbers, separated by periods or decimal points, in the 0–255 range. The address is converted by using a conversion table stored either on the user's computer or on a computer with which the local computer can communicate. For example, say you want to send an e-mail message to World Vision Canada, whose address is info@worldvision.ca. The network connection converts this to the IP address 205.189.149.31.

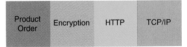

Figure C.8 The components of the connection layer for a message.

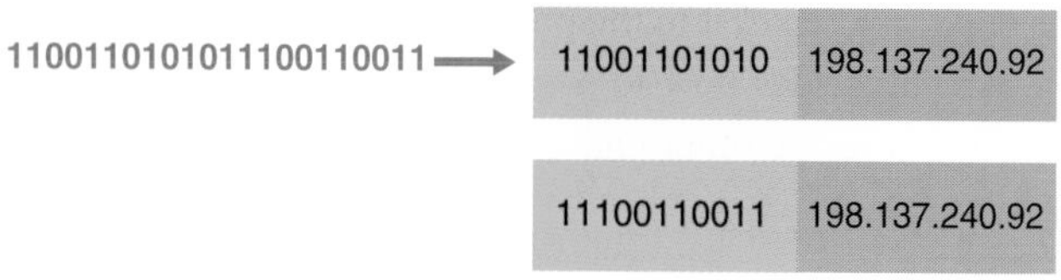

Figure C.9 Converting binary data into packets.

11001101010111001100 11 ⟶

| 11001101010 | 198.137.240.92 |

| 11100110011 | 198.137.240.92 |

Next, the network connection divides the message into smaller digital units called **packets**, each of which contains a specific number of bytes. At this step, each packet receives a sequence number and a destination address. Figure C.9 shows this process of converting binary digits to packets and adding the IP address to them.

After the networking software layer divides an Internet message into packets, the physical layer sends these packets over telephone lines. However, it uses an approach that differs from the method used to send voice and fax telephone calls. For voice and fax calls, the process creates, and keeps open, a complete path from the caller to the receiver for the duration of the call. Such an approach would be very inefficient for networks. Why? Network computers send large amounts of data quickly and then do not send any data for a while. For this, networks rely on a technology called packet switching.

Packet switching routes individual packets through the network based on their destination addresses. It thus allows the sharing of the same data path among many computers in the network. Further, if a computer on the network is inoperable, the packet finds another way to reach its destination. Packet switching is the key technology that makes the Internet so efficient.

When sending a group of data packets, like product orders or e-mail messages, to a computer with an IP address, software on the sending computer sends the packets to the nearest router for retransmission to other routers on the network. A *router* is a type of computer with the sole purpose of accepting packets and determining the best way to send them to the destination computer. That is, the router specializes in referring the packets to the least-congested network path to the eventual goal.

Because packets travel so fast over the Internet, delay time is more important than distance in determining total time to deliver a message. Sophisticated software carries out this process on the routers and speeds the data packets to their destination. Figure C.10 shows the process of sending data from one network to another on the Internet using intermediate routers. Note that the packets don't flow through all routers, just the ones that are necessary to get the message to the destination.

A packetized message is reconstructed using the sequence order that is attached to each packet. As a result, packets may follow differ-

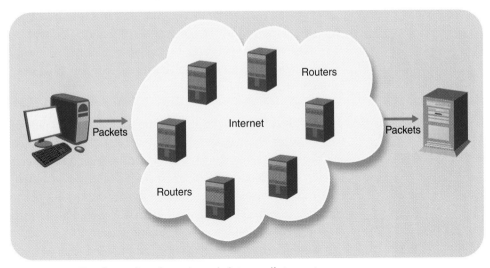

Figure C.10 The flow of packets through intermediate routers.

ent paths through the network, as well as arrive in a different order. As they arrive, the destination computer acknowledges received packets. If the sending computer does not get an acknowledgement that a packet has arrived within a certain timeframe, it automatically resends the unacknowledged packets. This ensures the receipt of all packets.

Have you ever tried to make a phone call using voice over IP (VoIP)? Was it a little choppy and out of sequence at times? This occurs because a phone call using VoIP relies on packet switching. Voice is broken into packets (just like data), routed by routers, and re-assembled at the destination. At times this results in poorer quality than calls placed using regular phone lines. Of course, providers of VoIP in Canada, such as Primus and Vonage, are finding ways of improving quality and offering their services at competitive prices.

DATA COMPONENT LAYER

Over a computer network, we can share any data that can be converted to electronic signals. The sending of data from one computer to another over a channel using electronic signals is known as *data transmission*. Data transmission is concerned with ensuring that the data are sent and received correctly and efficiently.

Data and information transmitted over networks travel over various media, including twisted pair wire, coaxial cable, fibre-optic cable, and microwave and satellite transmission. *Twisted pair*, which consists of twisted pairs of copper wires, is similar to the wiring used in much of the existing telephone system. Networks widely rely on it, both within and between locations.

Coaxial cable, which transmits cable television signals into your home, is also widely used in networks. In many areas, television

Copper wire

Glass fibre

Figure C.11 Coaxial cable compared with glass fibre cables.

cable is being converted to a type of cable capable of handling two-way signals instead of the one-way signals associated with television transmissions. This two-way cable enables the connection of home computers to ISPs at much faster speeds than those available with traditional telephone connections.

Fibre-optic cable is the newest medium and consists of hundreds of glass fibre strands that can transmit a large number of signals at extremely high speeds. The glass fibre strands also reduce the size of the cable required. However, individual computers are not set up to connect directly to fibre-optic cable, so it is often necessary to use twisted pair or coaxial cable for the last few feet to the computer. Figure C.11 compares copper wire with fibre-optic cables for transmitting the same volume of information.

Microwaves are high-frequency radio transmissions that can be sent between two Earth stations or between Earth stations and communications satellites. It is the method commonly used to transmit television signals. Direct broadcast *satellite transmisson* uses microwaves for one-way downloads of data to homes and offices. It provides a new way of carrying out transmission of data to a user, especially where traditional telephone lines do not exist or are difficult to install.

A variety of wireless technologies are also becoming popular as a way to provide mobile users with connections regardless of where they may be. The two most popular wireless methods of sending data rely on infrared light and radio. Infrared light wireless transmissions, like microwaves, require a line of sight. On the other hand, radio transmissions can pass through walls. However, security is a problem due to the radio waves going in all directions. (We discuss wireless networks in more detail in a later section.) Table C.3 compares the communication media used in the data component layer.

Table C.3	Comparison of Media[1]		
Media	**Cost**	**Error Rates**	**Speed**
Twisted pair	Low	Low	Low-high
Coaxial cable	Moderate	Low	Low-high
Fibre optics	High	Very low	High-very high
Radio	Low	Moderate	Low
Infrared	Low	Moderate	Low
Microwave	Moderate	Low-moderate	Moderate
Satellite	Moderate	Low-moderate	Moderate

1. Jerry Fitzgerald and Alan Dennis, *Business Data Communications and Networking*, 8th ed., New York: John Wiley, 2005, p. 85.

In addition to the media that transmit data, other aspects of the data component layer include the signal type and the data rate.

Signal Type

The **signal type** is how data are sent over the network. A signal can be digital or analog. Digital transmission sends bits as high and low electronic pulses. A computer can therefore transmit over a digital communications link without changing the data. On the other hand, analog signals transmit bits as wave patterns, which requires modifying data before transmitting them. Because most telephone and cable systems are analog, to transmit data, *modems* convert digital signals from the computer into analog signals for transmission over the communications link.

Telephone and cable modems convert between analog and digital forms of data using different methods. In a telephone modem, at the sender's end, the modem modulates the digital computer data or information into an analog form that can travel over standard telephone lines. At the other end, a modem demodulates the analog signal back into a digital form that the receiver's computer can understand. A cable modem modulates and demodulates the cable signal into a stream of data. In addition, cable modems incorporate a variety of other functions to allow the PC to be linked to a network.

Both analog and digital data transmission are frequently used. Table C.4 lists some advantages and disadvantages of each form of transmission. The choice of signal usually rests on which of the two is more efficient for the given application.

Table C.4	Analog vs. Digital Data Transmission	
	Analog	**Digital**
Advantages	• Reflect natural phenomena; sound, light, and electricity are all analog • Low-cost, existing infrastructure for analog transmission	• Less susceptible to noise, resulting in a lower error rate • Allows transmission of multiple signals over one line at the same time (called *multiplexing*) • Faster rate of transmission • Less-complex and lower-cost circuits
Disadvantages	• Difficult to design and analyze analog circuits • More susceptible to noise, distortion, and interference	• Analog phenomena require conversion to digital signals

Data Rate and Bandwidth Issues

The **data rate** is measured in bits per second (bps). For example, a telephone modem allows for a maximum data rate of 56 kbps. Even when using a 56-kbps modem, the actual data rate can vary depending on the quality of the telephone line. As a result, most knowledge-enabled professionals increasingly use other methods of transferring data, including digital subscriber lines, television (TV) cable, and the various T-carrier circuits.

A **digital subscriber line (DSL)** transmits computer data in a digital form along the same telephone line that analog voice communications uses. The **T-carrier circuits** are dedicated digital lines that a telecommunications company leases to users to carry data between specific points. Table C.5 lists the maximum data rates for various methods of transmitting data.

Transmission speed relates to how fast a single message can be transmitted between two nodes. *Transmission capacity* relates to how many messages can be sent over the connection simultaneously. While speed and capacity are not the same thing, they are highly related. A measure for one often proves indicative of the other. Much like our network of highways for automobile traffic, higher capacity (more lanes) usually means higher possible speeds.

The term *bandwidth*, often used in relationship to data rate, measures how fast data flow on a transmission path. With the increasing demand from users for the capability to view high-quality photos, graphics, and full-motion video on their computers, the competition to provide higher bandwidth access is becoming keen among telecommunications providers. The two extremes of bandwidth are baseband and broadband. *Baseband* carries only a single digital signal through the media. For example, your regular

Table C.5 Maximum Data Rates[2]		
Transmission Method	**Maximum Data Rate**	**Comments**
Standard telephone service	56 Kbps	Available everywhere.
Digital subscriber line (DSL)	6 Mbps in; 640 Kbps out	Becoming more available; does not slow down as more people sign up.
Cable	As high as 55 Mbps but averages between 200 Kbps and 2 Mbps	Cable must support two-way communication; available in many locations but slows down as more people use it in a specific location.
T-carrier circuits (T-1 to T-4)	1.544 Mbps–274 Mbps	Leased lines used for commercial telecommunication.

2. Jerry Fitzgerald and Alan Dennis, *Business Data Communications and Networking*, 8th ed., New York: John Wiley, 2005.

telephone line is a baseband medium. *Broadband* transmits a variety of different analog signals.

Broadband is really what makes Web-based services viable and attractive. To place orders on an e-commerce site, the data component layer must include the customer's modem and telephone line, or cable modem and cable. When the message reaches the customer's *Internet service provider* (*ISP*), the ISP's modem and hardware connections then handle the data. Without a high speed connection, popular applications like Myspace and gmail would not work well. Certainly without broadband it is impossible to take advantage of software downloads and new services such as VoIP. Bandwidth is a consideration in any e-commerce venture. Not only do the technical aspects of the website have to take bandwidth into account, the bandwidth of the target customers needs to be considered. It would be all well and good to have a fantastic video demonstrating your products on a website, but if a target customer does not have DSL or higher, they will not be able to view the video.

Until recently, Canada was a world leader in broadband adoption. Even though our adoption rates are at a plateau, we continue to lead the United States in percentage terms.[3] Research on Canadian broadband usage and its social and economic impact is being conducted. Does Canada's adoption of broadband enhance economic activities? Does it promote societal well-being or does it create a social divide between those who have high speed access and those who do not?[4] It is certain that consumers will continue to move from baseband to broadband in order to access the increasing number of Web services offered by businesses and other organizations.

Now that you have a better understanding of how networks operate, let's look next at how knowledge-enabled professionals use them.

Quick Test

Match the network layer with the appropriate hardware or software.

1. Application software layer	a. TCP/IP
2. Network connection layer	b. Fibre optics
3. Data component layer	c. E-mail software

Answers: 1. c; 2. a; 3. b

3. Organisation for Economic Co-operation and Development, "OECD broadband statistics, December 2005," http://www.oecd.org/document/39/0,2340, en_2825_495656_36459431_1_1_1_1,00.htm, retrieved July 31, 2006.
4. C.A. Middleton and C. Sorensen, "How connected are Canadians? Inequities in Canadian households' Internet access," *Canadian Journal of Communication*, 30(4), 2005, p. 463–483.

LOCAL AREA NETWORKS

Most organizations today use local area networks (LANs) to share information and resources among employees. Sharing information enables users to work with, and send, the same data or information files. Sharing resources involves the users' ability to share software and hardware.

Sharing software avoids the need for an organization to purchase a copy of a software package for every computer in the organization. Instead, the organization purchases *software licences* for their employees, which allow multiple persons to simultaneously use a software package. Sharing hardware allows the use of printers, disk storage, scanners, and so on through the network, rather than purchasing these devices for each user. Making hardware available through a LAN, especially highly specialized types of hardware, can significantly reduce an organization's costs.

Most LANs are client/server networks, although peer-to-peer networks can also implement LANs. Peer-to-peer networks cost significantly less than the dedicated server configuration, but until recently were not well suited for heavy-duty transaction processing. There are also significant security concerns about using a peer-to-peer network for working with sensitive material. In this Tech Guide, we concentrate our discussion on client/server LANs.

The vast majority of LANs use the **Ethernet protocol** to connect computers and move information between computers on the network by transmitting packets on a bus network. A *bus network* uses a main cable, called a *bus*, to connect all clients and servers on the network. With the Ethernet protocol, a computer on the network transmits a message that contains the address of the destination computer. Because all computers are free to transmit at any time, collision-detecting software must be in place. After detecting a collision, the software directs each computer to stop transmitting and wait a random length of time before re-transmitting its message. This system works well and is the basis for most LANs in operation today.

A client on a LAN can not only share information and software with other PCs on the same LAN but also communicate through gateways and bridges with other types of computers and with other LANs. A **gateway** is a combination of hardware and software that connects two dissimilar computer networks. The gateway allows a LAN user to access a mainframe network without leaving his or her PC. Similarly, a gateway between a LAN and a WAN enables a LAN user to send e-mail over the WAN. In contrast, a **bridge** connects two similar networks. For example, if a bridge connects two LANs, computers on each LAN can access the other network's file server without making any physical changes to the data.

WIRELESS LANS

As its name implies, **wireless LANs (WLANs)** replace the usual LAN cabling between computers with wireless transmissions. They are becoming increasingly popular as mobile users need to connect to their local network and, possibly, from there to the Internet. WLANs eliminate the need for cable in remote areas, provide an inexpensive alternative to shared printing, and connect two networks separated by some obstacle, such as a highway or wall, through which cable cannot run.

Knowledge-enabled professionals use WLANs to increase the efficiency of many activities in the workplace, including the following:

- Pricing, labelling, handling orders, and taking inventory from anywhere in a store, and then communicating that information directly to the back-office computer.
- Connecting a wireless device to a bar code scanner, to scan items in a warehouse and thereby produce a list of items and their locations.
- Requesting medical tests, checking the results, and then entering the information into a patient's electronic record from the patient's room.
- Checking e-mail on laptops and hand-helds from anywhere without having to be connected by wiring.

Wireless networking hardware uses radio frequencies to transmit information between individual computers, each of which has a wireless network adapter. The individual computers do not communicate directly with each other. Instead, they communicate with a wireless network hub or router. The hub or router bridges the wireless network to a traditional Ethernet as well as provides a shared Internet connection. Figure C.12 shows how a wireless LAN connects a number of laptops to a hub, which, in turn, connects to the organizational LAN.

The current popular standard for wireless networking supports a data rate of 11 mpbs, with a typical range through open air of about 200–1000 m. Nicknamed *Wi-Fi (wireless fidelity)* by the industry group that supports it, this approach to wireless LANs uses the IEEE 802.11b standard for short-range radio transmissions. However, the 802.11a and 802.11g standards may surpass it, since 802.11a allows for data rates of up to 54 mbs, but it is not directly compatible with the older 802.11b standard.

Figure C.12 Connection of laptops and PCs to the Internet through wireless LAN.

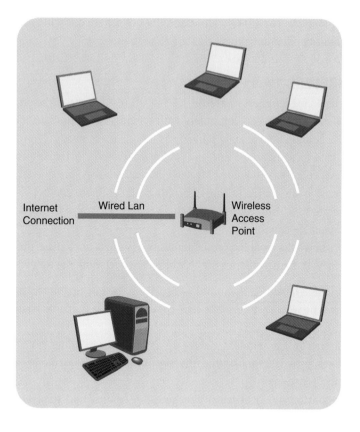

In addition, while faster, 802.11a does not cover as wide a range as the lower frequency standards. On the other hand, the newer 802.11g standard delivers data at 54 mbs on the same frequencies as 802.11b. This makes 802.11g devices backward-compatible with the older 802.11b hardware. The only disadvantage 802.11g has in relation to 802.11a is that it can be subject to more interference, as many other wireless devices (e.g., your household wireless phone) operate over the same frequencies.

Any company or individual that uses a wireless LAN should be concerned about security. Access to a wireless LAN must be restricted by using passwords or allowing only certain computer IP addresses, or both. WLANs are even vulnerable internally between a laptop and the router; there should be some form of encryption used to ensure that packets are not hacked.

BLUETOOTH AND PANS

One of the newest wireless technologies, developed by a consortium of companies including Nokia, Ericsson, and Motorola, is Bluetooth. Named after the tenth-century king who merged Denmark and Norway, **Bluetooth** is a form of **personal area network**

(PAN). PAN technology enables wireless devices, such as mobile telephones, computers, and PDAs, to communicate over a short distance—less than 10 m. By embedding a low-cost transceiver chip in each device, it allows total synchronization of wireless devices, without the user having to initiate any operation. The chips communicate over a previously unused radio frequency at up to 2 Mbps.

As envisioned by its developers, a knowledge-enabled professional would use a single device adhering to the Bluetooth protocol as a mobile telephone away from the office and as a portable telephone in the office. In addition, the device would work as a PDA and quickly synchronize information with a desktop computer (also containing a Bluetooth chip), or act as a remote control to initiate any number of other operations with other devices (with the appropriate chip). For example, a user could initiate sending or receiving a fax, or printing or copying a document, from anywhere in the office. Bluetooth thus enables pervasive connectivity between personal technology devices without the use of cabling.

Quick Test
Indicate whether the following statements are True or False.

1. The majority of local area networks uses the Jobs-McPherson protocol.

2. A gateway is another term used to describe a bridge.

3. The major technology used in PANs is Bluetooth.

Answers: 1. False; 2. False; 3. True

THE INTERNET: A NETWORK OF NETWORKS

Because of its tremendous growth over the last decade, the Internet is the subject of much discussion in newspapers, books, magazines, and movies. For many companies, the Internet is the basis for the widespread use of e-commerce. Without a doubt, the Internet is the most significant technology innovation to come along since the invention of the computer itself (over 60 years ago).

Originally developed in the 1960s and 1970s as a way of sharing information and resources among universities and research institutions, the Internet began its dramatic growth in 1991 when the

U.S. government opened the Internet for commercial use. This growth further accelerated with the introduction of the World Wide Web in 1994. Today, the Internet is growing so fast that no one can say exactly how many people are using it. We do know that the number of users surpassed 1 billion at the end of 2005 and is predicted to pass 2 billion by 2011.[5]

HOW DOES THE INTERNET WORK?

The Internet is not a single network, but rather a network of networks. In fact, the name Internet is a shortened version of the term *internetworking* because it allows users to work among multiple networks. To connect to the Internet, as Figure C.13 shows, your computer will usually first connect to a LAN through a network interface card (NIC) or to an ISP through a modem and telephone line. The LAN, mainframe, or ISP, in turn, connect to a regional network via a high-speed (T-1) telephone line. The regional network then links into the backbone of the Internet.

A **network interface card (NIC)** provides the physical connection between a computer and a local network. Most NICs come built into the computer with a jack into which a network cable can be plugged. Wireless NICs convert signals to radio waves that conform to standard wireless protocols and can be sent through the air. Wireless client devices can communicate directly with each other or over the network through a wireless *access point (AP)*.

Within each network, there is at least one **host computer** that connects to the Internet, with full two-way access to other computers

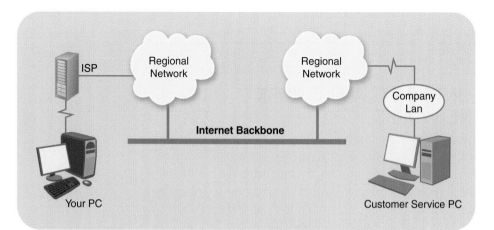

Figure C.13 Connecting a computer to the Internet through an ISP.

5. "Worldwide Internet Users Top 1 Billion in 2005," *Computer Industry Almanac*, January 4, 2006, http://www.c-i-a.com/pr0106.htm.

on the Internet and with a unique Internet address. In many cases, all computers in the network are host computers because all have Internet addresses, even if for only a short time, as with a dial-up system.

Each host computer that connects to the Internet uses the TCP/IP protocol for assigning addresses, and packet switching for exchanging information. By having all networks follow the same TCP/IP protocol, users on any network can exchange information with users on other networks, with little or no knowledge of their physical location or configuration.

TCP/IP rules also govern e-mail and other Internet addresses. An e-mail address consists of two parts: (1) the user name and (2) the server address. The user name is assigned to a person or organization that is connected to a server. The at symbol (@) separates the user name from the server address. The server address, also known as the *domain name,* consists of groups of letters separated by periods. Moving from right to left, this address goes from the most general (country name or organization type) to the most specific (computer name). The rightmost part of the address is known as the *top-level domain.* Note that these Internet addresses are easy-to-remember versions of the numeric IP addresses that actually identify computers on the Internet.

For example, Figure C.14 shows the e-mail address of the sales department for a fictitious company (WildOutfitters.com). In this example, the user name is *sales*, the server name is *wildoutfitters.com,* and the top-level domain is *com.* Because the WildOutfitters example is the general e-mail server, it has just the company name (WildOutfitters.com) as the server address. Other servers at WildOutfitters may have additional names to distinguish them from this server, say, returns.wildoutfitters.com for the e-mail server for the returns department, or www.wildoutfitters.com for the Web server.

sales @ wildoutfitters.com

User   Server name

Figure C.14 Components of an e-mail address.

In 2001, the Internet Corporation for Assigned Names and Numbers (ICANN), a not-for-profit company set up specifically to administer the domain name system, added seven new top-level domains. Table C.6 lists the top-level domains and the types of organizations that might use them.

How do you know if an e-mail or Web address is for a person or organization located outside Canada? For servers located in another country, a two-letter suffix may be used at the end of the server name as the top-level domain. For example, the server name for the University of Minho in Portugal is a minho.pt. Further, businesses often use a second-level domain name of "co" prior to the top-level domain corresponding to their country. For example, the Tanda Tula

Table C.6	Top-Level Domain Names	
Type of Organization	Designation	Example
Canadian-based	.ca	www.chapters.indigo.ca (Chapters and Indigo bookstores)
Educational institution	.edu	www.athabasca.edu (Athabasca University)
Commercial company	.com	www.ebay.com (eBay Auctions)
Not-for-profit organization	.org	www.aiesec.org (an international student organization)
Network provider	.net	www.nortel.net (Nortel Networks)
Government	.gc.ca	www.cra-arc.gc.ca (Canada Revenue Agency)
Aerospace organizations*	.aero	www.ba.aero (British Airways)
Businesses*	.biz	www.secor.biz (a Canadian strategy consultancy)
Co-operatives*	.coop	www.ontario.coop (a resource for co-operatives and credit unions in Ontario)
Various*	.info	www.vancouver.info (information about Vancouver, B.C.)
Museums*	.museum	www.naturalhistory.canada.museum/ (Canadian Museum of Nature)
Various*	.name	www.yourname.name
Professionals*	.pro	www.broadway.pro (Broadway theatre shows)

*These are some of the top-level domains approved by ICANN in 2001.

game preserve in South Africa's domain name is tandatula.co.za (where "za" is the top-level domain for South Africa). Many Canadian organizations prefer to distinguish themselves as Canadian by using the popular ".ca" top-level domain (e.g. www.cbc.ca).

USING THE INTERNET TO PERFORM KNOWLEDGE WORK ACTIVITIES

A number of software applications run on the Internet, such as the World Wide Web, e-mail, and chat rooms. All use the client/server approach, with each server on the network providing data and information to client computers connected to the network. The client computer must run two types of software to take advantage of the Internet: Internet conversion software and client software. The Internet conversion software enables the computer to work with Internet packets. Most operating systems, including Windows, come with this software built into the operating system.

Client software carries out the desired operation, such as sending e-mail, downloading files from or uploading files to a server, participating in discussion groups, working on someone else's computer, or accessing the World Wide Web. For example, to send e-mail, you would use an e-mail client to generate the message, which then goes to the Internet conversion software that translates it into a form that can be sent over the Internet. The most widely used Internet operations are as follows:

- E-mail (electronic mail)
- FTP (file transfer protocol)
- Newsgroups
- Telnet
- Internet relay chat
- World Wide Web

E-Mail

According to a Pew poll, e-mail over the Internet is the most popular application. Over half of the people interviewed claimed it as their number one on-line activity. E-mail has fundamentally changed the amount of personal and business communication that occurs. So what exactly is e-mail? E-mail is an asynchronous electronic method of exchanging information over a network. *Asynchronous* means that the sender and receiver are not communicating at the same time. Instead, one person sends a message, and the other person reads and replies to it at another time.

A special use of e-mail is for listservs. A *listserv* is server software that can broadcast an e-mail message from one member of a group to all other members. Group members simply subscribe to a listserv, and any messages sent to the listserv are automatically broadcast to the group members. Depending on how the listserv is set up, a member may be able to send messages to the listserv or may be able only to receive messages. Your instructor may have set up a listserv to which you subscribe. That way, he or she can communicate information to the entire class with one e-mail rather than sending it to a large group of e-mail addresses.

E-mail also has a number of commercial applications. Many companies use it as a powerful marketing tool. Incoming e-mail can provide them with queries about their products, information about problems with products, or suggestions for better ways to serve their customers. Companies can combine e-mails with other contacts to create mailing lists for either e-mail or postal mail (often referred to as *snail mail*) as a means of communicating with customers. On the other hand, customers expect companies to respond to e-mail queries, complaints, or comments. Failure by a company to respond to these messages can result in very unhappy customers. Companies are finding it necessary to develop systems of responding to incoming e-mail in addition to sending an auto-mated response that acknowledges receiving the customer's e-mail message.

Companies are also discovering that outbound e-mail can gener-ate revenue in ways never before considered. This includes sending special offers to customers who have purchased items on-line or who have sent a question via e-mail. For example, airlines regularly send notices of special fares that users can only purchase on-line. This has resulted in a significant increase in ticket sales, with almost no addi-tional cost to the airlines.

FTP

Companies and individuals frequently need to make software, data, or document files available to a wide audience over the Internet. For example, a software company may want to distribute to current users an upgrade of a software package that it markets. Or it may make a utility software package or data files freely available. In most cases, the best way to distribute files to a large audience is to place them on a **file transfer protocol (FTP)** server and have the users download them over the Internet.

Using an FTP site to download files is straightforward. You start FTP client software or a Web browser, enter the address of the FTP server that you want to use, and enter your user ID and password. At this point, you will see a list of directories or folders on the FTP server from which you can select files to download, as Figure C.15 shows. Downloading or uploading files with this client is a simple process of highlighting the file and clicking the upload or download arrow. Other systems allow you to drag-and-drop files between client and server windows.

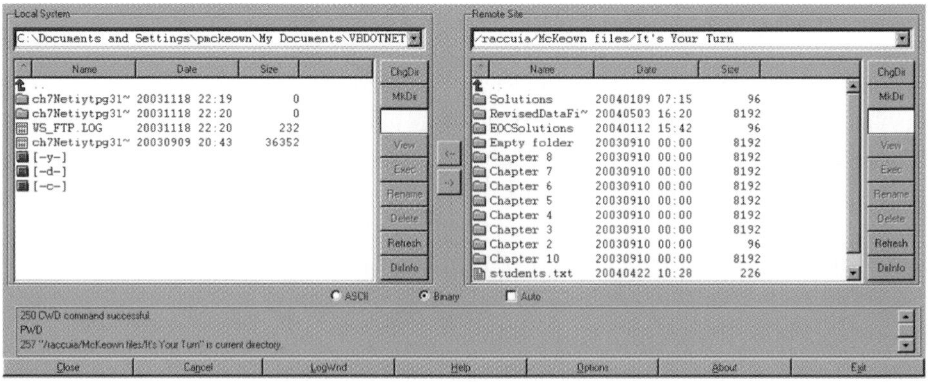

Figure C.15 Software for accessing an FTP server.

Telnet

One of the original purposes of the Internet was to allow researchers at one university to use a computer at another university. To make it possible to use a computer at a remote location, the telnet protocol was made a part of the Internet from the beginning. With the **telnet protocol**, you actually log on to a computer at a remote location and run the application there, with your computer acting as a terminal. The use of telnet has diminished greatly over the last few years as organizations have found ways to replace direct access to their computers with Web access, and because organizations have security concerns about telneting. Telneting does not provide any encryption or authentication capabilities and has been largely abandoned for a system called **Secure Shell (SSH)** provides all the functionality of telnet, with the addition of strong encryption to prevent sensitive data such as passwords from being intercepted and public key authentication to ensure that the remote computer is actually what it claims to be. However, telneting continues to be useful in locations where a slow Internet connection makes a typical e-mail client or even Web-based e-mail difficult to use. With telnet, or now more commonly SSH, a system administrator can log on to a remote system and perform any kind of maintenance or support required. This eliminates the need to be located at the same site as the system.

Newsgroups

The **newsgroups** Internet application is a vast number of discussion groups on a wide range of topics. A newsgroup consists of messages written on a series of news servers, each of which transfers messages to each other. This results in replicating all postings to one newsgroup on all the other news servers through the use of the *network news transfer protocol (NNTP)*. Typically, you use an e-mail client to access the newsgroups.

A tree structure of discussion topics organizes the groups. The first few letters of each newsgroup name indicates the major subject category. For example, *rec* refers to recreation and hobbies, *sci* references topics in science, *alt* refers to alternative topics (anything that's not mainstream), and so on. Each major heading has many subgroups, separated from the major heading by a period (e.g., soc.culture.australia).

Newsgroup users can post questions or comments to existing newsgroups, respond to previous posts, and create new newsgroups. Messages on newsgroups are *threaded* so that answers to or comments about a newsgroup message appear beneath it in a

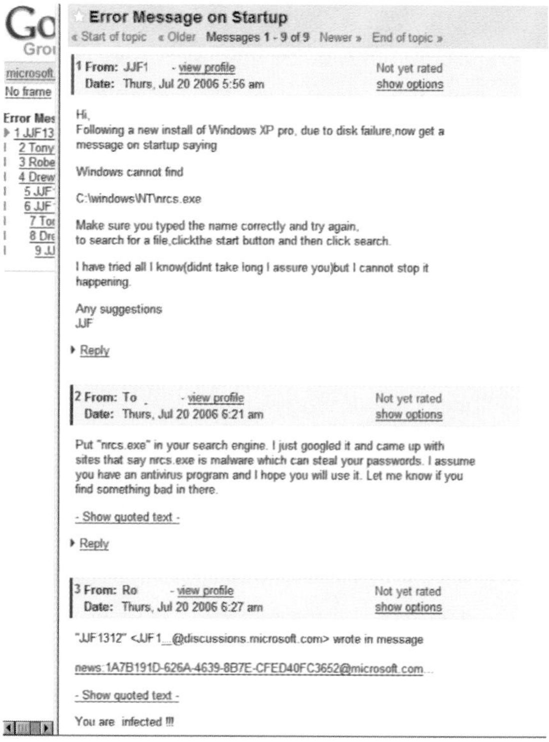

Figure C.16 The Microsoft Windows XP newsgroup.

list of messages, regardless of the data posted. This allows readers to easily follow a discussion.

Newcomers to newsgroups should become familiar with a newsgroup before posting to it by reading the newsgroup's *frequently asked questions (FAQ)* list. FAQ lists provide answers to the most frequently asked questions about a topic. Figure C.16 shows the Microsoft Windows XP newsgroup with a threaded discussion on replacing the main (mother) board on a computer (note that we deleted subscribers' names to protect privacy).

Many companies have begun to monitor newsgroups devoted to their products as a good source of customer feedback. Because bad news travels fast on the Internet, companies must quickly detect, and respond to, any emerging problems. In our example, Wild-Outfitters would probably want to monitor newsgroups dedicated to outdoor products, to find new ideas for marketing its products as well as to watch for negative or erroneous postings about them. They might also want to start a newsgroup to allow customers to ask questions and exchange information on hiking equipment with other customers.

Somewhat related to newsgroups are blogs. The word "**blog**" is derived from "Web log," a user-generated website written as a journal. Blogs can cover a variety of topics, including personal reflection, commentary on current affairs, movies, food, or games. Similar to newsgroups, blogs can contain opinions on products that companies should be aware of. In fact, several companies are creating blogs to discuss and promote their own products.

Internet Relay Chat

Internet relay chat (IRC) is a *synchronous* way to use the Internet to communicate. That is, IRC allows users to communicate back and forth at the same time, similar to a telephone conversation. Chat rooms and instant messaging are two widespread uses of IRC. With *chat rooms*, many individuals can send and receive messages simultaneously regarding a subject of interest to all of them; it is a group conversation. **Instant messaging (IM)** provides a private link between two individuals over which they communicate. Although instant messaging requires a server to create the initial link between the two users, once created, the link becomes automatic, does not require the server any more, and becomes a peer-to-peer network.

Note that chat rooms allow on-line discussions involving multiple persons, each adding his or her comments. It is a very popular way of interacting on-line, and provides a way of meeting other people on-line with similar interests. Meetings in a chat room have led to a number of relationships and even marriages. However, no one in the chat room has to provide evidence as to who they actually are. As a result, anyone using chat rooms should protect their own identity and be aware that others are doing the same. In same cases, individuals may be using chat rooms to lure unsuspecting people into dangerous situations.

Quick Test

Determine if the following statements are True or False.

1. The Internet is actually one single global network run by ICANN.

2. Newsgroups are a form of synchronous communications.

3. A domain name is always included as a part of the server address.

THE WORLD WIDE WEB

Of the six Internet operations listed earlier, the most recent is the World Wide Web (WWW), more commonly known as simply the Web. The Web is a body of software and a set of protocols and conventions based on hypertext and multimedia that make the Internet easy to use and browse. *Hypertext* links related information for which there is no hierarchy or menu system. **Multimedia** interactively combines text, graphics, animation, images, audio, and video displayed by and under the control of a computer.

Tim Berners-Lee, a computer scientist, developed the Web in 1989, at the European Laboratory for Particle Physics (CERN) in Geneva, Switzerland. He saw a need for physicists to be able to communicate with colleagues about their work while it was in progress, rather than waiting until a project was finished. To make this *real-time* communication possible, he wanted to create an interconnected web of documents that would allow a reader to jump between documents at will using hypertext links.

Although used only since the early 1990s on most computers, hypertext actually predates the use of personal computers. U.S. President Franklin D. Roosevelt's science advisor, Vannevar Bush, originally proposed the idea in a 1945 *Atlantic* magazine article entitled "As We May Think." Twenty years later, computer visionary Ted Nelson coined the term *hypertext.* However, hypertext remained a largely hidden concept until Apple Computers released its Macintosh HyperCard software in 1987.

As you can see, the Internet, and especially the World Wide Web, provide valuable tools and resources to knowledge-enabled professionals. So how do you access the Web? The client computer uses software called a *Web browser* (or simply, *browser*) that initiates activity by sending a request to a Web server for certain information.

USING BROWSERS TO ACCESS THE WEB

After using a browser to send a request to a Web server for information, the Web server responds by retrieving the information from its disk and then transmitting it to the client. Upon receiving the data, the browser formats the information for display. Web browsers use a graphical user interface (GUI) like that available on Microsoft Windows or the Apple Macintosh. With a GUI-based Web browser, you can perform various operations simply by pointing at menu selections or icons representing operations and clicking the mouse button; that is, point-and-click operations. For example, you can use a browser to navigate the Web by pointing at a hypertext link in the current document and clicking it. This operation causes the retrieval of the linked document, image file, or audio file from a distant computer and its display (or playing) on the local computer. You can also enter an address to retrieve a desired document or file.

When displaying information, the browser processes formatting instructions included in the text file retrieved from the server. For example, assume that the creator of a document stored on a Web server decides that a certain phrase should appear in italics when displayed. Instead of saving the file with an italics font, the server stores the text with tags of the form <i> and </i> that indicate the beginning and end of the text that will appear in italics when displayed.

The tags in World Wide Web documents are part of a special publishing language called *hypertext markup language (HTML)*. As such, the documents on the Web all have an .html (or .htm) extension. Documents on the Web are referred to as **web pages**, and their location is a **website**. Because HTML is standard for all computers, any Web browser can request an HTML document from any Web server. For instance, a browser running on a PC using Windows XP can access files created on a Macintosh, which are stored on a Linux-based server.

Web servers can also store multimedia files, which include digitized text, images, animation, video, and audio. The browser retrieves these files and displays them using appropriate software. The transfer of multimedia files from the Web server to the client browser is one of the key operations that sets the Web apart from the other Internet applications. Because multimedia enables us to view photographs, graphics, and videos and listen to music, it is a major reason for the phenomenal growth in the Web's popularity.

Figure C.17 shows a fairly simple web page. The underlined words indicates a hypertext link is beneath it. Also shown in this figure is the HTML source language, or source code, necessary to create the web page. Angle brackets (< >) enclose code tags, such as *title* to indicate the title of the page, *center* to centre the text, and *b* to make the text appear in boldface. Today you can create web pages with word-processing-like software such as Microsoft Front-Page and Netscape Composer, without knowing the details of HTML.

Browser Operations

A Web browser retrieves web pages from Web servers and displays them on a client computer. In addition to being electronic rather than physical, web pages differ from pages in a book or magazine in

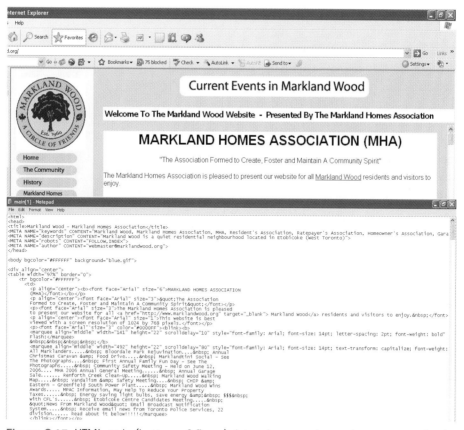

Figure C.17 HTML code (bottom of figure) determines a web page's appearance (top).

other ways. For example, although the amount of information on a physical page is restricted to the size of the paper page, a web page can extend beyond the area shown on a screen and include audio and video.

Many individuals, companies, and organizations have created websites that contain information about themselves and their activities. They continue to add more web pages every day. A specific address identifies each web page. In Web terminology, the address of a web page is referred to as its uniform resource locator. A *URL (uniform resource locator)* is a standard means of consistently locating web pages or other resources regardless of where the Internet stores them. For example, the URL of the first page for the WildOutfitters website might be

http://www.wildoutfitters.com/welcome.htm

Like every URL, this one has three parts: (1) the protocol, (2) the Internet address of the server that contains the desired resource, and

Protocol   Web server address   Path name

Figure C.18 The three parts of a URL.

(3) the path of the resource (sometimes hidden). Figure C.18 shows the three parts of the WildOutfitters welcome page address.

For Web resources, the protocol (also called the *service resource*) defines the type of resource being retrieved. The letters *http*, which, as we discussed earlier, stand for *hypertext transfer protocol*, identifies a web page resource. Some of the other allowable protocols include file, telnet, FTP, mailto, and news. Table C.7 lists these protocols (service resources) and their purposes.

The second part of the URL names the Web server, in this case, www.wildoutfitters.com. The third part of the URL is the *path* of the Web resource, which includes the name of the web page file plus its location in any directories or folders. In our example, the path of the web page document is simply the file name, *welcome.htm*. In many cases, the path name will be much longer because it includes the folder(s) that stores the web page.

For example, the URL of the website for the Information Technology and Strategic Management course offered at Ryerson University is

http://www.ryerson.ca/itm/Coursepdf/ITM700.pdf

In this URL, Coursepdf is a subfolder in the folder called "itm". Note also that this URL ends with a .pdf, indicating that this is a document. The complete path is interpreted as itm/Coursepdf/ITM700.pdf.

Many websites make use of index.html or default.html files to save people unnecessary typing. This also helps us to guess the URL of an organization's web page. For example, you would guess correctly if you tried http://www.dell.com/ to access Dell Inc.'s web page. In fact, most browsers now have built-in search engines that will search

Table C.7	Internet Protocols
Protocol	**Purpose**
http	Retrieve web pages
File	Retrieve files from local hard disk
telnet	Log on to a remote computer connected to the Internet
FTP	Download or upload files from an Internet FTP server
mailto	Send outgoing e-mail
News	Display newsgroup

for the *home* website if you simply enter the name. For example, entering *Dell* will result in finding and displaying matching websites, including the one shown on the previous page.

After entering a valid address for a resource, the next step is automatic: The browser software attempts to connect to the Web server at that address, find the page referenced in the address, and return it to the user's browser. If this operation is successful, then the Web browser displays the page on the screen; otherwise, it displays an error message.

The process of moving from one website or page to another one is known as surfing the Web. Web surfing can quickly become a time-consuming process as you follow links looking for information or a product to purchase. You can short-circuit this process to some extent by using one of the numerous Web search engines, into which you enter a query word or term and find pages or sites that match it. However, a problem with this approach is the large number of web pages that can be returned, many of which have nothing to do with the query you entered.

As you move from website to website, you may not be aware that something called a *cookie* is saved on your PC, A **cookie** is not an application or virus, but simply a data file that will be accessed by the related website the next time you visit it. This data file tells the website any preferences you have registered with them. Obviously there are privacy concerns associated with cookies, but they do make some websites very convenient to use since you do not have to re-register your information and preferences every time you visit. Every browser has the ability to reject cookies to prevent websites from installing them. However, if this function is enabled, many websites, especially those with shopping carts, will not work.

WIRELESS CONNECTIVITY TO THE WEB AND INTERNET

A number of mobile telephone companies have collaborated to create a special protocol, called **wireless application protocol (WAP)**, so their telephones can connect to the Internet. These companies—Ericsson, Nokia, Matsushita (Panasonic), Motorola, and Psion—have also created a company named Symbian (www.symbian.com) to develop and market an operating system named Symbian OS for their wireless devices. Symbian OS supports browsers and other software using WAP. Further, Symbian OS provides contacts information, messaging, browsing, and wireless telephone calls.

WAP has been transferred to some models of the PDAs running the Palm operating system, enabling them to take advantage of special WAP-based websites. These WAP-based websites *cannot* normally be viewed with the most popular browsers, Netscape and Internet Explorer. Instead, they have been specially configured for WAP devices connected to a WAP server.

Another popular use of connecting mobile telephones to a WAN is **short message service (SMS)**, which sends text messages of up to 160 characters to mobile telephones. SMS can send messages to a mobile telephone when it is not active and hold the message until it becomes active. The widest use of SMS is in systems that use the **global system for mobile communication (GSM) protocol**. It is also possible to send messages to GSM mobile telephone phones using a website. Between the use of SMS and GSM, over 430 *billion* messages were sent in 2002. A variant of SMS that allows images and audio to be sent via mobile devices is called multimedia messaging service (MMS). Many mobile telephones now have the ability to take photos and send them via the mobile network. Even more popular is the ability to download ring tones for mobile telephones to personalize telephone rings.

An increasingly popular device that leverages both WAP and SMS is the BlackBerry. The BlackBerry®, shown in Figure C.19, is produced by Research In Motion, a Canadian company based in Waterloo, Ontario. The BlackBerry enables e-mail capabilities, allowing users to access their e-mail virtually any time and any place they are able to connect to a wireless provider's network. Beyond personal applications, the business applications for WAP, SMS, and MMS are numerous:

Figure C.19 The BlackBerry is a popular device that leverages both WAP and SMS, allowing for "always on" e-mail capabilities.

- Using SMS to notify a salesperson about a request for information, along with a number to call
- Immediately sending a photo of a car accident to expedite an insurance claim
- Providing a service person with the name and location of their next service call that includes a link to an Internet site with a map to the location
- Using the company intranet via mobile phone to search for inventory while making a sale with a client

Quick Test

Fill in the blanks for the following statements.

1. The Web is a body of software and a set of protocols and conventions based on hypertext and _____ that make the Internet easy to use and browse.

2. The tags in World Wide Web documents are part of a special publishing language called _____.

3. Of the three parts of the URL, the _____ is sometimes hidden.

Answers: 1. multimedia; 2. HTML; 3. path

ROI STUDENT RETURN ON INVESTMENT SUMMARY

1. What is client/server architecture, and how does it work?

The most common architecture for computer networks is client/server architecture, in which each computer on the network is running either server software or client software, or both types of software simultaneously. Server software provides data or resources to other computers in the network. Client software requests services from the servers. Clients and servers can work in series, with the most common form being the three-tiered client/server architecture that uses a client, an application server, and a database server. It is possible for computers on a network to be both servers and clients; this is known as a peer-to-peer network.

2. How does the network layer model describe a wide area network?

The network layer model is used to understand the way networks operate. The layers define the standards with which each network must comply. The simplified model presented here consists of three layers: the application software layer, networking software layer, and data component layer. The application software layer specifies the software on each computer on the network that the user sees and uses to send and receive messages and data between computers, as well as the software necessary to encrypt the message or data streams. The networking software layer describes how the message from the application software layer is formatted according to whatever protocol will actually be used to send it over the network. For WANs, the Internet protocols (TCP/IP) and EDI protocols are important protocols in the network layer model. The data component layer describes the hardware and media (twisted pair, coaxial cable, and so on) over which a message is sent. Radio and infrared transmissions are now being used for wireless networks. Packets are transmitted over the Internet via a packet switching methodology that uses routers. Two other key considerations are the signal type—analog or digital, and the data rate—the rate at which bits are transmitted through the network.

3. How are local area networks configured?

The parts of a local area network include the server, client computers, cabling and hubs, the network operating system, and network interface cards (NICs). The cabling and hubs tie the server and client computers together. The network operating system directs the operations of the LAN and resides on both the server and the clients. Finally, the network interface card handles the electronic interface between the servers or clients and the rest of the network. The Ethernet protocol is used in the vast majority of LANs. Ethernet LANs have a bus physical setup and a hub usually handles interconnections. Wireless LANs (WLANs), in which the usual LAN cabling is replaced with wireless transmissions between computers, are becoming increasingly popular.

4. How does the Internet work?

The Internet is a network of networks that have agreed to use the TCP/IP protocols for addressing computers and sending packets over the network. There is no governing authority or central computer.

The six primary operations on the Internet are e-mail, FTP, telnet, newsgroups, and Internet relay chat (IRC). E-mail uses the simple mail transfer protocol (SMTP) to send asynchronous messages over the Internet to individuals and groups. A listserv is a method of easily sending e-mail messages to a group. FTP uses the file transfer protocol to transfer files between computers over the Internet. Telnet allows users to log on to a distant computer and to use software on that computer. Newsgroups enable users to engage in discussions on a global network of news servers. Finally, IRC enables users to communicate synchronously in chat rooms or through instant messaging.

5. What makes the World Wide Web valuable to knowledge-enabled professionals?

The World Wide Web (WWW), often referred to as the Web, is a body of software and a set of protocols and conventions based on hypertext and multimedia that make the Internet easy to use and browse. It is a client/server network by which the client browser software requests web pages created in hypertext markup language (HTML) from a Web server. Multimedia files are retrieved separately from text pages. Hypertext allows the user to jump within pages or from page to page. The address of the website is called a uniform resource locator (URL) and consists of a protocol, a Web server address, and the path of a web page.

KNOWLEDGE SPEAK

TECH GUIDE

TECH GUIDE D

The Details of SQL, Logical Modelling, and XML

WHAT WE WILL COVER

- Using SQL to Query Relational Databases
- Using Logical Modelling to Create a Relational Database
- Querying Multitable Databases
- Using XML for Data Transfer

ROI STUDENT RETURN ON INVESTMENT

Through your investment of time in reading and thinking about this guide, your return, or created value, is gaining knowledge. Use the following questions as a study guide.

1. How do knowledge-enabled professionals use SQL to query a single-table database?

2. How do knowledge-enabled professionals use logical modelling to create effective relational database systems?

3. How is SQL used to query multiple-table databases?

4. How do knowledge-enabled professionals use XML to transfer data between software applications?

In Chapter 5, we discussed how knowledge-enabled professionals use relational database systems as a way of organizing and accessing data. We also described how knowledge-enabled professionals use XML (extensible markup language) as a way of transferring data between software applications and for working with Web services. In this Tech Guide, we provide you with more information on both relational database systems and XML.

We start by describing the use of the SQL language to pose queries to a relational database to find needed data. We then discuss the concept of logical modelling, which guides setting up the tables in a relational database to allow easy data access (using SQL). Finally, we provide more details on how to use XML to describe and transfer data between applications.

USING SQL TO QUERY RELATIONAL DATABASES

The primary function of a database is to allow knowledge-enabled professionals to obtain information from it in a usable form. You will recall from Chapter 5 that a relational database is a database structured with tables that are related to one another so data can be stored and retrieved efficiently. These relations allow a user to run *queries* (questions) on the database to retrieve specific data. To query a relational database, many knowledge-enabled professionals use **Structured Query Language (SQL),** which is a computer language for manipulating data in a relational database. SQL queries also enable database users to add new records, or change or delete records in a database (instead of using commands from Microsoft Access or another software package). To demonstrate how to use SQL effectively, let's begin with a simple relational database example.

RELATIONAL DATABASE EXAMPLE

Recall the relational database that we used in Chapter 5 (WildOutfitters), shown here in Figure D.1. The database tables, Product and Vendor, are related through the **primary key**, a field that holds a unique value for each record. The VendorID is the primary key for the Vendor table. The Product table includes VendorID as a **foreign key**, to relate the two tables.

What types of queries would knowledge-enabled professionals, such as marketing analysts, use for this database? They might use a query to display all WildOutfitters products that sell for more than $100.00. Once a query has been used to find matching rows, the marketing analyst could then update a row, by making changes to the contents of one or more rows (e.g., modify prices), or to delete a row if it is no longer needed (e.g., discontinued products). It is also possible to add new rows to a table as WildOutfitters adds new products to its inventory.

ItemCode	ItemName	RetailPrice	ItemCost	VendorID
AM	Air Mattress	$100.00	$60.00	SFJ
BP	Backpack	$165.00	$80.00	BRU
CC	Child Carrier	$175.00	$85.00	SFJ
CK	Cookset	$50.00	$32.50	DOL
DP	Day Pack	$105.00	$60.00	WED
HB	Hiking Boots	$110.00	$50.00	DOL
PL	Propane Lantern	$35.00	$20.00	FEU
SB	Sleeping Bag	$100.00	$45.00	DOL
TT	Tent	$385.00	$110.00	WED
GC	Ground Cover	$20.00	$12.50	FEU

Product Table

VendorID	VendorName	Contact	PhoneNumber	Discount
BRU	Backpacks R' U	Nick Estelle	415-555-8328	5.00%
DOL	Doleman Manuf	George Burdell	770-555-4505	6.00%
FEU	Feuters Campin	Chris Patrick	406-555-2103	4.00%
SFJ	SFJ Enterprises	Ashley Hyatt	239-555-0308	5.00%
WED	Waters End	Todd Keegan	715-555-1212	7.00%

Vendor Table

Figure D.1 Related WildOutfitters database tables.

PRODUCT

ItemCode*
ItemName
RetailPrice
ItemCost
VendorID

Figure D.2 Single database table (in all capitals) with five fields.

QUERYING A SINGLE-TABLE DATABASE

A table is known more formally as an **entity**. All tables must be given an **identifier,** or a name, as must all fields in the database. In both cases, it is best to use descriptive names. Figure D.2 shows the Product entity with the fields shown earlier. Note that the table name is in all capitals to distinguish it from the field names. Note also that an asterisk denotes the primary key for this table, ItemCode.

So how would knowledge-enabled professionals use SQL to query this database table? Let's begin by looking at the general form of an SQL query to search for matching records:

SELECT *fields* FROM *tables* WHERE *fields match query condition*

Here, the SELECT keyword designates which fields to display as a result of the query, the FROM keyword designates which tables to search, and the WHERE keyword specifies the search criteria, or query condition, to use in finding records. Note that we use upper-case for keywords, to make them stand out, but otherwise case is not important when using SQL.

So to display the ItemCost for all records in the PRODUCT table that have an ItemCode of BP, the SQL query is

SELECT ItemCost FROM Product WHERE ItemCode = 'BP'

We enclose the BP ItemCode in single quotation marks to designate it as a character or text constant (double quotation marks can also be used). Numeric constants (such as the retail price or item cost) will not be enclosed in such quotation marks. For this query, and assuming the entire product table is shown in Figure D.1, the result will show $80.00.

In addition to the SELECT keyword, there are a number of other keywords that we can use to CREATE a table, to INSERT new records in a table, to DELETE records from a table, and to UPDATE one or more records in a table. We can also search for records that are *like* a specific condition as well as calculate sums, averages, and so on, for all records that match some criteria.

In the next sections we use several SQL commands with which you should become familiar, to increase your productivity as a knowledge-enabled professional.

USING SQL TO DISPLAY SPECIFIC INFORMATION

Let's begin by using SQL to display all of the table; that is, all fields for all of the records. In this case, the form of the SQL command is quite simple:

SELECT * FROM *TableName*

ItemCode	ItemName	RetailPrice	ItemCost	VendorID
AM	Air Mattress	$100.00	$60.00	SFJ
BP	Backpack	$165.00	$80.00	BRU
CC	Child Carrier	$175.00	$85.00	SFJ
CK	Cookset	$50.00	$32.50	DOL
DP	Day Pack	$105.00	$60.00	WED
HB	Hiking Boots	$110.00	$50.00	DOL
PL	Propane Lantern	$35.00	$20.00	FEU
SB	Sleeping Bag	$100.00	$45.00	DOL
TT	Tent	$385.00	$110.00	WED
GC	Ground Cover	$20.00	$12.50	FEU

Product Table

Figure D.3 WildOutfitters Product Table.

Here, the asterisk is a placeholder for all fields in the table. Figure D.3 shows the result of this SQL command for the Product table.

Displaying Selected Fields for all Records

Instead of displaying all fields for all records, we may only want to display a subset of the fields. The standard form of this query is

SELECT *FieldName1, FieldName2, . . .* FROM *TableName*

Note that you can include one or more field names in the list. For example, if we want to display just the item names and retail prices for all products sold by WildOutfitters, the SQL command would be

SELECT ItemName, RetailPrice FROM Product

Figure D.4 shows the resulting output, which displays all the products along with their retail prices.

If we want to display these records in some order other than in increasing order of the primary key, we can add the *Order By* clause to the SQL statement. The standard form of this query is

SELECT *FieldName1, FieldName2, . . .* FROM *TableName*
ORDER BY *FieldName*

In this case, the results of the query will be ordered according to the last field name mentioned. For example, to show the same list of items as before but now in increasing order of retail price, the SQL statement is

SELECT ItemName, RetailPrice FROM Product
ORDER By RetailPrice

ItemName	RetailPrice
Air Mattress	$100.00
Backpack	$165.00
Child Carrier	$175.00
Cookset	$50.00
Day Pack	$105.00
Ground Cover	$20.00
Hiking Boots	$110.00
Propane Lantern	$35.00
Sleeping Bag	$100.00
Tent	$385.00

Figure D.4 Result of query to display specific field names.

Displaying Selected Fields for Matching Records

In many cases, we may only want to display selected fields for records that match some condition. To do this, we need to use the WHERE keyword followed by some query condition involving one of six comparison operators: equals (=), greater than (>), less than (<), greater than or equal to (>=), less than or equal to (<=), or not equal to (<>), plus a field name and a value. The general form is

SELECT *FieldName1, FieldName2, . . .* FROM *TableName*
WHERE *Query Condition*

For example, assume that the marketing department at WildOutfitters wants to know the names and wholesale costs of products with an item cost greater than $50. To display the item name and item cost, the SQL statement is

SELECT ItemName, ItemCost FROM Product
WHERE ItemCost > 50

Here, using the WHERE keyword restricts which rows to display; that is, only those that have an ItemCost value greater than $50.00. In this case, this query would display the item name and item cost for the five products with an item cost over $50.00: Air Mattress, Backpack, Child Carrier, Day Pack, and the Tent.

It is also possible to combine conditions in a query by using the AND or OR operators, known as *compound operators.* The AND operator requires both conditions to be true, while the OR operator only requires that one or both of the conditions be true. For example, consider this query:

SELECT ItemName, ItemCost FROM product WHERE
ItemCost > 15 AND VendorID = "FEU"

The results of this query will show the name, cost, and vendor ID for any product with a cost greater than $15.00 from the vendor whose ID is FEU.

USING THE LIKE OPERATOR

Whenever you use the equals sign in a SELECT query, you are looking for an exact match. But what happens, for example, if you don't know the exact product name? Or if you're looking for information about a group of products? In that case, you should use the LIKE operator. The LIKE operator uses the **wildcard** character as a replacement for unknown or nonexisting characters in attempting to find matches to a group of characters (commonly referred to as a **character string**). The wildcard character is usually either the asterisk (*) in Microsoft Access or the percent sign (%) in other database mangement systems. The general form of this type of query is

SELECT *FieldName1, Fieldname2, . . .* FROM *TableName*
WHERE *FieldName* LIKE '*value*'

For example, to find the item names and retail prices of all types of backpacks offered by WildOutfitters, the query in Access is

SELECT ItemName, RetailPrice FROM Product
WHERE ItemName LIKE '*Pack*'

In this query, the wildcard character represents anything on either side of the word "Pack". The query results in this case will display records for the Backpack and the Day Pack.

INSERTING OR DELETING RECORDS

As we discussed earlier, you can use Microsoft Access or another relational database management package to add records to or delete records from a database table. It is also possible to carry out both of these operations using SQL. To insert a record into a table, you would use an SQL statement of the form

INSERT INTO *TableName* Values *(value1, value2, . . .)*

Note that, in this format, you must enter the values in the exact order as the fields in the record, separated by commas. If there are null or missing values, you must still enter the corresponding comma.

For example, to insert a new record for a heater with an item code of HH, a retail price of $75.00, and an item cost of $45.00 into the Product table of the WildOutfitters database, the SQL statement is

INSERT INTO Product Values('HH', 'Heater', 75, 45)

As above, note that we use single quotation marks to set off the two character strings in this query.

To delete an existing record from a database table, you would use an SQL statement in the form

DELETE FROM *TableName* WHERE *FieldName* = *value*

This will delete all records that match the criteria. For example, assume that WildOutfitters no longer carries the Ground Cover product and needs to remove it from the database. To do this, the SQL command is

DELETE FROM Product WHERE ItemCode = 'GC'

CHANGING VALUES WITH SQL

To change values in a row of a database, you can use the UPDATE and SET keywords in the form

UPDATE *TableName* SET *FieldName1* = *value*
WHERE *FieldName2* = *value;*

For example, assume the ItemCost for the tent has increased by 10 percent. To account for this increase in the database table, the SQL statement is

UPDATE Product SET ItemCost = ItemCost*1.1 WHERE
ItemCode = 'TT';

Executing this SQL statement will result in the ItemCost for the tent to increase from $110.00 to $121.00.

USING AGGREGATE FUNCTIONS IN SQL

Our final SQL operation is to use it to calculate certain values in the table using five different **aggregate functions**: COUNT, AVG, SUM, MIN, and MAX. As their names indicate, the purposes of these functions are to count the number of matching records, find their average value, sum the values, or find the minimum or maximum matching value, respectively. In each case, you must use a dummy field name for the result of the calculation.

The form for the AVG function is

SELECT AVG*(fieldname)* AS *DummyName* FROM *TableName*
WHERE *Query condition*

In this SQL statement, the AVG function finds the average of the values of the field name in parentheses, subject to the query condition. It then stores that value in the dummy name variable, which is displayed after running the query.

For example, to find the average retail price for all items in the Product table, the query is

SELECT AVG(RetailPrice) AS AvgPrice FROM Product

Running this query on the PRODUCT table shown in Figure D.4 results in displaying the average retail price of $124.50.

The SUM, MAX, and MIN functions have the same form as the AVG function. The COUNT function, however, uses a different form, as the following shows:

> SELECT COUNT(*) AS *DummyName* FROM *TableName*
> WHERE *Query condition*

For example, to count the number of items in the table with a retail price of more than $75.00, the SQL statement is

> SELECT COUNT(*) AS Over75Count FROM Product
> WHERE RetailPrice>75

The results of this query will display the number of items with a retail price of more than $75.00.

So far in our discussion of relational databases, we have been querying a single table using SQL. However, the real power of a relational database comes from the use of multiple tables. In the next section, we discuss how creating a database with multiple tables usually increases the productivity of knowledge-work activities.

Quick Test

For the Product table above, write queries to carry out the following operations.

1. Display the item name and retail price for all items with a retail price greater than $100.00.

2. Insert a new record for a product with ItemCode of 'CC,' an item name of 'Camp Chair,' an item cost of $95.00, and a retail price of $175.00.

3. Calculate the average item cost of all items in inventory.

Answers: 1. SELECT ItemName, RetailPrice FROM Product WHERE RetailPrice > 100; 2. INSERT INTO Product VALUES('CC', 'Camp Chair', 95, 175); 3. SELECT AVG(ItemCost) as AvgCost FROM Product

USING LOGICAL MODELLING TO CREATE A RELATIONAL DATABASE

Most relational databases include many tables, not just one. Why? To help you understand the reasons for this, consider the expanded version of the PRODUCT table, shown in Figure D.5. Note that we have now added information about the vendor that provides each product to WildOutfitters. Included in the vendor information are the vendor

ItemCode	ItemName	RetailPrice	ItemCost	VendorID	VendorName	Contact	PhoneNumber	Discount
BP	Backpack	$165.00	$80.00	BRU	Backpacks R' L	Nick Estelle	415-555-8328	5.00%
CK	Cookset	$50.00	$32.50	DOL	Doleman Manuf	George Burdell	770-555-4505	6.00%
HB	Hiking Boots	$110.00	$50.00	DOL	Doleman Manuf	George Burdell	770-555-4505	6.00%
SB	Sleeping Bag	$100.00	$45.00	DOL	Doleman Manuf	George Burdell	770-555-4505	6.00%
PL	Propane Lantern	$35.00	$20.00	FEU	Feuters Campin	Chris Patrick	406-555-2103	4.00%
GC	Ground Cover	$20.00	$12.50	FEU	Feuters Campin	Chris Patrick	406-555-2103	4.00%
AM	Air Mattress	$100.00	$60.00	SFJ	SFJ Enterprises	Ashley Hyatt	239-555-0308	5.00%
CC	Child Carrier	$175.00	$85.00	SFJ	SFJ Enterprises	Ashley Hyatt	239-555-0308	5.00%
DP	Day Pack	$105.00	$60.00	WED	Waters End	Todd Keegan	715-555-1212	7.00%
TT	Tent	$385.00	$110.00	WED	Waters End	Todd Keegan	715-555-1212	7.00%

Figure D.5 Using a single table to store data often results in redundancy.

name, the contact name and telephone number, and the discount given by the vendor if WildOutfitters pays its bill within 30 days of delivery.

In looking at Figure D.5, you can now probably see a big reason for not using a single table: *redundancy.* Note that the Product table now lists each vendor's name, contact, phone number, and discount rate multiple times. This redundancy can not only result in the database table taking up storage space (especially for a realistic-sized database table involving millions of records), but also causes problems, typically referred to as **anomalies**, when trying to insert new records, delete existing records, or update records. Therefore, to solve the problems associated with storing all the data in one table, relational databases are used.

As we discussed in Chapter 5, reducing data redundancy is one advantage of using a relational database. Other advantages include improving data access and sharing by using database standards; maintaining the integrity of the data by having security and controls to prevent errors, duplication, and unauthorized entry; and allowing configurable views of the data to match the user needs.

To create the appropriate relational tables, most knowledge-enabled professionals rely on logical modelling. *Logical modelling* provides tools to help analyze and understand what data are important, and the relationships between the data.

ENTITY-RELATIONSHIP DIAGRAMMING

The first step in logical modelling is to create an *entity-relationship diagram (ERD).* The ERD is uncluttered by attributes so businesses can focus on the "big picture;" that is, the entities and the relationships. Businesses then use the ERD to build a *relational data model,* which adds the attributes and helps to organize them prior to creating the database.

For example, let's use the information from Figure D.5 (the Product-Vendor information), picking out the entities and attributes, to create the ERD. We first need to think about what entities we need to consider. In this case, we can easily identify two entities:

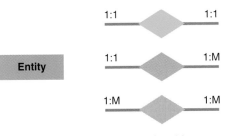

Figure D.6 Standard ERD symbols, where a diamond indicates a relationship.

PRODUCT and VENDOR. Now, using standard symbols, we can draw the entities and the relationships between the entities. Figure D.6 shows the standard symbols for an ERD. Note that 1:1 means one-to-one (a **one-to-one relationship**), and 1:M means one-to-many. The diamond indicates a relationship between two entities.

Figure D.7 shows the ERD for our example. In reading from left to right, you can see the ERD indicates that *one* vendor sells *many* products, while each product is sold by only one vendor. Note that the 1:M is next to the Product entity, as it includes *many* products.

Let's now think of another situation involving the Product table, one involving customers instead of vendors. If you think about it, a customer can purchase many products, and many customers can purchase the same product. As a result, the 1:M is next to both the Product and Customer entities. The ERD, shown in Figure D.8, includes what is known as a **many-to-many relationship** between the Customer and Product entities.

What happens when you have this type of relationship between entities? You have a problem, because many-to-many relationships violate logical modelling rules for creating a relational database. Specifically, it is not possible to create a primary key–foreign key relationship with a many-to-many relationship (primary and foreign keys are defined in Chapter 5). As a result, you need to draw a new **relational entity** to lie between the original two entities. As Figure D.9 shows, the relational entity is connected to each original entity by a one-to-many relationship, thereby transforming the original many-to-many relationship into two one-to-many relationships.

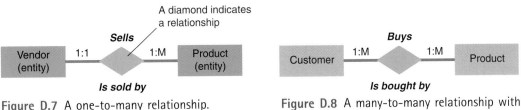

Figure D.7 A one-to-many relationship.

Figure D.8 A many-to-many relationship with no primary key–foreign key relationship.

This . . .

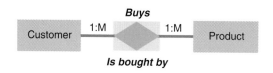

Many-to-many relationship (before transformation).

. . . Becomes this

Two one-to-many relationships with relational entity (after transformation)

Figure D.9 Converting a many-to-many (M:M) relationship into two one-to-many (1:M) relationships.

THE RELATIONAL DATA MODEL

After creating the ERD, the next step of logical modelling is to create the relational data model. Recall that this step "fills in the details" of the relationship between the entities. That is, a relational data model adds the attributes, as well as identifies primary and foreign keys. To see how to do this, let's convert the 1:M ERD (Figure D.7) into a data model.

As Figure D.10 shows, the symbols change when converting the ERD to a data model. The relationship symbol changes from a "labelled diamond" to a "line with crow's foot." The "crow's foot" is placed on the "many" side of the relationship. The data model also adds more detail to the entities, including a listing of the attributes (fields) for the entities and indicators for the primary and foreign keys. A simple rule of thumb for determining foreign keys is that the primary key from the "one" side of the relationship is used as a foreign key on the "many" side of the relationship.

What about the data model for the ERD for the M:M customer-product situation discussed above? We can use the same PRODUCT table, but now we need a CUSTOMER table that includes a customer's

Figure D.10 Data model for a one-to-many (1:M) relationship.

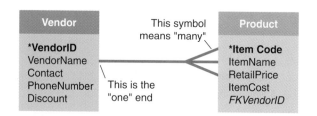

ID number, shipping address, city, province, postal code, and e-mail address. Figure D.11 shows the resulting entity, where the CustomerID field is the primary key.

Next, we need a PURCHASE table to convert the M:M relationship into two 1:M relationships. This entity will include the primary keys from both the CUSTOMER and PRODUCT tables (as foreign keys), as well as some unique identifier as its own primary key. The two foreign keys enable WildOutfitters to determine information on the buyer (customer) as well as information on the product purchased. Finally, we will also include the number of items purchased and the date of the purchase in this table. Figure D.12 shows the resulting entity.

Now, using the CUSTOMER, PRODUCT, and PURCHASE tables, we can create the data model that represents the purchase of a product by a customer. Note that the customer may purchase multiple products, and multiple customers can purchase the same product, by simply having one record in the PURCHASE table for each purchase. Figure D.13 shows the resulting data model, which matches the transformed M:M ERD shown in Figure D.8.

We have included the VendorID foreign key in the PRODUCT table, since it is also related to the VENDOR table. We can now combine both of these entity-relationships into one complete data model, as shown in Figure D.14. As this shows, by using logical modelling, organizations can effectively expand their databases along with their businesses.

A final consideration in creating a data model is that of **referential integrity**, which enforces consistency between linked tables. To understand referential integrity, you should think of the values stored in a foreign key as a reference to a record in another table. If, for some reason, that record does not exist, then there are problems. For example, if we try to add a record to the PRODUCT table that tries to reference a VendorID for a vendor that does not exist in the VENDOR table, then a message will warn us about it. Conversely, if we try to remove a vendor record from the VENDOR table and that vendor has products listed in the PRODUCT table, a warning message will also appear. This feature helps to maintain the overall integrity of databases.

CUSTOMER

*CustomerID
ShipAddress
ShipCity
ShipProvince
ShipPostal
EmailAddress

Figure D.11 CUSTOMER entity, where CustomerID is the primary key.

PURCHASE

*PurchaseID
FKCustomerID
FKItemCode
PurchaseDate
Number

Figure D.12 PURCHASE entity used to transform the M:M relationship into two 1:M relationships.

CUSTOMER	PURCHASE	PRODUCT
*CustomerID	*PurchaseID	*ItemCode
ShipAddress	FKCustomerID	ItemName
ShipCity	FKItemCode	RetailPrice
ShipProvince	PurchaseDate	ItemCost
ShipPostal	Number	FKVendorID
EmailAddress		

Figure D.13 Conversion of an M:M relationship into two 1:M relationships.

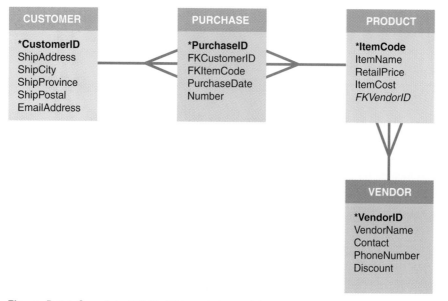

Figure D.14 Complete WildOutfitters data model.

After creating a relational database with two or more tables, we can use SQL to query it, in a manner similar to querying a single-table database.

Quick Test

Indicate whether the following statements are True or False.

1. Logical modelling helps to create anomalies in relational databases.

2. An ERD identifies the primary and foreign keys of entities.

3. Referential integrity enforces consistency between linked tables.

Answers: 1. False; 2. False; 3. True

QUERYING MULTITABLE DATABASES

In this section, we look at the most common operation on a two-table database: the Join operation. We then discuss how to use views to save queried results.

THE JOIN OPERATION

The **Join operation** creates a single table from two (or more) tables, after which you can use it to perform calculations and carry out

Query1 : Select Query

ItemCode	ItemName	RetailPrice	ItemCost	Product.VendorID	Vendor.VendorID	VendorName	Contact	PhoneNumber	Discount
BP	Backpack	$165.00	$80.00	BRU	BRU	Backpacks R' Us	Nick Estelle	415-555-8328	5.00%
HH	Heater	$75.00	$45.00	BRU	BRU	Backpacks R' Us	Nick Estelle	415-555-8328	5.00%
CK	Cookset	$50.00	$32.50	DOL	DOL	Doleman Manufac	George Burdell	770-555-4505	6.00%
HB	Hiking Boots	$110.00	$50.00	DOL	DOL	Doleman Manufac	George Burdell	770-555-4505	6.00%
SB	Sleeping Bag	$100.00	$45.00	DOL	DOL	Doleman Manufac	George Burdell	770-555-4505	6.00%
PL	Propane Lanter	$35.00	$20.00	FEU	FEU	Feuters Camping I	Chris Patrick	406-555-2103	4.00%
AM	Air Mattress	$100.00	$60.00	SFJ	SFJ	SFJ Enterprises	Ashley Hyatt	239-555-0308	5.00%
CC	Child Carrier	$175.00	$85.00	SFJ	SFJ	SFJ Enterprises	Ashley Hyatt	239-555-0308	5.00%
DP	Day Pack	$105.00	$60.00	WED	WED	Waters End	Todd Keegan	715-555-1212	7.00%
TT	Tent	$385.00	$121.00	WED	WED	Waters End	Todd Keegan	715-555-1212	7.00%

Record: 1 of 10

Figure D.15 Results of a Join query.

grouping of products. For our example, the SQL instruction to do this is as follows:

```
SELECT * FROM Product, Vendor WHERE
Product.VendorID = Vendor.VendorID
```

In looking at this query, note that because the field name for the foreign key in PRODUCT (VendorID) is the same as the primary key field name in VENDOR, we distinguish between them by combining the table name and the field name using a period; that is, Product.VendorID and Vendor.VendorID. Figure D.15 shows the result of this query.

While this looks very much like the single table we decided earlier to avoid, it does enable us to avoid update anomalies. Further, we can use the same approach as querying a single table to quickly do a number of things. For example, to list products, vendor name, and item cost in alphabetical order of item name, we could easily modify the previous query to the following:

```
SELECT ItemName, VendorName, ItemCost FROM Product,
Vendor WHERE Product.VendorID = Vendor.VendorID
ORDER BY ItemName;
```

It is also possible to carry out calculations and display them as the result of a join query. For example, each vendor offers a different discount to WildOutfitters for paying its bill within 30 days of receiving the merchandise. The net item cost then equals the item cost times (1 – discount). We can modify the previous SQL query to output the item name, vendor name, item cost, discount, and the net cost as follows:

```
SELECT ItemName, VendorName, ItemCost, Discount,
ItemCost*(1-Discount) as NetCost FROM Product,
Vendor WHERE Product.VendorID = Vendor.VendorID
ORDER BY ItemName;
```

The results of this query will list the products in order of vendor, as well as create a new field, NetCost, that will indicate the discounted cost.

CREATING VIEWS

With most relational database management systems, it is possible to save the queries you have created. Another name for a saved query is a **view**. However, note that these views are not actual tables, even though they might appear that way on the screen.

There are two main reasons for creating a view. First, it enables you to simplify query writing in the future. If you plan to reuse some aspect of a query, you can save it as a view and then use it by itself or as part of another query. For example, say we had saved a previous query as *TotalSold* and now only wanted to see the item names and revenue from this query. A new and simpler query to do this would be as follows:

SELECT ItemName, Revenue FROM TotalSold;

A second reason for using a view is for security. We can create a view only showing fields that we want others to see. That way, they cannot look at fields in the database, such as customer information, that may include confidential information.

Quick Test
Determine if the following statements are True or False.

1. The most common operation on a two-table database is the Intersection operation, which creates a single table from two (or more) tables.

2. A vision is another name for a saved query.

3. You must include table names when creating a multitable query.

Answers: 1. False; 2. False; 3. True

USING XML FOR DATA TRANSFER

Until now, we have limited our discussion to creating and using relational databases within an organization. However, most companies today require the ability to share data and resources over the Web. Although for many years companies have been using a system known as *electronic data interchange (EDI)*, EDI is expensive and has been found to be useful only to very large companies. With the rapid growth of the Internet, organizations have turned to the use of XML as a way of carrying out the same processes. An XML file can be processed purely as data by a program, it can be stored with similar data on another computer, or, like an HTML file, it can be displayed.

XML vs. HTML

A good way to understand XML is to compare it with HTML, the markup language that is the basis for the Web. First, you should recall that HTML is a *formatting language* that is meant to display numbers and text in a predefined way on a Web browser. As such, it does not have the structure to impart meaning to items like part numbers or prices. Because it is not a good idea to have computers to infer meanings from entries on web pages, HTML is not appropriate for transmitting large amounts of purchasing and shipping information over the Internet. HTML also has predetermined tags, which reduces its flexibility, and the only way you can retrieve information from it is to search for specific text.

XML solves these problems with HTML because it is a language that emphasizes the structure and meaning of data. This means that product information such as name, identifier, and price are easily transmitted using XML. XML is also flexible in that users can define their own tags. For example, a company could use XML to define tags that their trading partners can understand. This enables searches of the data using the meaning of the data instead of just using a text search. For example, the tag <PARTID> would indicate that the field that followed was a part number and it would be easy to find all part numbers by searching for this tag. An XML file can be processed purely as data by a program, it can be stored with similar data on another computer, or, like an HTML file, it can be displayed. For example, depending on how the application in the receiving computer wanted to handle the part number field, it could be stored or displayed, or some other operation could be performed on it, depending on the content of the field. Table D.1 compares XML with HTML.

Table D.1	Comparison of HTML and XML	
Feature	**XML**	**HTML**
Type of text	Structured with meaning defined	Formatted with meaning inferred
Definition of structure	User-defined	Predetermined
Retrieval	Context-sensitive	Limited
Searchability	Searchable by text or meaning	Searchable only by text or format
Hypertext linkage	Extensive	Limited

SETTING UP AN XML DOCUMENT

The first step to creating an XML file is to decide which tags to use to describe the data that are being transferred over the Internet. As with HTML, the tags are enclosed in angle brackets (<>). Each beginning tag *must* have an ending tag. For example, if using a <PARTID> tag to describe the part ID, then there *must* be a matching </PARTID> tag. These tags must come immediately before and after the data item, to ensure that there is no ambiguity or inconsistency about the description.

While current browsers are usually capable of determining the matching tags for each data item in an XML file, it is a better practice to provide a formal definition of all the data elements in the XML file. This can be done in one of two ways: the **document type definition** method or the **XML schema** method. Both can be incorporated into the XML file or created as separate files with DTD or XSD extensions, respectively. These files are then referred to by the XML file to define the XML tags it uses to describe the data.

Using a DTD or XSD file, a program called a *parser* in a Web browser can work with the tags that the document contains. For example, Figure D.16 shows an XML schema (XSD) file for a list of WildOutfitters' vendors. Note that the first line of this XSD file with the "<?xml . . .>" tag defines it as also being an XML file. The tags that begin with *xsd:* make up the formal definition of the data elements to be used in the matching XML file. Note also that the schema defines the names of tag elements in the XML file and their data type. For instance, the schema defines an element called CompanyName, which will contain text (string) information.

Figure D.17 shows a portion of the XML file that uses this schema. Note that the file line defines it as an XML file, and the third line references the schema (XSD) file shown in Figure D.16 (companynew.xsd).

```
<?xml version="1.0" encoding="UTF-8"?>
<xsd:schema xmlns:xsd="http://www.w3.org/2001/XMLSchema">
<!--Customer List-->
<xsd:element name="Customers">
 <xsd:complexType>
  <xsd:sequence>
   <xsd:element maxOccurs="unbounded" minOccurs="1" name="Company" type="companies"/>
  </xsd:sequence>
 </xsd:complexType>
</xsd:element>
<xsd:complexType name="companies">
 <xsd:sequence>
  <xsd:element name="CompanyName" type="xsd:string"/>
  <xsd:element name="Address" type="xsd:string"/>
  <xsd:element name="City" type="xsd:string"/>
  <xsd:element name="State" type="xsd:string"/>
  <xsd:element name="Zip" type="xsd:string"/>
 </xsd:sequence>
</xsd:complexType>
</xsd:schema>
```

Figure D.16 XML schema (XSD) file.

```
<?xml version="1.0" encoding="utf-8"?>
<?xml-stylesheet type="text/xsl" href="companynew.xsl" media="screen"?>
<NewDataSet xmlns:xsi="http://www.w3.org/2001/XMLSchema-instance" xsi:noNamespaceSchemaLocation="companynew.xsd">
    <Company>
        <CompanyName>ABC Metals</CompanyName>
        <Address>550 Montgomery Street</Address>
        <City>Minneapolis</City>
        <State>MN</State>
        <Zip>55402</Zip>
    </Company>
    <Company>
        <CompanyName>Backpacks R Us</CompanyName>
        <Address>122 Hilltop Avenue</Address>
        <City>Missoula</City>
        <State>MT</State>
        <Zip>59801</Zip>
    </Company>
    <Company>
        <CompanyName>Doleman Hiking Supplies</CompanyName>
        <Address>2532 Epson Blvd</Address>
        <City>Ocala</City>
        <State>FL</State>
        <Zip>34470</Zip>
    </Company>
    <Company>
```

Figure D.17 Portion of the XML file that uses the schema from Figure D.16.

The second line refers to a stylesheet (XSL) file (which we will discuss shortly). You can see these elements used to describe actual data starting with the fourth line, which has a < company > tag. It is fairly easy to see that the first company is named ABC Metals, located at 550 Montgomery Street in Minneapolis, Minnesota, 55402. Note that a tag </company > terminates the data for the first company.

To display an XML file in a more readable form on a Web browser, we need to use an XML **stylesheet (XSL) file.** This file uses a combination of HTML and XML tags. In our example, the XML file references it in the second line. Figure D.18 shows the actual companynew.xsl stylesheet file. Note that it is also an XML file, and the *xsl:* tags reference the stylesheet elements along with the HTML tags.

```
<?xml version="1.0" encoding="UTF-8"?>
<xsl:stylesheet version="1.0"
xmlns:xsl="http://www.w3.org/1999/XSL/Transform">
    <xsl:output encoding="UTF-8" indent="yes" method="html" version="1.0" />
    <xsl:template match="/">
    <html>
        <head>
            <title> Complete List of Vendors </title>
        </head>
    <body>
        <h1> Complete List of Vendors| </h1>
        <xsl:apply-templates select="NewDataSet" />
    </body>
    </html>
    </xsl:template>
    <xsl:template match="NewDataSet">
        <table border = '1'>
        <xsl:for-each select="Company">
            <tr>
                <td><xsl:value-of select="CompanyName" /></td>
                <td><xsl:value-of select="Address" /></td>
                <td><xsl:value-of select="City" /></td>
                <td><xsl:value-of select="State" /></td>
                <td><xsl:value-of select="Zip" /></td>
            </tr>
            </xsl:for-each>
        </table>
    </xsl:template>
</xsl:stylesheet>
```

Figure D.18 This stylesheet (XSL) file uses a combination of HTML and XML tags.

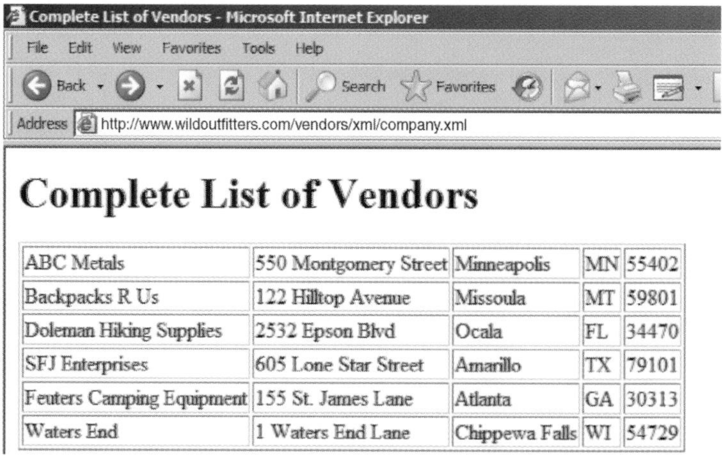

Figure D.19 How a browser displays the XML data from Figure D.18.

Complete List of Vendors

ABC Metals	550 Montgomery Street	Minneapolis	MN	55402
Backpacks R Us	122 Hilltop Avenue	Missoula	MT	59801
Doleman Hiking Supplies	2532 Epson Blvd	Ocala	FL	34470
SFJ Enterprises	605 Lone Star Street	Amarillo	TX	79101
Feuters Camping Equipment	155 St. James Lane	Atlanta	GA	30313
Waters End	1 Waters End Lane	Chippewa Falls	WI	54729

So what does the final result of these files look like on a Web browser? Figure D.19 shows the results.

Quick Test

Fill in the blanks for the following statements.

1. All XML files must include both beginning and _____ tags.

2. Unlike HTML, XML files provide _____ to the data.

3. A(n) _____ file is used to display an XML file in easily readable form.

Answers: 1. ending; 2. meaning; 3. stylesheet

(ROI) STUDENT RETURN ON INVESTMENT SUMMARY

1. How do knowledge-enabled professionals use SQL to query a single-table database?

The primary function of a database is to enable users to obtain information from it in a usable form. Users obtain information from a database by constructing and running queries or questions to the database. For a relational database, the queries are written in Structured Query Language (SQL), which is a computer language for manipulating data in a relational database.

The general form of SQL query to search for matching records is:

SELECT *fields* FROM *tables* WHERE *fields match query condition*

In the SQL statement, the SELECT keyword designates which fields to display as a result of the query, the FROM keyword designates which tables to search, and the WHERE keyword specifies the search criteria or query condition to use in finding records. In addition to finding data, SQL can be used to insert, delete, and update records in the database tables as well as carrying out calculations on records.

2. How do knowledge-enabled professionals use logical modelling to create effective relational database systems?

Logical modelling provides tools to help businesses analyze and understand what data are important and the relationships between the data by creating a picture of this world of data and relationships. An accurate logical model provides a business with a solid foundation upon which to build its database(s).

In logical modelling, the ERD focuses on the entities and the relationships. The Data Model adds the attributes and helps to organize them prior to creating the database. Primary and foreign keys are identified as well. The Data Model is built after the ERD by adjusting some symbols and adding more detail.

3. How is SQL used to query multiple-table databases?

The most common operation on a two-table database is the Join operation, which creates a single table from two (or more) tables. The general form of a two-table join is

SELECT*FROM *Table1, Table2* WHERE
Table1.Primary*Key* = *Table2.ForeignKey*

The Join operation is not restricted to just two tables; it is possible to carry out a three, four, or even more table join as long as all of the tables are related.

4. How do knowledge-enabled professionals use XML to transfer data between software applications?

XML uses tags to mark up content and/or data so that software applications can recognize it. Using XML, companies can define their own tags, which their trading partners can then understand. An XML file can be processed purely as data by a program, it can be stored with similar data on another computer or, like an HTML file, it can be displayed. The first step to creating an XML file is to decide on the tags that will be used to describe the data that are being transferred over the Internet. While it can be left to the browser to determine the matching tags, the best way to do this is to use Document Type Definition or an XML schema, either in the XML file or as a separate file that is referenced by the XML file. To display an XML file, a stylesheet (XSL) file can be used that converts it into HTML.

KNOWLEDGE SPEAK

TECH GUIDE E

The Technology of Teams

WHAT WE WILL COVER

- Why Do Organizations Use Teams?
- How People Work in Teams
- How Teams Develop
- Hallmarks of Highly Effective Teams
- Bringing It All Together

ROI STUDENT RETURN ON INVESTMENT

Through your investment of time in reading and thinking about this guide, your return, or created value, is gaining knowledge. Use the following questions as a study guide.

1. Why do organizations use teams to solve business challenges?
2. How do skills and roles work in concert to help people work better in teams?
3. What stages do teams naturally need to progress through in order to become high performing?
4. What are the critical success factors that characterize effective teams?
5. What tools do well-functioning teams apply to ensure their success?

In Chapter 4, we considered organizations as open systems. In this approach, organizations transform inputs into outputs (i.e., use business processes to create value) and achieve their goals given market opportunities, resource limitations, and the constraints of their competitive environment.

Think about how complex the modern business environment has become. New technologies and new knowledge emerge at a rapid pace, and new demands occur from stakeholders such as customers, shareholders, employees, and the government. Nothing stands still for very long in today's fast-paced world.

To draw on expertise from colleagues in various areas, organizations often use teams. Therefore, to be a better knowledge-enabled professional, you need to know some fundamentals about the

A special thanks to Carol-Ann Hamilton for co-authoring this Tech Guide.

"technology" of teams: how people work in teams, how teams develop, how teams succeed, and how terms collaborate. Let's consider the important question of the value created by using teams in an organizational context.

WHY DO ORGANIZATIONS USE TEAMS?

THE BUSINESS CASE FOR USING TEAMS

As Ashby's Law of Requisite Variety[1] implies, a complex and varied external environment demands a correspondingly varied and complex internal organizational environment. Ashby's Law means that in order to survive, businesses need to be as complex as their environment dictates. How does an organization meet this challenge and continue to succeed?

One way organizations meet this challenge is by hiring talented knowledge-enabled professionals who work primarily as individuals (see Figure E.1). These knowledge-enabled professionals possess the required expertise and skills to ensure the organization succeeds despite the complex environment it operates in. However, talented experts are a precious resource and may not always be available to work on every challenge that an organization faces at any point in time.

Few, if any, employees are experts in all areas of organizational knowledge, nor is this a feasible objective because of the cost and

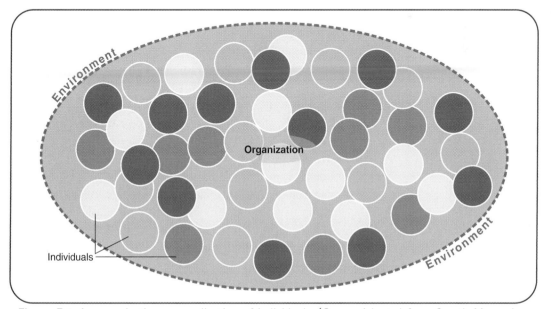

Figure E.1 An organization as a collection of individuals. (*Source:* Adapted from Gareth Morgan's *Images of Organizations, 2nd ed.*, Sage Publications, 1997, p. 112–113)

1. For more information, please see W. Ross Ashby, *An Introduction to Cybernetics*, London: Chapman and Hall, 1956. Internet (1999): http://pcp.vub.ac.be/books/IntroCyb.pdf.

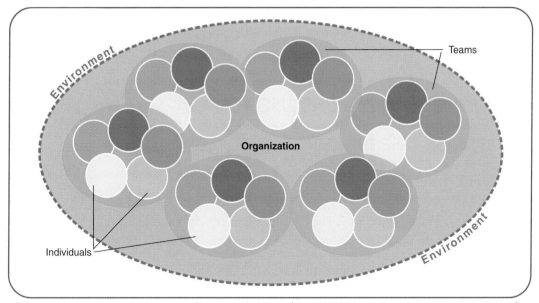

Figure E.2 An organization as a collection of teams. (*Source*: Adapted from Morgan, pp. 112–113)

time involved. For example, if an IS development expert is managing a financial systems development project, will this expert know how the system should account for the sale of tangible assets? This is likely outside the IS expert's usual area of expertise.

To solve this problem, organizations tap into the collective power of teams. As Figure E.2 shows, team members possess a more diverse and complementary set of knowledge, expertise, and skills than any single individual. This creates powerful synergies among team members and generally produces better results. In the case of the financial systems development project, the IS expert may be on a team with an accounting expert who will provide subject matter expertise to the team.

Consequently, most modern organizations succeed today through a blend of individual and team effort (see Figure E.3). As we will cover next, there are times when strong, high-potential employees working on individual goals and responsibilities is the best way for the organization to achieve its mandate. Generally speaking, though, if the organization has thoughtfully hired top talent, then a team of the right people working in an aligned fashion in the "right" direction will be greater than the sum of its parts.

TEAMS VS. WORK GROUPS

When you hear the word "team," what do you think of? Perhaps you think of your favourite sports team, or maybe you work part-time and belong to a team at work, or you may think of a sales team. Although there are many different definitions of **teams**, we'll use a

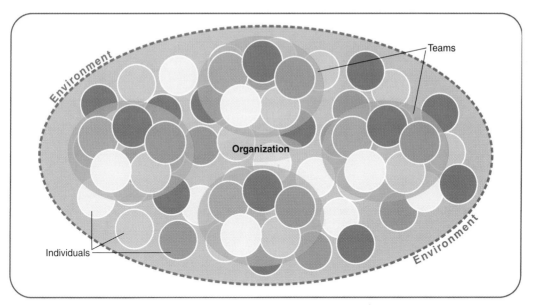

Figure E.3 An organization as a collection of teams and individuals. (*Source:* Adapted from Morgan, pp. 112–113)

slightly modified version from Jon R. Katzenbach's and Douglas K. Smith's best-selling book *The Wisdom of Teams:* "a [relatively] small number of *people with complementary skills* who *are committed to a common purpose, performance goals and approach* for which *they hold themselves mutually accountable.*"[2]

Throughout this guide, we will return often to the italicized concepts above. For the time being, think back to the "teams" in which you have been involved in the past and determine if they now meet our definition. Some may. Some may not.

A team is not just any group working together. No matter how much a leader might want to call a group of employees within a reporting relationship a team, this does not necessarily make them so. As Katzenbach and Smith point out, the entire workforce of any large and complex organization is *never* a team, despite how often that label is offered up. Table E.1 below illustrates how to tell the difference between **work groups** and teams.

Notice how a work group's performance is linked directly to what its members do individually. The best work groups come together to share information, viewpoints, and learning; to make decisions that help each person accomplish their own responsibilities; and to reinforce individual performance standards. The focus is always on singular goals and accountabilities. Work group members only take responsibility for their personal results. They do not focus on continuous performance improvements requiring the combined

2. Jon R. Katzenbach and Douglas K. Smith, *The Wisdom of Teams,* p. 45.

Table E.1 Not All Groups Are Teams: How to Tell the Difference[3]	
Work group	**Team**
Strong, clearly focused leader	Shared leadership roles
Individual accountability	Individual and mutual accountability
The group's purpose is the same as the broader organizational mission	Specific team purpose that the team itself delivers
Individual work products	Collective work products
Runs efficient meetings	Encourages open-ended discussion and active problem-solving meetings
Measures its effectiveness indirectly by its influence on others (e.g., financial performance of the business)	Measures performance directly by assessing collective work products
Discusses, decides, and delegates	Discusses, decides, and does real work together

work of two or more members. They operate independently, or at best, as a collection of individuals.

On the other hand, a team's performance includes both individual results and what we call "collective work products." A collective work product is what two or more members must work on together (e.g., interviews, surveys, experiments). A collective work product reflects the joint contribution of team members and requires that they collaborate and merge their efforts into a joint output. This suggests that team members operate interdependently rather than independently, which is another important distinction between a team and a work group.

TYPES OF TEAMS

Assuming the team is producing a collective work product through mutual accountability, shared contribution, group decision making, and best practice performance standards, there are many potential types of teams to which an employee can contribute. Just some of these include:

- **Independent:** The team is composed of individuals who perform basically the same actions. The work of one team member has little to no direct effect on the performance of the other team members.
- **Natural Work Group:** The team reports to the same manager, works in the same department, or works together in the same area to contribute to group goals.
- **Project:** The team comes together temporarily for a specific project or assignment and when completed, disbands.
- **Functional:** The team is composed of members from the same function or department, such as customer service.

3. Jon R. Katzenbach and Douglas K. Smith, "The discipline of teams," *Harvard Business Review*, March–April 1993).

- **Cross-Functional:** The team is composed of members from varying disciplines, such as sales, parts, and manufacturing, responsible for supporting a unit or position, such as a field service engineer.
- **Virtual:** The team works in various facilities or locations, coming together "virtually" through technology (e.g., conference calling, video conferencing, VoIP).

Rather than get caught up in specific terminology, what is important to note are the variety of teams to which a knowledge-enabled professional can belong. Team membership can enhance careers and bring other professional and personal benefits. Being part of a team can give you insight into the subject matter expertise of other functions, opportunities to develop additional skills and knowledge, along with personal growth and fulfillment as you learn to apply your skills and talents for the greater good.

Quick Test

1. Ashby's Law of Requisite Variety implies that:
   a. teams are required to consist of members from varying functions.
   b. organizations should be composed of teams of individuals.
   c. businesses need to be as complex internally as their external environment dictates.
   d. a knowledge-enabled professional should belong to a varied and complex array of teams.

2. True or False. A cross-functional team is composed of members from the same discipline.

3. Fill in the blanks. A team is a small number of people with _____ skills who are committed to _____ for which they hold themselves _____.

Answers: 1. c; 2. False; 3. complementary; a common purpose, performance goals, and approach; mutually accountable.

HOW PEOPLE WORK IN TEAMS

Now that you know why organizations deploy teams and how they are structured, we can look inside teams and see how individuals relate in order to get the job done. We must consider both their skills and assigned or adopted roles that will allow them to succeed.

SKILLS

A skill is an ability to accomplish a task. This ability is usually accompanied by a level of proficiency that enables an individual to accomplish skill-related tasks successfully (e.g., efficiently and effectively). Efficiency refers to producing an outcome with minimal waste or effort. Effectiveness is more about having a definite or desired effect. Both efficiency and effectiveness are needed to successfully apply a set of skills.

What are some skills that members might contribute to teams? In general, team skills fall into three areas:

- **Technical skills** include expertise or functional knowledge, such as a chartered accountant's accounting knowledge or an experienced programmer's IS knowledge.
- **Problem-solving skills** include investigating and analyzing as well as decision making and implementing. Teams must be able to identify problems and opportunities, evaluate their options, and then make appropriate decisions about how to move forward.
- **Interpersonal skills** are required for effective relationships between team members and include the ability to compromise and build consensus. Listening and supporting are two other essential interpersonal skills.

In organizational life, people are often hired (and promoted) primarily for their technical, or functional, skills and knowledge. These areas of expertise are referred to as "hard" skills, as they can be readily seen in actions performed on the job. Interpersonal skills are frequently referred to as "soft" skills, as they are perhaps less visible.

When it comes to teamwork, though, soft skills are more often the "make or break" point for an individual working on a team. While technical and problem-solving skills can be learned, it is more difficult to instill the attitudes that underpin positive interactions or interpersonal relationships. In this sense, organizations are wiser to hire (or compose) teams based on a superior interpersonal fit between the individuals and their responsibilities rather than always focusing on the hard skills required to do a job. Simply stated, it's easier to repair gaps in an employee's hard job-related skills than in their interpersonal abilities.

In the end, of course, it is best when a team is composed of members who have **complementary skills** from both areas. It is a matter of balance, which is a key contributor to solid team performance. For example, an effective software application design team might include software engineers (technical skills), a certified project manager (problem-solving, decision-making, and interpersonal skills), and sales and customer service representatives (interpersonal skills).

However, complementary skills of team members will not necessarily produce desired results if the members fail to understand their team roles.

TEAM ROLES

According to Dr. Meredith Belbin, a role is a "tendency to behave, contribute and interrelate with others in a particular way."[4] She has identified nine team roles, highlighted in Table E.2, that people tend

Table E.2	Belbin's Team Roles		
Category	Team-Role Type	Contributions	Allowable Weaknesses
Action-oriented roles	Shaper	Challenging, dynamic, thrives on pressure. Has the drive and courage to overcome obstacles.	Prone to provocation. Offends people's feelings.
	Implementer	Disciplined, reliable, conservative, efficient. Turns ideas into practical actions.	Somewhat inflexible. Slow to respond to new possibilities.
	Completer-Finisher	Painstaking, conscientious, anxious. Searches out errors and omissions. Delivers on time.	Inclined to worry unduly. Reluctant to delegate.
People-oriented roles	Coordinator	Mature, confident, a good chairperson. Clarifies goals, promotes decision making, delegates well.	Can often be seen as manipulative. Off-loads personal work.
	Teamworker	Co-operative, mild, perceptive, diplomatic. Listens, builds, averts friction.	Indecisive in crunch situations.
	Resource Investigator	Extroverted, enthusiastic, communicative. Explores opportunities. Develops contacts.	Overoptimistic. Loses interest once initial enthusiasm has passed.
Cerebral roles	Plant	Creative, imaginative, unorthodox. Solves difficult problems.	Ignores incidentals. Too preoccupied to communicate effectively.
	Monitor-Evaluator	Sober, strategic, discerning. Sees all options. Judges accurately.	Lacks drive and the ability to inspire others.
	Specialist	Single-minded, self-starting, dedicated. Provides knowledge and skills in rare supply.	Contributes only on a narrow front. Dwells on technicalities.

4. http://www.belbin.com

to assume in today's organizations. **Belbin's Team Roles** are categorized by action-oriented roles, people-oriented roles, and cerebral roles.

While it may be tempting to wonder if a particular role is better than another, this is just not appropriate. Although a Shaper could at first be perceived as more valuable than a Monitor-Evaluator, what do you suppose would happen if your team were only composed of Shapers and other action-oriented players?

Again, the key is balance. A team's strength lies in its diversity. Heavy weighting within a given team on only one or two roles will create a serious imbalance. Without the unorthodox Plant, confident Coordinator, strategic Monitor-Evaluator, disciplined Implementer, conscientious Completer-Finisher, enthusiastic Resource Investigator, challenging Shaper, co-operative Teamworker, or single-minded Specialist, the team is out of kilter.

Another widely accepted view of team roles divides roles into task (doing) and process (relating).[5] Some examples of each type follow:

Task (Doing)

- Elaborator: builds on suggestions from others
- Clarifier: gives relevant examples, restates the problem, and probes for meaning and understanding

Process (Relating)

- Tension Reliever: uses humour or suggests breaks
- Compromiser: is willing to yield a point of view
- Harmonizer: mediates/reconciles
- Encourager: uses praise and support
- Gatekeeper: keeps communication open and encourages others

The most successful teams enjoy a well-blended mix of all the potential role profiles. Each member values the variety of skill and expertise brought to bear by their teammates, and is in turn appreciated for their uniqueness. Contributory aspects of each role are highlighted; allowable weaknesses are minimized. If, by chance, the team lacks representation in a given role(s), members willingly step outside their comfort zones in order to adopt these missing strengths. They know that all qualities embodied by these team roles must be somehow factored into the way of working with one another.

5. Adapted from D. Hunter, A. Bailey, and B. Taylor, *The Zen of Groups*, Tucson, AZ: Fisher Books, 1995, p. 21–22.

On the other hand, high-performing teams avoid or certainly minimize the behaviours associated with the dysfunctional roles listed below:

- Aggressor: deflates others' status or disagrees aggressively
- Negator: criticizes or attacks others
- Blocker: holds onto attitudes, mentions unrelated experiences, or returns to already resolved topics
- Withdrawer: refuses to participate
- Recognition-Seeker: boasts or talks excessively
- Topic Jumper: changes the subject, sometimes frequently or randomly
- Joker: diffuses the energy by telling ill-timed or off-topic jokes

You will learn later in this guide how to effectively manage or eliminate these negative behaviours using practical tools such as a Code of Conduct, an important part of the technology of teams (which is described in the section Bringing It all Together).

THE WHAT AND HOW OF TEAMS

Working in concert, skills and roles are key ingredients to team success. Expressed a different way, skills are *what* each person brings to the table while roles are *how* every member executes their involvement. The "what" together with the "how" ensures effective, balanced performance.[6]

To illustrate, have you ever been part of a team where the intended outcome was accomplished, but the process left everyone dissatisfied? How did that feel? Something about *how* the result was reached left regret or anger. It could be that the team's leader treated people disrespectfully, or maybe the members did not get along. The process for accomplishing the goal may have been defective. Regardless of the cause, the experience is a negative one.

In turn, have you ever felt great about a team you were on, even though the end result was not attained? How did that leave you remembering the experience? Even though the how (as in team interactions and process) was satisfying, the *what* left something to be desired. At the end of the day, feeling good cannot fulfill a corporate mandate of successful outcomes, and this must be taken into account. However, leaving employees' self-esteem intact in those instances where failure is a part of the normal outcomes (as it will be from time to time) is an important behaviour.

---

6. Carol-Ann Hamilton and James Norrie, *The A to Z Guide to Soul-Inspiring Leadership*, Epic Press, 2003.

So only when both of these occur simultaneously do we have complete organizational performance, where the required outcomes are achieved and the team feels good about the way this was done. In an organizational context, this means true performance results from each team member pulling their weight in accordance with the organization's stated vision, mission, and values and the charter or goals for the specific team they are on.

Quick Test

1. Team skills generally fall into which of these three broadly categorized areas?
   a. functional, analytical, and relationship
   b. technical, problem-solving, and interpersonal
   c. technical, decision-making, and relationship
   d. functional, implementing, and interpersonal

2. True or False. A Gatekeeper is a task role that encourages communication from everyone.

3. Fill in the blanks. A skill is ____ the team member contributes, while their role is _____ they contribute.

Answers: 1. b; 2. False; 3. what, how.

HOW TEAMS DEVELOP

If complementary skills and roles are necessary for team success, how do team members first come together, then uncover what they each know how to do, and learn how to work effectively with each other? A good place to start is to consider what happens when people first form a team. According to Henry Ford, founder of the Ford Motor Co., "Coming together is a beginning, staying together is progress, and working together is success."

Successful teams don't just happen; they develop purposefully. Building a high-performing team takes time and effort. Each team develops differently and in its own time depending on a number of related variables including team composition, size, type, and mandate.

Something else of note is that in spite of the specific nature of any particular team, all teams are said to generally move through four or five core stages of development. Let's look at a couple of the more common models that represent team development. Perhaps the most widely accepted model of team development is **Tuckman's Stage Model**. You may have seen or heard variations of his model, which is often summarized by its five parts: "forming, storming, norming, performing, and adjourning."

Wherever possible, every team should aim to reach the performing stage, the ideal state where a team is fully developed, deployed, and productive. However, it is important to recognize that moving through the stages is not a linear, step-by-step process. Often teams move back and forth fluidly between the stages for any number of valid reasons. It is also implied that eventually the team completes its work and is likely disbanded, although in some instances this may occur only in a long-term context.

As an example of a triggering event that can cause movement within the stages, if a member leaves or is being added, this change in team composition and hence its dynamics may take everyone, even temporarily, from a norming or high-performing state back to the earlier forming and storming. Since teams are also surrounded by a broader organization, any external factors such as unexpected demands, market threats, or new information from regulators can cause shifts in performance. The mark of a high-functioning team is how quickly individuals and the total team can return to a

Table E.3 Tuckman's Stage Model of Team Development[7]	
Tuckman's Stages	**Associated Behaviours[8]**
Forming	• Politeness; tentative interactions • Attempt to define goals • Leadership and member roles emerge • Feelings of insecurity, anxiety, excitement
Storming	• Conflict emerges regarding roles, priorities, leadership • Ideas criticized • Competition between members • Feelings of resentment, hostility, and withdrawal
Norming	• Agreement on rules • Compromising, collaborating, co-operating • Sharing of information • More accepting of differences—cohesion—"we" feeling
Performing	• Group members work toward achieving their goals • Trust, flexibility, and interdependence • Decision making; problem solving
Adjourning	• Termination of duties and reduction of dependence • Completion of tasks and disengagement • Increased emotions, e.g., celebration, sorrow over parting

7. B. W. Tuckman, "Developmental sequence in small groups," *Psychological Bulletin* (1965), 63(6), p. 384–399; also B. W. Tuckman and Mary Ann C. Jensen, "Stages of small-group development revisited," *Group and Organization Studies*, Vol. 2 (1977), p. 419–427.

8. Adapted from M. Lankau, unpublished presentation, Department of Management, University of Georgia, 2000.

high-performing state and recover from the occurrence of either an internal or external event.

While Table E.3 lists each stage and its associated team member behaviours, let's further describe what happens at each stage of development.

FORMING

For many, the **forming** stage is an exciting one. Launching a team can feel like the beginning of a new adventure. Although team members may be eager to start, they are probably feeling somewhat unsure at the same time. The sooner the team can come to know one another's skills and expectations, and begin to define their tasks and roles, the sooner members will experience the possibility of eventually becoming a productive unit. Some testing of one another's commitment and attitude is normal at this point. It's just that the team cannot be allowed to linger unduly in this tentative state.

STORMING

Once team members get underway, they will likely find they are not collaborating at all, they just thought they were! If anything, the **storming** stage can bring a real sense of spinning their wheels, or even going backward. Little progress is being made as certain members compete for control. Many would like to avoid this stage altogether. They wish they could just move directly from forming to norming, where work proceeds effectively according to team norms. Skipping the storming stage is not possible, nor desirable. In fact, if natural conflict is not allowed to emerge at this early stage, it will either go underground (where it silently disrupts team functioning throughout its life cycle) or come back in a more entrenched form later (when the impact of unresolved issues is far more damaging to the final result). While uncomfortable for many, it is advisable to allow the storm clouds to gather and then to dissipate using the problem-solving and interpersonal skills described earlier.

NORMING

By the time the team reaches the **norming** stage, members have gotten to know one another and find they are now able to work effectively together. While some difficulties may yet present themselves, the team is generally making real progress toward its goal. Members are using one another's ideas, giving and receiving both positive feedback and feedback for improvement in the process. Individual differences are valued and harnessed. This stage marks the establishment of team ground rules and norms (standards for the work to be done as well as how it will be produced). Agreed-upon norms, such as respecting one another's needs and capabilities, are not only set, but adhered to.

PERFORMING

At the **performing** stage, the team is making progress toward its goal with efficiency and effectiveness. Members are legitimately excited about their accomplishments, as they use everyone's strengths to analyze and overcome obstacles. This stage has the quality of "full steam ahead" toward the destination. Feeling confident and competent, members take pride in their work, knowing they will reach their goal. If anything, a high-performing team looks for ways to continuously improve how members work together.

ADJOURNING

It is almost as though the **adjourning** stage marks a **transition**, defined by William Bridges as "the psychological process all people need to go through to come to terms with a new situation."[9] In this case, a new situation is the happy completion of the team's mandate as well as the need to disband this particular team configuration. As such, adjourning encompasses the three phases of **Bridges' Transitions Model**, namely Endings, Neutral Zone, and New Beginnings, as depicted in Figure E.4.

Bridges writes that the failure to account for the endings and losses that change produces is the single largest issue encountered by organizations in transition. So, too, would it be a sad ending if after all their hard work, the team members were not allowed to properly "complete" with one another. Endings are underpinned by the very

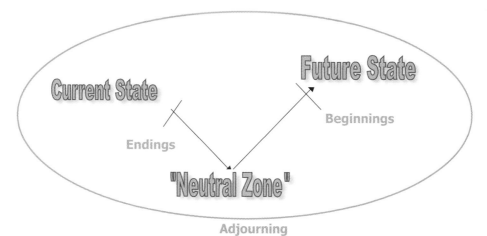

Figure E.4 William Bridges' Transitions Model (*Source:* Adapted from William Bridges, *Managing Transitions,* Perseus, 1991)

9. William Bridges, *Managing Transitions,* Cambridge, MA: Perseus, 1991, p. 3.

same emotions. Members must go through the "grieving" process of letting go of those they have come to know well and move into the ambiguous Neutral Zone (between assignments) in order to ready themselves for the New Beginning of the next team launch. The process of adjourning must be properly marked, offering room for both the sadness of closure and the rightful celebration of a job excellently done.

Although Tuckman's Stage Model is very popular and widely accepted in business, not everyone agrees with it. For example, some researchers in the field of leadership have suggested that not all teams must go through each stage in order to become high performing.[10] Others might question how it's possible to reach a truly high-performing level of development and sustain it for any period of time.

To both, we respond that the only way out is through. This essentially means the stages of development are a process through which all teams must journey and they cannot simply "get to it." Experiencing and resolving the natural dynamics of each stage is what builds the team's "muscles" for eventual success. Rushing toward the end goal all the time might actually burn a team out before it can get there and defeat the point of trying to create high-performing teams in the first place.

Speed is another matter. While each stage is necessary, a team need not spend undue time in any one stage. Especially when a team uses techniques to expedite their progress and agrees on their purpose early on, it is possible to quickly and effectively achieve high-performing status.

Quick Test

1. Match each stage of development with its appropriate descriptor:

i. forming	a. full steam ahead
ii. storming	b. transitions
iii. norming	c. spinning wheels
iv. performing	d. getting to know you
v. adjourning	e. making progress

2. True or False. Every team needs to go through the same five stages of development.

4. Fill in the blank. One of the most widely accepted models of team development is Tuckman's _____ of Team Development.

Answers: 1. i-d, ii-c, iii-e, iv-a, v-b; 2. True; 3. Stage Model

10. J. Beck, and N. Yeager, "Moving beyond team myths," *Training and Development*, 50(3), March 1996.

HALLMARKS OF HIGHLY EFFECTIVE TEAMS

By now you should have discovered that successful team development is not a given. It requires deliberate effort. Teams consist of individuals, each with their strengths and weaknesses, and each with their own goals (which may or may not be aligned with the team's goals). For instance, some team members seek membership in high visibility project teams simply to get promoted; they participate and perform only to the extent that this will help them gain their next high profile assignment. Do you recognize this behaviour? And what impact do you think it might have on a team you were on? To achieve a highly effective team, therefore, Katzenbach and Smith suggest that members accept mutual accountability; that is, the promises team members make to each other to be responsible for achieving the team's goals.[11] Ideally,

> highly effective teams are comprised of groups of committed individuals who trust each other, have a clear sense of their purpose about their work, are effective communicators within and outside the team, make sure everyone in the team is involved in decisions affecting the group, follow a process that helps them plan, make decisions, and ensure the quality of their work.[12]

Another important concept about teams is listening to each other for insights. The blending of multiple perspectives often offers teams a chance to make better decisions that incorporate a diversity of perspectives on a problem. In an earlier book by James Norrie, one of the authors of this text, the following equation was created:[13]

Organizational Agility = Quality of Insight + Speed of Execution

Essentially, if a team does not spend time developing its insights into the problem, the value of any solution, even one implemented quickly, is diminished and will be suboptimal in the end. Put another way, without the right directions, going fast just gets you to the wrong place faster! This creates an important distinction between simply having "speed" (going fast) vs. being "agile" (going fast appropriately and confidently knowing the direction is the right one for your organization and its customers or clients).

Several factors contributing to team development are listed in Table E.4.

---

11. Jon R. Katzenbach and Douglas K. Smith, *The Wisdom of Teams*, pp. 60–61.
12. R. S. Wellins, W. C. Byham, and J. M. Wilson, *Empowered Teams: Creating Self-directed Work Groups that Improve Quality, Productivity, and Participation*, San Francisco: Josey-Bass, 1991, p. 188.
13. Carol-Ann Hamilton and James Norrie, *The A to Z Guide to Soul-Inspiring Leadership*, Epic Press, 2003, p. 129.

Table E.4	Critical Success Factors in Team Development[14]

● Commitment
Team members see themselves as belonging to a team rather than as individuals who operate autonomously. They are committed to group goals above and beyond their personal goals.

● Purpose
The team understands how it fits into the overall business or the organization. Team members know their roles, feel a sense of ownership, and can see how they make a difference.

● Communication
Communication refers to the style and extent of interaction both among members and between members and those outside the team. It also refers to the way that members handle conflict, decision making, and day-to-day interactions.

● Involvement
Everyone has a role in the team. Despite differences, team members must feel a sense of partnership with each other. Contributions are respected and solicited, and a real consensus is established before committing the team to action.

● Process
Once a team has a clear purpose (why it's together and where it's going), it must have a process or means to get there. The process should include problem-solving tools, planning techniques, regular meetings, meeting agendas and minutes, and accepted ways of dealing with problems.

● Trust
Team members have faith in each other to honour their commitments, maintain confidences, support each other, and generally behave in a consistent and predictably acceptable fashion.

All six of these critical success factors must be present in order for a team to advance to higher levels of development. Especially if a team intends or needs to move quickly through the five stages of team development awareness and application of these factors can help them move more rapidly.

How these critical success factors influence performance varies depending on what stage the team is at. Since it is not unusual for a team to be strongest in one or two factors, being aware of how each factor contributes to success helps members decide what actions to take to improve their overall performance. Let's take a closer look at each factor.

COMMITMENT

When people are wholly committed to the team, they are willing to give it their all. Commitment is the essence of a team. Without it, groups remain a conglomeration of individuals. With it, they become a powerful unit of collective performance.

14. R. S. Wellins, W. C. Byham, and J. M. Wilson, *Empowered Teams: Creating Self-directed Work Groups that Improve Quality, Productivity, and Participation*, San Francisco: Jossey-Bass, 1991, p. 188.

Commitment lies at the heart of "owning" one's particular contributions. Commitment is what allows a team member to treat their mates with honour and trust, enacting their responsibilities almost like a legal contract that cannot and must not be violated.

We are referring to personal leadership here. Personal leadership has nothing to do with your job description. Have you ever known someone who holds a leadership title, but never gains followers? Others "walk their talk" everyday, inspiring everyone around them. What creates this difference? The answer is their personal integrity, attitude, beliefs, and values. The extent of personal leadership brought to bear is squarely within one's direct control. Personal character is what commitment is all about.

PURPOSE

A team's **purpose** is its reason for being. Without a clearly understood and agreed-upon purpose, team members don't know what they're supposed to do. With one in place, they can set and base short-, medium-, and longer-term goals in accordance with their larger purpose.

The best teams invest time and effort into exploring, shaping, and agreeing upon a purpose that belongs to them both collectively and individually. This "purposing" activity continues through the life of the team. In contrast, failed teams rarely develop a common purpose. Whether this is due to insufficient focus on performance, lack of effort, or poor leadership, they do not coalesce around a challenging aspiration.

The best teams also translate their common purpose into specific performance goals, like reducing the reject rate from suppliers by 50 percent. Indeed, if a team fails to establish specific performance goals or if those goals do not relate directly to their purpose, team members become confused, pull apart, or revert to mediocre performance. By contrast, when the team's purpose and goals operate in harmony and are combined with commitment, they become powerful engines of performance.

Purpose gives the team direction in the sense that members can align their decisions or resources with it. Purpose allows them to concentrate on what is most important. It also offers the team a sense of identity that encourages everyone to rally around the common purpose, thereby putting the team's needs ahead of their own.

COMMUNICATION

The importance of **communication** in business has been stated so often as to almost be overdone. Nonetheless, when it comes to teamwork, we can safely say you can never over-communicate. In fact, the three C's of teamwork could refer to Communicate, Communicate, Communicate. That's because communication is central to team effectiveness.

When communication is authentic, people exchange not only ideas but also feelings. Both are shared within an atmosphere of mutual trust and respect. Good communicators are therefore honest and sincere. They respect others' opinions and beliefs.

When team members communicate effectively, they resolve conflicts readily or even prevent them altogether. Constant communication also promotes continuous improvement and makes all members of the team feel their viewpoint is important.

INVOLVEMENT

Involvement is another factor central to the team's effective functioning. A body of thought suggests that the employee directly performing a particular job knows it best. The premise is, they are on the "frontlines" each day, and thus become deeply familiar with the issues, challenges, and inner workings of their function. By encouraging each person's involvement, the smart team benefits from the diverse skills and talents each member brings to the table. Involvement is what harnesses the value of these differences. Every person will look at problem solving and other challenges in their unique ways. By encouraging these varying contributions, a highly involved team becomes greater than the sum of its individual parts.

PROCESS

Process refers to how teams get things done (i.e., using well-defined procedures). Examples of processes include how a team identifies problems, analyzes data, makes decisions, develops solutions, or reaches agreement. Solid processes help teams reach their goals more effectively and efficiently. They further allow the team to plan and organize its work, which is especially helpful when under tight deadlines. Solid processes are what allow a team to uncover hidden agendas, because the team would have agreed to give everyone a voice in how they arrive at decisions and solutions. The tool called a Code of Conduct (under the section Bringing It All Together) is an excellent example of a process mechanism.

TRUST

Which comes first: trust or trust? This paradoxical question basically means, is trust given or earned? Do you know anyone who believes trust should first be granted and only taken back if it is broken in some way? Do you know anyone who believes that trust should only be accorded once earned or deserved? Either way, this subject of **trust** is a complex one because it tests the very belief systems of every team member.

Not surprisingly, many people enter new team situations somewhat cautiously because they are not sure whether those gathered can be entirely trusted. Compounding this reality is the degree to which team players have previously been on the receiving end of mistrustful behaviours. People cannot be *made* to trust one another.

Trust grows through shared purpose, process, involvement, and communication. That is why trust and commitment are so intertwined. Both climb as team members learn they can rely on one another. Promises are made and kept. Teammates are there for you when you need them. As trust builds, teams feel more comfortable to take risks and try new ideas. That is why anything a team can do to build trust sooner rather than later will stand them in good stead down the road.

Among the many benefits a team will realize by developing in all six critical success factors are reduced conflict, higher productivity, better quality, and greater job satisfaction for members. To summarize this discussion of the hallmarks of highly effective teams:

- High-performance teams find ways to become highly skilled in all six critical success factors.
- A team should (regularly) evaluate its strength or weakness in each factor.
- Effectiveness in one factor is closely related to effectiveness in the others.
- By focusing on all the success factors, a team can move more rapidly through the stages of team development.
- Teams work best when they combine the critical success factors with good interpersonal skills.
- As a team works on one factor, it should see improvement in the others.

Quick Test
Fill in the blanks.

1. Commitment is the _____ of a team.

2. A team's purpose is its _____.

3. The three C's of teamwork could refer to _____.

4. By encouraging each person's _____, the smart team benefits from everyone's diverse skills and talents.

5. Process refers to _____.

6. Trust grows through shared _____.

Answers: 1. essence; 2. reason for being; 3. communicate, communicate, communicate; 4. involvement; 5. how teams get things done; 6. purpose, process, involvement, and communication.

BRINGING IT ALL TOGETHER

CODES OF CONDUCT

As we have just learned, effective teams develop a strong commitment to a common approach, or how they will work together to accomplish their shared purpose. Just some of the many decisions that need to be made include who will do particular jobs, how the schedule of work will be set and followed, what skills need to be developed, and how the team will make decisions.

All members of a successful team must equally share workloads and contribute in specific ways to their end product. While the team's leader may at first be viewed as owning responsibility for the team's performance, this is not completely true. Yes, the leader must provide direction and take accountability for the final result. However, as Katzenbach and Smith articulate, no group ever becomes a team until it can hold itself accountable. It is the subtle yet critical difference between "the boss holds me accountable" and "we hold ourselves accountable." Without the attitude conveyed within the second phrase, there can be no team.

Only by going through the sometimes arduous exercise of openly and honestly exploring how this diverse collection of individuals will work effectively with each other is the groundwork laid for ultimate performance. In effect, the **Code of Conduct** that results from this commitment-building process becomes like a social contract that obliges team players to follow it. Because everyone has presumably been given a fair voice during these discussions, in "signing up" (often, literally) each person is really saying they are prepared to uphold their end of the bargain.

In this way, the Code of Conduct serves as a touchstone to which the team can regularly refer during its development to ensure it is on track. Indeed, it is highly advisable to review and stress the importance of these ground rules at each meeting, particularly early on in the team's development.

Following are some typical Do's and Don'ts that would characterize a team Code of Conduct in business:

DO

- Establish and follow clearly laid-out performance standards
- Define clear roles and goals
- Create and follow an agenda during meetings
- Give people the opportunity to openly and honestly express their concerns
- Include all team members in discussions and decisions
- Acknowledge the legitimacy of everyone's feelings
- Take advantage of everyone's individual strengths
- Keep a positive attitude
- Work out conflicts in a healthy manner
- Make decisions through consensus
- Focus on one issue at a time
- Be open to giving and receiving positive feedback and feedback for improvement
- Summarize and paraphrase discussions to ensure everyone is on the same page
- List ideas and decisions visibly so the whole team can see them
- Agree on who will do what by when
- Pay attention to opportunities for continuous improvement
- Incorporate "lessons learned" into the team's go-forward procedures

DON'T

- Participate in negative gossip or politics
- Assume things about others' motives
- Interrupt one another
- Criticize others' ideas
- Be closed-minded to alternative ideas and suggestions
- Jump too early to a particular conclusion
- Come unprepared to meetings
- Let people go off on tangents
- Withhold important or relevant information from the team
- Fail to alert the team if you are at risk of missing a deadline (that way, contingency plans can be instituted as soon as possible)

By now, you must have realized that becoming a highly productive team is a challenge, but not impossible. By using a process tool like the Code of Conduct to ensure that everyone participates openly and honestly as well as brings their full set of skills, knowledge, and talent to the table, virtually any team can become highly productive.

COLLABORATIVE TECHNOLOGIES

It would not be prudent of us to leave this guide without addressing the fundamentals of technology used to support teams. Collectively, these are often referred to as "collaboration tools" and range in cost, features, and complexity.

Of course, any good team member will ensure that they take advantage of the normal technology made available to them on the job. That is not what we are referring to here. Rather, we are addressing technology that is specifically designed and developed to help teams function better while doing their job.

Examples of this might include calendar systems (such as Outlook or Groupwise), e-mail, or perhaps specially designed parts of a corporate intranet aimed at supporting collaboration. Maybe it's a corporate directory system that helps team members get to know about each other before their first meeting or connect with an expert in a certain field. For instance, at IBM, an on-line internal database can help any team member locate an expert in any specialized area and quickly reach out to get the most up-to-date information. It could also include communication tools such as a BlackBerry, Web conferencing, MSN Messenger, or even something as simple as making sure that offices are equipped with speaker phones for multi-person conference calls.

Two very popular team collaboration technologies today are ProjectSpaces and Windows SharePoint. These Web-based tools allow teams, both internal and external to an organization, to share documents, use discussion boards, and chat and access integrated task lists and calendars. These tools are very powerful in that they offer the same capabilities to all team members and are highly effective in facilitating communication. Team members can no longer claim that they didn't know that a task was assigned to them, or they didn't know where to find a document, or that they weren't advised of an important meeting. These tools support not only business processes and workflow, but also work accountability and responsibilities.

The range of technologies available to support teams in your organization is only as large or as small as your imagination, time, and budget permit. Like anything else in business, technology can either be a help or a hindrance, much of which depends on how it is designed and deployed. However, what is certain is that technology is a factor in team performance and so having a technology strategy that addresses the needs of your organization's teams is essential.

CONCLUSION

Current thinking further emphasizes that rather than always working on so-called "weaknesses," it is more effective to build on strengths. For each of us, our innate strengths flow naturally and effortlessly. So why not harness those as opposed to the often-laborious effort involved in overcoming our areas for development? We hope this discussion will help you become a player who brings their best self to teams now and in the future.

At the end of this Tech Guide is the Nut Island Case Study, a classic from the *Harvard Business Review*, which brings together all the concepts we have illustrated throughout this guide on the technology of teams and helps you apply it in a real organization setting.

Quick Test

1. A Code of Conduct is:
   a. a legally binding contract created among team members.
   b. an ethical statement of philosophy about teamwork.
   c. a set of rules everyone in the organization follows.
   d. a "social contract" created among the team that helps members stay on track process-wise and interpersonally.

2. Which of the following is not an example of a Code of Conduct statement?
   a. Question each other through challenging, provoking comments.
   b. Actively seek out the opinions and perspectives of everyone.
   c. Make decisions through consensus.
   d. Pay attention to opportunities for continuous improvement.

Answers: 1. d; 2. a.

 STUDENT RETURN ON INVESTMENT SUMMARY

1. Why do organizations use teams to solve business challenges?

Given the increasing complexity of today's organizational environment (i.e., new technologies, new knowledge, new demands), it only makes good business sense to use teams to address a number of these issues. While corporations increasingly seek out talented knowledge-enabled professionals to help them solve problems despite a complex environment, these expert individuals may not always be available to work on every challenge. As well, no one can be specialized in all fields of knowledge. That's why organizations tap into the collective power of teams. Team members possess a more diverse and complementary set of knowledge, expertise, and skills than any single individual. A well-functioning team is truly greater than the sum of its parts.

2. How do skills and roles work in concert to help people work better in teams?

A skill is an ability to accomplish a task efficiently and effectively. Typical examples of skills members might contribute to teams include technical or functional, problem-solving, and interpersonal. However, even complementary skills of team members will not necessarily produce desired results if members fail to understand their team roles. Roles generally can be categorized as task/action-based or process/people-oriented. Successful teamwork demands a mix of all types of roles; no one role is better than another. Skills are, therefore, what each person brings to the table while roles are how every member executes their involvement. The "what" together with the "how" ensure balanced, complete performance.

3. What stages do teams naturally need to progress through in order to become high-performing?

Successful teams don't just happen; they develop. Building a high-performing team takes time and effort. Each team develops differently and in its own time depending on a number of variables, not the least of which are member composition, team type, and mandate. Despite their specific nature, teams are generally said to go through the stages of Forming, Storming, Norming, Performing, and Adjourning (Tuckman's Stage Model of Team Development). Moving through the stages is not a linear, step-by-step process. Internal and external events will "throw" a team back to an earlier stage of development, even temporarily. While some would like to advocate for skipping steps, resolving each stage's natural dynamics builds the "muscles" for success.

4. What are the critical success factors that characterize effective teams?

The six critical success factors of Commitment, Purpose, Communication, Involvement, Process, and Trust must be present in order for a team to advance to higher levels of development. Especially if a team intends or needs to move quickly through the five stages of development, awareness and application of these factors can help them move more rapidly. How these critical success factors influence performance varies depending on what stage the team is at. Since it is not unusual for a team to be strongest in one or two factors, being aware of how each contributes to success helps members decide what actions to take to improve their overall performance. All six factors are intertwined. These factors combined reduce conflict as well as increase productivity and quality.

5. What tools do well-functioning teams apply to ensure their success?

The core tool we examined in this Tech Guide is the Code of Conduct. Although it can often be a time-consuming and labour-intensive exercise to openly and honestly explore how a diverse collection of individuals will work effectively with each other, the resulting Code lays the groundwork for ultimate performance. Through this commitment-building exercise, team players become obliged to follow the Code of Conduct, because they have each been given a fair voice during the discussions. The Code, thus, serves as a touchstone to which the team can regularly refer during its development to ensure it is on track. It is highly advisable to review and stress the importance of these ground rules at each meeting, especially early on.

KNOWLEDGE SPEAK

KNOWLEDGE INTEGRATING CASE: NUT ISLAND EFFECT CASE STUDY[15]

Nut Island is a small peninsula in Quincy, Massachusetts, a city of 85,000 located about 15 kilometres south of Boston. The rickety Nut Island sewage treatment plant was decommissioned in 1997 and its core team was disbanded after 30 years of efforts that left Boston Harbour no cleaner than it was when the team came together in the late 1960s.

The Nut Island effect is a destructive organizational dynamic that pits a homogeneous, deeply committed team against its disengaged senior managers. Their conflict can be mapped as a negative feedback spiral that passes through five predictable stages:

1. Management, its attention riveted on high-visibility problems, assigns a vital, behind-the-scenes task to a team and gives that team a great deal of autonomy. Team members self-select for a strong work ethic and an aversion to the spotlight. They become adept at organizing and managing themselves. The unit develops a proud and distinct identity.

2. Senior management takes the team's self-sufficiency for granted and ignores team members when they ask for help or try to warn of impending trouble. When trouble strikes, the team feels betrayed by management and reacts with resentment.

3. An "us-against-the-world" mentality takes hold in the team, as isolation heightens its sense of itself as a band of heroic outcasts. Driven by the desire to stay off management's radar screen, the team grows skilful at disguising its problems. Team members never acknowledge problems to outsiders or ask them for help. Management is all too willing to take the team's silence as a sign that all is well.

4. Management fails in its responsibility to expose the team to external perspectives and practices. As a result, the team begins to make up its own rules. The team tells itself that the rules enable it to fulfill its mission. In fact, these rules mask grave deficiencies in the team's performance.

5. Both management and the team form distorted pictures of reality that are very difficult to correct. Team members refuse to listen when well-meaning outsiders offer help or attempt to point out problems and deficiencies. Management, for its part, tells itself that no news is good news and continues to ignore team members and their task. Management and the team continue to shun each other until some external event breaks the stalemate.

15. Paul F. Levy, "The Nut Island Effect: When Good Teams Go Wrong," *Harvard Business Review*, March 2001.

Case Questions

Before you read ahead as to how to stop the Nut Island Effect before it starts, answer the following:

1. What critical failures do you diagnose, based on the concepts in this Tech Guide?
2. Using what you have learned, what remedies would you prescribe to senior management?
3. How can you use this Nut Island Effect information in teams you participate on in the future?

Now, for the "preventive medicine." The Case Study goes on to talk about a fine line. The humane values and sense of commitment that distinguished the Nut Island team are precisely the kinds of values to encourage. The trick is to separate them from the isolation and lack of external focus that breeds counterproductive practices and, ultimately, failure.

As such, here are some suggested ways for a team or organization to avoid the Nut Island Effect:

- The first step is to install performance measures and reward structures tied to both internal operations and company-wide goals.
- Second, senior management must establish a hands-on presence by visiting the team. These occasions will be a chance to detect early warnings of problems and will give the team a sense they matter and are listened to.
- Third, team members must be integrated with people from other parts of the organization. This exposes team members to ideas and practices being used elsewhere, as well as encourages them to think in terms of the big picture.
- Finally, it would be helpful to periodically rotate new members into the team environment. This would not be done so frequently as to be disruptive, but often enough to discourage the institutionalization of bad habits.

CHAPTER MAP

Dear Instructors & Students:

In our experience teaching introductory IT to thousands of students in hundreds of classes at various institutions, we are aware that the individual approach used in any one class can vary. We also recognize that as students acquire knowledge, there may come a time when they wish to quickly locate and apply knowledge of a particular type to a situation that often arises outside of the IT classroom. To accommodate both of these needs, we have created the following Chapter Map that helps locate common IT and business concepts within each chapter.

We hope that this map will act as a useful reference for students and will enable instructors to define how they wish to progress through the text.

Chapter	Key Learning Themes	Technical Components	Business Components
Logon	• Becoming a knowledge-enabled professional • Applying technology in a business context • Spiral Model and CORE (Connectivity, On-line Security, Relationships, Ethics) approach to content	• Data • Information • Knowledge • Wisdom	• Creating business value • Competitive advantage • Continuous improvement
Chapter 1 Introduction to the Business Context	• Information technology's relationship to the business environment • Knowledge creation as an essential activity • Impact of the digital world on workers in the future	• Input-Process-Output • The Internet • Information systems • Types of information systems: CRM, DSS, TPS, ERP, MIS • E-commerce as a global phenomenon • Podcasting	• Drucker and knowledge workers • Knowledge replication and utility • Globalization • "Phishing" • Teams • Ethics
Chapter 2 Fundamentals of Information Technology	• Information technology components and terminology • Being familiar with IT to take advantage of opportunities and increase organizational efficiency	• Hardware/software basics • Network architecture: LAN, WAN, routers, hubs, NIC • CPU • Memory: RAM, ROM • Internet: TCP/IP, ISP, HTTP, HTML, XML • Storage technologies • Firewall basics • E-commerce infrastructure designs	• Device selection criteria • Advantages of being aware of information technology and options • Opportunities in e-commerce for market and process efficiencies • Teams • Software piracy • Flash mobs

Chapter	Key Learning Themes	Technical Components	Business Components
Chapter 3 Doing Knowledge Work to Create Business Value	• How technology enables key business activities across the value chain	• Structured Query Language (SQL) • DBMS • Search engines • Wireless security	• Decision making • Problem solving • Communication • Intellectual property rights • Technology for meetings
Chapter 4 Business Fundamentals and IT Strategy	• Strategic management and how IT can support strategy • Aligning business strategy and IT infrastructure, policies, and practices	• Cookies • Spyware • Enterprise resource planning (ERP) • Security risks and solutions • Instant messaging • On-line security	• Supply chain • Organization structure • Value chain/Porter's Five Forces Model • Strategy development • Privacy laws • Building competitive advantage using IT • Using IT for automating, infomating, and transforming business processes • Data ownership • Teamwork
Chapter 5 IT for the Organization	• How IT applications support businesses on a day-to-day basis • Using IT to connect employees to relevant data for business decision making	• Processors • Networks • Storage • DBMS • RDBMS • Intranet • TCP/IP • HTML/XML • Firewall • Document management system (DMS) • Knowledge management • Artificial intelligence • Collaborative software/groupware • Software suites • Middleware • Web services • ERP • Transaction processing: batch, on-line • Workflow management (WMS) • Business process management (BPM) • Decision support systems (DSS) • OLAP • Disaster recovery • Groupware • RFID	• Business intelligence for problem solving: data warehouses, data marts • Information integrity/information processing • Transaction processing (OLAP) • Functional information systems: marketing, HR, finance, accounting, manufacturing • Workflow management • Business process management

Chapter	Key Learning Themes	Technical Components	Business Components
Chapter 6 Creating IS Solutions	• How organizations can use IS to reach their goals • Dominant models and terminology in IS projects	• System development life cycle (SDLC) • System analysis and design • IS development terminology • Methodologies: Waterfall, evolutionary, prototyping, agile (RUP) • Entity relationship diagram (ERD) • Logical data model • Data flow diagram (DFD) • Unified Modelling Language (UML) • Project management software • Gantt chart • PERT • Integrated development environment (IDE) • Code generators • Computer aided software engineering (CASE) tools • Application security	• Feasibility study: IRR, NPV • Outsourcing: ASPs • Project management basics • Stakeholder analysis • Assessing and mitigating IT project risk • Teams
Chapter 7 E-commerce for Consumers and Organizations	• E-business and its impact on individual consumers and organizations and as a way of facilitating global commerce • Impact of the World Wide Web on existing business models and industries	• Authentication • Electronic data interchange (EDI) • Interorganizational systems (IOS) • Extranet • Wide area network (WAN) • Value added network (VAN) • Passwords	• Types of e-commerce: B2C, B2B, B2G, C2G, C2C • Electronic, downloadable products • Cost per click (CPC) • Information density • Mass customization • Personalization • How e-commerce changes competition • Co-operative websites • E-commerce strategy • Customer relationship management (CRM) • Privacy policies • Data security • Mobile commerce • E-commerce business models • E-procurement • Supply chain • On-line advertising • Virtual teams

Chapter	Key Learning Themes	Technical Components	Business Components
Chapter 8 E-commerce Technologies	• Technical evolution of the World Wide Web • Technology behind e-commerce	• HTTP • HTML and HTML forms • Cookies • Persistent data • Java Script • ActiveX • Plug-ins • Java applet • Server-side programming: CGI, PHP, .NET, Servlets • Open source software • Metatags • SSL/encryption • SET • XML • AJAX • SOAP • UDDI • WSDL	• E-commerce • Personalization • Search engine ranking • On-line ordering: shopping cart • On-line payment • Security • Web services use in business partnering and strategic partnerships • Teams through social networks • Data protection
Chapter 9 The Connected Enterprise: Business Partnering and Protecting	• Role of IT governance and corporate governance • Global laws and regulations on IT security • Globalization of business and IT through strategies such as offshoring, best-shoring, and outsourcing • Managing risk at the enterprise level	• Global information systems • Internet security issues • Simple security solutions (including password protections, encryption) • RFID	• Corporate governance • IT governance • Chief information officer (CIO) • IT governance contribution to business value (using Porter's model) • Offshoring, nearshoring, insourcing, onshoring • Sarbanes-Oxley Act • PIPEDA • Privacy Act • Enterprise risk management (ERM) • People-policy-technology framework • Data security
Logoff	• Case study: Canadian Idol • Review of the objectives of the book and Spiral Model • Importance of technology to business and society		• Convergence • Productivity zone
Tech Guide A Details of IT Hardware	• Vocabulary related to system hardware concepts and components • Information to make decisions on IT purchases	• Hardware devices: input and output • Memory: RAM, ROM • Storage • Microprocessor • Bits, bytes • Encoding: ASCII, Unicode, EBCDIC • CPU • Bandwidth • Megahertz	• IT purchasing decisions: evaluating strategic trade-offs for hardware choices

Chapter	Key Learning Themes	Technical Components	Business Components
Tech Guide B Details of Software	• How software contributes to knowledge work, efficiency, and effectiveness • Vocabulary of software-related terms	• Operating systems: Windows, UNIX, Macintosh • Kernel • API • DOS • I/O • Processing: multitasking, parallel • Application software: purchased and custom • DLL • Word processing • Spreadsheets • Database software • Presentation software • Web browser • Computer languages: Java, C, PHP, .NET, SQL • Open-source software	• Cost-benefit trade-offs of off-the-shelf vs. customized software
Tech Guide C The Details of Networking	• Network topologies and architectures and how they facilitate commonly used technology such as PCs, mobile phones, and the Internet	• Network architecture • Client/server: thin, fat • Three-tiered architecture • Peer-to-peer network • HTTP • TCP/IP • Packets/packet switching • Data transmission • Bandwidth • Local area network (LAN) • Ethernet • Wireless LAN • WiFi • Bluetooth • Personal area network (PAN) • Internet • NIC • Domain • FTP • Telnet • E-mail • Instant message (IM) • World Wide Web (WWW) • HTML • URL • Wireless application protocol (WAP) • Short message service (SMS) • Global system for mobile communication (GSM) protocol	

Chapter	Key Learning Themes	Technical Components	Business Components
Tech Guide D The Details of SQL, Logical Modelling, and XML	• Practical instruction for using SQL and XML • Relational databases and their application	• Structured Query Language (SQL) • Relational database • Primary and foreign keys • Entity relationship diagram (ERD) • Extensible Markup Language (XML) • EDI • HTML • Document type definition (DTD) • XML schema • XML stylesheet	
Tech Guide E Technology of Teams	• Why teams are critical in organizations • How teams develop, what type of roles people play, and how to create a high-performing team	• Collaboration tools	• Teams vs. work groups • Team roles, types of teams, and team development • How to produce highly effective teams • Creating and using a Code of Conduct

INDEX

PHOTO CREDITS

Chapter 1 Page 10 Photodisc/Getty Images; p. 19 Courtesy of SanDisk Inc.

Chapter 2 Page 36 Photodisc/Getty Images; p. 45 Courtesy of Hewlett-Packard Company, p. 46 (clockwise) Courtesy of Hewlett-Packard Company, Photodisc/Getty Images, TM & © 2007 Nintendo, used with permission; p. 47 (clockwise) Sam Ogden/Photo Researchers Inc., Thinkstock/Media Bakery, Photodisc/Getty Images; p. 48 Courtesy of Hewlett-Packard Company; p. 49, Courtesy of Hewlett-Packard Company; p. 50 Courtesy of Hewlett-Packard Company; p. 50 Courtesy of Hewlett-Packard Company; p. 57 (top) Courtesy of WestJet; (bottom) Courtesy of TELUS.

Chapter 3 Page 74 Photodisc/Getty Images.

Chapter 4 Page 114 Photodisc/Getty Images; p. 128 Thinkstock/Media Bakery.

Chapter 5 Page 148 Photodisc/Getty Images; p. 153 Copyright @Studio City/eStock Photo; p. 169 Reproduced with permission of the Minister of Public Works and Government Services Canada, 2006.

Chapter 6 Page 196 Photodisc/Getty Images.

Chapter 7 Page 250 Photodisc/Getty Images; p. 260 Courtesy of Mercedes-Benz Canada Inc.; p. 261 Amazon.ca; p. 262 Courtesy of VRBO.com.

Chapter 8 Page 292 Photodisc/Getty Images; p. 297 Intel Corporation; p. 300 Yahoo! Canada; p. 310 Microsoft Corporation; p. 311 Printed with permission from Yahoo.com; p. 312 Printed with permission from Yahoo.com; p. 320 Amazon.ca.

Chapter 9 Page 342 Photodisc/Getty Images; p. 359 Courtesy of Logitech.

Logoff Page 394 Courtesy of Bell Canada.

Tech Guide A Page 407 Corbis Digital Stock; p. 414 (top) Brand X Pictures/Media Bakery, (bottom) Medioimages/Media Bakery; p. 415 (top to bottom) Photodisc/Getty Images, Courtesy of Hewlett-Packard Company, Courtesy of Logitech, Cut and Deal/Media Bakery, Photodisc/Getty Images; p. 416 Courtesy of Logitech, Photodisc/Media Bakery, Courtesy of Hewlett-Packard Company; p. 420 ImageSource/MediaBakery; p. 425 Courtesy of Wacom Technology Corporation; p. 426 (top to bottom) Courtesy of Epson UK Ltd., Courtesy of Hewlett-Packard Company, Courtesy of Hewlett-Packard Company, Courtesy of Hewlett-Packard Company, Courtesy of Epson America Inc. System Device Group; p. 429 (top to bottom) Corbis Digital Stock, Corbis Digital Stock, Photodisc/Getty Images, Corbis Digital Stock, Corbis/Media Bakery, Courtesy of Hewlett-Packard Company.

Tech Guide C Page 493 The RIM and Black-Berry families of related marks, images and symbols are the exclusive properties of Research In Motion—used by permission.